Expert Oracle Enterprise Manager 12c

Kellyn Pot'vin
Anand Akela
Gokhan Atil
Bobby Curtis
Alex Gorbachev
Niall Litchfield
Leighton Nelson
Pete Sharman

Apress·

Expert Oracle Enterprise Manager 12c

ISBN-13 (pbk): 978-1-4302-4938-2

ISBN-13 (electronic): 978-1-4302-4939-9

President and Publisher: Paul Manning
Lead Editor: Chris Nelson
Technical Reviewer: Frits Hoogland
Editorial Board: Steve Anglin, Mark Beckner, Ewan Buckingham, Gary Cornell, Louise Corrigan, Morgan Ertel, Jonathan Gennick, Jonathan Hassell, Robert Hutchinson, Michelle Lowman, James Markham, Matthew Moodie, Jeff Olson, Jeffrey Pepper, Douglas Pundick, Ben Renow-Clarke, Dominic Shakeshaft, Gwenan Spearing, Matt Wade, Tom Welsh
Coordinating Editor: Jill Balzano
Copy Editor: Sharon Wilkey
Compositor: SPi Global
Indexer: SPi Global
Artist: SPi Global
Cover Designer: Anna Ishchenko

Distributed to the book trade worldwide by Springer Science+Business Media New York, 233 Spring Street, 6th Floor, New York, NY 10013. Phone 1-800-SPRINGER, fax (201) 348-4505, e-mail orders-ny@springer-sbm.com, or visit www.springeronline.com. Apress Media, LLC is a California LLC and the sole member (owner) is Springer Science + Business Media Finance Inc (SSBM Finance Inc). SSBM Finance Inc is a Delaware corporation.

For information on translations, please e-mail rights@apress.com, or visit www.apress.com.

Apress and friends of ED books may be purchased in bulk for academic, corporate, or promotional use. eBook versions and licenses are also available for most titles. For more information, reference our Special Bulk Sales–eBook Licensing web page at www.apress.com/bulk-sales.

Any source code or other supplementary materials referenced by the author in this text is available to readers at www.apress.com/9781430249382. For detailed information about how to locate your book's source code, go to www.apress.com/source-code/.

Contents at a Glance

Contents

About the Authors

Kellyn Pot'Vin is an Oracle ACE Director and senior technical consultant at Enkitec, managing Oracle and SQL Server. She specializes in environment optimization, tuning and creating systems that are robust and enterprise level. Kellyn works mostly on multiterabyte databases, including Exadata, and databases with driven performance involving solid-state disk solutions. Kellyn is deeply involved in the Oracle User Group community, speaking at conferences around the world, and is the director for the Rocky Mountain Oracle Users Group (RMOUG) Training Days conference, one of the largest regional conferences. Kellyn blogs at https://dbakevlar.com and is engrossed in social media. She can be found on Twitter under the handle @DBAKevlar, LinkedIn, and Facebook, where she often discusses her daily technical adventures since she works from home and doesn't have any coworkers to tell them to. She also heads up local and global Women in Technology (WIT) groups, mentoring fellow women in technical fields. Kellyn resides in Westminster, Colorado, with her partner, Tim Gorman, and her three children, Sam, Cait, and Josh.

Anand Akela is senior principal product marketing director for Oracle Enterprise Manager. He focuses on Oracle's enterprise cloud, virtualization, and infrastructure management offerings. Prior to his current role at Oracle, he worked at HP in various product marketing, product management, and engineering roles in the areas of systems management, servers, data center energy efficiency, and enterprise software.

Anand is an active participant in various data center industry consortiums and currently serves as chairman for the Data Collection and Analysis Work Group at The Green Grid. The Green Grid is a global consortium of IT companies and professionals seeking to improve energy efficiency in data centers and business computing ecosystems around the globe. Anand also serves as an advisor to PeersNet, a web services provider. Anand received his MBA from the Fuqua School of Business at Duke University and a BS in computer science from the University of Pune in India.

Gokhan Atil is an independent consultant who has been working in IT since 2000. He worked as a development and production DBA, trainer, and software developer. He has a strong background in Linux and Solaris systems. He's an Oracle Certified Professional (OCP) for Oracle Database 10g and 11g, and has hands-on experience with Oracle 11g/10g/9i/8i. He is an active member of the Oracle community and has written and presented papers at various conferences. He's also a founding member of the Turkish Oracle User Group (TROUG). He was honored with the Oracle ACE award in 2011. He has a blog in which he has shared his experience with Oracle since 2008: www.gokhanatil.com.

Bobby Curtis is a solution architect at BIAS Corporation in Atlanta, Georgia. He has been a database administrator for 11 of his 17 years in the IT industry, with experience in Oracle, MS SQL Server, MySQL, and Sybase. Bobby specializes in database implementation, configuration, and data integration for enterprise-level databases and monitoring tools. He is a member of the Georgia Oracle Users Group (GOUSER), Independent Oracle User Group (IOUG), and Oracle Developer Tools User Group (ODTUG). Bobby is also certified in Oracle GoldenGate, Oracle Enterprise Manager 11, Oracle Enterprise Manager 12c, and Oracle Exadata. He now puts particular focus on the Oracle Database Appliance.

Few DBAs are as well equipped as **Alex Gorbachev** to handle any kind of database scenario. Alex has architected and designed numerous successful database solutions addressing challenging business requirements. Alex is a respected figure in the Oracle world and a sought-after leader and speaker at Oracle conferences around the globe. He regularly publishes articles on the Pythian blog and runs online webinars. Alex is a member of the OakTable Network and an Oracle ACE Director.

Today, Alex is working at The Pythian Group. He started at Pythian in Ottawa, leading a team of database experts before moving to Australia to embrace the challenges of setting up company business in the East Asia/Pacific region. Now he's back in Ottawa as Pythian's chief technology officer, continuing to bridge the gap between business and technology. The search for the perfect fit between technology, engineering talents, and business processes is what keeps him up at night.

Niall Litchfield is a DBA of 15 years standing, with extensive experience running databases on various x86(64) platforms, and with a particular bias toward Microsoft Windows. Niall began professional life as a "bean counter" for KPMG and consequently is a DBA who respects auditors, mainly because they have to stand in unheated warehouses in the middle of winter watching other people count things, something he never wants to do again. His dad was a real engineer, crafting genuinely useful objects with fine tolerances, and that, coupled with an early experience in which he showed that the two competing macroeconomic theories of the time both explained actual behavior equally well, and that neither explained it adequately, rather explains his evidence-based approach to databases in general and performance tuning in particular.

Leighton Nelson is an Oracle Certified database administrator and is a Lead Oracle DBA at Mercy, Saint Louis. He has over ten years of experience working with Oracle database products and currently spends his time working on database management, performance tuning, high availability, and backup and recovery. Leighton is an active member of the Oracle community. He often speaks at regional conferences across the United States, including Oracle Open World and IOUG Collaborate. He currently serves as the Oracle RAC SIG US Events Chairperson and IOUG Liaison. In addition to his speaking engagements, Leighton shares his experience with working with various Oracle products by blogging at `blogs.griddba.com` and by tweeting at his twitter handle `@leight0nn`. Leighton resides in Saint Louis, MO with his wife Kerrine and their four sons Casani, Brandon, Justin and Matthew.

Pete Sharman is a Principal Product Manager with the Enterprise Manager product suite group in the Server Technologies Division at Oracle Corporation. He has worked with Oracle for the past 18 years in a variety of roles from Education to Consulting to Development, and has used Enterprise Manager since its 0.76 beta release. Pete is a member of the Oak Table Network, and has presented at conferences around the world from Oracle Open World (both in Australia and the US), RMOUG Training Days, the Hostsos Conference, Miracle Open World, and AUSOUG and NZOUG conferences. He has previously authored a book on how to pass the Oracle8i Database Administration exam for the Oracle Certified Professional program. He lives in Canberra, Australia, with his wife and three children.

About the Technical Reviewer

Frits Hoogland is an IT professional specializing in Oracle database performance and internals. Frits frequently presents Oracle technical presentations in the Netherlands, United Kingdom, United States, and other countries. In 2009 he received an Oracle ACE award from the Oracle Technology Network and a year later became an Oracle ACE Director. In 2010 he joined the OakTable Network. In addition to developing his Oracle expertise, Frits works with MySQL, PostgreSQL, and modern operating systems. Frits currently works at VX Company in the Netherlands.

■ ■ ■

CHAPTER 1

Enterprise Manager Cloud Control 12c Architecture

by Pete Sharman

Oracle Enterprise Manager Cloud Control 12c (referred to hereafter as *EM12c*) is the latest version of Oracle Corporation's end-to-end management tool for both Oracle and non-Oracle technology. Previously known as Oracle Enterprise Manager (OEM) or Oracle Enterprise Manager Grid Control, the tool has been around for quite some time now. The 12c release, though, is a landmark version that makes huge advances in terms of both the breadth and depth of its functionality. In many ways, this release has moved Enterprise Manager from being a database administrator's monitoring tool, to a tool that can be used to manage your entire data center. EM12c now covers several focus areas, including the following:

Framework and infrastructure: EM12c provides security, scalability, a rich user interface, the new Self Update functionality, and more.

Enterprise monitoring: You can monitor the status of your entire infrastructure, including databases, middleware, and applications. EM12c provides ways of notifying you when issues arise, resolving them, and reporting on them.

Cloud management: Managing the cloud is a hot topic in the industry today, and EM12c provides a range of solutions in this space, including chargeback/showback, policy-based resource management, and self-service provisioning.

Lifecycle management: Administering computing systems today requires many manual processes for the discovery, provisioning, patching, change management, and configuration management of those systems. EM12c automates many of these manual processes, freeing the administrator to spend more time on other, higher-priority tasks.

Database management: Managing databases has been a key feature of OEM since its first release. That continues in the EM12c release, including solutions around patching, upgrading, provisioning, performance tuning, data masking, and subsetting, as well as configuration and change management.

Middleware management: A key component of EM12c is providing comprehensive management capabilities across all of Oracle's middleware products (including WebLogic Server, SOA Suite, Identity Management, WebCenter, and Coherence), as well as non-Oracle middleware (such as IBM's WebSphere or JBoss Application Server).

Application management: Monitoring and management solutions for all the Oracle-provided applications (E-Business Suite, PeopleSoft, Siebel, JD Edwards, and Fusion Applications) come out of the box with EM12c, in addition to capabilities for managing your own custom-built or third-party applications.

Application performance management: EM12c delivers end-to-end monitoring of your applications, including real-user monitoring via Real User Experience Insight (RUEI) as well as synthetic-transaction monitoring via Service Level Management beacons. Other functionality introduced here includes the ability to monitor and trace business transactions, topology discovery, and Java and database monitoring and diagnostics.

Application quality management (AQM): Three areas of testing are provided—application testing via the Application Testing Suite product, infrastructure testing via Real Application Testing and Application Replay, and test data management functionality that includes test system creation, data masking, and data subsetting technologies.

Hardware and virtualization management: Complete lifecycle management is offered for both physical and virtual environments, including provisioning, patching, configuration management, administration, and monitoring. This includes managing systems running on Linux, Unix, Windows, and Oracle Virtualization Server (Oracle VM Server) operating systems, as well as providing insight into the server, network, and storage layers for systems built on top of Oracle Sun hardware.

Heterogeneous (non-Oracle) management: Supplying a range of extensions known as connectors and plug-ins (among others), EM12c provides capabilities to manage non-Oracle technology in addition to Oracle environments. These extensions could be built by Oracle, partners, or even customers themselves. They are based on the same management framework as the rest of the EM12c product, and so can be downloaded, imported, and deployed by the Self Update mechanism.

Coverage of all these focus areas adds up to a robust product for managing the complete data center. The rest of this book drills into the details of many of these areas. The remainder of this chapter introduces you to the basic architecture that you need to understand before delving further into the wonders of EM12c.

Architecture Overview

From an architectural perspective, EM12c is composed of five main parts:

- Cloud Control console
- Oracle Management Agent
- Oracle Management Service
- Oracle Management Repository
- Plug-ins

Let's look at each of these in more detail.

■ **Note**   A discussion of the licensing for EM12c is beyond the scope of this book. (An entire licensing document is available in the Enterprise Manager documentation at `http://docs.oracle.com/cd/E24628_01/license.121/e24474/toc.htm`.) However, it's worth noting that, in general, most of the basic functionality described here carries a restricted-use license and therefore is free. This restricted-use license refers specifically to Enterprise Manager, however, and many add-on options do come with license costs. Refer to the licensing documentation for full details.

The Cloud Control Console

The *Cloud Control console* provides the user interface that you use to access, monitor, and administer your computing environment. The console is accessed via a web browser, thus allowing you to access the central console from any location. You can customize the EM12c console much more than in previous releases, allowing you the following options:

- Choosing your home page from various predefined pages (or indeed setting any page you want to be your personal home page)

- Moving regions around on a target home page

- Adding regions that might be of more interest to you than the defaults

- Deleting regions that aren't of interest to you

The graphical user interface (GUI) provides a history of the most recent targets you have visited (the standard browser history is also available). In addition, you can mark pages as favorites and have them appear in a favorites list on the new menu-driven interface. Figure 1-1 shows an example of the default home page.

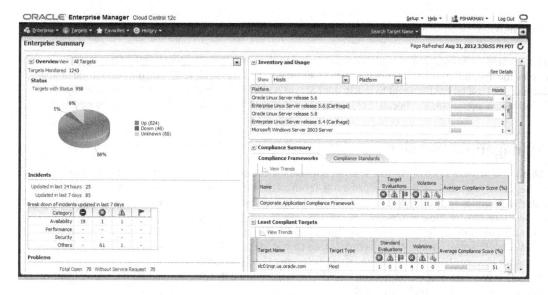

Figure 1-1. *The new default home page in EM12c*

Oracle Management Agents

An *Oracle Management Agent* (usually referred to as simply an *agent* or abbreviated to *OMA*) is generally installed on each host that is monitored in your computing environment. (EM12c also introduces the capability to manage environments remotely in some cases.) These agents are deployed from the console (see Figure 1-2), and then monitor all the targets that have been discovered by the agents. They are used to control blackouts on those targets, execute jobs, collect metrics, and so forth, and in turn provide details such as availability, metrics, and job statuses back to the Oracle Management Service.

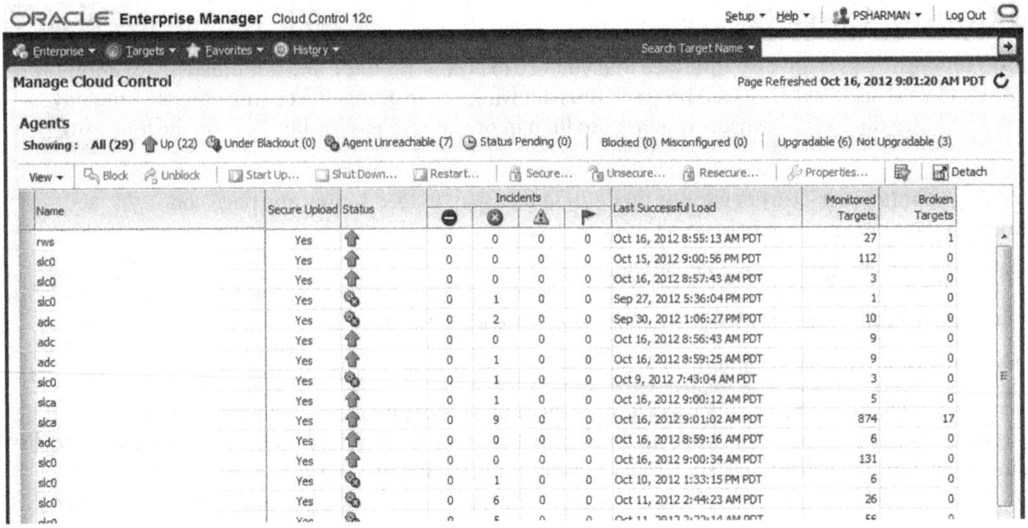

Figure 1-2. *User interface for managing agents within EM12c*

For the EM12c release, agents were completely rewritten from the ground up for greater reliability, availability, and performance (see the upcoming section on plug-ins for details of how this was achieved). The only downside of this change is that you must use an EM12c agent to talk to the EM12c Oracle Management Service. Backward compatibility between 12c and earlier agents was lost because of the number of changes that were made in the new release.

Oracle Management Service

The *Oracle Management Service (OMS)* is a web-based application that communicates with the agents and the Oracle Management Repository to collect and store information about all the targets on the various agents. (Note that the information itself is stored in the Oracle Management Repository, not the OMS.) The OMS is also responsible for rendering the user interface for the console.

The OMS is installed into an Oracle middleware home, which also contains the Oracle WebLogic Server (including the WebLogic Server administration console), an Oracle Management Agent for the middleware tier, the management service instance base directory, the Java Development Kit (JDK), and other configuration files. You can install the OMS into an existing WebLogic Server (WLS) configuration if it exists, but usually it is better from an availability perspective to have it installed in a dedicated WLS home.

Oracle Management Repository

The *Oracle Management Repository* (also called the *repository* or *OMR*) is an Oracle database that stores all the information collected by the various management agents. It is composed of database users, tablespaces, tables, views, indexes, packages, procedures, and database jobs.

Unlike the OMS, the installation process for the OMR requires that a database already exists for the repository. This means you need to have created the database somewhere in your environment prior to installing the OMS. Again, it is typically recommended for the repository to be created in a dedicated database.

Plug-ins

Plug-ins take on a whole new meaning in EM12c. In earlier releases, plug-ins were largely system-monitoring utilities used to monitor and manage non-Oracle (heterogeneous) software including databases and middleware. Partners or Oracle Corporation itself usually built them. Some technically savvy customers built their own as well, but there weren't many plug-ins overall.

In the EM12c release, a few of these monitoring plug-ins remain, but plug-ins have been greatly expanded to include every target type being managed. As such, there is now an Oracle database plug-in to manage Oracle databases, a Fusion Middleware plug-in to manage Oracle's middleware, a Fusion Application plug-in to manage Oracle's Fusion Applications product suite, and so on. Because new releases of the Oracle software will include plug-ins used to manage that software, this means EM12c (and later releases) will be able to monitor and manage those releases much more quickly than has been the case in the past. Plug-ins can be downloaded, applied, and deployed using the new Self Update functionality available from the Cloud Control console (if you have sufficient privileges to use it).

In addition, this modular plug-in architecture means that an agent is no longer configured to be able to monitor any target type. Now, an agent will download only the plug-ins that are needed for the targets that the agent is monitoring. This means the agents themselves are smaller than they were in previous releases. This change is one of the biggest improvements in the architecture of the EM12c release.

A High-Availability EM12c Configuration

In the most basic of EM12c installations, the OMS and the repository can be physically located on a single machine. However, Oracle recommends placing these two components on different machines. Figure 1-3 shows the simplest installation.

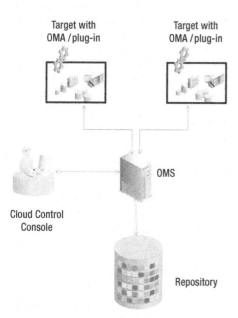

Figure 1-3. *Basic EM12c architecture*

Although this relatively simple architecture may be sufficient for an initial deployment, you might need to grow it into a more scalable, available architecture. There are four levels of deployment that you could use with EM12c to achieve higher scalability and availability. Of course, as in any architecture requiring both scalability and availability, trade-offs need to be made in terms of increasing cost as performance and availability increase.

Level 1

Figure 1-3 shows a *level 1* deployment. The OMS and repository are installed either on a single host or, more preferably, on two separate hosts. However, neither of these hosts has any failover configured.

Level 2

For *level 2*, the OMS is installed on shared storage and uses VIP-based (virtual IP–based) failover. The repository database is protected by using local physical standby database technology. Usually, this means that level 2 deployments use double the number of machines used by level 1. Level 2's active/passive configuration (albeit located locally rather than having remote passive sites), leads to a downtime window when failing over from the active site to the passive site. This architecture is shown in Figure 1-4.

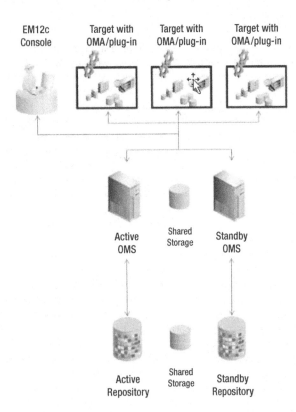

Figure 1-4. *Schematic diagram of a level 2 deployment*

Level 3

In a *level 3* configuration, the OMS is installed using an active/active configuration, requiring a local load balancer. The repository database is protected by both Real Application Clusters (RAC) and local Data Guard. This level is shown in Figure 1-5.

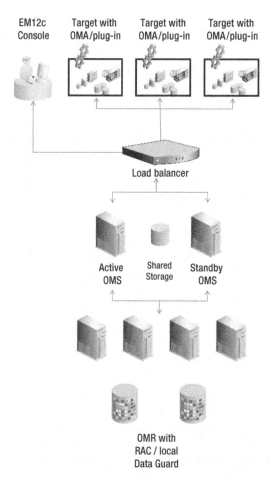

Figure 1-5. Schematic diagram of a level 3 deployment

Level 4

Level 4 is the deployment level providing the most scalability and availability. In this case, the OMS is running in an active/active configuration on a primary site (just like level 3), but additional standby OMS installations are at a remote site. (Note that because of network latency requirements between the OMS and the repository being less than 1 millisecond consistently, the remote site cannot be running an active OMS). This configuration requires a local load balancer at both the primary and standby sites. The repository database is again running on RAC, but in this case the standby RAC database is located at the disaster recovery site. As you can tell, this is quite a complex architecture, shown in Figure 1-6 (without all the lines of communication that would make it even harder to understand).

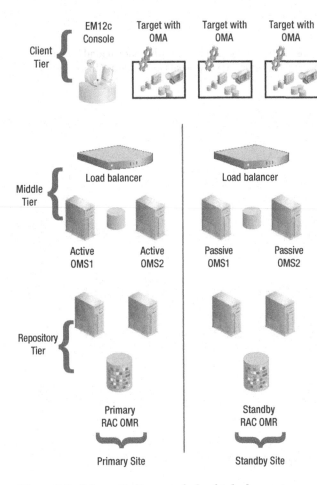

Figure 1-6. *Schematic diagram of a level 4 deployment*

You've now got the gist of the four possible deployment levels. Chapter 13 covers them in greater detail in the context of high availability. Also, be aware that it is possible to create configurations that do not match these levels exactly. Don't be too surprised if someday you see a configuration slightly different from what's just been described. EM12c provides you a great deal of flexibility.

The Software Library

Another important part of an Enterprise Manager installation is the Software Library. The Software Library is a storage area used for such things as patches, Self Update downloads, and gold images. It is depicted earlier, in the diagrams in the section "A High-Availability EM12c Configuration," as shared storage sitting between the OMSs. (Figure 1-5 shows it clearly. There you'll see the shared storage icon almost dead-center). To create the Software Library, you use the Software Library: Administration page, available from the Setup ➤ Provisioning and Patching ➤ Software Library menu path. The Software Administration page is shown in Figure 1-7.

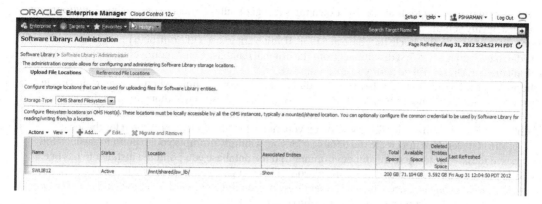

***Figure 1-7.** The Software Library: Admnistration page*

One important point to be aware of when creating your Software Library is that you need to ensure that the location you create the Software Library in is accessible from each OMS, if at some stage you believe your EM12c deployment will require some level of high availability. This can be achieved by using the same network file system (NFS) share mounted on each OMS, or any other technology that allows sharing file systems between machines.

The EM12c release includes several new features related to the Software Library:

- In this release, the Software Library becomes the single location for a lot more entities, such as directives and assemblies. (These new entities are explained in Chapter 5.) Many of these entities are self-updateable, so we now have integration with Self Update.

- Oracle has also expanded the storage-type support, so you now have support for NFS filesystems being shared between OMSs as well as any filesystem that we can reach (that is, agent filesystems can now be used to host the Software Library as well).

- Referenced locations are now supported for the Software Library, so if you have a centralized location for serving these entities that is separate from the OMS, you can now reference those via HTTP, NFS, and so forth. In this case, the OMS stores the metadata about where this referenced location is, and the software bits are stored externally.

- A range of other capabilities exist in this release. You can, for example, attach support notes or readme files to Software Library entities. The library includes improved search capabilities, and of course the new privilege model allows the use of fine-grained privileges for entity access.

Management Tools

So right about now, you're probably asking, "Well, what about all those other management tools that Oracle has?" Often you'll find there's some level of confusion about what all these tools are, how to differentiate between them, and of course when to use which one. Let's spend some time discussing that now.

First, the main point of differentiation between Cloud Control and the other Oracle management tools such as Database Control (DB Control) and Fusion Middleware Control (FMW Control) is the architecture. Cloud Control is designed to manage your entire data center, and as such it has a much more robust, multi-tier architecture than you'll find in the other tools.

Second, the other management tools are scaled-down tools that generally connect to only a single environment at a time, rather than giving you the much broader data center–wide vision of your environment. As an example, DB Control can connect to only a single Oracle database at a time. If you want to use DB Control to manage or monitor another Oracle database, you have to first disconnect from the original database before connecting to the new one. In fact, if you don't do that, Oracle will do it for you automatically.

Finally, there are some incompatibilities between the different tools. For example, when you create an Oracle database by using the Database Configuration Assistant (DBCA), you will be asked whether you want the database to be managed centrally (via EM12c) or locally (via DB Control). It's an either/or decision; you can't choose both. This incompatibility reaches its zenith with the OMR. When you install EM12c, you are prompted for the location of the repository. (The installer does not create the database for you; it simply prompts you to point to the location of an existing Oracle database somewhere in your environment.) If the database you point the installer to has been configured by DBCA to be locally managed by DB Control, you will in fact get an error from the installer indicating that the database is already locally managed. (The installer does give you the command to remove the DB Control configuration if you so choose, but won't actually execute the command for you.)

On a final note, at the time of writing this chapter, Oracle has announced that DB Control will be desupported in database releases after 11.2. Although we don't know yet what the new product will be called, Oracle notes, "In future Oracle Database releases, basic database management will be available through a streamlined management tool, while extensive management capabilities will exist through the latest Oracle Database plug-in deployed from Oracle Enterprise Manager Cloud Control" (see Note 1484775.1 on My Oracle Support for details).

Command-Line Tools

In addition to the GUI that most users of EM12c will use for their day-to-day work, Oracle provides two command-line tools that you need to become familiar with:

Enterprise Manager Command Line Interface (EMCLI): This tool is largely used for scripting operations that might need to be repeated. It is a tool often used by consulting companies that make a business out of configuring EM12c, who thus have a need to execute the same operations repeatedly across different customers. EMCLI can be installed on any computer (not necessarily the OMS or OMR) simply by downloading the tool via the Cloud Control Setup menu and then following the installation instructions. Not all operations that can be performed through the GUI can be performed with EMCLI, however.

Enterprise Manager Control (EMCTL): This utility is used for a variety of tasks, the most important of which are starting, stopping, and checking the status of the OMS, agent, and Cloud Control itself. It is also used to secure/unsecure agents and the OMS, starting and stopping blackouts and other operations.

Repository Users

In terms of database users, the most important user in an EM12c installation is the SYSMAN user. The SYSMAN user has been around for a number of releases now. It is basically the owner of the database schema containing the repository. In many ways, it is akin to the SYS user in an Oracle database, and as such, should not be used apart from the first time you create another Super Administrator account (see Chapter 4 for more details on Super Administrator accounts).

Apart from the SYSMAN account, other database users are created in the repository during repository creation or upgrade. These include the following:

- CLOUD_ENGINE_USER and CLOUD_SWLIB_USER are used to perform cloud operations.

- MGMT_VIEW is used for report generation.

- SYSMAN_APM, SYSMAN_MDS, and SYSMAN_OPSS are metadata schemas for Fusion Middleware components.

- SYSMAN_BIP is used for Business Intelligence (BI) Publisher integration.

- SYSMAN_RO is a general-purpose, read-only user.

Not much detail is provided in the Oracle documentation on these accounts. Suffice it to say, though, that these are all special accounts that you should not drop. Nor should you change their passwords.

Repository Views

Information about administrators, targets, metrics, blackouts, and jobs is all kept in the Oracle Management Repository in a group of repository views. Although the information in these views is obviously used by the Cloud Control console to display that information to you, it can also be used in other ways, primarily by a programmer building extensibility on top of the Enterprise Manager product. As a plug-in developer, for example, you may want to extend Enterprise Manager to manage your own, custom-developed targets, or indeed expand on the target types that Oracle provides out of the box. You may also want to write your own scripts to query historical data from these views, or build your own custom reports to run from SQL Developer or other products. Clearly, a chapter on the Enterprise Manager architecture is not the place to drill into gory details on how to do all these things, but it is worthwhile to understand what these repository views are and how to find more information about them.

The repository views are documented as part of the *Enterprise Manager Cloud Control Extensibility Programmer's Reference* (you can access this from the EM12c documentation located at http://docs.oracle.com/cd/E24628_01/ index.htm). Chapter 18 of that online reference details the use of those views, along with a complete listing of the views displaying the column names for each view.

Communication Flow

When you first start using a product such as Enterprise Manager Cloud Control 12c, one of the areas of greatest confusion is just how communications flow between the various parts of the product. Essentially, you need to understand three areas: the protocols involved, the ports that are being used, and whether firewalls are being used.

Protocols

Three main protocols are used to communicate between the components in an EM12c installation:

> *Hypertext Transfer Protocol (HTTP) or Hypertext Transfer Protocol/Secure (HTTP/S)*: These are the underlying protocols used by the World Wide Web. They define how messages are transmitted and formatted, as well as the actions that browsers and web servers take in response to different commands. HTTP and HTTP/S are used to communicate between the OMA, OMS, and OMR. For security reasons, Oracle typically recommends using HTTP/S rather than HTTP.

> *Java Database Connectivity (JDBC)*: This Java standard is used by the OMS to communicate with the repository, as well as to communicate with any database targets.

> *Internet Control Message Protocol (ICMP)*: This protocol is used by the OMS to communicate with a host, to check the status of the host. Essentially, a ping command is used to check its status.

Ports

During the EM12c installation, you are prompted to supply a list of ports for entities to communicate on. A default list is provided on the Port Configuration Details page, shown in Figure 1-8. The page displays a Recommended Port Range column. The first port number listed in this column is the default port. If for any reason the default port is already used when you are doing an installation, the next port number in the Recommended Port Range will be used. Post installation, you can also find the port numbers that were used in the `staticports.ini` file, located on the OMS host.

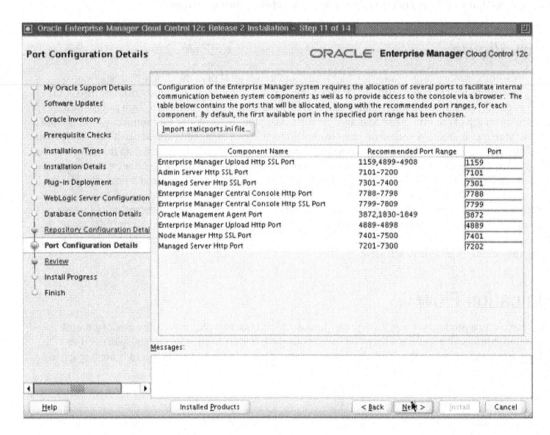

Figure 1-8. *The Port Configuration Details page*

Firewalls

In many cases, a business will require firewalls to be used to control both outgoing and incoming network traffic. This typically involves restricting either the availability of ports or the type of traffic that can pass through a particular port. Because this restriction can be difficult to set up, it is usually recommended that firewall configuration and enablement are left until after you have deployed your Enterprise Manager configuration. However, if the firewalls are already in place, you should open the communication ports you are planning to use until the installation is complete.

Pulling these three areas (protocols, ports, and firewalls) together, the default communication flows in an EM12c installation are shown in Figure 1-9.

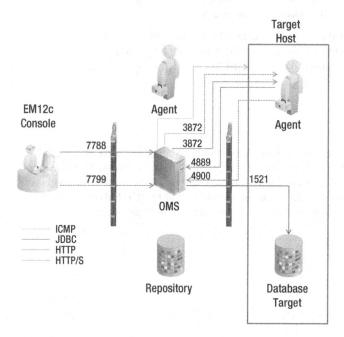

Figure 1-9. *Ports, protocols, and firewalls in an EM12c configuration*

Authentication in EM12c

With the new pluggable framework that is available to you in the EM12c release, you now have more options as far as authentication is concerned. The framework accepts a range of pluggable authentication schemes, enabling you to choose the methods that are most suitable to your environment. Because EM12c relies on Oracle's WebLogic Server for external authentication, any authentication method that WLS supports can be used to authenticate to EM12c. Supported authentication methods include the following:

Repository-based authentication: In this default authentication option that you might be familiar with from previous releases of Enterprise Manager, you are prompted for a username and password. Standard password options—such as password lifetime, password grace, number of failed attempts, and password complexity—are available with this authentication method.

Single sign-on authentication: If you use single sign-on (SSO) authentication in your enterprise, you can register those SSO credentials as an administrator in EM12c. You can then use those credentials to access the Cloud Control console.

Oracle Access Manager SSO authentication: Oracle Access Manager (OAM) is the SSO solution supplied with Oracle's Fusion Middleware product. Again, if you are using OAM SSO, you can register those credentials as an administrator in EM12c and use them to access the console.

Enterprise User Security authentication: EUS allows you to create and store enterprise users and roles as directory objects in a directory server compliant with the Lightweight Directory Access Protocol (LDAP). You can then use EMCTL to set some properties to allow you to drill into those databases without displaying the standard logon pages.

LDAP authentication: In previous releases of Enterprise Manager, LDAP authentication was allowed, but it was restricted to Oracle's LDAP solution, Oracle Internet Directory (OID). In the 12c release, that has now been extended to allow you to use Microsoft's Active Directory product in addition to OID.

Summary

This chapter has introduced you to the major architectural components of Enterprise Manager Cloud Control 12c: the Cloud Control console, the Oracle Management Agent, the Oracle Management Service, the Oracle Management Repository, and plug-ins. You've looked at options for deploying this architecture and the authentication methods you can use to connect to EM12c. This chapter also covered the protocols, ports, and firewalls used by EM12c, so you're now ready to drill into the installation of the product in more detail. That's the subject of our next chapter.

CHAPTER 2

Installation and Agent Deployment

by Gokhan Atil

In this chapter, you will learn how to create a repository database and install Oracle Enterprise Manager Cloud Control 12c. If you have any experience with installing Enterprise Manager Grid Control (the ancestor of Cloud Control), you'll see that EM12c comes with a smarter installation wizard, so the installation is much easier.

EM12c consists of three components: Oracle Management Service (OMS), Oracle Management Agents (management agents), and Oracle Management Repository (management repository).

This chapter's demonstration of the installation and agent deployment uses three servers:

> `cloudcontrol12.testdomain.com`: Oracle Management Service will be installed to this server.

> `repositorydb.testdomain.com`: This database server will host the management repository.

> `target.testdomain.com`: Management agents will be deployed to this target server.

All of these servers are running Oracle Linux 5.8 (64-bit) as well as the GNOME desktop environment and the X Window System.

Although you can install both the management repository and OMS on same server, we prefer to install the management repository on a separate server. If you're planning to install both on the same server, you should accommodate the requirements for both installations.

We recommend that you use a Domain Name System (DNS) server to solve the hostnames of the servers. If you do not have a DNS server, you need to enter the hostnames and corresponding IPs of all targets into `/etc/hosts` on the Oracle Management Server. You also need to enter the hostname/IP address of OMS into the `/etc/hosts` file on all target servers (to which you'll deploy the management agent).

It's also important to use fully qualified hostnames. A fully qualified domain name (FQDN) is a complete domain name for a server. It contains both a hostname and a domain name to specify its exact location in the DNS hierarchy. For example, `cloudcontrol12.testdomain.com` is a fully qualified hostname. At least ensure that your Oracle Management Server has a fully qualified hostname.

Oracle Enterprise Manager Cloud Control 12c can fetch the latest patch information from My Oracle Support for your servers and can create service requests for incidents. Therefore, we recommend that you enable Oracle Management Service to reach the My Oracle Support web site. If you don't want to allow your servers to directly access the Internet, you can set up a proxy server to make the My Oracle Support web site accessible to OMS.

Meeting Hardware Requirements

This section describes the hardware requirements for installing OMS, the management repository, and management agents.

Hardware Requirements for OMS

As you can see in Table 2-1, the hardware requirements for OMS depend on the number of targets you have and the number of agents you'll deploy.

Table 2-1. *Hardware Requirements for OMS*

	Small	Medium	Large
	1 OMS Fewer than 1,000 targets Fewer than 100 agents Fewer than 10 concurrent user sessions	2 OMSs 1,000–9,999 targets 100–999 agents 10–24 concurrent user sessions	3 or more OMSs 10,000 or more targets 1,000 or more agents 25–50 concurrent user sessions
CPU cores/host	2	4	8
RAM	6GB	8GB	16GB
Oracle WebLogic Server JVM heap size	1.7GB	4GB	8GB
Hard disk space	7GB	7GB	7GB

Hardware Requirements for Management Repository

Hardware requirements for the repository database also depend on the number of agents and targets, as shown in Table 2-2.

Table 2-2. *Hardware Requirements for the Management Repository*

	Small	Medium	Large
	1 OMS Fewer than 1,000 targets Fewer than 100 agents Fewer than 10 concurrent user sessions	2 OMSs 1,000–9,999 targets 100–999 agents –10–24 concurrent user sessions	3 or more OMSs 10,000 or more targets 1,000 or more agents 25–50 concurrent user sessions
CPU cores/host	2	4	8
RAM	6GB	8GB	16GB
Hard disk space	50GB	200GB	400GB

Hardware Requirements for Management Agents

Each agent deployment requires approximately 1GB of free hard disk space. Although management agents do not consume large amounts of CPU or RAM, we do not recommend deploying agents to systems with less than 512MB of RAM.

■ **Tip**   The hardware requirements in the preceding sections may change from version to version, so you should check the actual requirements in the Oracle Enterprise Manager Cloud Control Basic Installation Guide.

Installing Management Repository

In this section, you'll download and install Oracle Database 11gR2 on the server named repositorydb.testdomain.com.

It's possible to use one of the certified databases: 11.2.0.3, 11.2.0.2, 11.2.0.1, 11.1.0.7, or 10.2.0.5. If you already have a database server for the repository database, you can skip to the installation of Oracle EM12c.

■ **Tip**   You can find an up-to-date list of certified databases for Enterprise Manager Cloud Control on My Oracle Support: https://support.oracle.com/epmos/faces/CertifyHome. You may want to use an Oracle Real Application Clusters (RAC) database for high availability.

Using the Oracle-Validated RPM Package and YUM

In order to install Oracle Database 11gR2 on Oracle Linux, your system needs to meet a few prerequisites. Using the oracle-validated RPM package, you can complete most of the preinstallation configuration tasks including creating a user and groups. Using this package is the recommended way to install all the Oracle prerequisites on Oracle Linux. You can download the RPM package from the Oracle web site, or you can use the YUM package manager. Oracle provides a free public yum server that you can use even if you don't buy support from Oracle.

To use the Oracle public yum server, you first need to download and copy the appropriate yum configuration file in place, by running the following commands as ROOT:

- Oracle Linux 4, update 6 or newer

  ```
  [root@repositorydb ~]# cd /etc/yum.repos.d
  
  [root@repositorydb ~]# mv Oracle-Base.repo Oracle-Base.repo.disabled
  
  [root@repositorydb ~]# wget http://public-yum.oracle.com/public-yum-el4.repo
  ```

- Oracle Linux 5

  ```
  [root@repositorydb ~]# cd /etc/yum.repos.d
  
  [root@repositorydb ~]# wget http://public-yum.oracle.com/public-yum-el5.repo
  ```

- Oracle Linux 6

  ```
  [root@repositorydb ~]# cd /etc/yum.repos.d
  
  [root@repositorydb ~]# wget http://public-yum.oracle.com/public-yum-ol6.repo
  ```

Open the yum public-yum*.repo configuration file in a text editor. Locate the section in the file for the repository you plan to update from—for instance, [el5_base]—and change enabled=0 to enabled=1.

Save the file and start using yum:

```
[root@repositorydb ~]# yum install oracle-validated
```

For Oracle Linux 6, you need to install the `oracle-rdbms-server-11gR2-preinstall` package instead of the `oracle-validated` package:

```
[root@repositorydb ~]# yum install oracle-rdbms-server-11gR2-preinstall
```

You can also manually download the `oracle-validated` package for Red Hat Enterprise Linux 5 from the following link: `https://oss.oracle.com/el5/oracle-validated/`.

After you install `oracle-validated`, you need to set the password for the ORACLE user. Be sure that you also set up YUM and install the `oracle-validated` package for the OMS server.

Creating Oracle User and Groups

If you do not want to use the `oracle-validated` package, you can create the required groups and user manually. Log in as ROOT and run the following commands:

```
[root@repositorydb ~]# groupadd oinstall
[root@repositorydb ~]# groupadd dba
[root@repositorydb ~]# useradd -g oinstall -G dba oracle
[root@repositorydb ~]# passwd oracle
```

After the last command, enter the password for the ORACLE user.

Setting Kernel Parameters

The Oracle Database 11gR2 installer can detect and fix errors on kernel parameters, so you can run the installer and let it create scripts to set required parameters. If you want to configure kernel parameters without the help of the installer, make a backup of `/etc/sysctl.conf` and then use any text editor to edit the file so that it includes lines similar to the following:

```
fs.aio-max-nr = 1048576
fs.file-max = 6815744
kernel.shmall = 2097152
kernel.shmmax = 4536870912
kernel.shmmni = 4096
kernel.sem = 250 32000 100 128
net.ipv4.ip_local_port_range = 9000 65500
net.core.rmem_default = 262144
net.core.rmem_max = 4194304
net.core.wmem_default = 262144
net.core.wmem_max = 1048576
```

These are recommended values for Oracle Database. If any of the current values are bigger than the recommended value, use the bigger value.

■ **Tip** On 64-bit Linux systems, `kernel.shmmax` can be set to a maximum of 1 byte less than the physical memory.

Enter the following command to set the current values of the kernel parameters in /etc/sysctl.conf:

```
[root@repositorydb ~]# /sbin/sysctl -p
```

Creating Required Directories

The Oracle base directory must have at least 5GB of free disk space. Enter commands to the following to create the recommended subdirectories and set the appropriate owner, group, and permissions on them:

```
[root@repositorydb ~]# mkdir -p /u01/app/
[root@repositorydb ~]# chown -R oracle:oinstall /u01/app/
[root@repositorydb ~]# chmod -R 775 /u01/app/
```

Installing the Oracle Database Software

To install the database software, you need to download the installation files, unzip them, and then run the installer. All the steps are laid out in this section.

You can download the Oracle database software from the Oracle Technology Network (OTN). The software is available in zip files. Here's the link for Oracle Database:

```
www.oracle.com/technetwork/database/enterprise-edition/downloads/index.html
```

We also recommend downloading and installing the latest patch set of Oracle Database software from My Oracle Support.

After you download the installation files, copy them to a directory that the ORACLE user can access, and then switch to the ORACLE user and unzip them:

```
[oracle@repositorydb ~]$  unzip linux_11gR2_database_1of2.zip
[oracle@repositorydb ~]$  unzip linux_11gR2_database_2of2.zip
```

After unzipping the files, you will see a newly created directory named database. Open this directory and run the installer:

```
[oracle@repositorydb ~]$ cd database
[oracle@repositorydb ~]$ ./runInstaller
```

When the installer starts, complete the following steps:

1. The first installer step is Configure Security Updates, shown in Figure 2-1. You may prefer not to enter My Oracle Support (MOS) credentials because you will be able to follow all security updates by using Cloud Control. So deselect the I Wish to Receive Security Updates option and click Next. The installer warns about the importance of receiving critical security updates, but ignore the warning.

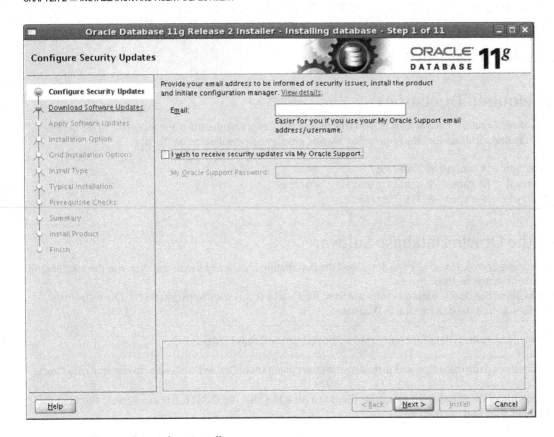

Figure 2-1. *The Oracle Database installer*

2. The Download Software Updates step, shown in Figure 2-2, appears. If your database
   server has Internet access, you should enter your MOS credentials to download and apply
   the latest patches. (In this example, we'll skip this step and apply critical patch set updates
   manually.) After selecting the appropriate option, click Next.

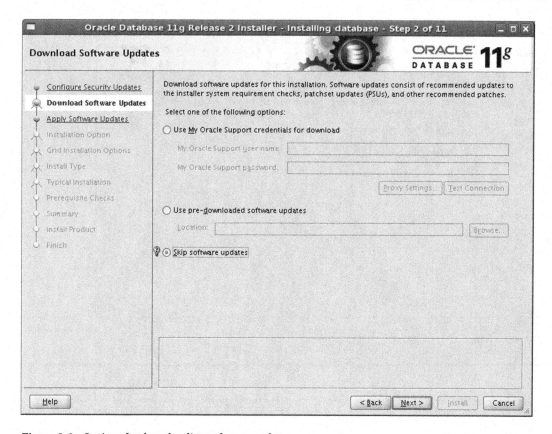

Figure 2-2. *Options for downloading software updates*

3. For the Select Installation Option step, shown in Figure 2-3, select Install Database Software Only. Then click Next.

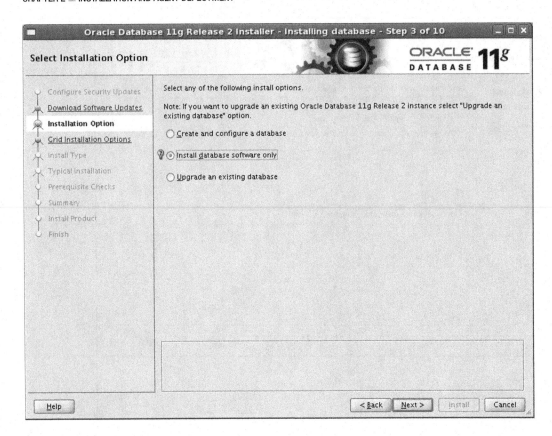

Figure 2-3. *Installation options*

4. In the Grid Installation Options step, shown in Figure 2-4, select Single Instance Database Installation. Then click Next. (If you wanted to create the OEM repository database as an Oracle RAC database, you would select the second or third option.)

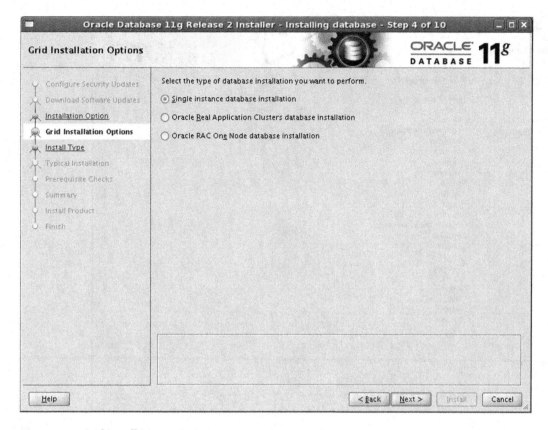

Figure 2-4. *Grid installation options*

> 5. Select English for the default language, as shown in Figure 2-5.

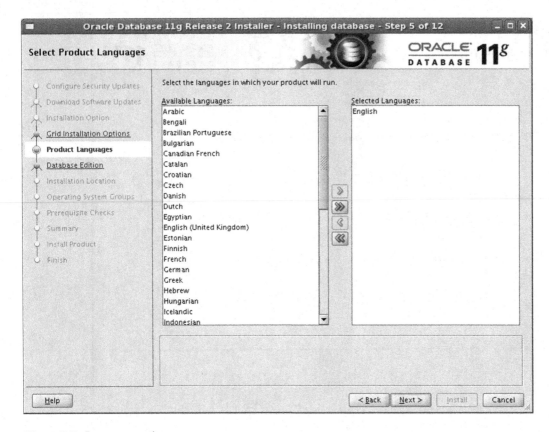

Figure 2-5. *Language options*

6. Now you're ready to select a database edition. This server will be used only as the repository database of Oracle Enterprise Manager Cloud Control, so you don't need to pay a license fee for Oracle Database. Select Enterprise Edition, as shown in Figure 2-6, and click Next.

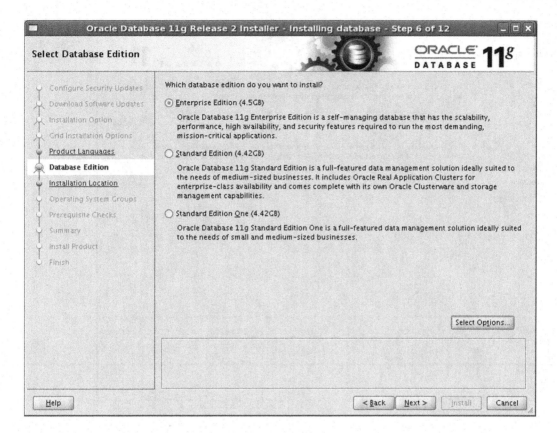

Figure 2-6. *Selecting the database edition*

7. The Specify Installation Location step appears, as shown in Figure 2-7. You created /u01/app for Oracle Database, so enter /u01/app/oracle for the Oracle base directory. The installer will determine the Oracle home according to the Optimal Flexible Architecture (OFA). Out-of-place upgrades have always been a best-practice recommendation, but starting with Oracle Database 11.2.0.2, patch set installations are all out of place by default. So you may prefer to enter the full version in the path, such as /u01/app/oracle/product/11.2.0.3/dbhome_1.

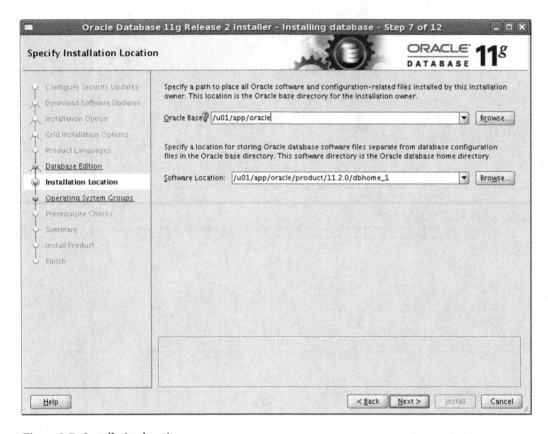

Figure 2-7. *Installation location*

8. Enter (or just accept) the Inventory Directory and click Next, as shown in Figure 2-8.

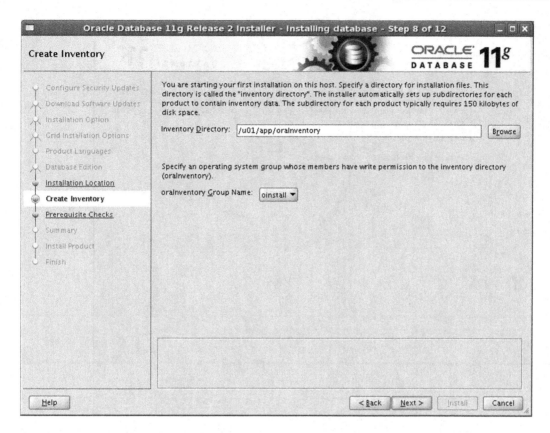

Figure 2-8. *Creating the inventory directory*

9. For the Privileged Operating System Groups step, shown in Figure 2-9, accept the defaults and click Next. Oracle checks the prerequisites in the following step. If it doesn't find any errors, the installer advances to the Summary step.

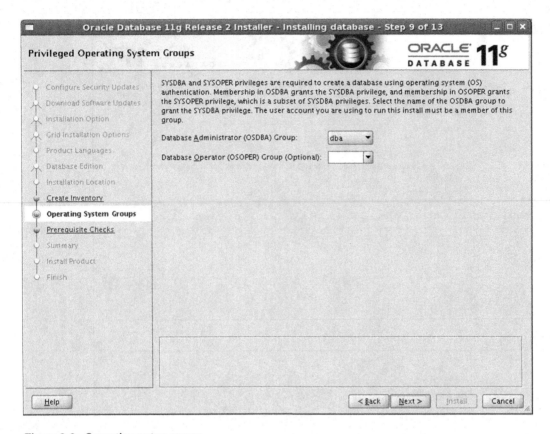

Figure 2-9. *Operating system groups*

10. Review the Summary screen, shown in Figure 2-10. Click the Install button if the information onscreen seems OK.

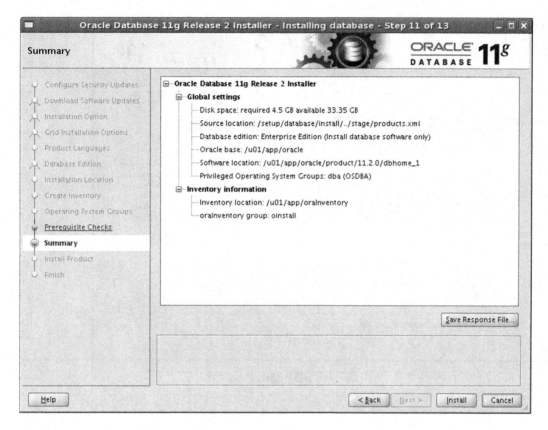

Figure 2-10. *Summary*

11. At the end of the installation, you need to execute some configuration scripts. Log in as ROOT to the server in another terminal session and run the scripts. Then click OK to finish the installation (see Figure 2-11).

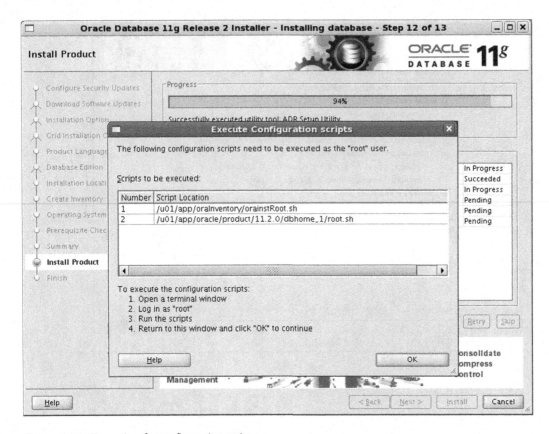

Figure 2-11. *Executing the configuration scripts*

Creating the Repository Database

Now that you have installed the Oracle Database software, you will create the management repository database. Connect to the repository server, set the Oracle home, and run dbca:

```
[oracle@repositorydb ~]$ . oraenv
ORACLE_SID = [oracle] ? oracle
ORACLE_HOME = [/home/oracle] ? /u01/app/oracle/product/11.2.0/dbhome_1
The Oracle base has been set to /u01/app/oracle
[oracle@repositorydb ~]$ dbca
```

When you run dbca, the Database Configuration Assistant Welcome screen appears. Click Next to pass the screen and then complete the following steps:

1. For the Operations step, shown in Figure 2-12, select Create a Database and then click Next.

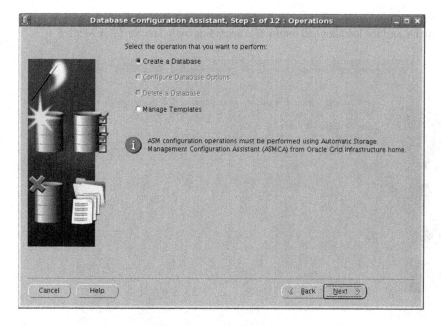

Figure 2-12. *Database Configuration Assistant*

2. For the Database Templates step, shown in Figure 2-13, you can select General Purpose or Custom Database. We recommend that you select Custom Database because it will prevent the installation of some SYSMAN objects in the database. Otherwise, you have to remove these objects from the database before you can use it as the management repository database. Click Next.

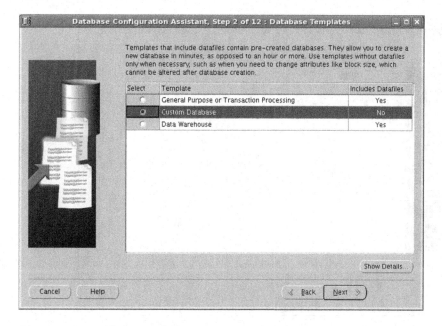

Figure 2-13. *Database templates*

3. The Database Identification step appears, as shown in Figure 2-14. Enter the global database name, and the installer will set the SID according to that name. Click Next.

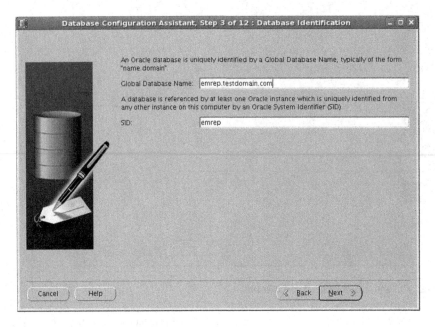

Figure 2-14. *Database identification*

4. For the Management Options step, shown in Figure 2-15, deselect Configure Enterprise Manager and then click Next.

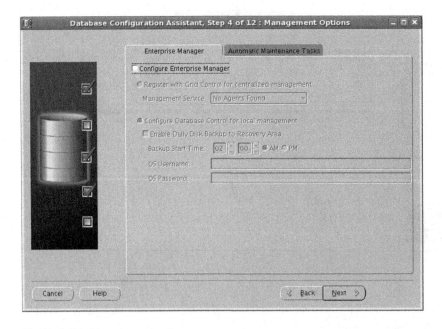

Figure 2-15. *Management options*

5. Enter the passwords for SYS and SYSTEM users in the Database Credentials step, shown in Figure 2-16, and then click Next. Oracle recommends entering a password with a minimum of eight characters, including at least one uppercase letter, one lowercase letter, and one digit.

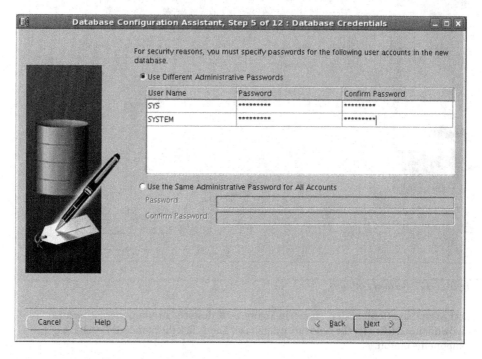

Figure 2-16. *Database credentials*

6. Accept the defaults for the database file locations and click Next.

7. You can enable archiving now in the Recovery Configuration step, shown in Figure 2-17, or you can enable it later. Set the Fast Recovery Area (FRA) destination and size, and then click Next.

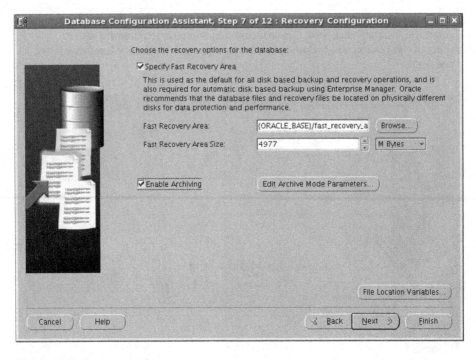

Figure 2-17. *Recovery options*

8. For the Database Content step, shown in Figure 2-18, deselect all components, because you do not need them for the repository database. Then click the Standard Database Components button.

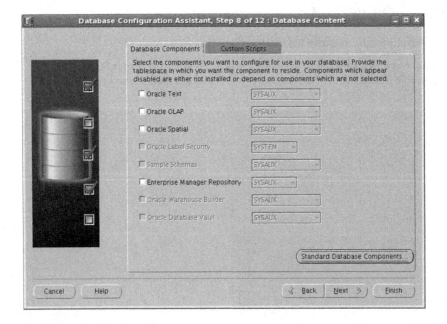

Figure 2-18. *Database content*

9. In the Standard Database Components dialog box, deselect Oracle Multimedia and Oracle
    Application Express, as shown in Figure 2-19. Click OK to close the dialog box and then
    click Next to advance to the next step.

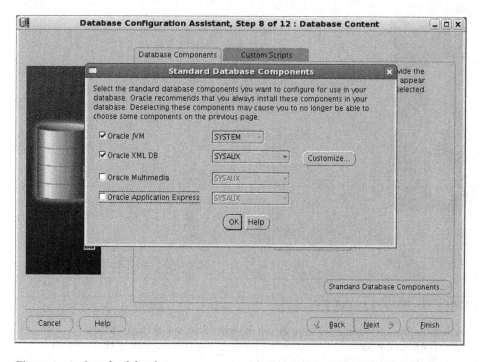

Figure 2-19. *Standard database components*

10. While setting the memory (see Figure 2-20), ensure that total memory (SGA_max_size +
    PGA_aggregate_target) set for the database will not exceed 75 percent of the total
    physical memory of the system. Otherwise, the system will start using the swap device. We
    recommendthat you do not use the memory_target parameter with Enterprise Manager.
    Next click the Character Sets tab.

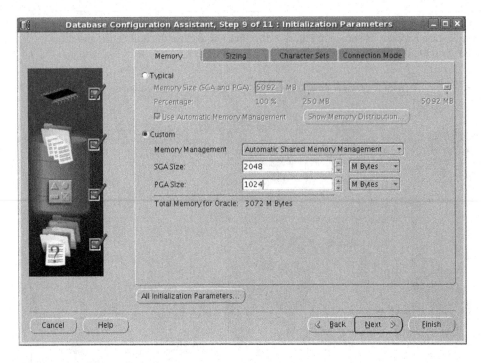

Figure 2-20. *Memory parameters*

11. For the Initialization Parameters step, shown in Figure 2-21, select Use Unicode (AL32UTF8). Set the National Character Set option to any UTF-supported character set, such as AL16UTF16 or UTF8. Then click Next.

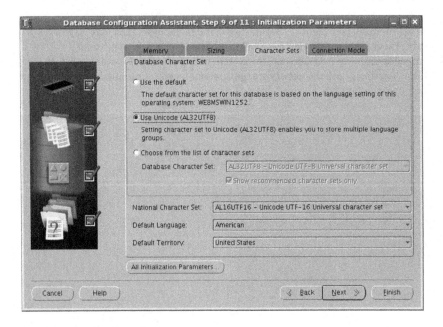

Figure 2-21. *Database character set*

12. The Database Storage step appears, as shown in Figure 2-22. The management repository's redo log file size should be a minimum of 300MB. Set the File Size option to 300MB for all three redo log groups, and then click Next.

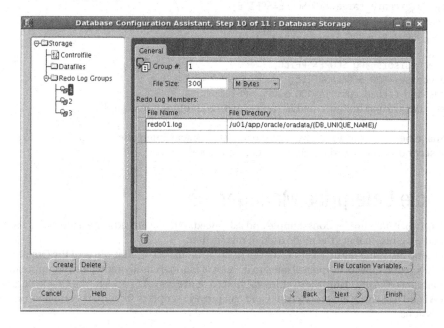

Figure 2-22. *Database storage*

13. Click the Finish button to review the configuration and create the database (see Figure 2-23).

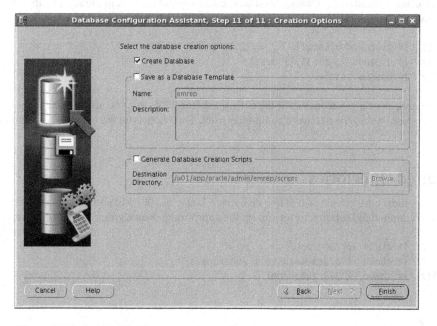

Figure 2-23. *Creation options*

After you create the database, connect to it by using SQL*Plus, run the following commands, and then restart the database:

```
ALTER SYSTEM SET pga_aggregate_target=1G SCOPE=SPFILE;
ALTER SYSTEM SET shared_pool_size=600M SCOPE=SPFILE;
ALTER SYSTEM SET job_queue_processes=20 SCOPE=SPFILE;
ALTER SYSTEM SET log_buffer=10485760 SCOPE=SPFILE;
ALTER SYSTEM SET open_cursors=300 SCOPE=SPFILE;
ALTER SYSTEM SET processes=500 SCOPE=SPFILE;
ALTER SYSTEM SET session_cached_cursors=200 SCOPE=SPFILE;
EXEC dbms_auto_task_admin.disable('auto optimizer stats collection',null,null);
```

Now that the management repository is ready, it's time to install Oracle Enterprise Manager. You'll do the rest of the operation on your second server named cloudcontrol12.testdomain.com.

Installing Oracle Enterprise Manager 12c

Enterprise Manager has two installation options: Simple and Advanced. When using advanced mode, it's possible to select the preconfigured plug-ins, so that's the mode used in this section.

We highly recommend installing the oracle-validated package on the server that will host the Oracle Management Service. If you don't install it, you will need to do a lot of manual configuration, including creating a user and setting kernel parameters. Despite using the oracle-validated or preinstall package, the Oracle Enterprise Manager Installation Wizard will check the prerequisites and can provide scripts to fix kernel parameters (and missing libraries) if it finds omissions.

Creating the Oracle User and Groups

If you didn't install the oracle-validated package, you should create the ORACLE user manually. Log in as the ROOT user and issue the following commands:

```
[root@cloudcontrol12 ~]# groupadd oinstall
[root@cloudcontrol12 ~]# useradd -g oinstall oracle
[root@cloudcontrol12 ~]# passwd oracle
```

After the last command, enter a password for the ORACLE user. As the ROOT user, you are allowed to choose any password, even one that doesn't obey the password complexity rules. The system will warn if you do so, but will let you proceed.

Creating Required Directories

The Oracle base directory must have at least 5GB of free disk space. Log in as ROOT and enter commands similar to the following to create the recommended subdirectories and set the appropriate owner, group, and permissions on them:

```
[root@cloudcontrol12 ~]# mkdir -p /u01/app/
[root@cloudcontrol12 ~]# chown -R oracle:oinstall /u01/app/
[root@cloudcontrol12 ~]# chmod -R 775 /u01/app/
```

Installing Oracle Enterprise Manager

You can download the Enterprise Manager Cloud Control software from OTN. The software is available in zip files. Here's the link for Oracle Enterprise Manager:

www.oracle.com/technetwork/oem/enterprise-manager/overview/index.html

After you download the installation files, copy them to a directory that the ORACLE user can access, and then switch to the ORACLE user and unzip them:

```
[oracle@cloudcontrol12 ~]$ unzip em12_linux64_disk1of2.zip -d cloudsetup
[oracle@cloudcontrol12 ~]$ unzip em12_linux64_disk2of2.zip -d cloudsetup
```

Make sure that no environmental variable related to the database (ORACLE_HOME, ORACLE_SID, or ORACLE_BASE) is set prior to installation. Oracle also recommends to set umask to 022. Change the directory to cloudsetup and run the installer:

```
[oracle@cloudcontrol12 ~]$ umask 022
[oracle@cloudcontrol12 ~]$ cd cloudsetup
[oracle@cloudcontrol12 ~]$ ./runInstaller
```

When the Enterprise Manager installer starts, follow these steps:

1. For the My Oracle Support Details step, shown in Figure 2-24, enter your credentials if you want to receive security updates. Then click Next.

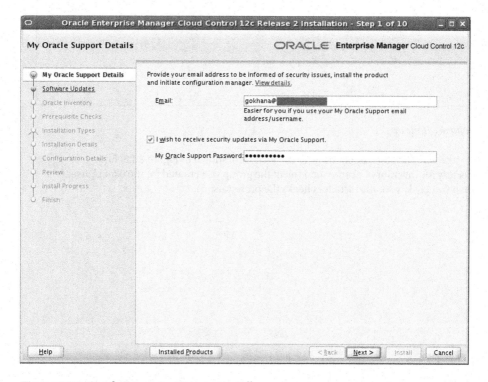

Figure 2-24. *Oracle Enterprise Manager installer*

2. In the next step, enter your My Oracle Support credentials (again) and then click Search for Updates. In this example, you can see that a patch is available (see Figure 2-25). You may see different patches in your situation. Click Next and then click OK to accept the warning about restarting the installer.

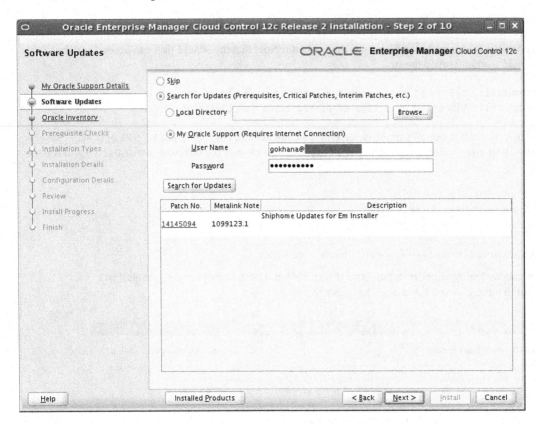

Figure 2-25. *Software updates*

3. After the installer restarts, continue to the next step, shown in Figure 2-26. Enter a directory for Inventory Location and select the group you created for the ORACLE user. When you click Next, the installer checks the prerequisites.

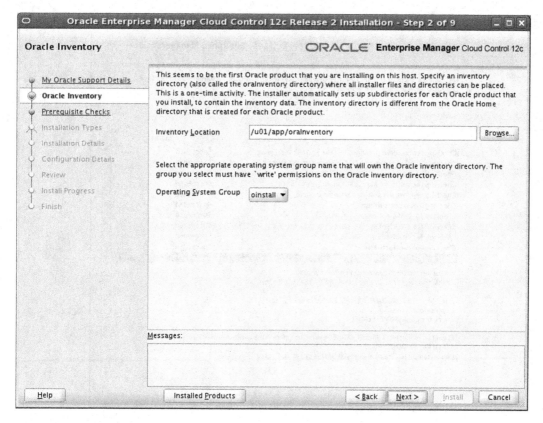

Figure 2-26. *Oracle inventory*

4. Make sure that all prerequisite checks have the status Succeeded, as shown in Figure 2-27, and then click Next.

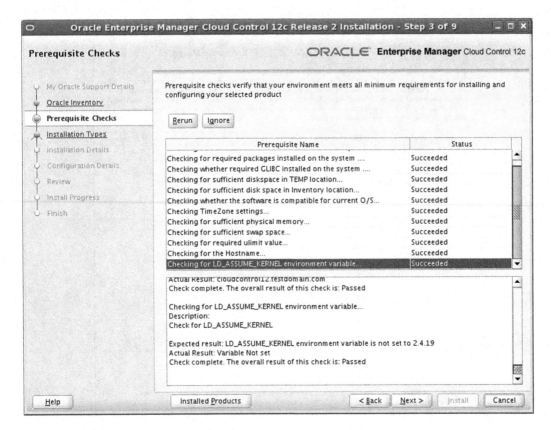

Figure 2-27. *Prerequisites check*

5. Select Create a New Enterprise Manager System and then select Advanced (see Figure 2-28). Click Next.

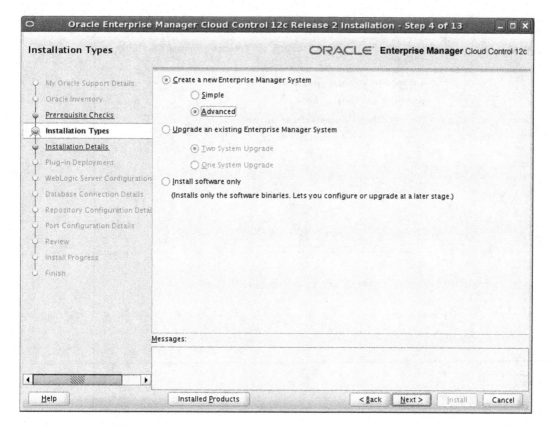

Figure 2-28. *Installation types*

6. For the Installation Details step, shown in Figure 2-29, enter the Middleware Home Location as /u01/app/Middleware, the Agent Base Directory as /u01/app/agent, and your Host Name. Then click Next.

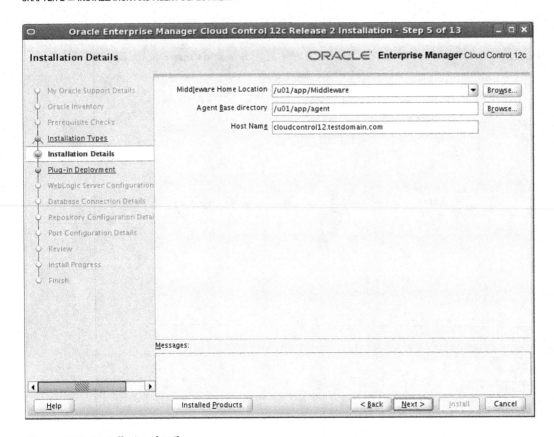

Figure 2-29. *Installation details*

7. In the Plug-in Deployment step, shown in Figure 2-30, select the management plug-ins you want to configure. It's also possible to add or remove the management plug-ins after you install Enterprise Manager. Click Next.

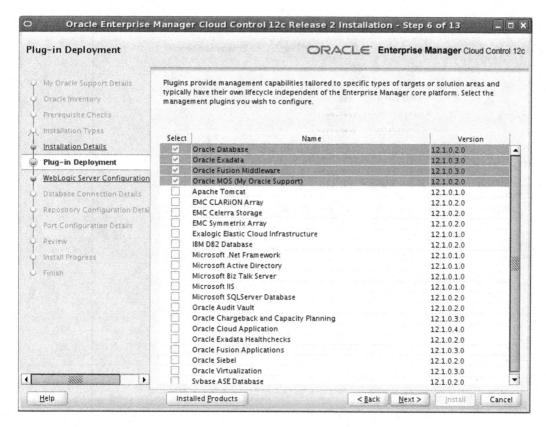

Figure 2-30. *Plug-in deployment*

8. The Oracle Management Service is the main application of the Enterprise Manager and it needs a WebLogic application server to run. In the next step, shown in Figure 2-31, choose a username and password for the WebLogic server and a password for the node manager. Please keep this information safe. It can be required to troubleshoot problems related to WebLogic. Click Next.

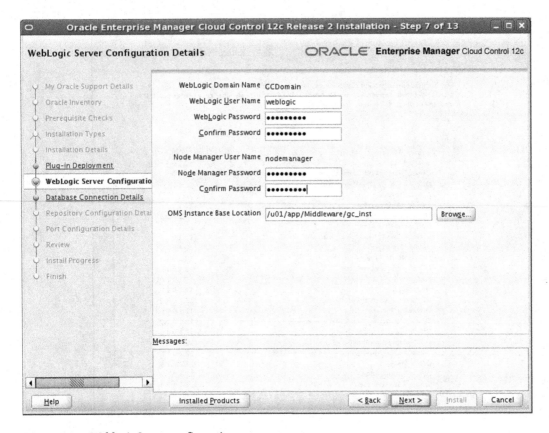

Figure 2-31. *Weblogic Server configuration*

9. Enter the connection info of the repository database and select the deployment size (see Figure 2-32). The installer checks the database settings according to the deployment size. Click Next.

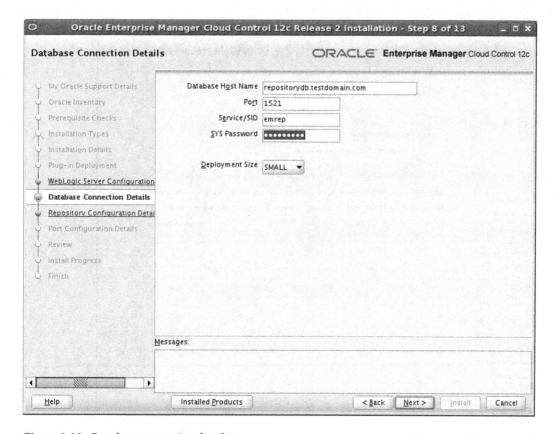

Figure 2-32. *Database connection details*

10. The installer creates the required database user and the tablespaces in the repository database. For the Repository Configuration Details step, shown in Figure 2-33, enter a password for the SYSMAN user, modify the directory locations if needed, and enter a registration password that will be used for securing agent communications. Click Next.

■ **Note** If you are configuring the management repository on a database that uses Oracle Automatic Storage Management (ASM) for storage, then when you specify the data file location, only the disk group is used for creating the tablespaces. For example, if you specify +DATA/mgmt.dbf, only +DATA is used for creating the tablespaces on ASM, and the exact location of the data file on the disk group is decided by Oracle Managed Files.

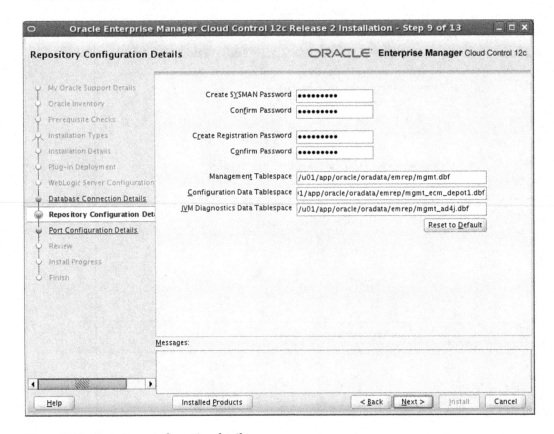

Figure 2-33. *Repository configuration details*

11. Check the ports that will be allocated for the Oracle Enterprise Manager (see Figure 2-34). You can modify them, but keep in mind that the port numbers must be higher than 1024 and lower than 65535.

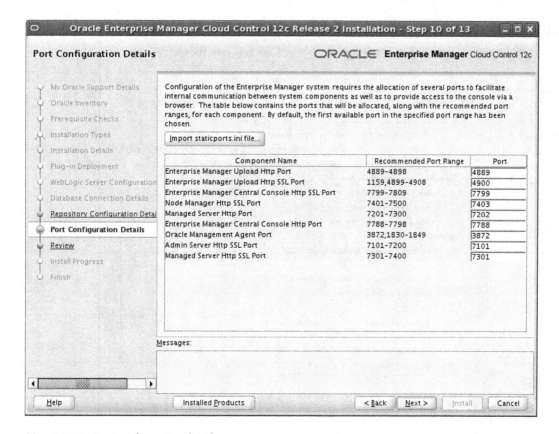

Figure 2-34. *Port configuration details*

12. Review the configuration (see Figure 2-35). When satisfied with the configuration, click Install to start the installation.

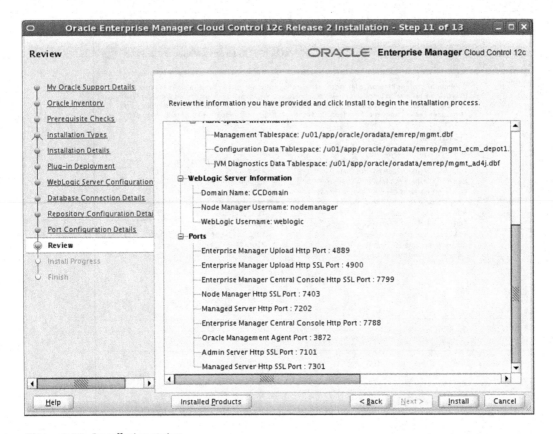

Figure 2-35. *Installation review*

13. At the end of the installation, you need to execute some configuration scripts. Log in as ROOT to the server in another terminal session and run the scripts (see Figure 2-36). Then click OK to finish the installation.

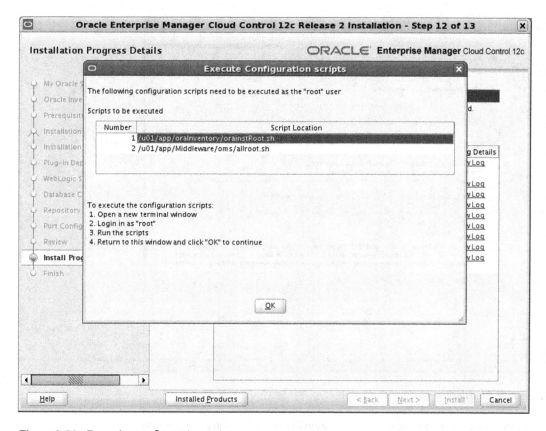

Figure 2-36. Executing configuration scripts

14. Review the information, as shown in Figure 2-37, and click Close to complete the Oracle Enterprise Manager Cloud Control 12c installation.

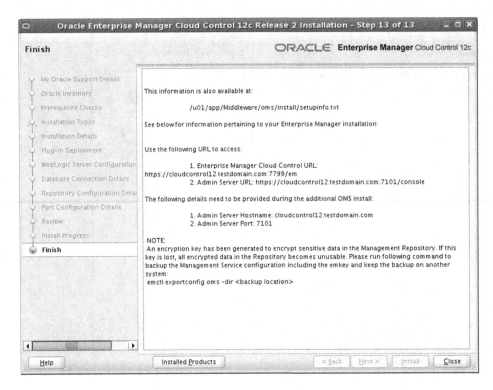

Figure 2-37. *Installation completed*

15.   You now can log in to Enterprise Manager Cloud Control, as shown in Figure 2-38.

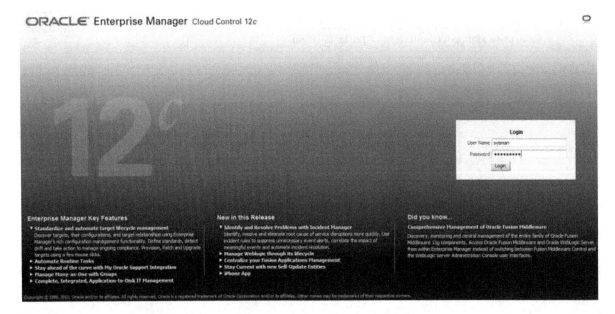

Figure 2-38. *Login screen of Oracle Enterprise Manager*

Deploying Management Agents

The Oracle Management Agent is one of the core components of Enterprise Manager Cloud Control. If you want to monitor a target (such as a database or an application server) running on a host, you need to convert the host to a managed host by deploying a management agent. Then you can discover the targets running on that host and add them to the Enterprise Manager system.

There are several ways to deploy agents:

- Using the Add Host Targets Wizard
- Using an RPM file
- Using the `AgentPull` script
- Using the `agentDeploy` script

The following sections describe these options.

Using the Add Host Targets Wizard

Using the Add Host Targets Wizard is the easiest way to deploy a management agent. It's especially useful for the mass-deployment of management agents. Oracle also recommends using this wizard. Follow these steps:

1. Log in to the Enterprise Manager Cloud Control console.

2. From the Setup menu, choose Add Target ➤ Add Targets Manually, as shown in Figure 2-39.

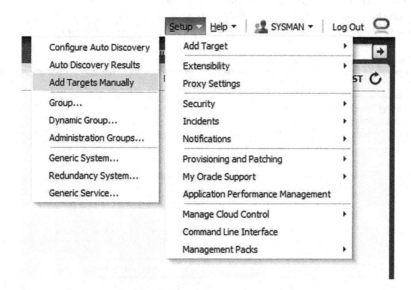

***Figure 2-39.** Add Hosts Wizard*

3. Select the Add Host Targets radio button and then click the Add Host button, as shown in Figure 2-40.

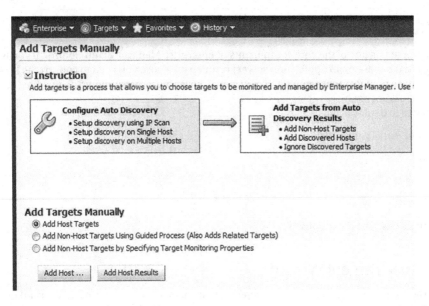

Figure 2-40. *Adding targets manually*

4. To be able to monitor the repository database, deploy a management agent to the
    repositorydb.testdomain.com server. Click the Add button with the plus sign, enter
    the hostname, and then select the OS of the target server. For this example, we installed
    Enterprise Manager on Linux x64 and didn't download any additional agent software, so
    for now, we can deploy agents only for Linux 64-bit servers (see Figure 2-41). Click Next.

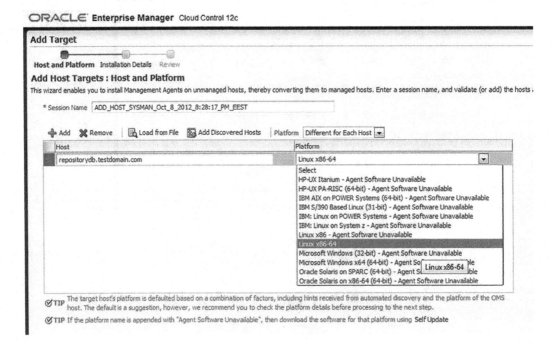

Figure 2-41. *Adding host targets*

5. Enter the directory where the agent software will be installed. Click the blue plus sign next to the Named Credential option to add a credential for the host. In the Create New Named Credential dialog box that displays, give the credential a meaningful name and then click OK to save it (see Figure 2-42).

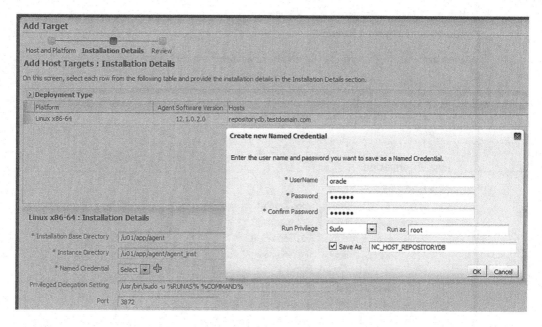

Figure 2-42. *Creating a new named credential*

6. Using named credentials provides an additional layer of security. An administrator can create named credentials for operators so they can use the login information without knowing the actual username and password associated with it. Click Next to review the configuration details, shown in Figure 2-43.

■ **Tip** Oracle recommends configuring privilege delegation (i.e., giving sudo permission to the management agent user).

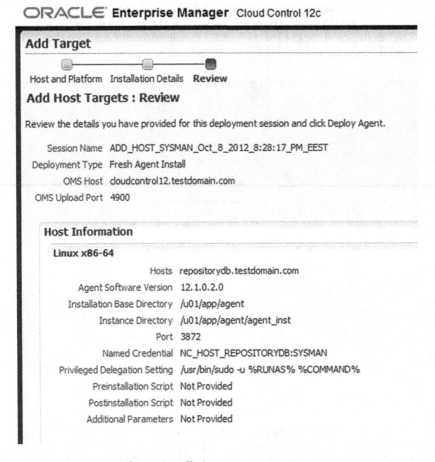

Figure 2-43. *Review of agent installation*

7. Click the Deploy Agent button in the upper right of the console to start the deployment process.

Agent deployment is completed (see Figure 2-44). Now you can add nonhost targets that are on this server (such as Oracle Database) to the Enterprise Manager system.

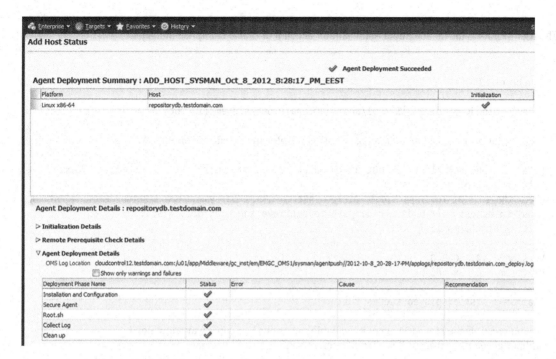

Figure 2-44. *Agent deployment summary*

As mentioned before, the Add Host Targets Wizard is the recommended way to deploy agents. However, if your target hosts do not have SSH service enabled, or if you want to delegate agent installation to system administrators, you may use other methods such as creating an RPM package of agents, or using AgentPull or agentDeploy scripts.

Using RPM

This section outlines the process for deploying the agent via RPM. Follow these steps:

1. To be able to create RPM packages, you need to create the directory /usr/lib/oracle on the OMS server, if it doesn't exist already. Log in as the ROOT user and run the following commands:

    ```
    [root@cloudcontrol12 ~]# mkdir /usr/lib/oracle
    [root@cloudcontrol12 ~]# chmod 777 /usr/lib/oracle
    ```

2. Install the rpm-build package on the OMS host:

    ```
    [root@cloudcontrol12 ~]# yum install rpm-build
    ```

3. Log in to the OMS host as the ORACLE user, and log in to the OMS using EMCLI:

    ```
    [oracle@cloudcontrol12 ~]$ /u01/app/Middleware/oms/bin/emcli login -username=sysman
    ```

■ **Note** The user SYSMAN is the default Super Administrator account of Oracle Enterprise Manager.

4. Synchronize EMCLI:

```
[oracle@cloudcontrol12 ~]$ /u01/app/Middleware/oms/bin/emcli sync
```

5. List the platforms for which the management agent software is available on the OMS host:

```
[oracle@cloudcontrol12 ~]$ /u01/app/Middleware/oms/bin/emcli get_supported_platforms
Getting list of platforms ...
Check the logs at /u01/app/Middleware/gc_inst/em/EMGC_OMS1/sysman/emcli/setup/.emcli/agent.log
About to access self-update code path to retrieve the platforms list..
Getting Platforms list  ...
------------------------------------------------
Version = 12.1.0.2.0
Platform = Linux x86-64
------------------------------------------------
Platforms list displayed successfully.
```

As you see, only the Linux x64 agent is available right now. You can always download additional agents by using the Self Update screen of Enterprise Manager.

6. Issue the following command to create and download the RPM file of the management agent from the Oracle Software Library to a directory on the OMS host:

```
[oracle@cloudcontrol12 ~]$ /u01/app/Middleware/oms/bin/emcli get_agentimage_rpm \
-destination=/home/oracle -platform="Linux x86-64" -version=12.1.0.2.0
...
Agent Image copied successfully...
Creation of RPM started...
RPM creation successful.
Agent image to rpm conversion completed successfully
```

7. You can copy the RPM put in the /home/oracle directory on the OMS server to the target system in order to deploy the agent. We assume that you have already created a user for the agent on the target system. If you installed the oracle-validated package on the target system, the ORACLE user and OINSTALL group are already created.

```
[oracle@cloudcontrol12 ~]$ scp oracle-agt-12.1.0.2.0-1.0.x86_64.rpm \
oracle@target.testdomain.com:/home/oracle/
oracle@target.testdomain.com's password:
oracle-agt-12.1.0.2.0-1.0.x86_64.rpm          59%  133MB  15.4MB/s  00:05 ETA
```

8. Log in as ROOT on the target system and install the RPM:

```
[root@target ~]# cd /home/oracle
[root@target ~]# rpm -i oracle-agt-12.1.0.2.0-1.0.x86_64.rpm
```

9. Now you need to edit the /usr/lib/oracle/agent/agent.properties file according to
    your Enterprise Manager installation and run /etc/init.d/oracle-agt:

```
[root@target ~]# vi /usr/lib/oracle/agent/agent.properties
OMS_HOST=cloudcontrol12.testdomain.com
OMS_PORT=7799
AGENT_REGISTRATION_PASSWORD=<registration_password>
AGENT_USERNAME=oracle
AGENT_GROUP=oinstall
AGENT_PORT=3872
ORACLE_HOSTNAME=target.testdomain.com
[root@target ~]# /etc/init.d/oracle-agt RESPONSE_FILE=/usr/lib/oracle/agent/agent.properties
```

10. Check whether the agent is up:

```
[oracle@target ~]$ /usr/lib/oracle/agent/core/12.1.0.2.0/bin/emctl status agent
Oracle Enterprise Manager Cloud Control 12c Release 2
Copyright (c) 1996, 2012 Oracle Corporation.  All rights reserved.
---------------------------------------------------------------
Agent Version      : 12.1.0.2.0
OMS Version        : 12.1.0.2.0
Protocol Version   : 12.1.0.1.0
Agent Home         : /usr/lib/oracle/agent/agent_inst
Agent Binaries     : /usr/lib/oracle/agent/core/12.1.0.2.0
Agent Process ID   : 5323
Parent Process ID  : 5283
Agent URL          : https://target.testdomain.com:3872/emd/main/
Repository URL     : https://cloudcontrol12.testdomain.com:4900/empbs/upload
Started at         : 2012-10-12 03:44:47
Started by user    : oracle
Last Reload        : (none)
Last successful upload                       : 2012-10-12 03:47:06
Last attempted upload                        : 2012-10-12 03:47:06
Total Megabytes of XML files uploaded so far : 0.01
Number of XML files pending upload           : 0
Size of XML files pending upload(MB)         : 0
Available disk space on upload filesystem    : 91.52%
Collection Status                            : Collections enabled
Heartbeat Status                             : Ok
Last attempted heartbeat to OMS              : 2012-10-12 03:47:00
Last successful heartbeat to OMS             : 2012-10-12 03:47:00
Next scheduled heartbeat to OMS              : 2012-10-12 03:48:00


---------------------------------------------------------------
Agent is Running and Ready
```

As you see, the agent is deployed and running successfully.

Using the AgentPull Script

To use the `AgentPull` script, follow these steps:

1. You need to create a user for the management agent, create the required directories, and give permission to the new management agent user. In this example, you will create the ORACLE user, so log in as ROOT and run the following commands:

   ```
   [root@target ~]# groupadd oinstall
   [root@target ~]# groupadd dba
   [root@target ~]# useradd -g oinstall -G dba oracle
   [root@target ~]# passwd oracle
   [root@target ~]# mkdir -p /u01/agent
   [root@target ~]# chown -R oracle:oinstall /u01/agent
   ```

   If there's already an ORACLE user (and you want to use it for the management agent), you don't need to drop and re-create it.

2. After you create the mandatory directories, open an X Window session as the ORACLE (management agent) user and download the `AgentPull` script from the OMS.

   If the target host runs on a Unix box, access the following URL from the host:

   ```
   https://<OMS_HOST>:<OMS_PORT>/em/install/getAgentImage
   ```

   For example:

   ```
   https://cloudcontrol12.testdomain.com:7799/em/install/getAgentImage
   ```

   If the destination host runs on Microsoft Windows, access the following URL from the host, which adds `?script=bat` to the end of the previous URL:

   ```
   https://cloudcontrol12.testdomain.com:7799/em/install/getAgentImage?script=bat
   ```

3. It's also possible to download the `AgentPull.sh` script with `curl` or `wget`. To download the script using `wget`, issue the following commands. Notice that you download `getAgentImage`, and then change the name to `AgentPull.sh`.

   ```
   [root@target ~]# wget https://cloudcontrol12.testdomain.com:7799/em/install/getAgentImage
   --no-check-certificate
   [root@target ~]# mv getAgentImage AgentPull.sh
   ```

   To download via `curl`, issue the following command:

   ```
   [root@target ~]# curl "https://cloudcontrol12.testdomain.com:7799/em/install/getAgentImage"
   --insecure -o agentPull.sh
   ```

■ **Note** The preceding wget and curl examples actually download a file named `getAgentImage`. The file is then renamed after the download (`wget`) or as part of the downlad process (`curl`). The file is renamed to `AgentPull.sh`.

---

4. Make the AgentPull.sh script executable:

    ```
    [oracle@target ~]$ chmod +x AgentPull.sh
    ```

5. Check available platforms:

    ```
    [oracle@target ~]$ ./AgentPull.sh -showPlatforms
    Platforms       Version
    Linux x86-64    12.1.0.2.0
    ```

6. To use the AgentPull script, create a response file—for example, agent.rsp (in any location on the destination host, preferably in the same directory as the AgentPull script):

    ```
    [oracle@target ~]$ vi agent.rsp
    LOGIN_USER=sysman
    LOGIN_PASSWORD=<sysman_password>
    PLATFORM="Linux x86-64"
    VERSION=12.1.0.2.0
    AGENT_REGISTRATION_PASSWORD=<registration_password>
    ```

7. Then run the AgentPull script:

    ```
    [oracle@target ~]$ ./AgentPull.sh RSPFILE_LOC=/home/oracle/agent.rsp AGENT_BASE_DIR=/u01/agent
    ```

8. After the script successfully completes, open a new terminal window, log in as ROOT, and run the configuration scripts (the locations of the scripts are written in the output of AgentPull.sh):

    ```
    [root@target ~]# /u01/agent/core/12.1.0.2.0/root.sh
    Finished product-specific root actions.
    /etc exist
    Finished product-specific root actions.
    [root@target ~]# /u01/app/oraInventory/orainstRoot.sh
    Changing permissions of /u01/app/oraInventory
    Adding read,write permissions for group,Removing read,write,execute permissions for world.
    Changing groupname of /u01/app/oraInventory to oinstall.
    The execution of the script is complete
    ```

After you execute the script, agent deployment is completed.

Using the agentDeploy Script

To deploy a management agent by using the agentDeploy script, follow these steps:

1. Create a user for the management agent, create the required directories, and give permission to the management agent user. We assume that you are creating the ORACLE user, so log in as ROOT and run the following commands:

    ```
    [root@target ~]# groupadd oinstall
    [root@target ~]# groupadd dba
    [root@target ~]# useradd -g oinstall -G dba oracle
    [root@target ~]# passwd oracle
    ```

```
[root@target ~]# mkdir -p /u01/agent
[root@target ~]# chown -R oracle:oinstall /u01/agent
```

If there's an already existing ORACLE user (and you want to use it for the management agent), you don't need to drop and re-create it.

2.   Log in to the OMS host as the ORACLE user, and log in to OEM using EMCLI:

```
[oracle@cloudcontrol12 ~]$ /u01/app/Middleware/oms/bin/emcli login -username=sysman
```

3.   Synchronize EMCLI:

```
[oracle@cloudcontrol12 ~]$ /u01/app/Middleware/oms/bin/emcli sync
```

4.   List the platforms for which the management agent software is available on the OMS host:

```
[oracle@cloudcontrol12 ~]$ /u01/app/Middleware/oms/bin/emcli get_supported_platforms
Getting list of platforms ...
Check the logs at /u01/app/Middleware/gc_inst/em/EMGC_OMS1/sysman/emcli/setup/.emcli/agent.log
About to access self-update code path to retrieve the platforms list..
Getting Platforms list ...
------------------------------------------------
Version = 12.1.0.2.0
Platform = Linux x86-64
------------------------------------------------
Platforms list displayed successfully.
```

5.   Download the management agent software to a directory on the OMS host:

```
[oracle@cloudcontrol12 ~]$ /u01/app/Middleware/oms/bin/emcli get_agentimage
-destination=/home/oracle -platform="Linux x86-64" -version=12.1.0.2.0
```

6.   The command downloads the core management agent software to the destination directory (/home/oracle). For example, for Linux x86-64, you will see the file 12.1.0.2.0_AgentCore_226.zip.

7.   Transfer this file to the target server:

```
[oracle@cloudcontrol12 ~]$ scp 12.1.0.2.0_AgentCore_226.zip \
 oracle@target.testdomain.com:/home/oracle/
```

8.   Log in to the target server and extract the zip file:

```
[oracle@target ~]$ unzip 12.1.0.2.0_AgentCore_226.zip -d agentsetup
Archive:  12.1.0.2.0_AgentCore_226.zip
  inflating: agentsetup/unzip
  inflating: agentsetup/agentDeploy.sh
  inflating: agentsetup/agentimage.properties
  inflating: agentsetup/agent.rsp
 extracting: agentsetup/agentcoreimage.zip
 extracting: agentsetup/12.1.0.2.0_PluginsOneoffs_226.zip
```

9. Enter the agentsetup directory and edit the agent response file:

    ```
    [oracle@target ~]$ cd agentsetup/
    [oracle@target agentsetup]$ vi agent.rsp
    ```

10. Enter the following values:

    ```
    OMS_HOST=cloudcontrol12.testdomain.com
    EM_UPLOAD_PORT=4900
    AGENT_REGISTRATION_PASSWORD=<registration_password>
    AGENT_INSTANCE_HOME=/u01/agent
    AGENT_PORT=3872
    b_startAgent=true
    ORACLE_HOSTNAME=target.testdomain.com
    s_agentHomeName="agent12gR2"
    ```

11. Run the agentDeploy.sh script to deploy the agent:

    ```
    ./agentDeploy.sh RESPONSE_FILE=/home/oracle/agentsetup/agent.rsp AGENT_BASE_DIR=/u01/agent
    ```

12. After the script successfully completes, open a new terminal window, log in as ROOT, and run the configuration script (the location of the script is written in the output of agentDeploy.sh):

    ```
    [root@target ~]#  /u01/agent/core/12.1.0.2.0/root.sh
    Finished product-specific root actions.
    /etc exist
    Finished product-specific root actions.
    ```

13. Check the agent's status:

    ```
    [oracle@target agentsetup]$ /u01/agent/core/12.1.0.2.0/bin/emctl status agent
    Oracle Enterprise Manager Cloud Control 12c Release 2
    Copyright (c) 1996, 2012 Oracle Corporation.  All rights reserved.
    ---------------------------------------------------------------
    Agent Version     : 12.1.0.2.0
    OMS Version       : 12.1.0.2.0
    Protocol Version  : 12.1.0.1.0
    Agent Home        : /u01/agent
    Agent Binaries    : /u01/agent/core/12.1.0.2.0
    Agent Process ID  : 14620
    Parent Process ID : 14578
    Agent URL         : https://target.testdomain.com:3872/emd/main/
    Repository URL    : https://cloudcontrol12.testdomain.com:4900/empbs/upload
    Started at        : 2012-10-12 06:10:12
    Started by user   : oracle
    Last Reload       : (none)
    Last successful upload                       : 2012-10-12 06:12:57
    Last attempted upload                        : 2012-10-12 06:12:57
    Total Megabytes of XML files uploaded so far : 0.01
    Number of XML files pending upload           : 0
    ```

```
Size of XML files pending upload(MB)      : 0
Available disk space on upload filesystem : 89.15%
Collection Status                         : Collections enabled
Heartbeat Status                          : Ok
Last attempted heartbeat to OMS           : 2012-10-12 06:13:26
Last successful heartbeat to OMS          : 2012-10-12 06:13:26
Next scheduled heartbeat to OMS           : 2012-10-12 06:14:26


---------------------------------------------------------------
Agent is Running and Ready
```

So the agent is installed and running.

Summary

In this chapter, you learned how to install the management repository and Oracle Enterprise Manager Cloud Control. You also learned various agent deployment methods. After deploying agents, you may discover targets (such as Oracle Database, Middleware, and applications) on hosts.

CHAPTER 3

Management of the OMS and Repository

by Pete Sharman

Now that we've covered the options for installing Enterprise Manager Cloud Control 12c, including agent deployment, it's time to look at what you need to do to maintain your EM infrastructure. As discussed in Chapter 1, Enterprise Manager is composed of three main moving parts: the Oracle Management Agent, Oracle Management Service, and Oracle Management Repository. Let's examine each in turn.

Oracle Management Agent

Agent management is one area that has become much more straightforward with the 12c release of Enterprise Manager. In previous releases, agent management had to be performed from the command line, through the EMCTL or EMCLI tools. Although in the 12c release you can still use the command line interfaces to manage your agents, much of the management can also be done through the Cloud Control console. This section covers the use of the console first, and then comes back to the command-line interfaces.

Agent Management with the Console

To access the agent management functionality from the Cloud Control console, from the Setup menu choose Manage Cloud Control ➤ Agents, as shown in Figure 3-1.

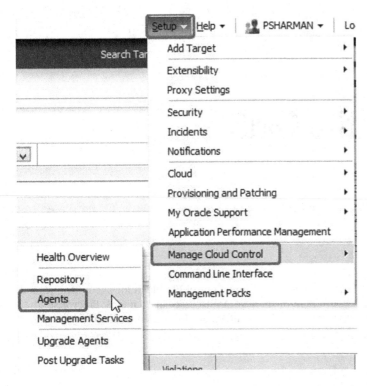

Figure 3-1. *Selecting agent management in the Cloud Control console*

This takes you to the Agents page, shown in Figure 3-2. By default, this page shows you the status of all the agents in your system, but you can select an option to show just those agents that are up, under blackout, unreachable, and so on.

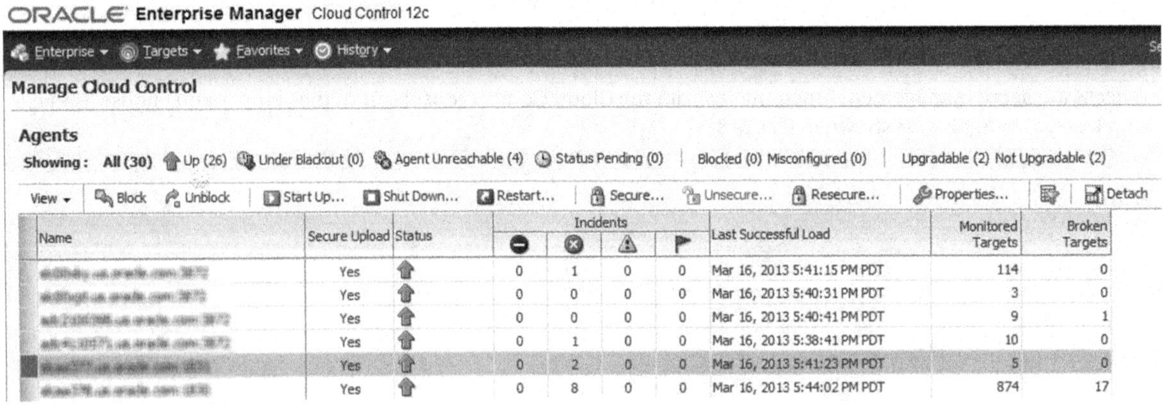

Figure 3-2. *The Agents page*

■ **Tip**   The values of Upgradable and Not Upgradable are present only if you have upgraded your OMS from 12.1.0.1 to 12.1.0.2. Upgrading the OMS, of course, does not upgrade the agents as well. However, you can mass-upgrade agents from the console in EM12c by clicking Upgradable, selecting the agents to upgrade, and clicking the Upgrade button.

You can also select specific agents (by holding down the Ctrl key while selecting) or a range of agents (by holding Shift while selecting) to perform operations on, such as starting, shutting down, securing, and so forth. These fairly straightforward operations are covered well in Oracle's documentation for the Enterprise Manager product, and so are not covered further here.

■ **Tip**   One trap that new users often fall into when first using the EM12c user interface is not clicking the correct part of the screen. Note that the agent names are hyperlinks, so clicking the name of an agent will take you to that particular agent's home page. If you want to select the agent and stay on this page to perform specific operations, either click the column to the left of the agent name, as seen in Figure 3-2, or click in the agent column but to the right of the hyperlink.

Controlling Multiple Agents at the Same Time

The ability to select multiple agents to perform operations on is one of the major enhancements from previous releases in this part of EM12c. This capability enables administrators to make changes to multiple agents at one time, instead of one by one. For example, let's say you want to change the upload interval at which a group of agents uploads accumulated data files to a smaller value, because these agents monitor your more critical systems. All you need to do is select the agents you want to modify and click the Properties icon, as shown at the right of Figure 3-2. This starts the Create 'Agents Configuration Operation' job workflow, as shown in Figure 3-3.

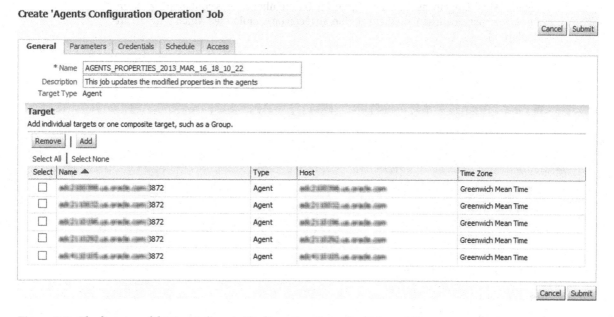

Figure 3-3. *The first step of the Create 'Agents Configuration Operation' job workflow*

Notice that none of the agents are initially selected. Therefore, you select the agents you want (or just click Select All to select all of them) and then click the Parameters tab. This brings up a long list of agent properties you can change, as shown in Figure 3-4. Scroll down to the UploadInterval parameter and enter a value in minutes for how frequently you want the agents to upload. In Figure 3-4, the value is set to upload every 5 minutes (from the default of 15 minutes).

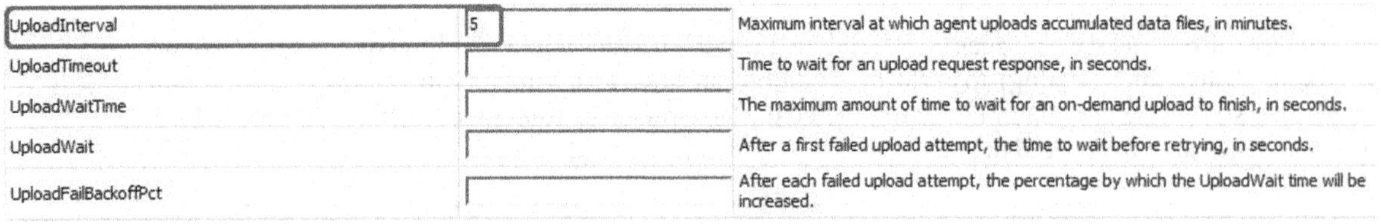

UploadInterval	5	Maximum interval at which agent uploads accumulated data files, in minutes.
UploadTimeout		Time to wait for an upload request response, in seconds.
UploadWaitTime		The maximum amount of time to wait for an on-demand upload to finish, in seconds.
UploadWait		After a first failed upload attempt, the time to wait before retrying, in seconds.
UploadFailBackoffPct		After each failed upload attempt, the percentage by which the UploadWait time will be increased.

Figure 3-4. *Changing the* UploadInterval *parameter*

You could schedule this to occur at a later time (for example, an allocated maintenance time) by using the Schedule tab. However, if you don't need to schedule this job to run later, you can simply click Submit. You are then returned to the Agents page and provided with an informational message that the job has been submitted, along with a link to check progress of the job.

Using an Agent's Home Page

From the Agents page just described, you can go to the home page for a specific agent, by clicking the agent name. (You can also reach an agent's home page by selecting the agent from the All Targets page.) The OMS makes a connection to the agent and displays a variety of more-detailed information for that specific agent, including the following:

> *Summary region*: This provides details such as the agent's availability and status. Of particular interest in this region is the list indicating which management plug-ins are deployed in this agent, as shown in Figure 3-5. (Remember, agents contain plug-ins only for targets that are present on the machine, so it can be useful to see which plug-ins are deployed.)

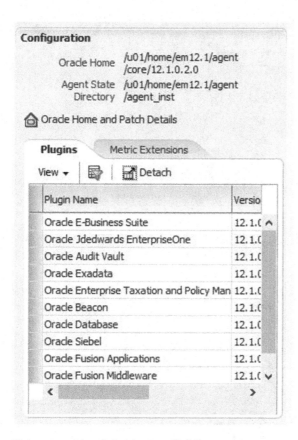

Figure 3-5. *List of plug-ins installed for an agent*

Monitoring region: This shows details of the targets being monitored by this agent, metric issues for these targets, and the top collections for them.

Performance and Usage region: This details how well the agent itself has been performing, as shown in Figure 3-6. You should be aware of several important items in this region:

- At first glance, the graphs can be confusing because the y axis seems to have no units of measurement. In fact, the units are there, just in the caption for each graph.

- The y axis is scaled, based on the results. That means that performance can look worse than it really is. For example, the upload rate in Figure 3-6 looks bad at first glance, but it reaches a maximum of just over 0.5 KB/sec, which is clearly not a problem!

- Sometimes you need to look at two graphs to see an issue. Using that same upload rate graph, performance is an issue only when the upload backlog (the graph to the right of the upload rate) is increasing while the upload rate isn't increasing.

- By looking at the Collection Performance graph, you can determine when an agent is reaching the maximum number of targets it can monitor. As you can see in the tip underneath the agent, when the value on the y axis approaches 100, the agent is reaching capacity. This is probably not something you'll see often. (The agent in this case was monitoring 114 targets, yet the percentage of the collection interval spent in execution is averaging slightly under 0.02, which is a long way off 100!)

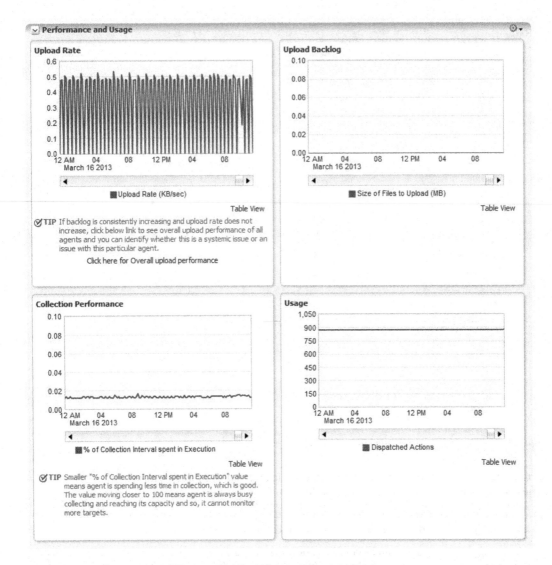

Figure 3-6. Performance and Usage region from the agent home page

Resource Consumption region: This provides information on the CPU and Java heap utilization for the agent, as shown in Figure 3-7. Again, this is something that usually should not be problematic, but having the information is useful in case you do see an issue here.

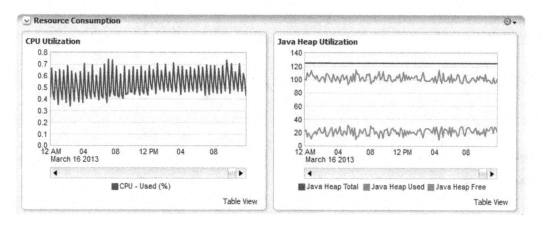

Figure 3-7. *The Resource Consumption region of the agent home page*

Incidents region: This displays the list of incidents recorded for the agent. (Incident management is covered in more detail in Chapter 12, and so is not covered here.)

The other area of interest on the agent home page is the Agent menu, shown in Figure 3-8. From here, the most interesting selections you can drill into are as follows:

Monitoring: This shows details of metrics, metric settings, metric collection errors, status and alert history, and blackouts, as well as providing access to the Incident Manager console.

Diagnostics: This links into the Support Workbench to allow you to package details of recent problems or incidents for uploading to My Oracle Support.

Control: This provides the relevant links to shut down or restart the agent, or to end a blackout.

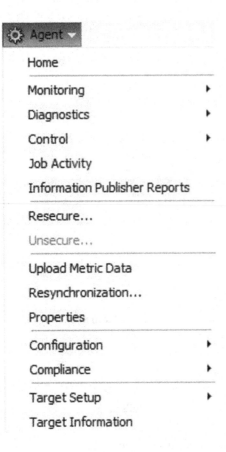

Figure 3-8. *The Agent menu from the agent home page*

Using the EM Agent Browser

The EM agent browser is another graphical user interface (GUI) that was developed several releases ago to access the agent while the OMS was being built. It was disabled by default in versions 10g and 11g, but seems to be available again in 12c. Whether that continues to be the case remains to be seen. Nevertheless, it can be very useful to you if your agent is stuck in a pending state (though that can also be cleared via the console) or if some metrics are not being collected.

To reach the agent browser, you use a URL of the form `https://<agent_host_name>:<agent_port_number>/emd/browser/main` (for example, `https://em12c.acme.com:3872/emd/browser`). You are then prompted for a user ID and password, either for the agent owner or root (in a Unix environment). That brings up a screen like that shown in Figure 3-9.

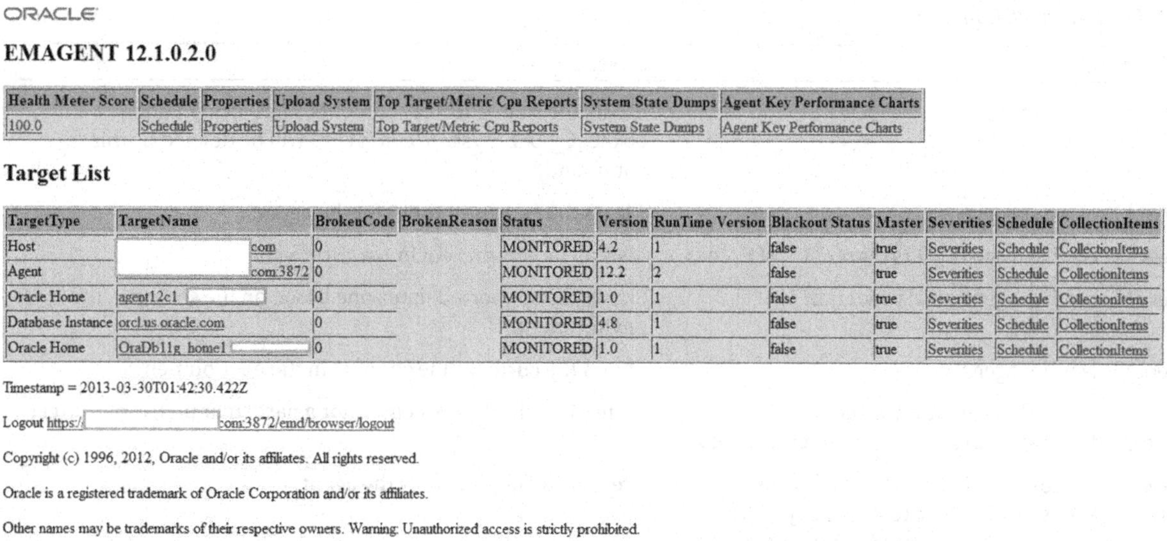

ORACLE

EMAGENT 12.1.0.2.0

Health Meter Score	Schedule	Properties	Upload System	Top Target/Metric Cpu Reports	System State Dumps	Agent Key Performance Charts
100.0	Schedule	Properties	Upload System	Top Target/Metric Cpu Reports	System State Dumps	Agent Key Performance Charts

Target List

TargetType	TargetName	BrokenCode	BrokenReason	Status	Version	RunTime Version	Blackout Status	Master	Severities	Schedule	CollectionItems
Host	com	0		MONITORED	4.2	1	false	true	Severities	Schedule	CollectionItems
Agent	com:3872	0		MONITORED	12.2	2	false	true	Severities	Schedule	CollectionItems
Oracle Home	agent12c1	0		MONITORED	1.0	1	false	true	Severities	Schedule	CollectionItems
Database Instance	orcl.us.oracle.com	0		MONITORED	4.8	1	false	true	Severities	Schedule	CollectionItems
Oracle Home	OraDb11g_home1	0		MONITORED	1.0	1	false	true	Severities	Schedule	CollectionItems

Timestamp = 2013-03-30T01:42:30.422Z

Logout https://com:3872/emd/browser/logout

Copyright (c) 1996, 2012, Oracle and/or its affiliates. All rights reserved.

Oracle is a registered trademark of Oracle Corporation and/or its affiliates.

Other names may be trademarks of their respective owners. Warning: Unauthorized access is strictly prohibited.

Figure 3-9. *The Agent browser*

Many of the `emctl` commands described in the upcoming section "The EMCTL Utility" are available via this browser interface as well. One of the more interesting ones is the command to take a system state dump for the agent, which can be particularly useful in debugging the status of a problematic agent. To take a system state dump, you simply click the link System State Dumps, as shown in Figure 3-9, and then click Perform System Dump in the window that opens. Be aware that this may take some time to generate, and it also generates quite a large XML file, which for space reasons is not shown here.

Agent Management with the Command Line

Of course, all the areas you just looked at are available from the command line as well. Enterprise Manager has two command-line interfaces: EMCTL and EMCLI. Let's look at each in turn.

The EMCTL Utility

The Enterprise Manager Control utility (EMCTL) is mainly used—surprise, surprise!—for control of the different parts of the EM infrastructure. Because this section is about the management agent, discussion is restricted here to functions used with the agent. You'll need to ensure that you're using EMCTL from the agent home page to use these commands. Use `emctl getemhome` to validate this, because it can be easy to get confused about which `emctl` you are using!

Many of the `emctl` commands remain unchanged from previous releases. Just for completeness, though, Table 3-1 shows a list of the more frequently used `emctl` commands for management agents.

Table 3-1. emctl Commands

Command	Description
emctl clearstate	Clears the state directory contents. Files located under $ORACLE_HOME/sysman/emd/state will be deleted by this command.
emctl clearsudoprops	Clears the sudo properties for the agent.
emctl config [agent] listtargets [<EM loc>]	Lists all targets present in targets.xml.
emctl config agent getSupportedTZ	Shows the supported time zone based on the setting in the environment.
emctl config agent getTZ	Shows the current time zone set in the environment.
emctl control agent runCollection <target_name>:<target_type> <metric_name>	Manually runs the collections for a particular metric of a target.
emctl deploy agent [-s <install-password>] [-o <omshostname:consoleSrvPort>] [-S] <deploy-dir> <deploy-hostname>:<port> <source-hostname>	Creates and deploys only the agent.
emctl dumpstate agent <component> . . .	Generates dumps for the agent, allowing you to analyze CPU or memory issues for the agent.
emctl gensudoprops	Generates the sudo properties of the agent.
emctl getemhome	Prints the agent home directory.
emctl getversion agent	Prints the version of the agent.
emctl listplugins agent	Lists plug-ins deployed on the agent, their versions, and installation directories.
emctl pingOMS [agent]	Pings the OMS to check whether the agent is able to reach the OMS, and waits for the reverse ping from the OMS so that the agent can say the pingOMS is successful.
emctl reload agent dynamicproperties [<Target_name>:<Target_Type>]...	Recomputes and generates dynamic properties for a specified target and generates the dynamic properties for the target.
emctl resetTZ agent	Resets the time zone of the agent. You need to do the following: 1. Stop the agent first. 2. Run this command to change the current time zone to a different time zone. 3. Restart the agent.
emctl secure agent [registration password]	Secures the agent against an OMS. This will prompt for the registration password.
emctl start agent	Starts the management agent.
emctl start blackout <Blackoutname> [-nodeLevel] [<Target_name>[:<Target_Type>]].... [-d <Duration>]	Starts blackout on a target.
emctl status agent	Shows the status of the agent.

(continued)

Table 3-1. (*continued*)

Command	Description
`emctl status agent cpu [-depth n	-full_cpu_report]`	Provides CPU statistics (either a top-n listing using `depth` or `full` details). Requires `topMetricReporter=true` to be set in `emd.properties`.
`emctl status agent dbconnections`	Shows the contents of the DBConnection Cache.
`emctl status agent jobs`	Shows the status of the jobs that are currently running.
`emctl status agent mcache <target name>,<target type>,<metric>`	Shows the metric names that have values in the metric cache.
`emctl status agent scheduler`	Shows all scheduled, ready, or running collection threads.
`emctl status agent -secure`	Shows whether the agent is running in secure mode, as well as the security of the OMS it is reporting to.
`emctl status agent target <target name>,<target type>,<metric>`	Shows detailed status of the specific targets in the order of target name, target type.
`emctl status blackout [<Target_name>[:<Target_Type>]]....`	Provides the status of the blackout of the target.
`emctl stop agent`	Stops the management agent.
`emctl stop blackout <Blackoutname>`	Stops the blackout that was started on a particular target. Only blackouts that are started by the EMCTL tool can be stopped using EMCTL.
`emctl unsecure agent`	Unsecures the agent. Generally, this isn't a recommended practice.
`emctl verifykey`	Verifies the communication between the OMS and agent by sending `pingOMS`.

When you run an `emctl` command, the output from that command is captured in the `emctl.log` file, located under the `$AGENT_HOME/agent_inst/sysman/log` directory. (Some commands also display their output to `stdout`.) More details on agent log and trace files are given in the upcoming section cleverly named "Agent Log and Trace Files."

The EMCLI Utility

Before you look at agent log and trace files in more detail, though, let's examine the other command-line utility for managing agents, the Enterprise Manager Command Line Interface utility (EMCLI). The EMCLI utility is mainly used for automating commands that need to be executed against a large number of targets, because scripting this can be much faster than selecting each target to process the operation on via the EM console.

As an example, let's say you have a group of Production databases called `ProdDB` that are administered by someone who is leaving the organization. If you have 500 databases in that group, you wouldn't want to update the `Contact` lifecycle properties one by one. Instead, you could do the following:

```
emcli set_target_property_value -property_records="ProdDB:composite:Contact:psharman"
-propagate_to_members
```

This changes the contact details to the psharman user ID for all 500 databases in one fell swoop.

One of the main advantages of using EMCLI over EMCTL, though, is that EMCLI has a client that can be installed on any system that can reach the OMS. That means it can be executed anywhere in your managed environment. Many Cloud Control administrators install EMCLI on their local machine, for example. EMCLI also allows you to call custom scripts such as TCL, Perl, SQL, or OS scripts.

From an architectural perspective, there are two parts to EMCLI. There is the EMCLI client (the part that you install where you want to) and an OMS extension, which is automatically installed in the OMS. The Java-based client sends command requests using emcli verbs to the OMS extension, which passes them on to the OMS to action. These verbs are plug-in extensions that contain the relevant command and options.

Installation of the EM CLI client is done by first downloading the EMCLI kit to the location where you want to install it. The kit can be downloaded from the EM console, by choosing Command Line Interface from the Setup menu, as shown in Figure 3-10.

Figure 3-10. *Accessing the EM CLI kit*

Once you have downloaded and installed the EM CLI kit, you have access to only a few of the basic verbs, such as help, login, logout, and setup. To set up the client completely, you need to execute the command emcli setup. At a minimum, you need to pass parameters for the EM console and username that you want to use for logging in with emcli (this username is the one you normally log into the console with), but I find it useful sometimes to include the -autologin parameter. This parameter ensures that you are automatically logged back in if your session times out.

■ **Caution** Use the -autologin parameter only if the workstation you are installing the client on is secured, particularly if the username you also pass in has Super Administrator–level access.

As an example, here's a command executed to complete setup on a local workstation:

```
$ ./emcli setup -url=https://em12.acme.com/em -username=psharman -autologin
```

Once the command completes, you will have access to all the verbs EMCLI recognizes. There are way too many to describe here, but executing the command `emcli help` will list them for you. It provides quite a long listing, so you may want to redirect the output to a file for easier perusal. You can get detailed help on any particular verb by passing that verb as an argument to the `help command`. For example, `emcli help setup` gives you more detailed help on the setup verb. There is also a complete manual on the EMCLI utility available in the EM12c documentation set (`http://docs.oracle.com/cd/E24628_01/em.121/e17786/toc.htm`).

Agent Log and Trace Files

When you install a management agent, you are prompted for an `AGENT_BASE` directory. This directory is similar to the `ORACLE_BASE` directory used in database installations. Underneath it, you will find the agent instance directory (`agent_inst`, which contains all the agent-related configuration files), as well as the management agent home. The management agent home will be `<AGENT_BASE>/core/12.1.0.2.0`. Obviously, the version number in the directory name reflects the version number for the agent, so depending on your installation, this number may differ from the example just given. Most of the agent log and trace files you will need are found somewhere under this management agent home directory. Some of the directories you may need to look at to find information are shown in Table 3-2. In this table, `<AGENT_HOME>` refers to the management agent home (for example, `<AGENT_BASE>/core/12.1.0.2.0`), while `<AGENT_INST>` refers to the agent instance directory (for example, `<AGENT_BASE>/agent_inst`).

Table 3-2. *Locations of Agent Log and Trace Files*

Type of Information	Location
Agent heartbeat history	`<AGENT_INST>/sysman/log/gcagent.log`
Agent startup information for both agent and watchdog	`<AGENT_INST>/sysman/log/emagent.nohup`
Agent trace files	`<AGENT_INST>/sysman/log/*.trc`
Configuration assistant errors	`<AGENT_HOME>/cfgtoollogs/cfgfw/CfmLogger_<timestamp>.log`
emctl command output	`<AGENT_INST>/sysman/log/emctl.log`
Errors on securing agent	`<AGENT_INST>/sysman/log/secure.log`
System state dumps	`<AGENT_INST>/sysman/emd/dumps/SystemDump_<number>.xml`

■ **Note** The watchdog referred to in Table 3-2 is the agent watchdog. When the agent is started, it also starts an agent watchdog process whose role is to monitor the agent and attempt to restart it should it fail.

You can control the number and size of these files by using an `emctl` command. By default, the agent writes only informational, warning, and critical messages to the trace file, but you can change the level of information written by using the following command:

```
$ emctl set property agent -name "Logger.log.level" -value "<LEVEL>"
```

where <LEVEL> is one of the following values—DEBUG, INFO, WARN, ERROR, or FATAL. Because this can generate large amounts of information, you can restrict that by setting different values for -name. However, it is best to do this only under guidance from Oracle Support, so contact them if needed.

Oracle Management Service

Let's move on now to discuss the Oracle Management Service (OMS). As mentioned in Chapter 1, the OMS is a web-based application that communicates with the agents and the Oracle Management Repository to collect and store information about all the targets on the various agents. The OMS is also responsible for rendering the user interface for the console. Like the agent, the OMS can be controlled via both the EM12c console and the command-line utilities. Let's start by looking at the console in more detail.

OMS Management with the Console

To manage the OMS from the console, you choose Setup ➤ Manage Cloud Control ➤ Management Services, as shown in Figure 3-11.

Figure 3-11. *Accessing the OMS from the EM12c console*

This takes you to the Management Services home page, shown in Figure 3-12.

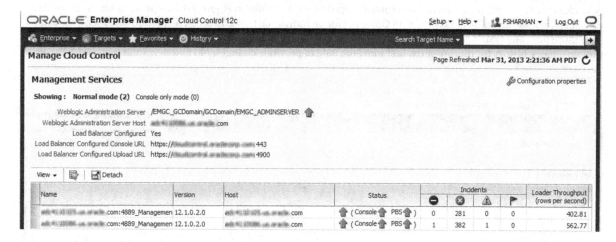

Figure 3-12. *The Management Services home page*

In this particular environment, we have two OMSs set up, with a load balancer controlling the connections to each one. There is actually more output to the right of this screen (CPU Usage, Heap Usage, and WebLogic Server) but it has been trimmed to fit on the page more easily.

By clicking Configuration Properties at the top lright you can alter the runtime behavior of the OMS by setting properties as needed. The default setting shows you all the nondefault properties, , but you can change that to All or Non Default at Management Server Instances by clicking the drop-down arrow on the right of the highlighted box, as seen in Figure 3-13.

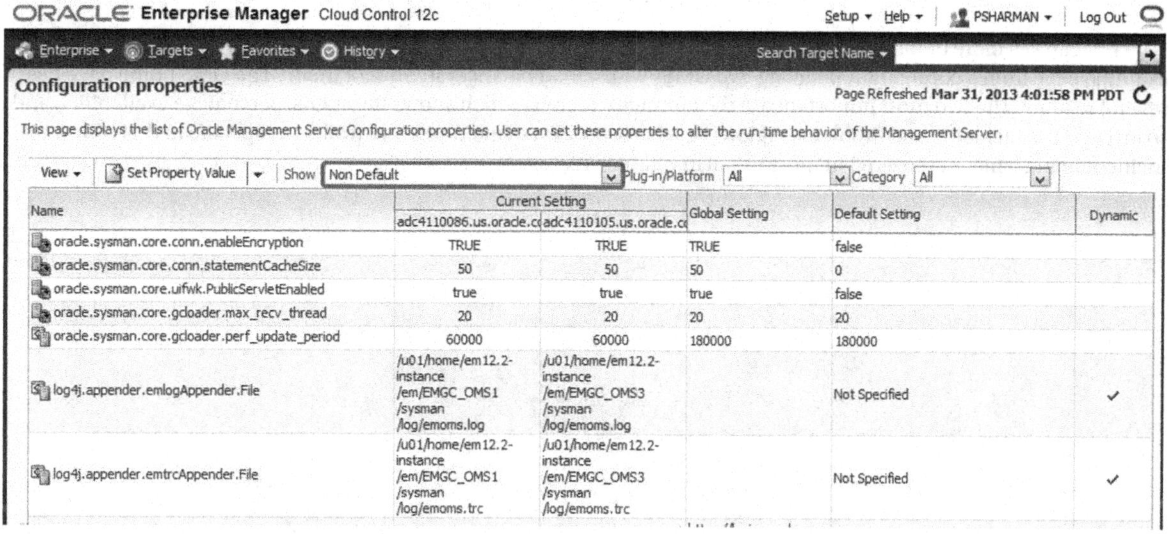

Figure 3-13. *Configuration properties for the OMS*

You can also click a property name to change it. For example, if you want to set up tracing between an agent (or group of agents) and the OMS to diagnose problems between them, you can click the property `oracle.sysman.core.gcloader.trace_agent`, and change the setting as appropriate, as shown in Figure 3-14. Depending on the property, you can either set this value globally (for all OMSs) or for an individual OMS. This can be particularly useful if you have more than one OMS and a problem occurs for just one of them. Note also (as highlighted in Figure 3-14) that you can see change history for this property, including the date of previous changes, old and new values, and who made the change.

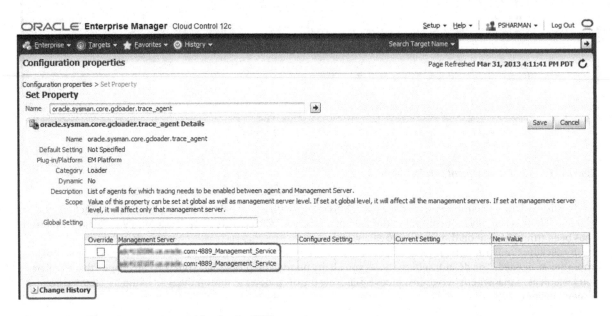

Figure 3-14. *Changing a property value for the OMS*

You can see more detail on each OMS by clicking its name to go to the OMS home page. Figure 3-15 shows an example page from a configuration having two OMSs with a load balancer in front of them . The OMS home page has several regions. The two most important are the Summary region (which shows the status, percentage availability, and so on) and the Incidents and Problems region (which shows a list of incidents and problems specific to this OMS). Incident management is covered in more detail in Chapter 12.

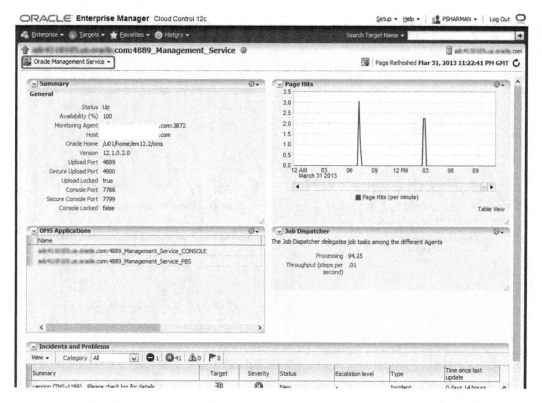

Figure 3-15. *OMS home page*

The other section of the page that is of interest is the Oracle Management Service at the top left. Many of these options are similar to those on the agent home page, so they are not covered here.

So right about now you might be wondering where all the start, stop, and status commands are available from. These commands would cause the console to become unavailable, because the OMS is also responsible for rendering the user interface. Therefore, these commands are executed via our old friend, EMCTL, which you'll look at in the context of the OMS shortly. Before you do so, however, there is one more part of the GUI that you need to look at for the OMS: the Health Overview page, shown in Figure 3-16. This page provides an overview of both the OMS and repository operations and performance. It is accessed by choosing Setup ➤ Manage Cloud Control ➤ Health Overview.

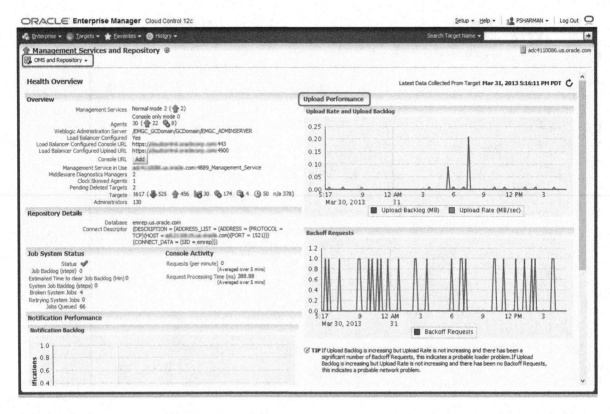

Figure 3-16. *Health Overview page*

The Health Overview page also has several useful regions. For a quick overview of the managed environment, the Overview region is quite useful, particularly for determining the number and status of all the targets being monitored. However, the most interesting part is the Upload Performance region, where you can identify probable loader problems and network problems. Also of interest is the OMS and Repository menu. This again has similar content to the equivalent menu on the OMS and Agents home pages, but there are a couple of other options that you don't see on those pages. The one that's of most relevance from the OMS perspective (others are covered in the equivalent repository section of this chapter) is the Add Management Service link, which starts the Deployment Procedure Manager to add an additional OMS to your existing system.

OMS Management with the Command Line

Let's start this section by discussing what's *not* available for managing the OMS from the command line anymore, and that's the OPMNCTL utility. Although the utility still exists, it has been superseded by the EMCTL utility. So let's look at that in more detail.

The EMCTL Utility

The EMCTL utility is used for many operations against the OMS, in a similar manner to the way it is used against the agent. Having said that, there are many emctl commands that will appear to operate against the repository when you issue them via the emctl command from the OMS home. That's because a lot of repository information (credentials, connectivity, and so forth) is also stored in the OMS to enable it to connect to the repository and do its work, so these commands are basically synchronizing between the two.

Table 3-3 lists some of the more commonly used emctl commands from the OMS home.

Table 3-3. *OMS emctl Commands*

Command	Description
emctl abortresync repos (-full|-agentlist "agent names") -name "resync name" [-sysman_pwd "sysman password"]	Aborts the currently running repository resynchronization operation. Use the full option to stop a full repository resynchronization. Use the agentlist option to stop resync on a list of agents.
emctl config oms -change_repos_pwd [-change_in_db] [-old_pwd] [-new_pwd] [-use_sys_pwd [-sys_pwd]]	Changes the repository password.
emctl config oms -change_view_user_pwd [-sysman_pwd] [-user_pwd] [-auto_generate]	Changes the password of the MGMT_VIEW user. -auto_generate generates a random password.
emctl config oms -list_repos_details	Shows the repository details in the OMS.
emctl config oms -store_repos_details (-repos_host -repos_port -repos_sid | -repos_conndesc) -repos_user [-repos_pwd] [-no_check_db]	Changes and stores repository information in the OMS.
emctl delete property [-sysman_pwd "sysman password"] -name	Removes the property from the emoms.properties file for the given property name.
emctl dump oms	Dumps all node manager logs, admin server logs, managed server logs, sysman logs, and stack trace files.
emctl dump omsthread	Dumps thread that is causing CPU spin.
emctl exportconfig oms [-sysman_pwd] [-dir] [-keep_host]	Exports the configuration from the primary management service.
emctl get property [-sysman_pwd "sysman password"] -name	Gets the property value from the emoms.properties file for the given property name.
emctl importconfig oms -file	Imports the exported configuration on the standby management service.
emctl list oms	Gives the OMS name configured in that local Oracle home.
emctl list properties [-sysman_pwd "sysman password"] [-module]	Lists all the properties set from the emoms.properties file.
emctl resync repos -full -name "<resync name>"	Initiates repository resync from one of the OMS Oracle homes.
emctl secure lock [-upload] [-console]	Restricts HTTP access (that is, allows only HTTP/S access) to the management service.

(continued)

Table 3-3. (*continued*)

Command	Description

`emctl secure oms [-sysman_pwd ] [-reg_pwd ]`
`[-host ] [-slb_port ] [-slb_console_port ]`
`[-reset] [-console] [-lock] [-lock_console]`
`[-secure_port ] [-upload_http_port ] [-root_dc ]`
`[-root_country] [-root_email ] [-root_state ]`
`[-root_loc] [-root_org ] [-root_unit ]`
`[-wallet -trust_certs_loc ] [-wallet_pwd ]`
`[-key_strength ] [-cert_validity ] [-protocol ]`
	Enables the OMS to accept upload requests from agents and console requests in HTTP/S mode.

`emctl secure setpwd [authpasswd] [newpasswd]`	Creates a new agent registration password.
`emctl secure unlock [-upload] [-console]`	Allows nonsecured HTTP access to the OMS.
`emctl set property [-sysman_pwd "sysman` `password"] -name -value[-module (default emoms)]`	Sets the property values in the `emoms.properties` file.
`emctl start oms`	Starts the OMS in the following order: 1. Start OPMN and OHS if not already up. 2. Start the Node Manager if not running. 3. If running on Admin Server, start it (if not already up). 4. Start the managed server through Node Manager.
`emctl status oms`	Provides the status of the OMS. Use `-details` to get detailed information (including secure status and protocols used).
`emctl statusresync repos -name "resync name"`	Lists the status of the given repository resynchronization operation.
`emctl stop oms [-all] [-force]`	Stops the OMS in the following order: 1. Stop the OHS. 2. Stop the OPMN. 3. Stop the managed server. Using `-all` stops the OMS in the following order: 1. Stop the OHS. 2. Stop the OPMN. 3. Stop the managed server. 4. Stop the Admin Server if running. 5. Stop the Node Manager. If either stop command does not shut down the relevant processes, use `-force` to forcefully stop them.

OMS Directories

The OMS is installed into an Oracle middleware home, which may also contain the Oracle WebLogic Server (including the WebLogic Server administration console), an Oracle management agent for the middleware tier, the management service instance base directory, the Java Development Kit (JDK), and other configuration files. Some of these directories may be located outside the middleware home, depending on decisions you make at installation time. You need to be familiar with the important directories to configure, maintain, and troubleshoot the OMS. It's probably easiest to look at this diagrammatically, so start by looking at Figure 3-17, which shows you the default middleware home directory structure on an example environment.

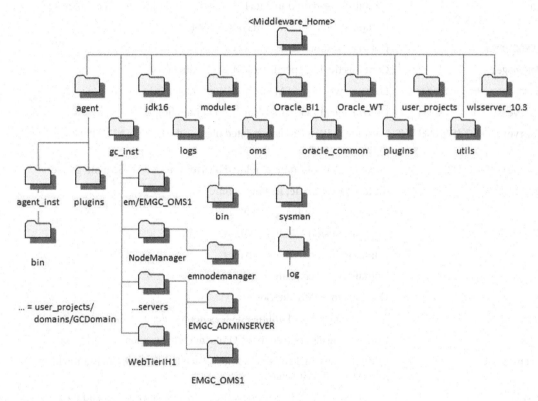

Figure 3-17. *OMS directory structure*

Table 3-4 explains what each of these directories is used for.

Table 3-4. *OMS Middleware Home Directories and Their Uses*

Directory	Description
agent	Contains agent code and configuration files
agent/agent_inst	The <AGENT_HOME> directory
agent/agent_inst/bin	Contains the executable code for the agent running on the OMS
agent/plugins	Contains configuration data for metadata plug-ins installed on the agent
gc_inst	Default location for OMS_INSTANCE_HOME
gc_inst/em/EMGC_OMS1	Default location for EM_INSTANCE_HOME
gc_inst/NodeManager	Contains the EM-specific NodeManager directory
gc_inst/NodeManager/emnodemanager	Location where the EM-specific NodeManager is installed
gc_inst/...servers	Default location for the WebLogic Domain home
gc_inst/...servers/EMGC_ADMINSERVER	Location of WLS Domain–related files for the EMGC_ADMINSERVER managed server
gc_inst/...servers/EMGC_OMS1	Location of WLS Domain–related files for the EMGC_OMS1 managed server
gc_inst/WebTierIH1	Middleware WebTier instance home
jdk16	Contains JDK configuration files
logs	Contains Fusion Middleware files
modules	Contains Fusion Middleware files
oms	Contains OMS code and configuration files
oms/bin	Contains the OMS binaries
oms/sysman	Contains a variety of utilities such as RepManager
oms/sysman/log	Contains log files related to the OMS, including component_info.log
Oracle_BI1 [optional]	Contains the Oracle Business Intelligence Publisher configuration files, if BI Publisher is installed
oracle_common	Contains common files used by the OMS, Oracle WebTier, and WebLogic Server
Oracle_WT	Contains Oracle WebTier configuration files
plugins	Contains configuration files for metadata plug-ins installed on the OMS
user_projects	Contains Fusion Middleware files
utils	Contains Fusion Middleware files
wlserver_10.3	Contains Fusion Middleware files

OMS Log and Trace Files

There are six main log and trace files used for troubleshooting issues with the OMS. These are located under the OMS instance base directory (gc_inst in Table 3-4). These files are as follows:

- emctl.log contains output from emctl commands.

- emctl.msg is generated when the OMS restarts because of critical errors.

- emoms.log, the log file for the console, contains information created when the OMS performs an action (such as starting or stopping) or generates an error.

- emoms.trc contains more-detailed tracing information to support troubleshooting errors.

- emoms_pbs.log contains errors or warnings for background modules such as the event and job systems.

- emoms_pbs.trc contains more-detailed tracing information to troubleshoot problems with background modules.

As you might imagine, these files can quickly increase in size over time. Thankfully, the files have a predefined maximum size before the OMS rolls information to a new file. The old versions of the file can be identified as EM places a number in the name. For example, in my environment I can see the following files under the log directory:

```
[oracle@server log] ls -al
total 101600
drwxr----- 2 oracle oinstall    4096 Mar 30 22:38 .
drwxr----- 3 oracle oinstall    4096 Sep 19  2012 ..
-rw-r----- 1 oracle oinstall 5242789 Mar 18 01:08 emoms-156.log
-rw-r----- 1 oracle oinstall 5242789 Mar 18 01:08 emoms-156.trc
-rw-r----- 1 oracle oinstall 5241643 Mar 19 16:15 emoms-157.log
-rw-r----- 1 oracle oinstall 5241643 Mar 19 16:15 emoms-157.trc
-rw-r----- 1 oracle oinstall 5242832 Mar 21 08:27 emoms-158.log
-rw-r----- 1 oracle oinstall 5242832 Mar 21 08:27 emoms-158.trc
-rw-r----- 1 oracle oinstall 5241829 Mar 22 14:52 emoms-159.log
-rw-r----- 1 oracle oinstall 5241829 Mar 22 14:52 emoms-159.trc
-rw-r----- 1 oracle oinstall 5242518 Mar 24 13:55 emoms-160.log
-rw-r----- 1 oracle oinstall 5242518 Mar 24 13:55 emoms-160.trc
-rw-r----- 1 oracle oinstall 5236550 Mar 26 06:45 emoms-161.log
-rw-r----- 1 oracle oinstall 5236550 Mar 26 06:45 emoms-161.trc
-rw-r----- 1 oracle oinstall 5242710 Mar 28 01:34 emoms-162.log
-rw-r----- 1 oracle oinstall 5242710 Mar 28 01:34 emoms-162.trc
-rw-r----- 1 oracle oinstall 5242442 Mar 28 20:46 emoms-163.log
-rw-r----- 1 oracle oinstall 5242442 Mar 28 20:46 emoms-163.trc
-rw-r----- 1 oracle oinstall 5242752 Mar 30 22:38 emoms-164.log
-rw-r----- 1 oracle oinstall 5242752 Mar 30 22:38 emoms-164.trc
-rw-r----- 1 oracle oinstall 4709623 Apr  1 21:56 emoms.log
-rw-r----- 1 oracle oinstall 4709623 Apr  1 21:56 emoms.trc
```

You can control the number and size of these files by using an emctl command. The exact command varies depending on which file you want to control. You can also control which information goes into emoms.trc. By default, the OMS writes only warning and critical messages into the trace file, but you can change the level of information written there by using the following command:

```
$ emctl set property -name "log4j.rootCategory" -value "<LEVEL>, emlogAppender, emtrcAppender"
-module logging
```

where <LEVEL> is one of the following values—INFO, WARN, ERROR, or DEBUG. Because this can generate large amounts of information, you can restrict that by setting different values for -name. However, it is best to do this only under guidance from Oracle Support, so contact them if needed.

Oracle Management Repository

Let's move on now to discuss the Oracle Management Repository. As mentioned in Chapter 1, the Oracle Management Repository (OMR, or more commonly, just the repository) is an Oracle database that stores all the information collected by the various management agents. It is composed of database users, tablespaces, tables, views, indexes, packages, procedures, and database jobs. Like the agent and the OMS, the repository can be controlled both via the EM12c console and command-line utilities. Let's start by looking at the console in more detail.

Repository Management with the Console

To manage the repository from the console, you choose Setup ➤ Manage Cloud Control ➤ Repository, as shown in Figure 3-18.

Figure 3-18. *Accessing the repository home page*

This brings you to the repository home page, shown in Figure 3-19. (Note that the page title remains Management Services and Repository, as it did when accessing the OMS home page, but the regions shown are all applicable to the repository.). Notice in this figure that the Details link has been clicked in the Repository Details region to display all the sessions accessing the repository.

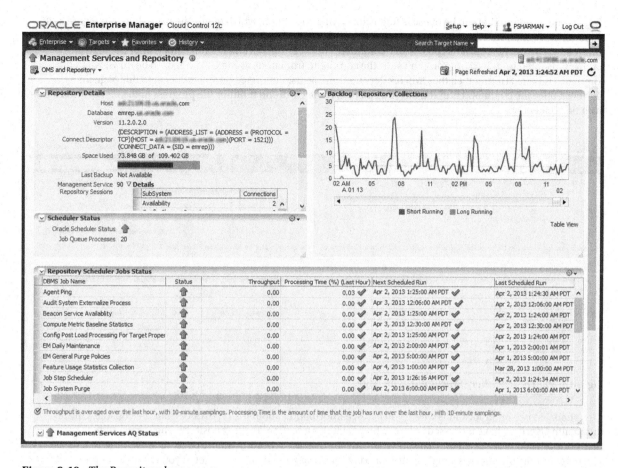

Figure 3-19. *The Repository home page*

There's not really a lot you can do on this page; it's used more for a quick glance and making sure things are OK. Some things to typically check here include the following:

- Is there still space available? Checking the Space Used bar will quickly tell you that.

- Is the backlog of repository collections increasing? This isn't a common problem. It may spike occasionally, as you can see in the example in Figure 3-19, but in general, it's not an issue.

- Is the Oracle Scheduler status OK? The green arrow here is generally enough, but if there are problems, you can look at the Repository Scheduler Job Status region for more-granular details.

- Is the Management Services AQ Status OK? Again, checking that the arrow is green is usually sufficient. If it's not, you can expand that region for more details.

From the OMS and Repository drop-down menu toward the top left of the screen, there are a couple of options specific to the repository. One of those is called just Repository, and it simply displays the page seen in Figure 3-19 (so it's really of use only if you've been looking at the OMS home page, which has the same menu).

The other option that can be of use is Repository Synchronization, which opens the page shown in Figure 3-20. Hopefully, you shouldn't need to use this very often. It's basically used to monitor resynchronization operations (initiated via an `emctl resync repos -full` command) between agents and the repository, after the repository has been restored from backup. You can't start the command from here, as the OMS needs to be down when the command is issued (remember, the OMS renders the console user interface, so you can't get to this page then). However, once the command is executed, you can restart the OMS and monitor the progress of the resynchronization from this screen.

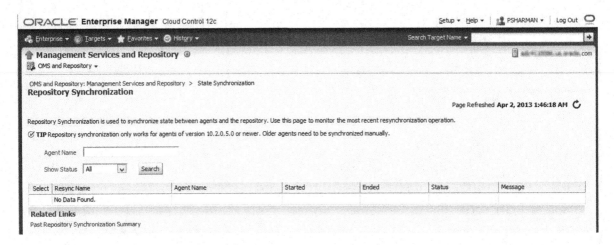

Figure 3-20. *The Repository Synchronization page*

There are two other locations where you can see information about the repository from the console. One is the Health Overview page discussed before, which includes a section on the repository. The information there really doesn't add more detail to what you've already seen on the repository home page, so let's ignore that for now. The other option, of course, is simply to drill into the repository as a database target. If you know the name of the repository database, you can simply type it into the Search Target Name field at the top-right side of the screen. Alternatively, you can simply click Targets ➤ Databases and then click the database name. That takes you to the standard Database home page, shown in Figure 3-21. Most of these features are ones you should probably be already familiar with from previous releases, even if the user interface is unfamiliar. (By the way, just in case you've picked up on the seeming lack of backup for the repository in these screenshots, it's a fairly ad-hoc system running in NOARCHIVELOG mode, so I just use cold backups via `tar` when necessary.)

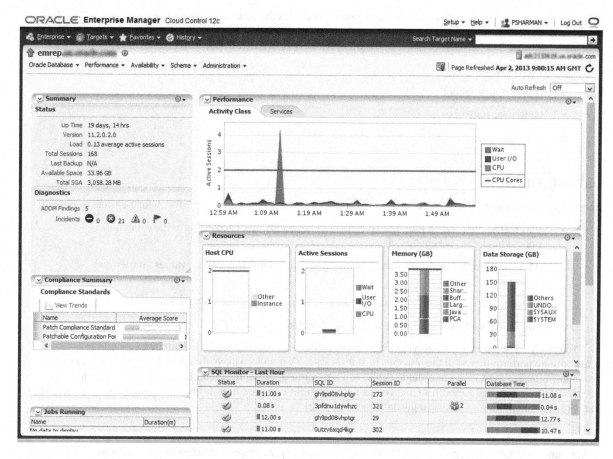

Figure 3-21. *Database home page for the repository*

Repository Management with the Command Line

In earlier sections, you've seen that agent and OMS management from the command line is largely performed using the EMCTL and EMCLI utilities. Management of the repository from the command line is different. It's really just another Oracle database (albeit one with a special use), so the command-line interface for repository management is the DBA's old friend, SQL*Plus. As this book isn't aimed at DBA 101–level skills, this section does not take you through the process of starting or stopping the repository. The only things you need to be aware of here are these:

- You should stop the OMS (using an `emctl stop oms` command) prior to stopping and restarting the repository database.

- You should also ensure that the listener is started before the repository database is started.

Having said that, you do need to be aware of some other areas that you can manage from within SQL*Plus for the repository, particularly around space consumption and performance considerations. In this section, you'll learn about the following:

- Data retention
- Queue management
- Optimizer statistics
- Repository views

Data Retention

Enterprise Manager gathers a lot of data. This data is processed and aggregated in the following lifecycle by default:

- Raw metric data, which is uploaded by the management agent according to the collection policy you define, is kept for 7 days.
- After 7 days, only hourly summaries (maximum, minimum, and average values for metrics) are kept.
- These are kept by default for 31 days, after which only daily summaries are kept.
- Finally, the daily summaries are kept for 12 months.

You likely will want to review these policies. In particular, a common task carried out by target administrators is to compare performance with the previous business cycle. It's therefore likely that you would want raw metrics available for longer than 7 days in order to drill down into more-granular data. Similarly, you might want to keep hourly data for more than a month so that you can, for example, compare month-end data between months. Finally, many organizations choose to keep daily data for many years.

■ **Caution**   Enterprise Manager uses partitioning in the repository database to maintain metric and other data. This would normally be an added feature as far as licensing is concerned, but provided you use only the Partitioning option for Enterprise Manager base tables, you do not need to pay extra. Please do *not* relink Oracle without partitioning, as I had one customer do who was concerned about extra licensing costs. You will seriously break the repository if you do!

Enterprise Manager archives old data by dropping aged-out partitions for the metric tables. The retention policy can therefore be set by modifying the number of partitions to keep. Enterprise Manager provides a stored procedure to perform exactly this task. Listing 3-1 implements a retention policy of 10 days for detail data, 40 days for hourly data, and 3 years for daily data.

Listing 3-1. Modifying EM Retention Policies

```
BEGIN
        sysman.gc_interval_partition_mgr.set_retention('SYSMAN','EM_METRIC_VALUES',10);
        sysman.gc_interval_partition_mgr.set_retention('SYSMAN','EM_METRIC_VALUES_HOURLY',40);
        sysman.gc_interval_partition_mgr.set_retention('SYSMAN','EM_METRIC_VALUES_DAILY',36);
END;
/
```

■ **Note**   The table `EM_INT_PARTITIONED_TABLES` contains the default retention times for various interval-partitioned tables supplied as part of the repository.

Queue Management

Enterprise Manager makes significant use of Oracle's in-database queuing technology (Oracle Streams Advanced Queuing, commonly referred to as AQ). This technology can require some care and maintenance to ensure that performance remains at optimal levels. This is especially true if you chose to implement an Oracle Real Application Clusters solution for your repository database. AQ queues are implemented using a variety of database technologies, including index-organized tables. If message dequeuing does not take place efficiently or completely, then over time the underlying data structures may grow significantly, and message enqueue and dequeue times may increase.

Enterprise Manager uses queues heavily, specifically for metric load and upload and for notifications. The first indication you will likely have of a problem in this area will be that there is a persistent and increasing upload backlog, or a delay in notifications. Unfortunately, both of these symptoms can also have other causes.

The initial database setup for Oracle Enterprise Manager doesn't specifically configure the database as per the general guidance for AQ. In particular, AQ will benefit from a dedicated memory pool called the Streams pool. In a default installation, you will likely find this pool size unset, and so only a minimal memory allocation will be used for Advanced Queuing. I recommend you set the initialization parameter `STREAMS_POOL_SIZE` to a value of 100MB as a starting point (the AQ documentation suggests 20MB, but in my experience, that is undersized for busy systems). You can monitor memory usage of the streams pool by using the query in Listing 3-2.

Listing 3-2. Memory Usage of the Streams Pool

```
SELECT name,round(sum(bytes)/1024/1024,1) memory_mb
FROM v$sgastat
WHERE pool = 'streams pool'
GROUP BY name;
```

If you chose a RAC implementation for your repository database, you may also wish to configure instance affinity for your queue tables to minimize intra-instance block pinging. You should, of course, verify with Oracle Support that any such modification to the queue definition will be supported. In order to perform this task, you will need the `AQ_ADMINISTRATOR_ROLE` role and execute rights on the `SYS.DBMS_AQADM` package. You assign a preferred instance by using code like that in Listing 3-3.

Listing 3-3. Altering a Queue Table's Instance Affinity

```
BEGIN
        SYS.DBMS_AQADM.ALTER_QUEUE_TABLE(
        queue_table => 'SYSMAN.EM_CNTR_QTABLE',
        primary_instance => 1);
END;
/
```

■ **Note**   Setting the instance affinity controls only which QMN process consumes messages and doesn't prevent other instances from using the queue.

Optimizer Statistics

One of the core tasks for an administrator of any Oracle database is ensuring that the optimizer has representative statistical data about the objects that database applications access in order to determine the cost of, and therefore optimize, execution plans appropriately. In the absence of representative statistics, Oracle is much more likely to choose inefficient access paths. To this end, Oracle supplies a built-in statistics-gathering job for Enterprise Manager repository statistics maintenance. This job implements a statistics-gathering policy that allows for more flexibility than the database built-in stats-gathering job.

The job is controlled by the contents of the EM_STATS_MONITOR table, which contains a subset of the tables used by Enterprise Manager together with preference values to supply to the DBMS_STATS package. In this release, the only preferences overridden by the stats-gathering job are the percentage of changed rows required before an object is considered stale and the granularity at which to gather statistics.

This single scheduler job is logically organized into two separate statistics-gathering activities:

- A daily run, which ensures that all stale Enterprise Manager object stats are updated

- A second bi-hourly run, which considers the top stale objects in the EM_STATS_MONITOR table for stats collection

The daily task runs between midnight and 1 AM in the time zone of the database server. The second job runs every 2 hours and is designed to meet the following objectives:

- Ensure that volatile tables have current statistics

- Ensure that provision is made for site-specific needs

In the case of the bi-hourly collection, it may well be that the statistics-gathering regime is overly aggressive. Few sites will really need bi-hourly runs against repository tables. You may, therefore, wish to modify the schedule of the EM_GATHER_SYSMAN_STATS scheduled task, but if you do so, make sure that it still executes between midnight and 1 AM so as to ensure that the overnight collection still occurs.

Repository Views

When all is said and done, Enterprise Manager stores its data in a set of tables. Access to these base tables is provided by a set of repository views, which have been documented in Chapter 18 of the *Oracle Enterprise Manager Cloud Control Extensibility Programmer's Reference* (available online at http://docs.oracle.com/cd/E24628_01/doc.121/e25161/views.htm#sthref1292). Note that this reference is to the 12.1.0.2 version of the documentation. If you are still on 12.1.0.1, you need to look at Chapter 17 of the equivalent document.

■ **Note**   Some of the views you may be interested in are documented in the Extensibility Development Kit (EDK), so you may also need to install that to see the documentation for those views. That's done by selecting the Setup menu from the console, choosing Extensibility ➤ Development Kit, and following the instructions documented there.

Obviously, with a product as large as Enterprise Manager, there are an equally large number of views that you can look at, so all are not documented here. The important thing to be aware of is how to find more information on them, and that's all documented in the aforementioned chapter. Depending on your requirements, you may also want to investigate the use of BI Publisher, the new reporting capability with EM12c that allows highly formatted custom reports against the EM repository. (Again, EM includes a restricted-use license for BI Publisher for use against the EM repository. Use against other data sources will require a BI Publisher license.)

■ **Tip** I'm continually amazed by how few people know about these views, so take the time to examine the Oracle documentation and become familiar with them. In particular, look at the example usage documented at the end of Chapter 18 in the *Oracle Enterprise Manager Cloud Control Extensibility Programmer's Reference.*

Troubleshooting

There is one more utility that you should be familiar with, which is used for troubleshooting across all three layers of the stack. That tool is EMDIAG. EMDIAG is a collection of scripts and tools designed to help troubleshoot and diagnose problems with EM. Each EM tier has a specific kit: AGTVFY for the agent tier, OMSVFY for the OMS tier, and REPVFY for the repository tier, each of which will identify known issues by looking for known problem signatures. Oracle Support has an EMDIAG Master Index note (Note 421053.1) that explains how to download, install, and use each kit. Be sure to download the correct version for EM12c.

Each kit is a set of commands that you can use for displaying information about the setup, configuration, and use of a relevant tier, or to dump objects. They can even be used when the tier itself is not running (or indeed when it is broken). When you run these commands, you can pass a level from 0 to 9 into them like this:

```
$ ./agtvfy verify all -level 2 details
```

When a command takes a level as a parameter, you should start with the lowest value (0), fix issues that are reported from that command, and then run it again at the next highest level. Levels from 0 to 4 report functional issues, 6 to 8 are reporting issues, and 9 is for internal diagnostics. You should run the reports at level 9 only under guidance from Oracle Support. Just as an example, here's the sort of difference you can expect between (for example) level 2 and level 9 when running REPVFY:

■ **Note** This is a purposefully badly set up environment. Hopefully, you won't see anywhere near this level of problems!

```
$ ./repvfy verify all -level 2 details

Please enter the SYSMAN password:

-- ------------------------------------------------------------------- --
-- REPVFY: 2013.0327    Repository: 12.1.0.2.0    04-Apr-2013 16:14:52 --
-- ------------------------------------------------------------------- --

verifyAGENTS
0001. Agents without a host target: 2
1005. Active Agents with clock-skew problems: 1
2001. Managed Agents without a managed ORACLE_HOME: 2
verifyASLM
verifyAVAILABILITY
verifyBLACKOUTS
verifyCAT
verifyCORE
0003. Invalid objects in EM schemas: 2
verifyECM
```

```
verifyEMDIAG
1001. Undefined verification modules: 1
verifyEVENTS
verifyEXADATA
verifyJOBS
verifyJVMD
verifyLOADERS
verifyMETRICS
verifyNOTIFICATIONS
verifyOMS
verifyPLUGINS
verifyREPOSITORY
verifyTARGETS
1003. Discovered entities on Agents not linked to a plugin: 5
1014. Admin group properties with non-used values in leaf groups: 100
2004. Targets without an ORACLE_HOME association: 2
2006. Targets with missing ORACLE_HOME target: 1
2007. Targets with unpromoted ORACLE_HOME target: 1
2010. Targets with hostname and agent name mismatch: 141
verifyUSERS
```

■ **Note**   The line 1001. Undefined verification modules: 1 is a bug in this particular version of REPVFY and should be ignored.

```
$ ./repvfy verify all -level 9 details

Please enter the SYSMAN password:

-- ---------------------------------------------------------------- --
-- REPVFY: 2013.0327    Repository: 12.1.0.2.0    04-Apr-2013 16:18:28 --
-- ---------------------------------------------------------------- --

verifyAGENTS
0001. Agents without a host target: 2
1005. Active Agents with clock-skew problems: 1
2001. Managed Agents without a managed ORACLE_HOME: 2
6006. Deployed Agent plugins lower than OMS plugin: 8
verifyASLM
verifyAVAILABILITY
8001. Composite availability errors: 1
verifyBLACKOUTS
verifyCA
8002. Broken corrective actions: 1
verifyCAT
verifyCORE
0003. Invalid objects in EM schemas: 2
verifyECM
verifyEMDIAG
1001. Undefined verification modules: 1
```

verifyEVENTS
verifyEXADATA
verifyJOBS
verifyJVMD
verifyLOADERS
verifyMETRICS
7005. Metric errors with newer data collections: 3
8001. Targets with response metric errors: 83
verifyNOTIFICATIONS
verifyOMS
verifyPLUGINS
verifyRCA
verifyREPOSITORY
6001. Unanalyzed tables: 10
6005. Tables with locked statistics: 4
6017. Database Timezone mismatch: 1
6023. Missing OMS exportconfig: 1
6037. PLSQL tracing enabled: 24
6039. Newer version available for deployed OMS plugin: 7
6041. AWR retention less than 2 weeks: 1
6042. Timezone mismatch between database and scheduler: 1
7001. Recyclebin not empty: 6
8001. Repeating worker task errors: 3
verifyTARGETS
1003. Discovered entities on Agents not linked to a plugin: 5
1014. Admin group properties with non-used values in leaf groups: 100
2004. Targets without an ORACLE_HOME association: 2
2006. Targets with missing ORACLE_HOME target: 1
2007. Targets with unpromoted ORACLE_HOME target: 1
2010. Targets with hostname and agent name mismatch: 141
6001. Non-standard hostnames discovered: 2
6002. OMS mediated targets without backup Agent: 17
7001. Orphan pending delete targets: 2
7004. Targets in stuck delete pending due to duplicate deletes (13462085): 1
7005. Old unpromoted targets: 412
7006. Duplicate ORACLE_HOME targets: 7
8002. Broken targets: 19
verifyUPGRADE
verifyUSERS
6001. Non-standard EM system administrators accounts: 2
8001. Blocked EM administrators accounts: 5

Summary

This chapter has taken you through some of the main care and feeding areas for your EM12c infrastructure, both from the console and the command-line utilities. Now that you feel more comfortable with managing your EM infrastructure, you're ready to become more familiar with the console itself. That's the subject of our next chapter.

■ ■ ■

CHAPTER 4

Interacting with the EM12c Console

by Niall Litchfield

Oracle Enterprise Manager is a product of many capabilities, but this book focuses on technology management and administration. To that end, Enterprise Manager must make administration and management tasks simpler, more consistent, and faster than the task would be when just utilizing the raw capabilities of the underlying technology. This chapter will help you achieve this by introducing you to Enterprise Manager's main user interface, the web console.

This chapter consists, therefore, of the following components:

- A brief history of the limitations of previous releases

- An overview of how EM12c addresses those limitations

- A review of the menu structures that you will use to navigate the console

- A brief discussion of the customization facilities supplied with the product

Along the way, you will learn how to configure Enterprise Manager to interact effectively with Oracle's support portal, My Oracle Support. You will also learn how to configure notifications and control the use of additional cost management packs, and will become familiar with the console as your administration home.

A Brief History of EM

Oracle Enterprise Manager started life in July 2002 as Java-based client application for managing Oracle Database 9.2. With the release of Oracle Database 10g, this application was reimagined as a web-based management interface, largely focused on the database, but with the ability to manage Oracle databases that spanned multiple physical hosts—the g in 10g stood for *grid* and the database-centric management product was to become known as Enterprise Manager Grid Control. Grid Control provided database administration staff with three key features that were a significant advantage in managing clustered environments, and in managing a variety of databases across an enterprise. These were as follows:

- An administrator could manage distributed environments as one rather than as a collection of targets.

- The state of the whole Oracle database estate could be seen in a single screen.

- It introduced the ability to manage target types other than just the Oracle Database, especially to the growing Oracle Application Server market.

These advantages significantly improved the life of an administrator compared with the previous fragmented, host-based management that tended to dominate the database world at the time. There was, of course, one other advantage that made Enterprise Manager Grid Control attractive to organizations running Oracle its implementation required (and still requires) no additional license cost.

■ **Tip** Enterprise Manager does make easily available several additional cost features, either embedded in the base product or sold separately. You will look at how to control management access later in the chapter. It is important to be clear that when using, for example, the Performance pages discussed in Chapter 9, you are using a separately licensed feature and not the free base product. As you will see when we discuss management pack access, you can use the Packs for This Page link to determine the necessary license for any currently active page.

As Oracle expanded its product offering through the 2000s into middleware, applications, and beyond, it became apparent that an enterprise-wide management tool would be a great advantage, and a source of additional revenue for Oracle. Each of the products that Oracle sold, however, tended to have both built-in management capabilities and internal teams that were experts in the management of their particular technology stack. Oracle settled on a solution by ensuring that the existing teams developed management functionality for their product within the Enterprise Manager product stack.

As we approached the end of that decade, Oracle's former database management product had become a fully fledged enterprise technology management product, allowing management of all Oracle products and a few third-party products via a centralized management console. There were, however, at least two structural problems with the product as it matured:

- Technology stack
- Interface

Technology

The technology stack in use for the 10.x series of Enterprise Manager was Oracle's old J2EE application server platform, Oracle Internet Application Server. Oracle had effectively given up on this platform a couple of years previously with the purchase of the BEA WebLogic product line. The 11.x release of Grid Control migrated the existing Grid Control product to the newer WebLogic technology stack, and integrated the database-derived Grid Control interface with the newly developed Fusion Middleware Control that used Oracle's own Application Development Framework (ADF). Enterprise Manager since 11g, therefore, has used the software stack shown in Figure 4-1. This architecture is likely to be current for at least the next five years.

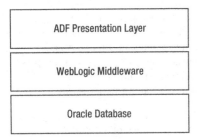

Figure 4-1. Oracle Enterprise Manager technology stack

However, all the technologies that Grid Control is able to manage advance, and all at different rates, and in some cases at rates and directions outside the control of Oracle Corporation. The monolithic design of previous Enterprise Manager releases meant that the product was, almost by design, permanently behind the release cycle of monitored products. This situation meant that customers could patch monitored targets to address production issues and then find that they could not obtain support for monitoring issues because the patched release was not certified with the enterprise management product. Oracle has addressed this issue, and others, with the plug-in architecture of EM12c.

■ **Note** We are familiar with a project to implement Oracle Enterprise Manager 11g for a UK-based enterprise with an installed estate of RAC, WebLogic, SOA, and E-Business Suite. EM 11g was specifically chosen because of its support for SOA, which was a key technology for the client. However, EM certification permanently lagged behind the SOA releases, and this led to significant support issues for the client when Oracle Support would not take service requests because the four-digit version number of the WebLogic server was one patch set ahead of the certified version. We expect the plug-in nature of support for managed targets to address this issue.

Interface

The visual interface for Grid Control had always been in the hands of the development teams providing the underlying management functionality. This had two large consequences. First, the interface design was, to put it charitably, old-fashioned. The original product was released in early 2004, which almost certainly means that it started development life sometime between 2001 and 2003. It's worth remembering what web interfaces were like in the early part of this century; the Grid Control product had usability issues, but it was by no means alone. Figure 4-2 shows the old-style interface, essentially a white page full of links arranged broadly by feature area.

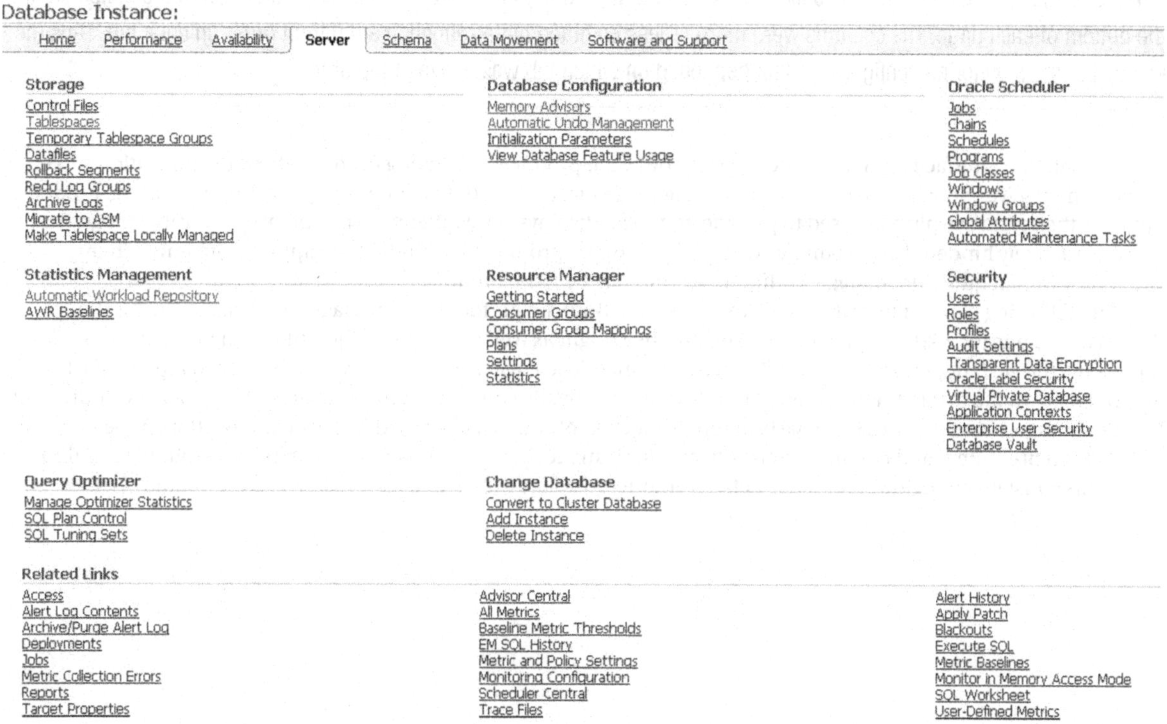

Database Instance:

| Home | Performance | Availability | **Server** | Schema | Data Movement | Software and Support |

Storage
Control Files
Tablespaces
Temporary Tablespace Groups
Datafiles
Rollback Segments
Redo Log Groups
Archive Logs
Migrate to ASM
Make Tablespace Locally Managed

Statistics Management
Automatic Workload Repository
AWR Baselines

Query Optimizer
Manage Optimizer Statistics
SQL Plan Control
SQL Tuning Sets

Related Links
Access
Alert Log Contents
Archive/Purge Alert Log
Deployments
Jobs
Metric Collection Errors
Reports
Target Properties

Database Configuration
Memory Advisors
Automatic Undo Management
Initialization Parameters
View Database Feature Usage

Resource Manager
Getting Started
Consumer Groups
Consumer Group Mappings
Plans
Settings
Statistics

Change Database
Convert to Cluster Database
Add Instance
Delete Instance

Advisor Central
All Metrics
Baseline Metric Thresholds
EM SQL History
Metric and Policy Settings
Monitoring Configuration
Scheduler Central
Trace Files

Oracle Scheduler
Jobs
Chains
Schedules
Programs
Job Classes
Windows
Window Groups
Global Attributes
Automated Maintenance Tasks

Security
Users
Roles
Profiles
Audit Settings
Transparent Data Encryption
Oracle Label Security
Virtual Private Database
Application Contexts
Enterprise User Security
Database Vault

Alert History
Apply Patch
Blackouts
Execute SQL
Metric Baselines
Monitor in Memory Access Mode
SQL Worksheet
User-Defined Metrics

Figure 4-2. Old-style interface

A good GUI has, among other things, the following characteristics:

Clarity: It's easy to find what you want.

Consistency: Similar tasks are done in similar ways.

Efficiency: Tasks are quickly and easily achieved.

Grid Control was a letdown in all of these areas, primarily because of its interface design and poor navigation in the product. The prime paradigm for the database pages was that of a categorized list of links. This led to a text-heavy set of pages with links sometimes located in surprising places—for example, the AWR interface, which you might expect to find on the Performance tab, was in fact located on the Server tab of the main database management screen. Overall, the choice and layout of links was more reminiscent of small, community ad sites such as Craigslist rather than a task-oriented management application.

This decision mattered, probably more than the designers imagined, because of the principle that a good UI should be clear. The old Grid Control interface left even experienced hands at times clicking from tab to tab and link to link, trying to find pages that they knew were listed somewhere. The product was also littered with odd artifacts that were never really addressed; for example, the server management screen for databases had two distinct links labeled JOBS that would take the user to separate pages, one for the database scheduler and one for the Enterprise Manager scheduler. There was no link to the job scheduler with which most DBAs of the time were familiar, DBMS_JOB.

■ **Note** One particularly annoying aspect of the Grid Control interface was the inconsistent arrangement of columns at the bottom of each page. The columns were more or less common but arranged in a different order on each tab. Thus the location of the monitoring configuration link depended on which tab was active at the time.

Second, the interface design was inconsistent between products. Switching from database to application server management gave you whole new interface paradigms. For example, context menus appeared in parts of the product but not others, and the plug-ins used to provide graphical displays were different. This inconsistency in appearance and style actively hindered users familiar with one part of the product from finding the appropriate functionality when they were required to manage a different technology with the product.

The following figures illustrate these problems well. Both are performance management pages, one for the database and one for a J2EE application server, but they might as well come from different products. Figure 4-3 represents the current performance of a database instance. The page uses area charts extensively to represent CPU and I/O load on the instance and to categorize current activity. By contrast, Figure 4-4, which is the nearest equivalent WebLogic page, primarily uses line charts to represent current activity, allows extensive customization of the information presented, and has an entirely different look and feel. For administrators with responsibility for multiple areas, this constant changing of interface actively interfered with the effectiveness with which they could operate.

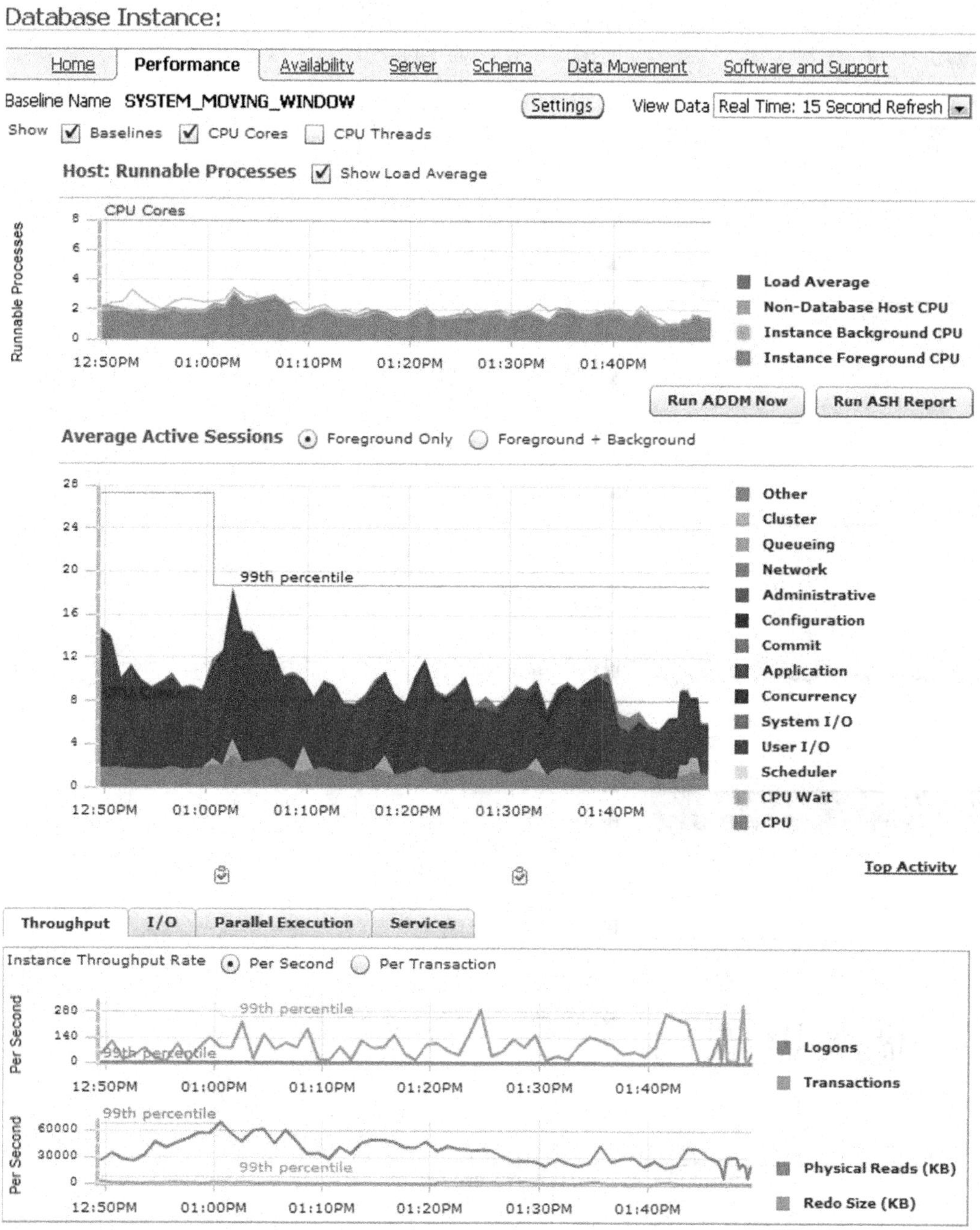

Database Instance:

| Home | Performance | Availability | Server | Schema | Data Movement | Software and Support |

Baseline Name **SYSTEM_MOVING_WINDOW**   (Settings)   View Data Real Time: 15 Second Refresh ▾

Show ☑ Baselines   ☑ CPU Cores   ☐ CPU Threads

Host: Runnable Processes ☑ Show Load Average

- Load Average
- Non-Database Host CPU
- Instance Background CPU
- Instance Foreground CPU

(Run ADDM Now)   (Run ASH Report)

Average Active Sessions ⦿ Foreground Only   ◯ Foreground + Background

- Other
- Cluster
- Queueing
- Network
- Administrative
- Configuration
- Commit
- Application
- Concurrency
- System I/O
- User I/O
- Scheduler
- CPU Wait
- CPU

Top Activity

| Throughput | I/O | Parallel Execution | Services |

Instance Throughput Rate ⦿ Per Second   ◯ Per Transaction

- Logons
- Transactions
- Physical Reads (KB)
- Redo Size (KB)

Figure 4-3. *Database Performance home page*

103

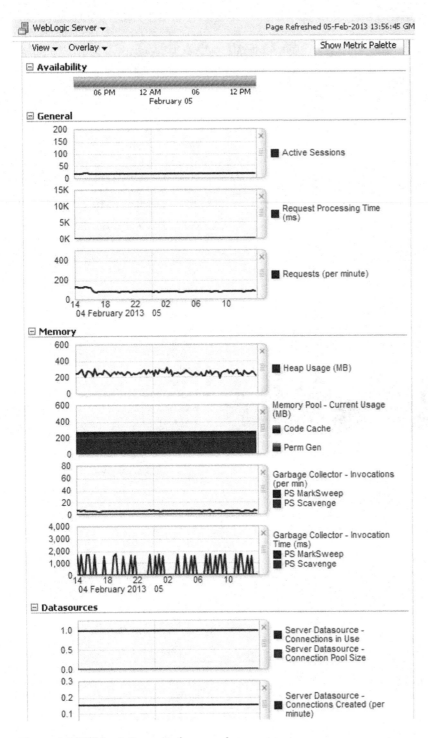

Figure 4-4. *WebLogic Server Performance home page*

Like many other web developers of the time, those responsible for Grid Control had to contend with a variety of browsers with a range of capabilities. However, as you have seen, Oracle's product had significant shortcomings in the areas of consistency and efficiency—the core features of an excellent GUI. These are all addressed by the Cloud Control release.

Cloud Control

At this point, you are probably wondering why this chapter has spent several pages on previous releases. This material is presented so you have the appropriate background to help you understand the design decisions of the Enterprise Manager team in creating the interface for this new product, which can seem overwhelming and overly complicated at first. The EM12c user interface has been entirely redesigned from the ground up, and addresses almost all of the concerns surrounding the previous generations of the product. This inevitably means that even experienced administrators must face a learning curve. Helping you through this curve is the main focus of this chapter.

■ **Note** The only areas of EM12c that could still use significant improvement are browser compatibility (Google Chrome/Chromium has some rendering issues, for example) and integration with browser navigation—for example, the Back button.

Cloud Control uses the following main UI features to allow the user to interact efficiently, clearly, and consistently with the product. The primary navigation element is no longer the hyperlink, but a menu system, combined with various wizards for multistep tasks. The net result of all this work is that it is now much more appropriate to describe Enterprise Manager as a web-based application rather than as a web-based management interface.

Cloud Control provides three distinct menu bars:

- Cloud Control menu bar (Figure 4-5)

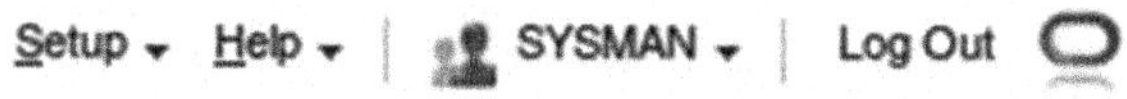

Setup ▾   Help ▾ | ▮▮ SYSMAN ▾ | Log Out ⬭

Figure 4-5. Cloud Control menu bar

- Navigation menu bar (Figure 4-6)

Figure 4-6. Navigation menu bar

- Target Management menu bar (Figure 4-7)

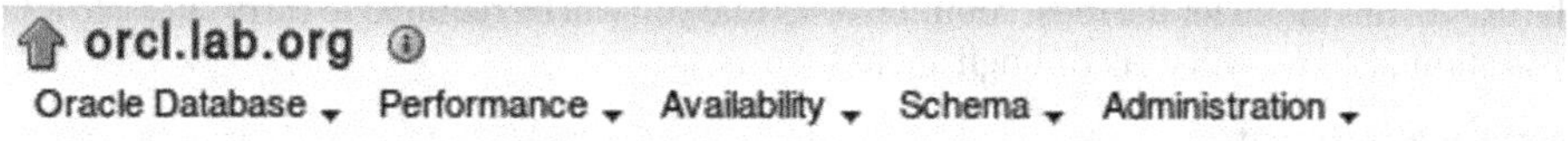

⬆ **orcl.lab.org** ⓘ
Oracle Database ▾   Performance ▾   Availability ▾   Schema ▾   Administration ▾

Figure 4-7. Target Management menu bar

The following sections discuss the roles that each menu bar plays in your operation of the Cloud Control product. Once you have established a clear understanding of these roles, the location of any given feature should be clear, and the way in which you interact with that feature should be consistent and effective.

■ **Note** There are no documented names for these menu bars in the Oracle documentation, so these terms are used throughout this chapter.

Cloud Control Menu Bar

The Cloud Control menu bar, located at the top-right side of the screen, is used for managing Cloud Control itself. This menu bar contains a useful Help menu and a short menu for personalizing system options for your administration account. However, the primary menu is the Setup menu. You will use this menu extensively to manage access and operation of the Enterprise Manager installation. The Setup menu is divided into five sections, as shown in Figure 4-8.

Figure 4-8. Setup menu

The Setup menu illustrates some of the issues the application designers have had rationalizing and streamlining the application, and we expect further work in this area as the product matures. The menu does provide access to all of the system-wide features that you need in order to set up and maintain the Enterprise Manager application in one location, but there is no clear rationale for the location of some of these items. Rather than running through the menu item by item, we will look at the uses of this menu for the most common tasks that you will be required to carry out as an administrator.

The administration tasks we will walk through are as follows:

- Security management

- My Oracle Support integration

- Network proxy configuration

- Configuration of notifications and alerts

- Controlling management pack access

We do not cover incident management (see Chapter 12 for that), or more-advanced features such as product extensibility and the command-line interface. This chapter is intended primarily to orient you to the basic layout of the console and the essential operations you will initially perform.

Security Management

Starting with this release, Oracle has centralized a lot of the security management in the product. To operate effectively, you will need to spend some time configuring the credentials that you require. In particular, you will need to administer the areas of security included in Table 4-1.

Table 4-1. *Securable Items Within Cloud Control*

Area	Purpose	Example
Enterprise Manager administrator	User access to EM	SYSMAN
Enterprise Manager roles	Rights within EM	PUBLIC
Named credentials	Target access	NC_DB_ORCL_SYS
Preferred credentials	Target access	NC_DB_ORCL_SYSTEM
Monitoring credentials	Agent access to targets	DBSNMP

In addition, you will probably want to set up a privilege delegation scheme so that necessary rights for administration are cascaded through a simple hierarchy of roles and rotation of agent registration passwords. These items, however, are highly dependent on the organization and security requirements of the enterprise for which you work and so lie outside the scope of this book.

The core concept here is that of named credentials. These preconfigured authentication credentials allow users and administrators to access various managed targets in a secure fashion without remembering a plethora of username/password combinations. The time you spend setting these up will seem rather tedious, especially in a large environment, but it is well worth it in terms of time saved in day-to-day operations and in allowing end users appropriately privileged access without disclosing passwords. You should set up the named credentials by using an account that is unlikely to be removed. (For example, you could use SYSMAN to own all named credentials and then grant access to named administrators.) This concept of a credential set to which administrators have access is a big step forward in security and will likely be welcomed by your internal security administrators. On the downside, you are likely to end up having to walk them through this process and explain access control, which is now more complicated than previously.

■ **Tip** We strongly suggest that you implement a naming convention for credentials, because you will have a lot of credentials to manage. One example is to use NC_<TARGETTYPE>_<TARGETNAME>_<USER> to indicate the user and targets to which the credentials apply. This works for an environment in which passwords differ between targets, but your setup may vary.

The first security administration task is to add administrator accounts. Once this is done, you can define and assign roles and set up access.

Adding an Administrator

This section outlines the process for adding a new administrator account. If you haven't yet created a dedicated administration account for yourself, you might want to follow along with the following exercise.

You will need the items of information shown in Table 4-2. You may want to make a table like this for your own use when adding administrators.

Table 4-2. *New Administrator Details*

Item	Purpose	Example
Username	Identify the user	JOE_DBA
Password	For authentication	Welcome1
E-mail address	Mail for notifications	joe.dba@lab.org

Follow these steps to add a new administrator account:

1. To start the wizard, choose Setup ➤ Security ➤ Administrators. A screen displays, listing all the administration accounts on the system. If this is the first administrator that you add, you'll see the page in Figure 4-9.

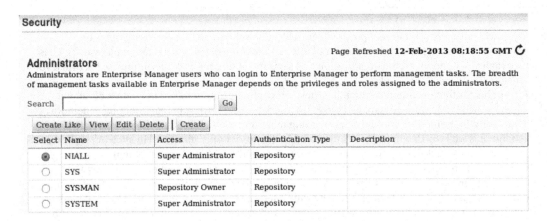

Figure 4-9. *Security Wizard*

2. Click the Create button. Then fill in the basic details about the administrator, as shown in Figure 4-10. (This is where your table will come in handy.) Note that adding the e-mail address will automatically create a 24×7 notification schedule. You will adjust this later.

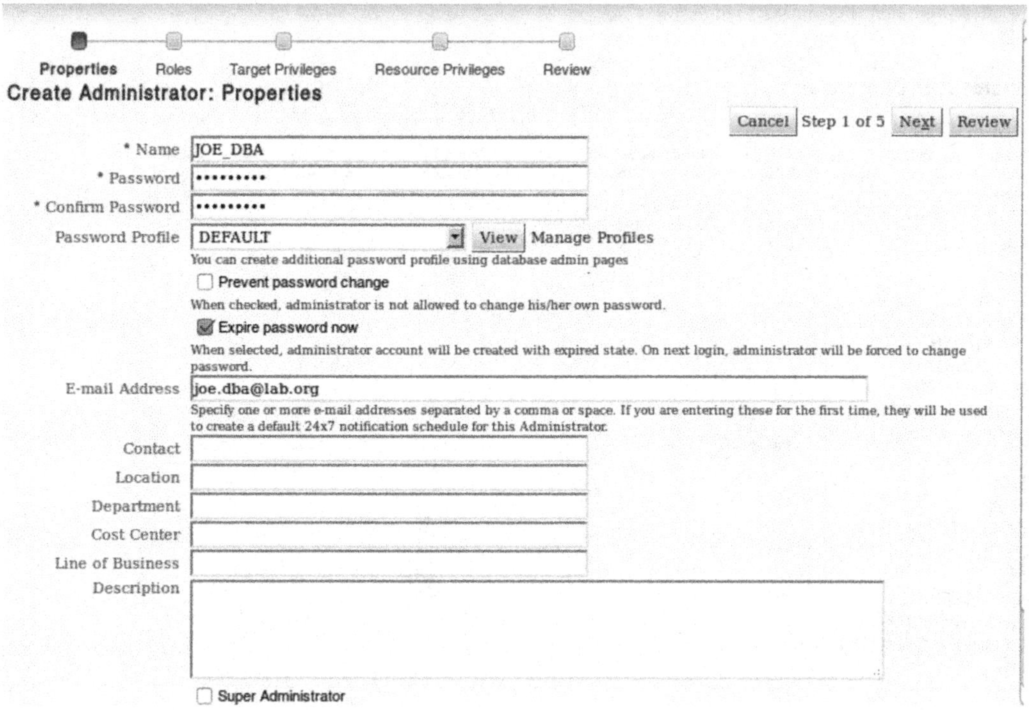

Figure 4-10. *Administrator details*

3. Click Next. Then select the Enterprise Manager roles that this administrator will take. You will learn more about roles in the next section. For now, notice that the range of roles is extensive and introduces role-based management for a wide variety of administration tasks. In this example, just use the default roles that come with the product (see Figure 4-11). Each repository-based user that you create is actually a database account on the repository database. You can manage profiles and resources by using the built-in resource and profile management of the database.

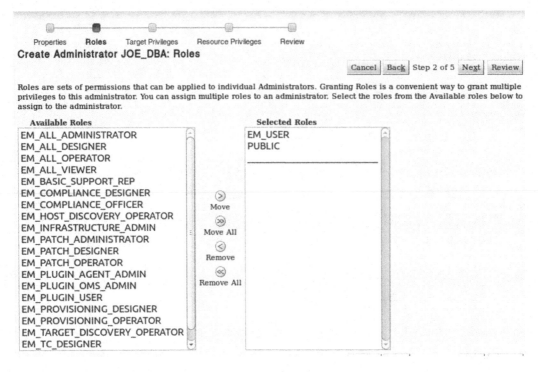

Figure 4-11. *Adding roles*

■ **Tip**   At the very least, we suggest utilizing the password complexity and expiration options of the database to ensure that your EM administrator accounts follow your corporate policies.

---

4.   For now, click Next. You are presented with the screen in Figure 4-12, in which you can assign privileges for the user, both across the enterprise and to specific targets.

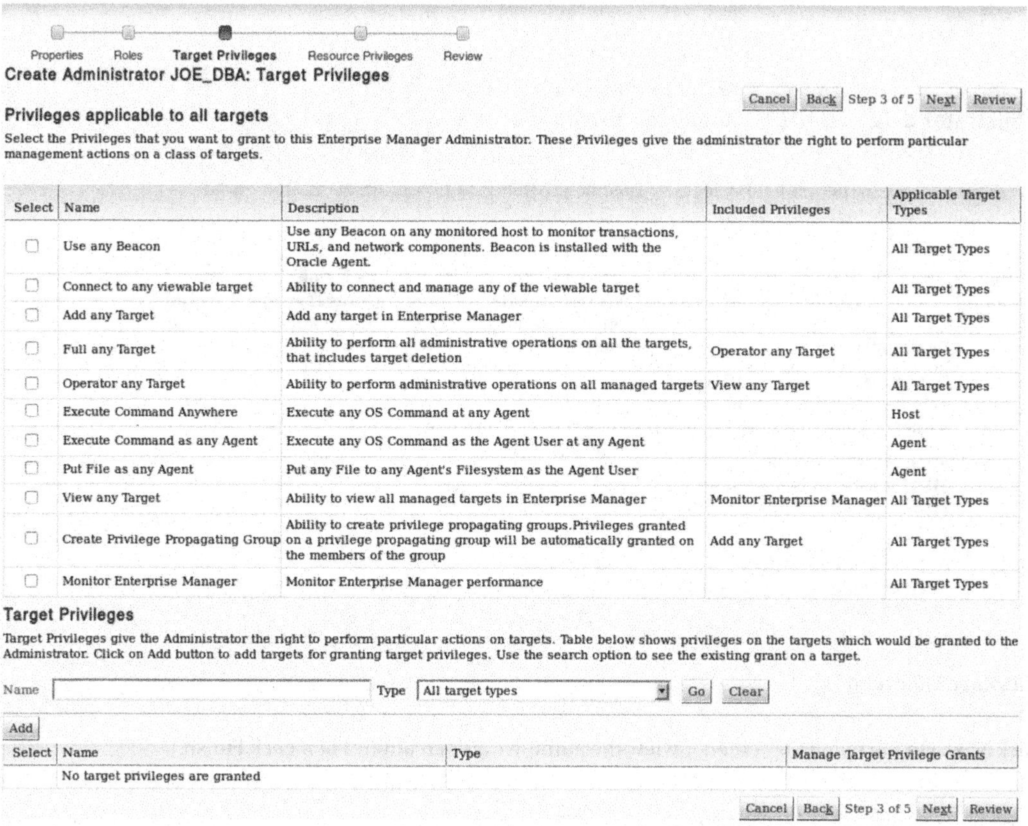

Properties   Roles   **Target Privileges**   Resource Privileges   Review

Create Administrator JOE_DBA: Target Privileges

Cancel   Back   Step 3 of 5   Next   Review

Privileges applicable to all targets

Select the Privileges that you want to grant to this Enterprise Manager Administrator. These Privileges give the administrator the right to perform particular management actions on a class of targets.

Select	Name	Description	Included Privileges	Applicable Target Types
☐	Use any Beacon	Use any Beacon on any monitored host to monitor transactions, URLs, and network components. Beacon is installed with the Oracle Agent.		All Target Types
☐	Connect to any viewable target	Ability to connect and manage any of the viewable target		All Target Types
☐	Add any Target	Add any target in Enterprise Manager		All Target Types
☐	Full any Target	Ability to perform all administrative operations on all the targets, that includes target deletion	Operator any Target	All Target Types
☐	Operator any Target	Ability to perform administrative operations on all managed targets	View any Target	All Target Types
☐	Execute Command Anywhere	Execute any OS Command at any Agent		Host
☐	Execute Command as any Agent	Execute any OS Command as the Agent User at any Agent		Agent
☐	Put File as any Agent	Put any File to any Agent's Filesystem as the Agent User		Agent
☐	View any Target	Ability to view all managed targets in Enterprise Manager	Monitor Enterprise Manager	All Target Types
☐	Create Privilege Propagating Group	Ability to create privilege propagating groups. Privileges granted on a privilege propagating group will be automatically granted on the members of the group	Add any Target	All Target Types
☐	Monitor Enterprise Manager	Monitor Enterprise Manager performance		All Target Types

Target Privileges

Target Privileges give the Administrator the right to perform particular actions on targets. Table below shows privileges on the targets which would be granted to the Administrator. Click on Add button to add targets for granting target privileges. Use the search option to see the existing grant on a target.

Name [   ]   Type [All target types ▾]   Go   Clear

Add

Select	Name	Type	Manage Target Privilege Grants
	No target privileges are granted		

Cancel   Back   Step 3 of 5   Next   Review

Figure 4-12. *Target privilege assignment*

5. Click Next. The configuration screen shown in Figure 4-13 presents you with the various Enterprise Manager Resource types that the administrator can manage. For example, you can ensure that the administrator can view and edit patching plans for deploying patches across the enterprise.

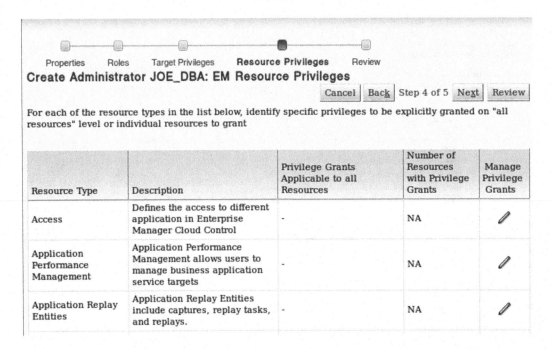

Figure 4-13. *Resource allocation*

6. Click Next. On the following screen, review the administrator creation. Then click Finish.

Creating a Role for Access Control

Once you have your administrator accounts set up correctly and have tested login access for the users themselves, you should use Enterprise Manager roles to configure role-based access control. On the Role Management home page, you will see the built-in EM12c roles and the various management operations that you can carry out.

A *role* is a named set of privileges, both on targets and on Enterprise Manager functionality. Thus, a role could define, for example, the rights necessary to manage a particular target type, or to perform an Enterprise Manager operation such as requesting a new self-service database. In addition, roles can contain other roles. Role design is, therefore, a core part of any effective Cloud Control deployment, but will be dependent on the specifics of your enterprise.

You will walk through an example by creating a database administrator role that will have rights appropriate for this job role. You can follow along in the next exercise. As you will see, the wizard allocates privileges in the following order: Roles, Target, Resource.

■ **Tip** In general, try to define roles that match job roles or tasks in your organization. In addition, use an appropriate naming convention—for example, you might use the LDAP directory group names that define your operating system security.

To create your Database Administrator role, perform the following steps:

1. On the Role Management page, click Create. The wizard in Figure 4-14 appears. Avoid the temptation to skip adding a description. Future administrators will be greatly aided by a useful description that indicates the privileges wrapped up in the role as well as the business purpose for which it was designed.

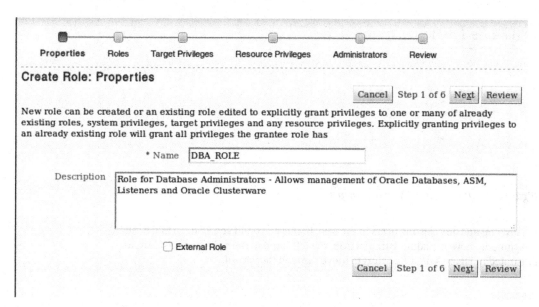

Figure 4-14. *Role Creation Wizard—step 1*

2. Click Next. Then add the EM12c roles that you require. In this example, you add the discovery operator roles, as well as the patch administrator role that allows full administration of the patch lifecycle (see Figure 4-15).

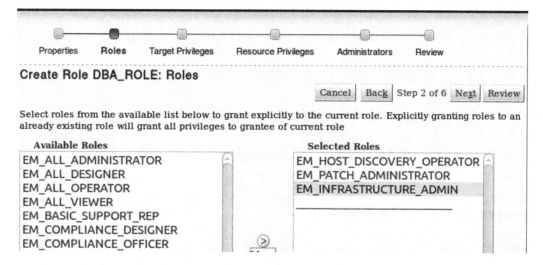

Figure 4-15. *Role Creation Wizard—step 2*

3. Click Next. The resource management right allocations screen opens. The critical section of this screen, shown in Figure 4-16, is on the far right and is labeled Manage Privilege Grants. Click the pencil icon for each category of privilege and assign rights individually. In this case, add all rights under the Target Discovery Framework to allow your DBA to manage target discovery.

Figure 4-16. *Role Creation Wizard—step 3*

4. Finally, you add any existing users to the role. In this case, add Joe_DBA. To make the assignment, move the administrators from the left-hand to the right-hand list box, as illustrated in Figure 4-17. Click Next to move through the wizard.

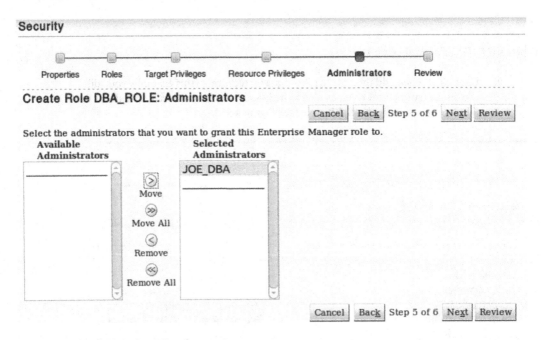

Figure 4-17. *Role Creation Wizard—step 4*

5. Finally, click Review and then Finish, and you have created your new role.

■ **Note**   Oracle provides the PUBLIC role specifically for customization suitable for all users of the EM installation.

Configuration of Support Integration

Enterprise Manager is closely integrated with the My Oracle Support site available to all customers with a support contract. It isn't uncommon to find customer sites that do not set up this integration, however. This is a significant mistake. Fortunately, the Cloud Control menu bar makes the required tasks straightforward.

Configuring integration with My Oracle Support offers the following key advantages that will make your life supporting Oracle significantly easier:

- Enhanced incident and problem reporting

- Access to the support knowledge base from within Enterprise Manager

- Patch lifecycle management

Integration with support requires the following to be set up, access from the OMS to the My Oracle Support site, proxy configuration, and My Oracle Support credentials. In addition, you can optionally assign managed targets to different customer support identifiers (CSIs) by linking them to an administrator account for that CSI.

Proxy Configuration

In most organizations, access to the Internet from the corporate network is controlled by the use of a proxy server. This server is designed as an intermediary to both facilitate and control access to resources on the Internet. In this case, the resources you require access to are the My Oracle Support web portal and the various Oracle and third-party servers that provide services that Oracle customers can request as part of a support contract. In this section, you will walk through a proxy configuration. If your organization has a proxy server that automatically authenticates users via a Microsoft Active Directory domain, you will probably want to read the upcoming section "Using the NTLMAPS Proxy" as a workaround.

Configuring Proxy Server Access

Complete the following steps to configure the proxy server:

1.   Select Proxy Settings from the Setup menu. The screen in Figure 4-18 appears.

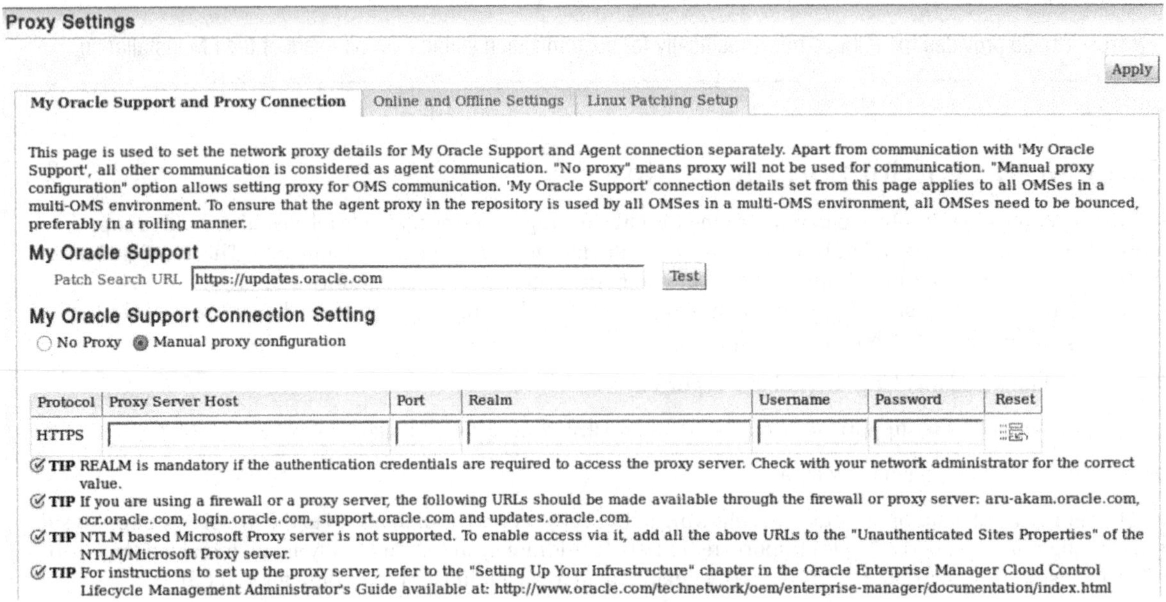

Proxy Settings

Apply

| My Oracle Support and Proxy Connection | Online and Offline Settings | Linux Patching Setup |

This page is used to set the network proxy details for My Oracle Support and Agent connection separately. Apart from communication with 'My Oracle Support', all other communication is considered as agent communication. "No proxy" means proxy will not be used for communication. "Manual proxy configuration" option allows setting proxy for OMS communication. 'My Oracle Support' connection details set from this page applies to all OMSes in a multi-OMS environment. To ensure that the agent proxy in the repository is used by all OMSes in a multi-OMS environment, all OMSes need to be bounced, preferably in a rolling manner.

My Oracle Support

Patch Search URL [https://updates.oracle.com]   Test

My Oracle Support Connection Setting

○ No Proxy ◉ Manual proxy configuration

Protocol	Proxy Server Host	Port	Realm		Username	Password	Reset
HTTPS							

✔ **TIP** REALM is mandatory if the authentication credentials are required to access the proxy server. Check with your network administrator for the correct value.

✔ **TIP** If you are using a firewall or a proxy server, the following URLs should be made available through the firewall or proxy server: aru-akam.oracle.com, ccr.oracle.com, login.oracle.com, support.oracle.com and updates.oracle.com.

✔ **TIP** NTLM based Microsoft Proxy server is not supported. To enable access via it, add all the above URLs to the "Unauthenticated Sites Properties" of the NTLM/Microsoft Proxy server.

✔ **TIP** For instructions to set up the proxy server, refer to the "Setting Up Your Infrastructure" chapter in the Oracle Enterprise Manager Cloud Control Lifecycle Management Administrator's Guide available at: http://www.oracle.com/technetwork/oem/enterprise-manager/documentation/index.html

Figure 4-18. Proxy details

2. Enter the details of your proxy server, or the NTLMAPS proxy you have configured as an alternative, together with any necessary authentication. Test access to updates.oracle.com using the Test button.

3. You will also likely want to ensure that Agent to OMS communication *doesn't* use the proxy. To do this, choose the No Proxy option at the bottom of the page, as shown in Figure 4-19.

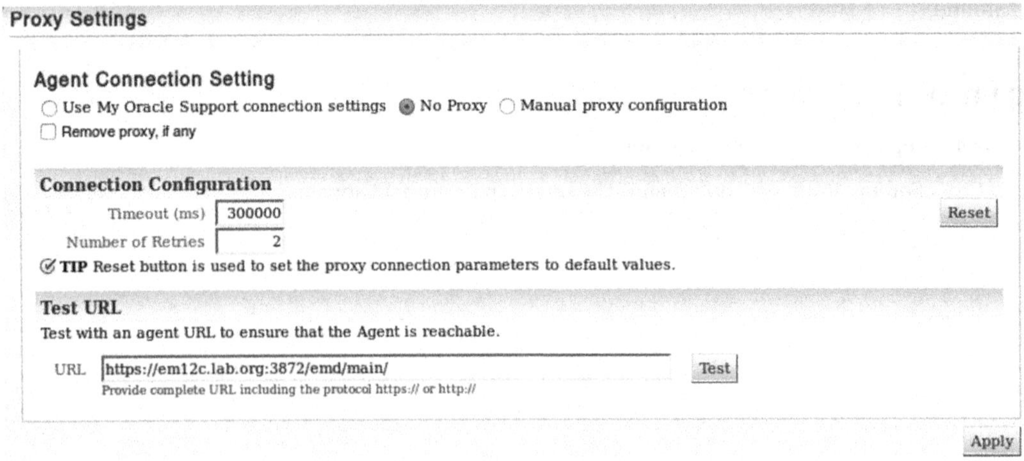

Proxy Settings

Agent Connection Setting

○ Use My Oracle Support connection settings ◉ No Proxy ○ Manual proxy configuration
☐ Remove proxy, if any

Connection Configuration

Timeout (ms) [300000]   Reset
Number of Retries [2]

✔ **TIP** Reset button is used to set the proxy connection parameters to default values.

Test URL

Test with an agent URL to ensure that the Agent is reachable.

URL [https://em12c.lab.org:3872/emd/main/]   Test
Provide complete URL including the protocol https:// or http://

Apply

Figure 4-19. Excluding agents from proxy access

4. The final step is to configure MOS credentials. This can and should be done for SYSMAN, perhaps using a generic account owned by the organization (for example, em@lab.org). This can be done by using the Set Credentials menu option shown in Figure 4-20.

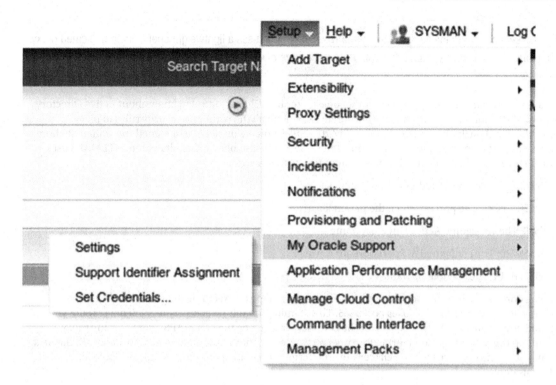

Figure 4-20. *Configuring My Oracle Support credentials*

■ **Note** If you have multiple CSIs with Oracle, perhaps because you are a third-party support company, you can assign different CSIs to various targets, and then each administrator will be able to obtain support on only the systems they are entitled to in accordance with their contract. You set this up via the Support Identifier Assignment option.

Although simple proxy authentication using challenge/response is simple to set up, over the years there have been a number of bugs associated with proxy configuration in Enterprise Manager. The product is definitely improving in this regard; however, you may still have problems authenticating to enterprise proxy servers that use NTLM to automatically authenticate users—a fairly common configuration given the ubiquity of Active Directory in the marketplace as an authentication repository. This is because NTLM proxy servers are not supported by Cloud Control. Instead, the official Oracle recommendation is to allow various oracle.com sites to be exempt from the corporate proxy configuration.

Using the NTLMAPS Proxy

The NTLM Authentication Proxy Server (NTLMAPS) is a proxy server—essentially a smart Python script and some open source NTLM libraries that redirect requests for Internet URIs to an upstream or parent proxy server. It adds appropriate browser headers if required and, crucially for EM12c purposes, authenticates correctly against the upstream proxy server with NT credentials. The project which is licensed under the GNU General Public License and so is cost free can be found at http://ntlmaps.sourceforge.net/.

> ■ **Caution**   This section covers the setup of an alternative solution that uses a lightweight open source dedicated proxy. If you choose to use this option, make sure that you gain the consent of your network administrators.

This means we can run our own proxy server that doesn't require Cloud Control to know about Active Directory authentication and still authenticate against the corporate proxy with all the corporate security rules in place. To install, download and unzip the distribution to /opt/ntlmaps. If you are on RedHat or something similar, Python is already available as part of the standard distribution. Otherwise, you'll also need to install Python. NTLMAPS uses a configuration file, server.cfg. You'll need to enter values for the following:

- PARENT_PROXY: The IP address of the parent server

- PARENT_PORT: The port on which the parent listens

- USER: The configured Active Directory name

- PASSWORD: The configured AD password for the user

- NT_DOMAIN: The NT domain name

Once this is done, start the proxy server manually for the time being by executing the supplied script, python main.py. By default, NTLMAPS uses port 5865. This should probably be acceptable. Whichever route you take, you should now configure Internet access for the OMS server(s) using the NTLMAPS address as the proxy address in step 2 in the preceding "Configuring Proxy Server Access" section. Once the proxy is working OK, the next step is to configure a Linux service by using chkconfig. The script I use is an open source script available in the code repository for this book.

Notifications

One of the major roles for Enterprise Manager is to trigger alerts when managed targets encounter an event that requires attention. Classic examples of this occur when a web server is down or when a data store is running out of space as data is added. Enterprise Manager splits this task into two distinct phases: alerting and notification. Both areas are configurable from the Cloud Control menu bar.

The alert phase is concerned with recording the occurrence of a particular event, usually driven by a certain metric. This information becomes visible on the target home page after processing by the management server. The fact that alerts fire but do not necessarily raise alarms for administrators is a common cause of confusion for users new to the product.

The notification phase, by contrast, is the process of sending the details of the alert by some method to allow an appropriate administrator to respond to the alert condition. For example, a DBA might be paged to let her know that a database's system tablespace is dangerously low on space and that she should add space to the tablespace urgently. Notifications traditionally take place via e-mail, but they can also be routed via SNMP, perhaps to an operational control center, by PL/SQL procedures that a DBA or database developer might write or by running an operating system command (perhaps a shell script) on the management server.

Once you have successfully installed Enterprise Manager and while logged in using the SYSMAN account, one of your first tasks should be to add a notification method that can be used to notify the administrators you set up. In this example, you will use e-mail, because that is by far the most common method encountered in real installations. To start the process, choose Setup ➤ Notifications ➤ Notification Methods, as shown in Figure 4-21.

Notification Methods
Customize Email Formats...
My Notification Schedule
Notifications
Provisioning and Patching
My Oracle Support

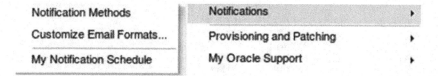

Figure 4-21. *Notification methods*

The screen in Figure 4-22 then displays. You can use this screen to set up the details of the corporate e-mail server(s), together with any authentication credentials that are required. The mail servers that you use *must* be configured to allow SMTP communication. You will probably need to ask your mail administrator which to use, because many corporate e-mail configurations allow only SMTP from specific servers, and they may require the account that you configure to authenticate to be a member of a specific group.

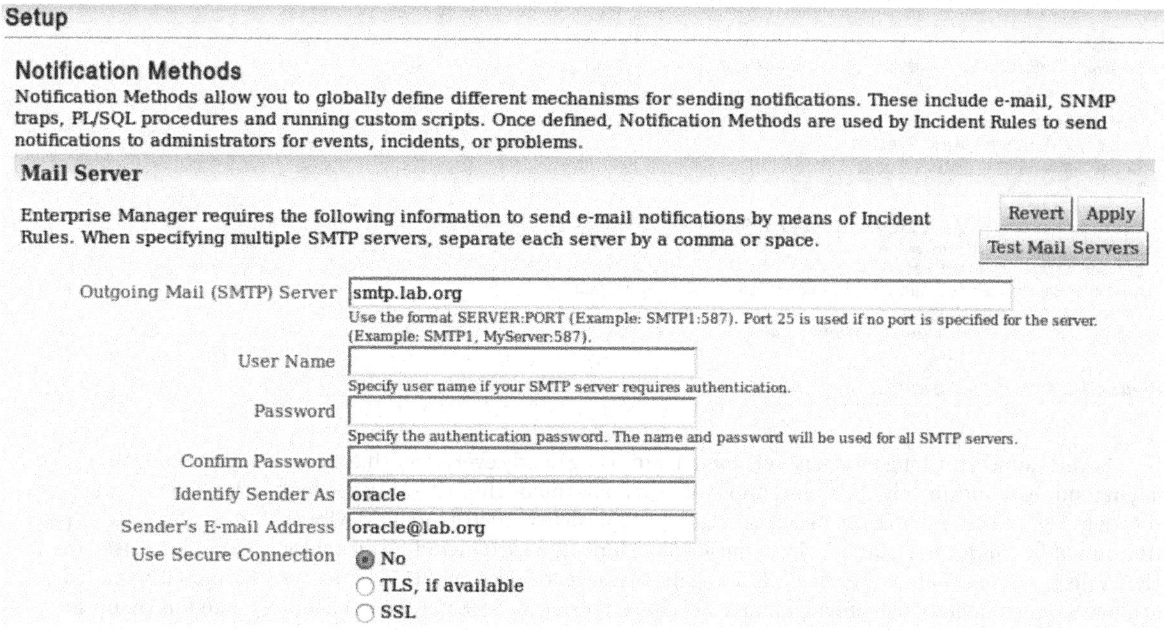

Setup
Notification Methods
Notification Methods allow you to globally define different mechanisms for sending notifications. These include e-mail, SNMP traps, PL/SQL procedures and running custom scripts. Once defined, Notification Methods are used by Incident Rules to send notifications to administrators for events, incidents, or problems.
Mail Server
Enterprise Manager requires the following information to send e-mail notifications by means of Incident Rules. When specifying multiple SMTP servers, separate each server by a comma or space.
Revert
Apply
Test Mail Servers
Outgoing Mail (SMTP) Server
smtp.lab.org
Use the format SERVER:PORT (Example: SMTP1:587). Port 25 is used if no port is specified for the server. (Example: SMTP1, MyServer:587).
User Name
Specify user name if your SMTP server requires authentication.
Password
Specify the authentication password. The name and password will be used for all SMTP servers.
Confirm Password
Identify Sender As
oracle
Sender's E-mail Address
oracle@lab.org
Use Secure Connection
No
TLS, if available
SSL

Figure 4-22. *SMTP server details*

By default, Enterprise Manager provides two e-mail templates for delivering notification of events. These are known as long- and short-format e-mails. You will probably want to customize these, especially to ensure that your e-mail client has rules configured to process the e-mails efficiently. To customize the e-mail format, you choose Customize Email Formats from the Notifications submenu (shown earlier in Figure 4-21). This presents you with the screen in Figure 4-23, which defaults to showing the long format for metric alerts, though you can change this with the drop-downs at the top of the screen.

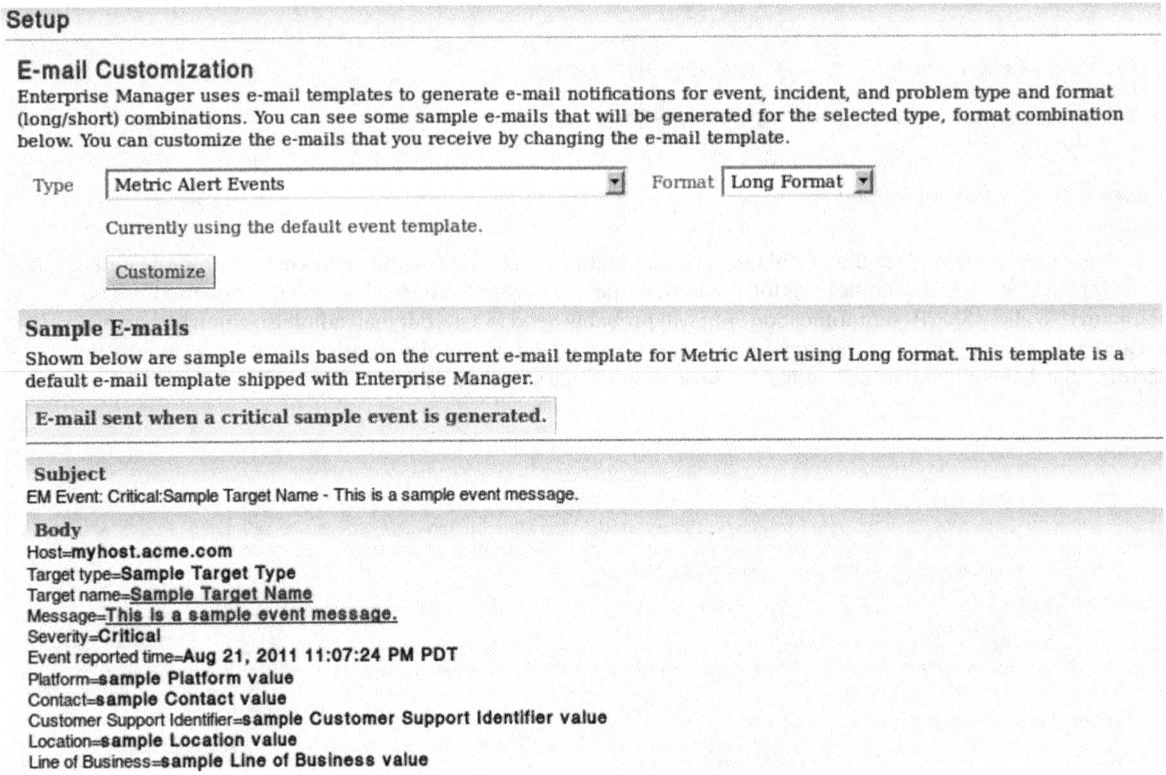

Setup

E-mail Customization

Enterprise Manager uses e-mail templates to generate e-mail notifications for event, incident, and problem type and format (long/short) combinations. You can see some sample e-mails that will be generated for the selected type, format combination below. You can customize the e-mails that you receive by changing the e-mail template.

Type | Metric Alert Events ▾ | Format | Long Format ▾ |

Currently using the default event template.

[Customize]

Sample E-mails

Shown below are sample emails based on the current e-mail template for Metric Alert using Long format. This template is a default e-mail template shipped with Enterprise Manager.

> **E-mail sent when a critical sample event is generated.**

Subject
EM Event: Critical:Sample Target Name - This is a sample event message.

Body
Host=**myhost.acme.com**
Target type=**Sample Target Type**
Target name=**Sample Target Name**
Message=**This is a sample event message.**
Severity=**Critical**
Event reported time=**Aug 21, 2011 11:07:24 PM PDT**
Platform=**sample Platform value**
Contact=**sample Contact value**
Customer Support Identifier=**sample Customer Support Identifier value**
Location=**sample Location value**
Line of Business=**sample Line of Business value**

Figure 4-23. *E-mail customization*

As you can see, the long format is well named, providing nearly every available piece of information that you might require. Unfortunately, it's almost impossible to read. You might then choose to look at the short format, shown in Figure 4-24, especially if these messages are to be delivered to a mobile device such as a cell phone or pager. Unfortunately, this format takes brevity to the absolute limit, not even including the metric details that caused the alert. This is a design feature specifically limiting the message to fewer than 155 characters. This limit is intended to allow SMS sending, though provider limits and character sets for SMS may be more limited than this (many for example, limit you to 140 characters). You will undoubtedly, therefore, wish to customize one or the other of these formats for production use.

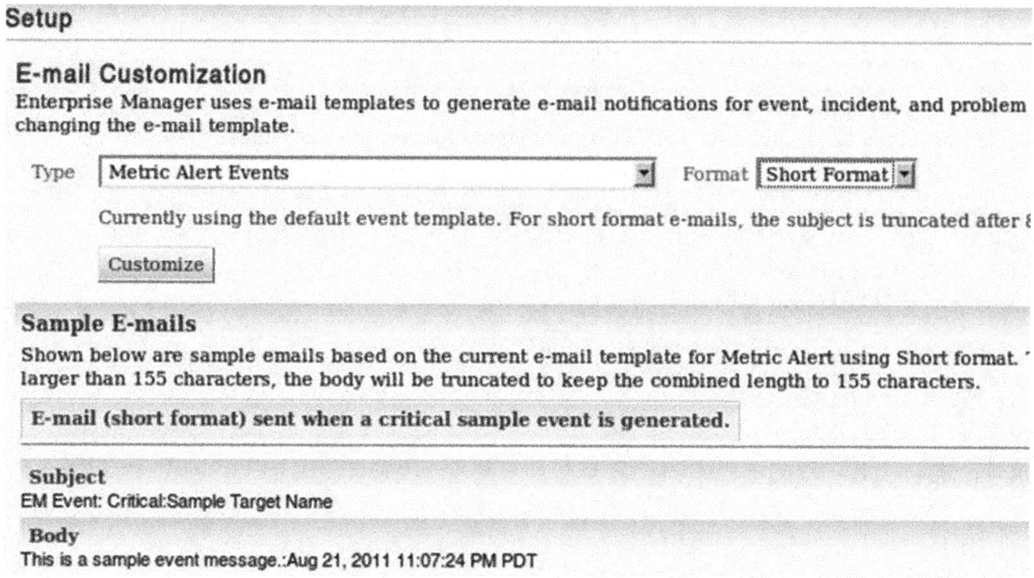

Setup

E-mail Customization

Enterprise Manager uses e-mail templates to generate e-mail notifications for event, incident, and problem changing the e-mail template.

Type [Metric Alert Events ▾]   Format [Short Format ▾]

Currently using the default event template. For short format e-mails, the subject is truncated after £

[Customize]

Sample E-mails

Shown below are sample emails based on the current e-mail template for Metric Alert using Short format. ' larger than 155 characters, the body will be truncated to keep the combined length to 155 characters.

E-mail (short format) sent when a critical sample event is generated.

Subject
EM Event: Critical:Sample Target Name

Body
This is a sample event message.:Aug 21, 2011 11:07:24 PM PDT

Figure 4-24. Short-format notifications

■ **Tip**   We suggest you start with the short format and expand it, rather than removing from the long format.

Customization is a relatively simple process, consisting of configuring a mix of plain text and placeholders that are substituted at runtime with attributes from the alert (for example, target name or alert timestamp). Comments can be prefixed with the -- character combination in the same way that SQL statements can. In addition, conditional logic can be applied in order to include relevant details, perhaps if this is a repeat notification. There is as yet no capability for creating new alert templates, so you are stuck with the two mail formats. This limitation can, however, be effectively worked around by careful use of the conditional logic feature together with appropriate attributes. For example, it is possible to define different short-response templates for Production and QA based on target deployment type. Figure 4-25 shows an example defining all alert types, including repeats for Production but only one regular mail for QA.

Subject

```
-- Enterprise Manager default event template

-- Subject of an e-mail is rendered in one line.
-- The resulting text from the following logic will be concatenated together into one line.

-- Production
[IF ORCL_GTP_DEPLOYMENT_TYPE EQ "Production"]
Production Alert:
[IF NOTIF_TYPE EQ "NOTIF_REPEAT"]
  \[[REPEAT_LABEL] #[REPEAT_COUNT]\]
[ENDIF]
-- if it is an email for success or failure of corrective action
-- show the name and execution status of the corrective action
[IF NOTIF_TYPE EQ "NOTIF_CA"]
   CA:[CA_JOB_NAME]:[CA_JOB_STATUS]
[ELSE] -- Email for regular events
   [SEVERITY]:[TARGET_NAME]
[ENDIF]
[ENDIF]
-- QA
[IF ORCL_GTP_DEPLOYMENT_TYPE EQ "QA"]
QA Alert:
-- Email for regular events only
   [SEVERITY]:[TARGET_NAME]
[ENDIF]
```

Figure 4-25. Use of conditional formatting logic

Management Pack Access

One of the major objections customers often have to implementing Oracle Enterprise Manager is the perceived cost involved. This is despite the fact that Enterprise Manager itself is a completely free product. The product does, however, expose in an easy-to-use fashion premium functionality that is licensed by target. This functionality is contained in management packs. Because the GUI makes it simple for administrators to access functionality for which they are not licensed, one of the tasks you should perform fairly shortly after implementation is to configure management pack access for your targets. This is done from the Cloud Control menu.

To begin the process, choose Management Packs from the Setup menu. Its submenu has four options, shown in Figure 4-26.

Show Management Pack Information

Management Pack Access

License Information

Packs for this Page

Figure 4-26. Management pack configuration menu

The Management Pack Access option allows you to enable—or more important, disable—premium functionality for which you haven't paid and are therefore not entitled to use. Figure 4-27 shows the screen that displays the options.

Management Packs

Management Pack Access

Enterprise Manager provides central management for your entire Oracle environment. Some premium functionality contained within this release of Enterprise Manager requires a separate Oracle license. Use target based access to enable or disable access for each target or use pack based batch update to enable or disable selected packs for all targets associated with the specified target type.

View Options

Choose from the below options to view management pack access information.
- ◉ Licensable Targets
- ○ All Targets (Licensable targets and all dependent targets)

Pack Access ◉ Target Based ○ Pack Based Batch Update ○ Auto Licensing
✅ **TIP** Enabling or disabling packs will affect pack-related management access for dependent targets.

Search Database ▾ [   ] Go   Revert Apply

Name ▲	Type	Host	Oracle Cloud Management Pack for Oracle Database	Database Diagnostics Pack	Oracle Database Lifecycle Management Pack	Data Masking Pack	Test Data Management Pack	Database Tuning Pack	Pack Access Agreed
em12db.lab.org	Database Instance	em12c.lab.org	☑	☑ 📝	☑	☑	☑	☑ 📝	☐
orcl.lab.org	Database Instance	sandbox.lab.org	☑	☑ 📝	☑	☑	☑	☑ 📝	☐

✅ **TIP** In Oracle Database 11g, you need to set the initialization parameter 'control_management_pack_access' to   Revert Apply
disable or enable Database Diagnostic and Tuning Packs.
✅ **TIP** For a detailed description of above functionality and where they can be used within the product refer to the Oracle Database Licensing Information document, the Oracle Application Server Licensing Information document or the Oracle Enterprise Manager Licensing Information document.

Figure 4-27. *Restricting access to management packs*

The Management Packs submenu's License Information item takes you to a long list of the various management packs and plug-ins you can buy to aid in the administration and management of Oracle products. These packs and plug-ins extend the functionality of Enterprise Manager and/or the base product in order to provide an enhanced management experience.

In addition, the submenu's Packs for This Page option now provides a pop-up detailing the management packs that are needed to access a given EM page. This feature is available throughout the product. For example, clicking this menu option on the Database Performance home page produces the dialog box shown in Figure 4-28.

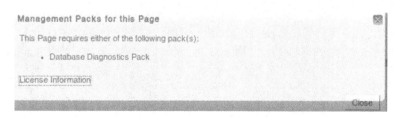

Figure 4-28. *Packs for This Page example showing required management packs*

■ **Note** The Packs for This Page feature regrettably doesn't provide pack access information at the same granular level as enabling the textual management pack labels did in previous releases.

Navigation Menu Bar

The Navigation menus, used for navigating the console interface itself, are located in the blue navigation bar at the top of each screen. There are four menus, which allow for quick navigation to the following:

- Enterprise-wide locations
- Target-based administration pages
- Saved locations (or favorites)
- Visited locations (or history)

The menu bar appears as in Figure 4-29. In addition, the Navigation bar also contains a search box on the right side of the screen (not shown in the figure).

Figure 4-29. Navigation menu bar entries

These menus are always available to you, no matter where you have navigated within the product. The chief advantage of this is that you will always have a consistent method available for navigating quickly and easily to the location of your choice.

Enterprise Menu

The Enterprise menu, shown in Figure 4-30, contains the items you need for an overall view of the health of your enterprise, as well as various items that don't naturally fit into the target-based menu.

Figure 4-30. The Enterprise menu

Next you'll learn about the menu's various options, and then take a little time to look at the reporting options that are available to you.

Exploring the Enterprise Menu

The Summary item takes you to the overall summary view of the enterprise, which gives at-a-glance current-state information for all managed targets to which you have access. For those familiar with previous product releases, this is the traditional home page.

The Monitoring submenu provides you with several enterprise-wide options for reviewing and standardizing monitoring and management across the enterprise. So, for example, this menu is the starting point for defining monitoring templates and corrective actions. This area is covered in Chapter 7. For now, note that this submenu provides a route to one-stop configuration of monitoring and automatic fault correction.

The Job submenu is the interface for the built-in Enterprise Manager job scheduler. This centralized job scheduling system allows you to run a variety of standardized jobs on managed targets across your enterprise. For example, it is possible to define standardized Recovery Manager (RMAN) backup scripts and deploy the same script across all databases in the enterprise. The job interface is covered in Chapter 11.

■ **Tip** You will have to decide whether the EM12c job system provides enough flexibility and reliability in your environment, or whether alternative job scheduling systems meet your requirements. In general, if you have an existing enterprise scheduler, we would recommend using that. If you have the usual collection of somewhat uncontrolled shell scripts, we would suggest that EM12c provides an opportunity for centralization and simplification.

The Reports submenu is designed to help you produce reports based on the centralized repository data that you accumulate through the operation of Oracle Enterprise Manager. This information provides much of the additional value of a centralized repository for management data. We cover the detailed functionality of this menu at the end of this section.

The next submenu is Configuration, which allows you to collect and compare configuration details for the managed targets in your organization. This allows you to ensure that, for example, you have the same operating system package versions installed on two similar hosts. This menu is where the configuration management capabilities of the product show through.

Next is the Compliance submenu. *Compliance* refers to the extent to which the actual configuration of a particular target conforms to a predefined standard for that type of configuration item. This area of the product has seen some significant improvement with 12c. In previous releases, all that could be achieved was to compare a managed target against a single, uneditable, predefined set of best practices. This had significant drawbacks, either because the predefined policy was too restrictive or because it wasn't restrictive enough. The best example of the latter is an organization that is subject to Payment Card Industry (PCI) standards. Figure 4-31 shows the Compliance submenu.

Dashboard

Results

Library

Real-Time Observations

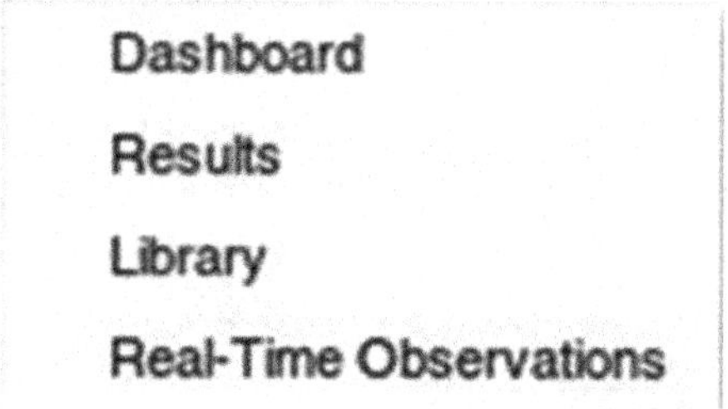

Figure 4-31. *The Compliance submenu*

A full coverage of target compliance is beyond the scope of this chapter. There are some basic concepts to get you started, however. Oracle envisages that, in line with industry practice, you define a set of standard practices (for example, that you will use Automatic Storage Management (ASM) for your database storage requirements, or that database listeners won't use the default port of 1521). These are managed individually as compliance standard rules. You then group a set of related rules into a corporate standard for, typically, a target type. So you might roll up your ASM standard together with a standard that states you will not use bigfile tablespaces and one that requires locally managed tablespaces with a uniform extent size into a Database Storage Standard. Finally, you can group related standards into a compliance framework. In our example, we might create a storage standard as described earlier, and a database password standard to comply with corporate password policy. These can then both be grouped together to form a Database Compliance framework for your organization. As of this release, the standards and policy rules are editable for your organization. In addition, Oracle ships several compliance frameworks with supporting standards and rules.

■ **Note** This one change means that the compliance capability of Enterprise Manager that was rarely used in previous releases should now be on your to-investigate list.

The rules, standards, and frameworks that you create form a Compliance Library. You can review this from the Library link in the Compliance menu. Enterprise Manager then allows you to ensure compliance in two ways. First, a compliance score is calculated as a weighted average of the results of evaluating your compliance standard rules against a managed target. This score shows up on the target and enterprise home pages. Second, a compliance officer can view target status interactively and use the Enterprise Manager reporting framework to maintain corporate assurance that standards are being complied with, and that variations from standards are addressed, either by corrective action or by documentation of the reasons for noncompliance.

The Enterprise menu's Provisioning and Patching option is the entry point to EM's provisioning and patching capabilities. As those capabilities are covered in Chapter 6, we do not go into that functionality here.

The next item is called Quality Management, but this is, in my view, a misnomer. The submenu shown in Figure 4-32 contains links to a variety of added-value options for the Database and WebLogic products. As these items are separately licensed, we don't cover these in this introduction to the Enterprise Manager interface.

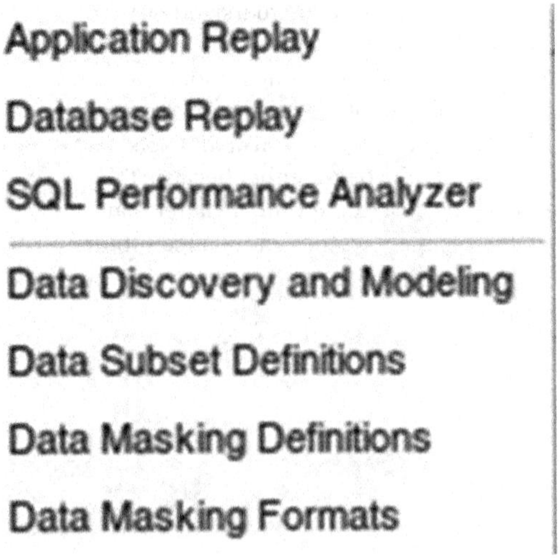

Application Replay

Database Replay

SQL Performance Analyzer

Data Discovery and Modeling

Data Subset Definitions

Data Masking Definitions

Data Masking Formats

Figure 4-32. *Quality management*

The last item we will look at in any detail is the My Oracle Support submenu. This provides access to four commonly used areas of Oracle's online support tool. These are Service Requests, Knowledge Base, Certification Information, and the My Oracle Support community forums. For any of these to work, you need to have configured support integration as described earlier. I personally use only the Service Requests option, because the other informational areas (knowledge base and community content) are, once My Oracle Support connectivity is established, directly searchable from the search box at the top right of the Navigation bar.

■ **Note**   One aspect of the support integration that may surprise you is that support pages are displayed from the now-retired Flash interface to My Oracle Support. We expect this to change in future updates to the product.

Finally, at the foot of the menu, looking suspiciously as through the designers couldn't find a better place, are the Chargeback and Consolidation Planning features. These advanced features are outside the scope of this chapter.

Overall, the Enterprise menu gives you access to product- or enterprise-wide functionality and is the place you should look for configuring or accessing enterprise management functionality. Before you leave this section, though, you'll look at the reporting capabilities of the product in a little more depth.

Configuring Reports

Enterprise Manager is in a transitional stage at the time of this writing, moving away from Information Publisher, which was the technology available in prior releases, towards Business Intelligence Publisher reporting, which offers greatly enhanced formatting, scheduling, and distribution options. With 12c Release 2, you have two distinct options, the first is a link to Information Publisher reports. (These are the only option available prior to 12c Release 2), but have been superseded by BI Publisher Reports. Oracle provides an embedded license for BI Publisher with Enterprise Manager, and this is clearly the way forward. At the moment, however, there are some restrictions, which we hope to see relaxed in future releases.

Currently, only BI Publisher 11.1.0.6 (yes, that's four decimal places of release number) is supported, and then only when loaded into the same WebLogic domain as Cloud Control. For all practical purposes, this means that you will either have to extend the domain to include a new BI Publisher server, or install BI Publisher onto the existing OMS servers. Either of these is a significant investment in complexity and management—and indeed come with additional CPU, memory, and disk requirements. Hopefully, in the future, the reliance on the same domain can be relaxed, and the BI Publisher templates can be installed either into an existing corporate BI Publisher environment or a stand-alone BI Publisher instance. Finally, Oracle currently offers no guarantee of backward compatibility for BI Publisher reports that you develop. This book, therefore, does not cover BI Publisher reports because we consider these restrictions to mean that it would be unwise to adopt BI Publisher at the time of writing.

If Information Publisher reports are chosen, you will be presented with a list of predefined reports, organized by category, which will look something like the alphabetically presented list in Figure 4-33.

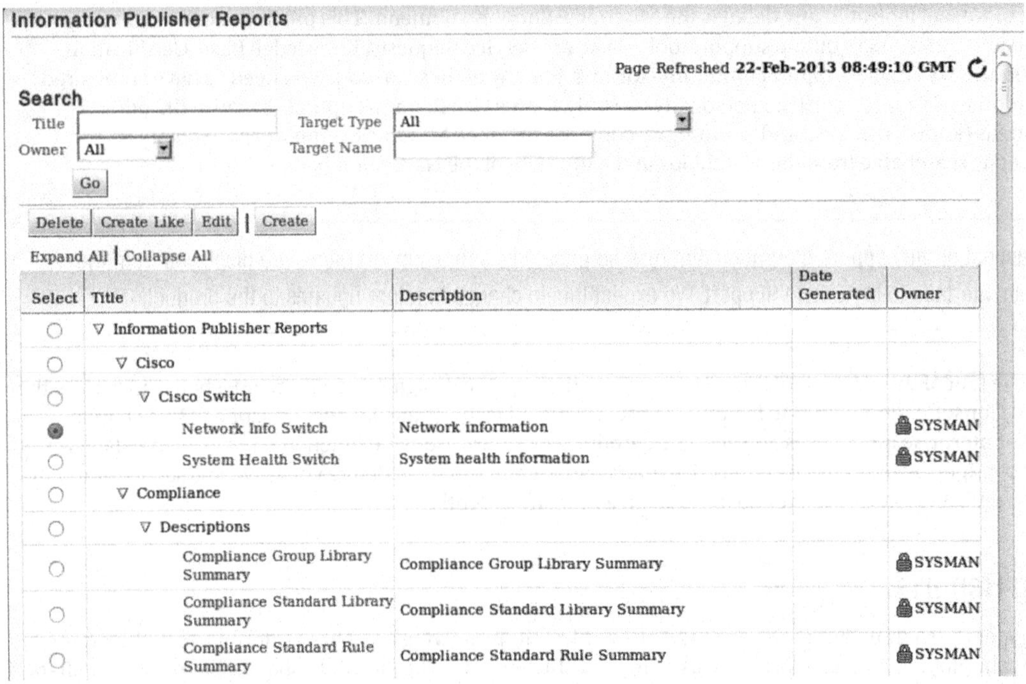

Figure 4-33. *Information Publisher out-of-the-box reports*

These reports are grouped in predefined categories. The complete list is shown in Figure 4-34. To produce this listing, choose Collapse All and then click the arrow next to Information Publisher Reports.

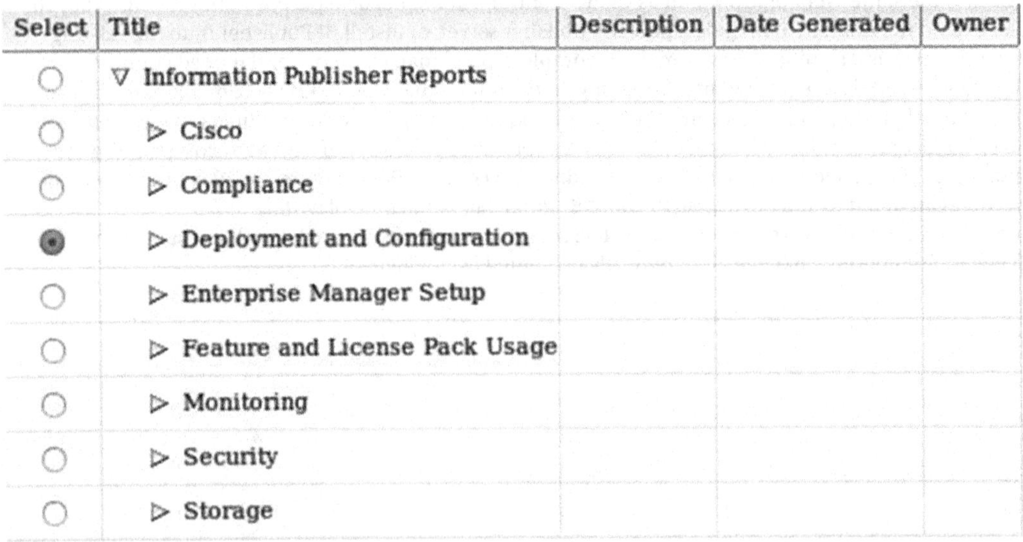

Figure 4-34. *Available report categories*

You cannot edit the predefined reports, but you can use the Create Like functionality to produce customized versions. To illustrate this principle, you will use the built-in Oracle Database Monthly Space Usage Report as the basis of a new daily space usage report. To find the report, expand the reports list so it looks like Figure 4-35.

Select	Title	Description	Date Generated	Owner
○	▽ Information Publisher Reports			
○	▷ Cisco			
○	▷ Compliance			
◉	▷ Deployment and Configuration			
○	▷ Enterprise Manager Setup			
○	▷ Feature and License Pack Usage			
○	▷ Monitoring			
○	▷ Security			
○	▽ Storage			
○	▷ Oracle Database Space Issues			
○	▽ Oracle Database Space Usage			
○	Oracle Database Space Usage	Displays space usage for an Oracle Database, its tablespaces and datafiles.		🔒 SYSMAN
○	Oracle Database Space Usage (Group)	Displays space usage and tablespace full alerts for each Oracle Database in a group.		🔒 SYSMAN
○	Oracle Database Tablespace Monthly Space Usage	Displays monthly space usage details for the tablespaces in an Oracle Database.		🔒 SYSMAN
○	Oracle Databases With Tablespace Space Used (%) Alert Enabled for Undo or Temporary Tablespaces (Group)	Displays databases in a group with the Tablespace Space Used (%) alerts enabled for any Undo or Temporary tablespace. This report can be useful in environments where DBAs do not want to get alerts for any Undo or Temporary tablespaces. It helps DBAs identify databases to run an EM job to disable the alerts if desired.		🔒 SYSMAN

Figure 4-35. Space Usage Report customization

Select the Monthly Space Usage Report and click Create Like. You will see a screen like the one in Figure 4-36. You can customize all the editable properties of this report and you *must* customize the report title.

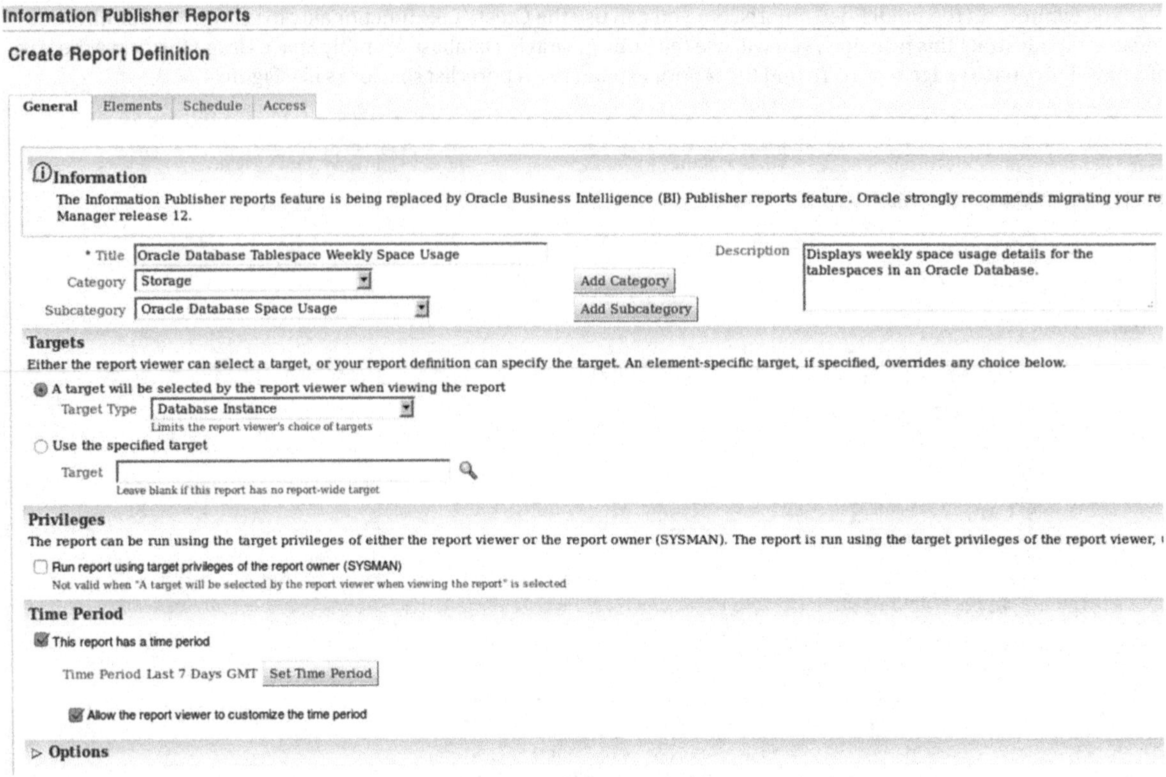

Information Publisher Reports

Create Report Definition

General	Elements	Schedule	Access

ⓘ **Information**

The Information Publisher reports feature is being replaced by Oracle Business Intelligence (BI) Publisher reports feature. Oracle strongly recommends migrating your re
Manager release 12.

* Title [Oracle Database Tablespace Weekly Space Usage]

Category [Storage ▼]   [Add Category]

Subcategory [Oracle Database Space Usage ▼]   [Add Subcategory]

Description [Displays weekly space usage details for the tablespaces in an Oracle Database.]

Targets

Either the report viewer can select a target, or your report definition can specify the target. An element-specific target, if specified, overrides any choice below.

◉ A target will be selected by the report viewer when viewing the report

Target Type [Database Instance ▼]
Limits the report viewer's choice of targets

○ Use the specified target

Target [   ] 🔍
Leave blank if this report has no report-wide target

Privileges

The report can be run using the target privileges of either the report viewer or the report owner (SYSMAN). The report is run using the target privileges of the report viewer, (

☐ Run report using target privileges of the report owner (SYSMAN)
Not valid when "A target will be selected by the report viewer when viewing the report" is selected

Time Period

☑ This report has a time period

Time Period Last 7 Days GMT [Set Time Period]

☑ Allow the report viewer to customize the time period

▷ **Options**

Figure 4-36. *Initial report settings*

Update all the existing references to *Monthly* to refer to your new analysis period (in this example, you would use *Weekly*). In addition, choose Set Time Period and change from 31 days to 7. When you have finished, the report should resemble Figure 4-37.

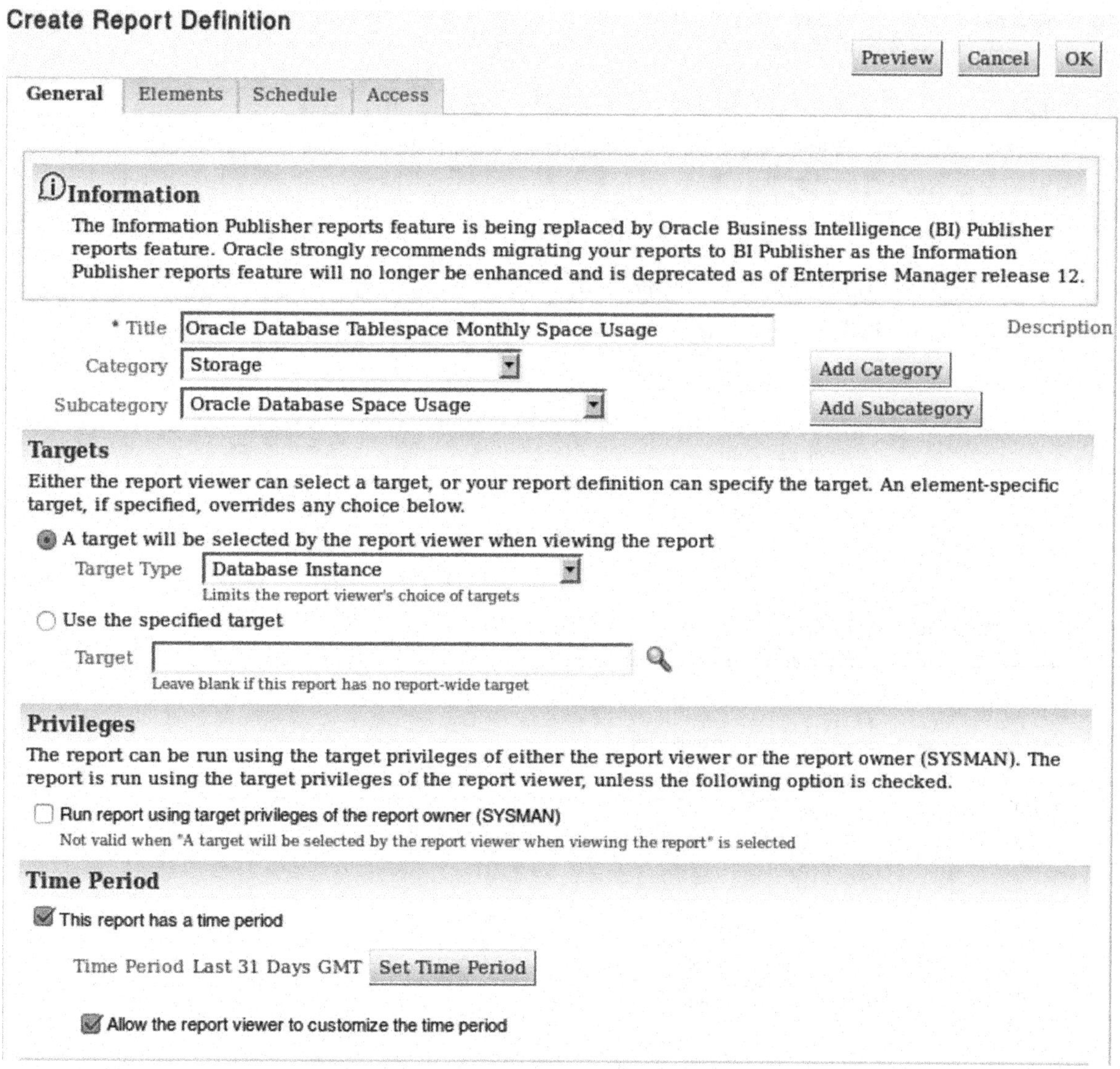

Create Report Definition

Preview | Cancel | OK

General | Elements | Schedule | Access

ⓘ**Information**

The Information Publisher reports feature is being replaced by Oracle Business Intelligence (BI) Publisher reports feature. Oracle strongly recommends migrating your reports to BI Publisher as the Information Publisher reports feature will no longer be enhanced and is deprecated as of Enterprise Manager release 12.

* Title	Oracle Database Tablespace Monthly Space Usage		Description
Category	Storage ▼	Add Category	
Subcategory	Oracle Database Space Usage ▼	Add Subcategory	

Targets

Either the report viewer can select a target, or your report definition can specify the target. An element-specific target, if specified, overrides any choice below.

◉ A target will be selected by the report viewer when viewing the report

Target Type | Database Instance ▼
Limits the report viewer's choice of targets

○ Use the specified target

Target | [   ] 🔍
Leave blank if this report has no report-wide target

Privileges

The report can be run using the target privileges of either the report viewer or the report owner (SYSMAN). The report is run using the target privileges of the report viewer, unless the following option is checked.

☐ Run report using target privileges of the report owner (SYSMAN)
Not valid when "A target will be selected by the report viewer when viewing the report" is selected

Time Period

☑ This report has a time period

Time Period Last 31 Days GMT | Set Time Period

☑ Allow the report viewer to customize the time period

Figure 4-37. Weekly Space Management Report

Next, ignore the Elements tab for the moment and then click Schedule. This tab allows you to configure the report to run weekly on a Sunday and e-mail to an appropriate address (see Figure 4-38). This scheduling of reports so that they are in the in-box of administrators or management is a big advantage of centralizing the reporting functionality along with the management repository. I suggest that you save copies of sent reports and purge after a sensible timeframe that allows comparison across time so that you can answer questions such as "What happened at this time last year?"

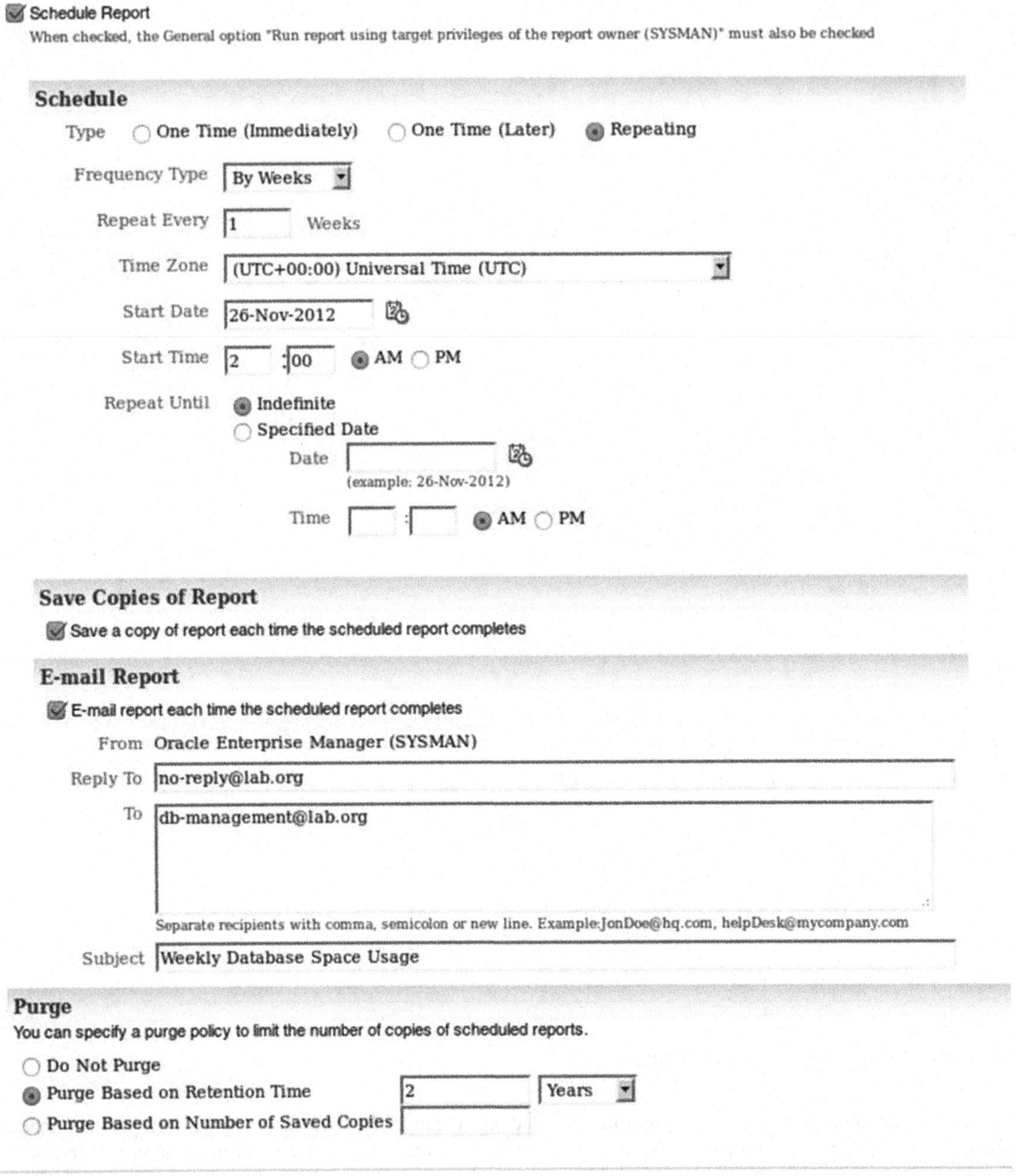

☑ Schedule Report

When checked, the General option "Run report using target privileges of the report owner (SYSMAN)" must also be checked

Schedule

Type   ○ One Time (Immediately)   ○ One Time (Later)   ◉ Repeating

Frequency Type   [By Weeks ▾]

Repeat Every   [1]   Weeks

Time Zone   [(UTC+00:00) Universal Time (UTC) ▾]

Start Date   [26-Nov-2012] 📅

Start Time   [2] : [00]   ◉ AM ○ PM

Repeat Until   ◉ Indefinite

           ○ Specified Date

           Date [   ] 📅

            (example: 26-Nov-2012)

           Time [ ] : [ ]   ◉ AM ○ PM

Save Copies of Report

☑ Save a copy of report each time the scheduled report completes

E-mail Report

☑ E-mail report each time the scheduled report completes

From   Oracle Enterprise Manager (SYSMAN)

Reply To   [no-reply@lab.org]

To   [db-management@lab.org]

      Separate recipients with comma, semicolon or new line. Example:JonDoe@hq.com, helpDesk@mycompany.com

Subject   [Weekly Database Space Usage]

Purge

You can specify a purge policy to limit the number of copies of scheduled reports.

○ Do Not Purge

◉ Purge Based on Retention Time   [2]   [Years ▾]

○ Purge Based on Number of Saved Copies [   ]

Figure 4-38. Two-year retention of Weekly Space reports

Targets Menu

The Targets menu gives you, as the name suggests, quick access to summary information about targets by type. The available target types vary according to the plug-ins you chose to install. Figure 4-39 shows an example.

All Targets	Ctrl+Shift+T
Groups	
Systems	
Services	
Hosts	
Databases	
Middleware	
Business Applications	
Composite Applications	

Figure 4-39. Targets menu

The All Targets option, or keyboard shortcut, takes you to a searchable list of targets organized in various ways. The screen looks similar to Figure 4-40.

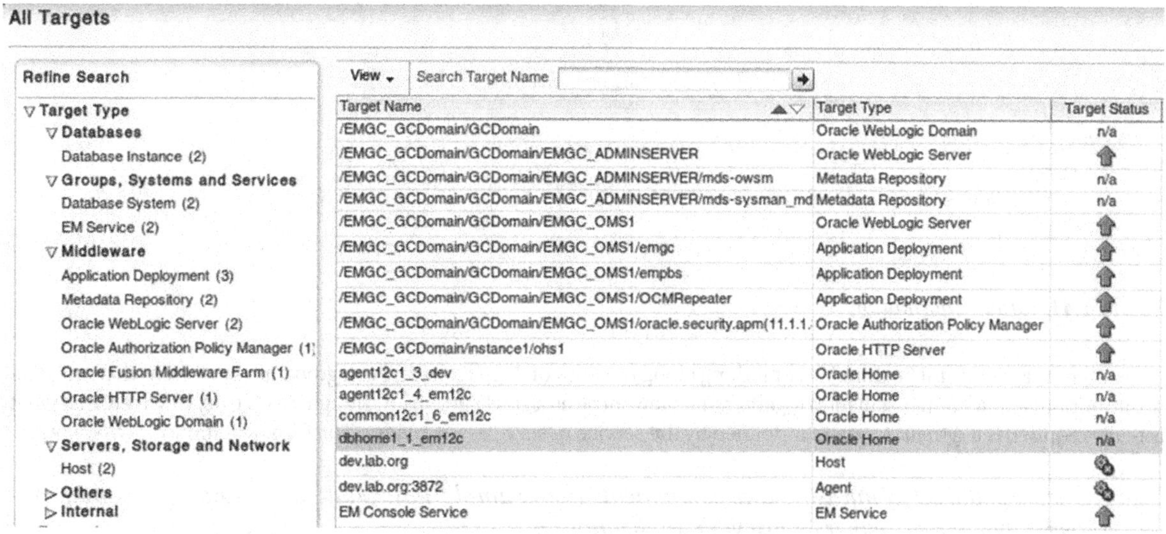

All Targets

Refine Search	View ▾ Search Target Name		
	Target Name ▲▽	Target Type	Target Status
▽ Target Type	/EMGC_GCDomain/GCDomain	Oracle WebLogic Domain	n/a
▽ Databases	/EMGC_GCDomain/GCDomain/EMGC_ADMINSERVER	Oracle WebLogic Server	⬆
Database Instance (2)	/EMGC_GCDomain/GCDomain/EMGC_ADMINSERVER/mds-owsm	Metadata Repository	n/a
▽ Groups, Systems and Services	/EMGC_GCDomain/GCDomain/EMGC_ADMINSERVER/mds-sysman_md	Metadata Repository	n/a
Database System (2)	/EMGC_GCDomain/GCDomain/EMGC_OMS1	Oracle WebLogic Server	⬆
EM Service (2)	/EMGC_GCDomain/GCDomain/EMGC_OMS1/emgc	Application Deployment	⬆
▽ Middleware	/EMGC_GCDomain/GCDomain/EMGC_OMS1/empbs	Application Deployment	⬆
Application Deployment (3)	/EMGC_GCDomain/GCDomain/EMGC_OMS1/OCMRepeater	Application Deployment	⬆
Metadata Repository (2)	/EMGC_GCDomain/GCDomain/EMGC_OMS1/oracle.security.apm(11.1.1.	Oracle Authorization Policy Manager	⬆
Oracle WebLogic Server (2)	/EMGC_GCDomain/instance1/ohs1	Oracle HTTP Server	⬆
Oracle Authorization Policy Manager (1)	agent12c1_3_dev	Oracle Home	n/a
Oracle Fusion Middleware Farm (1)	agent12c1_4_em12c	Oracle Home	n/a
Oracle HTTP Server (1)	common12c1_6_em12c	Oracle Home	n/a
Oracle WebLogic Domain (1)	dbhome1_1_em12c	Oracle Home	n/a
▽ Servers, Storage and Network	dev.lab.org	Host	🔗
Host (2)	dev.lab.org:3872	Agent	🔗
▷ Others	EM Console Service	EM Service	⬆
▷ Internal			

Figure 4-40. All Targets option

In addition to searching by target type, you can view targets by software version, target status, hardware platform, or operating system. This screen is faster if you want to review several targets of the same type or status; if you are searching for a specific target, you would likely do better to use the standard search box on the Navigation bar, which will achieve the same result.

The next section of the menu covers groups, services, and systems, which are three ways of viewing and managing a collection of managed targets as one. You will need to understand the differences and uses of each of these constructs in order to make effective use of the platform.

A *group* is a logical organization of a set of targets. For example, you might classify all production databases as a group, or all hosts in a specific data center. The effective use of groups is covered in Chapter 7. For now, all you need to know is that you can group logically related items and then view summary information about the group rather than the individual targets. Figure 4-41 shows the sort of information you will see by default for a group (in this case, of database instances).

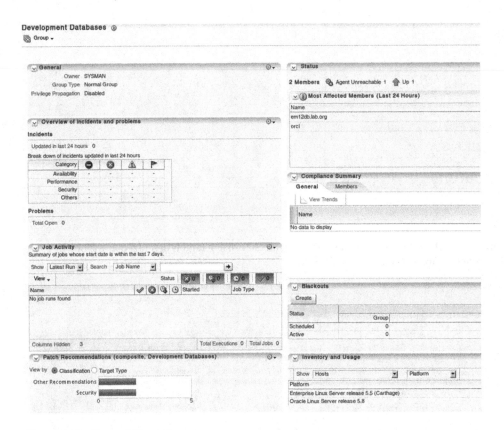

Figure 4-41. *Group information*

You may at this point be thinking something along the lines of, "That's great; I can group all the devices that make up my important application installation together and view these as a single group." Although this is true, it is likely that what is really required is a *system*. A system is defined by the service or services it provides. The formal definition is as follows:

> *A system is the set of infrastructure components (for example, hosts, databases, and application servers) that work together to host your applications.*

Systems come in several flavors, according to the services they provide. If you navigate to the systems page, you will see several predefined systems, including the WebLogic domain that runs the Enterprise Manager Service. Systems management is a comprehensive area of management and configuration, since Enterprise Manager allows you to define interdependencies and component roles and so on. The power of defining systems correctly comes into its own with the root-cause analysis and service-level analysis that Enterprise Manager offers for managed systems. The home page for a database system looks like Figure 4-42 (we use the Enterprise Manager repository database system, so you can compare it with your installation).

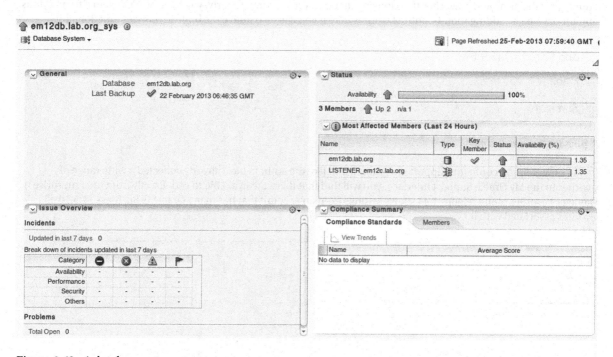

Figure 4-42. *A database system*

Services is the final menu option in this group and the basis of the service-level management capabilities of Enterprise Manager. A *service* is simply defined as the provision of a useful function to one or more users. This is pretty similar to the widely used ITIL definition, which focuses on the delivery of useful outcomes to customers. Systems as previously defined can deliver services, but you can also define services that are not based on systems (perhaps you don't own or monitor the IT infrastructure that provides them). The exact list of types of services available for monitoring in Enterprise Manager depends on the plug-ins in your installation.

The next set of menu items simply consists of home pages for the various managed target types for which you have monitoring configured. For example you might have entries for Hosts, Databases, and Middleware. Clicking any of these entries simply takes you to a view of your managed estate, filtered for all targets of the specified type. Each page allows you to view existing targets of that specific type, add new ones by way of the discovery process, or remove old ones at the end of the target's useful life.

■ **Tip** If your job role is as a dedicated administrator for a specific type of target—for example, if you are a Fusion Middleware administrator—you are better off choosing and, if necessary, customizing an appropriate home page.

Finally, in this menu you have links to applications that are under management. These are not supplied target types, but rather are built up by you from monitored components. This functionality is complex and site- and application-specific. The subject is covered in the documentation set *Oracle®Enterprise Manager Cloud Control Getting Started with Oracle Fusion Middleware Management,* available at http://docs.oracle.com/cd/E24628_01/install.121/e24215/bussapps.htm#sthref170.

Favorites Menu

The next menu looks at first sight redundant. This is the Favorites menu, which initially looks like Figure 4-43. As such, it duplicates the in-browser favorites functionality that you already have. Clearly, you likely will not gain a tremendous amount of value by adding Cloud Control favorites here if you can also utilize the built-in browser functionality.

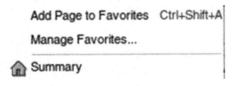

Figure 4-43. Favorites menu

    If, however, you configure support integration, and like the authors have already collected a wide range of favorites in the My Oracle Support interface, you will find that these are available to you directly from the Enterprise Manager Favorites menu. Figure 4-44 shows settings from an account that has many Oracle E-Business 11.5.10 favorites associated with it.

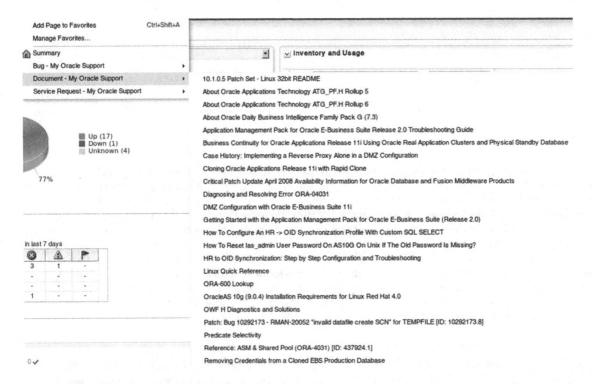

Figure 4-44. Displaying My Oracle Support favorites in EM

History Menu

The History menu merely gives you access to a history of recently accessed pages. This helps when using a browser Back button would take you through a task flow rather than to a genuine previous page. Other than this, we can find no use for the menu that the browser history doesn't give.

Search Box

On the right-hand side of the Navigation bar is a search box that allows you to search both Enterprise Manager and My Oracle Support (MOS) directly from within the product interface. The search box's default scope is Search Target Name, but the drop-down list enables you to change the scope to, for example, Oracle patches or the My Oracle Support knowledge base. As an example, suppose you cannot recall exactly how the ADR retention policies work in recent versions of Oracle Database. You surmise that this information ought to be available in the knowledge base within MOS. You therefore select Search Knowledge Base from the drop-down menu and enter a query, as shown in Figure 4-45.

Figure 4-45. *Searching the knowledge base from within Cloud Control*

Assuming that you have configured support access, you will be taken to the results of your query. In our case, the exact document we want is the first hit (see Figure 4-46). You can, if necessary, modify your search criteria in the normal MOS way to narrow down or expand your results.

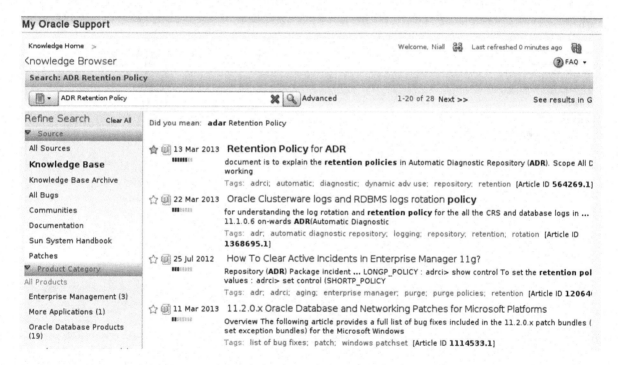

Figure 4-46. *Knowledge base search results in Enterprise Manager*

The range of sources for the search drop-down corresponds directly to the list of searchable sources in the My Oracle Support Flash interface.

Target Management Menu Bar

All of the menu items discussed previously are available throughout Enterprise Manager and provide the consistent, coherent, and always available navigation paradigm for the management product. Additionally, each plug-in, whether supplied by Oracle or a third party, is responsible for providing management menu bars for the target types for which it provides manageability services. To illustrate the general features, we will use the Oracle Database plug-in because we assume most readers are somewhat familiar with database administration. Each managed target type provides menus on its target-specific menu bar, some of which will be consistent with the menus presented here, and some of which will be target-type specific and expose manageability interfaces appropriate to that target type alone.

As you recall from the introduction, previous Enterprise Manager releases had somewhat inconsistent interfaces, with the design down to individual product groups and a variety of paradigms employed, from the database team's list of links to the highly menu-driven approach adopted by the Fusion Middleware team. With this release, the individual products utilize the approach pioneered by the Fusion Middleware team. The home page for a database target, for example, looks like Figure 4-47.

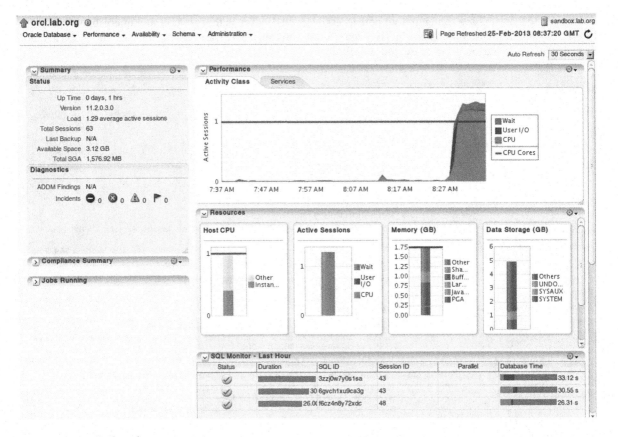

Figure 4-47. *Database home page*

The Target Management menu bar for an Oracle database has five submenus: Oracle Database, Performance, Availability, Schema, and Administration. These are illustrated at the top of Figure 4-47.

The leftmost menu, known as the *target type menu,* is common throughout the product and gives access to various configuration items for the target. It is always labeled for the target type (Oracle Database, WebLogic Server, and so on). Any further menus are the responsibility of the plug-in for that target type. To illustrate this, compare the Database home page with that for the Enterprise Manager WebLogic Administration Server, shown in Figure 4-48. The menus for performance, availability, and so on have been lost, because the manageability for these features is exposed in a different way by the underlying product. However, the target type menu is still there, this time labeled WebLogic Server.

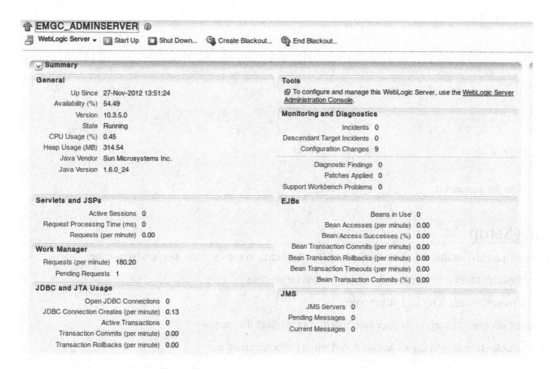

Figure 4-48. *Home page for a WebLogic administration server*

The target type menu items, as shown in Figure 4-49, are designed for quick access to controlling the monitoring, configuration, and reporting for the target. Here you can change or set up both monitoring and alerting. In addition, the menu may offer the ability to control the state of the target—for example, to shut it down—as well as various informational and reporting options. The following sections discuss key options from this menu.

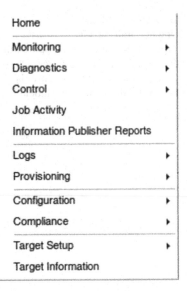

Figure 4-49. *The target type menu*

Monitoring Setup

The Monitoring submenu contains at least the following items relating to metric collection and reporting:

> *User Defined Metrics*: User-created metrics for this target type
>
> *All Metrics*: All metrics for this target type
>
> *Metric Collection Settings*: Whether and how often to collect the metric
>
> *Metric Collection Errors*: Errors encountered when collecting metrics

Figure 4-50 shows the Monitoring submenu for a WebLogic server, illustrating these and WebLogic-specific options. The use of these options is reasonably self-explanatory, while the actual metrics vary by target type. Figure 4-51 shows the result of selecting All Metrics for a database target. This gives you access to the full range of metrics available for this target. We have sorted by category to make the list easier to view, because databases have a very large number of potential metrics.

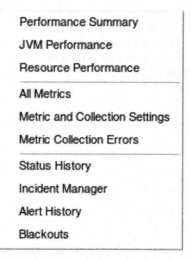

Performance Summary

JVM Performance

Resource Performance

All Metrics

Metric and Collection Settings

Metric Collection Errors

Status History

Incident Manager

Alert History

Blackouts

Figure 4-50. *The Monitoring submenu*

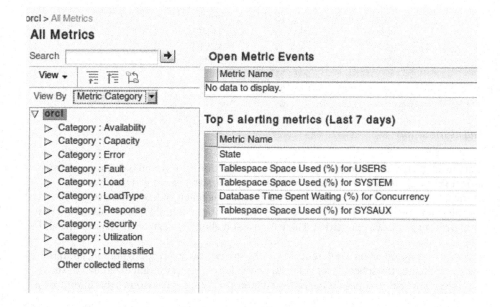

Figure 4-51. *Available metrics for a database target*

■ **Note**   We also get an immediate trend for top-five alerting metrics plus any open metric events. This is a neat improvement on the way the same information was presented previously.

If you expand the Capacity category and click on a tablespace used metric, you see the common metric configuration page, shown in Figure 4-52, allowing you to set the frequency of collection and upload interval. This functionality is common to all metrics for all managed targets. A management metric in this case is just a data point of interest—for example, the amount of free space in an Oracle tablespace. The metrics are collected by the agent at the configured frequency and uploaded every so many collections (in this case, every time).

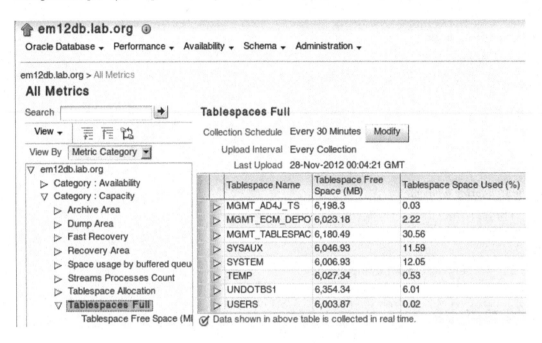

Figure 4-52. *Tablespaces Full metric details*

The available metrics vary by target type, but the configuration of the collection and upload is common across the product. The prime reason, of course, for collecting metrics is to allow analysis and alerting to take place. In Enterprise Manager, for historic reasons, *alerting* has a specific technical meaning that is different from common English usage. Specifically, an alert occurs when a metric crosses a threshold set by an administrator (this may have to occur for several collections in a row to avoid false positives). There is no association between an alert occurring and an administrator being notified.

The Metric and Collection Settings menu offers a different view of the metric collection configuration, grouping metrics by type, and allowing you to change the schedule for collecting the value of the metric and to define thresholds for that metric that represent warning or critical states for the collected metric. Figure 4-53 illustrates this interface for a database target.

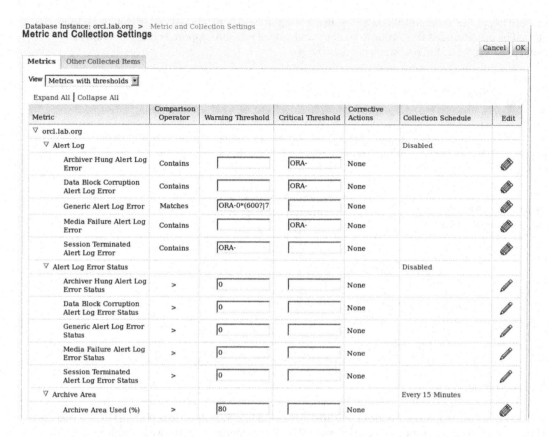

Database Instance: orcl.lab.org > Metric and Collection Settings
Metric and Collection Settings

Figure 4-53. *Metric and collection settings*

Notifications are configured on a per administrator basis by using the Setup menu located on the Cloud Control menu bar described earlier. The configuration of alert thresholds on a per target basis can be performed here.

■ **Note** As described in Chapter 7, you will mostly use monitoring templates to set alert thresholds. The Monitoring menu provides a method to override these where necessary. Once you have set up your metrics and your alerting, make sure to periodically review the target for any metric collection errors using the Metric Collection Errors menu item.

Diagnostics

Some, but not all, target types use the Diagnostics submenu to give you access to the Oracle Support Workbench and Health Check monitors. I expect the range of targets supplying this submenu to grow with time. This provides a handy way to package your support incidents and upload them to support, as well as to compare the existing state of your infrastructure with published Oracle practices.

For a database target, this submenu allows access to the Support Workbench, which allows you to package incidents detected by the Advanced Diagnostic Repository and upload these to support. Figure 4-54 shows an ORA-0600 error appearing for an EM repository database target.

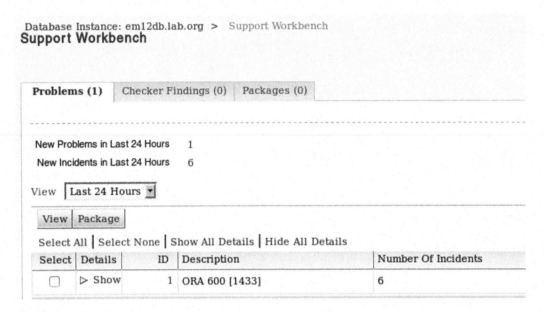

Figure 4-54. *Support Workbench*

This interface allows you to manage an incident with support and integrate the progress of that incident against the managed target. The full screen provides a graphic view of incident timelines and the way in which ADR has linked incidents to problem records (see Figure 4-55).

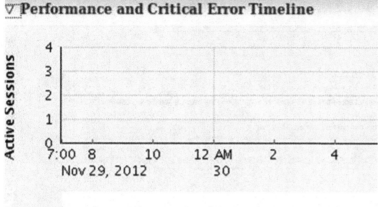

Incidents (6)

164377	ORA-600 [1433] [60]
164617	ORA-600 [1433] [60]
164649	ORA-600 [1433] [60]
164201	ORA-600 [1433] [60]
164489	ORA-600 [1433] [60]
	There are more incidents ...

▽ **Performance and Critical Error Timeline**

Figure 4-55. Incident occurrence

Target State and Notification Control

The Control submenu gives you two basic functionalities and should be available for all target types (see Figure 4-56). The first is the ability simply to start or stop the managed target by using the target-specific appropriate procedures. Just below this, though, is the ability to set or manage blackouts. A *blackout* is a predefined period during which normal monitoring and alerting is suspended, and optionally during which management tasks do not run. The blackout feature allows you to take account of planned downtime (for example, for monthly operating system security patch application without receiving a blizzard of notifications of target state-change alerts as the managed hosts shut down and restart).

Startup/Shutdown

Create Blackout...

End Blackout...

Figure 4-56. The Control submenu

Clicking Create Blackout opens the Create Blackout wizard, shown in Figure 4-57. As you can see, the blackout functionality is quite extensive and can apply to composite targets (most commonly a host and all targets running on that host).

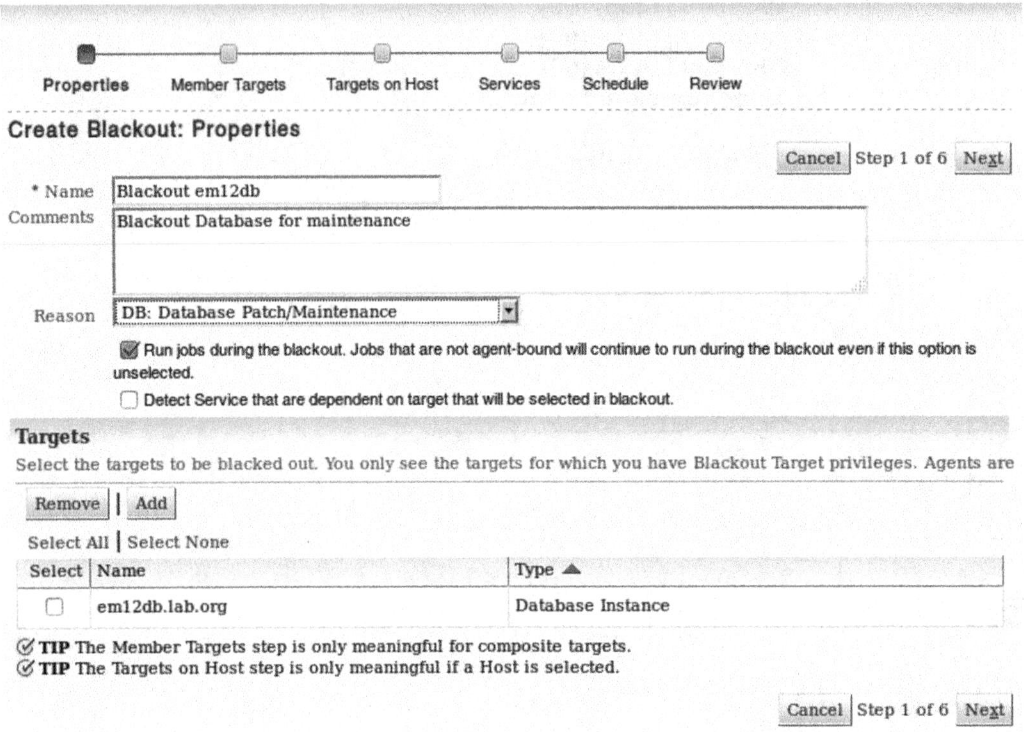

Figure 4-57. *Create Blackout welcome screen*

> ■ **Tip** Don't use blackouts to hide alerts that you don't want or know how to investigate. This *always* leads to missing alerts that you should have picked up. Instead, use blackouts only for planned maintenance.

Log Review

The target type menu also provides a handy Logs submenu for reviewing the system logs associated with various targets (see Figure 4-58). The menu itself is common to all targets, but the available level of detail depends on the nature of the target and the plug-in designer. In the case of a database, for example, the Logs submenu gives you access to review the alert.log file, to review all recorded errors, and to manage trace files.

Text Alert Log Contents

Alert Log Errors

Archive/Purge Alert Log

Trace Files

Figure 4-58. *Database diagnostic log access*

By contrast, a web server target simply provides a single Logs option that allows you to search for and view log messages based on criteria (see Figure 4-59).

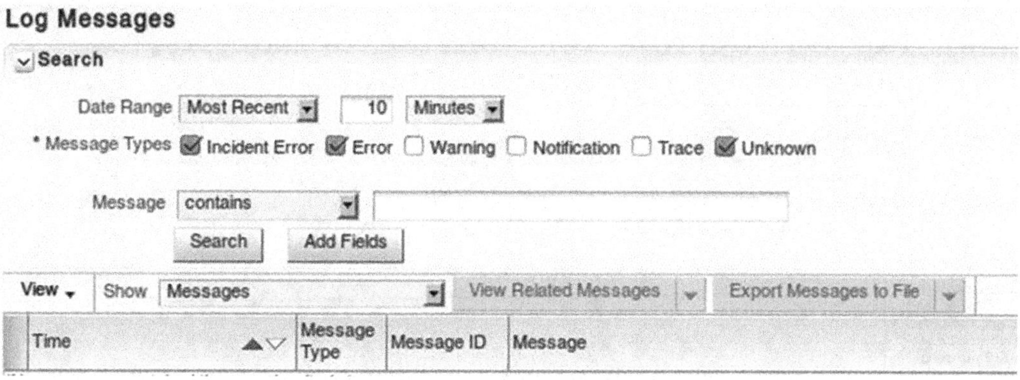

Log Messages

Figure 4-59. *Searching application server logs*

Target Setup

One place that you will definitely spend some time is in the Target Setup submenu, shown in Figure 4-60. This is where you will configure both the monitoring credentials and the metadata about the target, which you can use for grouping and access control.

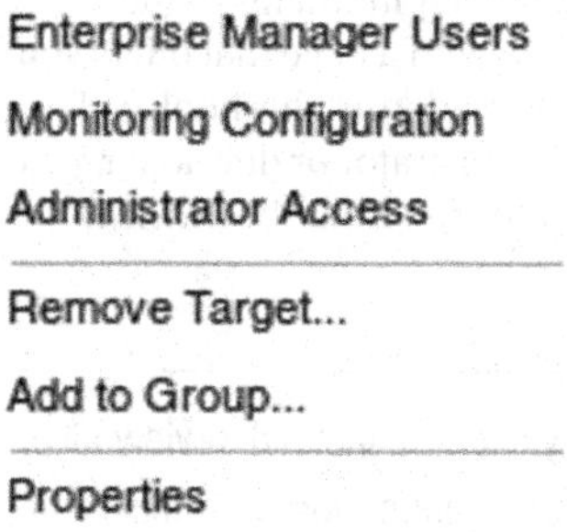

Enterprise Manager Users

Monitoring Configuration

Administrator Access

Remove Target...

Add to Group...

Properties

Figure 4-60. *Target Setup submenu*

To configure the account with which you monitor a target, select Monitoring Configuration. The actual details supplied vary by target type. Figure 4-61 shows the screen for a database target. As you can see, you are required to enter the monitoring account details (in the case of a database, Username, Password, Port, Role, and SID/Service_Name).

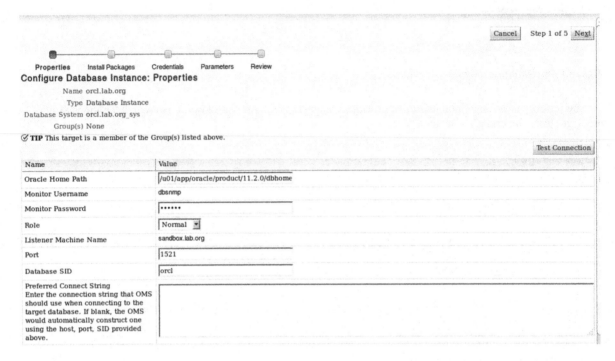

Figure 4-61. *Required database monitoring details*

Similarly, for other targets you will likely need names, passwords, and ports for the monitoring of the individual target-monitoring infrastructure.

Customization

The first indication that you will have that Cloud Control is designed to be customized to the requirements of the individual administrator comes at the very first login. After logging in, you will be presented with a page that offers you the chance to choose a home page based on one of a number of predefined job roles. Most readers of this book will probably want to choose one of two of the choices. If you primarily work as a database administrator or developer, you will likely choose the *Databases* page. If you work in operations or support, you may want to start from the *Incidents* page, which is focused for staff managing operational incidents in the enterprise.

■ **Note**   You don't have to choose any home page at this stage, and we recommend that you don't. Instead, review all of the available pages for an appropriate starting point for your role. You can then tailor your home page more specifically at a later point.

As the primary audience for this book consists of database professionals, we concentrate on the database-specific pages as an example for this section, unless otherwise noted. However, everything said here applies throughout the product. Figure 4-62 illustrates the home page for a database target.

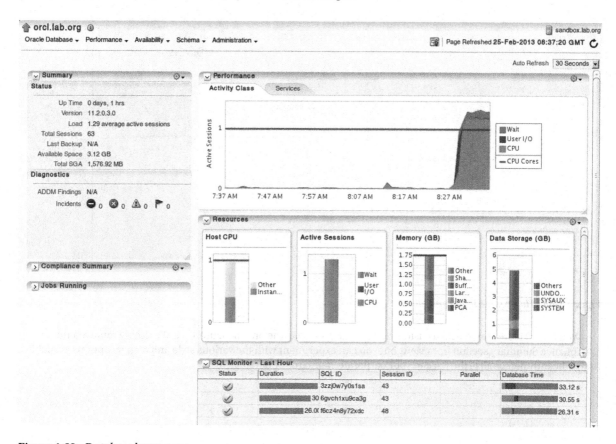

Figure 4-62. *Database home page*

Each page in Enterprise Manager is divided into several regions. Each region can be further customized by the end user. As an example, we will take the Database Summary region and remove the compliance summary, which is not hugely helpful.

To start the customization, click the Personalize This Page icon, located at the top right, next to the last refresh time for the page (see Figure 4-63). This will add menus to the page, allowing you to customize the page and each region. In this case, click the spanner icon at the top-right side of the Summary region.

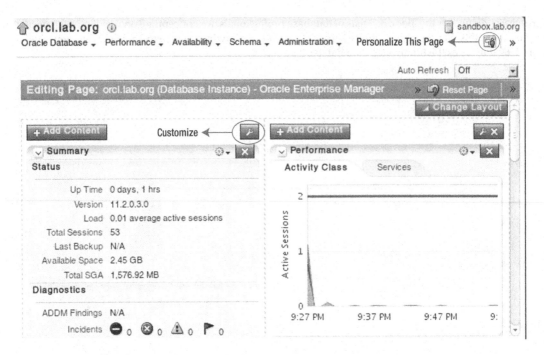

Figure 4-63. *Home page in Editing mode*

You are then presented with a customization dialog box like the one in Figure 4-64. We simply removed the Compliance Summary section from view, but you can experiment with the various style and display options available to significantly personalize the page to your corporate standards or personal taste.

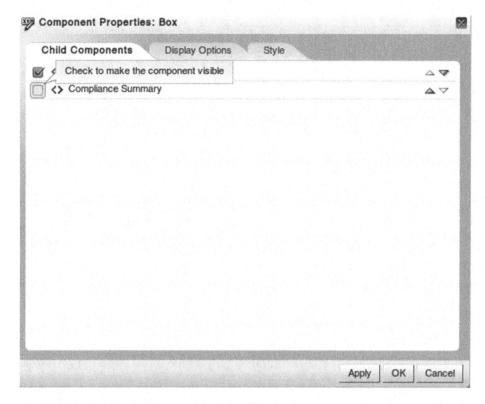

Figure 4-64. *Customizing the Summary component*

You should be aware that the options for customizing pages depend on the plug-in supplying the page. Thus the exact customization options may vary among apparently similar regions.

Summary

This chapter introduced you to the new interface and some of the basic tasks that you need to master in order to derive the manageability benefits of the Enterprise Manager product. You have learned about the roles of the Cloud Control, Navigation, and Target Management menus. Along the way, you have learned how to set up Enterprise Manager security, set up the powerful integration with My Oracle Support, and configure notifications. You've taken a brief tour around the navigation functionality. Finally, you've looked at the target setup functionality and learned how to configure monitoring and review diagnostic logs.

■ ■ ■

CHAPTER 5

Cloud Lifecycle Management

by Bobby Curtis and Anand Akela

Oracle Enterprise Manager 12c Cloud Control promises to deliver greater adaptability for dynamic business needs, significant operational efficiencies, and lower overall operational costs. For an organization to achieve these goals, we need to have a comprehensive and complete management solution. Without the cloud lifecycle management components of EM12c, these promises cannot be realized and enterprises may not derive maximum value out of their cloud computing infrastructure. The components in cloud lifecycle management allow organizations to be flexible with their architecture and derive greater business value from stretched resources. The tools covered by cloud lifecycle management include the following:

- *Self Service portal*: Allows administrators to configure the cloud and perform various operations such as defining policies associated with the cloud, exposing the cloud to users, deciding the total amount of resources that each user can reserve, and defining policies for the system.

  Chargeback: Allows enterprise organizations to allocate the costs of the Information Technology resources to the people, departments, or organizations that consume them.

  Consolidation Planner: Allows enterprise organizations to map managed servers to consolidated resources, such as Oracle Exadata or Oracle Virtual Machine, and to plan consolidation by using metrics and configuration data stored in the Oracle Management Repository.

Before we dive into these cloud lifecycle management tools using EM12c, let's review what cloud computing really is.

What Is Cloud Computing?

Although you can find many definitions of cloud computing, the National Institute of Standards and Technology (NIST) published one of the most complete and credible definitions in September 2011.[1]

According to NIST, "Cloud computing is a model for enabling ubiquitous, convenient, on-demand network access to a shared pool of configurable computing resources (for example, networks, servers, storage, applications, and services) that can be rapidly provisioned and released with minimal management effort or service provider interaction."

In this section, we'll add some details to this general definition. First, we'll review the essential characteristics of cloud computing. Then we'll look at the basic cloud computing service and supported deployment models.

---

[1]The NIST definition of Cloud Computing: http://csrc.nist.gov/publications/nistpubs/800-145/SP800-145.pdf

Essential Characteristics

According to the NIST, cloud computing has five essential characteristics. Let's look at each in some detail:

On-demand self-service: Cloud consumers should be able to consume the cloud services on demand, without requiring human interaction with the cloud service provider.

Broad network access: Cloud services should be accessed over the network and through various commonly used interfaces (for example, the Web, mobile devices, software clients, and so forth).

Resource pooling: Cloud providers pool computing resources to efficiently serve multiple consumers.

Rapid elasticity: Cloud services should be elastically provisioned and released to meet the business demand.

Measured service: Cloud resources should be monitored for usage and can later be reported, with users potentially billed for the utilized service.

The NIST definition also lists three *service models* (software, platform, and infrastructure) and four *deployment models* (private, community, public, and hybrid) that, combined, categorize ways to deliver cloud services. These are discussed in the following sections.

Service Models

For the cloud to be a viable option for any enterprise organization, that organization needs to choose which service model to provide. A *service model* is an approach that can be used to satisfy a specific requirement. Within the cloud architecture, three primary service models can be used— Software as a Service (SaaS), Platform as a Service (PaaS), and Infrastructure as a Service (IaaS):

Software as a Service (SaaS): In this model, the consumer of cloud services uses the software application. The consumer does not manage or control any of the underlying infrastructures to include network, servers, application servers, operating systems, storage, or even individual application capabilities, with the possible exception of limited user-specific application configuration settings. SaaS examples include the Web-based e-mail services provided by Yahoo!, Google, and other vendors.

Platform as a Service (PaaS): In this model, the consumer of the cloud builds and operates end-user applications leveraging the software platform—including database, middleware, programming languages, libraries, services, and tools—offered by the cloud provider. The consumer does not manage or control the software platform or the underlying infrastructure including network, servers, operating systems, or storage, but has control over the deployed applications and possibly configuration settings for the application-hosting environment. PaaS examples include Google Apps, which enables customers to work from a platform while being mobile.

Infrastructure as a Service (IaaS): In this model, the consumer of the IaaS cloud has the responsibility to manage the software platform (database, middleware, tools, and so forth) and develop and operate the end-user applications. The consumer does not manage or control the underlying cloud infrastructure but has control over operating systems, storage, and deployed applications, and possibly limited control of select networking components (for example, host firewalls). Amazon Elastic Compute Cloud, which provides developers with servers and databases, is an example of IaaS.

Deployment Models

In addition to describing service models, NIST also lists four models for deploying cloud services. Let's look at them quickly:

Public cloud: The cloud provider builds and operates the cloud infrastructure for use by the general public. This infrastructure exists on the premises of the cloud provider, and the provider manages the access control and potential pay-per-use model for consumers.

Example: Box and Dropbox offer a certain amount of online storage for free to the public, and charge for storage beyond that limit.

Private cloud: The cloud infrastructure is provisioned for exclusive use of lines of business or branches within a single organization. Usually the IT department of the organization builds and operates the private cloud (or enterprise private cloud).

Example: Oracle Global IT offers development and testing cloud infrastructure for Oracle employees worldwide. However, in some cases the cloud infrastructure may be owned and operated by a third-party vendor that manages the private cloud exclusively for a single organization.

Community cloud: The cloud infrastructure is provisioned for exclusive use by a specific community of consumers from organizations that have shared goals and concerns.

Example: Many federal and state organizations share resources through a cloud infrastructure.

Hybrid cloud: Organizations may decide to deploy certain key applications and data in their private cloud, but other applications in a public cloud. In case of a disaster or heavy demand on the applications in the private cloud, organizations may decide to temporarily move part of their workload to the public cloud. This process of temporarily extending to a public cloud from a private cloud during peak load is called *cloud bursting*. Hybrid cloud infrastructure is a combination of a private and public cloud (and/or community cloud) that is connected by standard or proprietary technology for data and application portability.

Enterprise Private Cloud

The rest of this chapter focuses on enterprise private cloud infrastructures managed by EM12c. However, a public, community, or hybrid cloud infrastructure provider can also decide to use EM12c for managing their entire cloud lifecycle. For example, Oracle uses EM12c to manage its public Oracle Cloud.

As mentioned earlier, the IT department of an enterprise usually becomes the cloud service provider in charge of the enterprise private cloud and its associated deployment model.

As you can see in Figure 5-1, the cloud users in the business units get more value when they move horizontally from IaaS to PaaS and then to SaaS. IaaS cloud users within the enterprise are responsible for databases, middleware, and development and operation of end-user applications on top of the cloud infrastructure offered by their IT department. If the IT department offers PaaS, cloud users will be responsible only for development, testing, and operations of their applications, while IT takes care of management and operations of the software platform and the underlying infrastructure. Enterprise IT departments will have more up-front investment in establishing a PaaS or SaaS model than an IaaS model.

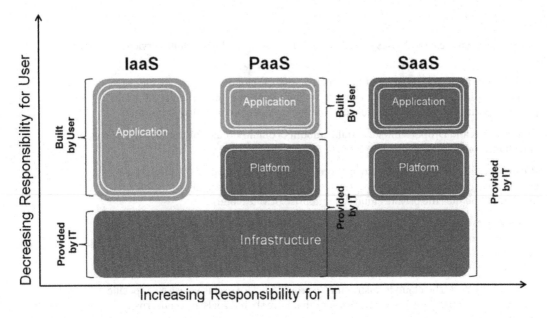

Figure 5-1. *Cloud service models deployed in an enterprise private cloud*

So far, you have seen an overview of cloud computing, its key characteristics, and its delivery and deployment models. Although cloud computing offers great efficiency, flexibility, and cost savings, the benefits for an enterprise private cloud can be maximized only if the enterprise can manage the complete cloud lifecycle across the whole technology stack. Let's look at the cloud lifecycle in detail and see how Oracle Enterprise Manager can help gain total control over the phases of that lifecycle.

Complete Cloud Lifecycle Management

To achieve the best value from the cloud infrastructure, it is important to have end-to-end management and automated workflows for various activities during all the phases of the cloud life cycle—from planning and setting up the cloud, to end-user self-service provisioning and de-provisioning of applications, to metering and charging back for the cloud resource usage (see Figure 5-2).

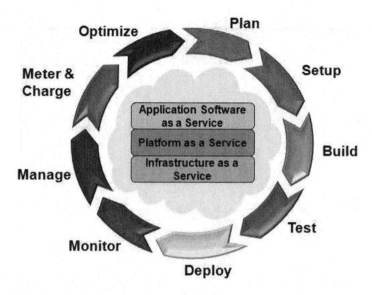

Figure 5-2. *Complete cloud lifecycle*

EM12c helps you manage the entire cloud lifecycle from a single tool. Let's look at the phases of this lifecycle in more detail.

Planning the Cloud

Moving to the cloud from your existing IT infrastructure is transformational in nature. It requires extensive planning to consider various design and operational criteria for successful deployment and operation of the cloud infrastructure.

First, you need to determine all the applications and infrastructure assets in the environment. You also need to understand the relationships between them so you can decide what to keep as is, what to update, and what to retire. Consolidating your applications and underlying infrastructure before, or as part of, moving to the cloud is considered an industry best practice. Over the years, data centers have accumulated excess servers that occupy rack space, consume a lot of power for cooling, and require system maintenance such as patching, and many of them are underutilized.

EM12c provides automated capabilities that allow IT departments to discover existing applications and infrastructure assets along with the relationships between them. This blueprint of the data center provides a baseline for cloud transformation planning. Additionally, EM12c offers a tool called Consolidation Planner, discussed in detail later in this chapter, that can simulate various consolidation scenarios based on usage data stored in OEM's repository and projected capabilities of future consolidation platforms. In the example shown in Figure 5-3, databases running on seven servers are being analyzed for consolidation to a quarter rack of Oracle Exadata.

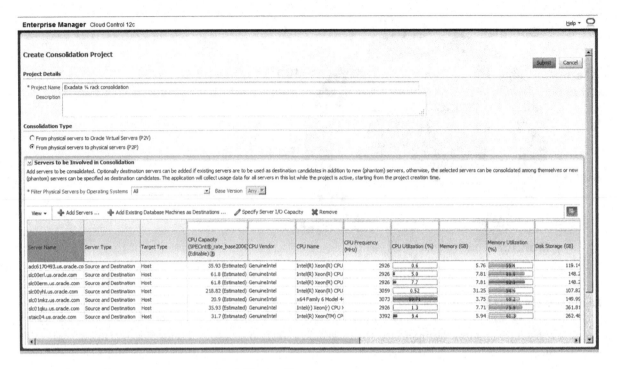

Figure 5-3. *Oracle Enterprise Manager Consolidation Planner*

The advisories from the Consolidation Planner tool can also consider technical and functional constraints—for example, production and testing cannot be colocated. With Consolidation Planner, a company's IT department could identify underutilized servers and find a way to consolidate them to free up as many as possible, at the same time maintaining current service levels. This type of elaborate scenario planning can mitigate many of the cloud transformation risks. You can have the confidence that applications will perform fine after the consolidation. Consolidation Planner is discussed in more detail later in this chapter.

During the planning phase, you also need to choose the cloud service delivery model (that is, IaaS, PaaS, or SaaS) that aligns best with the enterprise's business needs. IaaS can be a good starting point when your business units don't necessarily have a standardized application development platform and are just looking to IT to provide a compute infrastructure for their diverse applications and development environment. As we discussed earlier, enterprises can get more value by delivering a PaaS cloud to their enterprise users. Cloud users can just focus on developing, testing, and deploying their applications on enterprise private PaaS, delegating the operations and maintenance to IT. Enterprises can benefit from enhanced security and compliance while maximizing component reuse, flexibility, and control.

Setting Up the Cloud

After you baseline the IT assets, decide what to upgrade or retire as part of the cloud transformation, and finalize the cloud service delivery model, you need to set up and configure the cloud. This requires not only adding a self-service portal in front of the existing IT infrastructure, but also setting up broad network access, resource pooling, rapid elasticity, and measured service. You not only set up virtualization infrastructure, but also can also pool resources in a physical infrastructure. For example, you can have database consolidation in a PaaS cloud running on the top of an Oracle Exadata system.

To accommodate various cloud services (DBaaS, MWaaS, or IaaS), Oracle Enterprise Manager supports rich resource models for the cloud—right from applications to disks in storage infrastructure, for both physical and virtualized infrastructure. You can create zones that are logical groupings of a set of resources required for services provided by the cloud infrastructure. For example, a MWaaS user can worry only about middleware zones or domains and not worry about the underlying infrastructure. You could set up zones based on organizational structure, region, or whatever criteria enterprises choose when using the Self Service portal of Oracle Enterprise Manager. EM12c supports bare-metal provisioning of hypervisors and operating systems. During the cloud setup process, Enterprise Manager can also help integration with best-of-breed networking and storage technologies from vendors such as F5 Networks, NetApp, Hitachi, and Fujitsu. Let's walk through the IaaS setup process.

You start setting up the IaaS cloud by selecting the machine sizes. As shown in Figure 5-4, you could also add a custom machine size to meet your business needs and select that for your cloud.

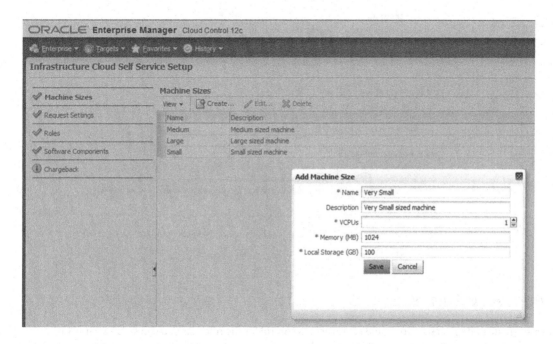

Figure 5-4. *Adding a custom machine size*

After you select the machine size, you can define the settings for infrastructure requests for the IaaS users. As you can see in Figure 5-5, you can indicate whether someone can reserve the cloud resources, how long the resource can be requested, whether the management agent should be configured, and more.

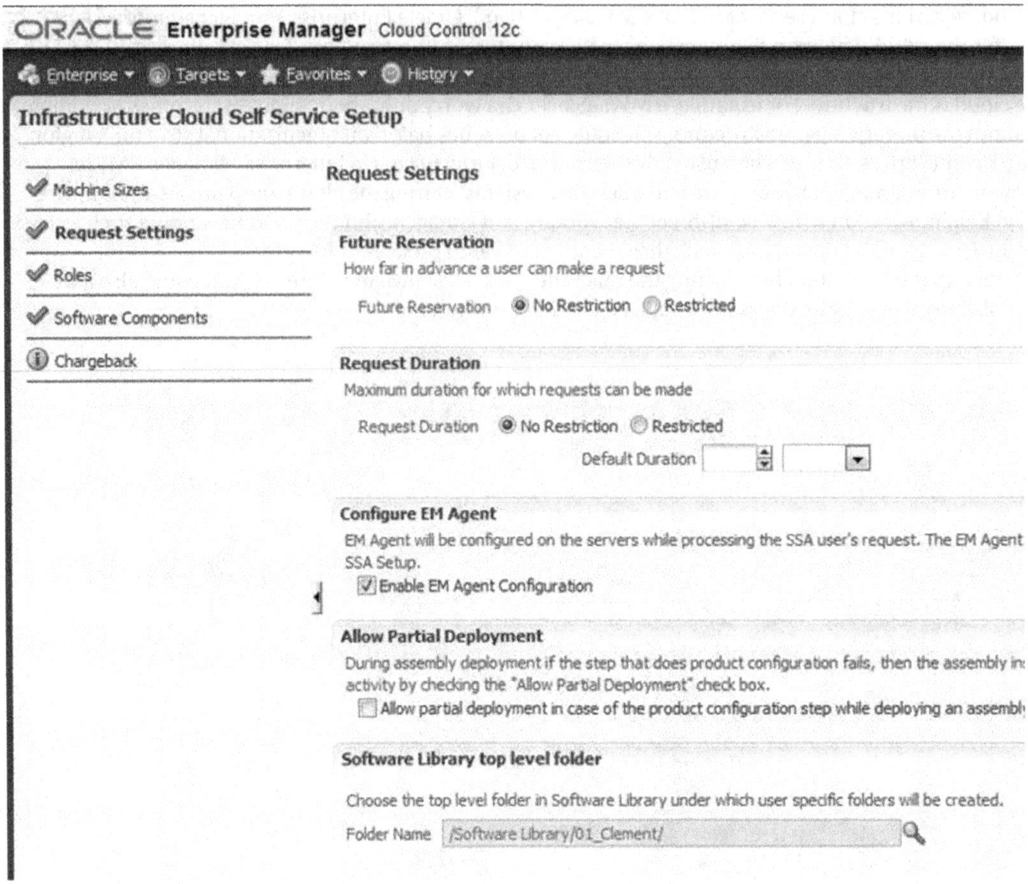

Figure 5-5. *Defining settings for requests*

You can also create and select user roles and set up access control for the roles. As you can see in Figure 5-6, you can assign quotas, zones, and network profiles to the roles.

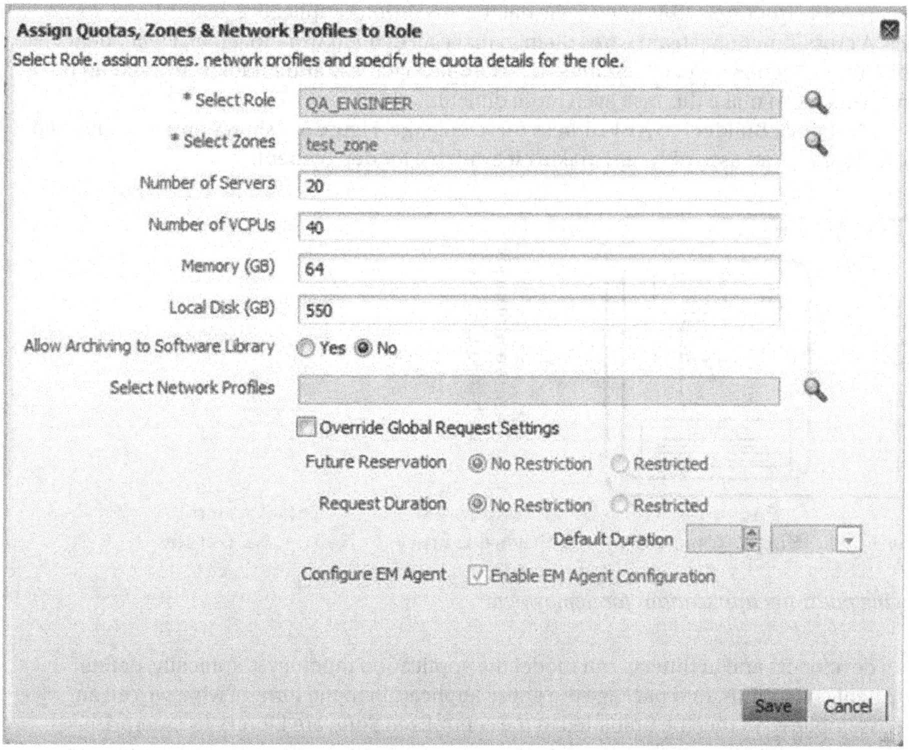

Figure 5-6. *Configuring roles*

You can also add software components to the infrastructure while setting it up. Finally, you could set up the chargeback and metering parameters for infrastructure resources during the setup phase and publish the infrastructure cloud resources for usage by cloud users. Oracle Enterprise Manager helps set up the database or middleware cloud out of the box in addition to the infrastructure cloud example shown here.

There can be different administration tasks and roles during the cloud setup phase. The cloud administrator can be someone who sets up the cloud infrastructure including systems, database, or any other cloud resource offered as a service. A self-service administrator can be the administrator at the business units or any other cloud tenant who sets up the quota and roles for their users.

Some of the typical tasks associated with cloud administrators are provisioning bare-metal hypervisors, configuring storage arrays and the network, creating server pools, and defining zones based on functional and operational boundaries. They also configure the policies and access control of the Software Library for the cloud users.

Self-service administrators define allowable VM sizes, assign quotas to users/roles, define access boundaries, map roles to zones, set up chargeback plans, and make software available for deployment by self-service users of the cloud.

EM12c supports these typical roles and their common activities out of the box. As you saw in Figure 5-6, these roles and policies for users can be customized if needed during the cloud setup process via the Self Service portal. The customized setup of cloud, user roles, and policies helps automate the provisioning of the resources depending on the cloud service models. The same automation technology, leveraged by the Self Service portal for provisioning the resources, is also available via command-line APIs called EMCLI (not discussed in this book).

Building the Cloud

After your cloud admins have set up the shared resources, self-service admins in the business units or other cloud user organizations will need to build the complete infrastructure, where they will ultimately deploy their business applications.

Usually IT sets up hardware infrastructure. DBAs deploy the databases. Various application teams build, test, and deploy their applications. A cross-functional team wires them to make all of them work together. Dependency between application components and deployment constraints (for example, database and middleware) should be in different network segments, which can make this task even more difficult.

EM12c and Oracle Virtual Assembly Builder (OVAB) address this challenge. Figure 5-7 shows the steps followed in packaging multi-tier applications into an assembly and making it available for deployment.

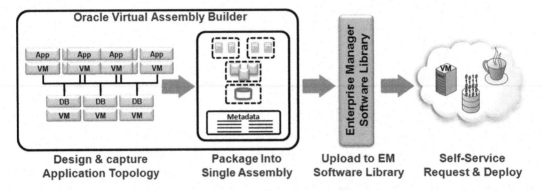

Figure 5-7. *Steps for packaging multi-tier applications for deployment*

Using OVAB, application developers and architects can model the application topology graphically, define all dependencies and deployment constraints, and package the entire application in the form of what we call an *application assembly*. These assemblies can then be uploaded to the centralized Software Library in Enterprise Manager for self-service deployments. An entire multi-tier application (including various application components, middleware software, databases, operating systems, and the virtual machines containing all of them) can be packaged together in an assembly. The assembly is then published into the Enterprise Manager Software Library, as shown in Figure 5-8, and made available to the users of the cloud for deployment via the Enterprise Manager Self Service portal. This can reduce the time needed for application deployments, from months and days to hours and minutes. The resulting standardization in software stack minimizes compliance risks and operational downtime.

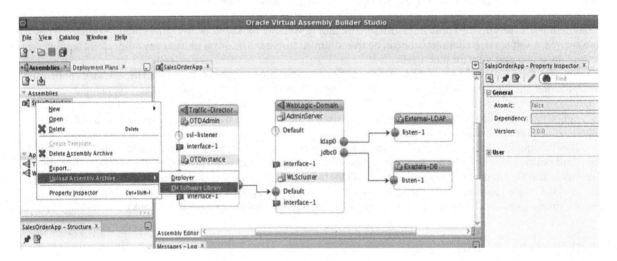

Figure 5-8. *Uploading the assembly to the Enterprise Manager Software Library*

Oracle plans to offer assemblies for all its products, which will allow you to deploy any Oracle product, including packaged applications, in a few clicks. Oracle Enterprise Manager can notify you of the availability of new assemblies so you can download them if you are interested.

Testing in the Cloud

Applications, as parts of assemblies or by themselves, need to be tested before they can be deployed into production. Applications need to be tested for functionalities as well as for performance during potential heavy loads. Oracle Enterprise Manager 12c Application Testing Suite, which includes Oracle Functional Testing, Oracle Load Testing, and Oracle Test Manager, offers a comprehensive testing solution for your Oracle applications, middleware, and databases.

Before you deploy the application in production, it is important to test it at full load to ensure that the application will be able to handle that load during its peak activity period. The Oracle Enterprise Manager load-testing tool allows you to simulate heavy loads with different combinations of concurrent users of different modules. The result from load testing is presented as a graphical report, similar to that shown Figure 5-9.

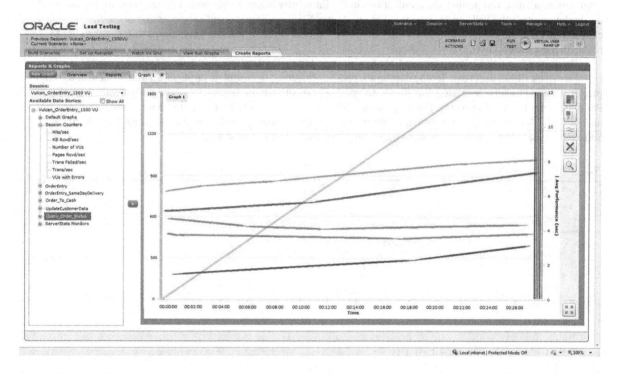

Figure 5-9. *Oracle Enterprise Manager load -testing report*

A unique aspect of the testing solution is the ability to capture a production load and replay it in a test environment, allowing you to test your application with a real production workload. This technology has been available as the Oracle Real Application Testing feature for some time with the Oracle database. EM12c introduced a similar solution for automated application testing called Application Replay. Unlike traditional application testing tools, Application Replay uses real production workloads to generate a load against applications under testing and does not require any script development or maintenance. It provides a best-of-breed approach for validating application infrastructure changes for all your Web and packaged Oracle applications.

Test data management is critical in a cloud environment but often gets overlooked. It is important that you protect critical and sensitive data when you allow users to provision applications and databases on demand via a self-service portal. The data-masking feature of Oracle Enterprise Manager testing suite can discover the data model interdependencies and "mask" any sensitive information to protect it. Data-masking templates with predefined sensitive columns and masking formats are also available for Oracle E-Business Suite and Fusion applications.

The data subsetting feature of EM12c lets you create smaller databases with subsets of application data that are relationally consistent so you can perform realistic testing and development by using just a small percentage of production data.

The Oracle Enterprise Manager testing suite also leverages the deep diagnostic capabilities built into the technology layers and provides prescriptions for remediation. All of these testing capabilities can really help you minimize the risk for downtime of applications deployed in the cloud.

Deploying the Cloud

After you build, test, and publish the applications in the Enterprise Manager Software Library, they are available for deployment via the Self Service portal of EM12c. As per NIST, on-demand self-service is one of the five key characteristics of the cloud. It provides a layer of abstraction that hides the underlying complexities of the cloud platform from the end user.

The out-of-box Self Service portal in EM12c, shown in Figure 5-10, allows cloud users to deploy a wide range of cloud services. Cloud users can deploy databases, Java applications, or complete application assemblies on the cloud platform listed in a service catalog that shows everything published in the Enterprise Manager Software Library. For deployment requests, users can specify the underlying resources (CPU, memory, database, WebLogic domain, and so forth) that they need for their applications, and Enterprise Manager will automatically provision them. Self-service users can also define policies based on schedule or performance metrics.

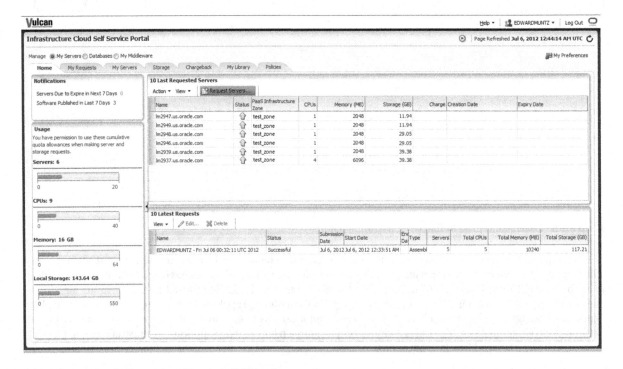

Figure 5-10. Oracle Enterprise Manager's Self Service portal

In addition to the deployment via the Self Service portal, cloud users can also use Oracle Enterprise Manager command-line APIs for deploying applications or application assemblies.

Monitoring the Cloud

After the cloud infrastructure is built and applications are deployed in it, you need to monitor the applications and underlying cloud infrastructure during ongoing operation. Oracle Enterprise Manager helps enterprises monitor complete cloud stacks, from applications to the storage disk, as shown in Figure 5-11.

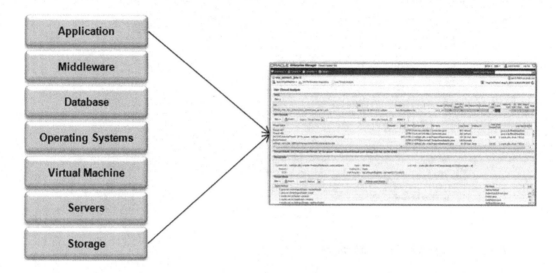

Figure 5-11. *Complete cloud stack monitoring by Oracle Enterprise Manager*

Applications and the underlying infrastructure need to be monitored at different levels and by different cloud roles that we discussed earlier. Table 5-1 summarizes monitoring tasks performed by various users of Oracle Enterprise Manager.

Table 5-1. *User Roles and Their Monitoring Tasks*

Roles	Monitoring Tasks
Cloud admin	Monitor cloud requests Monitor the health of the overall cloud service Monitor patch Track compliance
Self-service admin	Monitor application SLAs Monitor business transactions and metrics Monitor end-user experience
Self-service user	Monitor own requests Monitor own apps, VMs, databases Monitor quota, chargeback, etc.

The cloud admin (the administrator of the cloud infrastructure) monitors the health of the overall cloud application-to-disk stack by using Oracle Enterprise Manager to track resource flux, tenants, policy violations, and other incidents. The Oracle Enterprise Manager Incident Manager, shown in Figure 5-12, provides cloud administrators with a single interface that can be used to view, manage, resolve, and track all types of issues that have occurred within their monitored environments. Incident Manager is covered in more detail in Chapter 12.

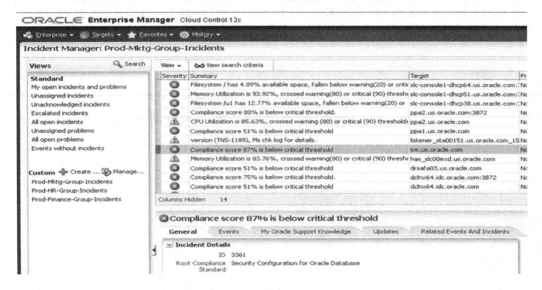

Figure 5-12. *Oracle Enterprise Manager Incident Manager*

In addition, the cloud administrator performs ongoing monitoring of requests and failure rates and identifies potential performance bottlenecks to remediate. Cloud administrators can automatically monitor cloud targets by using an administration group that defines dynamic criteria to group together cloud targets and auto-assign monitoring settings and policies. These groups can be created based on properties such as location, department, test, or production.

Self-service admins, who administer the common resources used by application owners at the line of businesses, monitor the application stack, the service levels and dependencies on the infrastructure, the end-user experience, and many other areas.

Self-service users or application owners monitor the health and quota aspects for their own applications hosted in the cloud environment. They can perform basic monitoring of provisioned resources including virtual machines, hosts, and databases. They can also monitor the end-user application experience.

Chapter 7 provides more details and best practices for the monitoring and management phases.

Managing the Cloud

You just learned about cloud monitoring, which is a process of being aware of the state of the applications and underlying cloud infrastructure. Monitoring typically results in uncorrelated sets of data. *Cloud management* is a set of functionalities and processes that use this data to deliver a desired objective for the cloud infrastructure and the applications deployed in the cloud. It involves managing and allocating cloud resources to produce useful outcomes.

EM12c provides comprehensive cloud stack management and business-driven application management functionalities. The Enterprise Manager approach is to move away from bolt-on and piecemeal management; embed management into the core solution; and deliver a complete, unified, and integrated solution for managing the entire stack. With EM12c, you have a single point of control for the entire infrastructure stack, including performance management, configuration management, and automated lifecycle operations such as provisioning and patching.

The other important aspect of Enterprise Manager is that it provides unparalleled depth when it comes to managing Oracle software. Oracle designs and instruments its products that power the cloud, for manageability. New Enterprise Manager features are developed along with the Oracle products and tested to ensure that they reduce complexity, enhance automation, optimize performance, and increase availability of the cloud environment.

Oracle Enterprise Manager enables you to build and manage a cloud that is optimized for the Oracle applications that power many of your business processes and services. Many custom applications are built using an Oracle middleware solution; a cloud powered by Oracle Enterprise Manager can not only run your mission-critical applications, but also provide you deep insight into the business services delivered by those applications. We call this approach *business-driven application management*, and it has three key capabilities:

- *User experience management* helps you monitor the experience of business users. Oracle Enterprise Manager Real User Experience Insight monitors network traffic to provide a complete and accurate view of who your users are, where they are located, what they are doing, and whether they are getting the desired service levels. This solution works with both custom and packaged applications. Out-of-the-box prebuilt knowledge modules for Oracle applications allow you to monitor business processes and activities quickly. Figure 5-13 shows the dashboard of Oracle Enterprise Manager Real User Experience Insight.

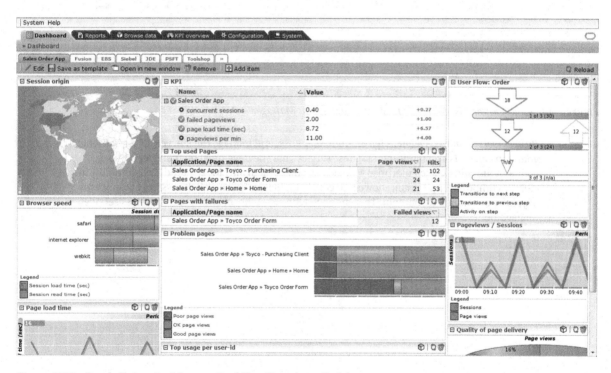

Figure 5-13. *Oracle Enterprise Manager Real User Experience Insight*

- *Business transaction management* gives you visibility into transactions that are executing across multiple components in the application. If your application is deployed in the cloud as an assembly, Enterprise Manager Business Transaction Manager can give you visibility into transactions across individual components of the assembly. It can even monitor transactions across assemblies or application components using external services. Figure 5-14 shows Business Transaction Manager.

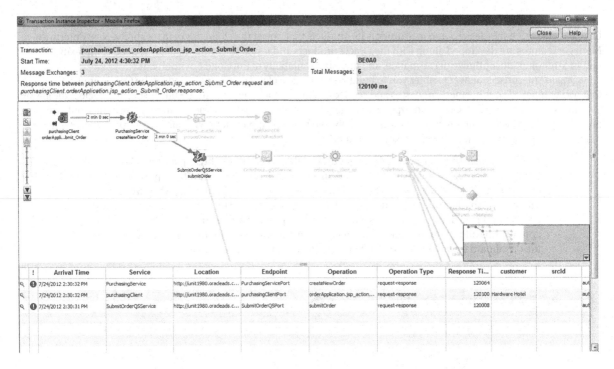

Figure 5-14. *Oracle Enterprise Manager Business Transaction Manager*

- *Business service management* helps monitor, diagnose, and manage the lifecycle of services that your transaction is executing across. These services may be developed on many technology components, and Oracle Enterprise Manager supports them all. EM12c introduced the ability to create a composite application, shown in Figure 5-15, that represents all the system components of your application environment. This enhanced the capability of end-to-end business service management.

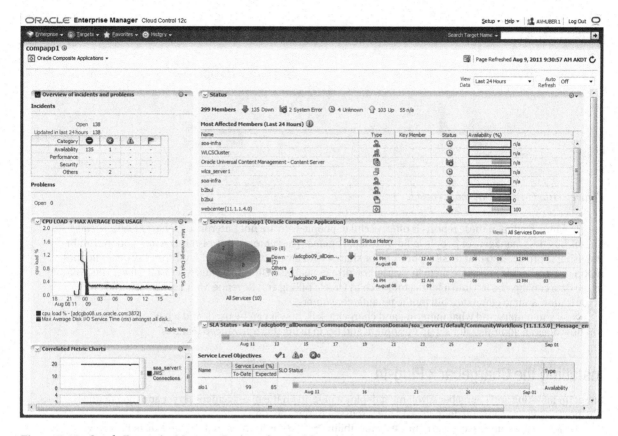

Figure 5-15. *Oracle Enterprise Manager Business Service Manager*

Metering and Chargeback

One of the key characteristics of a cloud is the ability to measure the usage of cloud resources and report or potentially bill for the utilized services. While cloud and self-service access bring a lot of flexibility and agility, they also brings some challenges.

As cloud users start sharing the cloud platform or infrastructure resources, you need to have accountability of the usage; otherwise, resources will be overused by some, while others won't get resources when they are needed. To mitigate this, enterprises need to measure the resource usage and optionally charge back to the tenants. Though an IT organization may not actually charge its lines of business, usage reporting provides a transparent mechanism for budgeting resources and optimizes the cloud platform on an ongoing basis.

Understanding Metering and Chargeback

EM12c offers a sophisticated and flexible Metering and Chargeback mechanism whereby you can define models based on fixed cost, configuration (such as version, licenses), or utilization, or a combination of these (see Figure 5-16). This feature enables you to meter resources at various levels—for example, host/VM level, database, and middleware. It is well integrated with LDAP so that you can traverse the organizational hierarchy and generate the consumption report at various levels.

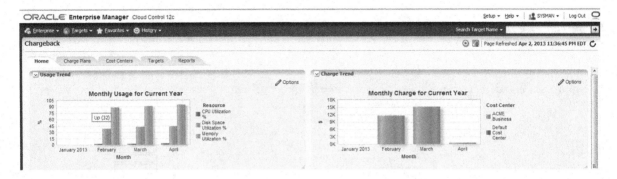

Figure 5-16. EM12c Chargeback console

The information in these reports is often useful to people who are not Enterprise Manager users, such as line-of-business managers or people in finance departments. Therefore, an out-of-the-box integration with BI Publisher is provided so that these reports can be shared with a variety of users. BI Publisher can generate these reports on a schedule and share them in a variety of formats such as PDF, HTML, and Microsoft Office. The resource usage data can then be fed into a billing tool such as Oracle Billing and Revenue Management, should any organization want to generate a bill for the tenants/consumers.

Now you understand what metering and chargeback is, how it can be used, and what features are available. But how does an administrator set up this option and begin using these advanced features?

Installing the Chargeback Plug-In

To set up metering and chargeback, you must deploy a plug-in on the management server and then define six tasks. The plug-in deployment and defined tasks are discussed in this section.

To access the plug-ins, choose Setup ➤ Extensibility ➤ Plug-ins from the right-hand side of the screen. This brings you to the page shown in Figure 5-17, where all available plug-ins are listed.

Plug-ins

This page displays the list of plug-ins available, downloaded and deployed in the Enterprise Manager environment. Plug-in lifecycle actions s

Actions ▼   View ▼   ⬛ Deploy On | ▼ ⬛ Undeploy From | ▼ ⬛ Check Updates   ⬛ Deployment Activities

Name	Version			Management Agent with Plug-in
	Latest Available	Latest Downloaded	On Management Server	
▷ 📁 Databases ⓘ				
▷ 📁 Middleware ⓘ				
▷ 📁 Servers, Storage and Network ⓘ				
🗗 Exalogic Elastic Cloud Infrastructure	12.1.0.1.0	12.1.0.1.0		0
🗗 Oracle Audit Vault	12.1.0.2.0	12.1.0.2.0		0
🗗 Oracle Beacon	12.1.0.2.0	12.1.0.2.0	12.1.0.2.0	1
🗗 Oracle Big Data Appliance	12.1.0.1.0			0
🗗 Oracle Chargeback and Capacity Planning	12.1.0.3.0	12.1.0.3.0	12.1.0.3.0	0
🗗 Oracle Exadata	12.1.0.3.0	12.1.0.3.0	12.1.0.3.0	0
🗗 Oracle Exadata Healthchecks	12.1.0.3.0	12.1.0.2.0		0

Figure 5-17. Oracle Chargeback and Capacity Planning plug-in availability

To deploy the Oracle Chargeback and Capacity Planning plug-in, you need to know the repository SYS password. Provide the password and continue with the deployment (see Figure 5-18).

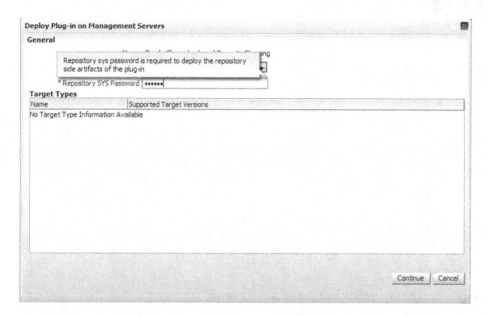

Figure 5-18. *Providing the repository SYS password for deployment*

■ **Note** If the plug-in is deployed on the management server, the deployment will require downtime. Ensure that you have a backup of the repository and configuration of the management server before deploying. You'll see a message similar to the following.

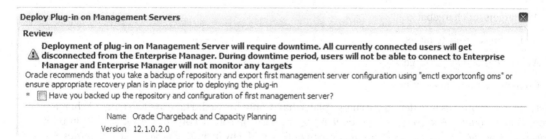

You will not be able to deploy until you select the check box confirming that you have made a backup of the repository and management server.

After the deployment is complete, two new menu items are displayed on the Enterprise menu: Chargeback and Consolidation Planner (see Figure 5-19). This means the deployment of the plug-in was successful, and you can now utilize the functionality associated with the Chargeback plug-in. You will also notice that functionality for Consolidation Planner has been enabled; this feature is discussed later in this chapter.

Figure 5-19. *Enterprise menu options for Chargeback and Consolidation Planner*

Configuring Metering and Chargeback

Once the Chargeback functionality is enabled within EM12c, it is time to focus on the six tasks required to successfully set up chargeback for your environment:

1. Define charge plans.

2. Create cost centers.

3. Add targets for chargeback.

4. Assign cost centers to targets.

5. Assign charge plans to targets.

6. Configure chargeback settings.

The first step in this process is to define the charge plans that should be used. There are two types of charge plans: universal and extended. A *universal charge plan* uses three basic metrics to compute resource consumption: CPU, memory, and storage. An *extended charge plan* enhances this model by including target-specific metrics to determine usage rates.

To determine the appropriate charge plan, you have to decided on a case-by-case basis whether the universal charge plan (CPU, memory, and storage) will be enough to meet the organization's needs. If more than the core three metrics are needed, the extended charge plan should be applied.

To define a charge plan, you choose Enterprise ➤ Chargeback to access the Charge Plans tab within the Chargeback interface. For a universal charge plan, it is easy to set the rate that is charged by highlighting and then editing the metric (see Figure 5-20). An extended charge plan can be created or edited immediately below the universal charge plan.

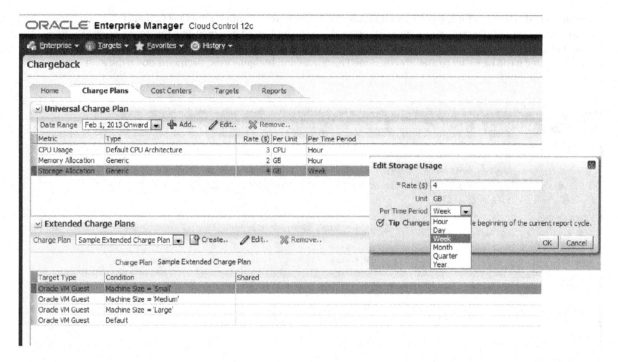

Figure 5-20. *Universal and extended charge plans can be edited on the same screen of the charge plan configuration interface*

The next step in configuring chargeback is to set up the cost centers for the organization. *Cost centers* are the vehicles used to aggregate charges. A cost center can be an individual, departments within the organization, or a multi-tiered business hierarchy that spreads the charges across an enterprise. To create a business hierarchy, set up cost centers and assign users to the business units. Additionally, a business hierarchy can be implemented by importing an organization's hierarchy from an LDAP server.

To add a cost center, click the Cost Centers tab and then click the Add button. This opens the New Cost Center dialog box, shown in Figure 5-21. Here you can enter the name of the cost center as well as its display name and level. If existing cost centers are available, the new cost center can be added as a "member of" one of those cost centers.

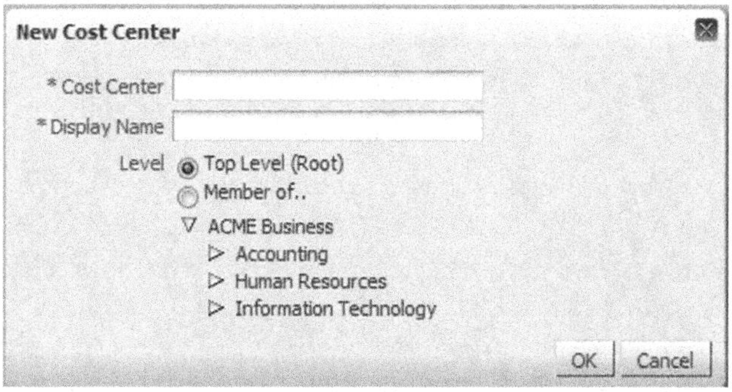

Figure 5-21. *Adding a new cost center*

Once a cost center is added, it will show up under the Cost Center column on the Cost Centers tab. If you added sub–cost centers as members of an existing cost center, these can be viewed by expanding the tree view (see Figure 5-22). As you will notice, this can become a complex architecture of cost centers to manage. However, by diligently laying out your cost center, it will be easier to identify consumed resources and budgetary requirements down the road.

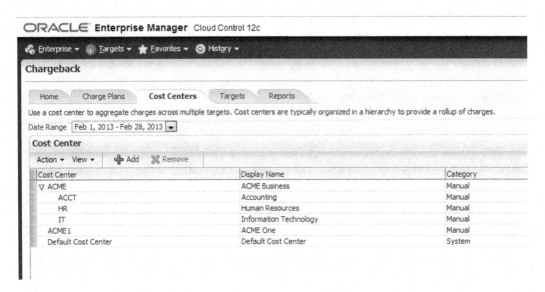

Figure 5-22. *Examples of cost centers defined*

As mentioned earlier, you could also import an LDAP hierarchy for your cost centers. This can be done from the Cost Center table, through the Action menu by selecting LDAP Settings (see Figure 5-23). There are a few, well-known LDAPs that are supported with EM12c:

- Oracle Internet Directory

- Microsoft Active Directory

- Sun iPlanet

- Novell eDirectory

- OpenLDAP

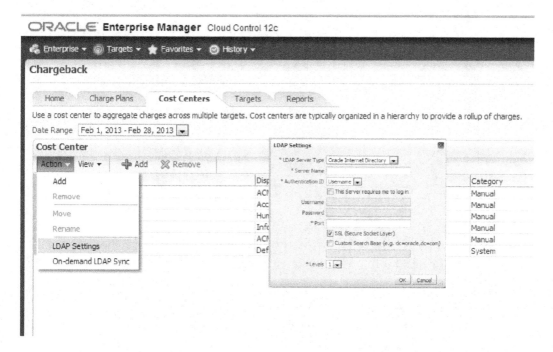

Figure 5-23. *Importing the LDAP hierarchy*

When using an LDAP to build the cost center hierarchy, the LDAP will overwrite the manually entered cost centers of the same name while maintaining target assignments. When an LDAP is successfully imported, it will generate a scheduled job that will run each reporting cycle to sync the cost centers with the LDAP. On-demand sync can be performed with the Action menu as well.

After setting up the cost centers, you need to assign targets for chargeback. To add targets, you must have the ADD_CHARGEBACK_TARGET role. This role allows you to add any target monitored by EM12c that qualifies for chargeback support. If this role is not granted to you, the Add Targets button will be disabled.

■ **Note**   In addition to the ADD_CHARGEBACK_TARGET role, two other roles may be needed by a user looking into chargeback. The VIEW_TARGET role allows you to see chargeback data related to a specific target. The VIEW_ANY_TARGET role allows you to see chargeback data related to any target.

For targets to be assigned to a chargeback plan and to a cost center, the target first has to be monitored by Enterprise Manager. Then on the Targets tab in the chargeback interface, you will be able to add targets by using the Add Targets button. Clicking the Add Targets button brings up the dialog box to add a target, as shown in Figure 5-24. Initially, this dialog box will be empty. Targets can be added by clicking the Target Selector button.

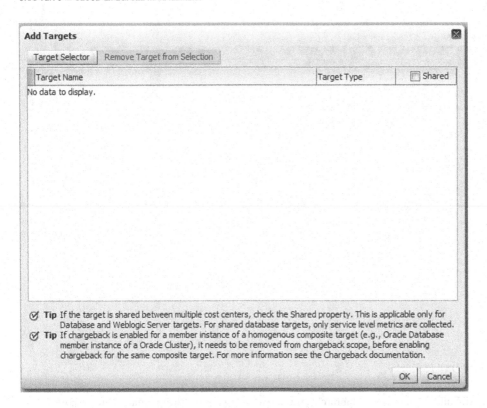

Figure 5-24. *Add Targets dialog box*

Clicking the Target Selector button brings up the functionality to search for the target that you would like to add (see Figure 5-25). By default, all target types are listed. As with many of the search options within Enterprise Manager, you select the target type and search for the target you want. Once you select your target, click Select and then OK to add it to the targets that can be assigned charge plans and a cost center.

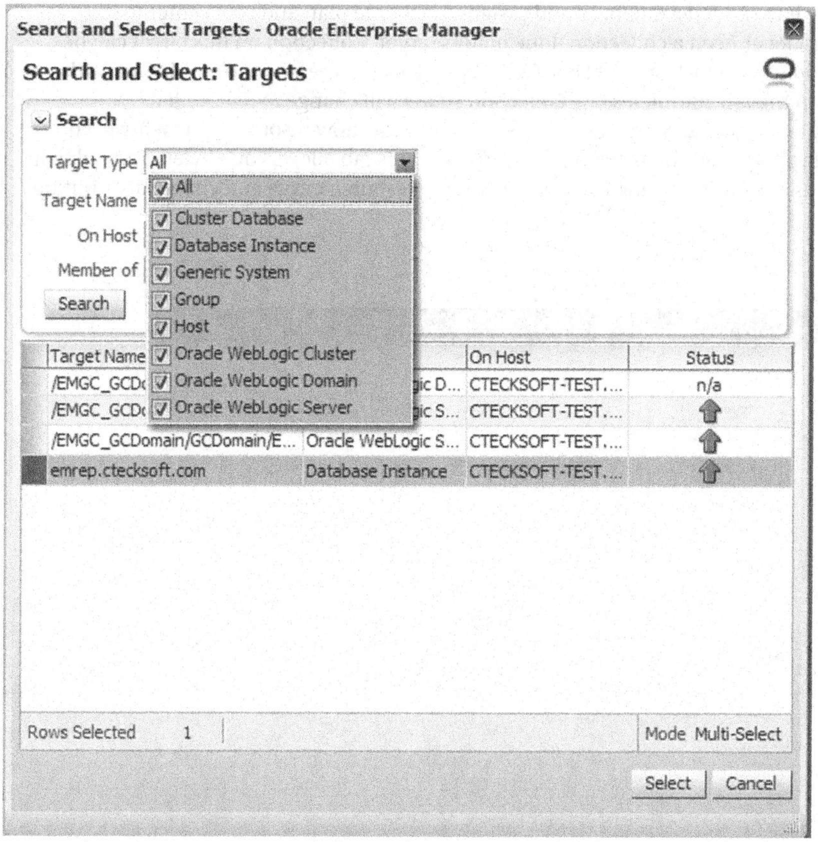

Figure 5-25. *Selection of targets for chargeback and cost centers*

After the target is added to the list of targets eligible for chargeback and cost center assignment, you can add the charge plan and cost center that was set up previously by clicking the Assign buttons above the list (see Figure 5-26). Many of the commands that are done via buttons for adding and removing targets, assigning plans, and assigning cost centers can also be done from the Action menu.

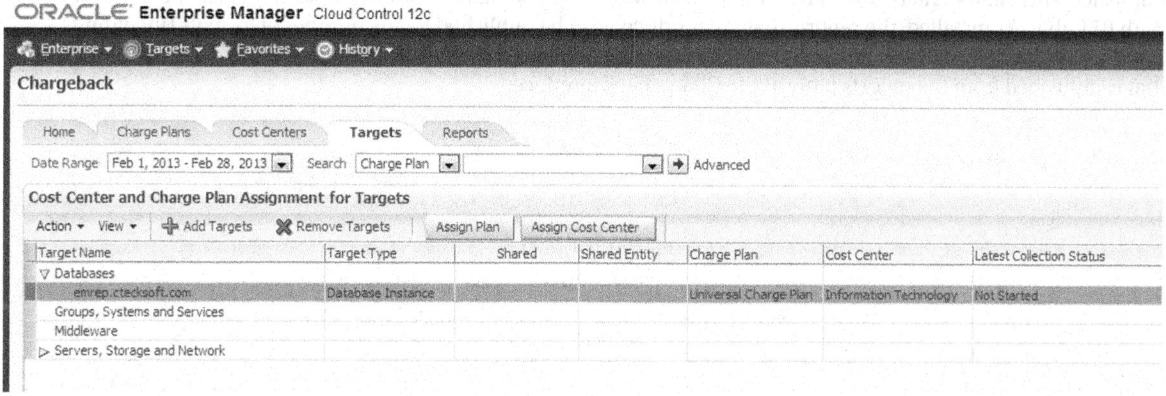

Figure 5-26. *Target added with charge plan and cost center*

As you can see in Figure 5-26, we have added a database and assigned a charge plan and cost center to it. You will notice, though, that there has never been a collection done on this target. Collection on this target can be done manually via the Action menu option of On-Demand Data Collection. This will create a job within Enterprise Manager that runs immediately. When the job completes, the collection status will change to Succeeded.

After some time, it will be handy to identify and provide reports that will show how resources are being used. This can be done on the last tab of the chargeback interface, the Reports tab. This tab allows you to view and publish chargeback reports that can be used as a powerful analytical tool for tracking resource usage and charge distributions (see Figure 5-27).

Figure 5-27. *Chargeback report view*

The Reports tab shows a lot of detail for resources. In Figure 5-27, you see a breakout by cost center and target type. Further to the right, you will see a breakout by resource. At the bottom of the screen, in the Details section, is a table that provides detailed information about resources that have been configured. Everything on the reports table is searchable and reportable at the top of the screen.

In addition to the report provided on the Reports tab, reports can be pushed with Oracle Business Intelligence (BI) Publisher. This allows Enterprise Manager to provide more-sophisticated reports in formats that can be e-mailed. With BI Publisher installed, the reports that are produced can be published to any number of formats (including HTML, PDF, Word, Excel, and PowerPoint) by clicking the Publish Report button. Figure 5-28 shows a sample report that is published from the reports table in the Chargeback interface.

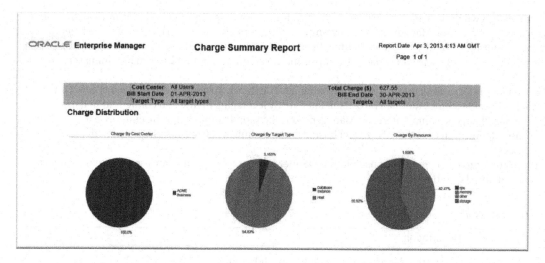

Figure 5-28. *Published report with BI Publisher*

The Chargeback module is and can be a powerful tool for an IT department. With the capacity to implement charge plans and cost centers, and then apply them to targets and provide reports to end users, the Chargeback module is a necessity for any cloud environment.

Optimizing the Cloud

The cloud infrastructure and the applications deployed on that infrastructure need to be optimized for performance, energy efficiency, user experience, and operational costs. Rich cloud management functionalities of Oracle Enterprise Manager help you rediscover assets, review application performance, and fine-tune various phases of the cloud lifecycle based on the information and intelligence collected during ongoing operations of the cloud. Starting from the setup phase—where you can scale up or down the machine sizes, change the quota or zone assignment, or fine-tune the policy for cloud resources—enterprises can decide to make changes to applications within an assembly or in the deployment of cloud resources in order to optimize the cloud. Enterprise Manager also provides a rich performance management database that provides a historical view of cloud performance to help you optimize it. Chapter 9 covers performance pages and optimization in more detail. Capabilities of the operating systems, database, and middleware layers help in continuous optimization of the cloud environment.

Throughout this chapter, we have talked about the many lifecycle stages for managing a cloud environment. As we pointed out earlier, Consolidation Planner is installed along with the Chargeback plug-in. Consolidation Planner can be used for not only cloud environments, but also traditional IT environments to help organizations shrink their overall enterprise footprint. Let's take a look at Consolidation Planner now.

Consolidation Planner

While the Chargeback module is good at helping organizations or service providers identify potential revenue from used resources, Consolidation Planner allows these same organizations a way to drive down internal costs associated with running noncloud or cloud resources. Every enterprise data center grows steadily over time, and addition of servers is needed to satisfy increasing business demands. This growth typically results in the increase of rack space and the power needed for cooling and maintenance of systems to include security and patching.

To combat these growth trends, many enterprises are increasingly investigating and investing in virtualization technology, such as Oracle Virtual Machine, by moving physical servers to virtual ones. The goal of these types of moves is to consolidate shared hardware while retaining the benefits of isolation that virtual machines provide. Consolidation in this way enables the enterprise to free up as many servers as possible while maintaining service-level agreements.

Consolidation Planner enables enterprises to match managed servers with generic physical machines, Oracle Exadata, or Oracle Virtual Machines they can be consolidated to. By leveraging metric and configuration data collected from managed targets within Enterprise Manager, Consolidation Planner helps the enterprise to determine the optimum consolidation scenarios that also reflect business and technical constraints associated with the consolidation process.

Each consolidation project defined in Consolidation Planner has key concepts that are essential to the project. These concepts are defined in Table 5-2.

Table 5-2. *Key Concepts for Consolidation Planner*

Concept	Description
Source server	An existing server considered for consolidation.
Destination server	An existing or yet-to-be-purchased server that a source server will be consolidated to. Also thought of as the consolidation target.

Consolidation project	Defines the scope of a potential consolidation effort
	
	• Type of consolidation
	    • Physical to virtual (physical to Oracle Virtual Machine)
	    • Physical to physical
	• The preliminary set of candidate source servers to consider consolidating from
	• The preliminary set of candidate target servers to consider consolidating to
	• The duration over which data used to generate consolidation scenarios will be collected for the source server

Consolidation scenario	Scenarios that are generated based on the input provided. Inputs provided to a scenario include the following:
	
	• The source server resource requirements that a destination server must meet, including one or more of the following:
	    • CPU
	    • MemoryDisk I/O
	    • Network I/O
	    • Disk storage
	• Any business, compliance, or technical constraints that must be considered
	• The destination server to consider in the scenario

Now that you know the key concepts for Consolidation Planner, it is important to also understand a few constraints you should be aware of. These constraints center on the source server and the destination server.

Source server constraints are based on compatibility or exclusivity. Servers are considered compatible if certain properties and configuration values match. These properties include the following: lifecycle status, department, and location. As an example, a property may need to be set when source servers must remain within a specific location or geographical area. Additionally, source servers can be defined by configuration values that include the following: network domain, system vendor, system configuration, CPU vendor, CPU name, and operating system. Finally, source servers can be mutually exclusive. This means that they can be excluded from the consolidation scope because they do not fit within Oracle best practices. To exclude matching servers, set either or both of the following conditions: Nodes of a RAC Database, Nodes of an Oracle Cluster.

Destination servers can be scoped out against new or existing candidate servers. The constraints associated with destination servers are primarily expressed as a percentage of the CPU and memory resource utilization—that is, how much of either resource type can be used by the destination server.

Now that we have defined source and destination servers, you're ready to take a closer look at how to define a consolidation project and evaluate the scenarios.

Consolidation Planner is installed as part of the plug-in that includes the Chargeback module. To access Consolidation Planner, choose Enterprise ➤ Consolidation Planner. This opens the Consolidation Planner module. If this is a new implementation of Consolidation Planner, no projects will be defined. Figure 5-29 illustrates how to open the Consolidation Planner.

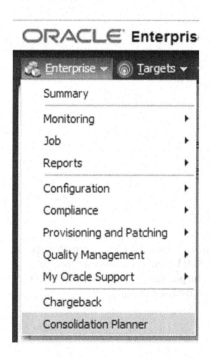

Figure 5-29. *Enterprise menu options for Consolidation Planner*

On the Consolidation Planner home page, you will find a list of projects that are defined along with menu items that can help in defining new projects, create scenarios, report on projects, and delete projects. Figure 5-30 shows a newly implemented Consolidation Planner with one project. We will walk through creating a new project for consolidating a physical server to an Oracle Virtual Machine.

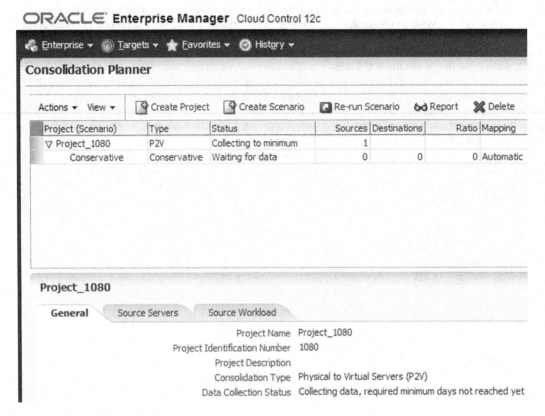

Figure 5-30. *Newly implemented Consolidation Planner with project*

On the Consolidation Planner page, to create a new project, the administrator needs to click the Create Project button. This brings up the Create Consolidation Project details page (see Figure 5-31). Here the administrator can define all aspects of the project, such as the type of consolidation that is going to be performed, servers involved in the consolidation, length of data collection, and any preconfigured scenarios if they have been defined.

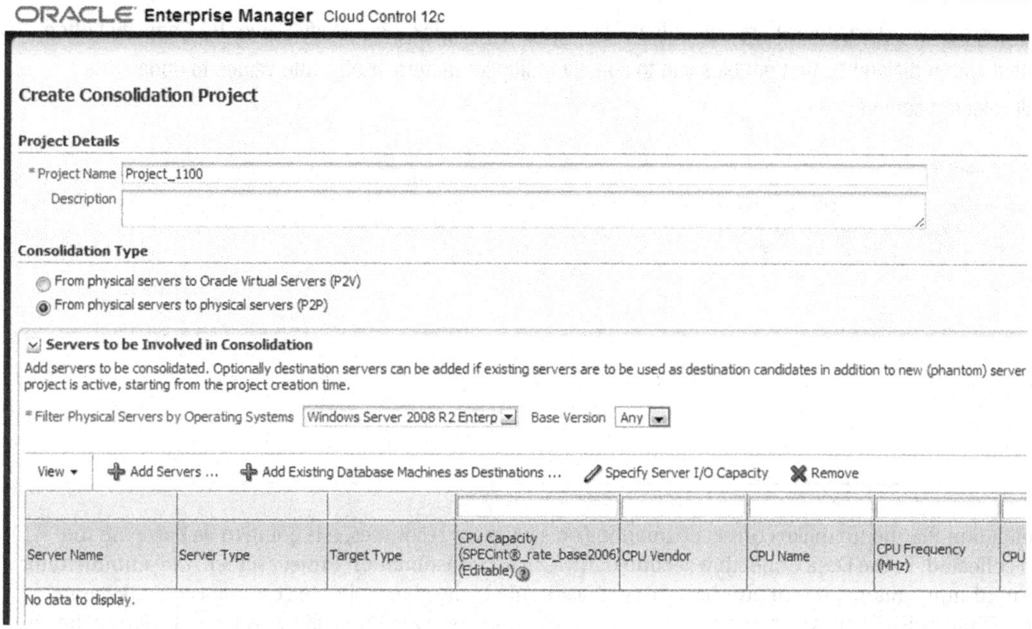

ORACLE Enterprise Manager Cloud Control 12c

Create Consolidation Project

Project Details

* Project Name Project_1100

Description

Consolidation Type

○ From physical servers to Oracle Virtual Servers (P2V)

● From physical servers to physical servers (P2P)

☑ **Servers to be Involved in Consolidation**

Add servers to be consolidated. Optionally destination servers can be added if existing servers are to be used as destination candidates in addition to new (phantom) server project is active, starting from the project creation time.

* Filter Physical Servers by Operating Systems Windows Server 2008 R2 Enterp ▾   Base Version Any ▾

View ▾   ➕ Add Servers ...   ➕ Add Existing Database Machines as Destinations ...   ✏ Specify Server I/O Capacity   ✖ Remove

Server Name	Server Type	Target Type	CPU Capacity (SPECint®_rate_base2006) (Editable) ⓘ	CPU Vendor	CPU Name	CPU Frequency (MHz)	CPU

No data to display.

Figure 5-31. *Create Consolidation Project screen*

This screen is full of information needed to define a consolidation project. The first item that has to be decided is the type of consolidation that is going to be done. The two options are Physical to Oracle Virtual Machine (P2V) and Physical to Physical (P2P). Next, we have to choose what servers are going to be involved in the consolidation. When adding a target for consolidation, first we have to add a source server. We also have the option of adding existing virtual servers as destinations if needed. After the source target or OVM destination is added, you'll see a lot of estimates that are specific to that source or destination server (see Figure 5-32).

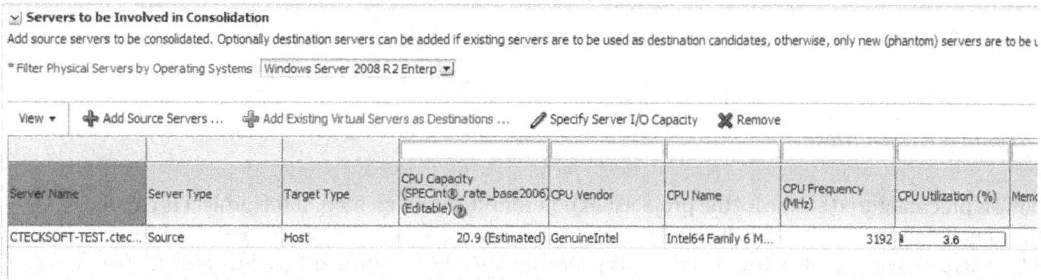

☑ **Servers to be Involved in Consolidation**

Add source servers to be consolidated. Optionally destination servers can be added if existing servers are to be used as destination candidates, otherwise, only new (phantom) servers are to be u

* Filter Physical Servers by Operating Systems Windows Server 2008 R2 Enterp ▾

View ▾   ➕ Add Source Servers ...   ➕ Add Existing Virtual Servers as Destinations ...   ✏ Specify Server I/O Capacity   ✖ Remove

Server Name	Server Type	Target Type	CPU Capacity (SPECint®_rate_base2006) (Editable) ⓘ	CPU Vendor	CPU Name	CPU Frequency (MHz)	CPU Utilization (%)	Mem
CTECKSOFT-TEST.ctec...	Source	Host	20.9 (Estimated)	GenuineIntel	Intel64 Family 6 M...	3192	3.6	

Figure 5-32. *Source server added for consolidation*

■ **Note** Specifying server I/O capacities are estimates with Oracle. If you click the Specify Server I/O Capacity button, you'll be presented with a dialog box that enables you to specify multiplier factors or absolute values to update the capacities for all selected servers.

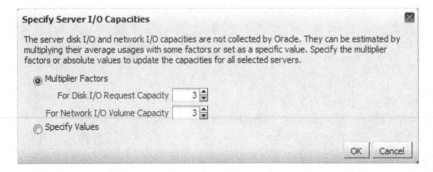

For Consolidation Planner to make correct estimations on savings or resources, it is going to be based on the amount of data collected. In the Data Collection section of the Create Consolidation Project screen, the administrator can specify the minimum and maximum number of days that should be used to estimate consolidation. Like many other tasks within Enterprise Manager, the collection of data is handled by a job that will be created. As part of the data collection, the option to start data collection immediately or later can be specified.

The last step in creating a consolidation project is to specify whether the project should use any preconfigured scenarios. By default, no scenarios are selected. However, a preconfigured scenario can be selected from three options; these scenarios use the metric for CPU, Memory, and Disk Storage to analyze the consolidation project. Figure 5-33 provides the breakdown of these scenarios.

Add Pre-Configured Scenarios

Select one or more pre-configured scenarios in the below table to be evaluated along with the project creation.

Name	Description	Type	Constrained Resources	Destination Resource Limit (%)
Conservative	A conservative pre-configured scenario analysis.	Conservative	CPU, Memory and Disk Storage	70
Medium	A medium pre-configured scenario analysis.	Medium	CPU, Memory and Disk Storage	80
Aggressive	An aggressive pre-configured scenario analysis.	Aggressive	CPU, Memory and Disk Storage	90

Figure 5-33. *Preconfigured scenarios*

After selecting a preconfigured scenario, the project can be submitted and created. If the project is created successfully, the Consolidation Planner page will reflect the project being created and the current status of the project. At the bottom of the screen, you will also notice three tabs providing specific information on the project. These tabs are General, Source Servers, and Source Workload.

The General tab gives you all the specific information related to the project, including the project name, identification number, consolidation type, and current status of data collection. The Source Servers tab gives you information similar to that presented when adding the source targets to the project. Items such as CPU utilization, memory utilization, and disk storage are presented. What is interesting on this tab is the information that is provided by telling you the start and end dates of data collection. The Source Workload tab gives you a 24-hour view, in a table format, of the resources that are being measured for consolidation (see Figure 5-34). These can be viewed by using the Resource Type drop-down menu.

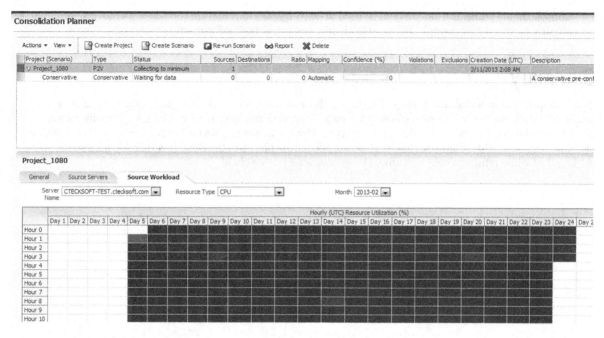

Figure 5-34. *Consolidation Planner with project information*

Once the project is done gathering information needed to project consolidation efforts, a report can be generated by clicking the Report menu item on the Consolidation Planner screen. Much like the Chargeback report, the Consolidation Project report will be displayed within the browser. With Oracle BI Publisher installed in Enterprise Manager, the option to publish reports will be available, allowing the administrator to publish consolidation reports to end users. Figure 5-35 shows a sample report that is published from the report table in Consolidation Planner.

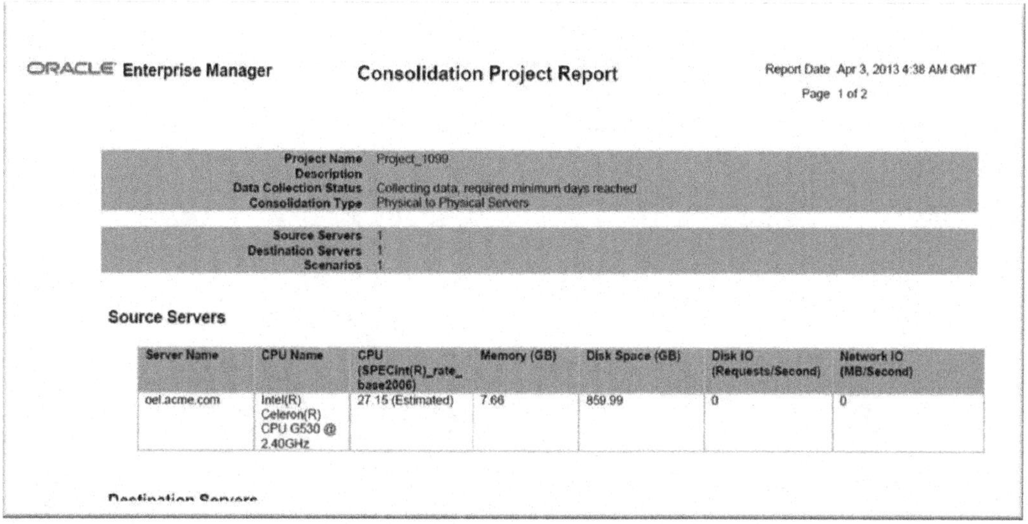

Figure 5-35. *BI Publisher report for the consolidation project*

Consolidation Planner is a tool that can be used to help organizations that are considering a move to the cloud or new physical hardware (for example, Exadata) to identify and shrink their infrastructure footprint.

Summary

In this chapter, you reviewed cloud computing, its key characteristics, and its delivery and deployment models. You also learned that in order to get the best out of your cloud infrastructure, it is important to efficiently manage all phases of the cloud lifecycle. You can't have a very good solution just for provisioning or monitoring, for efficient cloud management. EM12c lets you gain total control over all the phases of the cloud lifecycle, allowing you to achieve the highest return on your investment in an enterprise private cloud.

■ ■ ■

CHAPTER 6

Software Library, Patching, and Provisioning

by Bobby Curtis

One of the main benefits of using Oracle Enterprise Manager 12c is its ability to help database, system, and application administrators save time and automate the processes required to manage the Oracle database lifecycle. Patching and provisioning of resources is essential to daily operations and maintenance of critical business systems across the enterprise. Through the Database Lifecycle Management Pack, administrators are given tools to help eliminate manual and time-consuming tasks related to discovery, initial provisioning, patching, configuration management, and ongoing change management. In this chapter, you will take a look at the Software Library and the components of the Database Lifecycle Management Pack needed to implement the patching and provisioning options for EM12c.

Software Library

One of the core features in EM12c is the *Oracle Software Library*. This is the core repository that stores software entities such as agent software, patches, virtual appliance images, gold images, application software, and their associated scripts. Additionally, the Software Library allows you to maintain versions, maturity levels, and states of the various software entities stored. Figure 6-1 gives you the general look and feel of the Software Library console.

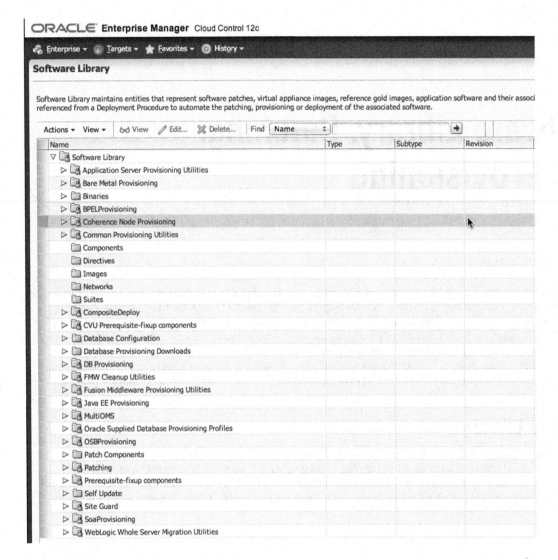

Figure 6-1. *Software Library console*

To access the Software Library console page, you choose Enterprise ➤ Provisioning and Patching ➤ Software Library. In the Software Library console, there are two types of folders: the folders marked with a lock are Oracle-owned folders, and folders without a lock are user-owned folders. (Folders with and without locks can be seen in Figure 6-1.)

Oracle-owned folders (and subfolders) are those that ship with EM12c by default. These folders will appear in the Software Library console after the Software Library is configured. User-owned folders are top-level folders that users create to organize the software entities within the Software Library.

■ **Note**   The Software Library, once configured, contains a series of numbered directories that can be confusing to look at when first reviewed. According to the Oracle Enterprise Manager team, the numbered folders in the Software Library structure were designed to keep everyone focused on the GUI interface.

Using the Software Library yields a lot of advantages for administrators, including the following:

- Facilitates patching and provisioning tasks in both modes, online and offline

- Supports referenced file locations, allowing administrators to leverage existing IT infrastructures (file servers, web servers, and storage systems) to store and stage software entities for patching and provisioning activities

- Allows for organization of software entities into logical folders for efficient management

As mentioned earlier, the Software Library is the core repository for everything within EM12c, when it comes to patching and provisioning. We have briefly discussed how to get to the Software Library console, the types of folders that can be configured within the library, and its advantages. What we haven't discussed yet is how to configure the Software Library so it can be used. Let's take a look at that now.

Configuring the Software Library

Before you can start using the Software Library, you must set it up through the Software Library Administration console. A Software Library must consist of at least one upload file location on the host where the Oracle Management Server (OMS) is running. A storage location in the Software Library represents a directory that is either uploaded to the library or generated and saved by some user-owned processes.

There are three options for upload file locations when configuring the Software Library: an OMS Shared Filesystem, OMS Agent Filesystem, or Referenced File Location. These are the only supported storage options for setting up the Software Library. Let's take a quick look at these options:

> *OMS Shared Filesystem*: This location is required to be shared (or mounted) across all the OMS hosts.

> *OMS Agent Filesystem*: Using this option, ensure that you have a preferred or name credential for the OMS host set.

> *Referenced File Location*: This option allows you to leverage the organization's existing IT infrastructure for sourcing software binaries and scripts. Referenced File Locations support three storage options:

> - *HTTP*: An HTTP storage location represents a base URL that acts as the source of files that can be referenced.

> - *NFS*: An NFS storage location represents an exported filesystem directory on a server. The server does not need to be the OEM host target.

> - *Agent*: An agent storage location is similar to the OMS Agent Filesystem option, but an OEM agent can monitor any host. The agent can be configured to serve the files located on that host.

To configure the Software Library, you need to decide on the upload file location. In many of the configurations I have done, I use the OMS Shared Filesystem for the Software Library, because it is simple to set up and is local to the OMS. Let's take a look at how to set up this type of share for the Software Library.

■ **Note**   When setting up the Software Library, no matter the type of location you use, the question of size comes to mind. How large is the Software Library supposed to be? What do I need to preallocate for the Software Library? You should allocate as much space as you think is going to be used. I've always recommended a starting size between 5GB and 50GB. This is due to the agent software needing to be downloaded into the Software Library before deployment.

To access the Software Library Administration console, you choose Setup ➤ Provisioning and Patching ➤ Software Library. Figure 6-2 shows the menu path to this location.

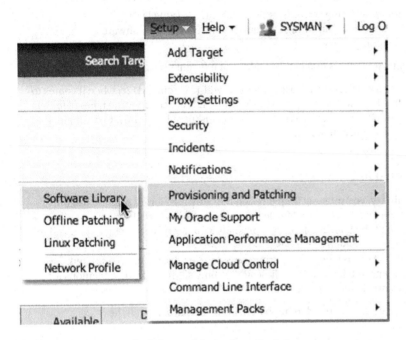

Figure 6-2. *Accessing the Software Library from the Setup menu*

In the Software Library Administration console, you will immediately see two tabs that help you distinguish between the upload locations on the OMS and the referenced locations. To set up an OMS Shared Filesystem location, you need to stay on the Upload File Locations tab. Here, the Storage Type drop-down menu gives you the option of either an OMS Shared Filesystem or an Agent Shared Filesystem (see Figure 6-3).

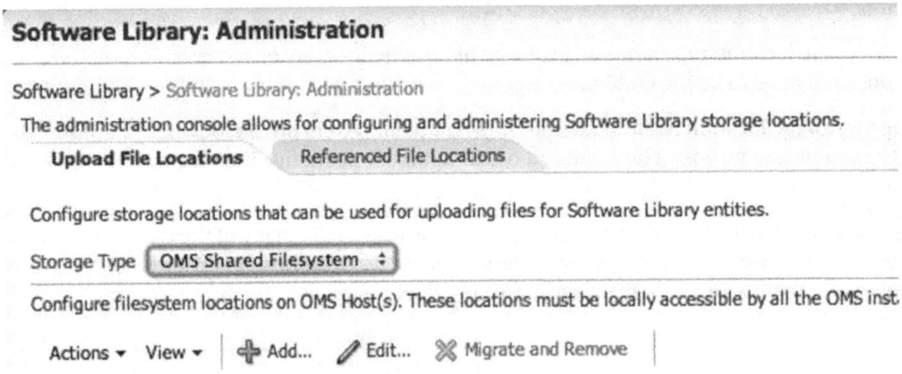

Software Library: Administration

Software Library > Software Library: Administration

The administration console allows for configuring and administering Software Library storage locations.

Upload File Locations   Referenced File Locations

Configure storage locations that can be used for uploading files for Software Library entities.

Storage Type   [OMS Shared Filesystem ♦]

Configure filesystem locations on OMS Host(s). These locations must be locally accessible by all the OMS inst.

Actions ▾   View ▾ | ⊹ Add...   ⬦ Edit...   ✖ Migrate and Remove |

Figure 6-3. *Software Library Administration console*

Now, because you are going to use the OMS Shared Filesystem for our Software Library, you need to ensure that you have a location on the local host to store the Software Library. Once this directory structure has been identified, you can add the filesystem to OEM. While in the Software Library Administration console, click the Add menu option. This opens a dialog box that allows you to name the Software Library and identify the location on the OMS server (see Figure 6-4).

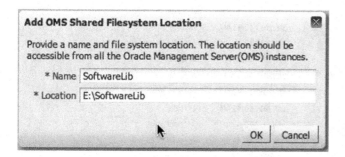

Figure 6-4. *Adding an OMS Shared Filesystem location*

Click the OK button, and the creation of the Software Library begins. The library lists the location that you created with the Add menu command and the status of library, as shown in Figure 6-5.

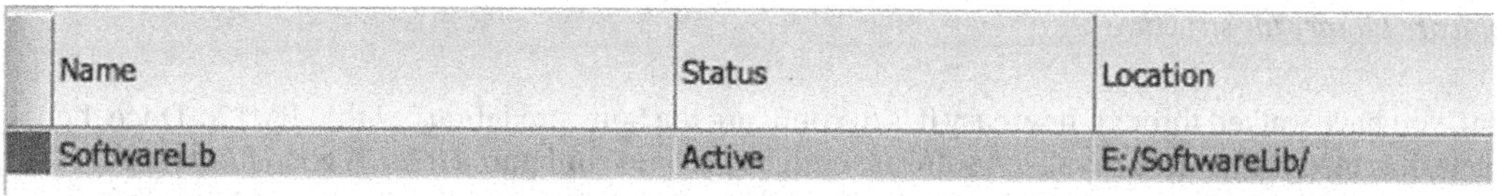

Name	Status	Location
SoftwareLb	Active	E:/SoftwareLib/

Figure 6-5. *Software Library name, status, and location*

As I mentioned earlier, if you were to go and look at the location where the Software Library populates its initial entries, you would see only a bunch of folders with numbers. This is designed to keep the Software Library clean and prevent anyone from modifying the library from outside OEM. Figure 6-6 gives an example of the file structure.

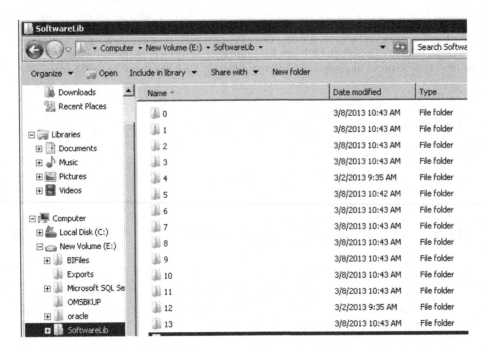

Figure 6-6. *Software Library file structure*

At this point, you have walked through how easy it is to configure the Software Library within EM12c. Once the library is complete, it is ready to be used for all the software entities that you configured it for. A good first test of the Software Library is to download the agent software that you will need for your enterprise systems. Agent software download and installation was covered in Chapter 2.

Using Software Library Entities

Now that the Software Library is configured, you want to use the entities that can be found in the library. To do this, you need to access the Software Library home page by choosing Enterprise ➤ Provisioning and Patching ➤ Software Library, as shown in Figure 6-7.

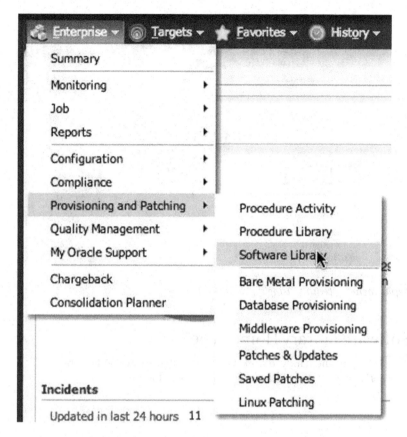

Figure 6-7. *Software Library home page*

When working with entities in the Software Library, it is important to remember that there are two, broadly classified types: Oracle-owned entities and custom entities. Each entity has its own purpose and usage within the Software Library. Table 6-1 describes these entity types.

Table 6-1. *Entities in the Software Library*

Types	Description
Oracle-owned entities	These entities are available by default on the Software Library home page, once the Software Library is configured.
Custom entities	The Software Library users create these entities.

Numerous lifecycle management tasks make use of the entities in the Software Library. Such tasks include patching and provisioning deployment procedures, which are covered later in this chapter. Figure 6-8 shows how patching and provisioning deployment procedures use the Software Library.

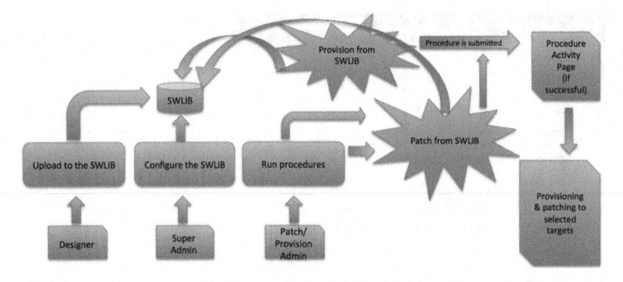

Figure 6-8. Patching and provisioning deployment procedures using the Software Library

Performing Tasks via the Software Library Home Page

When on the Software Library home page, it is helpful and handy to work with entities that are available to the Software Library user. The tasks that can be performed from the library home page are as follows:

- Organizing entities

- Creating entities

- Customizing entities

- Managing entities

As you look at these tasks, keep in mind that managing entities within the Software Library is initially simple. However, depending on the complexity of your organization and environment, the Software Library can become time-consuming to maintain. Knowing what the Software Library will be used for will help simplify maintenance tasks.

Organizing Entities

Organizing entities within the Software Library is simply a process of creating folders within the library. The folder structure can be as simple or as complex as your organization would like to make it. Figure 6-9 shows an example.

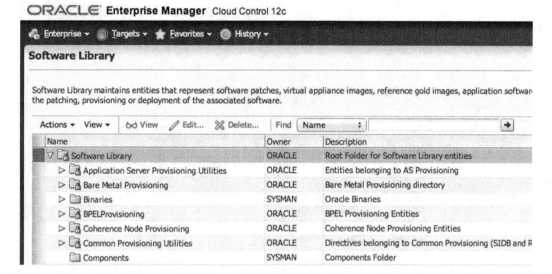

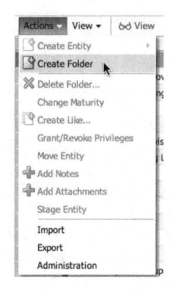

Figure 6-9. Software Library home page

From the Actions menu on the menu bar, you choose Create Folder, as shown in Figure 6-10. Note that additional commands from this menu are grayed out. These commands can be performed on existing folders after they are created. For now, let's focus on the Create Folder command.

Figure 6-10. Create Folder menu command

After selecting the Create Folder command, a dialog box appears, allowing you to specify the name of the folder (see Figure 6-11). Additionally, you can provide a description of the folder. These details will show up in the Software Library and help you quickly identify the folder you created. Notice that the Parent Folder option is grayed out. This is the default behavior. The text in this box will change based on the selection you make in the folder structure below it. By default, the parent folder is /Software Library.

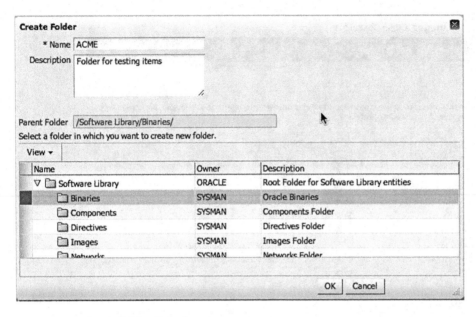

Figure 6-11. *Create Folder dialog box*

Click OK. If the folder is created successfully, you will receive a confirmation, as shown in Figure 6-12. You will also be able to see the folder in the tree structure under the folder you specified as the parent folder.

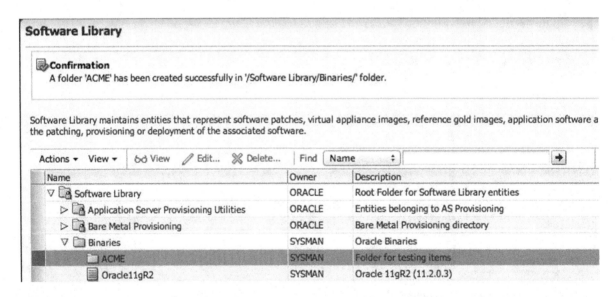

Figure 6-12. *Folder created in the Software Library*

■ **Note**   After a folder is created, the only person with the privilege to delete that folder is its owner or a Super Administrator.

Creating Entities

Entities are certified software binaries that are stored in the Software Library. An entity can be any software that includes patches, virtual appliance images, reference gold images, application software, and their associated directive scripts. As noted earlier, there are two, broadly defined entity types: Oracle-owned and custom. From within the Software Library, you can create two basic types of custom entities:

- Generic components
- Directives

Let's take a look at how to create both types within the Software Library.

Creating Generic Components

Generic components consist of a broad range of software items that can be created as entities. These entities enable you to define an installation process that will be used within the lifecycle framework for patching or provisioning. The list of generic components includes the following:

- Configuration template
- Database template
- Generic component
- Installation media
- Java EE application
- Oracle Application Server
- Oracle Clusterware Clone
- Oracle Database Software Clone
- Oracle Middleware Home Gold Image
- PDB template
- WebLogic domain provisioning profile

To create generic components in the Software Library, you need to select a custom folder that is not an Oracle-owned folder. You need to create this custom folder if it has not already been established (see the "Organizing Entities" section earlier). After you have selected the custom folder in the Software Library, the Actions menu's Create Entity option and associated submenus become enabled. Choose Actions ➤ Create Entity ➤ Component, as shown in Figure 6-13. The submenu items Directives and Bare Metal Provisioning are also available; we will discuss directives shortly. Provisioning of bare metal systems is not discussed in this chapter, because it is outside the scope of database patching.

Figure 6-13. *The Actions* ➤ *Create Entity options*

Selecting the Component option opens a dialog box where you can select the type of component you want to create. As listed earlier, there are many options. Choose the entity you would like to create and then click Continue, as shown in Figure 6-14.

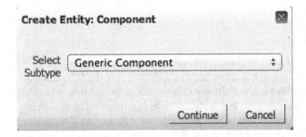

Figure 6-14. *Choosing the type of component*

Clicking the Continue button takes you to the Create Generic Component: Describe page, shown in Figure 6-15. On this page, you can define specifics such as the component's name, description, and other attributes. You can also add attachments to the component if desired. Attachments can be anything from a readme file to licensing information. If you are going to add attachments, make sure the files are 2MB or smaller. Additionally, you can add notes about the component. However, be cautious, because notes cannot be removed.

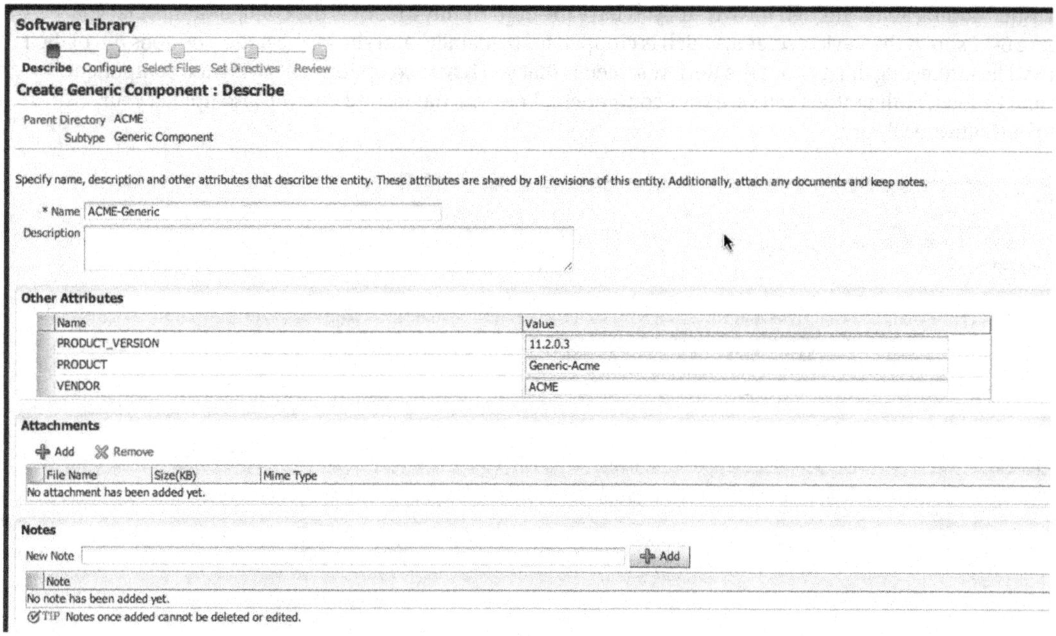

Figure 6-15. *Describing the component*

What you will notice about this page is that Oracle Enterprise Manager places you into a wizard to help you create the component. There are four additional steps that may or may not have to be configured. It all depends on what you are trying to do with the component. What is interesting at this point is that on the Set Directives screen, shown in Figure 6-16, you can add directives to tell the component to follow specific steps. We will dive more into directives in a moment.

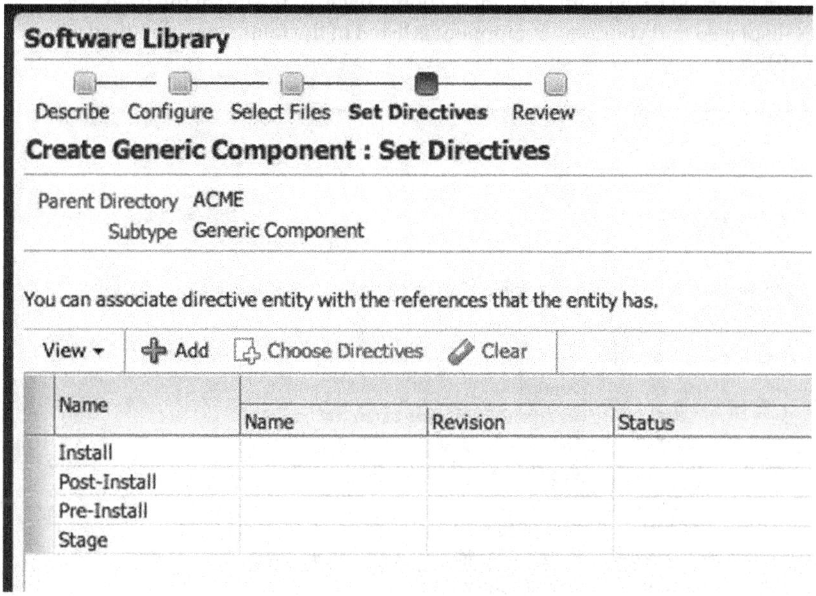

Figure 6-16. *Setting directives*

When finished adding items through the wizard, you have the opportunity to review the configurations that you provided. Figure 6-17 shows the Review screen, which is cropped for readability and shows the option buttons out of their normal context. The interesting thing about the Review screen is that you have two options for saving the component: Save, or Save and Upload. Both buttons will save your component; however, the second one will also upload your component to the Software Library.

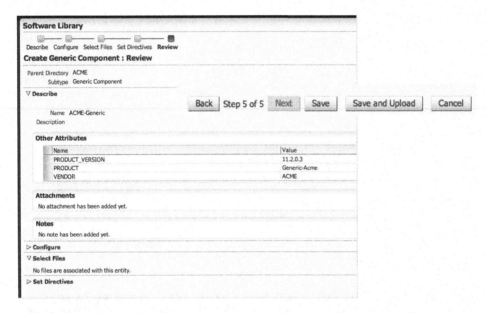

Figure 6-17. *Reviewing and saving the generic component*

The Save and Upload button automatically uploads your new component to the Software Library. After the component is saved to the library, you are returned to the Software Library home page. At the top of the page, you can see that a confirmation message is displayed and your new component is listed in the folder you identified when creating the component (see Figure 6-18).

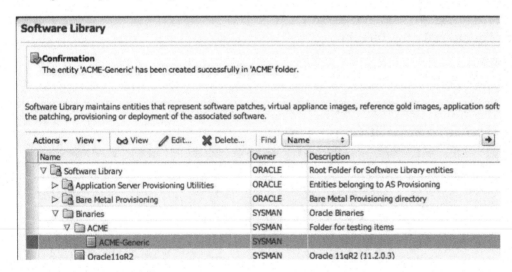

Figure 6-18. *Confirmation of the created generic component and its location*

Creating DirectivesDirectives:

Now that you understand what generic components are, let's take a look at directives. *Directives* are entities in the Software Library that represent a set of instructions that can be performed. These entities are used to associate scripts with software components and images. These scripts contain the directions on how to interpret and process the contents of a particular software component or image.

When setting up directives, you have to use the same interface as you use for generic components. To create a directive, you start at the Software Library home page (choose Enterprise ➤ Provisioning and Patching ➤ Software Library). Remember, in order to create a new directive, you need to select a custom folder that is not owned by Oracle.

To start creating a new directive, you will use the Actions menu in the Software Library. This is the same menu that you used to create a generic component. However, this time you choose Actions ➤ Create Entity ➤ Directive, as shown in Figure 6-19.

Figure 6-19. *Creating a new directive*

The Create Directives wizard then displays. First, the wizard wants you to describe the type of directive this is going to be by placing you on the Describe page, shown in Figure 6-20. The only required information on this page is the Name, Description, and Other Attributes for the entity. As with generic components, you can associate files and notes with the directive by adding files or notes in the Attachments and Notes areas.

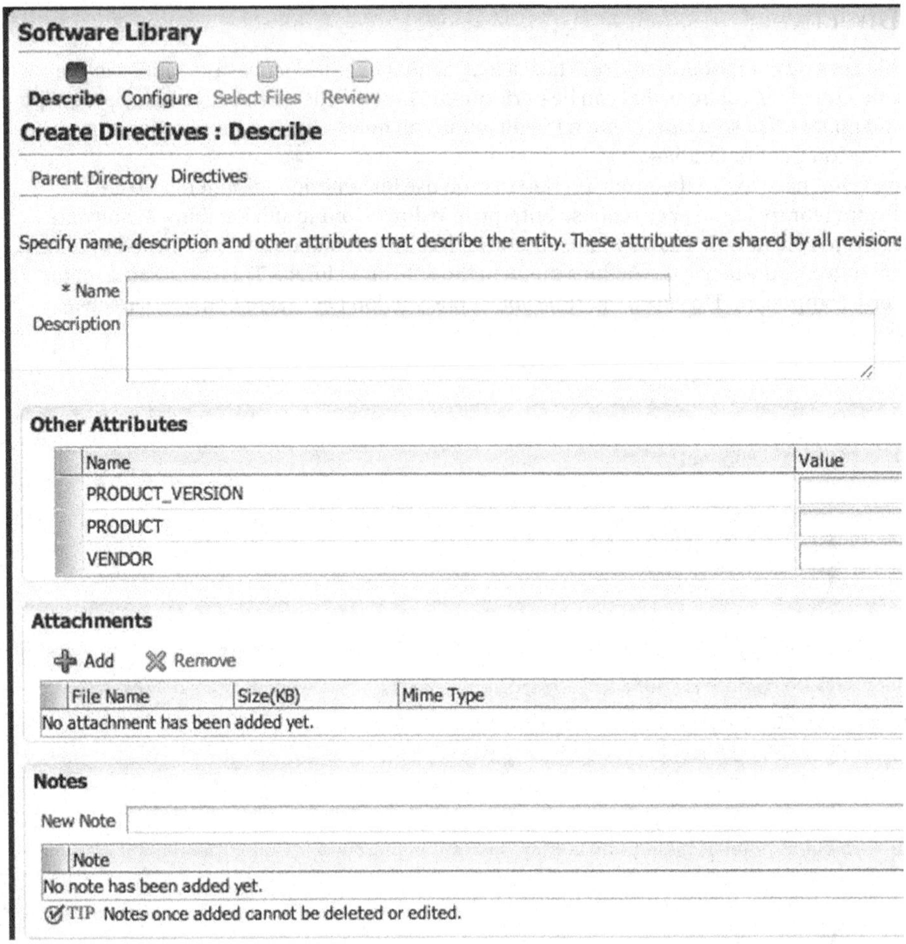

Figure 6-20. Describing the directives

The other thing you may notice are the wizard steps at the top of the page. There are fewer steps required to create a directive than a generic component. Fill in the required fields and then click Next to move to the next screen of the wizard.

As noted earlier, directives are entities that perform a set of instructions on a software package within the Software Library. On the Configure page, shown in Figure 6-21, you have the option of adding command-line arguments and properties associated with the directive. If you have nothing to add for command-line arguments, or the type of properties you want, you can click Next.

Software Library

Describe **Configure** Select Files Review

Create Directives : Configure

Parent Directory Directives

Configure Directive.

☑ **Command Line Arguments**

Specify command line arguments to be passed to the Directives. Each entry represen "./test.sh -user={username}", argument prefix will be "-user=" and property name w

✎ Edit... ✖ Remove ➕ Add

Argument Prefix	Property Name	Argument Suffix
No arguments are defined.		

Command Line

☑ **Configuration Properties**

Shell Type | Perl ▲▼ |

Run Privileged ☐

Figure 6-21. *Configuring the directives*

Command-line arguments are just that—arguments that can be passed as if you were using a script. Arguments can include variables that can be set later, a prefix, and suffix. The prefix and suffix text are appended before and after the property value to produce the command-line argument.

■ **Note** The following is a command-line argument example:

`./test.sh -user={username}`

The prefix is `-user=`, and the property is `username`.

To set up a command-line argument, you click the Add button. A dialog box appears, allowing you to configure the argument prefix, property name, and argument suffix, as shown in Figure 6-22. The nice thing about this dialog box is that it tells you specifically what you need to provide, unlike other dialog boxes.

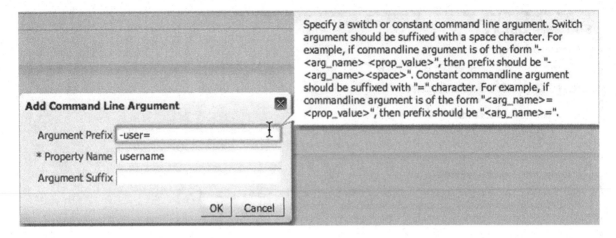

Specify a switch or constant command line argument. Switch argument should be suffixed with a space character. For example, if commandline argument is of the form "-<arg_name> <prop_value>", then prefix should be "-<arg_name><space>". Constant commandline argument should be suffixed with "=" character. For example, if commandline argument is of the form "<arg_name>=<prop_value>", then prefix should be "<arg_name>=".

Figure 6-22. *Adding command-line arguments*

After all the arguments that you want set are in place, click OK. This adds the argument to the Configure page. As you add more arguments, the command line starts to build under them. Figure 6-23 shows that we added two arguments, and the command line is created for us.

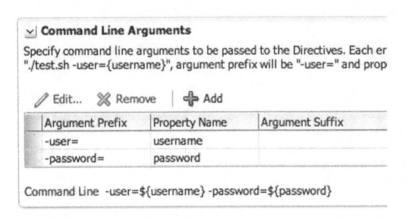

Figure 6-23. *Command line built with arguments added*

After all the arguments are added for the directive, you need to tell the directive what type of script will be running. This is accomplished on the same page, in the Configuration Properties section. You need to tell the directive that you will use either Perl or Bash. Additionally, if the script needs to run with elevated privileges, you can direct that by clicking the Run Privileged box. Figure 6-24 shows the Run Privileged check box selected for a Bash script.

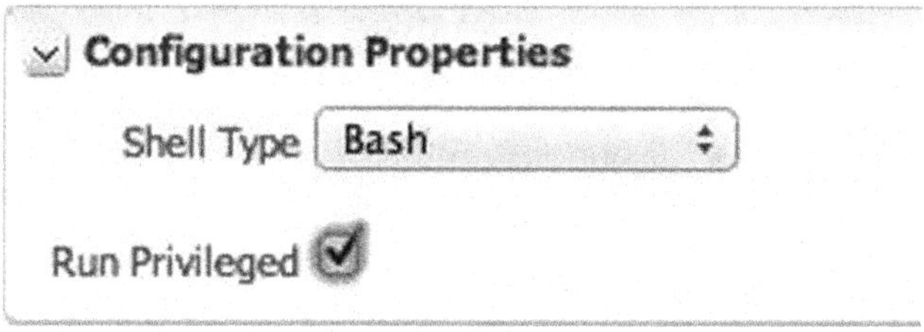

Figure 6-24. *Configuration properties for a directive*

Now that you have configured all the items you would like on the Configure page for the directive, you can move on by clicking Next. The wizard brings you to the Select Files screen.

On this screen, you are presented with two radio buttons, which enable you to either upload the files needed for the directive or to refer to them by location. These two options are much like the options you had when initially creating the Software Library; the same rules apply:

> *Upload Files*: Use this option if you want to upload some entity files from the local filesystem or agent machine to the selected destination location.

> *Refer Files*: This option allows you to enter the source location details, since you are not uploading anything to the Software Library.

Select the Upload Files option, as shown in Figure 6-25.

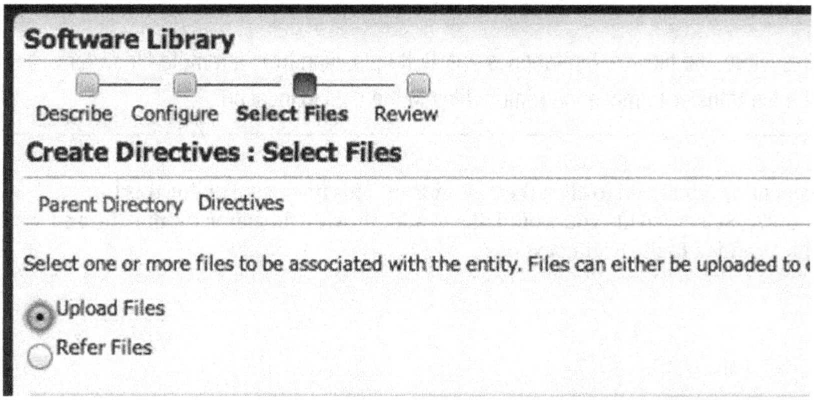

Figure 6-25. *Selecting files to upload*

Next you need to select the destination location. Select the magnifier icon next to the upload location under Specify Destination. This opens the dialog box where you can choose either an OMS Shared Filesystem or an OMS Agent Filesystem. What appears by default is the location specified when setting up the Software Library (see Figure 6-26). Select the Software Library and click OK.

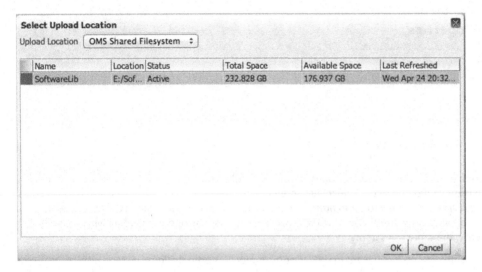

Figure 6-26. *Selecting the upload location*

Next you need to specify our source files. These are the script files that are needed for the directive to perform its job. These files can be uploaded either from the local host or from a remote host via a remote transfer process such as secure copy.

■ **Note**   If uploading from the local filesystem, the file size limitation is 25MB. If uploading from a remote filesystem, the Save and Upload action will submit a file transfer to move the remote files to the upload location.

To add files in the Specify Source location, you need to click the Add button. This opens the dialog box for selecting and adding a file (see Figure 6-27). Select the file you would like to add, provide the name for the file, and click OK. By default, the name of the file is added to the Name text box.

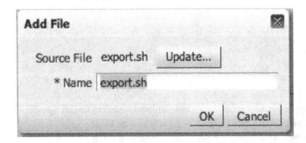

Figure 6-27. *Adding a file to the directive*

After you click OK, the file is added to the Specify Source section of the Select Files page, shown in Figure 6-28. Notice that the name, size, and mime type are listed for the file. If there is more than one file for this directive, a drop-down box enables you to select the main file. In this example, you are using only one file; by default, that will be the main file. Click Next to complete the creation of the directive.

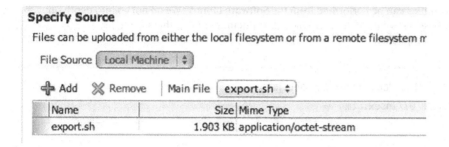

Figure 6-28. *Specifying source files*

When the directive is complete, the wizard drops you back in the Software Library with a confirmation message stating that the creation was successful. At this point, you will be able to find the directive you created. Figure 6-29 displays the confirmation message.

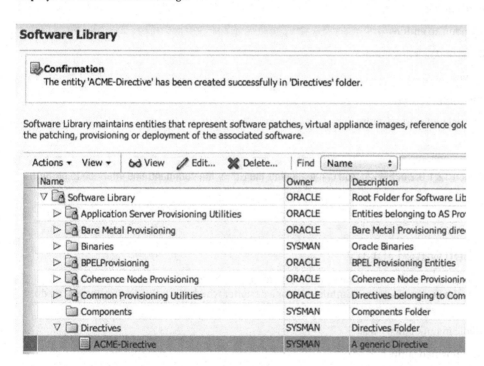

Figure 6-29. *Completion of a new directive*

After the directive is completed, it is like any other entity in the Software Library. It can be viewed, edited, or deleted by the owner who created it or by a Super Administrator.

Maintaining Entities in the Software Library

As with any software, maintenance tasks need to be attended to. The entities in the Software Library are no exception. We have discussed how to create and add both a generic entity and a directive entity. Now you're ready to learn about maintaining the entities.

Many maintenance tasks on entities can be performed from the Software Library. We do not go into depth on these here. More information on these tasks can be found in the Oracle documentation; this section provides only a listing of items that can be accomplished.

■ **Note**   Oracle documentation for EM12c Cloud Control is located here:
http://docs.oracle.com/cd/E24628_01/index.htm.

Maintenance tasks for entities are as follows:

- Granting or revoking privileges
- Moving entities
- Changing entity maturity
- Adding notes to entities
- Adding attachments to entities
- Viewing, editing, and deleting entities
- Searching entities
- Exporting/importing entities
- Staging files associated with an entity

■ **Note**   Starting with version 12.1.0.2 of EM12c, you can use either the GUI or the command-line interface to perform the preceding tasks.

Maintaining the Software Library

Just as we maintain the entities in the Software Library, we have to maintain the health and functionality of the Software Library itself. Only the Software Library administrator or a designer who has administration access can do the following:

- Perform periodic maintenance tasks
- Reimport Oracle-owned entity files
- Remove (and migrate) the Software Library storage location
- Purge deleted entity files
- Back up the Software Library

All of these tasks are critical to the proper functioning of the Software Library.

Performing Periodic Maintenance Tasks

To keep the Software Library functioning properly, the following tasks must be performed on a regular basis:

- Refreshing the Software Library to compute the free and used disk space
- Purging deleted entities to conserve disk space
- Checking the configured Software Library locations to ensure that they are accessible

Reimporting Oracle-Owned Entity Files

Reimporting Oracle-owned entity files is not a periodic activity. This process should be used only when needing to recover metadata files that are owned by Oracle. This should be done in only two situations:

- If you delete the filesystem location where the metadata was imported
- If the import job submitted while creating the first upload location fails

To reimport the metadata of Oracle-owned files, access the Software Library Administration page under Setup. From the Actions menu, choose Re-Import Metadata, as shown in Figure 6-30. This submits a job that will reimport the metadata.

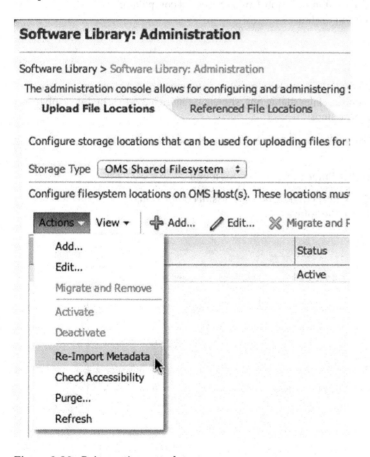

Figure 6-30. *Reimporting metadata*

■ **Note** Reimporting metadata applies only to the Oracle-owned files, which means all entity files that ship with the OEM product by default. User-owned entity metadata cannot be recovered through the Re-Import functionality.

Removing (and Migrating) the Software Library Storage Location

There may come a time when you need to move the Software Library from its current storage location to a new location. This can happen for any number of reasons. For example, you might need more storage space.

Only Software Library Storage Administrators have the required permissions to delete a storage location. Before a storage location can be deleted, you will be prompted to choose an alternate location to migrate the files to. Next, a migration job will be submitted and the current location will be marked inactive. After the migration job is complete, the old storage location will be deleted.

To delete the current storage location, you follow these steps:

1. Access the Software Library Administration page (Setup ➤ Provisioning and Patching ➤ Software Library).

2. Select the storage location. Then click Migrate and Remove.

3. In the confirmation box, click Remove to submit the job. Upon successful completion, the old storage area will be removed from the table.

Purging Deleted Entity Files

Starting with EM12c, entities can be purged from the Software Library when no longer needed. The purge jobs can now be scheduled, as well, in the Purge Deleted Entities Files dialog box, shown in Figure 6-31. To schedule a job to purge entities from the Software Library, follow these steps:

1. Access the Software Library Administration page (Setup ➤ Provisioning and Patching ➤ Software Library).

2. Select the storage location and then click Purge from the Actions menu.

3. Enter all the details needed for the job and click OK. Upon successful completion, all deleted entities will be removed from the Software Library.

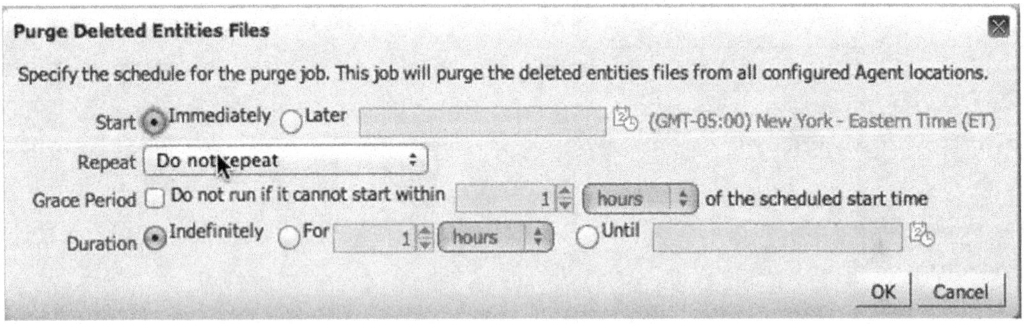

Figure 6-31. *Scheduling a purge of entities*

Backing Up the Software Library

Until now, we have spent a lot of time defining the Software Library, what it is used for, and how to add entities to it. Since we have spent a lot time setting up the Software Library, the last thing we want to do is back it up. However, just like any other Oracle product, backups are critical to ensure recoverability in the event of a disaster.

Backing up the Software Library is actually done when you back up the Oracle Enterprise Manager itself. Backing up the Oracle Enterprise Manager is covered in detail in Chapter 13.

Patching

Patching is one of the most important phases in the lifecycle of a product. It enables us to keep our software products updated with bug and security fixes. Throughout the year, Oracle releases several types of patches to help maintain our products. However, patching also has always been the most challenging lifecycle phase, because it often is complex, risky, time-consuming, and requires downtime for applications. Although we can use several approaches to patching our databases, the challenge of minimizing downtime or outages unfortunately remains the same.

In this section, you will learn how patches should be managed within EM12c. Additionally, you will look at configuring Enterprise Manager to use My Oracle Support and review the overall process of patching within the Enterprise Manager environment.

Patch Management

Before diving into the new features of patch management within EM12c, you need to understand the challenges that were faced before. Table 6-2 lists the patching approaches and their associated challenges.

Table 6-2. *Current Patching Tools and Challenges*

Approach	Description	Challenges
OPatch	Oracle proprietary tool that is installed with Oracle products such as the Oracle Database, Oracle Management Agent, SOA, and so on	• Difficult to identify the patches to be rolled out • Patches only one Oracle inventory-backed product at a time • Offers limited support to handle pre- and post-patching scripts
Custom scripts	User-created scripts developed around OPatch, SQL*Plus, and so on	• Difficult to identify the patches to be rolled out • Can be used only on a single server • Requires significant maintenance overhead to meet the new version and configuration needs
Deployment procedures	Default procedures for automating patching operations	• Confusion over which deployment procedure to select • Limited scope of validating the patches and targets selected in a deployment procedure • Separate deployment procedures for patching in rolling and parallel mode • Difficult to handle patch conflicts

Oracle Enterprise Manager addresses the challenges listed in Table 6-2 with its much-improved patch management solution that delivers maximum ease with minimum downtime. The new patch management solution offers the following benefits:

- Integrated patching workflow with My Oracle Support Therefore, you see recommendations, search patches, and roll out patches all using the same user interface.

- Complete, end-to-end orchestration of patching workflow using *patch plans,* including automated selection of deployment procedures and analysis of the patch conflicts. Therefore, minimal manual effort is required.

- Clear division of responsibilities between designers and operators - Designers can focus on creating patch plans, testing them on a test system, and saving them as patch templates. Operators can focus on creating patch plans out of the template for rolling out the patches on a production system.

- Easy review of patches for applicability in your environment, validation of patch plans, and automatic receipt of patches to resolve validation issues.

- Saving successfully analyzed or deployable patch plans as patch templates, which contain a predetermined set of patches and deployment options saved from the source patch plan.

- Out-of-place patching for stand-alone (single-instance) database targets and Oracle Grid Infrastructure targets that are part of Oracle Exadata.

- Flexible patching options such as rolling and parallel, both in offline and online mode.

Configuration of My Oracle Support

Before we can truly discuss some of the new patching options, Oracle Enterprise Manager (OEM) has to be integrated with My Oracle Support (MOS). Oracle has done a good job of integrating the two interfaces, making it easier for us to find patches within MOS from the Oracle Enterprise Manager interface.

To set up My Oracle Support within Oracle Enterprise Manager, our MOS credentials need to be added to OEM. This can be accomplished by choosing Setup ➤ My Oracle Support ➤ Set Credentials, as shown in Figure 6-32.

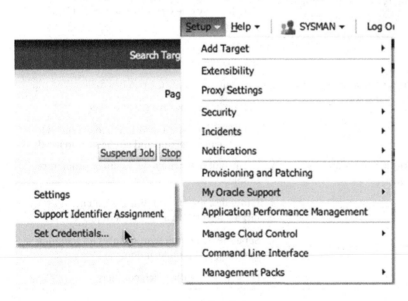

Figure 6-32. *Setting credentials for My Oracle Support*

Clicking this menu command lands you on the My Oracle Support Preferred Credentials page. Here you enter your single sign-on login needed for MOS, as shown in Figure 6-33. Then click Apply. (Next to the Apply button is the Remove button. If you want to remove your MOS credentials from OEM, the Remove button does that.)

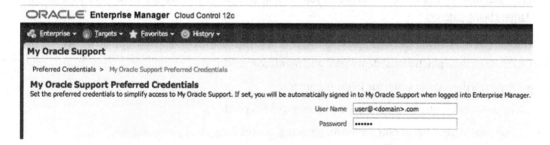

Figure 6-33. *Setting My Oracle Support preferred credentials*

After adding your MOS account information to OEM, you can begin to look for patches and updates from within Enterprise Manager.

Patch Plans

Patch plans help you create a consolidated list of patches that you want to apply as a group to one or more targets. Patch plans have states that map to key steps in the deployment process. Oracle Enterprise Manager supports creating patches in two forms:

- Patch sets
- Patches (one-off)
  - Interim patches that contain a single bug fix or a collection of bug fixes provided as required.
  - Diagnostic patches, intended to help diagnose or verify a fix or a collection of bug fixes.
  - Patch set updates (PSUs).
  - Critical patch updates (CPUs), now known as security patch updates (SPUs).

■ **Note**   You cannot add both patch sets and patches to the same patch plan. Instead, you can have a patch plan for patch sets and another patch plan for patches.

Patches can be added to a target in a plan only if the patch has the same release and platform as the target to which it is being added. A warning will be raised if you try to add a patch that is different from the product associated with the target. However, the warning will not prevent you from adding the patch to the plan. You can include any patch for any target in a patch plan. The plan will validate any patches against your environment and check for conflicts with the installed patches.

Depending on the patches added to the patch plan, Oracle automatically selects the appropriate deployment procedure to be used for applying the patches.

By using patch plans, we can simplify the identification and deployment of patches for many environments. This greatly increases our flexibility in patching by helping us identify any potential conflicts before actually patching environments.

■ **Note** Patch plans are currently not available for patching hardware systems or operating systems. If patching an Oracle Grid Infrastructure target, which is part of Oracle Exadata, you can add only one patch (Oracle Exadata) per patch plan. For all other targets, you can add as many patches as you want, as long as the patches are of the same release and platform as the targets being patched.

There are two basic types of patch plans: deployable and nondeployable.

- A patch plan is deployable when the following are true:
  - It contains only patches of the same type (homogenous patches).
  - It contains targets that are supported for patching, are similarly configured, and are of the same product type, platform, and version.
  - There are no conflicts within the plan.
- Any patch plan that does not meeting the preceding conditions for deployment is a nondeployable plan. Any patch plan that is nondeployable cannot deploy patches using the patch plan. You can perform some analysis and checks, download patches, and manually apply them.

Creation of a Patch Plan

Now that you understand what a patch plan is and the two types of plans, let's quickly walk through creating a patch plan for applying a CPU patch. In this section, you'll walk through all the steps needed to create a patch plan that can be used for either a patch set or one-off deployment.

Setting Up the Patch Plan

To create a patch plan, you need to start on the Patches & Updates page in Oracle Enterprise Manager. Navigate to this page by choosing Enterprise ➤ Provisioning and Patching ➤ Patches & Updates, as shown in Figure 6-34. This page looks exactly like the My Oracle Support (MOS) page. The only difference is that the page is being accessed from within Enterprise Manager.

Figure 6-34. *Patches & Updates from the Enterprise menu*

On this page, you will start creating the patch plan by looking at Patch Recommendations (see Figure 6-35).

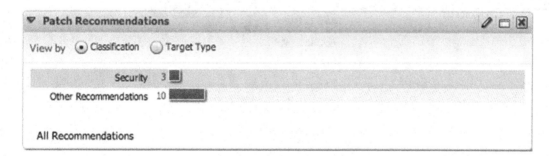

Figure 6-35. *Patch recommendations on the Patches & Updates page*

■ **Note** Unless you have created patch plans in the past, the Plans section on the Patches & Updates page will be empty.

This section of the page contains two radio buttons. By default, the Classification button is selected. What is more important within this dialog box are the recommendations that Oracle is making. In the example shown in Figure 6-36, it appears that we have security patches waiting. Let's add these to a plan.

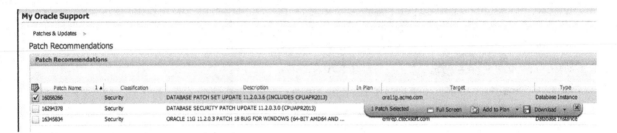

Figure 6-36. Patch Recommendations screen

Click the Security link, and you are taken to the Patch Recommendations page shown in Figure 6-36. This page provides a list of patches that are recommended, along with the target they are recommended for. Select the check box next to the patch name, and a dialog box opens, enabling you to download the patch directly to your desktop or to add it to a patch plan.

Because you are going to add this patch to a patch plan, click the Add to Plan drop-down menu, as shown in Figure 6-37. This menu enables you to add the patch to a new or existing plan. Choose the Add to New option, and a dialog box opens, allowing you to name the plan (see Figure 6-38).

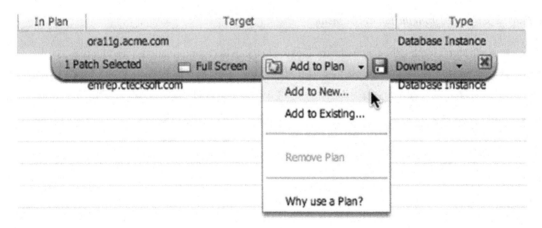

Figure 6-37. Add to Plan menu

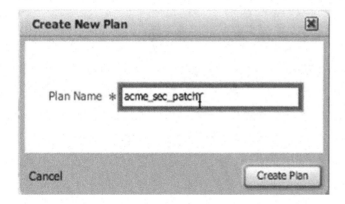

Figure 6-38. *The Create New Plan dialog box*

Name the plan and click Create Plan. If you want to add more than one patch, select both the patches first and then add them to the plan.

■ **Note**   Patches can be added to the plan later, if needed.

Reviewing the Plan and Deployment

After the plan has been created, you can review it by clicking View Plan. You can also view the plan from the Patches & Updates page; the new plan is listed in the Plans window, shown in Figure 6-39. Clicking the plan name enables you to review the plan in detail.

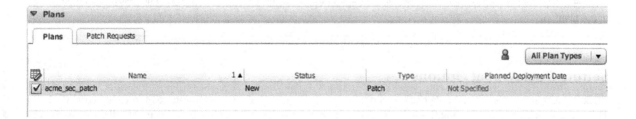

Figure 6-39. *Reviewing the plan from Patches & Updates*

Remember, a patch plan is nothing but a collection of patches that you want to apply to a target or targets. The plan review is a five-step process, which you can view on the left side of the screen. By default, the review starts on step 2, where you can add patches to the plan if desired (see Figure 6-40). If you take a step back and click step 1, Plan Information, you can modify the name of the plan, set a deployment date, and add a plan description. You can also add permissions to the plan that will either grant Full or View permissions to various Enterprise Manager roles.

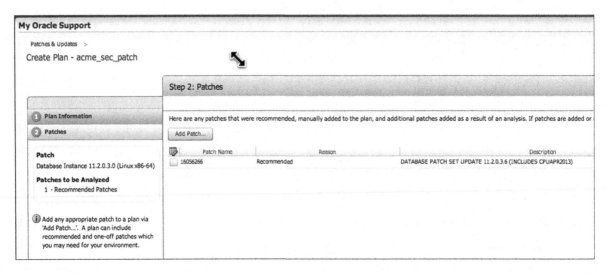

Figure 6-40. *Step 2 of reviewing the plan*

Adding Patches

You add patches to the plan in step 2 by clicking the Add Patch button. After the analysis, the result may require patches to be added to the plan.

You will notice that the plan is deployable (although this is not shown in Figure 6-40, this indication appears at the top-right corner). If there is nothing you want to change or add within the plan, you can click Review and end the wizard without doing steps 3 through 5.

■ **Note** The Full permission allows for the role to validate the plan. The View permission does not allow validation of the plan.

Setting Deployment Options

Clicking Next at the bottom of the Patches screen takes you to step 3, Deployment Options, as shown in Figure 6-41. This screen contains a lot of configurable items that may or may not have to be changed. Reviewing all these options is critical for a successful patch plan.

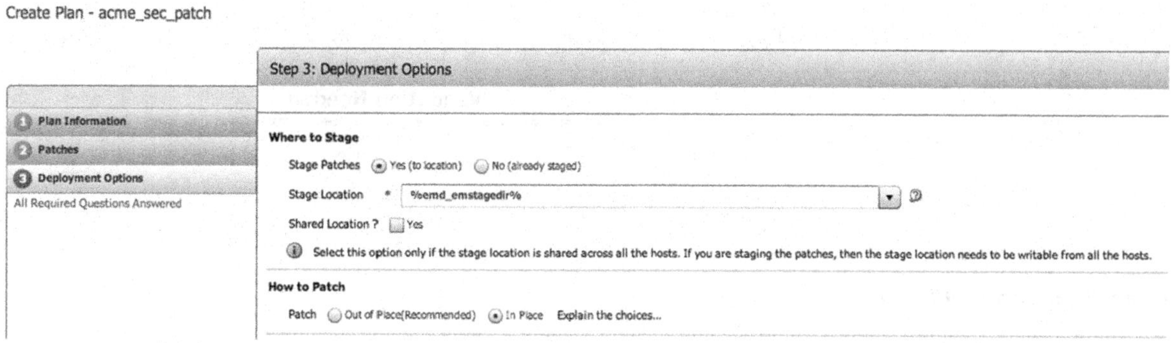

Create Plan - acme_sec_patch

Figure 6-41. *Deployment options (partial screen)*

In the Where to Stage option, you can specify the location where the patch is either downloaded to and/or stored for patching purposes. By default, patches will be downloaded and stored at the location specified by %em_emstagedir%. The staging location for the patches needs to be writable by the host, which is going to access the patch.

The How to Patch section provides two options for patching: Out of Place and In Place. The hyperlink to the side explains each choice:

> *Out of Place*: Uses less downtime and keeps your old Oracle home available for recovery

> *In Place*: Requires bringing down all databases in the Oracle home during installation of the patches

Both are good choices, depending on your required service level agreements (SLAs) or organizational policies. Oracle recommends out-of-place patching, because it basically clones your existing Oracle home and gives you the ability to back out any changes you do not want by returning to the old Oracle home.

Additional sections on the Deployment Options page are What to Patch, Customization, Recoverability, Rollback, and Oracle Home Credentials. Each section needs to be reviewed and verified prior to completing the review of the patch plan.

Validating the Patch Plan

After verifying and configuring all options in step 3, click Next to move to step 4, Validation. In this step, Oracle Enterprise Manager checks the patches in the plan against previously installed patches for conflicts. This check is performed against the target inventory for conflicts. The validation takes many factors into account, and may take more than 10 minutes to complete. These validations include checks against the Oracle home for readiness, space requirements for the home, OPatch version validation, and other checks such as cluster node connectivity (if patching a RAC environment).

Figure 6-42 shows what the screen looks like before validation is done. Click the Analyze button to begin the validation of the patches against targets for the patch plan. While the validation is running, you can move off this screen and return to it later.

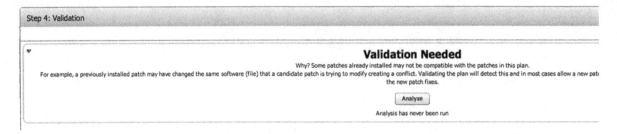

Figure 6-42. *Step 4: Validation*

After the validation starts, the message above the Analyze button changes, providing additional information on the process. You can get a detailed view by clicking Show Detailed Progress Here. You may notice that the analysis includes quite a few checks: verifying that the targets are supported for patching; verifying normal and elevated user credentials; verifying target tools, commands, permissions, and upgrades to OPatch; staging the selected patches; and then running the prerequisite checks for patching. If all the prerequisites pass, the patch is seen as Ready for Deployment.

Any issues that the patching may have will show up at this point. For example, if a patch conflict exists, a replacement or merge patch may be required. If a replacement or merge patch is not available, you can request such a patch directly from this screen.

If any issues need to be resolved, they will be listed under the Issues to Resolve heading. Anything that the analysis recommends to be added will be listed under Added from Analysis. General messages will be under Informational Messages. After reviewing all these messages, you can click the Review button.

Reviewing and Deploying the Plan

At this point, you are ready to move directly to step 5, Review & Deploy. You can reach this step by either clicking the Review button in step 4 or clicking Review & Deploy on the left side of the screen.

On the Review & Deploy page, the patch plan is described in detail along with the targets that will be affected by the plan. If additional targets have been discovered after the analysis, they will be added to the Impacted Targets list. In our case, two additional listeners were found and added, because they run out of the same Oracle home that we are preparing to patch.

The patches that are going to be applied to the Oracle home are listed on this page as well. The important thing to look for is a status of Conflict Free. In our case with CPUAPR2013, we have no conflicts with the patch. Figure 6-43 shows a subset of the Review & Deploy screen indicating that the plan is ready for deployment.

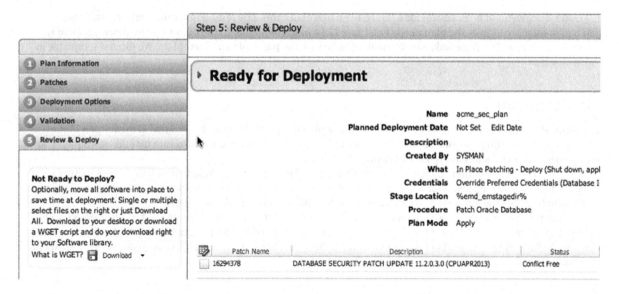

Figure 6-43. *The Review & Deploy step*

Earlier, in step 3, you configured the patch plan to use in-place patching. This means that an outage will occur after this patch plan is deployed. Click the Deploy button to immediately start the deployment of the patch. The screen changes to Deployment in Progress. A background job starts, and the database is taken offline for patching.

After the deployment is complete, the Review & Deploy screen will show a status of Deployment Successful, as shown in Figure 6-44. If a deployment is not successful, the Review & Deploy screen will indicate that the deployment failed and provide information related to the failure.

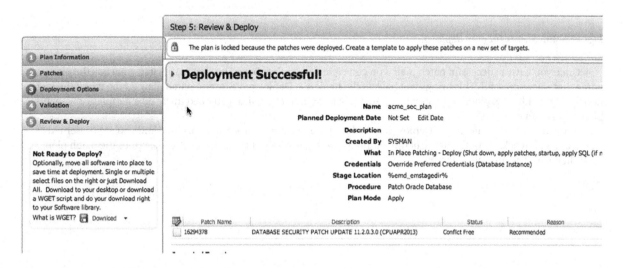

Figure 6-44. *The deployment is successful*

After a deployment is successful for a target, the patch plan cannot be reused for additional targets. To use the patch plan for more targets, the plan needs to be saved as a patch template. At the bottom of the Review & Deploy screen is the Save as Template link, which enables you to save the patch plan as a template. We discuss templates in the next section.

Plan Templates

As previously mentioned, a patch plan can be saved as a plan template. This can be initiated at the bottom of the Deployment Successful page. Before you can create a plan template, you need to make sure that the patch plan you want to use was successfully analyzed and deployed.

As with any type of template, there will be no target associated with the template, which makes the template available to be applied against multiple targets. Inside the plan template, the Create Plan button can be used to create a new plan based on the template and can be repeatedly applied against multiple targets.

Before you create a template, you need to make sure that the patch plan you want to use has been successfully deployed. This can be done from the Patches & Updates page, accessed by choosing Enterprise ➤ Provisioning and Patching ➤ Patches & Updates. On this screen, all the patch plans are listed in the Plans list. What you are looking for is a status of Deployed Successfully, as shown in Figure 6-45.

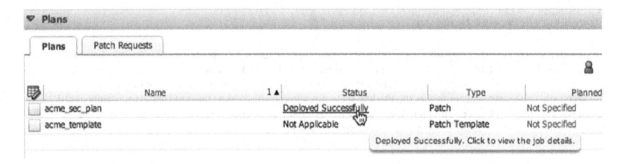

Figure 6-45. *Successful plan deployment*

Once you have a successful patch plan, you can create a template based on that plan. First, you click the plan name that was successful. This brings you back to the Review & Deploy page for the patch plan. At the top of the page, notice a lock with an explanation about the plan being locked. At this point, you need to create a template to use this plan against other targets.

At the bottom of the Review & Deploy page is the Save as Template link. Click this link, and you are presented with a dialog box asking for the name of the template (see Figure 6-46). Enter a name that describes the patch plan that will be used against other targets.

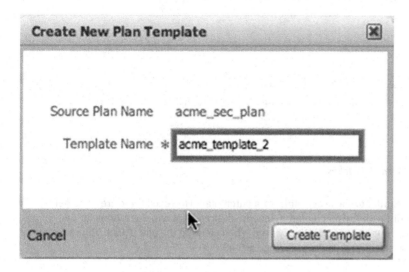

Figure 6-46. *Create New Plan Template dialog box*

Click the Create Template button, and the template is created. At the top of the Patches & Updates screen, you can see a message that states it has been created. This same message contains a View Template link. Click that link to access the Edit Template Wizard. This wizard is similar to the Create Plan Wizard discussed earlier. There are only three steps to editing a template.

The first step is Plan Information. On this page, you can add or modify the template name, set a plan deployment date, and add a description (see Figure 6-47). Click Next to move on to the next step of the wizard.

My Oracle Support

Patches & Updates >   Create Plan - acme_sec_plan >
Edit Template Wizard - acme_template_2

Step 1: Plan Information

Plan Information

Templates are useful for applying a successful patch plans to multiple targets. Use the **Create Plan button to create a new plan based on this template.**

Overview

Name *	acme_template_2
Planned Deployment Date	Not Set
Description	
Created By	SYSMAN

Figure 6-47. *The first step of the Edit Template Wizard: Plan Information*

The second step of the template wizard lists the patches associated with the template. Because the patch plan has already been successfully deployed, the patches have already been added to the template. It is not possible to add more patches to a template; any new patches have to be applied and validated through the patch plan process. Figure 6-48 shows the patches added to the template. Click Next at the bottom of the screen.

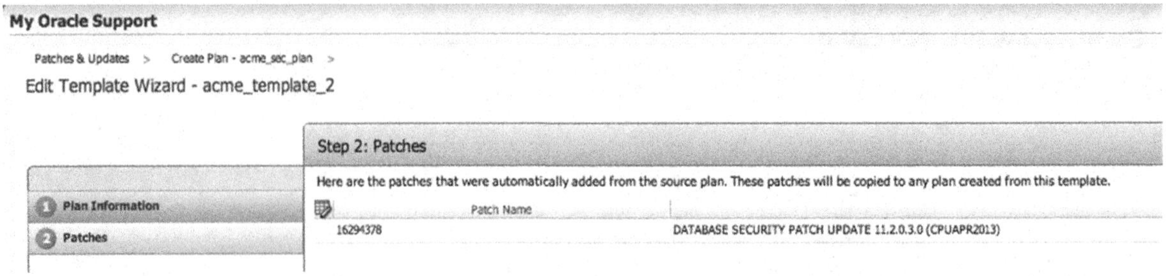

Figure 6-48. *Step 2 of the Edit Template Wizard: Patches*

Step 3 provides deployment options similar to those available for a patch plan. However, there are no targets associated with the template. Just as you did with the patch plan, select the desired deployment options for the template. These options are taken from the options you previously used when creating the patch plan. You can keep what you previously selected or make new selections, as shown in Figure 6-49.

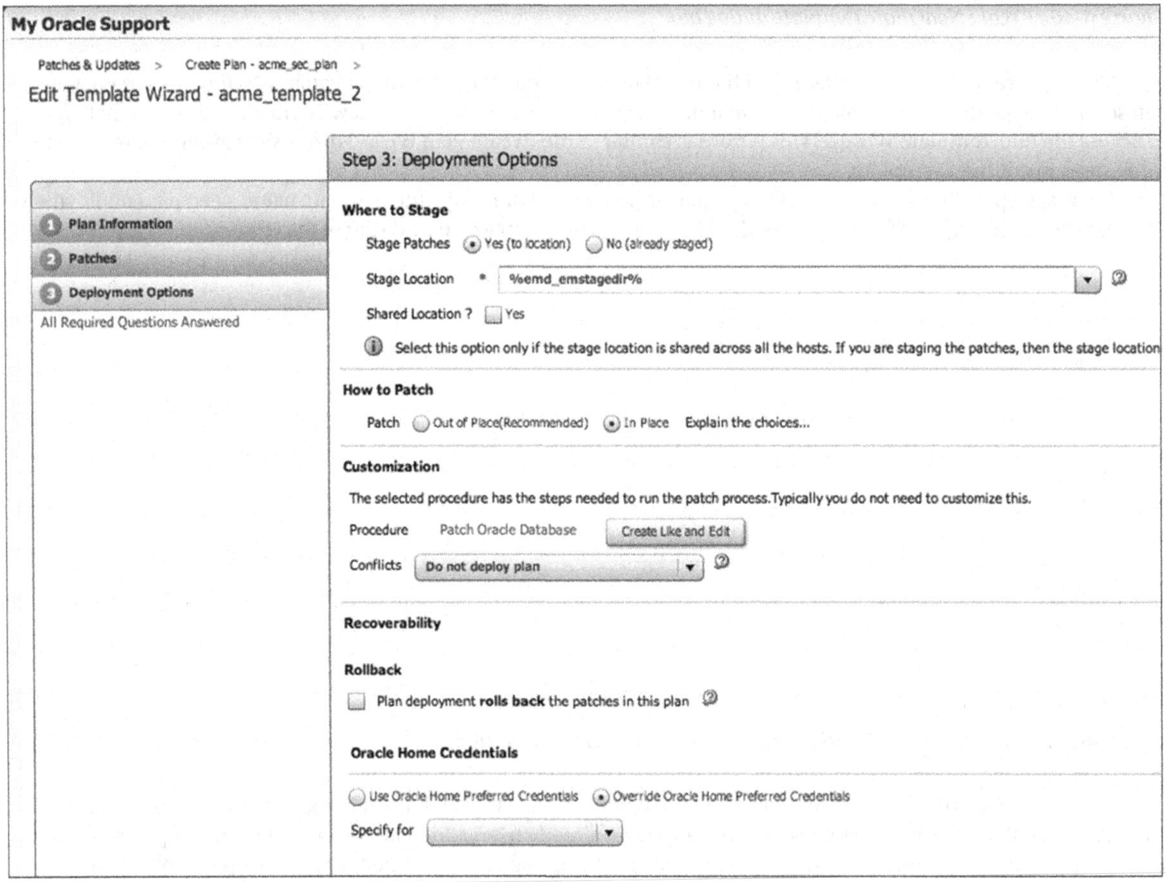

Figure 6-49. *Step 3 of the Edit Template Wizard: Deployment Options*

When you are finished making selections, click Exit Wizard at the bottom of the page. This brings you back to the Deployment Successful page. At this point, you need to return to the Patches & Updates page to see whether the template is listed in the Plans window (see Figure 6-50).

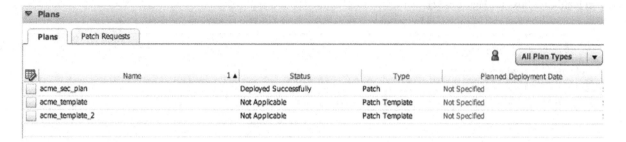

Figure 6-50. *Plans window listing templates*

Saved Patches

The patches that are deployed using patch plans or templates are stored in the Software Library. You can see what patches are stored in the Software Library from the Saved Patches location: choose Enterprise ➤ Provisioning and Patching ➤ Saved Patches. Figure 6-51 shows the listing of saved patches currently in the Software Library.

Select	Patch Number	Created On	Type	Release	Platform	Product	Description	Metadata Available	Downloaded	Size(KB)	ReadMe
☐	6880880	Dec 16, 2012	Patch	11.1.0.0.0	Linux x86-64	Universal Installer	OPatch patch of version 11.1.0.9.10 for Oracle software releases 11.1.0.x (DECEMBER 2012)	N	Y	31780	ReadMe
☐	2617419	Oct 1, 2009	Patch	10.1.0.2	Generic Platform	Universal Installer	OPATCH FOR EM	N	Y	354	ReadMe
☐	4898608	Dec 17, 2009	Patch	10.2.0.4	Generic Platform	Universal Installer	OPatch for EM	N	Y	1371	ReadMe
☐	4898608	Dec 17, 2009	Patch	11.1.0.0.0	Generic Platform	Universal Installer	OPatch for EM	N	Y	1473	ReadMe
☐	6880880	Dec 16, 2012	Patch	11.1.0.0.0	Microsoft Windows x64 (64-bit)	Universal Installer	OPatch patch of version 11.1.0.9.10 for Oracle software releases 11.1.0.x (DECEMBER 2012)	N	Y	30632	ReadMe
☐	12426828	May 26, 2011	Patch	10.3.5	Generic Platform	Oracle WebLogic Server	SMARTUPDATE 3.3 INSTALLER PLACEHOLDER	N	Y	20222	ReadMe
☐	6880880	Apr 15, 2013	Patch	11.2.0.0.0	Linux x86-64	Universal Installer	OPatch patch of version 11.2.0.3.4 for Oracle software releases 11.2.0.x (APRIL 2013)	N	Y	31790	ReadMe
☐	6880880	Apr 15, 2013	Patch	11.2.0.0.0	Microsoft Windows x64 (64-bit)	Universal Installer	OPatch patch of version 11.2.0.3.4 for Oracle software releases 11.2.0.x (APRIL 2013)	N	Y	30582	ReadMe
☐	16294378	Apr 17, 2013	Patch	11.2.0.3.0	Linux x86-64	Oracle Database	DATABASE SECURITY PATCH UPDATE 11.2.0.3.0 (CPUAPR2013)	N	Y	3828	ReadMe
☐	16056266	Apr 17, 2013	Patch	11.2.0.3.0	Linux x86-64	Oracle Database	DATABASE PATCH SET UPDATE 11.2.0.3.6 (INCLUDES CPUAPR2013)	N	Y	31400	ReadMe
☐	6880880	Dec 16, 2012	Patch	11.1.0.0.0	Linux x86	Universal Installer	OPatch patch of version 11.1.0.9.10 for Oracle software releases 11.1.0.x (DECEMBER 2012)	N	Y	31780	ReadMe

Figure 6-51. *Saved patches in the Software Library*

On the Saved Patches page, you can perform various operations. You can manually upload and remove patches if needed. You can also access the readme files for the associated patches. These features make it easier to work with offline patching if there is no connection to the Internet from the Oracle Management Server and need to download the patches manually.

For more information on offline patching, refer to the *Oracle Enterprise Manager Lifecycle Management Administrator's Guide 12c Release 2 (12.1.0.2)* at the following URL:

```
http://docs.oracle.com/cd/E24628_01/em.121/e27046/pat_mosem_new.htm#BABBIEAI
```

Additional Patching Procedures

Additional patching procedures can be used for deployments of patches. You can access these procedures by choosing Enterprise ➤ Provisioning and Patching ➤ Procedure Library and then searching for patches in the Search Text Fields text box (see Figure 6-52).

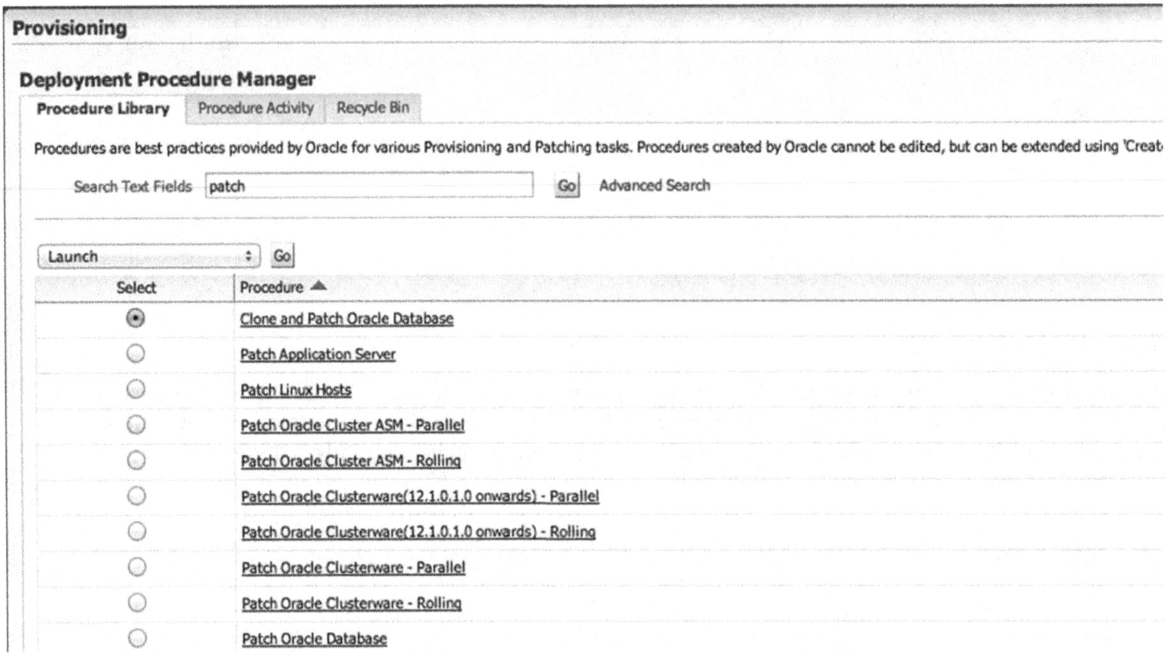

Figure 6-52. *Procedure Library (partial listing)*

As you can see, many additional patching procedures are available, such as Clone and Patch Oracle Database, Patch Application Server, and parallel and rolling patches. With all these options, Oracle Enterprise Manager is a valuable tool in helping administrators patch their environments.

Roles Needed for Patching

EM12c supplies some new roles out of the box that are specific to patching: EM_PATCH_ADMINISTRATOR, EM_PATCH_DESIGNER, and EM_PATCH_OPERATOR. These roles need to be granted to the administrators who are responsible for patching activities.

To view these roles within Oracle Enterprise Manager, choose Setup ➤ Security ➤ Roles. Then search for the keyword *patch*. This brings up all the roles associated with patching (see Figure 6-53).

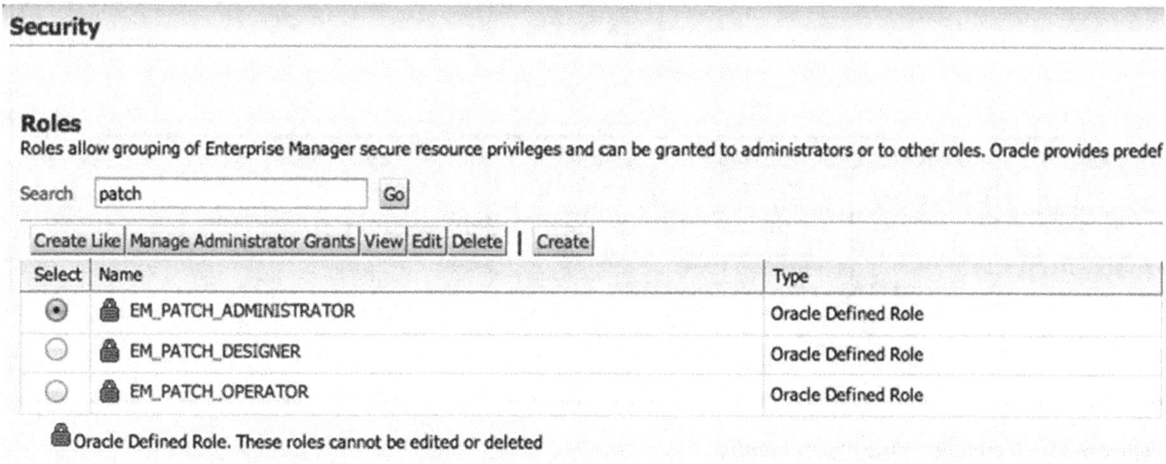

Security

Roles

Roles allow grouping of Enterprise Manager secure resource privileges and can be granted to administrators or to other roles. Oracle provides predef

Search [patch] [Go]

[Create Like] [Manage Administrator Grants] [View] [Edit] [Delete] | [Create]

Select	Name	Type
⦿	🔒 EM_PATCH_ADMINISTRATOR	Oracle Defined Role
○	🔒 EM_PATCH_DESIGNER	Oracle Defined Role
○	🔒 EM_PATCH_OPERATOR	Oracle Defined Role

🔒 Oracle Defined Role. These roles cannot be edited or deleted

Figure 6-53. *Patching roles located under Security*

Let's take a look at these roles as defined for patching:

> EM_PATCH_ADMINISTRATOR: This is the role for creating, editing, deploying, deleting, and granting privileges for any patch plan in Enterprise Manager. This role can also grant privileges to other administrators after creating them. This is a full privilege access role to any patch plan and template within Enterprise Manager. This role should be given out on a limited basis.

> EM_PATCH_DESIGNER: This role can create and view any patch plan. This role is normally used in the identification of patches across the patching lifecycle (development, testing, and production). This role would be assigned to a senior DBA in an organization. This role has the ability to create patch plans and templates and grant privileges to those plans to EM_PATCH_OPERATORS.

> EM_PATCH_OPERATORS: This is a role for deploying patch plans. This role is very limited in that is can only deploy patch plans. It has no privileges to create or modify any patch plans or templates. This role is ideal for junior DBAs of an organization.

These new patching roles enable administrators to provide a division of work between many layers of a department while making sure that patches are applied on a consistent schedule.

Provisioning

Provisioning is another important part of the lifecycle offered with Cloud Control. It allows us to provision database options, such as single-instance Oracle databases and Oracle Real Application Cluster databases; extend or delete nodes from Real Application Clusters, Oracle Real Application Clusters One; and upgrade single-instance databases in an automated manner.

Overview of Database Provisioning

First, let's take a general look at database provisioning. Figure 6-54 shows the provisioning solution in a hierarchical view.

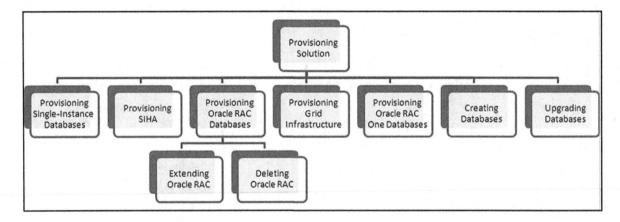

Figure 6-54. *Hierarchical view of provisioning*

There are a few features that you need to understand before moving on. These features are the following:

Designer and operator roles: Cloud Control offers designer and operator roles for administrators for provisioning. These clearly defined roles give you the capability to lock down the deployment procedure inputs to provide standard deployment configurations.

Locking-down feature in the designer role: This feature of provisioning enables the designers to lock down a set of variables, such as host target, credentials, and the Oracle home to be provisioned in the deployment procedure. This enables the standardization and minimizes errors in the configurations for mass deployments. The operator can deploy the procedure that was saved by the designer in the procedure library.

Provisioning profiles and database templates: Provisioning profiles are used in provisioning to ensure standardization in deployments and minimize errors.

Creating databases using Cloud Control: You can create databases directly from the Cloud Control console. This is to ensure that databases can be provisioned and created from a single interface.

Easy-to-navigate database provisioning wizards: Designers and operators can easily use and navigate through the Database Provisioning Wizard in Cloud Control.

Self Update: The Self Update feature is used to automatically download and install updates to your provisioning entities.

Database Provisioning console for all database provisioning activities: The Database Provisioning console is the central starting point for database provisioning activities. The console displays information about provisioning setup, profiles, deployment procedures, and any information about getting started with provisioning.

To access the Database Provisioning console, you choose Enterprise ➤ Provisioning and Patching ➤ Database Provisioning. You will notice additional provisioning options for Bare Metal and Middleware; these are used to provision servers and middleware targets. Just to be clear, we are focusing on database provisioning in this chapter. Figure 6-55 shows the upper portion of the Database Provisioning console.

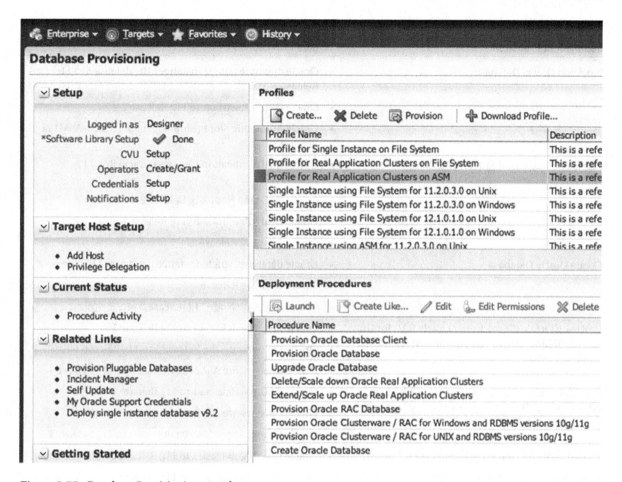

Figure 6-55. *Database Provisioning console*

Supported Targets and Deployment Procedures

Now that you have a starting point for database provisioning, what can you provision? How do you provision? Cloud Control enables you to perform database provisioning by using deployment procedures. A *deployment procedure* is a set of predefined steps that run in sequence to complete the provisioning tasks. Table 6-3 lists procedures that are offered and used to provision databases from within Cloud Control.

Table 6-3. *Deployment Procedures used for Database Provisioning*

Deployment Procedure	Targets Provisioned
Provision Oracle Database	• Oracle database (single instance) 10g Release 1 to 11g Release 2
	• Oracle Grid Infrastructure 11g Release 2
	• Oracle Automatic Storage Management (Oracle ASM) 11g Release 2
Provision Oracle Real Application Clusters	• Oracle Real Application Clusters (Oracle RAC) 11g Release 2
	• Oracle RAC One Node 11g Release 2
	• Oracle Grid Infrastructure 11g Release 2
	• Oracle ASM 11g Release 2
Create Oracle Database	• Oracle database (single-instance database) 11g Release 2
	• Oracle RAC 11g Release 2
	• Oracle RAC One Node 11g Release 2
Provision Oracle Clusterware / Oracle RAC for Unix and RDBMS versions 10g/11g (applicable for Unix platform)	• Oracle RAC 10g Release 1 to 11g Release 1
	• Oracle Clusterware 10g Release 1 to 11g Release 1
	• Oracle Clusterware ASM 10g Release 1 to 11g Release 1
Provision Oracle Clusterware / Oracle RAC for Windows and RDBMS versions 10g/11g (applicable for Windows platform)	• Oracle RAC 10g Release 1 to 11g Release 1
	• Oracle Clusterware 10g Release 1 to 11g Release 1
	• Oracle Clusterware ASM 10g Release 1 to 11g Release 1
Extend/scale up Oracle Real Application Clusters	• Oracle RAC 10g Release 1 to 11g Release 2
Delete/scale down Oracle Real Application Clusters	• Oracle RAC 10g Release 1 to 11g Release 2
Provision Oracle Database Client	• Oracle Database Client 10g Release 2 to 11g Release 2

With the deployments procedures that are in Table 6-3, there are a variety of use cases. There are far too many to discuss in this chapter, so we will focus on a single-instance Oracle database provisioning for the remainder of this chapter.

Setup for Database Provisioning

Using the Provisioning options in Oracle Enterprise Manager Cloud Control, you can provision Oracle databases, Oracle Real Application Clusters databases, and Oracle Real Application Clusters One databases by using templates, installation media, database entities, or provisioning profiles to standardize deployments.

Creating a Provision Profile

A *provision profile* is an entity that contains software bits and configuration details. When a profile is created from an existing installation, it provides flexibility in cloning of an Oracle database. We can create database templates by using provisioning profiles. Using a provisioning profile enables standardization within deployments. Provisioning profiles reduce the need to reschedule deployments by avoiding errors and increase efficiency of deployment procedures. Let's review how to create a provision profile.

To create a provision profile, you need to access the Provision Database console by choosing Enterprise ➤ Provisioning and Patching ➤ Database Provisioning. At the top of the Profiles section is a Create button. Click this button, shown in Figure 6-56, to start the Database Provisioning Profile Wizard, a four-step wizard that walks you through the creation of a provisioning profile.

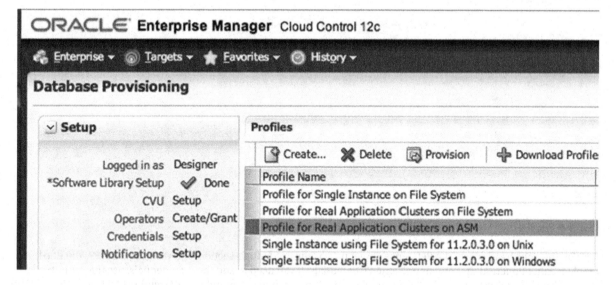

Figure 6-56. *Clicking the Create button*

The Database Provisioning Profile Wizard starts at step 1, which asks for a reference target (see Figure 6-57). This is the target you want to use to build the provisioning profile. Click the search icon and select the target you want to use. Then click Next to move on.

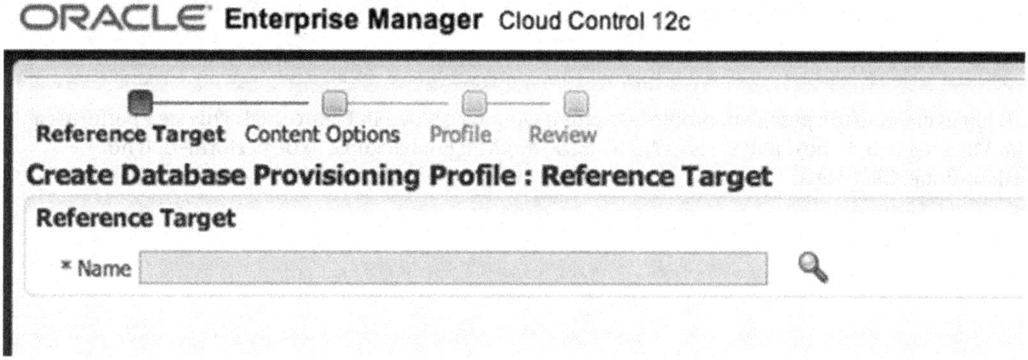

ORACLE Enterprise Manager Cloud Control 12c

Reference Target   Content Options   Profile   Review
Create Database Provisioning Profile : Reference Target
Reference Target

  * Name

Figure 6-57. *Reference target*

Now you are presented with components specific to the target. These components will be included in the provision profile (see Figure 6-58). Depending on the reference target, you can choose to either leave these items or remove them from the profile.

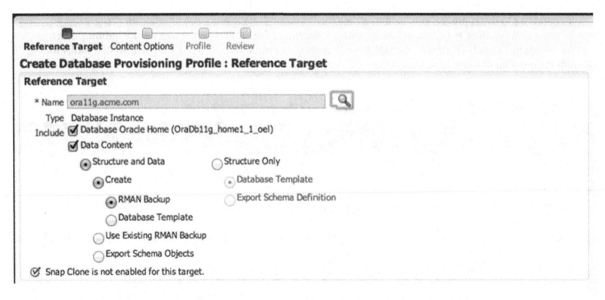

Figure 6-58. *Reference target components*

On the right-hand side of the Reference Target page is the Credentials section, shown in Figure 6-59. You need to select either Preferred Credentials or Named Credentials. If you need to add these credentials, use the Setup ➤ Security function. Chapter 4 covers how to add credentials to the security modules. If everything is set, click Next.

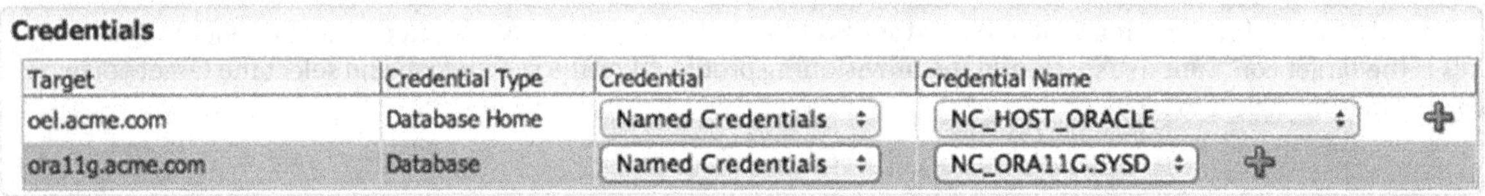

Credentials				
Target	Credential Type	Credential	Credential Name	
oel.acme.com	Database Home	Named Credentials ⊕	NC_HOST_ORACLE ⊕	✛
ora11g.acme.com	Database	Named Credentials ⊕	NC_ORA11G.SYSD ⊕	✛

Figure 6-59. *Credentials section*

The second step in creating the provision profile is Content Options, shown in Figure 6-60. This step performs a backup using RMAN, if needed. If the database is in ARCHIVELOG mode, a hot backup can be performed. If not, a cold backup will be done. Click Next.

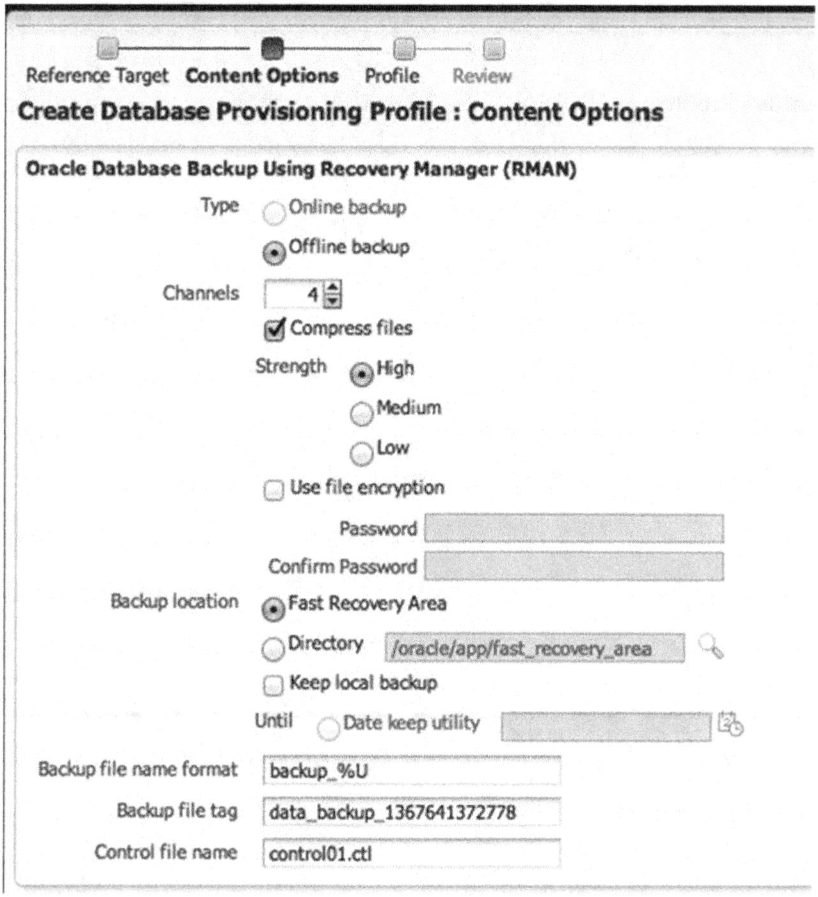

Figure 6-60. *Content options*

The Profile page, shown in Figure 6-61, is the third step in creating a provision profile. At this point, you can edit or retain the defaults on the page. The storage location for this profile is also defined in the Software Library Storage section. This shows that we will be storing this provision profile in the Software Library for later use. Not listed in Figure 6-62 is the schedule and working directory windows. These areas can be changed as needed. Click Next.

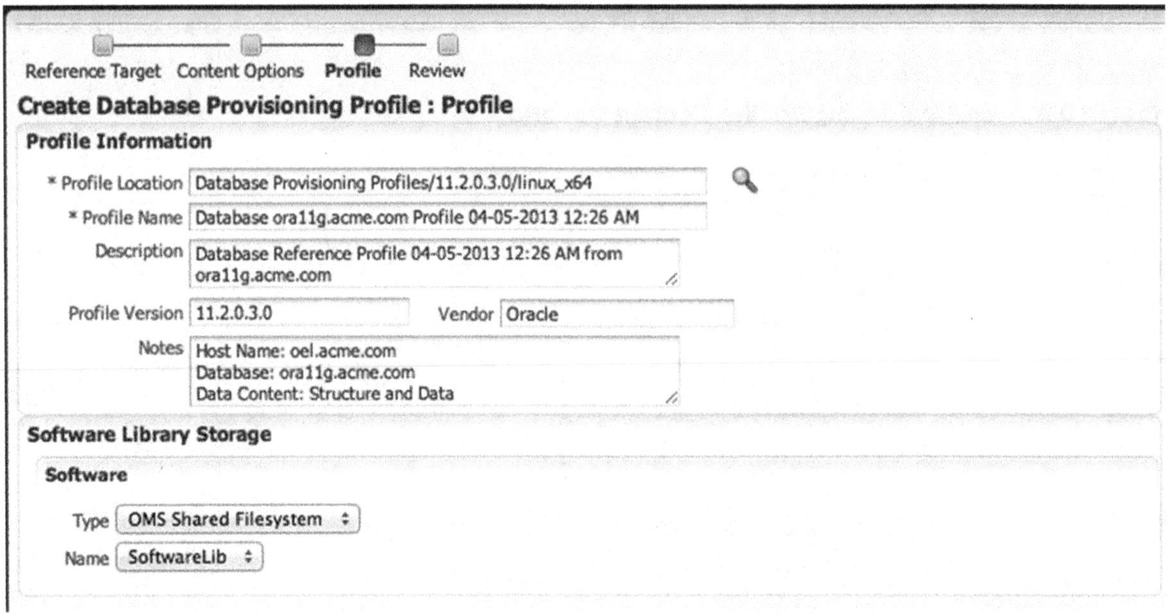

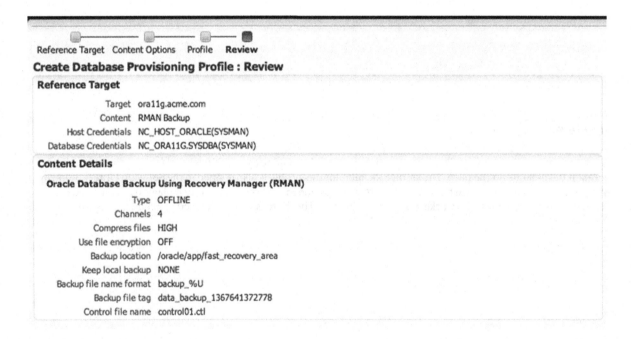

Figure 6-61. Profile page

Figure 6-62. Reviewing the profile

The final step is the Review page, shown in Figure 6-62. As with other review pages, you can review your choices here before hitting Submit. Click Submit to create the profile.

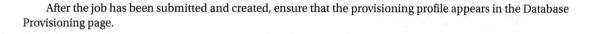

After the job has been submitted and created, ensure that the provisioning profile appears in the Database Provisioning page.

■ **Note**   The provisioning job that is submitted will create the gold image of the database that was selected for the profile.

Creating Installation Media

Another way to provision an Oracle database is to upload the installation media into the Software Library. The installation media can then be pushed out to target systems by using deployment procedures. Let's look at how to create and upload installation media to the Software Library.

Before you can upload installation media into the Software Library, you need to download the media from Oracle. Media files can be downloaded from the Oracle Technology Network (OTN), My Oracle Support (MOS), or Oracle's E-Delivery portal.

■ **Note**   From the Oracle Technology Network, anyone can download the software. If you have a valid customer support identifier (CSI), you can access E-Delivery and download from there, as well.

You need to pull down the zip files for the Oracle database to a temporary directory on the host you are working from. These files are located on disk 1 and disk 2 of the media downloaded from Oracle. Then follow these steps:

1. After the files from disk 1 and 2 are downloaded, navigate to the temporary location where they were saved. These files need to be unzipped by using a zip tool that is available on the system. Then combine these two files into a single zipped file.

2. Open the Software Library by choosing Enterprise ➤ Provisioning and Patching ➤ Software Library. In the Software Library, select the directory where you want to create the installation media for the database.

3. With the directory selected for the binaries, you need to create a new entity under this folder. From the Actions menu in the Software Library, choose Create Entity, as shown in Figure 6-63.

Figure 6-63. Creating a new entity in the Software Library

4. Next you need to upload the installation media as a new entity in the Software Library.
    This process is similar to the steps used earlier in this chapter, except you choose
    Installation Media when selecting the component (see Figure 6-64). Click Continue.

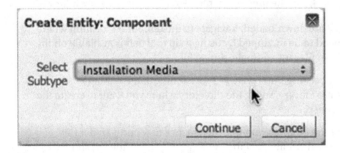

Figure 6-64. Creating an installation media entity

5. On the Describe page, the only input required for Installation Media is the name. All other
    information on this page is optional. Click Next.

6. On the Configure page, you indicate the components of the installation media, as shown
    in Figure 6-65. These settings cannot be changed after the media has been uploaded to the
    Software Library. Click Next.

Software Library

Describe **Configure** Select Files Review

Create Installation Media : Configure

Parent Directory Media
        Subtype Installation Media

Installation Media Component

Select Product, Platform and Version for the Installation Media you want to upload to Software Library.

* Product | Oracle Database ⬍ |

* Platform | Linux x86–64 ⬍ |

* Version | 11.2.0.3.0 ⬍ |

Figure 6-65. Specifications for the installation media components

7. Next is the Select Files page, where you will select the single zip file created earlier for the database binaries. By default, the Upload Files option is selected. Under the specified destination, we need to select the upload location where we want to place our zip file. Click the search icon to open the Select Upload Location dialog box, shown in Figure 6-66.

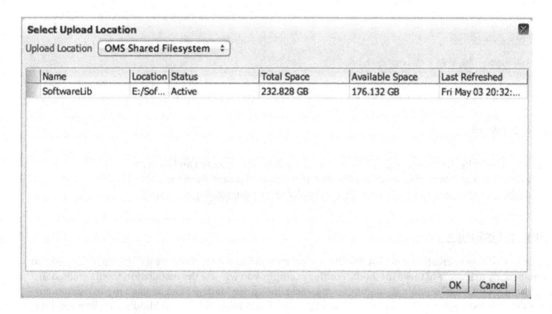

Select Upload Location   ⊠

Upload Location | OMS Shared Filesystem ⬍ |

Name	Location	Status	Total Space	Available Space	Last Refreshed
SoftwareLib	E:/Sof...	Active	232.828 GB	176.132 GB	Fri May 03 20:32:...

OK   Cancel

Figure 6-66. Selecting the upload location

8. Since we have only one Software Library, click OK. The location selected will be reflected on the Select Files page. Then in the Specify Source section, click the Add button and select the zip file that you would like to upload to the Software Library (see Figure 6-67). Click Next.

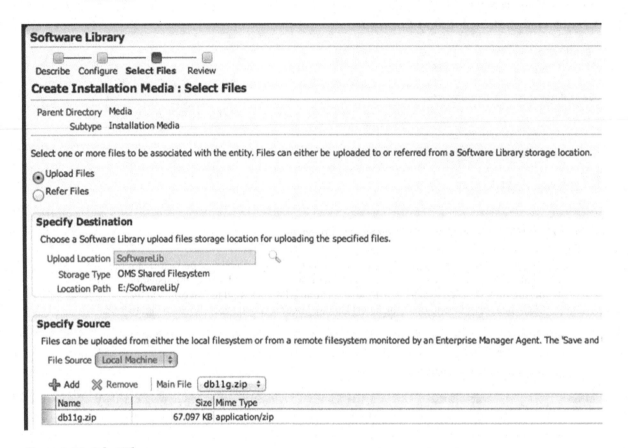

Figure 6-67. *Select Files page*

9. Finally, on the Review page, you can review all the options you selected and then click Save and Upload. This uploads our zip file into the Software Library. After the upload is complete, you just need to verify that the file is uploaded where you expected it to be.

Provisioning a Database

Thus far, you have seen how to create a provision profile and create installation media. Now let's take a look at how to provision a database by using one of these methods. For this example, you will use the installation media created in the "Creating Installation Media" section. Remember that Oracle Enterprise Manager can be used to provision many types of targets through tools such as Database Provisioning, Bare Metal Provisioning, and Middleware Provisioning. To get started in the provisioning of a database, you need to open the Database Provisioning console; choose Enterprise ➤ Provisioning and Patching ➤ Database Provisioning.

From the Database Provisioning page, you will use deployment procedures to provision a database. Because we are provisioning a single database, select Provision Oracle Database and click the Launch button, as shown in Figure 6-68. At this point, the provisioning wizard for Oracle database launches.

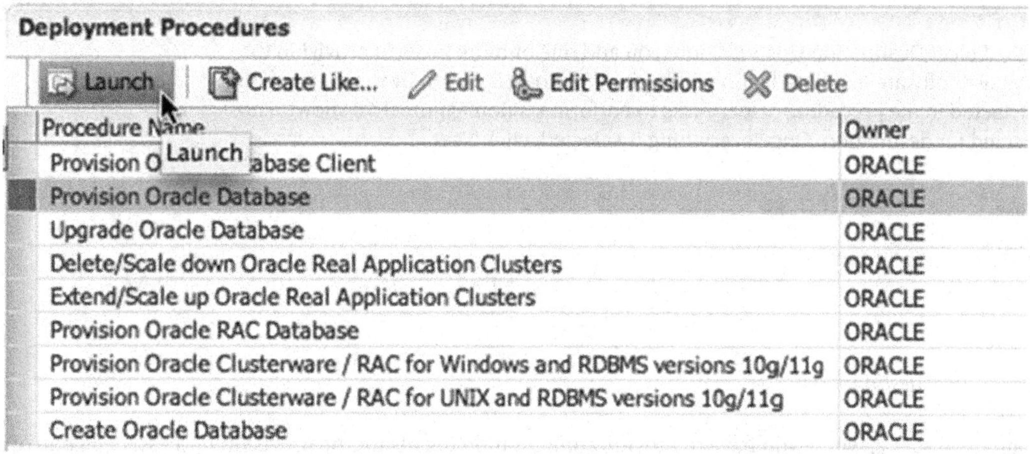

Figure 6-68. *Select and launch the Provision Oracle Database deployment procedure*

When the Provision Database wizard starts, you can see that it is similar to many other wizards within Oracle Enterprise Manager. This wizard is a five-step process, with the first step enabling you to select the host where you want to provision a database. Here are the steps of the wizard:

1. On the Select Host page, you have the option of using a provision profile. By default, this option is set to None. Because we are using installation media to provision a database, you do not need to select a provisioning profile.

2. The next two sections on the Select Hosts page are important to provisioning a database. In the Select Tasks to Perform section, you choose a platform and a version, and whether to install Grid Infrastructure and deploy database software. The Version drop-down box provides all the versions of Oracle that are supported for provisioning (see Figure 6-69).

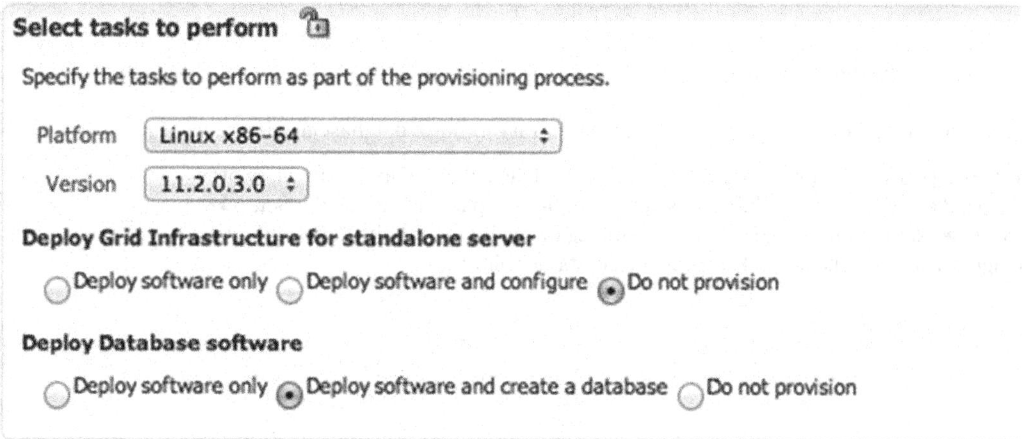

Figure 6-69. *Selecting tasks to perform*

■ **Note**　Oracle Enterprise Manager Cloud Control 12c Bundle Patch 2 Update 1 contains the plug-ins and support for upcoming releases of Oracle products.

---

3. In the Select Destination Hosts section, you add one or more hosts to provision the database software to. The selection of destination hosts is driven by the platform that is selected in the preceding Select Tasks to Perform section. Figure 6-70 shows a host selected for destination. Once everything is selected, click Next.

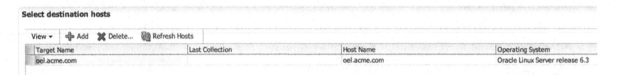

Select destination hosts

Target Name	Last Collection	Host Name	Operating System
oel.acme.com		oel.acme.com	Oracle Linux Server release 6.3

View ▾　✚ Add　✖ Delete...　Refresh Hosts

Figure 6-70. *Selection of destination hosts*

Now you end up at step 2, where you have to provide configuration details for the provision process. Each one of these tasks needs to be completed and checked off before you can move to step 3 (see Figure 6-71).

Select Hosts　**Configure**　Custom properties　Schedule　Review

Provision Oracle Database : Configure

Configure

Use the following sections to provide configuration details for the various tasks that will be performed as part of this provisioning operation.

Task No.	Task	Status
1	Setup hosts	
2	Deploy software	
3	Create databases	
4	Compliance Standards	

Figure 6-71. *Providing configuration details*

The tasks outlined on the Configure page are required for provisioning a database to a host:

1. The Setup Hosts task allows us to set normal and privileged usernames and passwords to be used against the host. These passwords can be set up in advance under Setup ➤ Security ➤ Named Credentials or created during the task. Once all the passwords are configured, a green check mark appears in the status column.

2. The second task is to specify the software that you want to deploy. Click the Deploy Software link, and you are taken to a single-step wizard where you can specify the source, destination, and additional parameters for this deployment (see Figure 6-72). To deploy the database software, you need to select the software to deploy. Click the search tool in the Source section and then select the software from the Software Library. Next, provide the details for the deployment, such as destination and any additional parameters needed for deployment. Click Next.

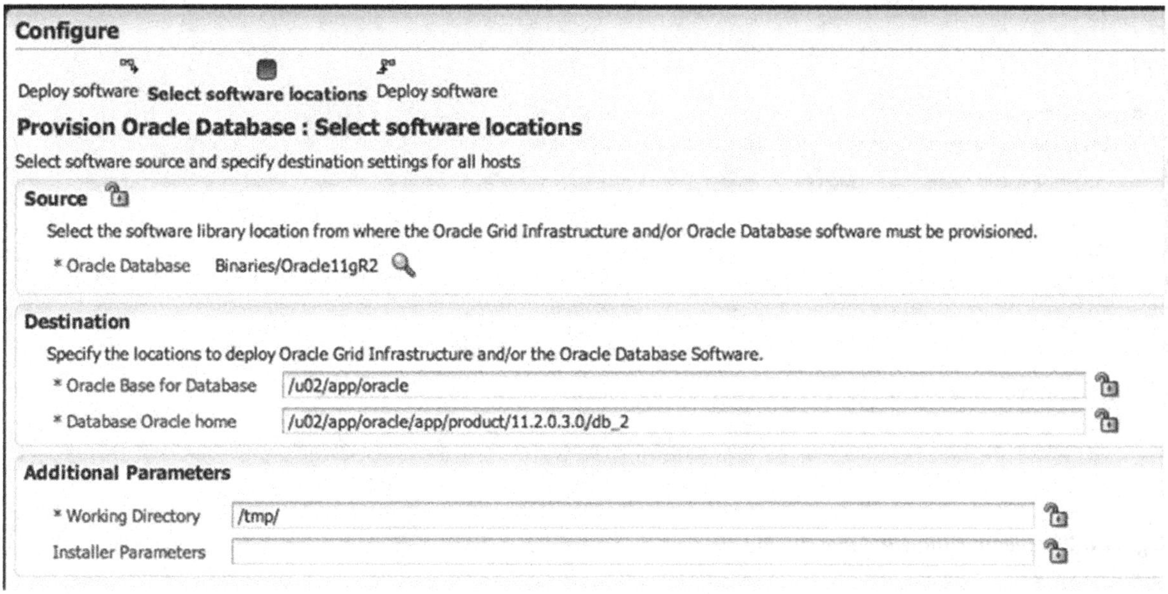

Configure

Deploy software **Select software locations** Deploy software

Provision Oracle Database : Select software locations

Select software source and specify destination settings for all hosts

Source

Select the software library location from where the Oracle Grid Infrastructure and/or Oracle Database software must be provisioned.

* Oracle Database   Binaries/Oracle11gR2

Destination

Specify the locations to deploy Oracle Grid Infrastructure and/or the Oracle Database Software.

* Oracle Base for Database   /u02/app/oracle

* Database Oracle home   /u02/app/oracle/app/product/11.2.0.3.0/db_2

Additional Parameters

* Working Directory   /tmp/

Installer Parameters

Figure 6-72. *Selecting software locations*

3. The third task in the configuration to provision a database is the Create Database task. Just as in the first two steps, you click Create Database to start the wizard. This six-step wizard is similar to the Oracle Database Configuration Assistant, but this one is inside Oracle Enterprise Manager. Click Next to walk through the wizard and configure many items such as SID and passwords, as shown in Figure 6-73.

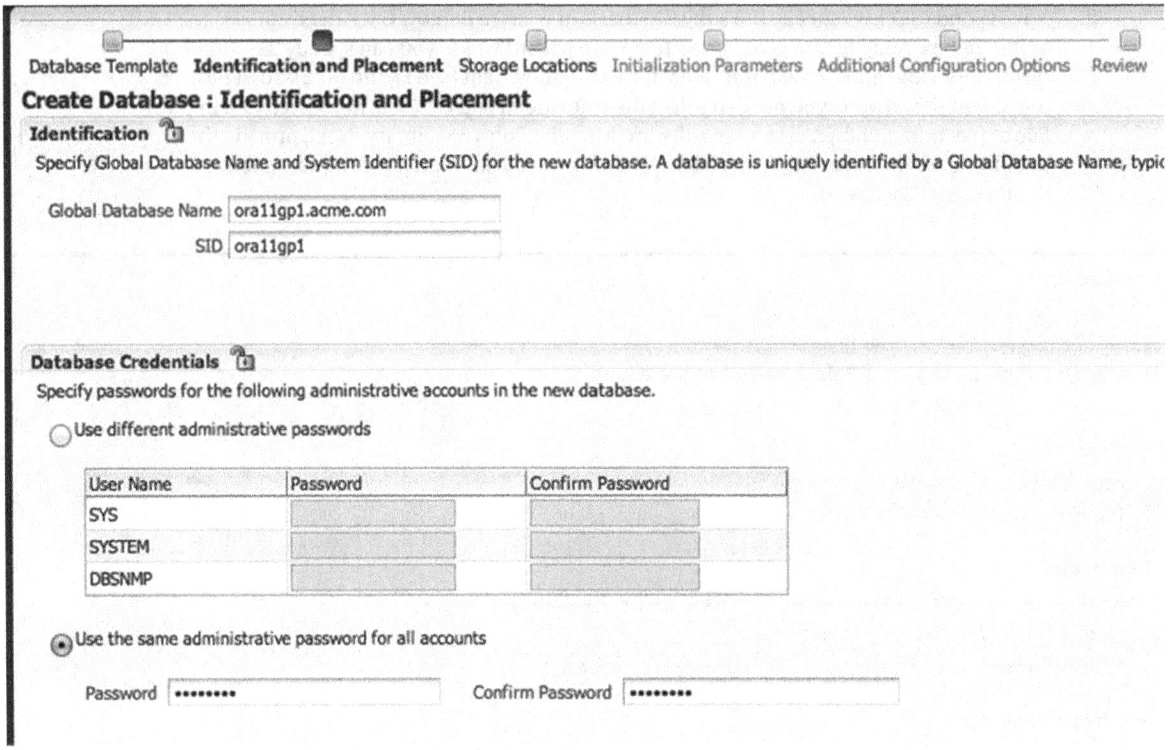

Figure 6-73. Identification and placement

4.   The last of the four tasks is Compliance Standards. Click Compliance Standards to access
      its one-step wizard. Here you assign a compliance standard to the new database. This
      greatly speeds up the configuration of databases to internal compliance standards
      (see Figure 6-74). For this example, select None and click Next.

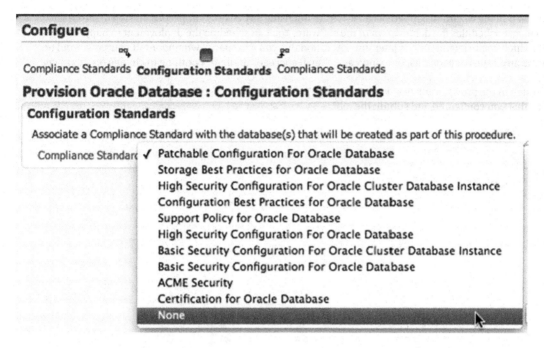

Figure 6-74. *Setting configuration standards*

■ **Note**   For more information on compliance configuration within the Oracle Enterprise Manager, please see the Oracle documentation.

5.   Once everything is configured, as shown in Figure 6-75, you can move on to the next steps in the wizard. Click Next.

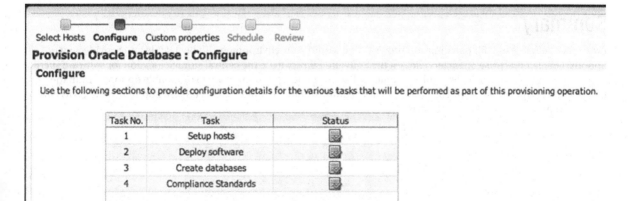

Figure 6-75. *Configuration is completed*

The third step in the wizard is skipped because we are not using any custom properties. In step 4, the Oracle Enterprise Manager schedules the deployment of the software. You can schedule the deployment to happen immediately (which is the default) or at a later time. Additionally, you can specify whether notifications should be used to indicate any issues or concerns, or to indicate when it succeeds. If there is nothing to change on this page, click Next.

The final step in the provisioning of a database is step 5, the Review step (see Figure 6-76). From here you can see all the options that you configured and submit the job.

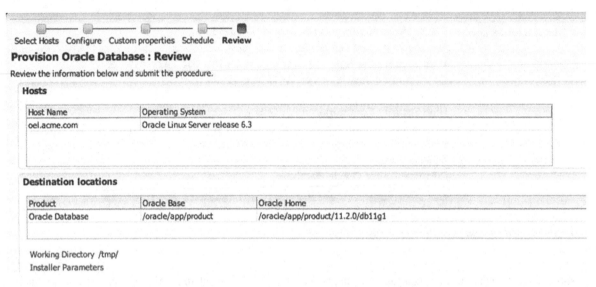

Figure 6-76. Reviewing options for provisioning the Oracle database (partial screen)

After submitting the job, you will be taken to the Provisioning page, where you can monitor the job. This page is loaded with a lot of valuable information. You can either stay on this page or move away and work on something else while the database is provisioned.

Summary

EM12c is a valuable tool for patching and provisioning within your environment. To be flexible and provide a lot of options, Oracle Enterprise Manager relies on the Software Library to be the central storage location for software such as patches, and to install software and gold images. Patching and provisioning are two valuable options within the lifecycle of Enterprise Manager. The options enable administrators to quickly patch old environments and provision new environments very quickly and securely.

CHAPTER 7

■ ■ ■

Managing and Monitoring Best Practices

by Leighton Nelson

Oracle Enterprise Manager Cloud Control 12c is built from the ground up to manage and monitor your enterprise infrastructure and applications across the entire IT stack. To effectively manage your environment, various techniques and best practices should be followed. Monitoring your environment ensures that no component goes unwatched. By using events, metrics, and incidents, you can provide yourself a comprehensive picture of the environment at any point in time.

This chapter presents some of the best practices to apply to monitoring and managing your environment with EM12c. The following best-practice areas are discussed:

- Metric thresholds
- Monitoring templates
- Administration groups
- Template collections
- Synchronization schedules
- Incident management

Metric Thresholds

Metric thresholds are the main features when it comes to monitoring. They enable you to be proactive so you can identify issues and address them in a timely manner. Enterprise Manager Cloud Control includes many types of metrics, which can be used for monitoring targets. Several classes of metrics are available, depending on the type of target. Metric thresholds should be configured so that alerts are triggered and sent via notifications to administrators.

Two levels of severity are associated with metric thresholds: *warning* and *critical*. For example, you may set a metric threshold for a tablespace in the database to send a warning alert when the tablespace becomes more than 80 percent full. Then you might set another threshold to send a critical alert when the tablespace becomes more than 95 percent full. A warning threshold will allow enough time to address issues before they become critical. Critical alerts would indicate an impending problem and require immediate action.

When defining your thresholds, first determine the important components on which thresholds should be set. This could include database instances, listeners, and filesystems. Metrics can then be selected from EM12c for each target type.

To view all metric thresholds and their values for a database instance, follow these steps:

1. From the Oracle Database drop-down menu, choose Monitoring ➤ All Metrics, as shown in Figure 7-1.

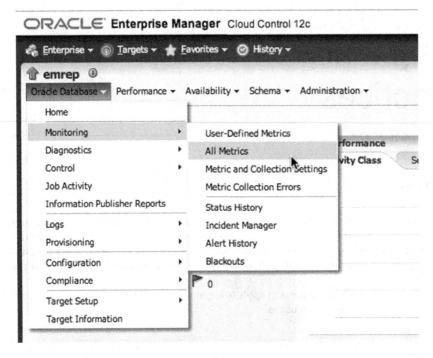

Figure 7-1. *Viewing a list of metric thresholds*

2. A display of metrics and thresholds similar to that in Figure 7-2 displays. Set thresholds only for the metrics that you care about. Selecting too many metrics could generate a lot of "white noise" and cause critical alerts to be overlooked. You should also disable metrics that you don't need for reporting or monitoring purposes in order to reduce storage consumption.

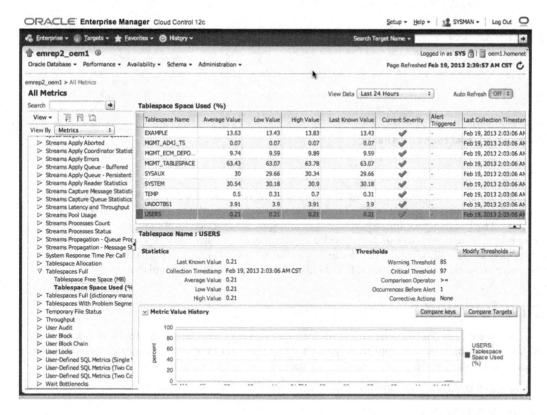

Figure 7-2. *Database metrics and their current threshold settings*

Threshold values should be obtained by gathering data during performance or load testing. View the available metric history to obtain these values while the performance is acceptable. Also define metrics for target availability such as database instance status. The values selected for critical thresholds should be chosen conservatively so that you are alerted under only extremely serious conditions, such as when a tablespace is over 97 percent full.

To set values for a metric, follow these steps:

1. Click a metric category such as Tablespaces Full. These categories are listed to the left in Figure 7-2.

2. Click a specific metric such as Tablespace Space Used (%).

3. Click the Modify Thresholds button. You should see a dialog box like the one in Figure 7-3.

Modify Thresholds

Data available from Feb 19, 2013 1:16:16 AM CST to Feb 19, 2013 2:33:06 AM CST

Warning Threshold	90	High Value 0.22	Time in warning (%) 0
Critical Threshold	99	Low Value 0.21	Time in critical (%) 0
Occurrences Before Alert	1	Average Value 0.21	Number of warning events 0
	Test Thresholds		Number of critical events 0

Figure 7-3. *Entering threshold values for a metric*

4. Enter the values for the metric.

EM12c includes out-of-the-box thresholds that can be used as the basis for your own monitoring. Customize these as necessary to ensure that they meet service-level agreements for your business. Thresholds can then be fine-tuned over time if they are not meeting requirements, or in response to service-level changes.

While the one-by-one method in this section provides a quick way to set thresholds for a single target, the method becomes increasingly difficult and time-consuming as the number of targets across the enterprise increases. Thus, my recommended method of setting metric thresholds is to employ monitoring templates.

Monitoring Templates

Monitoring templates are collections of metric thresholds for a specific target type. Metric thresholds should be set on monitoring templates, which are then applied to one or more targets. For example, a monitoring template can be created for production database instances that may include the following metrics and warning/critical thresholds:

- Tablespace Space Used (%) > 80/97

- Archive Area Space Used (%) > 75/90

- Dump Area Used (%) > 90/95

- Status = DOWN

The monitoring template can then be applied to all production database instances, easing the task of standardizing your monitoring settings. Separate monitoring templates can be created for each target type. For example, you can create a listener template, a host template, and so forth.

The metric thresholds set in your monitoring templates should not be fine-grained, but rather broad enough to meet general service levels for the majority of targets. If finer granularity is required, additional templates can be created and applied to those targets that require them. Think in terms of creating the minimum number of templates to cover the maximum possible targets. Don't gratuitously create more templates than you need, because it's just more work then to manage them. Create what you need, but no more than you need.

To create a monitoring template, follow these steps:

1. Run the Enterprise Manager Cloud Control console.

2. Choose Enterprise ➤ Monitoring ➤ Monitoring Templates, as shown in Figure 7-4.

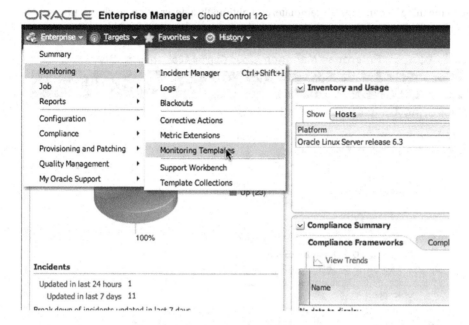

Figure 7-4. *Preparing to create a new monitoring template*

3. The Monitoring Templates page opens. Click the Create button to create a template.

4. Choose a representative target for the monitoring settings that you want to create, as shown in Figure 7-5. This target will be used as the basis for metrics and policies in the monitoring template. For example, to create a Database Instance monitoring template, select an existing database instance target from which to copy existing monitoring settings. Alternatively, you may select a target type and enter the settings manually.

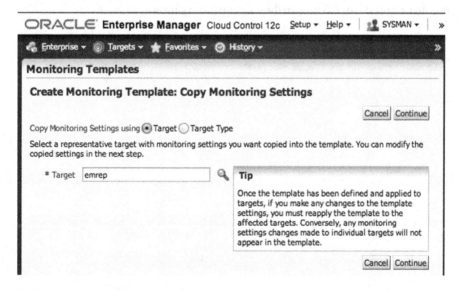

Figure 7-5. *Creating a monitoring template*

5.   Enter a meaningful name for the template, and optionally a description, as shown in
      Figure 7-6. (Writing a short description to jog your memory later is a good idea.)

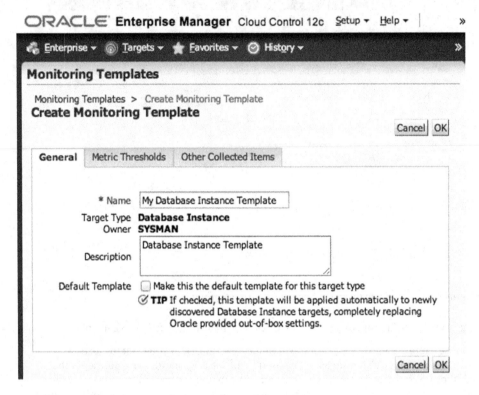

Figure 7-6. *Naming your template*

6.   Click the Metric Thresholds tab to open the data entry area shown in Figure 7-7.

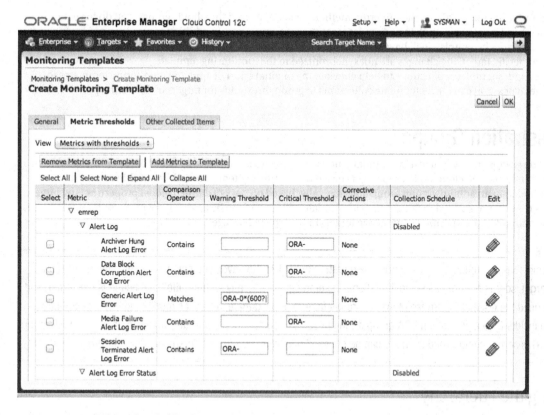

Figure 7-7. *Specifying threshold values*

7. Enter or modify the values for the metrics that you want to set. Select only the metrics that you care about. Remember, values for the metrics should be set according to your operational goals. You can also remove selected metrics altogether if you don't want them to be collected. If a threshold value is not set for a metric, no alerts will be sent for the metric.

In addition to specifying thresholds for your metrics, you can modify the collection schedules for the metrics if those schedules are not in line with your operating goals. For example, the Archive Area Used (%) metric collection schedule by default is set to collect every 15 minutes. If your database instance has a high transaction rate that generates a lot of archive redo logs, you may want to modify the collection schedule for the metric to collect at 10-minute intervals instead. Click the link in the Collection Schedule column to modify the schedule. Figure 7-8 shows a close-up of an Archive Area threshold. The Every 15 Minutes link is what you would click to modify the schedule.

▽ Archive Area				Every 15 Minutes	
Archive Area Used (%)	>	80	None		✏✎

Figure 7-8. *Click the Every 15 Minutes link to modify the schedule for checking Archive Area thresholds*

Create additional monitoring templates for each target type that you wish to monitor. In a RAC environment, you might create templates for listener, cluster database, ASM instance, and host.

While monitoring templates are the preferred method for standardized threshold settings, you do have the additional overhead involved in applying a template to different target types. In addition, if you change a metric in a monitoring template, the template will have to be reapplied to its targets. Conversely, if metric threshold values are changed for a specific target, the changes are not synchronized to the monitoring template.

EM12c provides template collections to help alleviate the manual effort of applying monitoring templates to different target types. You can create template collections to group thresholds for targets of different types.

Administration Groups

Administration groups allow you to easily automate the management and monitoring of targets by applying metrics, compliance standards, and cloud policies to targets based on monitoring template collections. Members are dynamically added to an administration group automatically, based on a set of defined global properties. Any target that matches the criteria is added to the group, and template collections can be associated with those targets. As a best practice, use administration groups for managing targets in Enterprise Manager.

■ **Tip** Administration groups are a wonderful, new feature in EM12c. However, you can assign only one notification group per target, so this feature has some limitations. In some cases, you may want multiple notifications per target, and for that you need the original Enterprise Manager groups feature. For example, a target's monitoring requirement might be to assign incidents to a production DBA group during business hours, and to generate e-mails to an on-call DBA group after hours. This sort of complicated scenario can be satisfied only with the original Enterprise Manager groups feature.

Planning the Hierarchy

Before administration groups are created, you should plan your administration group hierarchy. This hierarchy comprises different, logically divided targets arranged in one or more levels based on global target properties. You may also specify multiple target types that define an administration group.

It is important that the hierarchy be planned so that it is in line with your organization's operational and monitoring standards. You should have an understanding of how targets are monitored so that similarly managed targets are grouped together. For example, you may want to create a group for Production targets and another group for Non-Production targets based on the *LifeCycle Status* property. In addition, you may want to create other levels in the hierarchy that are subgroups of Production and Non-Production based on the following target properties:

- Department
- Line of business
- Location
- CSI number
- Cost center
- Contact

The decision of whether to create more levels in the hierarchy should depend on the monitoring characteristics of the intended groups. For example, do you need to maintain separate metrics for HR and Sales groups, or can they be monitored using similar metrics? The diagram shown in Figure 7-9 is an example of an administration group hierarchy based on the LifeCycle Status, Location, and Line of Business target properties.

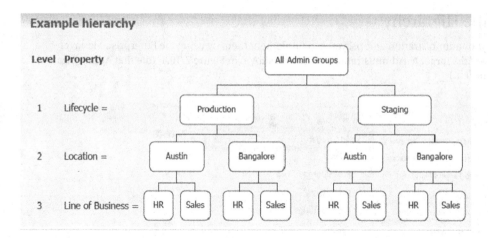

Figure 7-9. *Administration group hierarchy with three levels based on Lifecycle, Location, and Line of Business properties*

There can be only one administration group hierarchy. This limit of one prevents conflicts that would arise from multiple hierarchies. Furthermore, a target can belong to only a single group in the hierarchy.

A target cannot be added directly to a group. Instead, group membership is determined by the target's properties (for example, LifeCycle Status). These properties can be set at target discovery and promotion time, or at a later time if the targets have already been discovered. Target properties can be set by using the Enterprise Manager console or the emcli command-line interface with the set_target_property_value verb. For more information about the emcli commands, see Chapter 2 of the *Oracle Enterprise Manager Command Line Interface* documentation.

■ **Tip**   Think of planning your hierarchy in terms of two steps: 1) Define your hierarchy. 2) Assign properties to your targets. The "magic" happens then, as your targets are automatically slotted into your hierarchy at the appropriate levels.

After targets join the administration groups, you can associate template collections so that each group's members have similar metrics, policies, and standards. Template collections are a set of template metrics composed of several target types. They are discussed later in the chapter.

Separate template collections should be created for each administration group. Before creating administration groups, you should first create monitoring templates. Each monitoring template is specific to a single target type. Therefore, you will need to create a template collection consisting of several monitoring templates: one for each target type. For example, a Production Targets administration group consisting of hosts, listeners, database, and ASM instances will require a template collection consisting of four distinct monitoring templates.

If the administration group hierarchy consists of more than two levels, the order in which template collections are applied is important. Template collections at the leaf levels override metrics from the parent levels. Each group will have its own template collection, and those from the parent levels are propagated to their respective subgroups.

After template collections have been applied, you should associate the collections with the groups. This ensures that each group contains a standard set of metrics, standards, and policies. Once that is done, the targets are synchronized so that any future changes to monitoring templates are automatically applied to the associated targets.

Implementing the Hierarchy

Once you have defined your administration groups, you can implement them by using the Enterprise Manager console. Choose Setup ➤ Add Target ➤ Administration Groups, as shown in Figure 7-10. (Note that Administration Groups is displayed to the left.)

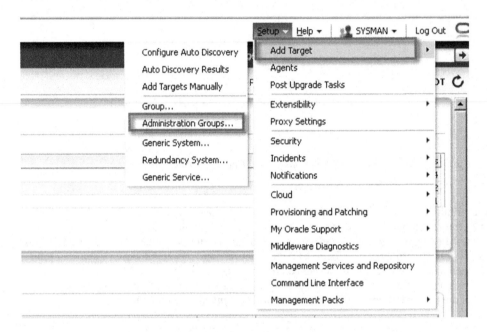

Figure 7-10. *Choosing to add administration groups*

Within the administration group home page (shown in Figure 7-11), you can now define the group hierarchy determined in the planning phase. You can also create template collections and associate them with the administration groups. Click the Hierarchy tab to define the hierarchy.

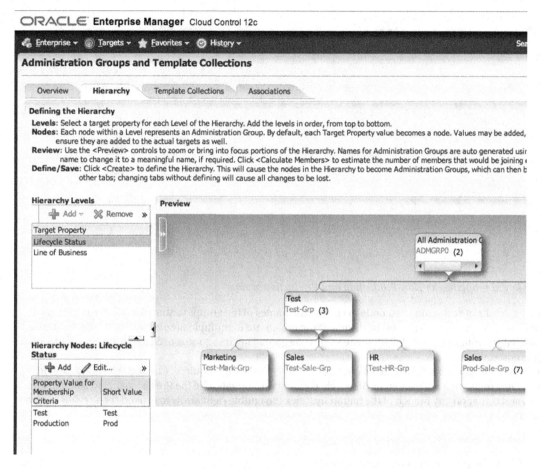

Figure 7-11. *Creating an administration group hierarchy based on LifeCycle Status from the Enterprise Manager console*

Levels are added from top to bottom. Click Add (+) under the Hierarchy Levels section on the left and select a global property that will be used to define the administration group. In Figure 7-11, you see that the LifeCycle Status property denotes the divisions under the administration group, and the Line of Business property denotes the next level of division. By default, those two choices cause a node for each group to be automatically created based on the predefined values for LifeCycle Status.

■ **Note**   If the Target Type property is used to create an administration group, include database, listener, and ASM in the same group instead of three separate groups.

If the intention is to have a single Production Target group and a Non-Production group, some of the groups can be merged. For example, merging Production and Mission Critical into one group called Production and then merging Development, Test, and Staging into a Non-Production Targets group will result in the hierarchy shown in Figure 7-12.

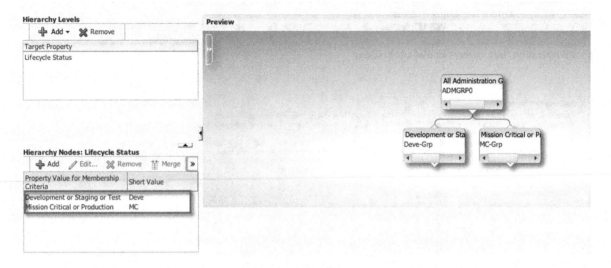

Figure 7-12. Merged properties for Non-Production and Production groups

Click on the details of each group in a node to change the names of the groups to something more meaningful than the autogenerated names they take on by default. If the targets are in multiple time zones, set the time zone for each group as well. All subgroups will default to the same time zone. The time zone is used for group charts and job scheduling purposes.

Repeat the process just described to create any additional levels that are required. Create the levels identified during the planning phase that are needed to effectively manage your targets. Use the Preview panel to zoom in and zoom out, pan and center on any branch of the hierarchy. Click the double right arrow to expand the Preview controls, shown in Figure 7-13.

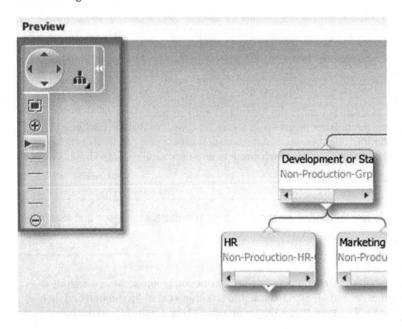

Figure 7-13. Preview controls for panning, zooming, and layout

Review the administration group hierarchy carefully after it has been defined. Once it has been created, you can modify only the target property values, which will result in the hierarchy expanding or shrinking in the same level.

Consider experimenting with different hierarchy organizations in a test Enterprise Manager environment. That gives you a chance to review your monitoring and management strategy before taking it to production.

If target properties have already been set prior to creating the administration group hierarchy, you can click the Calculate Members button to have the groups automatically populated. Once you are satisfied with the hierarchy, click the Create button.

■ **Caution**   If you want to add or remove target properties after the hierarchy has been created, the administration group will have to be deleted and re-created.

Joining Administration Groups

The next step is to set those target properties defined in the administration group hierarchy on the targets. This can be done by using the Enterprise Manager console. Or, you can chose the command-line approach using emcli and the set_target_property_value command. If you are setting properties for a small number of targets, use the console. Otherwise, EMCLI is recommended for setting the properties for batches of targets.

To determine which targets have their properties set, go to the All Targets menu. The default view shows the Target Name, Target Type, Target Status, and Pending Activation columns. Click the View drop-down, as shown in Figure 7-14, to add columns that correspond to target properties of the administration groups.

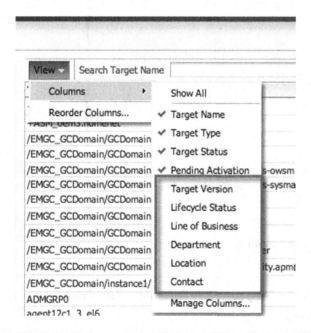

Figure 7-14. *Customize the All Targets view to display additional target properties*

To set the target properties for nondatabase targets using the console, right-click the target name and choose Target Setup ➤ Properties. For database instances, right-click the target name and choose Oracle Database or Cluster Database, and then Target Setup and Properties. As seen in Figure 7-15, the administration group properties and values chosen for the hierarchy are displayed above the table of all target properties. Click the Edit button to edit the properties.

■ **Note**   The display of values chosen above the table of target properties is a feature available starting in version 12.1.0.2.0.

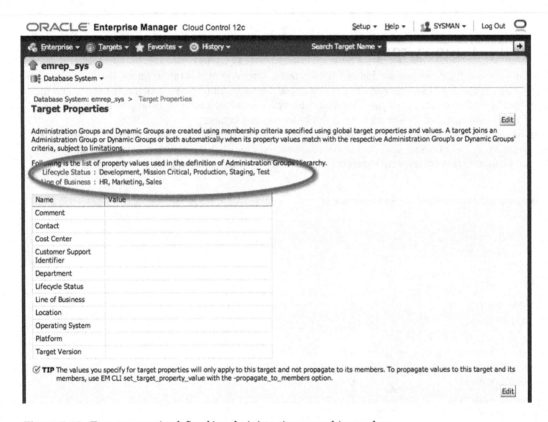

Figure 7-15. *Target properties defined in administration group hieararchy*

■ **Note**   Set target properties during target addition or promotion. Doing so ensures that members will join the administration groups automatically after they have been created.

Target properties set on noncluster aggregate targets are not automatically applied to member targets. This is to prevent ambiguity if the target already belongs to another administration group. To set target properties for noncluster aggregate targets, use `emcli` with `set_target_property_values` and the `–propagate_to_members` option. That way, members of the aggregate also join the same administration group.

■ **Note** Noncluster aggregate targets include the Database System target type, which consists of database instances, listeners, ASM instances, and high-availability services. Cluster targets such as database clusters, host clusters, and redundancy systems will automatically inherit the target properties for both current and new members.

Any new members of an aggregate will require that their target properties be set manually. The example to follow shows how to propagate the LifeCycle Status and Line of Business target properties to the emrep_sys aggregate:

```
$ emcli set_target_property_value -property_records
  ="emrep_sys:oracle_dbsys:LifeCycle Status:Production" -propagate_to_members
```

This command will cause members of the emrep_sys aggregate (database instance, listener, and ASM) to have identical LifeCycle Status and Line of Business properties.

When using emcli, the target properties are case-sensitive. For example, setting a property using Lifecycle Status instead of LifeCycle Status (note the uppercase *C*) will generate an error. To see the valid list of target properties that can be set for a particular target, issue the emcli get_target_properties command with the target_type option. The following example shows all valid properties for the oracle_dbsys aggregate target:

```
$ emcli get_target_properties -target_type="oracle_dbsys"
CommentContact
Cost Center
Customer Service Identifier
Department
LifeCycle Status
Line of Business
Location
Operating System
Platform
Target Version
Target properties fetched successfully
```

Be sure to visit each target you plan to monitor, and be sure to set for that target each of the properties used to build your administration group hierarchy. Any target whose properties are not set will not be part of an administration group, and therefore will not be monitored using the defined monitoring standards.

MULTIPLE TARGETS

When setting target properties for multiple related targets, you can use emcli with the aggregate/cluster target name to simplify the process. For example, to set the same Line of Business property for the database instance, listener, ASM home, and Oracle home for the orcl_sys database system in one command, you would do the following:

```
emcli set_target_property_value -property_records
  ="orcl_sys:oracle_dbsys:Line of Business:Marketing" -propagate_to_members
```

Template Collections

As mentioned earlier, *template collections* are used to provide a consistent set of metrics to a group of similar targets. Monitoring templates are created by target type, and are bundled together to form a template collection. A separate collection should be created for each node in the hierarchy. For example, a Production Targets group would be associated with a Production Targets template collection consisting of monitoring metrics of different target types. Once these templates have been associated, Use of template collections helps you to automate the deployment of monitoring standards using the metric thresholds and policies defined in the monitoring templates.

To create a template collection, choose Setup ➤ Add Targets ➤ Administration Group. Click the Template Collections tab to create the collections, as shown in Figure 7-16. This assumes that you have already created your monitoring templates for your targets. See the *Oracle Enterprise Manager Cloud Control 12c Administrator's Guide* for details on setting up monitoring templates.

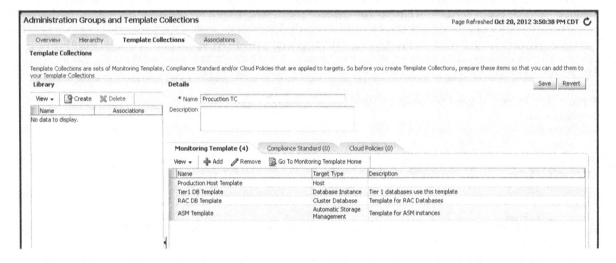

Figure 7-16. *Adding template collections*

There should be one monitoring template for each target type in the administration group node. Monitoring templates should be carefully designed so as to provide effective monitoring while reducing white noise. Review the monitoring templates after they have been created to ensure that key components are being monitored.

After all required template collections have been created, click the Associations tab to associate each node in the hierarchy with a template collection starting at the second level (the level after the All Administration Group). All targets that are members of the node as well as targets within the subgroups will inherit the metrics of the templates. You can see that this association of nodes with template collections greatly enhances the ability to automatically enforce standards within the IT infrastructure. Review each node in the hierarchy to verify that the state has a valid association. Look for the words *Valid Association*, as shown in Figure 7-17.

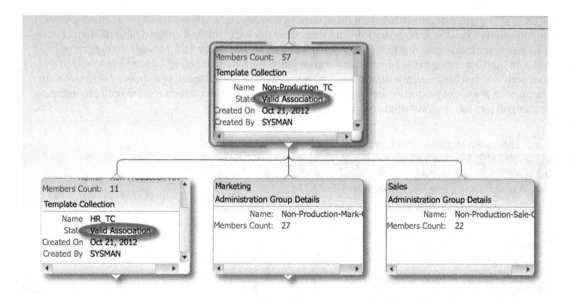

Figure 7-17. *Template collection associations applied to the Non-Production_TC and HR_TC groups*

The Non-Production_TC and HR_TC nodes in Figure 7-17's hierarchy have valid associations, while the Marketing and Sales groups have no valid associations. This is because the Sales and Marketing groups have inherited the Non-Production_TC template collection that has been directly associated with the Non-Production group. There is no template collection directly associated with Marketing, nor with Sales. The HR_TC group, however, *has been associated* with its own template collection. Thus, it shows the Valid Association status.

It is important to understand that the aggregate metrics are applied based on the combination of monitoring templates. If HR_TC has metrics in common with the top-level Non-Production group, those in the lower level take precedence. Use the View Aggregate Settings option shown in Figure 7-18 to see all the metrics that will be applied to the targets.

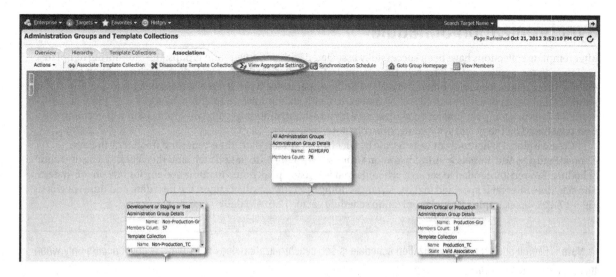

Figure 7-18. *Accessing the View Aggregate Settings option from the Administration Groups and Template Collections page*

Check if there are targets that are not being monitored using the standards defined via administration groups and template collections. Click the Actions drop-down menu at the top left of the Associations tab, and then choose Unassigned Targets Report, as shown in Figure 7-19. You will then be shown the targets that are missing one or more properties defined according to the administration group hierarchy. Remember, all targets have to match all membership criteria defined for the administration group hierarchy. That means that if you choose *LifeCycle Status* and *Line of Business* as the target properties for the administration hierarchy, then targets require both properties to be set before they will join an administration group.

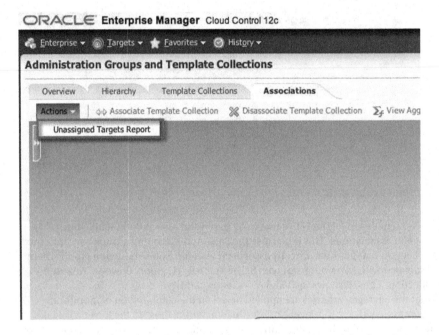

Figure 7-19. *How to access the Unassigned Targets Report option from the administration group*

Synchronization Schedule

After template collections have been successfully associated with administration groups, the monitoring templates are immediately applied to the targets in the administration groups. If there are pending synchronization operations, the synchronization schedule comes into effect. Pending operations typically result from changes to a monitoring template that is part of a template collection associated with an administration group. In addition, if there are modifications to a template collection associated with an administration group, synchronization will occur on the next date based on the global synchronization schedule.

Create a global synchronization schedule by specifying the start date, time zone, and frequency in days. Choose Setup ➤ Add Targets ➤ Administration Groups. Select the Associations tab, and then click Synchronization Schedule. It is recommended to set up a schedule that is outside peak hours to minimize any impact on the system. The schedule interval is specified in days, so any pending operations will occur on the next date and time specified. Figure 7-20 is an example of a synchronization schedule set for 12:01AM daily.

■ **Note** Even though the synchronization schedule is set, synchronization does not always occur. It occurs only when there are pending operations.

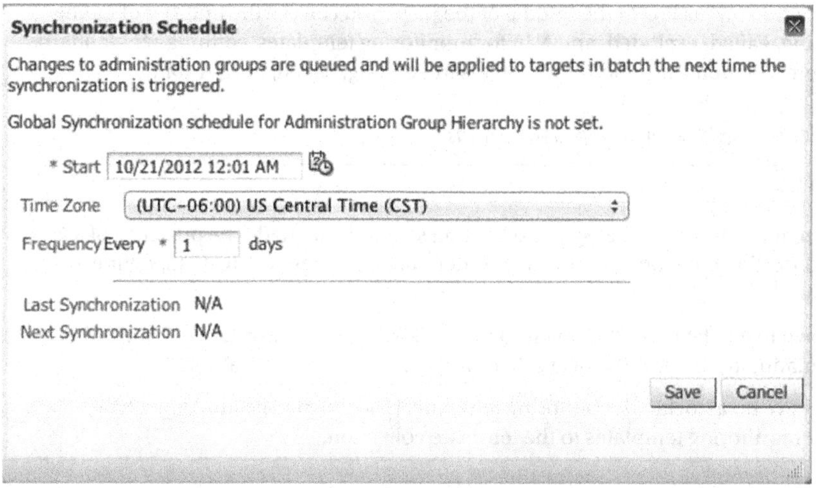

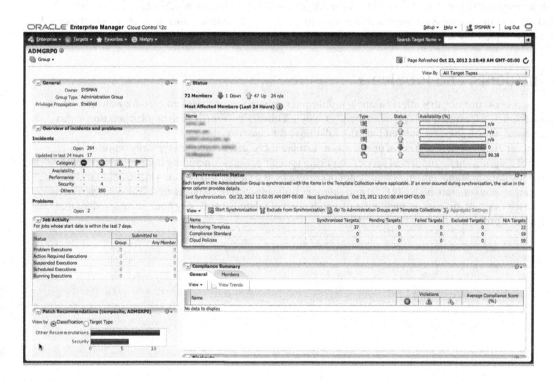

Synchronization Schedule

Changes to administration groups are queued and will be applied to targets in batch the next time the synchronization is triggered.

Global Synchronization schedule for Administration Group Hierarchy is not set.

* Start   10/21/2012 12:01 AM

Time Zone   (UTC-06:00) US Central Time (CST)

Frequency Every * 1   days

Last Synchronization   N/A
Next Synchronization   N/A

Save   Cancel

Figure 7-20. *The Global Synchronization Schedule setup page in Enterprise Manager Cloud Control 12c*

Once the synchronization schedule has been created and has successfully completed at least once, you can periodically check the Synchronization Status region of the topmost administration group (see Figure 7-21). That region displays the synchronization status of all targets in the hierarchy.

Figure 7-21. *The Synchronization Status in Administration Group page*

In Figure 7-21, in the Synchronization Status box in the middle of the page, you can see the number of targets with statuses of Synchronized, Pending, Failed, Excluded, and N/A for monitoring templates, compliance standards, and cloud policies. Follow the recommendations in Table 7-1 for targets in Pending, Failed, or N/A status.

Table 7-1. *Recommendations for Action Based on Synchronization Status*

Synchronization Status	What to Do
Pending Targets	Ensure that you have a global synchronization schedule defined. The presence of a Next Synchronization date indicates that one is defined. If you see N/A instead, define a schedule.
Failed Targets	Drill down to get details of the specific failures. Fix them where possible. Then either resync manually, or allow the next scheduled synchronization to take place.
N/A Targets	Targets have no associated monitoring template. Drill down to get the target type, and add monitoring templates to the template collection.

Incident Management Recommendations

Monitoring the database environment also means making sure that if any of your targets encounter any issues, you are made aware of them quickly—ideally before any of your clients become aware. It also means that if any operations occur that are of interest (normal or otherwise), that they will be addressed as needed.

What about impending problems? We need to be made aware of these too, and resolve them before they become disasters. EM12c provides the tools for the solution in the form of events, incidents, rules, and rule sets. In this section, you will see how to effectively employ these features to simplify and automate the monitoring requirements.

Events, Incidents, and Problems

An *event* is a discrete occurrence that affects a single monitored target in Enterprise Manager—for example, when a listener goes down or a filesystem fills up or an archiver hangs. Other occurrences such as job operation status changes (completed, failed, stopped, suspended) also fall under the category of events.

An *incident* can be thought of as a set of one of more correlated events. An incident typically represents the occurrence of a significant disruption of service requiring specific actions—including tracking, assignment, escalation, and resolution. Management of significant occurrences as a single unit is done via incidents and not events. A host target may generate high CPU (%) and memory utilization events (see Figure 7-22). A single event occurrence by itself may not indicate an incident, but a collection of related events may point to an incident that describes a resource problem.

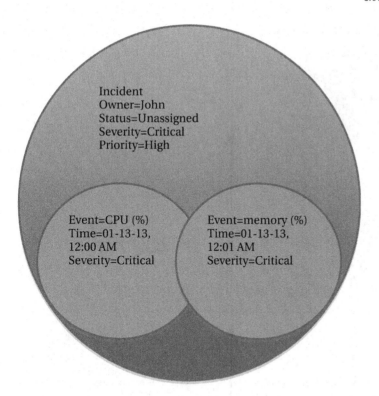

Incident
Owner=John
Status=Unassigned
Severity=Critical
Priority=High

Event=CPU (%)
Time=01-13-13,
12:00 AM
Severity=Critical

Event=memory (%)
Time=01-13-13,
12:01 AM
Severity=Critical

Figure 7-22. *Incident/event relationship for multiple events*

In addition to events and incidents, there is the concept of *problems*. Problems can be viewed as the source or root cause of incidents. They currently manifest themselves as errors in Oracle software. Problems are outside the scope of this discussion, as they can really be anything that causes an interruption or degradation of service. Rodents running loose under your server room floor, for example, can be a problem if they chew through wires and cause downtime.

■ **Note**   One of the challenges of a DBA's job is to constantly deal with problems that cannot all be foreseen. Indeed, the presence of a heretofore new problem is part of the "spice" that makes DBA work enjoyable and rewarding. Yet at the same time, we strive for the routine. Such is the inherent tension in our line of work.

Effectively managing incidents helps us to achieve better operational efficiency, helping us take control of the overall health of our system. Using a centralized incident management console allows us to view, manage, diagnose, and resolve incidents from a single location. A complete discussion of incident management is handled in Chapter 12. The diagram in Figure 7-23 shows the workflow of events and incidents using EM12c.

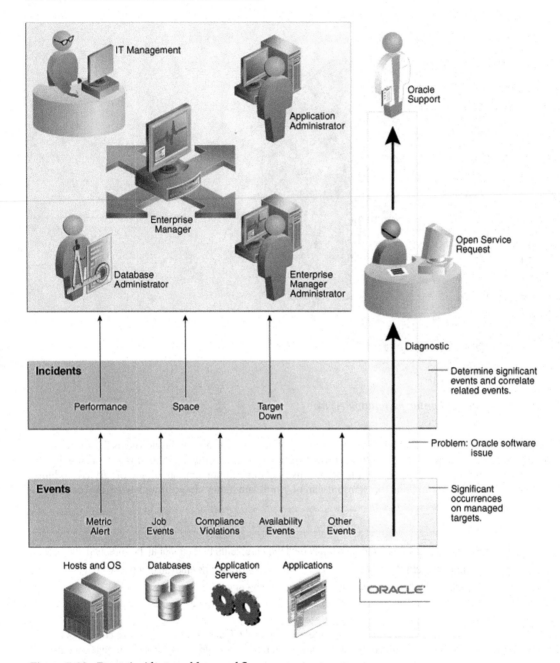

Figure 7-23. *Event, incident, problem workflow*

Rules and Rule Sets

Now that you understand events and incidents, you can begin to look at how to use them. *Rules* tell us the action or actions that should be performed when an event or incident meets certain criteria. These actions include sending an e-mail or page, opening a service-desk ticket, escalating the incident, or even generating another incident.

You can also specify different actions to take depending on the severity of the event. For example, if a Filesystem Space Used (%) rule generates a *warning* event, you may wish to send an e-mail notification. Then, if the same rule generates a *critical* event, you may send a page notification, to wake up the on-call DBA.

Many other actions can be performed for each type of rule. Table 7-2 summarizes each type of rule, and their usages for different scenarios.

Table 7-2. *Rule Types and Their Best Uses*

Type of Rules	Best Used to . . .
Event rule	• Create incidents based on events
	• Create help-desk tickets for incidents
	• Send events to third-party management systems
	• Send e-mail for specific events of interest (for example, send e-mail to business users if target is down)
Incident rule	• Automate incident workflow operations (for example, assign incident)
	• Send notifications on incidents
	• Create help-desk tickets for incidents (for example, create ticket if incident is escalated to level 2)
Problem rule	• Automate problem workflow operations (for example, assignment, prioritization, and so forth)
	• Send notifications on problems

Individual rules can be combined into sets for easier management. Rule sets possess the following attributes:

Name: An identifier for the rule set

Description: A brief statement of the rule set's purpose

Applies To: A list of objects to which the rules in the set apply

Owner: The administrator in Enterprise Manager who created the rule set

Enabled: An indicator of whether the rule set has been applied

Type: Denotes an Enterprise or Private rule set

Think about the order of rules within a rule set, and group similar rules together. Consider rules to create incidents, perhaps by sending an e-mail or creating a trouble ticket. Also consider rules to manage incidents, perhaps by escalating them. Duration-based rules should be put last.

Groups and systems should be used as targets for rule sets. It is recommended to use administration groups if they have been defined. Your defining an administration group hierarchy will enable rules to be applied automatically to new targets as they are added to administration groups by specifying their target properties.

Rules for the same group should be combined into one rule set. For example, in Figure 7-24, the PROD-GROUP rule set is applied to all targets whose LifeCycle Status = 'Production'.

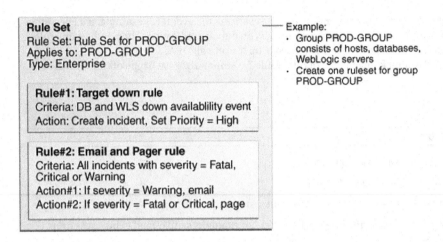

Figure 7-24. *Rule set application*

You can, and should, automatically create incidents by using rules. You will want to set up rules in your rule set that will create incidents based on events. These rules should be defined first in the rule set.

Enterprise Manager comes with out-of-the-box rule sets that create incidents for some significant events such as target down or target unreachable. One such rule set is named *Incident Management Ruleset for All Targets,* shown in Figure 7-25.

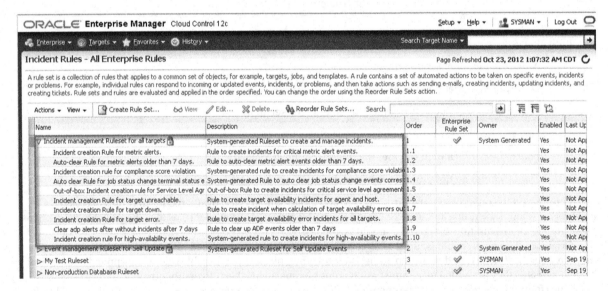

Figure 7-25. *Out-of-the-box rule set named Incident Management Ruleset for All Targets, as seen in the Enterprise Manager console*

Avoid using the out-of-the-box rule sets. Instead, create your own based on these stock rule sets by using the Create Like option in the Enterprise Manager console. Once you have created your rule set, you can disable the out-of-the-box rule sets.

Metric Collection Errors

The users monitoring a target should be configured so that their passwords do not expire or get locked. That's because expired or locked passwords result in metric collection errors. For example, the database user configured to monitor the database instance and cluster database targets by default is the DBSNMP user. Starting in Oracle Database 11g, the DBSNMP profile settings are configured to expire passwords after 180 days. So after six months, your ability to monitor goes away. Don't let that happen.

Create a separate profile that disables password expiration, and assign that profile to the monitoring user. For example, you can create a profile named DBSNMP_MONITOR, and assign that profile to user DBSNMP. Then make sure the profile allows unlimited password lifetime.

Enterprise security policies sometimes mandate changing passwords for such accounts. Such policies can be inconvenient, but they are a fact of life. You will need to change passwords on the required schedule. Then ensure that you update target monitoring properties so that they are continuously monitored. It's ideal if you can script or otherwise automate password resets, and also the needed updating of monitoring properties that is subsequent to them.

Summary

You have seen that Enterprise Manager Cloud Control 12c provides a standardized monitoring solution for IT infrastructure and applications. It provides increased operational efficiency by automating the workflow of assigning targets to groups, applying templates, and managing target memberships. With proper planning of standards and operational procedures, Enterprise Manager also provides significant benefits to administrators by enabling consistent event, incident, and problem management through rule sets. Finally, you have learned best practices for the aforementioned features that will make managing and monitoring your environment even more seamless when using EM12c.

■ ■ ■

CHAPTER 8

Managing Engineered Systems

by Bobby Curtis and Anand Akela

Oracle engineered systems are sets of pre-integrated hardware and software aimed at reducing the complexity and cost of enterprise infrastructures while increasing the productivity and performance of critical business systems. A few of the engineered systems are designed for specific functions within the enterprise. For example, the Oracle Exadata Database Machine was originally designed for data warehousing, yet its current release has been expanded to support both data warehousing and online transaction processing (OLTP). Other engineered systems serve a more general purpose. For example, the Oracle Database Appliance provides a two-node Real Application Cluster s(RAC)–ready solution for small to medium businesses.

Engineered systems include the complete hardware infrastructure (such as servers, storage, and networking) that would normally be separate entities in traditional configurations. These engineered systems also come with a complete software stack that runs the system out of the box. The unification of hardware and software at this level allows for fast implementation cycles.

In this chapter, you will take a look at engineered systems and how they can be managed with Oracle Enterprise Manager 12c, as well as how these systems can be viewed and monitored.

Types of Engineered Systems

Before you dive into how to manage engineered systems, let's look at a summary of the engineered systems that Oracle provides:

> *Oracle Exadata Database Machine*: Provides extreme performance, by off-loading queries to the storage-cell layer, for all database applications including OLTP and data warehousing. Ideal platform for consolidating database workloads to the private cloud or to a data center.

> *Oracle Exalogic Elastic Cloud*: Provides blazing-fast performance for enterprise applications (Java, Oracle applications, or third-party applications) and middleware to help businesses perform faster, whether in the data center or in the cloud.

> *Oracle SPARC SuperCluster T4-4*: Provides a general-purpose solution that delivers high performance, availability, scalability, and security across Oracle and third-party applications. Ideal for consolidating diverse environments, this engineered system is powered by the new SPARC T4 processor and Oracle Solaris 11. Offers the benefits of both the Oracle Exadata Database Machine and Oracle Exalogic Elastic Cloud in a single engineered system.

> *Oracle Database Appliance*: Provides an excellent in-the-box solution for midrange database workloads. Designed to help the small to midsize businesses or individual business units deploy an enterprise-level solution in record time.

Oracle Exalytics In-Memory Machine: Provides the first engineered system for in-memory analysis for business intelligence (BI) modeling, forecasting, and planning applications, along with advanced data visualization for actionable insight to large data sets.

Oracle Big Data Appliance: Provides optimized hardware and software to deliver a complete, easy-to-deploy solution for acquiring, organizing, and loading unstructured data into Oracle Database.

Sun ZFS Storage Appliance: Provides robust, efficient, and fast data storage for customers using network-attached storage (NAS) for enterprise applications, virtualization, private/public cloud deployments, storage consolidation, and data protection.

Engineered Systems Lifecycle

Oracle Enterprise Manager provides comprehensive management of Oracle engineered systems throughout the lifecycle of the applications or databases deployed on these systems. There are four stages in the engineered systems lifecycle, as shown in Figure 8-1:

- Planning and setup of the engineered systems
- Testing the engineered systems for deployment
- Managing for optimal performance and efficiency
- Maintaining for compliance and functionality improvements

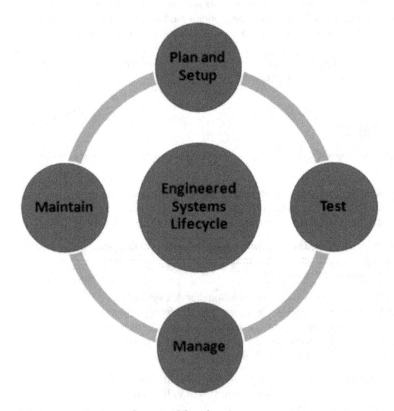

Figure 8-1. *Engineered systems lifecycle*

Although all the Oracle engineered systems share this lifecycle and can be managed from Oracle Enterprise Manager 12c, the examples throughout this chapter are for the Oracle Exadata Database Machine.

Supported Hardware and Software

Before delving into the various phases of the engineered system lifecycle, it is good to understand which hardware and software is supported by EM12c. The following Exadata Database Machine configurations are supported with plug-ins for 12.1.0.1, 12.1.0.2, and 12.1.0.3:

- V2
- X2-2
- X2-8
- X3-2
- X3-8
- Partitioned

Parts of the supported configurations are the components that come with the Exadata Database Machine. These components are supported in EM12c:

- Exadata Storage Server Software 11g Release 2 (11.2.2.3.0 through 11.2.3.2)
- InfiniBand Switch Release 1.1.3.0.0 to 1.3.3.2.0
- Integrated Lights Out Manager (ILOM), 3.0.9.27.a r58740
    - ILOM IPMItool Release 1.8.10.3 (for Oracle Linux)
    - ILOM IPMItool Release 1.8.10.4 (for Oracle Solaris)
- Avocent MergePoint Unity KVM Switch Release 1.2.8
- Power Distribution Unit Release 1.04
- Cisco—Cisco IOS Software, Catalyst 4500 L3 Switch Software (cat4500-IPBASE-M), Version 12.2(46)SG, RELEASE SOFTWARE (fc1)

With every new revision of an Oracle product, some items become desupported. The Exadata Database Machine has a few desupported hardware components. The following hardware configurations have been desupported with Oracle Enterprise Manager 12c or 12c Bundle Pack 1 (BP1):

- V1 hardware
- Super Clusters
- Expansion rack
- Multirack Exadata Database Machine

▪ **Note**   In the Exadata plug-in releases 12.1.0.1 and 12.1.0.2, using client network hostnames for compute nodes as Oracle Enterprise Manager target names is not supported. This is supported in the 12.1.0.3 plug-in.

With the evolution of technology, hardware standards change and provide new ways of performing tasks. Engineered systems, especially the Oracle Exadata Database Machine, are susceptible to these changes. EM12c's plug-in architecture was designed to work with not only the software stack but also the hardware stack. Moving forward, this plug-in architecture will allow for changes in existing engineered systems and future releases of the hardware.

Planning and Setup Phase

After an Oracle Exadata Database Machine arrives on site and has been acclimated to its surroundings, it can be configured with the network. The next task is to set up monitoring for the machine with EM12c.

■ **Note** The Oracle Exadata Database Machine is a complex piece of enterprise infrastructure. Its compact design makes it susceptible to condensation if it is not acclimated to its environment. We recommend letting it sit on site for 48 to 72 hours before plugging it in for configuration.

Although EM12c can monitor Exadata out of the box, you still need to plan and configure monitoring before deploying applications to the Exadata and using its capabilities. Typically, the following steps are performed in order to configure the Exadata for proactive monitoring:

1. Install the management agents to compute nodes.

2. Launch autodiscovery.

3. Specify component credentials.

4. Review configurations and complete setup.

After following these simple steps to discover Oracle Exadata Database Machine components, the configuration can be completed in a few minutes.

Installing the Management Agent

As with anything in Oracle Enterprise Manager, the first step starts with deploying the management agents to the Oracle Exadata compute nodes and then pushing the Oracle Exadata plug-in to the agents.

■ **Note** Oracle Exadata monitoring, like monitoring any other target in EM12c, is done through a set of plug-ins that is deployed at the management server and the agents.

Figure 8-2 shows how the EM12c agent interacts with the Exadata plug-in and other components of the Exadata Database Machine.

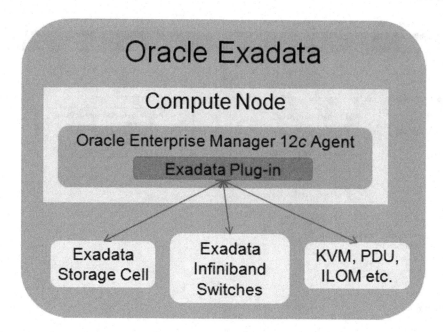

Figure 8-2. Oracle Enterprise Manager 12c agent and Exadata plug-in

Deploying the management agent to the compute nodes is done the same way as deploying the agent through Oracle Enterprise Manager for any other host target. The preferred method is to push the agent from Enterprise Manager. This process is discussed in more detail in Chapter 2.

Launching Autodiscovery

Once the management agents and Exadata plug-ins have been deployed, you can perform automatic discovery of targets to pull the Exadata components into EM12c.

As with many targets types in EM12c, there is a wizard-driven discovery for Exadata. Exadata hardware can be added automatically through this wizard. To access the wizard from the Enterprise Manager home page, choose Setup ➤ Add Targets ➤ Add Targets Manually. The page that you land on should look like Figure 8-3.

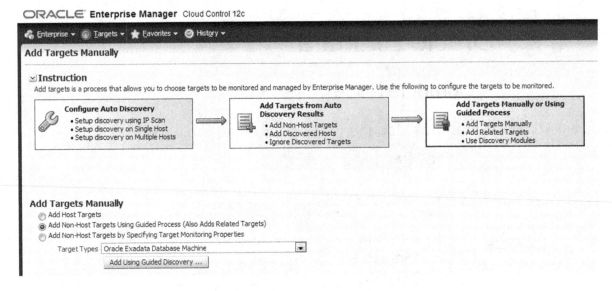

Figure 8-3. *Add Targets Manually page*

Once on the Add Targets Manually page, select the radio button for adding a Non-Host target. This enables you to then select the Oracle Exadata Database Machine option from the drop-down menu. Finally, click the button to use the guided discovery process.

This takes you to the Oracle Exadata Database Machine Discovery page, shown in Figure 8-4. Here you have the option of either adding a new database machine with associated hardware or discovering newly added hardware. After selecting an option, click the Discover Targets button.

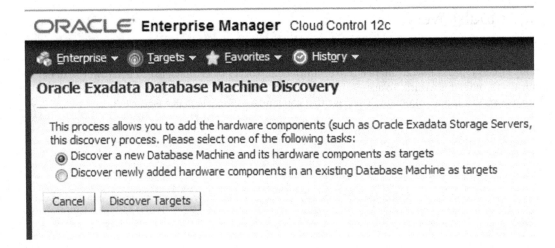

Figure 8-4. *Oracle Exadata Database Machine Discovery page*

Specifying Component Credentials

After clicking the Discover Targets button, EM12c launches the Database Machine Discovery Wizard, shown in Figure 8-5. The wizard will walk you through the ten steps needed to add an Exadata Database Machine to EM12c. During each of the discovery steps, the user is requested to provide login credentials for the various Oracle Exadata components such as Exadata cells and InfiniBand switches.

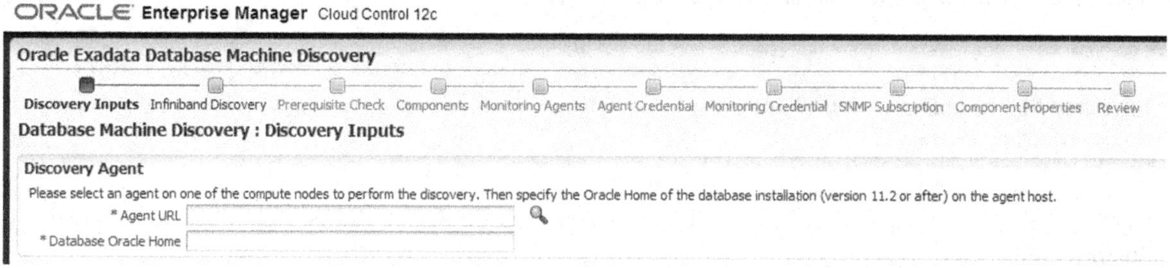

Figure 8-5. *Database Machine Discovery Wizard*

As you work through the discovery wizard, on the SNMP Subscription step (Figure 8-6), it is best to enable SNMP subscriptions on the cell and InfiniBand switch targets. This allows the management agent to automatically receive SNMP traps from the components being monitored.

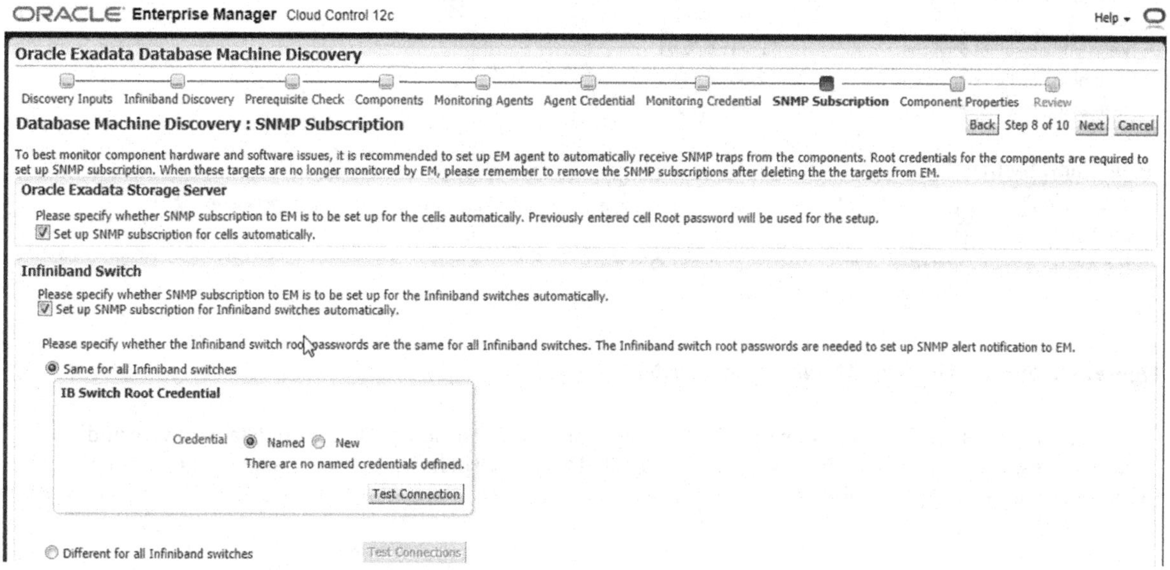

Figure 8-6. *SNMP Subscription step*

Reviewing Configuration and Completing Setup

Finally, when the wizard completes, you will be on the Review screen, shown in Figure 8-7. Verify all information before clicking Submit and finishing the discovery wizard. You then land on the Target Creation Summary page; click OK. This brings you to the Target Promotion page, where the targets are now displayed as managed targets.

Oracle Exadata Database Machine Discovery

Discovery Inputs   Components   Monitoring Agents   Agent Credential   Component Credential   Component Properties   **Review**

Database Machine Discovery : Review

The following options are selected:

- The monitoring agents are automatically selected.
- The monitoring agents have the same credential.

Please verify the following information. You can click on Back to revise the inputs or click on Submit to complete the discovery process.

Compute Node

The following compute nodes will be added as members of the Database Machine target.

Host Name
hostname1.mycompany.com
hostname2.mycompany.com

Oracle Exadata Storage Server

The following Exadata Storage Servers will be added as managed targets. The cells have the same credential.

Cell Name	Management IP
hostname2.mycompany.com	12.345.678.01
hostname3.mycompany.com	12.345.678.02
hostname4.mycompany.com	[IP Address]

Infiniband Switch

The following Infiniband switches will be added as managed targets. The Infiniband switches have the same credential.

Infiniband Switch Name	Description
IB-switch-name1.mycompany.com	Sun DCS 36 QDR switch
IB-switch-name2.mycompany.com	Sun DCS 36 QDR switch

Figure 8-7. *Exadata Database Machine Discovery Review page*

After the Exadata monitoring is set up, EM12c can provide a unified view of Oracle Exadata hardware and software, as shown in Figure 8-8. You can also see a detailed view of all of its components, such as the InfiniBand switches, storage cells, and so forth.

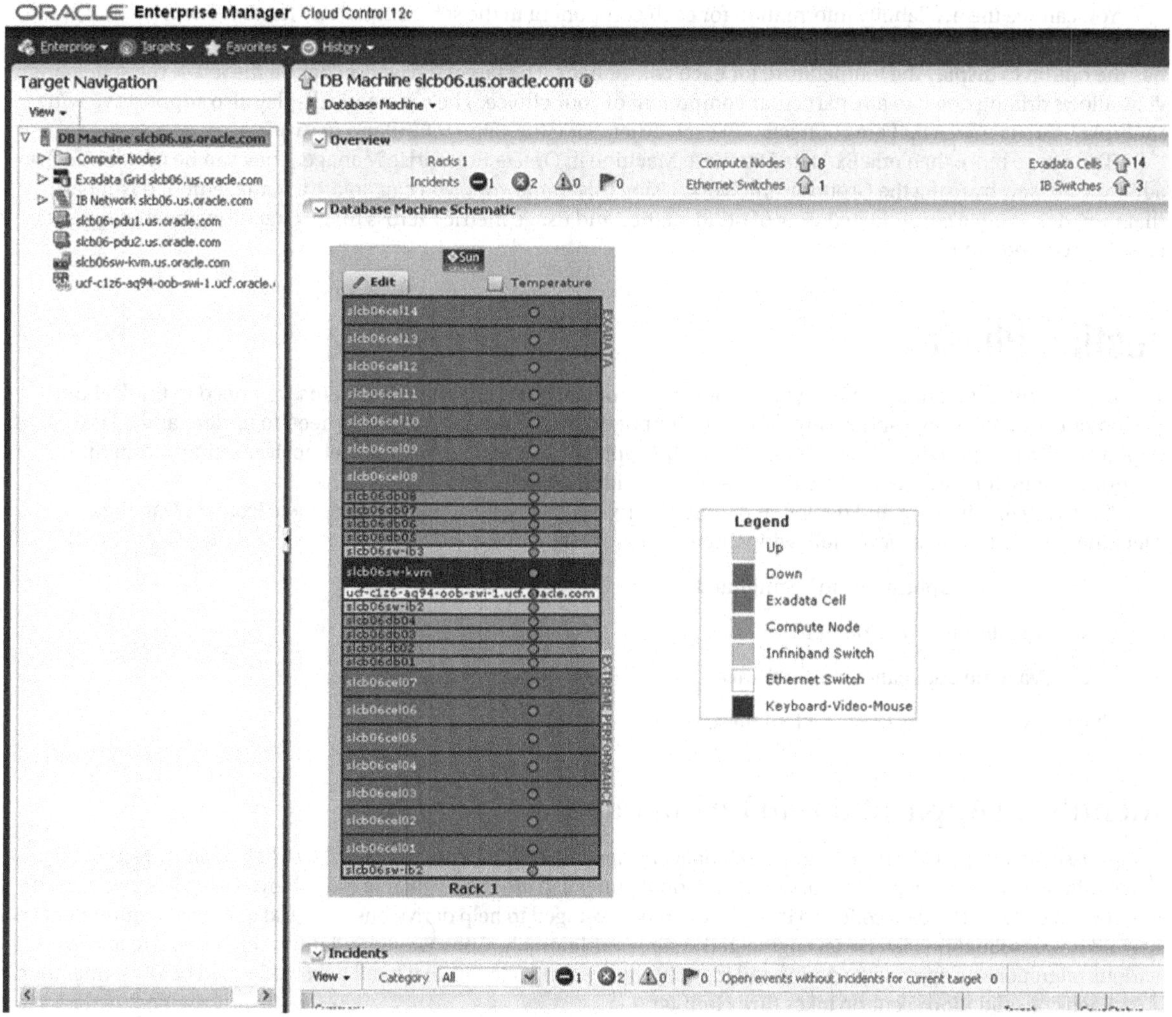

Figure 8-8. Oracle Exadata schematic view

■ **Note**   In addition to the automatic discovery process, an automation kit is available to help speed up the discovery. This kit simplifies the process of deploying the agent on each of the compute nodes by allowing the agent to be pushed to all compute nodes in one go.

More information on downloading and configuring the automation kit can be located in Doc ID: 1440951.1 in My Oracle Support.

You can see the availability information for each component in the schematic view. The Overview section at the top shows the summary of incidents and availability information for all targets within the database machine. It also has the option to display the temperature for each component. The target navigation bar on the left of the schematic view allows drilling down to any particular component of your choice. The schematic display also supports viewing multiple Exadata nodes that are connected to each other using the same InfiniBand network.

If you have more than one Exadata Database Machine in Oracle Enterprise Manager, they can be monitored from a high-level view by using the Groups framework. Using this framework, you can create a management dashboard that provides a single consolidated view of performance and usage metrics across many Oracle engineered systems and their components.

Testing Phase

When you're migrating or upgrading your applications to the Oracle engineered systems, you need to think about any potential impacts on response time and throughput of the application. Also, you need to understand all the dependencies and potential risks that may affect the application and plan for comprehensive testing within the environment to mitigate any of those risks associated with the migration.

For a typical migration and deployment onto an engineered system, such as the Oracle Exadata Database Machine, you could consider the following three-step process:

1. Identify applications to be migrated.

2. Create a test environment.

3. Validate application performance.

The following sections cover each of these steps.

Identifying Applications to Be Migrated

As discussed in Chapter 5, Oracle Enterprise Manager Consolidation Planner can be used to help identify resources that could benefit from consolidation. Consolidation Planner can also be a valuable tool when looking to move to an engineered system. The data collected by EM12c can be leveraged to help derive business and technical requirements to validate consolidation plans to an engineered system. Additionally, Consolidation Planner can be used to analyze various migrations or upgrade scenarios and identify application concerns that need to be addressed before a migration. Each consolidation scenario takes three inputs:

- Details of the pre-consolidation environment

- Technical, business, or compliance constraints

- Details of the destination environment

■ **Note**　When creating a consolidation project as outlined in Chapter 5, you can optionally choose to generate three preconfigured consolidation scenarios to add to the project. These out-of-the-box scenarios represent conservative, aggressive, and medium consolidation schemas.

Once you have a consolidation project (P2P) created for moving a physical machine to an Exadata Database Machine, you can create a custom scenario to identify any applications that may be affected by the consolidation. In order to create a scenario, you have to use Consolidation Planner, which is accessible from the Enterprise menu. Once Consolidation Planner is open, highlight the desired P2P project and click the Create Scenario menu item, as shown in Figure 8-9. This opens the Create Scenario Wizard to allow a customer scenario to be defined.

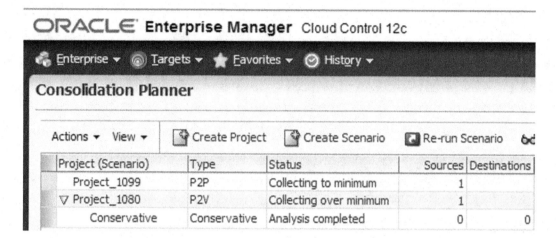

Figure 8-9. *Creating a scenario from Oracle Consolidation Planner*

When the Create Scenario Wizard starts, the default name of the scenario will be similar to the name of the project that it is associated with.

The first step of the Create Scenario Wizard is Resources, shown in Figure 8-10. Here you can specify scenario details, such as the name and description. You can also specify the resource requirements. Resource type(s), applicable days, time intervals, and the consolidation algorithm for estimating resource requirements can be defined as well. After providing all the resource requirements, click the Estimate Requirements button to show the requirements for the source server(s).

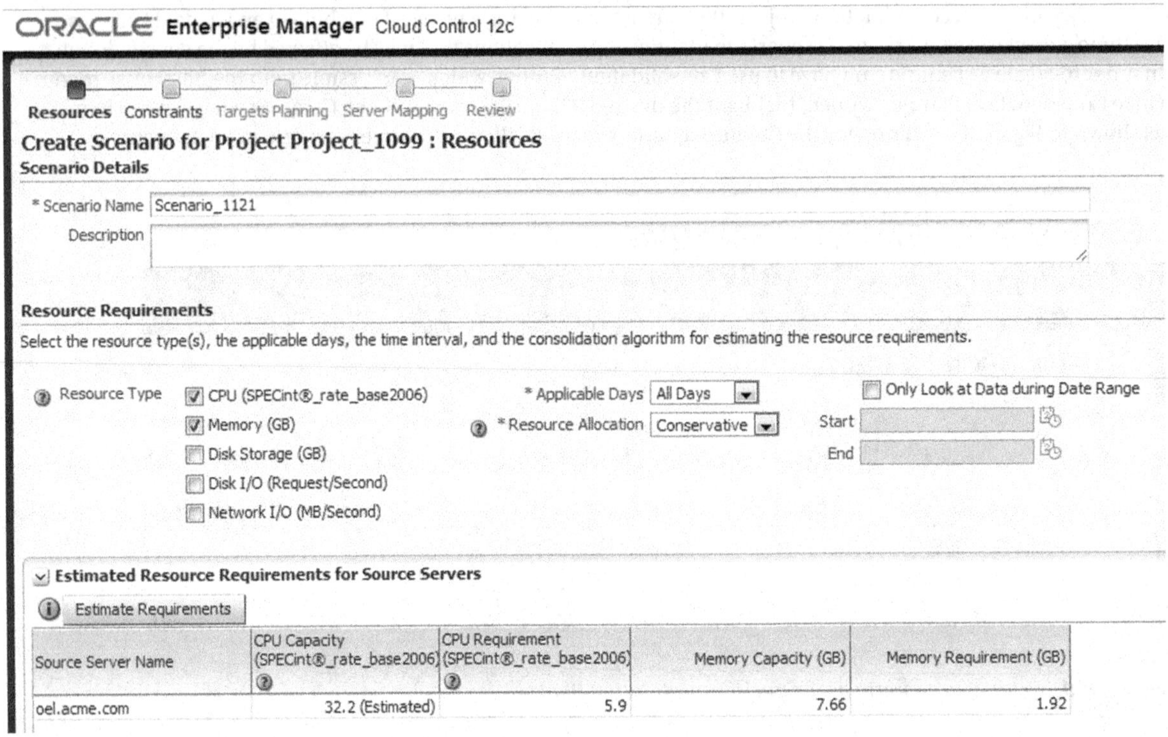

ORACLE Enterprise Manager Cloud Control 12c

Resources Constraints Targets Planning Server Mapping Review

Create Scenario for Project Project_1099 : Resources

Scenario Details

* Scenario Name Scenario_1121

Description

Resource Requirements

Select the resource type(s), the applicable days, the time interval, and the consolidation algorithm for estimating the resource requirements.

Resource Type ☑ CPU (SPECint®_rate_base2006)   * Applicable Days All Days ▾   ☐ Only Look at Data during Date Range
                ☑ Memory (GB)   * Resource Allocation Conservative ▾   Start
                ☐ Disk Storage (GB)   End
                ☐ Disk I/O (Request/Second)
                ☐ Network I/O (MB/Second)

▽ Estimated Resource Requirements for Source Servers

ⓘ Estimate Requirements

Source Server Name	CPU Capacity (SPECint®_rate_base2006)	CPU Requirement (SPECint®_rate_base2006)	Memory Capacity (GB)	Memory Requirement (GB)
oel.acme.com	32.2 (Estimated)	5.9	7.66	1.92

Figure 8-10. Defining resources in the Create Scenario Wizard

As you move through the wizard, you need to select servers that are compatible only with each other. Servers that are compatible should be consolidated together. On the Constraints screen, you have the options of specifying server properties, server configurations, and conditions that are requirements within your consolidation plan. Once all the constraints have been specified, the Preview Effect of Constraints option will be enabled and you will be able to see any incompatible servers. Figure 8-11 shows the Constraints screen with constraints defined.

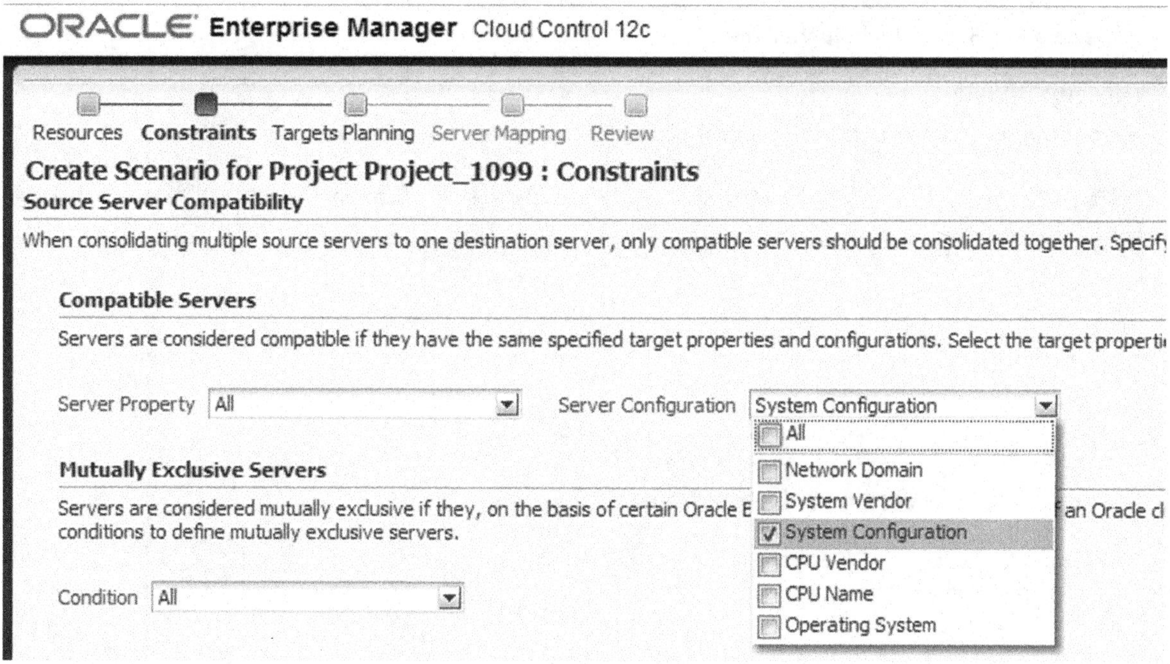

Figure 8-11. *Specifying constraints in the Create Scenario Wizard*

Clicking the Preview Effect of Constraints button opens a dialog box that shows the servers that are incompatible with the target server, as you can see in Figure 8-12. If there are any incompatible servers, adjust the constraints until there are none.

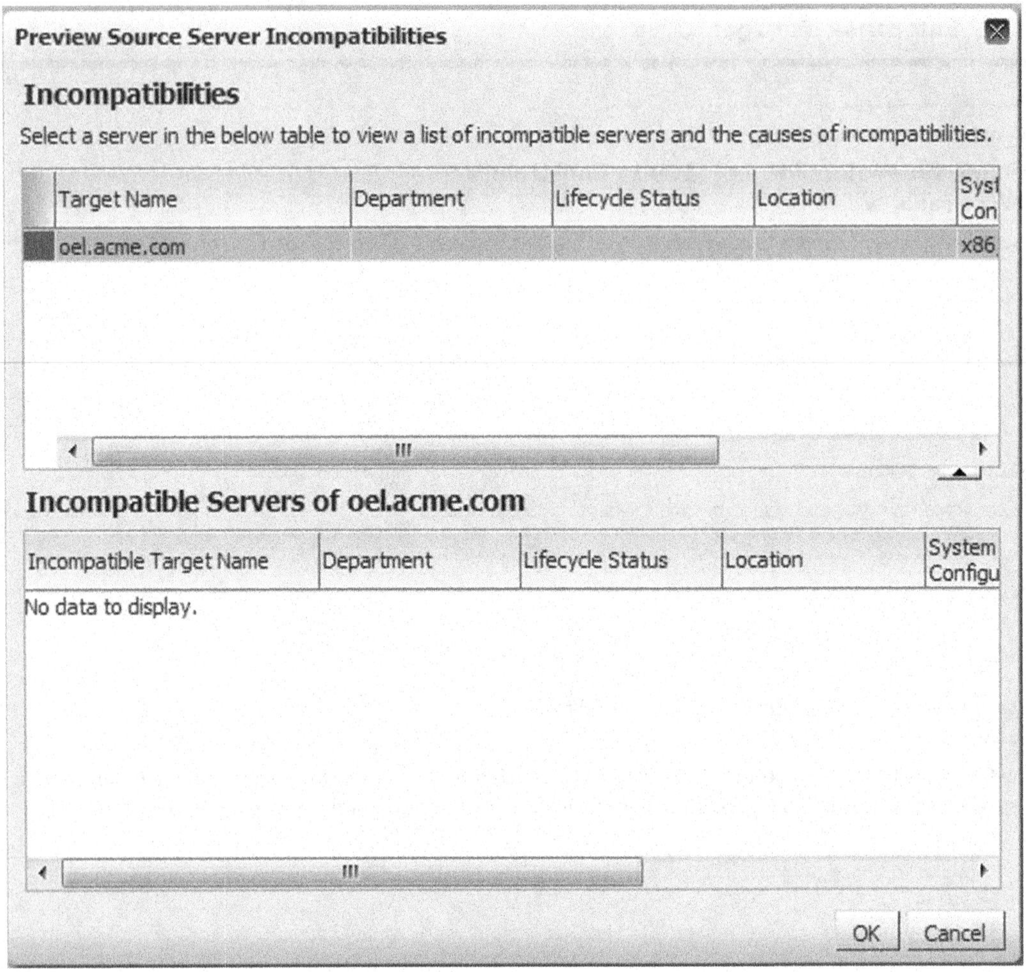

Figure 8-12. *Incompatibilities of servers*

After resolving any incompatibilities, the wizard moves you to the Targets Planning screen. Here you can identify destination candidates for the consolidation. By default, Oracle Enterprise Manager assumes you want to consolidate to a half-rack of Exadata Database Machine. Other options are available for Exadata Database Machine, along with generic servers or even using existing servers. In sticking with your examples of Exadata Database Machine, let's go with a full rack, as shown in Figure 8-13. On this screen, you can allocate the maximum resource utilization on the destination servers.

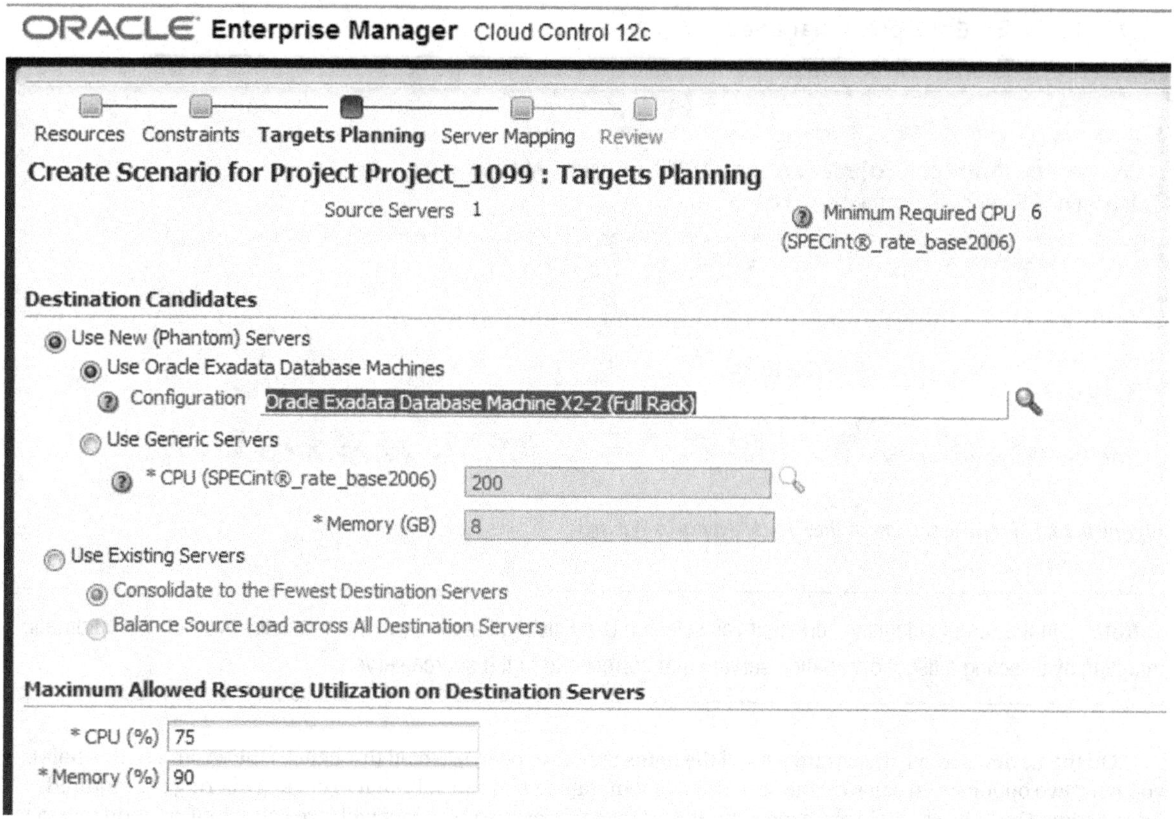

Figure 8-13. *Setting options for destination servers in the Create Scenario Wizard*

Once you have selected your planned target, it is time to map the source server to the destination servers. Since you stayed with the example of Exadata Database Machine, the Create Scenario Wizard is using automapping for our destination server (see Figure 8-14).

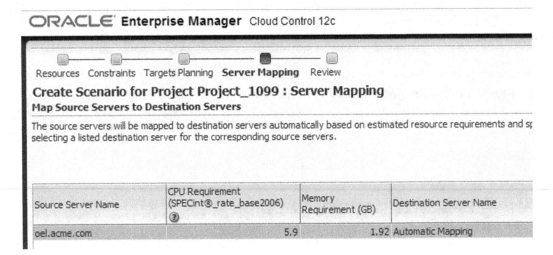

Figure 8-14. Mapping servers in the Create Scenario Wizard

■ **Note** On the Targets Planning screen, if you selected Use Existing Servers, you can manually override the automatic mapping by selecting a list of destination servers that correspond to the source servers.

On the Review screen, the wizard lists all the items that have been selected throughout the wizard. At this point, you have two options: you can save the scenario as a template or you can submit it to begin gathering the required information. Once the scenario has been submitted, Oracle Enterprise Manager will give you a confirmation message, as shown in Figure 8-15.

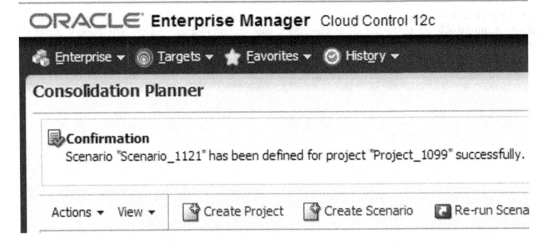

Figure 8-15. Confirmation of the submission

After the scenario job is completed, Consolidation Planner will generate a report and recommend an optimal consolidation plan. As you can see in Figure 8-16, it also details how consolidated workloads would perform on target servers.

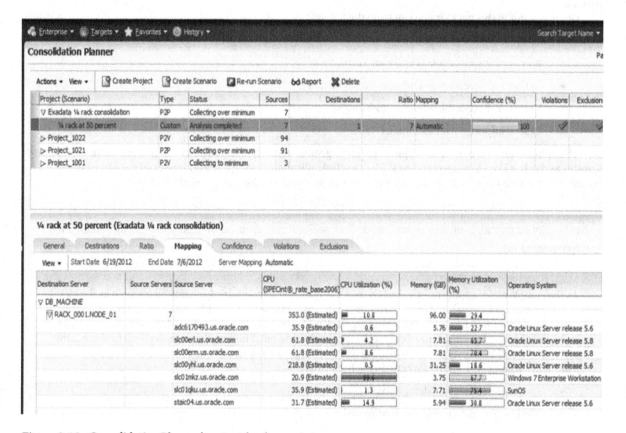

Figure 8-16. *Consolidation Planner's output for the scenario*

Just as Consolidation Planner is good for identifying how to consolidate physical resources to virtual ones, this valuable tool provides important information that can be helpful when considering moving physical servers to newer physical servers. Making a move to any engineered system by using Consolidation Planner can easily be scoped, identified, and executed with confidence.

Creating a Test Environment

After your scenario has completed running and yielded results that are acceptable, it is time to identify the applications to move and the details of the engineered system where the application will be moved to. You will need to create a test environment, which should mirror your target destination to some degree, to test and mitigate all potential risks associated with the migration.

As in any testing environment, storing a lot of data can be expensive, so idea subsets of data should be used. Oracle has developed two approaches to this concern: the Test Data Management Pack and the Oracle Application Testing Suite.

The Test Data Management Pack allows for data subsetting, data discovery, and modeling. The data subsetting functionality enables you to create a referentially intact subset of data on production, development, and test systems. Subsetting data for testing purposes makes testing easier by allowing you to select a percentage, 1% or 5%, of data required.

Other features in this pack enable you to do the following:

- Create/edit subset definitions

- Preview the subset details and space estimates

- Define and execute pre- and post-subset scripts

- Execute the subset definition across targets

- Export/import subset definitions

The second option is the Oracle Application Testing Suite, which is an extension to EM12c and enables the same features as the Test Data Management Pack. The Oracle Application Testing Suite addresses all the same concerns and provides a complete suite to create the test environment and perform the tests as needed.

▓ **Note**   More information on Oracle Application Testing Suite can be found at `http://otn.oracle.com` under Enterprise Manager.

As the complexity of applications increases, especially in shared computing environments such as the cloud, access to sensitive data increases. Access to this data, such as social security numbers, can be limited by masking it between environments. The Oracle Data Masking Pack replaces the original sensitive data with realistic-looking scrubbed data that has the same type of characteristics as the original. This enables organizations to share fully masked data and still be in compliance with both internal corporate governance and government regulations.

The Data Masking Pack enables you to do the following:

- Create or use masking definitions

- Mask real application testing workloads

- Define format libraries for reuse

- Export/import masking templates

- Export/import format libraries

EM12c, through the Data Masking Pack, introduced the ability to discover data dependency and modeling. This functionality allows you to discover data models and sensitive data in your environment so that you can protect them through data masking. Using Oracle's FAST (Find, Assess, Secure, and Test) methodology to implement data masking, you can create a test environment on Oracle Exadata that has all the sensitive information masked before proceeding with the next step of validating the performance of the system.

Additional data-masking features enable you to do the following:

- Create/edit application data models

- Manually define applications, schemas, and tables

- Use out-of-the-box metadata collection drivers for customer and packaged applications

- Define sensitive columns manually or by using sensitive column discovery

- Classify sensitive columns by sensitive types

- Define and manage sensitive types

- Export and import application data models

- Verify and associate definitions with multiple targets

These management packs allow you to define and extract test data that can be used in creating environments for testing on a variety of engineered systems and generic system platforms. Overall, these management packs help in defining, refining, and giving realistic testing results for migrations and consolidation efforts.

Validating Application Performance

After establishing your testing environment, you need to perform tests to validate that performance is acceptable compared to current production loads. Three tools that Oracle has developed to help with validating application performance are Database Replay, SQL Performance Analyzer, and SQL Tuning Sets. All of these capabilities are part of the Real Application Testing (RAT) suite. RAT is an option available with Oracle Database. RAT offers an ideal solution for validating production load performance in test environments.

The Database Replay feature provides the ability to capture production workloads, including online and batch workloads, and replay them against a test environment. It enables DBAs to test system changes, dependencies, and timings without the use of customized testing scripts. This saves both time and effort by reducing the time it takes to test, hence reducing overall testing cost. EM12c supplements RAT functionality by simplifying the process of saving and transferring the captured workload and performance data to the test system, setting up the test system, and replaying them via its central console.

■ **Note**   In order to use the features of Real Application Testing (RAT), you must purchase licenses. The only exception is SQL Tuning Sets, which can be licensed under either Oracle Tuning Pack or RAT.

EM12c also introduced Application Replay, functionality similar to Database Replay, for the middle tier. Application Replay provides the most efficient, optimized, and highest-quality testing for validating application infrastructure changes for all Web and packaged Oracle applications.

The SQL Performance Analyzer helps to predict and prevent SQL execution performance problems. It provides a detailed view of the impact of environment changes by running the SQL statements serially before and after the changes. It also generates a clear, detailed report outlining the impact on the workload due to the system change as well as the set of regressed SQL statements. The Oracle Enterprise Manager 12c Tuning Advisor supplements SQL Performance Analyzer and provides recommendations to optimize and tune the SQL statements for the best possible performance.

SQL Tuning Sets are groupings of SQL statements that serve as input to Automatic Database Diagnostic Monitor (ADDM)), SQL Tuning Advisor, or SQL Access Advisor. They are database objects that include one or more SQL statements with their associated execution statistics and context. These tuning sets are used to help the DBA perform automatic tuning of SQL statements and they can be exported to test systems where they can be evaluated and improved.

The three tools discussed in this section—Database Replay, SQL Performance Analyzer, and SQL Tuning Sets—were produced by Oracle to provide a methodological way for testing database loads. These tools work well individually. And together they provide a powerful way to monitor any environment, especially engineered systems.

Management Phase

After the database or application has been deployed in production, it's important to ensure that the applications perform optimally and meet the service levels expected. The integrated view of Oracle Exadata's hardware and software components in the EM12c console allows DBAs to navigate from the database performance page to the Oracle Exadata system health page. When Exadata is running correctly without issues, the system health button attached to the database is green. When Oracle Enterprise Manager detects an error, the system health button turns red, indicating a problem may be impacting the database availability.

There can be many reasons (for example, load imbalance, ASM-related problems, cell failures, cell configuration issues, or network-related failures) that can impact Exadata performance. EM12c can help troubleshoot and diagnose those problems in Exadata and other engineered systems. Automatic Database Diagnostic Monitor (ADDM) and Automatic Workload Repository (AWR) functionalities of the database are key tools to performance analysis with the Exadata Database Machine.

ADDM is a core part of the diagnostic infrastructure in the Oracle database. ADDM starts off with the analysis of snapshots based on key workload metrics taken within the database. These snapshots include critical performance information pertaining to the database kernel and the database workload as well as at the operating system level. ADDM runs on a regular basis, and it analyzes this information and makes recommendations on problems that it identifies.

For example, when there are SQL load issues, the SQL Advisors make recommendations on how to tune the SQL statements. Also when there are I/O or CPU issues, ADDM gives advice on system resource optimization. And if you are running a RAC, ADDM analyzes your complete RAC infrastructure, including the interconnect, and offers advice on how to improve overall performance.

AWR is a built-in repository, contained within the SYSAUX tablespace, that every Oracle database maintains about operational statistics. AWR is the foundation for all self-management functionality in the Oracle database. It is the primary source of information that keeps historical information on the Oracle database and how it is being used. The AWR repository and associated snapshots enable the database to make decisions that are specifically tailored for the environment it is operating in.

EM12c introduced a new tool to explore the Active Session History (ASH) data. ASH Analytics allows DBAs to analyze performance data across various performance dimensions. This ability to create filters on various dimensions really simplifies the identification of performance issues.

■ **Note**   Active Session History (ASH) is a PL/SQL package that has to be installed before it can be used. More information on ASH can be found in Chapter 9.

As shown in Figure 8-17, the drop-down menu of ASH Analytics allows administrators to explore performance data by using predefined performance dimension hierarchies.

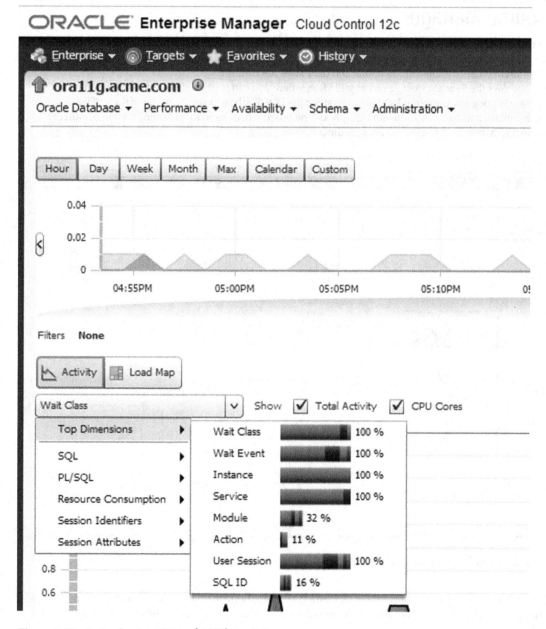

Figure 8-17. *Active Session History (ASH) Analytics*

The ASH Analytics feature can be used on any Oracle 11g database running on an Oracle Exadata Database Machine or on a non-Oracle platform. For example, by using the Wait event dimension, you can zero down onto Oracle Exadata specific wait events and resolve performance-related issues.

I/O Resource Manager

The Exadata I/O Resource Manager (IORM) is another key capability of Oracle Exadata that guarantees a database gets the minimal amount of I/O as defined in the resource plan at each storage server. Let's take an example of an Exadata environment where multiple applications and databases are running.

Figure 8-18 shows the Exadata storage server grid view, where you can see that the IORM is not enabled and the CRM database is not getting enough I/O resources since the DW database is hogging a lot of them. The DW database is a legitimate database, and you can't simply kill the process because it's consuming a lot of resources. You will need to find a more creative way to address the problem.

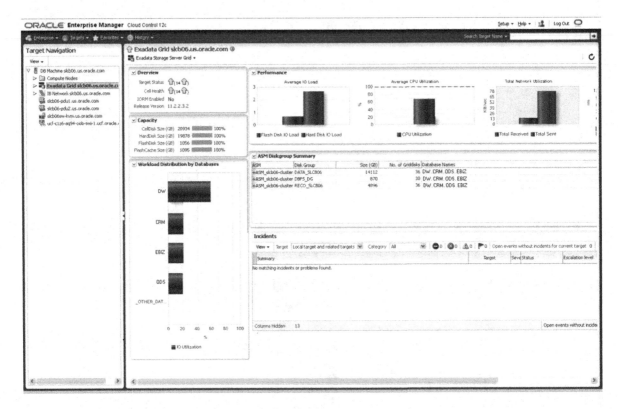

Figure 8-18. *Exadata storage server grid with IORM not enabled*

In Exadata, you can manage the allocation of I/O resources by enabling the IORM. You could configure the I/O allocation manually to allocate a fixed amount of I/O resources. You could also select predefined templates with fixed I/O allocations.

As you can see in Figure 8-19, we currently have IORM disabled; additionally, we do not have any internal interdatabase plans or disk I/O objectives enabled. To enable IORM, you need to change the desired setting and then click the Update All button. This enables all the changes selected, and the Exadata will start allocating resources by the defined I/O resource plan. There are predefined I/O templates that can be implemented as well.

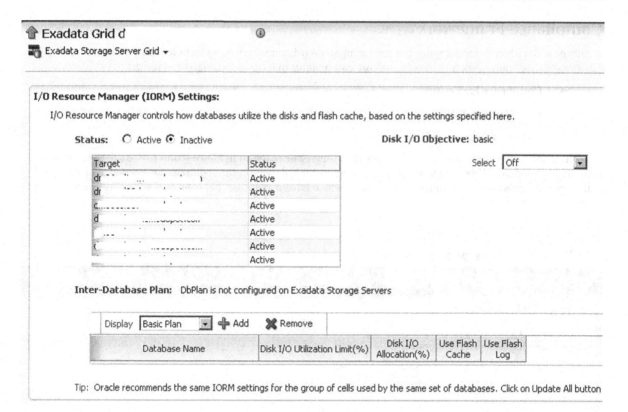

Figure 8-19. IORM settings

After enabling the IORM and allocating the resources needed, any performance bottlenecks should dissipate. When setting up an IORM plan, makes sure that the percentages allocated to resources meet service-level agreements (SLAs) that have been defined.

Maintenance Phase

After the application is deployed to production on an Oracle engineered system and you have ensured that the resources are optimally shared or assigned to databases, you also need to maintain the configuration within the environment. EM12c helps you ensure compliance across all components by using the Compliance Framework to evaluate the hosts and databases. The Compliance Framework proactively looks at the monitored environment and notifies you of potential environmental issues and associated patches needed.

Along with the Compliance Framework within EM12c, other robust solutions exist for maintaining the monitored environment configuration:

- Comprehensive Configuration Management

- Defect Diagnostics

- Automated Patching Solution

Although you will find a lot more details about these EM12c features in the rest of the book, let's look at them in little more detail in the context of Oracle engineered systems.

Compliance Framework

EM12c provides a hierarchical approach to managing standards across targets to include Exadata Database Machines. The Compliance Framework consists of three core components that can be managed and reused:

- Compliance Framework
- Compliance standards
- Compliance rules

The Compliance Framework is used to provide an aggregate of the compliance scores that are derived from the compliance standards. There can be more than one framework, depending on requirements needed to be complied with. Figure 8-20 shows the Compliance Dashboard, which is used to ensure that compliance is being followed with associated scores.

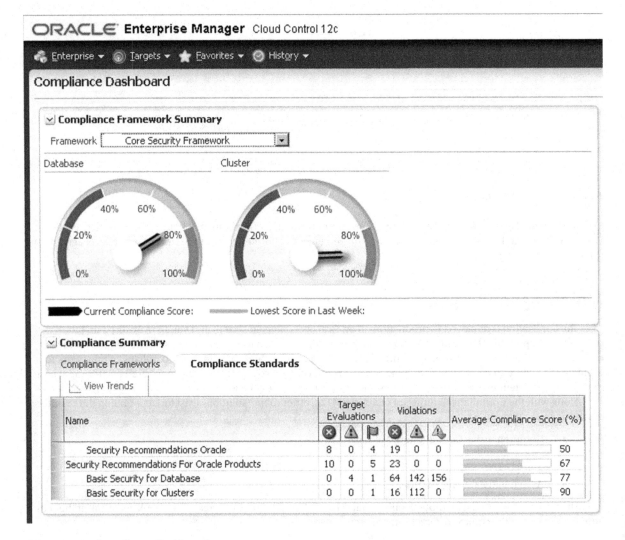

Figure 8-20. *Compliance Dashboard*

The compliance standards are the only part of the Compliance Framework that is associated with a managed target. The compliance rules are rules that are associated with the compliance standard. Once the compliance standard is associated with a target, the rules within the standard are executed against the target and stored in the Oracle Management Repository.

The results of the associated framework can be viewed from a high level on the Compliance Dashboard, as shown in Figure 8-20. For a more detailed view of the results, these compliance standards can be drilled into from the dashboard. Figure 8-21 show a more detailed view of the Security Recommendations Oracle standard.

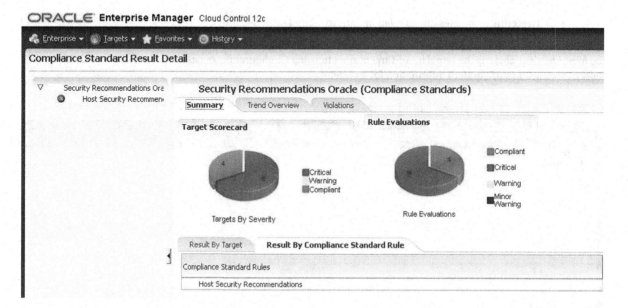

Figure 8-21. *Compliance standard result detail*

The Compliance Framework's associated standards and rules are a good way to keep a high-level view on the configurations within the infrastructure. This framework can be applied across all versions of hardware, including Oracle engineered systems.

Configuration Management

EM12c offers configuration management capabilities for Exadata, other engineered systems, and generic systems. Configuration management enables you to collect detailed information from a target, which is normally a large and rarely changing collection of information with nontrivial structure. These collections are collected rarely when compared to performance metrics. Configuration data should be affected only by administrators explicitly making changes to the target. Examples of changes that an administrator can make are patching or reconfiguring the target, such as changing file permissions on the Oracle home directory.

Configuration management within EM12c provides a number of features, including these:

- Infrequent collection of a relatively large set of related configuration data (daily)

- On-demand refresh and scheduled refresh of the configuration information

- Comparison of configurations to discover how they differ across targets

- Storage of configurations in the management repository as saved snapshots for later viewing, comparison, and other operations related to configurations

- Export of configurations into files and importing such files back into Enterprise Manager as saved snapshots

- Historical change tracking

- Powerful searches across all the configuration information in the enterprise or a subset of targets

- Triggering associates due to relationships to related targets

When looking for configurations through the Enterprise Manager user interface, configuration information can be found by right-clicking the target in All Targets and choosing Configuration ➤ Last Collected. Figure 8-22 illustrates how to access the configuration information for a target.

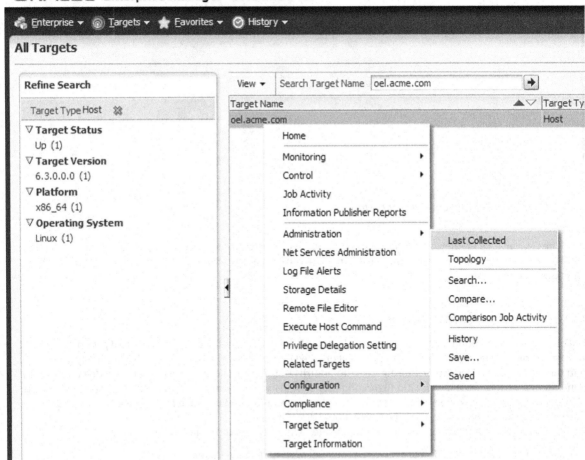

Figure 8-22. *Accessing configuration data*

Once you are on the last configuration page for the target, you are presented with a navigation tree on the left side of the screen and a series of tabs on the right side. These structures enable you to navigate the current configuration information associated with the target. Each target type will present a different navigation tree; the tab on the right will stay the same. Figure 8-23 shows an example of the latest configuration for an Oracle 11g database.

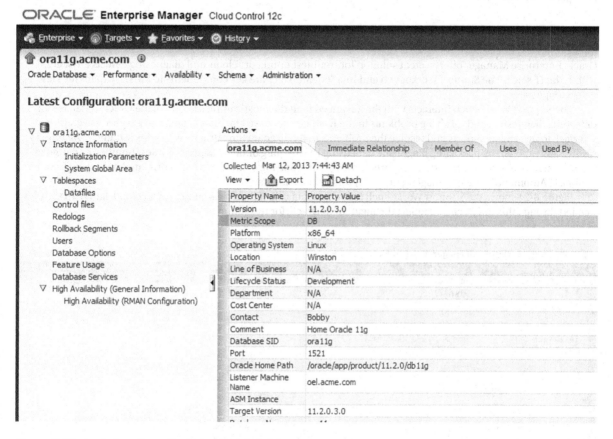

Figure 8-23. *Lastest configuration for an Oracle database*

When looking at the configuration for a database, a DBA can monitor and enforce the configurations of parameters associated with the initialization file (spfile), OS parameters, and cell configuration within Exadata or any other database. Configuration enforcement can be done by comparing two hosts that have the same configuration to identify any issues on one of the hosts. Comparison of configurations can also be done against a target's saved configuration, considered the gold standard, to determine whether any drift exists within the target's configuration.

■ **Tip**   Comparing target configurations or using a gold image for comparison requires a large amount of data. It is best to run comparisons during nonpeak hours.

Oracle Enterprise Manager can also compare the configurations of multiple Exadata Database Machines. Capabilities such as change history tracking or configuration management inventory help with configuration compliance as well. Oracle Enterprise Manager continuously captures the change events in the Oracle Exadata and can also generate comprehensive reports for configuration changes with details including what, when, and where the changes were done and by whom.

On many levels, change management can be used to identify current settings, compare changes, and track changes back to when they changed. Change management is a tool that not only DBAs, but also the whole IT department, will love.

Defect Diagnostics

Oracle Enterprise Manager offers a great solution for troubleshooting problems and diagnosing defects anywhere within the IT stack. The Support Workbench and Incident Manager are key components to EM12c capabilities for defect diagnostics.

The Support Workbench interacts with the advanced fault diagnostic infrastructure of the Oracle database for detecting, diagnosing, and resolving problems in the Exadata Database Machine. It offers an easy-to-use graphical interface to investigate reports and resolve the problems in the Exadata infrastructure. It helps minimize the time to resolve any problem by packaging diagnostic data using IPS, helping obtain a support request number, and uploading the IPS package to Oracle Support. It supports viewing and reporting of incidents with correlated packaging from the database, Automatic Storage Management (ASM) through to Exadata.

Figure 8-24 shows the Support Workbench for an Exadata cell. If there was an issue, you could gather all the files needed through this interface and report the incident to Oracle for resolution.

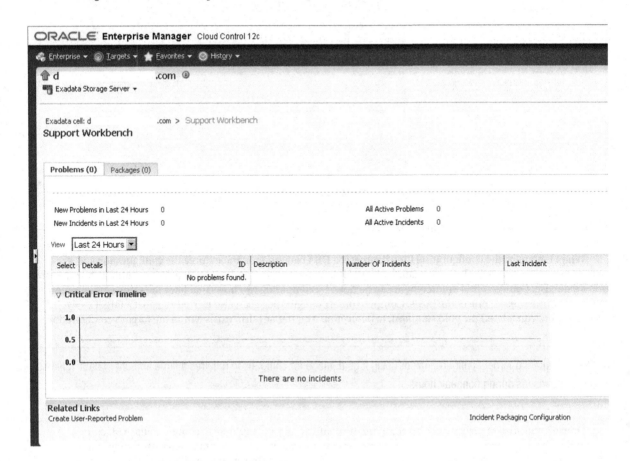

Figure 8-24. Support Workbench for an Exadata cell

One of the best features that EM12c has introduced is a centralized incident console called Incident Manager. Incident Manager enables the administrator to track, diagnose, and resolve incidents that can be an event or closely correlated events that represent an observed issue. Figure 8-25 shows the main console for Incident Manager.

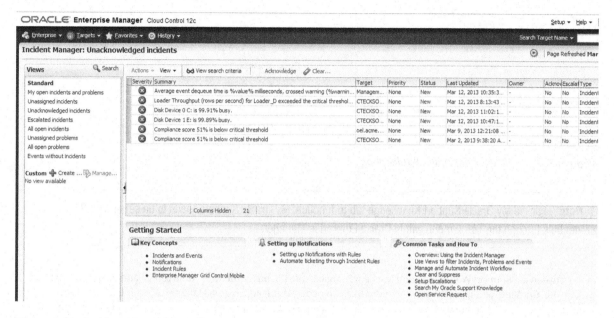

Figure 8-25. *Incident Manager console*

The goal of incident management is to enable administrators to monitor and resolve service disruptions as quickly and efficiently as possible. Instead of managing the numerous discrete events that may occur due to any service disruptions, incident management allows you to manage a smaller number of more meaningful incidents based on business priority.

Incident Manager also leverages My Oracle Support knowledge base articles and documentation to accelerate the problem diagnosis and resolution. Additionally, Incident Manager now allows you to assign ownership, acknowledge an incident, set priority for an incident, track an incident's status, and escalate or defer the incident. Using help-desk connectors, Incident Manager can also generate notifications of an incident or open a help-desk ticket.

Figure 8-26 shows the subsection where additional information of the incident can be viewed. The tabs within this section provide general information on the incident, associated events, associated MOS notes, updates that have happened to the incident, and whether any other related events have happened.

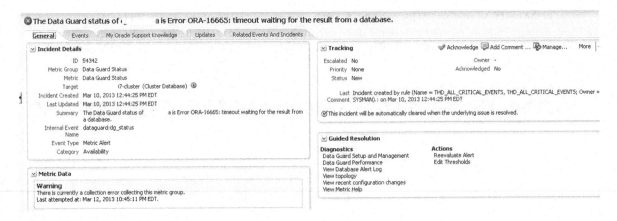

Figure 8-26. *Incident Manager detail subsection*

■ **Note**   For the My Oracle Support Knowledge tab to function, My Oracle Support needs to be set up with MOS credentials through the Setup menu within Oracle Enterprise Manager.

Between the Support Workbench and Incident Manager, EM12c has come with some robust and flexible options for identifying, troubleshooting, and resolving issues that can occur within an Exadata Database Machine. These diagnostic tools can be taken further and used with the help-desk ticketing software by extension with management connectors.

Automated Patch Management

To minimize application downtime, it is important to make sure that all recommended patches are applied in a timely manner. Patching can be a complex and time-consuming activity. EM12c addresses this concern by automating the deployment of patches, using the Lifecycle Management Pack, to ensure that patches are applied to your Oracle Exadata Database Machine or any other engineered systems. The Lifecycle Management Pack automates the deployment of Oracle patches for Oracle databases and infrastructure components including Grid Infrastructure (Clusterware, ASM, and Oracle RAC).

With the integrated interface to My Oracle Support, Oracle Enterprise Manager can analyze, recommend, and download the patches needed for your environment. You can then apply them to your test environment and promote them to a staging area, deploy them into production, and verify that they were applied correctly.

In environments where Oracle Real Application Clusters are deployed, certain patches can be applied in a rolling fashion to each node in the cluster to eliminate the need for downtime to patch. Real Application Cluster deployment procedures are used to orchestrate shutdown, patching, and startup across nodes in a rolling manner to minimize downtime.

Summary

EM12c offers comprehensive management capabilities of engineered systems. Although the applications and databases run on the engineered systems pretty similarly to how they do on a stand-alone system, the tighter integration of hardware and software brings additional administration and management capabilities. Oracle Enterprise Manager addresses those capabilities and provides seamless management from a single console that manages the complete Oracle stack throughout the IT lifecycle.

CHAPTER 9

■ ■ ■

Performance Pages and ASH Analytics

by Kellyn Pot'vin

Monitoring performance through the Top Activity feature has been one of the most utilized aspects of the Enterprise Manager since its introduction in Oracle 9i. Increased integration of optimization features as part of the existing and new performance pages in the EM12c console was one of the major accomplishments in the new release to answer the demand of more-complex database and cloud environments.

These accomplishments also include more-efficient data reporting in Top Activity, and new opportunities to utilize Active Session History (ASH) data with performance graphs in the form of ASH Analytics and Real-Time Automatic Database Diagnostic Monitor (ADDM). New advisor and reporting options from within the Top Activity and ASH Analytics interfaces exist, whereas in the past you would have been forced to leave the current performance page or open a secondary browser window or look to other tools to address issues.

Once logged into the EM12c database target interface, you can click Performance and choose various options to view activity in the database. This chapter covers the main performance categories that provide benefits in the following areas:

- Host performance home
- Performance home
- Top Activity
- ASH Analytics
- SQL Monitor
- SQL tuning options
- Advisors home
- Real-Time ADDM
- ADDM comparison reporting

Licensing Requirements

You must be aware of licensing requirements with Automatic Workload Repository (AWR), ASH, and ADDM. Ensure that you are licensed for Oracle's Diagnostic and Tuning Management packs before utilizing these performance reporting features.

Licensing information can be accessed through the EM12c console by clicking Setup ➤ Management Packs. You can view information for the individual page, for the environment as a whole, or for specific management packs/features. Figure 9-1 shows this menu hierarchy.

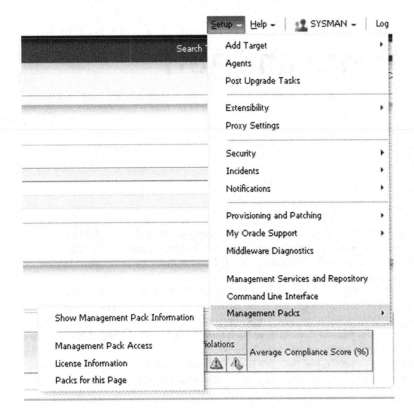

Figure 9-1. *The management pack and licensing information for any EM12c page or feature is readily available from the Setup menu in the console*

■ **Tip**   Administrators can gain access to any management packs used for any EM12c feature within a console page by clicking Setup ➤ Management Packs ➤ Packs for This Page.

With licensing out of the way, you can focus on performance data and the many options available through the EM12c console. The most common interface utilized for performance data is at a target level, often involving a single instance or cluster database.

Host Performance

A host target's performance information can be accessed from the EM console page by choosing Targets ➤ Hosts and then selecting the desired host. You can inspect basic performance metrics such as CPU utilization, memory utilization, filesystem usage, and network utilization, as shown in Figure 9-2.

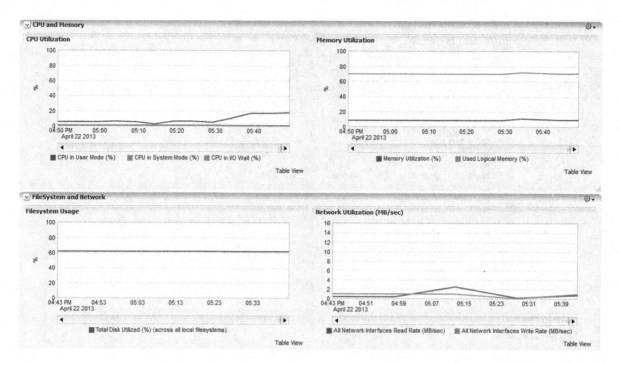

Figure 9-2. *Host performance information—note the spike in network utilization after 1:44 PM in the bottom-right graph*

In the left pane, you can view full summary information regarding the host status, incidents, configuration, and job activity.

Any fluctuations in CPU usage and memory are displayed, along with filesystem usage and network utilization. For each of the four areas (CPU, Memory, Filesystem, and Network), you can also view the data in a table format, as shown in Figure 9-3. To access this format, you click the Table View link at the bottom right of any graph. The tabular representation can be inspected for out-of-the-ordinary values that may not show as clearly in a graphic interface, or the data can be copied and pasted to a CSV or Microsoft Excel file.

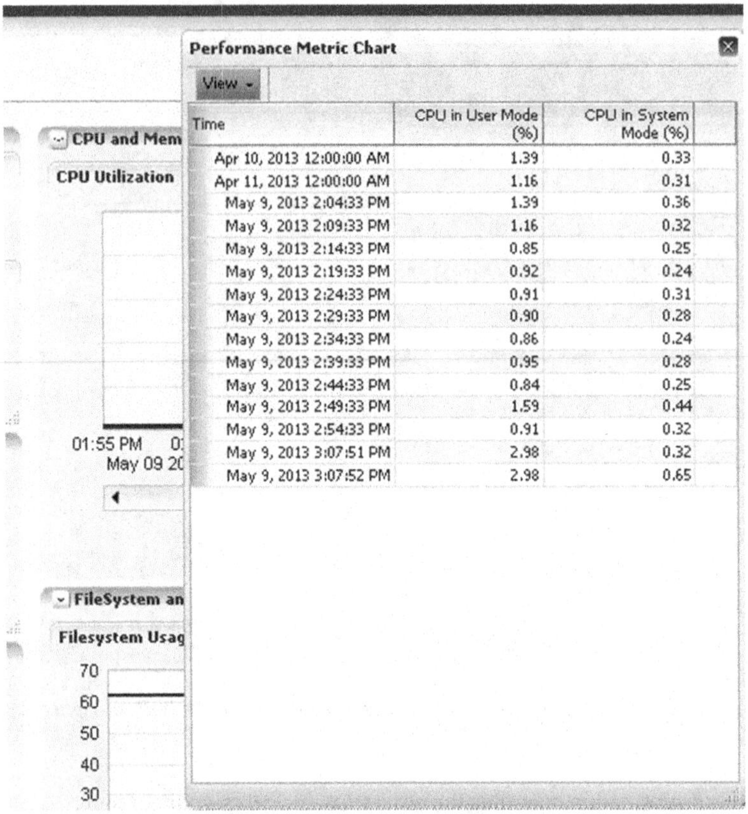

Performance Metric Chart

View ▾

Time	CPU in User Mode (%)	CPU in System Mode (%)
Apr 10, 2013 12:00:00 AM	1.39	0.33
Apr 11, 2013 12:00:00 AM	1.16	0.31
May 9, 2013 2:04:33 PM	1.39	0.36
May 9, 2013 2:09:33 PM	1.16	0.32
May 9, 2013 2:14:33 PM	0.85	0.25
May 9, 2013 2:19:33 PM	0.92	0.24
May 9, 2013 2:24:33 PM	0.91	0.31
May 9, 2013 2:29:33 PM	0.90	0.28
May 9, 2013 2:34:33 PM	0.86	0.24
May 9, 2013 2:39:33 PM	0.95	0.28
May 9, 2013 2:44:33 PM	0.84	0.25
May 9, 2013 2:49:33 PM	1.59	0.44
May 9, 2013 2:54:33 PM	0.91	0.32
May 9, 2013 3:07:51 PM	2.98	0.32
May 9, 2013 3:07:52 PM	2.98	0.65

CPU and Mem

CPU Utilization

01:55 PM   0:
May 09 20

FileSystem an

Filesystem Usag

70
60
50
40
30

Figure 9-3. *Tabular display of performance metric charts in the host performance page*

Each of these panes can be adjusted to display in any order you choose. Simply right-click the View Actions menu at the top right of each window to organize the performance summary view to your preference.

Performance Home

The database performance home offers a compact view of runnable processes, by CPU, including any baselines that are included for an individual database target. The performance home can be accessed in various ways, depending on the home page chosen by the administrator/user, but is always available once logged into EM12c by clicking Targets ➤ Databases and choosing a database. The Performance tab is the second from the left in the EM console database controls for the database home page (see Figure 9-4) and includes options for viewing, diagnosing, and inspecting database performance.

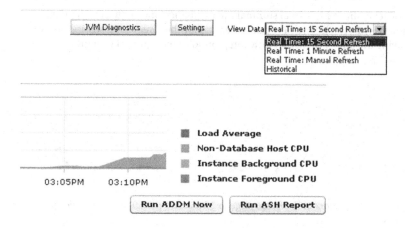

Figure 9-4. *CPU usage across a database server in an Oracle 11g environment, currently set to 15-second refresh intervals, but demonstrating how to change to extended update intervals*

The performance home, unlike the Top Activity performance page, is a summary of the database performance and is not specific to database performance, but overall performance of the database environment, including host and system info.

■ **Tip** Historical data from this section will be based on CPU data only. If you want more-specific data on database usage, you must go to Top Activity. For less-aggregated data, refer to ASH Analytics, which is discussed later in this chapter.

The performance home grid data can be viewed and refreshed in 15-second intervals, 1-minute intervals, or manually, or you can choose a historical view. Baselines can be included or excluded in the graph, along with load averages. Options to run JVM Diagnostics, ADDM, or ASH reports are available from this section.

The main area is broken down into high-level database wait information. This view displays information about not just CPU usage, but CPU usage outside the database and the system load average.

By clicking the Settings button, shown in the upper right of Figure 9-4, you can change the chart default settings from CPU based to display I/O chart information or baseline values (see Figure 9-5).

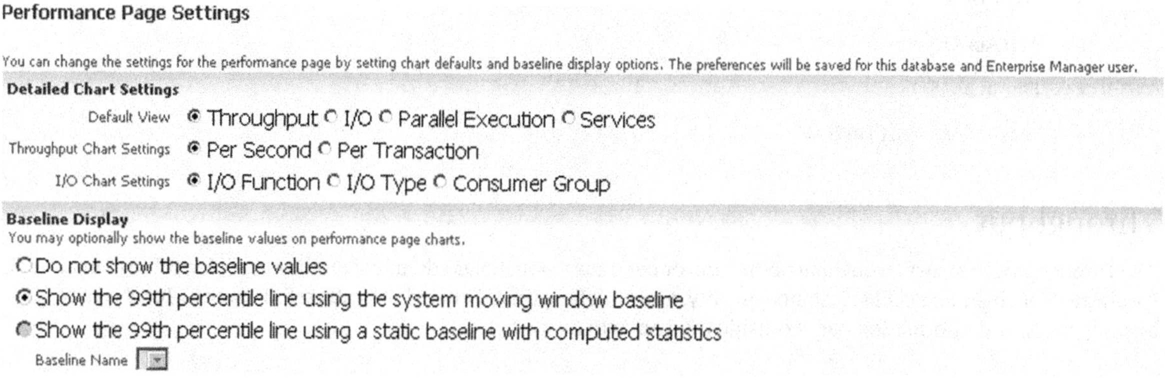

Performance Page Settings

You can change the settings for the performance page by setting chart defaults and baseline display options. The preferences will be saved for this database and Enterprise Manager user.

Detailed Chart Settings

    Default View   ⦿ Throughput ○ I/O ○ Parallel Execution ○ Services

Throughput Chart Settings   ⦿ Per Second ○ Per Transaction

    I/O Chart Settings   ⦿ I/O Function ○ I/O Type ○ Consumer Group

Baseline Display
You may optionally show the baseline values on performance page charts.

○ Do not show the baseline values

⦿ Show the 99th percentile line using the system moving window baseline

○ Show the 99th percentile line using a static baseline with computed statistics

    Baseline Name ☐▼

Figure 9-5. *Changing the default performance home chart settings*

In Figure 9-6, the administrator has switched from high-level summary performance information to detailed performance information (not to be confused with ASH). This view can either display the foreground sessions only or include background sessions. At times, having the ability to display only foreground or background wait information is very valuable.

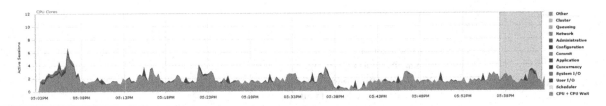

Figure 9-6. *The Average Active Sessions pane of the performance home page in EM12c, demonstrating an average load involving both CPU and some I/O waits*

■ **Tip** When diagnosing performance issues, inspecting just the foreground sessions and then inspecting both foreground and background sessions can help distinguish problems such as poor ETL batch load design or an issue with cursors not being closed correctly.

From the Average Active Sessions pane, you can quickly assess the performance statistics of the database. By clicking one of the links at the bottom of the main page, you can access the Top Activity page to perform a more detailed investigation.

Links can include the following:

- Top Segments
- Cluster Cache Coherency (in RAC)
- Interconnects (in RAC)
- Parallel Execution
- Database Locks
- SQL Monitoring
- Top Consumers
- Top Activity
- Duplicate SQL
- Instance Activity (in RAC)

Throughput

The Throughput tab shows throughput per second or per transaction. It has additional monitoring links to Top Consumers, Duplicate SQL, Instance Locks, Instance Activity, and SQL Response Time. These tabs relink back to Top Activity, locking pages, and information pages outside the Top Activity area.

I/O

The I/O tab has graphs for I/O latency in milliseconds and I/O in megabytes per second by I/O Function, Type, or Consumer Group (see Figure 9-7). There is a button to take you through a graphical interface to quickly perform I/O calibration (DBMS_RESOURCE_MANAGER.CALIBRATE_IO), needed if the database is going to utilize Auto DOP (degree of parallelism).

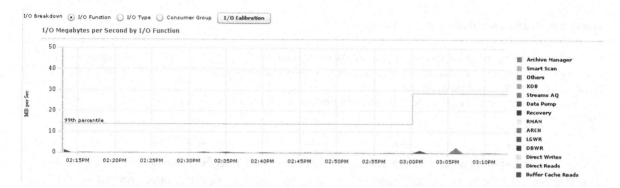

Figure 9-7. *I/O in megabytes during a data pump operation from the performance home page*

Parallel Execution

The Parallel Execution tab, shown in Figure 9-8, shows pertinent information regarding active serial/parallel sessions. In addition, a second graph shows the coordinator and slave sessions for each parallel execution, and a third graph shows DDL, DML, and queries parallelized in the database environment.

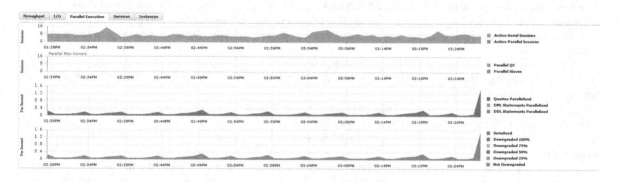

Figure 9-8. *An example of parallel execution shown from the performance home, detailing parallel usage from many levels*

Services

If services are in use for the database environment, they will be available in the Services tab, shown in Figure 9-9. The data displays in a standard grid performance graph, identifying each service and its resource usage by color and by name.

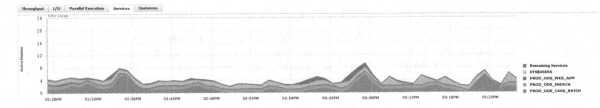

Figure 9-9. *Example of services and resource usage*

Upon viewing the magnified legend, it is simple to see that the `App1_Prod_Orcl` service is utilizing the most resources in the environment. The remaining services are quite similar in resource usage and in no way match the sizeable impact of the application service.

This information can then be used to help isolate performance issues by service, helping to narrow down optimization exercises.

■ **Note** The Instances tab will show only if accessing a Real Application Cluster (RAC) environment. Without this feature, there is no reason for the tab and it won't show in the performance home page. All RAC environments that were available at the time of this writing involved Release 2 Exadata, and no actual instance information was shown in the interface. This may be a bug in the current Exadata release, or this tab may function in only non-Exadata environments.

Top Activity

The Top Activity page has been the cornerstone of the Enterprise Manager environment from its initial release. Administrators could review the data displayed and have a graphical representation of the wait events in the database—a simple view of database usage. From easily understood color descriptions for waits groups, an administrator could often identify performance issues and pinpoint areas of concern without advanced knowledge of performance optimization.

With the release of EM12c, the Top Activity page has been enhanced to offer more-definitive performance data, simple interface options that tie in the Top Activity interface to the performance reports (such as ASH, AWR, and advisor opportunities), and detailed session history.

The Top Activity page is the second choice in the Performance drop-down menu at the top left of the performance page view (available once the administrator has logged in to a database target). The interface has remained greatly unchanged since its initial appearance in Enterprise Manager 10g, so even those new to EM12c find the interface easy to navigate.

The upper pane of the Top Activity page, shown in Figure 9-10, provides a quick view of wait activity and active sessions in the database environment. The legend to the right indicates what each color represents on the screen, and a timeline is shown across the bottom.

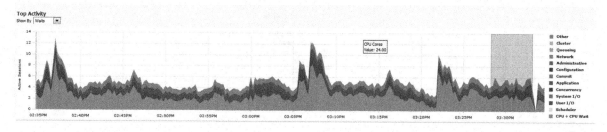

Figure 9-10. *Top Activity graph for EM12c, demonstrating higher than normal I/O waits*

The legend on the right consists of links for the wait events, shown for each color. Clicking any of these opens the Active Sessions page for that wait event, as shown in Figure 9-11. You can then lock in on a given wait event to gather more details.

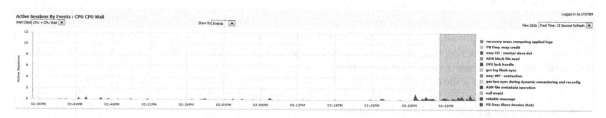

Figure 9-11. *Wait events highlighted for CPU + CPU Wait*

By hovering over the wait event, the resource usage in the graph for that specific wait are highlighted. Upon clicking the CPU + CPU Wait option, for example, you are connected to the page displaying the detail information on all sessions experiencing waits for CPU + CPU Wait, as shown in Figure 9-12.

Top SQL: CPU CPU Wait

Actions Schedule SQL Tuning Advisor ▾ Go

Select All | Select None

Select	Activity (%) ▾	SQL ID	SQL Type	Service	Instance
☐	41.18	3bka6xq476fnt	SELECT	.world	d011
☐	14.71	1uyp1pq4w60h7	SELECT	.world	d011
☐	8.82	adfpkwrb7pn7f	SELECT	.world	d011
☐	8.82	ga9v6nn3u1b3r	SELECT	.world	d011
☐	5.88	6h5ng67gfsvrb	SELECT	.world	d011
☐	5.88	gza99tjrbyk29	SELECT	.world	d011
☐	5.88	ac5d9k0xxt25z	SELECT	.world	d011
☐	2.94	f1y9kbhh6v9sv	SELECT	.world	d011
☐	2.94	bhjxxwujr3ac3	SELECT	SYS$USERS	d011
☐	2.94	8vh9 1ssy2k5j9	SELECT	.world	d011

Actions Schedule SQL Tuning Advisor ▾ Go

Total Sample Counts 34

Top Sessions: CPU CPU Wait

View Top Sessions ▾

Activity (%) ▾	Session ID	User Name	Program	Service	Instance
40.00	281	DBSNMP	OMS	.world	d011
3.75	4783	DBSNMP	(PZ99)	.world	d012
3.75	4534	DBSNMP	(PZ99)	.world	d011
3.75	4534	DBSNMP	(PZ99)	.world	d011
2.50	4783	DBSNMP	(PZ99)	.world	d012
2.50	4783	DBSNMP	(PZ99)	.world	d012
2.50	4534	DBSNMP	(PZ99)	.world	d011
2.50	4534	DBSNMP	(PZ99)	.world	d011
2.50	4783	DBSNMP	(PZ99)	.world	d012
1.25	2039	SYSTEM	OMS	.world	d011

Total Sample Count: 80

Figure 9-12. *Displaying only wait information for SQL ID and sessions that are experiencing waits for CPU and Waiting for CPU*

The grayed area in the Top Activity graph, shown earlier in Figure 9-10, is then detailed in the lower sections of the Top Activity page, defaulting to Top SQL and Top Sessions (see Figure 9-13). Note that each of the wait areas to the left of each SQL ID in the left panel and each Session ID in the right panel are color coded in green, to show that they are CPU wait events.

Top SQL: User I/O

Actions | Schedule SQL Tuning Advisor ▼ Go

Select All | Select None

Select	Activity (%) ▼	SQL ID	SQL Type	Service	Instance
☐	14.52	ajjxx1aha8rv3	SELECT	PROD_	d012
☐	11.29	0v8n8nxxud43x	SELECT		d011
☐	8.06	c1injkc3c5gzq	SELECT	PROD_	d012
☐	6.45	60bkct5vhrt91	SELECT	PROD_	d012
☐	6.45	1qsddgscpr3wx	SELECT	PROD_	d012
☐	4.84	164c7g55w5xf7	SELECT	PROD_	d012
☐	4.84	7j79xarz29bqh	SELECT	PROD_	d011
☐	4.84	fkz7nbvcavr906	SBLECT	PROD_	d012
☐	4.84	7fglrpd5jhx74v	SELECT	PROD_	d012
☐	4.84	8d85jqbb61bef	SELECT	PROD_	d011

Actions | Schedule SQL Tuning Advisor ▼ Go

Total Sample Count: 62

Top Sessions: User I/O

View | Top Sessions ▼

Activity (%) ▼	Session ID	User Name	Program	Service	Instance
11.29	281	DBSNMP	OMS	.world	d011
8.06	2264	2USR	JDBC Thin Client	PROD_	d012
8.06	2785	3USR	JDBC Thin Client	PROD_	d012
4.84	261	DM	sdpka@cspr f03.classifiedventures.com (TNS V1-	PROD_	d012
4.84	10	CUSR	JDBC Thin Client	PROD_	d011
4.84	1515	CUSR	JDBC Thin Client	PROD_	d011
4.84	5791	MSUSR	JDBC Thin Client	PROD_	d011
3.23	533	CUSR	JDBC Thin Client	PROD_	d012
3.23	1785	CUSR	JDBC Thin Client	PROD_	d012
3.23	528	RUSR	JDBC Thin Client	PROD_	d012

Total Sample Count: 62

Figure 9-13. *Top SQL and Top Sessions, demonstrating an I/O issue in a database environment*

Top SQL Pane

The Top SQL section is broken down by percentage of activity, SQL ID (unique identifier for the SQL statement), and the type of SQL performed. Note that in the example shown in Figure 9-13, an apparent high I/O resource statement is being executed by two sessions. As the percentage is displayed against the rest of the database sessions, the overall impact of the wait events is clearly shown.

At this point, you have the option to schedule a SQL Tuning Advisor or create a SQL tuning set from the drop-down below the Top SQL banner. Clicking any the SQL IDs opens the SQL Details page, which provides detailed information regarding the individual SQL statements.

SQL Details Page

The I/O issue demonstrated in SQL ID `cwu5p1yyp1p40` referenced back in Figure 9-12 is actually the SQL statement behind a tablespace data pump job. Clicking this SQL ID in the Top SQL section opens a second details page that provides detailed information regarding performance, statistics, explain plan, tuning history, and SQL monitoring (see Figure 9-14). The bottom pane of the page is controlled by a series of tabs that display different details regarding the statement. You can inspect each tab and research the data displayed to provide value to the issue at hand. At the top right, you can use buttons to refresh, create a SQL worksheet, perform JVM Diagnostics, or create a SQL Details active report.

Top Activity > SQL Details: cwu5p1yyp1p40

SQL Details: cwu5p1yyp1p40

Switch to SQL ID [ ] Go

Text

```
BEGIN
SYS.KUPW$WORKER.MAIN('SYS_EXPORT_TABLESPACE_01', 'SYSTEM', 0);
END;
```

Figure 9-14. *Top Activity, Top SQL details, with the example of a data pump statement, identified by SQL ID*

SQL Activity

The entry point for the SQL Details page is the SQL Activity tab. This view, offering the last hour's activity of the SQL ID under investigation, along with the statement information and wait history, is displayed clearly in a standard graph view (refer ahead to Figure 9-16). The SQL shown in the example is for a data pump job on the SYSTEM tablespace.

For procedural calls, it is extremely helpful to be able to tie the background SQL process back to its parent. To locate this from a SQL ID shown in the EM console, the following query can help:

```
select o.owner, o.object_name, o.object_type, s.program_line#
from v$sql s, dba_objects o
where sql_id = '<SQL_ID>'
and s.program_id=o.object_id;
```

The procedure or package, along with the line that the SQL call sourced from, will then be returned, thus quickly letting you know the source. This can be run from a SQL *Plus session. If you prefer to run it from the EM12c console, this can be accomplished by clicking Performance ➤ SQL ➤ Run SQL.

The interface offers a simple option to execute a SQL statement or load a SQL script. Input the login to be used to execute the script (see Figure 9-15).

Run SQL

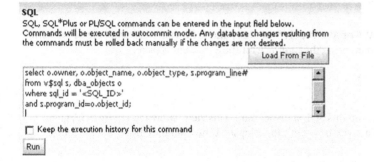

Figure 9-15. *The Run SQL interface inEM12c, which allows SQL to be executed directly from the console*

■ **Tip** If you run SQL from the EM12c console on a regular basis, it is best to ensure that the Host and Database Preferred credentials are set up to reduce issues with failed executions.

Once executed, the following information is returned:

```
OWNER        OBJECT_NAME        OBJECT_TYPE        PROGRAM_LINE#
-----------------------------------------------------------------
USER1        GET_NEW_FUNC       FUNCTION           9
```

The preceding information shows the object name, the object type, and the line number. This data can be used to quickly identify where the problem is in the code. The SQL Details Activity tab, shown in Figure 9-16, offers a SQL-specific view of Top Activity data, eliminating all other SQL waits and SQL executions, other than the one SQL ID in question. The grayed area can be moved anywhere within the timeline shown to highlight waits within the SQL activity. As this is SQL activity vs. session activity, the sessions executing the SQL in the Details page are shown at the bottom, along with percentage of activity, the session ID (SID) if the session is part of a parallel process, the QC SID (including all parallel sessions for the user executing the SQL), the program the SQL is part of, and whether there is a plan hash value that the SQL is identified with.

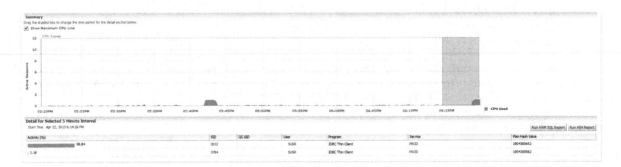

Figure 9-16. *Activity tab of the SQL Details page*

You can execute an HTML version of an AWR or ASH report from this pane to further investigate the activity and database performance by clicking a SQL ID and entering the interface for the SQL Details page.

SQL Statistics

The first tab in the SQL Details page, Statistics, contains SQL statistics data. This view, shown in Figure 9-17, gives active session information, breaking down the activity by waits, time, elapsed time (database time vs. CPU time), execution statistics, and cursor statistics.

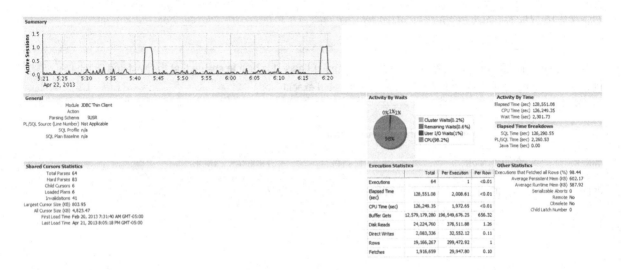

Figure 9-17. *Statistics activity in the SQL Details page*

SQL Plan

The Plan tab provides the actual explain plan for the SQL ID detailed, either in graphical or tabular format. The tabular version, shown in Figure 9-18, offers a drop-down menu if more than one hash plan value is available for the SQL statement. Basic plan information is shown, such as the parsing schema, optimizer mode, source of the statement, and capture time.

Operation	Object	Predicate	Pruning	Operation Cost	Estimated Rows	Estimated Bytes
⊟ SELECT STATEMENT						
⊟ NESTED LOOPS					120	12K
⊟ HASH JOIN OUTER		⚲			6	510
⊟ HASH JOIN OUTER		⚲		1	6	330
TABLE ACCESS FULL	SYS.TS$	▽		2	6	150
⊟ VIEW					2	60
⊟ HASH GROUP BY				1	2	40
⊟ VIEW	SYS.DBA_DATA_FILES				2	40
⊟ UNION-ALL						
⊟ NESTED LOOPS					1	353
⊟ NESTED LOOPS					1	339
⊟ NESTED LOOPS					1	326
FIXED TABLE FULL	SYS.X$KCCFN	▽			1	310
⊟ TABLE ACCESS BY INDEX ROWID	SYS.FILE$	▽		1	1	16

*Statistics Activity **Plan** Plan Control Tuning History SQL Monitoring*

Data Source Cursor Cache   Capture Time Apr 22, 2013 6:24:27 PM GMT-05:00   Parsing Schema DBSNMP   Optimizer Mode ALL_ROWS
Additional Information
◯ Graphical ◉ Tabular

Figure 9-18. *Tabular representation of an explain plan for a statement from the SQL Details page*

Also provided in the EM12c console version of the tabular plan are the type of waits by legend color in the Optimization Cost section. You can also see the rows, along with a graph line to quickly access the number of rows expected to be returned, and the bytes, again displayed with a visual indicator of the number of bytes expected. You can click any of the indicators in the Predicate column (highlighted in Figure 9-18) to view predicates and filters and more-detailed information on the step in question.

The graphical version of the Plan tab in SQL Details provides a visual display of the explain plan (see Figure 9-19). This is a step-by-step path of the statement, displaying joins, loops, and group objects through the SQL execution.

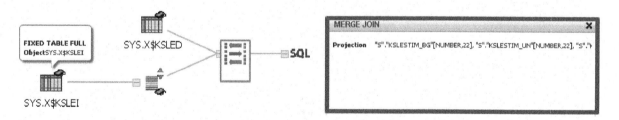

Figure 9-19. *Graphical explain plan for a statement, demonstrating a merge join highlighted in the console pane*

Projections, definitive column joins, and even bloom filters are shown when highlighting sections of the explain plan's graphical format. The buttons at the upper right in Figure 9-19 enable you to change the display to a vertical map from horizontal, perform a rewrite, or print out the explain plan graphic. The zoom bar on the left, under the Graphical and Tabular radio buttons, enables you to zoom in and out as needed.

SQL Plan Control

The Plan Control tab is available for advanced features such as SQL profiles, SQL patches, and SQL plan baselines. This pane is helpful in quickly determining whether a baseline is locking the plan into a potential suboptimal explain plan version, and whether a SQL profile or SQL patch is in place controlling the choice the optimizer makes for the SQL detailed in the pane. As with all tabs in the SQL Details page, you can easily execute a SQL worksheet or schedule a SQL Tuning Advisor from the bottom right of the panel.

■ **Note** Because the SQL Tuning Advisor is so readily available and automated with nightly runs, SQL profiles are becoming database standards. This combination of hints, outlines, and stats, connected to a statement through its SQL ID, provides the DBA with a quick solution to nagging problems when complex issues exist in a process. As a SQL profile is connected only through the SQL ID, any change to the SQL statement stops the SQL profile from functioning.

SQL Tuning History

The Tuning History tab supports the Plan Control section of the SQL Details page, offering historical information regarding previous advisor tasks against the SQL detailed or any ADDM findings during the historic period in question. If a SQL Tuning task has been executed against the SQL ID, it will show in the history, and a link is available to view details on the findings, even if the plan was not implemented.

SQL Monitoring

The SQL Monitoring tab gives a micro-view of what is offered in the full SQL Monitor (covered in full detail later in this chapter). This grants a clear view of what SQL is being executed for the session, along with completed SQL in previous executions for the session involved, how long each execution elapsed, I/O requests, and start/finish times (see Figure 9-20).

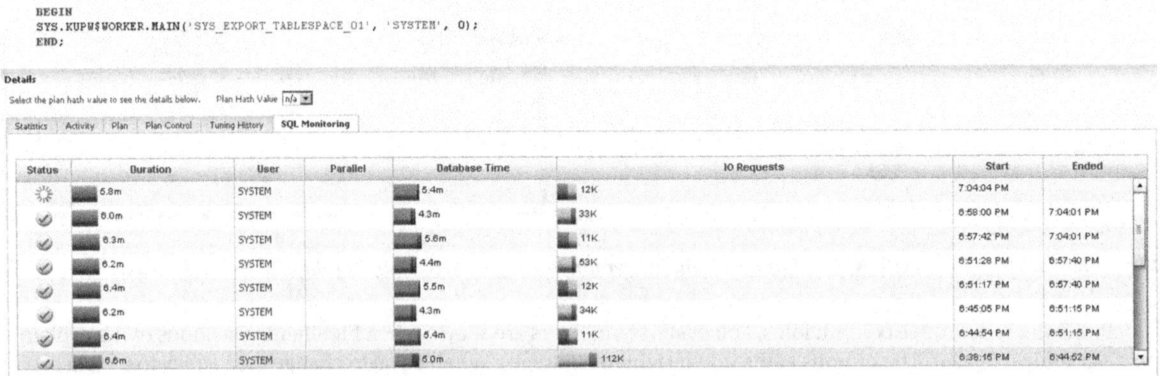

Figure 9-20. SQL Monitoring view of a data pump process

Each of these tabs offers valuable information when inspecting a SQL statement for optimization opportunities, baseline information, explain plan stability, and resource usage. By utilizing this small section of the Top Activity page, the administrator can provide great insight quickly into any SQL statement captured.

Top Sessions Pane

Top Sessions encompasses the bottom-right pane of the Top Activity page by default. Although this section can be changed to display top information regarding services, modules, actions, clients, files, objects, or PL/SQL (see Figure 9-21), session information is the main data that is found most useful by administrators.

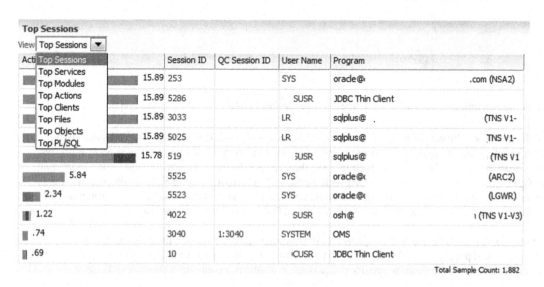

Figure 9-21. *Top Sessions of the Top Activity page, along with the drop-down list of other Top options*

In this pane, you can not only highlight wait events that are color coded to match the legend in the Top Activity graph, but also access links to each of the SIDs and usernames. The program executing the session is also displayed prominently to the right, helping to quickly distinguish the session.

As this page is distinguished by session information, clicking any SID opens the Session Details page.

Session Details Page

The Session Details page, unlike the SQL Details page, breaks down data at the session level. The tabs for this page are General, Activity, Statistics, Open Cursors, Blocking Tree, Wait Event History, Parallel SQL, and SQL Monitoring. Just as with the SQL Details page, the Session Details page defaults to the Activity tab, shown in Figure 9-22.

Figure 9-22. *Session Details page, showing an active query execution by SID*

The Activity tab shows the wait activity of the session, by color, along with the type of wait in a legend to the right side of the graph. From the right-hand corner of the page, you can enable tracing or kill the session, along with changing the refresh interval of the graph. At the bottom of the page is information regarding the 5-minute interval, highlighted in gray within the graph timeline, along with the SQL ID, which links to the SQL Details page for the statement executing during the timeline highlighted, along with the plan hash value and module information. If more than one statement is executed during the 5-minute window, all SQL IDs will be displayed in the detailed section for the interval.

The General tab, shown in Figure 9-23, displays all information regarding the session from the Top Activity page. The Session Details page, as with the SQL Details page, can be reached numerous ways from within the EM12c console, providing quick access from performance pages to the console to provide data about specific sessions.

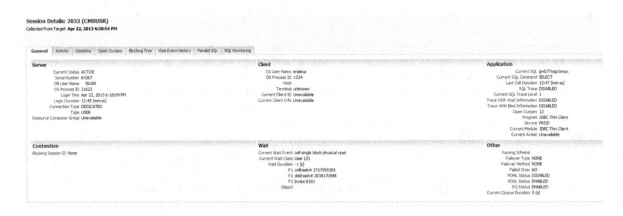

Figure 9-23. *General information in the Session Details page*

The Session Details page, shown in Figure 9-24, displays the server-level information, including the OS process ID (PID), the client information, the application, any blocking that has occurred, and waits. Another section includes parallel execution information.

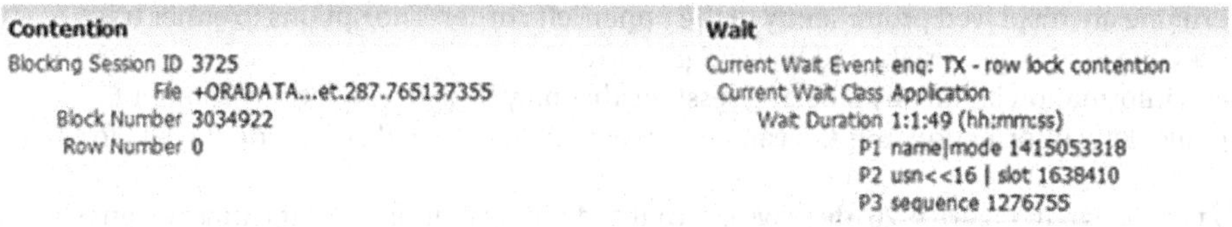

Contention

Blocking Session ID 3725
  File +ORADATA...et.287.765137355
  Block Number 3034922
  Row Number 0

Wait

Current Wait Event enq: TX - row lock contention
Current Wait Class Application
Wait Duration 1:1:49 (hh:mm:ss)
  P1 name|mode 1415053318
  P2 usn<<16 | slot 1638410
  P3 sequence 1276755

Figure 9-24. *Blocking session for a Session Details General page*

The Statistics tab displays all statistical information regarding the session, physical and logical waits, detailed CPU usage information, gets, and buffer information. Table 9-1 shows detailed Statistics tab information.

Table 9-1. *Detailed Information on the Statistics Tab from the Session Details Page*

Name	Delta	Current	Rate
Logical read bytes from cache	7059480576	2.23292E+12	1203662464
Index fetch by key	2133336	461521952	363740
Session logical reads	861753	272791968	146931
Consistent gets	861753	272791936	146931
Consistent gets from cache	861753	272573472	146931
Consistent gets-examination	719763	184395184	122721
Buffer is pinned count	617903	245734928	105354

The Statistics tab contains no drill-downs or links, but it does offer the opportunity to enable tracing to collect deeper session-level data or to kill the session.

The Open Cursors tab, shown in Figure 9-25, is extremely helpful in identifying cursor- or mutex-level performance issues in a session. The pane quickly displays the cursor and count, led by the SQL ID, which will again link to the SQL Details page to identify any issues in the cursor SQL.

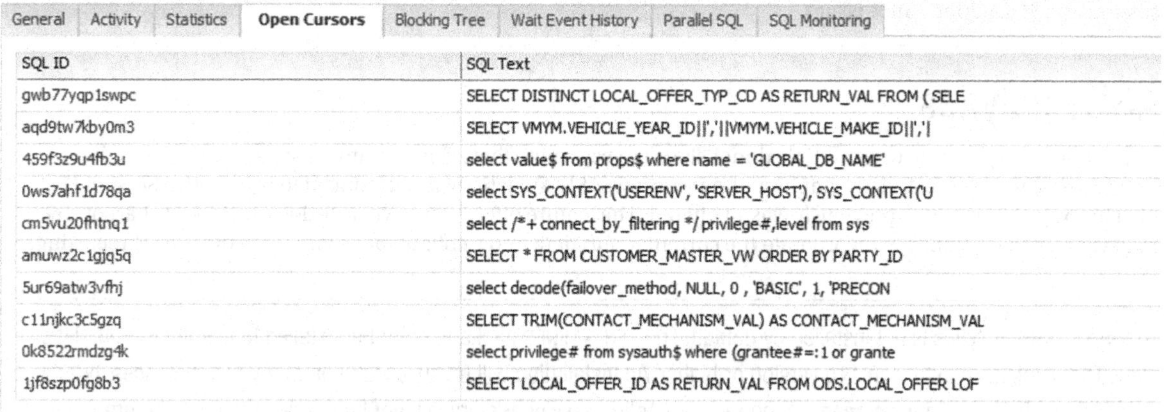

General	Activity	Statistics	**Open Cursors**	Blocking Tree	Wait Event History	Parallel SQL	SQL Monitoring

SQL ID	SQL Text
gwb77yqp1swpc	SELECT DISTINCT LOCAL_OFFER_TYP_CD AS RETURN_VAL FROM (SELE
aqd9tw7kby0m3	SELECT VMYM.VEHICLE_YEAR_ID||','||VMYM.VEHICLE_MAKE_ID||','|
459f3z9u4fb3u	select value$ from props$ where name = 'GLOBAL_DB_NAME'
0ws7ahf1d78qa	select SYS_CONTEXT('USERENV', 'SERVER_HOST'), SYS_CONTEXT('U
cm5vu20fhtnq1	select /*+ connect_by_filtering */ privilege#,level from sys
amuwz2c1gjq5q	SELECT * FROM CUSTOMER_MASTER_VW ORDER BY PARTY_ID
5ur69atw3vfhj	select decode(failover_method, NULL, 0 , 'BASIC', 1, 'PRECON
c11njkc3c5gzq	SELECT TRIM(CONTACT_MECHANISM_VAL) AS CONTACT_MECHANISM_VAL
0k8522rmdzg4k	select privilege# from sysauth$ where (grantee#=:1 or grante
1jf8szp0fg8b3	SELECT LOCAL_OFFER_ID AS RETURN_VAL FROM ODS.LOCAL_OFFER LOF

Figure 9-25. *Open cursors for ongoing processes from the Session Details page*

The session ID and username are displayed prominently in the upper-left corner. The options to either trace or kill the session are, again, available at the upper-right and lower-right corners.

The Blocking tab displays information about any blocking sessions that may be active in the environment. Because of the complexity of blocking information, this tab can take an extended time to display, but the data found in the pane is quite valuable.

The Wait Event History tab, shown in Figure 9-26, displays the wait event information, with the most recent wait event at the top. Displayed are the wait class, the actual wait event, and the P1, P2, and P3 text, all linking to detailed data about the wait information (data resulting from dba_hist_active_sess_history). The option to trace or kill the session is again offered at the top and bottom of the right-hand side.

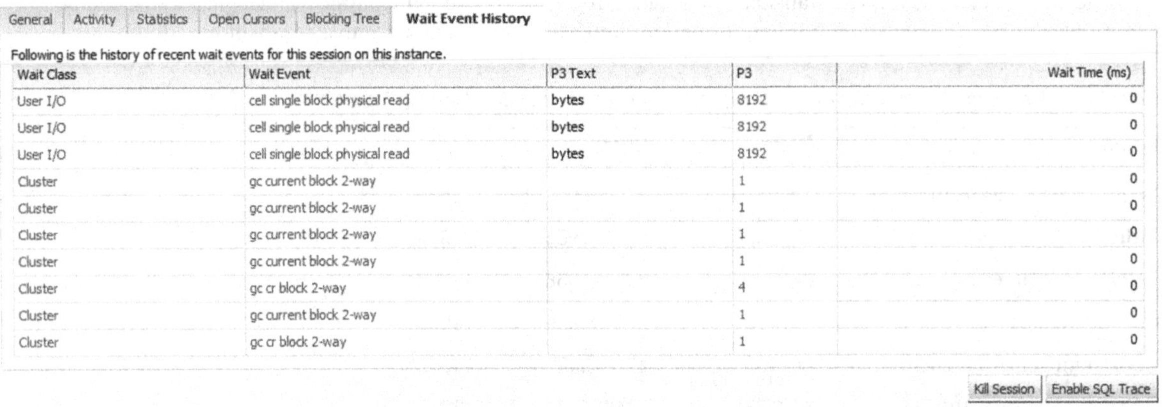

| General | Activity | Statistics | Open Cursors | Blocking Tree | **Wait Event History** |

Following is the history of recent wait events for this session on this instance.

Wait Class	Wait Event	P3 Text	P3	Wait Time (ms)
User I/O	cell single block physical read	bytes	8192	0
User I/O	cell single block physical read	bytes	8192	0
User I/O	cell single block physical read	bytes	8192	0
Cluster	gc current block 2-way		1	0
Cluster	gc current block 2-way		1	0
Cluster	gc current block 2-way		1	0
Cluster	gc current block 2-way		1	0
Cluster	gc cr block 2-way		4	0
Cluster	gc current block 2-way		1	0
Cluster	gc cr block 2-way		1	0

Kill Session | Enable SQL Trace

Figure 9-26. *Wait information from the Session Details page's Wait Event History tab*

The Parallel SQL tab shows data regarding any parallel execution information the session is involved in—including whether the session belongs to the coordinator or a slave, and if a slave, the producer or consumer of the parallel process.

The SQL Monitoring tab is available only for Oracle Database versions 11g Release 1 for the command-line data, and 11g Release 2 for the HTML version of the reports. This tab appears grayed out in environments that do not have this feature set up or available.

The Top Activity area of the performance pages in the EM12c console has a user-friendly interface for the seasoned administrator with previous Enterprise Manager experience and new, detailed information to assist with session and SQL performance issues.

ASH Analytics

Analyzing performance across multiple dimensions is a capability that administrators have searched for in the Enterprise Manager Top Activity graphs without success. ASH Analytics was introduced to offer Active Session History data in a visual format that previously wasn't offered. The feature offers recursive drill-downs, stacked chart or tree map views, and the ability to incorporate the current report data into a collaborative view with other ASH reporting.

■ **Note** ASH Analytics is not installed by default. The ASH_VIEWER package must be installed to use the ASH Analytics view. The database must be an 11g version or higher. An installation will be successful on many 10g instances, but no data will be displayed on the screen, as the required Active Session History will not be available to fulfill the graphs.

The main ASH Analytics screen shows data displayed by Average Active Sessions (AAS), viewed by graph or load map. Numerous drill-down opportunities exist in the main performance view, allowing for distinct research areas to be investigated.

The upper display of the ASH Analytics main page, shown in Figure 9-27, can be changed to display data by hour, day, week, or month. Alternatively, you can customize the display to show more-pertinent data to the monitoring task.

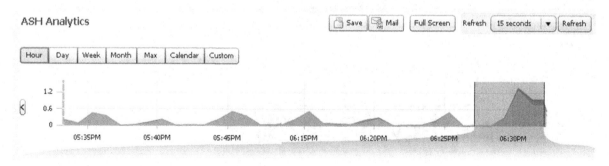

Figure 9-27. *ASH Analytics main performance graph*

■ **Note** If choosing the Max display type for ASH Analytics, the data will be displayed differently than how other wait event types commonly would be displayed. Ensure that you understand how choosing Max will impact the data dispersion in the graph and load map so that an inaccurate diagnosis does not occur.

Being able to save ASH Analytics data locally to a file or to e-mail an HTML report are valuable options if you need to retain the data or provide information to key members of the team. From the main view, you can also expand the window to full screen and change the refresh interval. Arrows at the left and right of the timeline enable you to easily maneuver to earlier timelines or future ones if refreshes have been stopped.

The gray highlighted section in the window, as shown in Figure 9-27, quickly draws the administrator's eye down, further detailing a 5-minute sample of ASH data to the graph, including wait events and defaulting with Wait Class events.

The lower Activity pane of the ASH Analytics page, shown in Figure 9-28, displays data in a format similar to Top Activity, but the data is based on the V$ACTIVE_SESSION_HISTORY view and has more performance data available for access from the links shown.

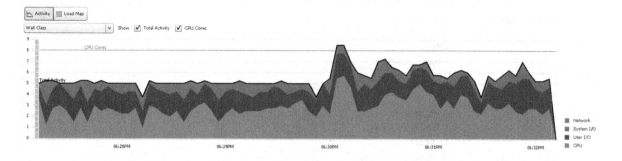

Figure 9-28. *The Activity pane for ASH Analytics*

The SQL ID section at the lower left links to the SQL Details page. The User Session section on the right links to the Session Details page. The drop-down Wait Class options are extensive, as seen in Figure 9-29.

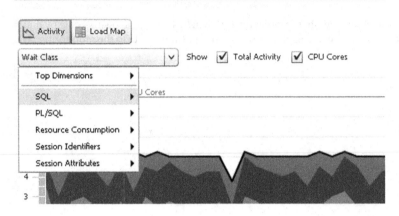

Figure 9-29. *The drop-down menu options for the ASH Analytics Wait Class*

SQL can be broken down in many ways within the ASH Analytics Activity view. The options are shown in Table 9-2. Depending on the needs of the administrator, the order of the presentation can be changed.

Table 9-2. *The Wait Class Options and Suboptions*

Option	Suboptions
SQL	SQL ID
	Top Level SQL ID
	SQL Force Matching Signature
	SQL Plan Hash Value
	SQL Plan Operation
	SQL Plan Operation Line
	SQL Opcode
	Top Level SQL Opcode
PL/SQL	PL/SQL
	Top Level PL/SQL
Resource Consumption	Wait Class
	Wait Event
	Object
	Blocking Session
Session Identifiers	Instance
	Service
	User Session
	Parallel Process
	User ID
	Program
	Session Type
Session Attributes	Consumer Group
	Module
	Action

Each of these options gives a unique view of waits and/or resource usage in the environment. You can choose the combination that best suits the situation at hand and then view the data to investigate the issue.

You can choose the Top Level SQL ID, subsequently creating a very different view of the database performance, and showing the percentage impact from the statement having that ID. See Figure 9-30.

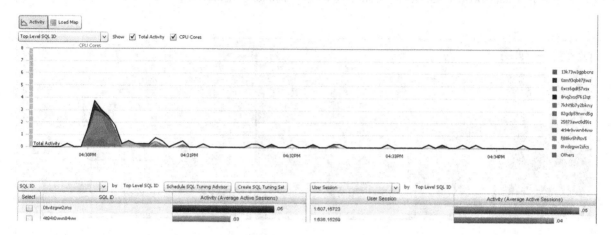

Figure 9-30. *Top-level SQL ID activity in ASH Analytics*

The percentage of impact of SQL ID cwu5p1yyp1p40 in Figure 9-30 is clearly demonstrated in the graph, which shows that two user sessions were executing the statement throughout the timeline. This can be assumed by the associated colors from the graph that identify the SQL ID and the user session, but also can be verified by clicking each of the links to the user sessions, which will then show the SQL ID okwk7211pw296 identified with each.

The example in Figure 9-31 still displays the overall total activity as a black line in the graph. The system response time per call, which encompasses usage by two CPUs, also shows a small "blip" of activity when ASH data samples are rolled up into the AWR.

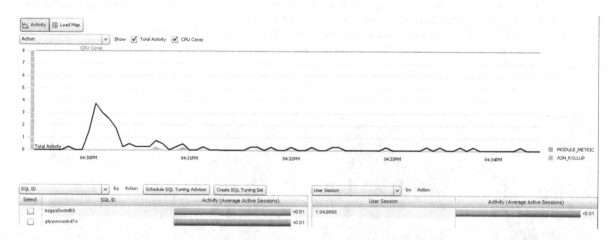

Figure 9-31. *ASH Analytics, graphing by action, showing system response time, DB wait time and ASH roll-up*

The Load Map

The load map, shown in Figure 9-32, is the second choice for viewing data from ASH Analytics. The Activity graph is the view most administrators are familiar with from years of Enterprise Manager experience. The load map is a new way to display all data found in ASH Analytics, but often more clear for nonadministrator groups.

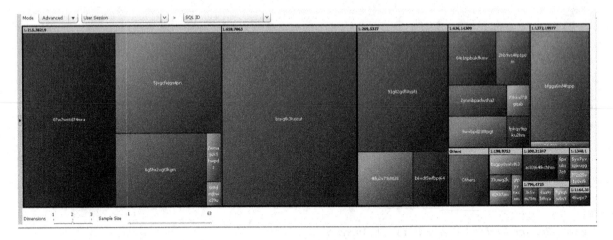

Figure 9-32. An ASH Analytics advanced load map displaying wait class and SQL ID

▧ **Tip**   The load map view is often lost on the administrator, who is familiar with and has training to understand data displayed from Top Activity. The load map displays performance data in a way that has more visual impact.

The load map in Figure 9-32 shows SQL ID csu5p1yyp1p40 as almost 50 percent of the resource usage in the environment. For a nonadministrator, this representation provides a clearer picture of the SQL affecting performance than a graph display of the same data, which might very well be misleading.

The same load map can then be changed to display the SQL IDs, but this time sorted by user session. Figure 9-33 shows the same load as in Figure 9-32, but the percentages are broken out by user session first, and then by SQL ID within each session.

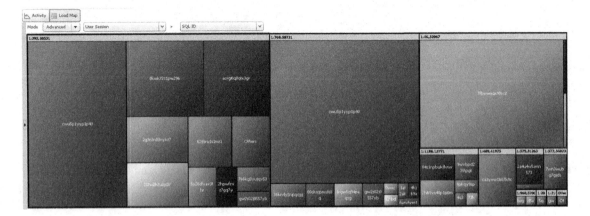

Figure 9-33. An ASH Analytics advanced load map, displayed by user session and SQL ID

Dimensions for the same load map can be adjusted, and sample size can be changed (see Figure 9-34).

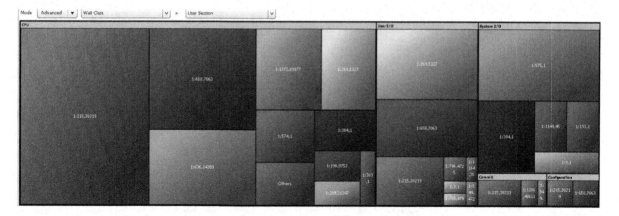

Figure 9-34. *An ASH Analytics load map with diminished dimensions and sample size*

The example in Figure 9-34 displays only the user session information. If you use an advanced load map setting and limiting the samples to three, you can display even smaller subsets of sample information.

By then increasing to three dimensions, building each of these dimensions by wait class, SQL ID, and client, you can create a load map that shows the SQL ID as the header in each section, along with client information and then the wait class indicator (see Figure 9-35).

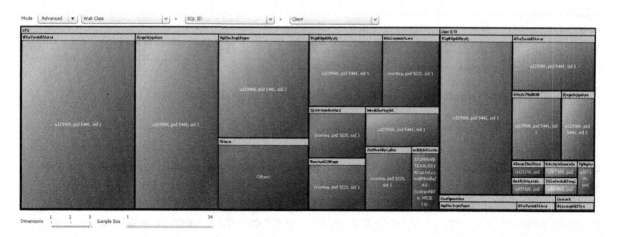

Figure 9-35. *ASH Analytics, displaying an advanced, three-dimension load map*

ASH Analytics is the future of Top Activity. With the advancements in ASH expected in future releases of Oracle, ASH Analytics will continue to provide more-enhanced performance data for the Oracle database environment.

SQL Monitoring

SQL Monitor, introduced in Oracle 11g, has been hailed as one of the best new features. The graphical display of SQL Monitor within Enterprise Manager offers a secondary view to session data in the database (see Figure 9-36).

Monitored SQL Executions

Active in last 6 hours ▼

Status	Duration	SQL ID	User	Parallel	Database Time	IO Requests
✓	7.0s	fj88kr5hftsv5			7.5s	
✓	7.0s	86qju9kg1u1by			7.4s	
✓	23.0s	694u1un2sh6q0			23.1s	7,742
✓	8.0s	cu61hq059cf8k	SYSTEM		9.2s	3,271
✓	7.0s	gps62djw0x9mu	SYSTEM		7.8s	2,566
✓	8.0s	4t94r0vwn84vw			8.2s	
✓	15.0s	14ts7q78gf051			13.1s	
✓	8.0s	4t94r0vwn84vw			8.5s	

Figure 9-36. *SQL executing in the SQL Monitor*

Data, ordered by active sessions displayed at the top, is followed by an active duration window, SQL ID, user info, database time, I/O wait info, start time, end time, and SQL text in the main monitoring view, as shown in Figure 9-37. The page also offers links for SQL ID and user sessions to the Monitored Executions page.

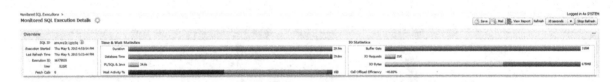

Figure 9-37. *The top section of the SQL Monitor, the Monitored SQL Execution Details page*

■ **Tip**   If there is one view that an administrator should consider giving view-only access to for monitoring activity in a database environment, the SQL Monitor is it. This view is exceptionally easy to use and offers incredibly valuable information regarding activity and performance. The SQL Monitor view offers quick access to alert the developer or analyst when something may be amiss that would be less likely to escalate to an incident in the EM12c, but may still require an administrator's assistance. In the development lifecycle, this can offer members of the database team another way to visually monitor what is occurring during both development and testing phases.

Whereas Top Activity and ASH Analytics share detail pages for SQL ID and user sessions, SQL Monitor shares session details only with user sessions and CPU usage. For SQL ID, the SQL Monitor has its own performance page data based on the execution of DBMS_SQLTUNE.REPORT_SQL_MONITOR by the EM12c console to populate the main SQL Monitoring page.

Figure 9-38 is a graphical representation of this report as report_level=>'ALL' is executed by the EM12c console. This same report can be executed using the package from the command line as well, but the EM12c SQL Monitor interface conveniently populates and displays the data in a user-friendly format for the administrator.

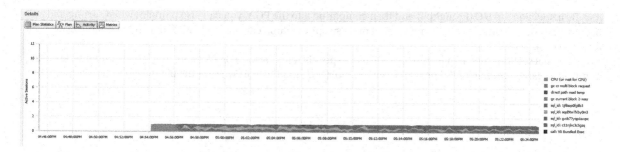

Figure 9-38. *The lower pane of the Monitored SQL Executions Details report by the SQL Monitor for SQL_IDs involved in the snapshot*

The view can be adjusted to show SQL-specific metrics, as shown in Figure 9-39, by simply clicking the Metrics button in the upper-left corner. The data can be incredibly detailed and valuable when investigating an impacting SQL statement.

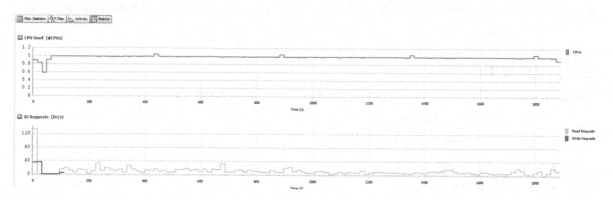

Figure 9-39. *Metric usage from the same report time as the SQL Monitor report in Figure 9-37, indicating CPU and I/O read and write requests in bytes*

Whereas Figure 9-39 shows CPU and I/O read and write requests from the report, Figure 9-40 shows the results of I/O throughput and PGA usage. This data shows the CPU usage and waits for CPU by the statement. By taking this data and intersecting the high/low points, you can build a clear picture of how the read and write requests are affected by CPU usage and CPU waits.

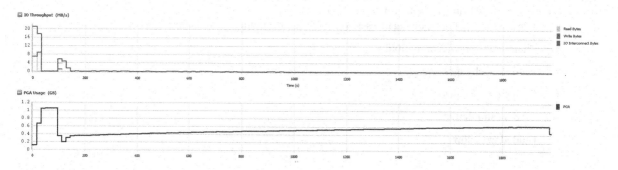

Figure 9-40. *SQL Monitor demonstrating I/O throughput by reads and writes in bytes*

By inspecting the I/O throughput and then comparing it to the PGA, you can also pinpoint when sorting and hashing may occur within the PGA and when it may "swap" to temp, (causing higher I/O due to temp tablespace reads/writes).

The final section, shown in Figure 9-41, displays specific temp usage. For DSS and OLAP environments, knowing temp usage can be very helpful. The SQL Monitor displays this in the SQL Monitor detail report.

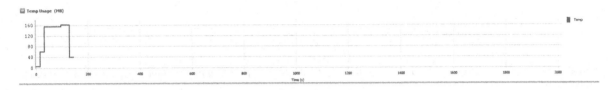

Figure 9-41. *Temp usage from the SQL Monitor report, displayed in a graph*

Using these specific SQL Monitor graphs offers high-level images detailing valuable usage areas outside of just monitoring database activity from the SQL perspective. Whereas an administrator might query over a period of time any of these areas or a combination of them, SQL Monitor is always available and clearly graphs out the recent usage for each.

SQL Performance

The SQL submenu within the database target home page has numerous options, including these:

- SQL Performance Analyzer
- SQL Access Advisor
- SQL Tuning Advisor
- SQL Tuning Sets
- SQL Plan Control
- Optimizer Statistics

SQL Performance Analyzer

The SQL Performance Analyzer, although easily accessible through the Performance drop-down, is part of the Advisor Central provision of EM12c features. The Analyzer provides a simple wizard to test and analyze how changes to a database environment will affect a SQL tuning set.

This enables you to test the following in a session-level environment, without affecting users:

- Changes in version compatibility
- Parameter changes
- Optimizer statistics
- Exadata simulation
- Guided workflow

SQL Performance Analyzer tasks can be created by clicking any of the links and working through the wizards. The tasks are then scheduled as an EM Job in the EM12c environment. You may check the status by manually refreshing the interface view or by leaving the View Data option at its default, which uses a 15-second interval.

SQL Access Advisor

The SQL Access Advisor provides a graphical interface for evaluating existing objects in the database for efficiency or recommending new objects that may increase performance through physical optimization options. Figure 9-42 shows the initial advisor options available from the interface.

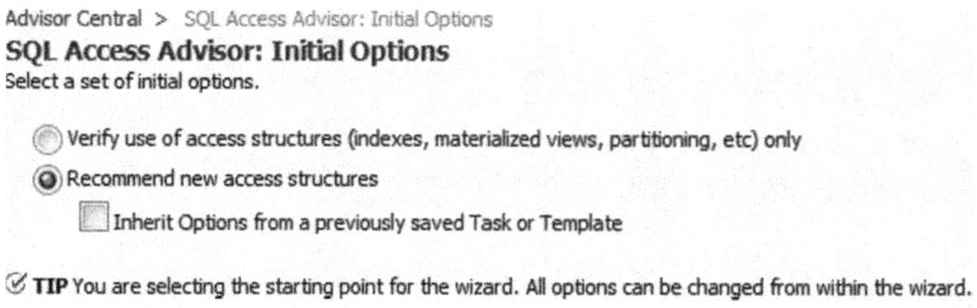

Advisor Central > SQL Access Advisor: Initial Options
SQL Access Advisor: Initial Options
Select a set of initial options.

- Verify use of access structures (indexes, materialized views, partitioning, etc) only
- ● Recommend new access structures
    - ☐ Inherit Options from a previously saved Task or Template

☑ **TIP** You are selecting the starting point for the wizard. All options can be changed from within the wizard.

Figure 9-42. The SQL Access Advisor performance options for database targets

The SQL Access Advisor (accessible from the Performance drop-down, but part of the Advisor Central features) has two options. The first inspects current objects and makes recommendations based on what is already present in the system. The second option inspects historical SQL for recommendations on indexes and materialized views that could assist in performance gains. As with any advisor, you must review and verify the SQL Access Advisor recommendations before implementing them.

SQL Tuning Sets

A *SQL tuning set* is a collection of SQL statements, which can be bound by executing schema, application module/action, or a set of bind variables, cursor fetches, execution count, command type, or optimizer cost.

SQL tuning sets can be migrated to other databases, allowing the administrator to perform tuning tests on other environments. Production performance issues can be migrated to a secondary stage environment to duplicate the issues experienced and resolution scenarios tested.

■ **Note** Understanding the SQL is essential for an administrator who wants to understand usage and optimization in their database environment. The SQL Tuning Advisor and the SQL Access Advisor utilize SQL tuning sets to give the best advice on optimizing the Oracle environment.

SQL Plan Control

Another option for controlling performance is to create and store SQL plans. SQL plans are one of the features utilized by SQL profiles and can be viewed in the SQL Plans section by clicking Performance ➤ SQL ➤ SQL Plan Control from the Database performance home page (see Figure 9-43).

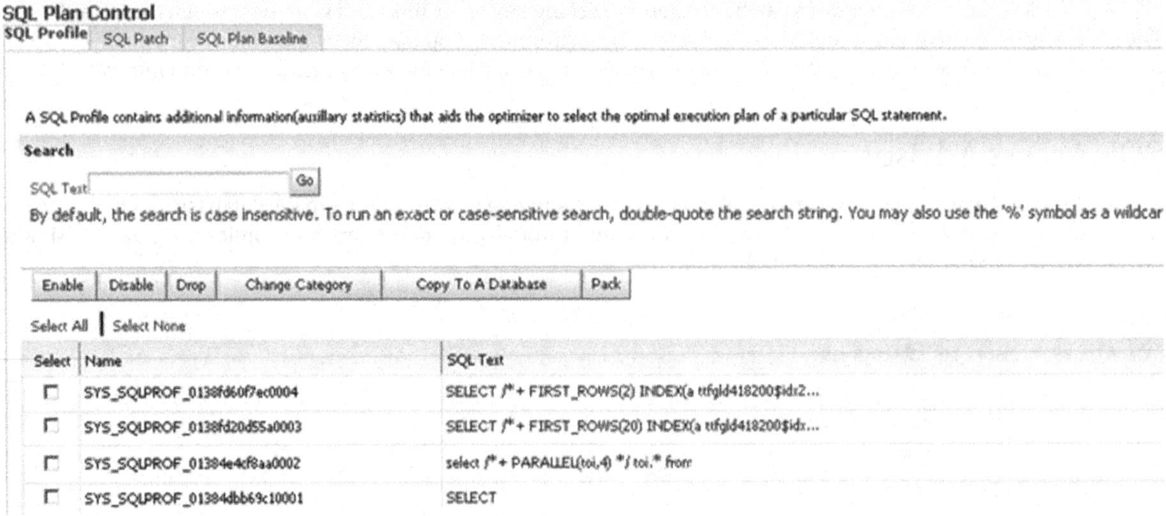

SQL Plan Control

SQL Profile   SQL Patch   SQL Plan Baseline

A SQL Profile contains additional information(auxiliary statistics) that aids the optimizer to select the optimal execution plan of a particular SQL statement.

Search

SQL Text [   ] [Go]

By default, the search is case insensitive. To run an exact or case-sensitive search, double-quote the search string. You may also use the '%' symbol as a wildcar

| Enable | Disable | Drop | | Change Category | | Copy To A Database | | Pack |

Select All | Select None

Select	Name	SQL Text
☐	SYS_SQLPROF_0138fd60f7ec0004	SELECT /*+ FIRST_ROWS(2) INDEX(a ttfgld418200$idx2...
☐	SYS_SQLPROF_0138fd20d55a0003	SELECT /*+ FIRST_ROWS(20) INDEX(a ttfgld418200$idx...
☐	SYS_SQLPROF_01384e4cf8aa0002	select /*+ PARALLEL(toi,4) */ toi.* from
☐	SYS_SQLPROF_01384dbb69c10001	SELECT

Figure 9-43. *SQL plans created as part of SQL profiles*

The benefit of having one view for all plan control is that if a statement has changed and there is a question about whether plan control is in place, the DBA can easily access and verify from the panel instead o having to search for the SQL ID.

Optimizer Statistics

Statistics are the core of Oracle's Cost-Based Optimizer (CBO.) As an administrator deepens their knowledge of performance and optimization, their knowledge of statistics must increase as well. EM12c offers a number of graphical user interfaces to lessen demands on command-line requirements, but the knowledge of how statistics help the CBO make optimization choices is a key to any Oracle database specialist's skill set.

Graphic options to gather, restore, lock, and manage statistics are a powerful tool in the hands of an administrator. The Performance drop-down menu of the database target in EM12c enables you to set default options for optimizer statistics, along with addressing performance issues with the CBO (see Figure 9-44).

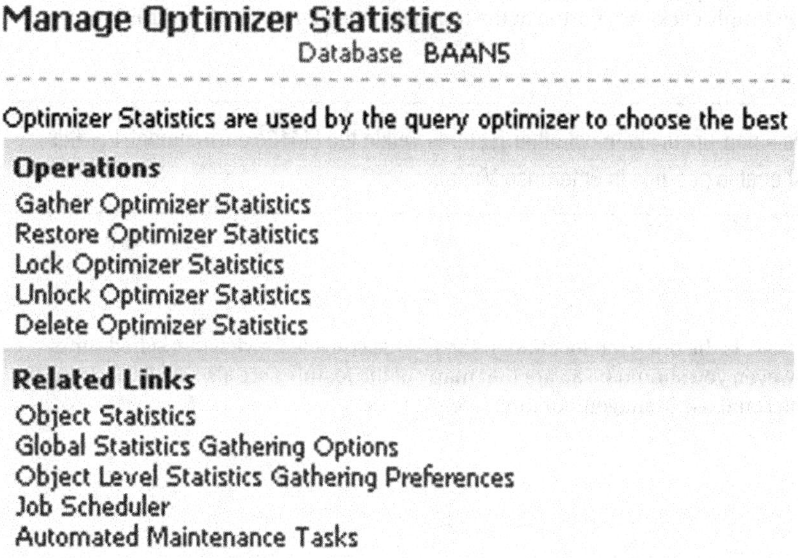

Manage Optimizer Statistics

Database BAAN5

Optimizer Statistics are used by the query optimizer to choose the best

Operations

Gather Optimizer Statistics
Restore Optimizer Statistics
Lock Optimizer Statistics
Unlock Optimizer Statistics
Delete Optimizer Statistics

Related Links

Object Statistics
Global Statistics Gathering Options
Object Level Statistics Gathering Preferences
Job Scheduler
Automated Maintenance Tasks

Figure 9-44. Managing optimizer statistics in the EM12c Performance console

Each of the links accesses a different area for managing database statistics. This includes operational tasks. From a lower section, you can access object-level and global-level statistics, along with scheduling and automating.

Cloud Control SQL History

The Cloud Control SQL History, unlike history from other SQL, includes SQL executed by EM12c for managing and monitoring the database environment. The view provides not just SQL_TEXT, but the start time, the duration and the URL (see Figure 9-45). The URL is extremely valuable, as it is descriptive enough to inform you which EM12c feature was responsible for the SQL executed.

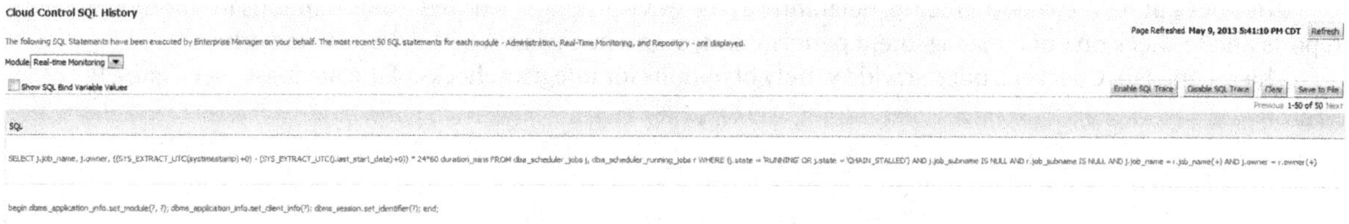

Figure 9-45. Information regarding a SQL statement from the cloud control that was issued by the SQL Monitor in EM12c

You can also issue an EM12c operation-specific trace if concerned about performance or investigating an issue. You can enable or disable the trace by simply clicking a button at the top-right side of the Cloud Control SQL History interface.

■ **Note**   Cloud Control SQL History is a pop-up, unlike most other features within the EM12c environment. For this feature to function correctly, you must enable pop-ups in Enterprise Manager.

Advisor Central

The Advisor home, shown in Figure 9-46, is the one-stop location in the EM12c console for viewing, scheduling, and managing Oracle's advisors. However, you should be aware that many of the features are also available from the Performance drop-down menu in the Database Management interface.

Advisor Central

Advisors | Checkers

Advisors

ADDM   Automatic Undo Management
Memory Advisors   MTTR Advisor
SQL Advisors   SQL Performance Analyzer

Advisor Tasks

Search

Select an advisory type and optionally enter a task name to filter the data that is displayed in your results set.

Advisory Type   Task Name   Advisor Runs   Status

All Types   ▼   Last 31 Days ▼   All   ▼   Go

By default, the search returns all uppercase matches beginning with the string you entered. To run an exact or case-sensitive match, double quote the search string. You can use the wildcard symbol (%) in a double quoted string.

Results

View Result | Delete | Actions| Re-schedule   ▼   Go

Select	Name	Advisory Type	Instance	Description
◉	ADDM:2921611025_9307	ADDM	All	ADDM auto run: snapshots [9306, 9307], , database id 2921611025

Figure 9-46. *Advisor Central, displaying the tab options and main advisors available*

Advisor Central has a two-tab setup, defaulting to the Advisors page. This page offers options to run ADDM reports and to check on undo management performance, segment advisors, SQL Advisors, and others.

The second tab, Checkers, offers a wide variety of options for integrity checks of the database (see Figure 9-47).

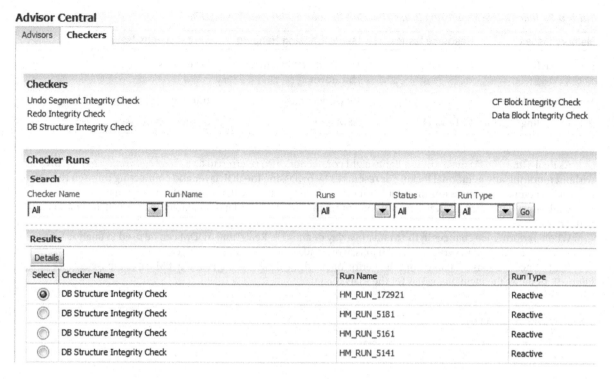

Figure 9-47. Advisor Central's database integrity checker options

The Performance section of each database target in the EM12c console offers incredible insight into the database, along with optimizing options for its long-term health.

Emergency Monitoring

Emergency Monitoring enables you to monitor basic processing and database information of an unresponsive database. The proprietary mechanism is available through EM12c and the Enterprise Manager Command Line Interface (EMCLI) and allows the administrator to diagnose performance issues, conduct hang analysis, and kill blocking sessions.

Emergency Monitoring requires SYSDBA access and DB Host access for the Oracle user to successfully implement.

Real-Time ADDM

A troubling scenario for an administrator is a hung database. The conundrum of deciding whether to quickly bounce the database—thereby removing the obstacle causing the hang situation but often losing all valuable data to diagnose the cause—has resulted in Oracle offering Real-Time ADDM.

Real-Time ADDM offers real-time analysis of a slow or hung database system and diagnoses deadlocks, performance impacts, and resource contention (see Table 9-3). The Real-Time ADDM feature uses DB Time as the basis for all performance measurements. It also identifies any configuration changes that have occurred, weighing both sets of metrics to report and compare.

Table 9-3. *Inaccessible Monitoring Issues That Can Be Solved with Real-Time ADDM*

Memory Issues	Resource Issues	Issues Causing Hanging	Miscellaneous Issues
Library cache	I/O waits	Unscheduled instance shutdown	Deadlocks
Memory allocation	Memory paging	Blocking issues	Interconnect issues
PGA extending	CPU waits	ASM issues	Sessions/processes

As Real-Time ADDM makes only a lightweight connection, also referred to as a *direct connection to the SGA* without requiring any additional locking or resources by bypassing the SQL layer and connecting through the agent, it is able to complete connections that would otherwise be impossible with traditional connection types.

Real-Time ADDM can analyze data returned numerous ways to the database, including the SQL layer and JDBC connection.

When performance changes in the matter of a day or an hour, Real-Time ADDM can be used to analyze what changes were made, and to verify new batch jobs, workloads, or configuration changes.

Real-Time ADDM is available from the Performance drop-down menu from any EM12c database target. Figure 9-48 shows the login dialog box for the ADDM console.

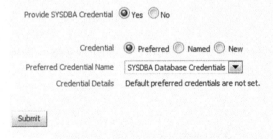

Figure 9-48. *Logging in to the Real-Time ADDM console requires SYSDBA credentials*

The analysis can be performed on a single instance, RAC environment, or even an engineered system, such as Exadata.

The Top Activity view, shown in Figure 9-49, displays about 1 hour of data, along with approximately 10 minutes of previous ASH data, so you can inspect for issues that are the cause of a database hang.

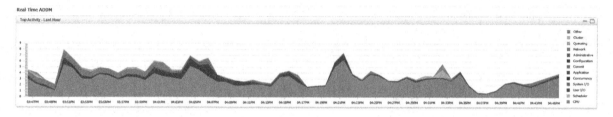

Figure 9-49. *Top Activity view through Real-Time ADDM*

The top section appears very similar to Top Activity, but is actually sourced from ASH data. To start the Real-Time ADDM analysis, you click the Start button, shown in Figure 9-50.

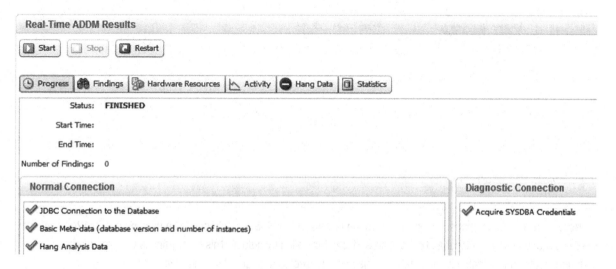

Figure 9-50. *Real-Time ADDM analysis interface for EM12c*

If the database is in a hung state, the status will be shown, notifying of the database's inability to accept connections. Real-Time ADDM will proceed with verifying credentials, providing connection options to be used, and performing hang analysis.

The report generated is displayed in six tab views, including the Progress tab, General Findings, Hardware Resources (detailing any hardware issues that are discovered), Activity (providing analysis of database sessions), Hang Data (providing information specific to the cause of the database hang), and Statistics (providing details on the analysis report).

The option to save or e-mail the results in HTML format is available at the upper-right corner of the Real-Time ADDM interface.

ADDM Comparison Report

Often the administrator is faced with performance differences in two time periods, when none should occur. The ability to perform a cause-to-effect analysis for two ADDM reports is available as part of the ADDM comparison report.

The ADDM comparison report is available by choosing Performance ➤ AWR ➤ Compare Period ADDM for any database target. After clicking the link, you will be asked to submit information about the begin time and end time for the timeline in question (see Figure 9-51). In the lower section, you then choose a base period for comparison from drop-down options that include the preceding time period, the previous day, or the previous week.

Run Compare Period ADDM

Step 1: Select a Comparison Period

Instance   All ▼

Begin Time   May 8, 2013 3:01:18 PM 📷

End Time   May 8, 2013 5:01:42 PM 📷

☑ **TIP**   Time will be adjusted to the capture time of the closest snapshot

Step 2: Select a Base Period

Instance   All ▼

◉ Offset

Offset   Preceding Period ▼

| Preceding Period |
| One Day |
| One Week |

◯ Baseline

Baseline   INDOW ▼

◯ Customize

Begin Time   📷

End Time   📷

☑ **TIP**   Time will be adjusted to the capture time of the closest snapshot

Figure 9-51.   Choosing options for a comparison ADDM report

■ **Note**   The ADDM comparison report requires the installation of PL/SQL packages to be used by the EM12c agent user on the target to perform the comparison report and is not installed by default. This installation is performed as an EM Job and can be implemented immediately or scheduled to execute at a later date and time.

In the example in Figure 9-52, the options are shown for choices in comparisons of an ADDM report. The latest offset, a baseline or a custom begin and end time can be chosen.

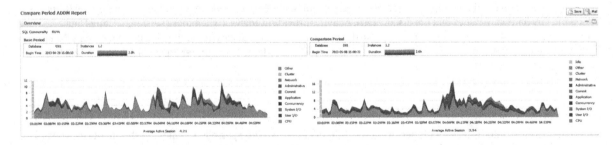

Figure 9-52.   ADDM comparison report activity

Below Detail for Selected 30 Minute Interval, you can locate the time of the section detailed in the bottom panes of the Top Activity graph. Using this information, you then can click Compare Period ADDM to identify any specific activity that was out of ordinary for the timeline of concern (see Figure 9-53).

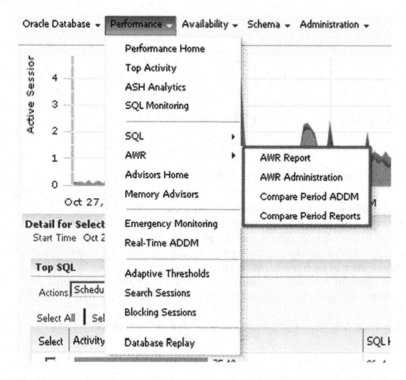

Figure 9-53. *Locating ADDM comparison reports in the EM12c database target interface*

Choosing a timeline that matches the scenario from Figure 9-52 to grant us the clearest view of the problem is essential.

As the Top Activity starts at 11:30 PM and is for a 30-minute period, the appropriate choice for an accurate comparison is to also match this in the ADDM Begin Time and set the End Time to 30 minutes later, resulting in an end-time "starting minute" of 11:59 PM.

As the night of the activity is on a Saturday, and the goal is to know what has changed from the hour previously, we will compare it to the preceding period.

Figure 9-54 shows the resulting settings for the Comparison ADDM Report fields.

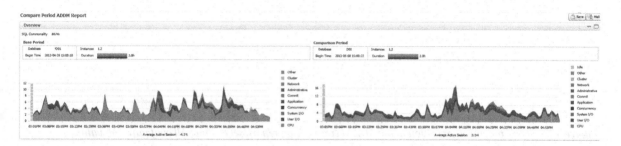

Figure 9-54. *Comparison timelines and baselines*

Clicking Run executes the ADDM comparison report. The report first indicates the commonality of the two timelines (see Figure 9-55).

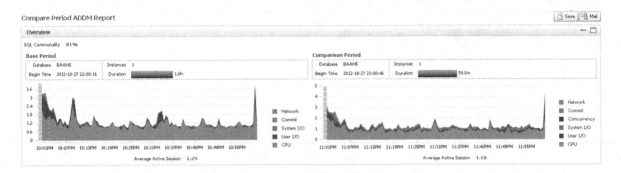

Figure 9-55. *An ADDM comparison report, comparing the previous hour with an hour of higher usage*

Note that the duration of the comparison is for the entire 1-hour snapshot, even though time was entered for a half hour. If snapshot intervals are set to occur more often than the default (1 hour), the ADDM comparison will show results for the minimum number of snapshots required to cover the beginning and end time chosen.

Inspecting the left-hand values in the graph, you must note that the average sessions shown is not a one-to-one representation between the graphs, but independent of each session to best demonstrate the data for each period used in the comparison. Each period graph also contains its own legend for wait event types, to the right of each graph.

The bottom of each graph clearly shows the average active sessions, along with buttons at the top right to save or e-mail the graphs in HTML format.

The Details pane in the bottom section of the ADDM comparison report is divided into three sections: Configuration, Finding, and Resource.

Configuration

The Configuration section of the ADDM comparison report presents information regarding physical configurations, parameter settings, and session parameters that may have impacted the difference in the periods compared (see Figure 9-56).

Name	Host/Instance	Base Period	Comparison Period
▼ DATABASE			
▼ Database Block Size			
	database	8KB	8KB
▼ Number of Instances Analyzed			
	database	1	1
▼ Number of Instances			
	database	1	1
▼ bitmap_merge_area_size			
	database	1MB	1MB
▼ cluster_database			
	database	FALSE	FALSE
▼ compatible			
	database	11.2.0.0.0	11.2.0.0.0

Figure 9-56. *The Configuration section of the ADDM comparison report, set to show All configuration values*

You can show just differences (by default) or show all configuration values. If a review of all configuration values is warranted, this does offer a quick review of the parameter settings and session values.

Finding

The Finding section presents each Performance Difference type, percentage of impact, and then the percentage of impact it created for each base period (see Figure 9-57). Since these values can be positive for one period and negative for another, you should note the totals for the change impact and ensure that the change impact is clearly understood for the comparison period in case the problem was one that had escalated over multiple time periods. If escalation did occur, the change impact percentage could be misleading, and the overall impact to the environment over a larger period of time should be taken into consideration.

Figure 9-57. *Findings for the ADDM comparison report, showing both improvement and degradation in performance between the two periods of the comparison*

For each Performance Difference, detailed information is displayed below the Details pane. As performance regression was discovered for Top Segments by User I/O, the following findings resulted:

- Individual database segments responsible for significant User I/O and Cluster waits were found.

- Impact changed from 0.04 active sessions to 0.1 active sessions, by –5%.

Resource

The Resource detail reports on differences in CPU, memory, I/O, and interconnect (if RAC is involved). This data can be represented in either a graphical form, shown in Figure 9-58, or in a tabular report, shown in Figure 9-59.

Figure 9-58. *Tabular representation of detail data on memory differences between two ADDM timelines in a comparison report*

Figure 9-59. *Graphical representation of detail data on I/O difference between two ADDM timelines in a comparison report*

With this detailed data, you can quickly assess that there was a 75 percent jump in memory usage and a significant difference in data-file single-block read latency between the two timelines used in the comparison.

As with other reports in the EM12c interface, there is an option to save or e-mail an HTML report for later review or to retain for historical reference.

Summary

As the need for automating and optimizing the database and its environment increases, the importance of the Enterprise Manager 12c performance console will increase in demand as well. Top Activity will slowly migrate to ASH Analytics, with its robust, transparent, and effective reporting. The opportunities to gather data from a simple and efficient graphical interface and provide effective optimization recommendations and monitoring provide the clear direction for enterprise-level database control.

■ ■ ■

CHAPTER 10

Metric Extensions and Management Plug-ins

by Alex Gorbachev

The 10g and 11g versions of Oracle Enterprise Manager introduced some basic features aimed at helping the product become an enterprise manageability and monitoring framework. However, OEM was, above all, a manageability tool built for Oracle products, with some features extending its capabilities to other target types not supported out of the box. Oracle Enterprise Manager Cloud Control 12c has been completely rearchitected from the ground up to be, first of all, a framework for enterprise manageability. Nearly all functionality for management and monitoring of specific Oracle and third-party products has been built on top of that framework as plug-ins.

Just like previous versions of OEM, EM12c provides options for users and product vendors to extend its capabilities in two basic ways. The first part of this chapter presents the simplest: metric extensions. The second part covers the basics of management plug-in development as well as some advanced features.

I recommend that you try the hands-on examples as you read through this chapter, and have the EM12c extensibility documentation handy as a reference. Full topic coverage would require a book of its own, and this chapter is more of an introduction to extending EM12c.

However, don't skip this chapter even if you don't expect to develop plug-ins yourself. Knowledge of EM12c internals will help you better understand how EM12c works. Ultimately, this will enable you to become more productive and find the environment more intuitive to use.

Metric Extensions

Metric extensions in EM12c replace user-defined metrics (UDMs) that were initially introduced in OEM 10g and are now deprecated in 12c. Compared to UDMs, metric extensions provide much more flexibility in data collection and are easier to deploy and manage at scale.

As you should already know by now, each monitored target comes with a set of predefined metrics that are designed by the plug-in creator (which could be Oracle or a third-party vendor). For example, host targets collect CPU utilization metrics, and Oracle Database targets collect physical IO metrics, among others. Usually these metrics will be enough, but at times you might want to collect more metrics than are available out of the box in order to monitor conditions specific to your environment or applications.

Metric extensions are run by an agent from the host that the agent is deployed on. While you are creating and managing metric extensions centrally by using the OMS, they need to be distributed to the agents that monitor targets where metric extensions are deployed to. That's done automatically as soon as a metric extension is deployed on the first target of an agent.

The development lifecycle of metric extensions is a little more involved compared to the old-style UDMs, but that's what makes metric extensions simpler to manage at scale in a multiuser environment. To access the Metric Extensions home page, choose Enterprise ➤ Monitoring ➤ Metric Extensions. There you will see a quick overview of the metric extensions development lifecycle, as shown in Figure 10-1.

***Figure 10-1.** Metric extension development lifecycle*

Your First Metric Extension

Let's create a sample metric so you can see the process in action. Let's say you need to monitor how close the sessions in your database get to the maximum number of open cursors per session. That maximum is controlled by the open_cursors init.ora parameter. You can use the query in Listing 10-1 to return the percentage of open cursors in terms of the defined maximum.

***Listing 10-1.** SQL for Open Cursors Metric Extensions*

```
SELECT ROUND (c.open_cursors / p.value * 100) open_cursors_pct
  FROM (SELECT   sid, COUNT (*) open_cursors
            FROM v$open_cursor
        GROUP BY sid
        ORDER BY 2 DESC) c,
      v$parameter p
 WHERE p.name = 'open_cursors' AND ROWNUM = 1
```

Creating the New Metric Extension

To create this metric, click the Create button on the Metric Extensions home page, just above the table listing available metric extensions. If the button is grayed out and not clickable, you don't have permission to create new metric extensions. You need to have the Create Metric Extension privilege granted by your EM Super Administrator. This privilege is assigned while creating or editing an EM user from the Resource Privileges screen, in the row Metric Extensions Resource. There is only one relevant privilege: Create Metric Extension. This privilege allows you to create and import new metric extensions.

After you click the Create button, the new Metric Extensions Wizard appears. Figure 10-2 shows the wizard's General Properties tab.

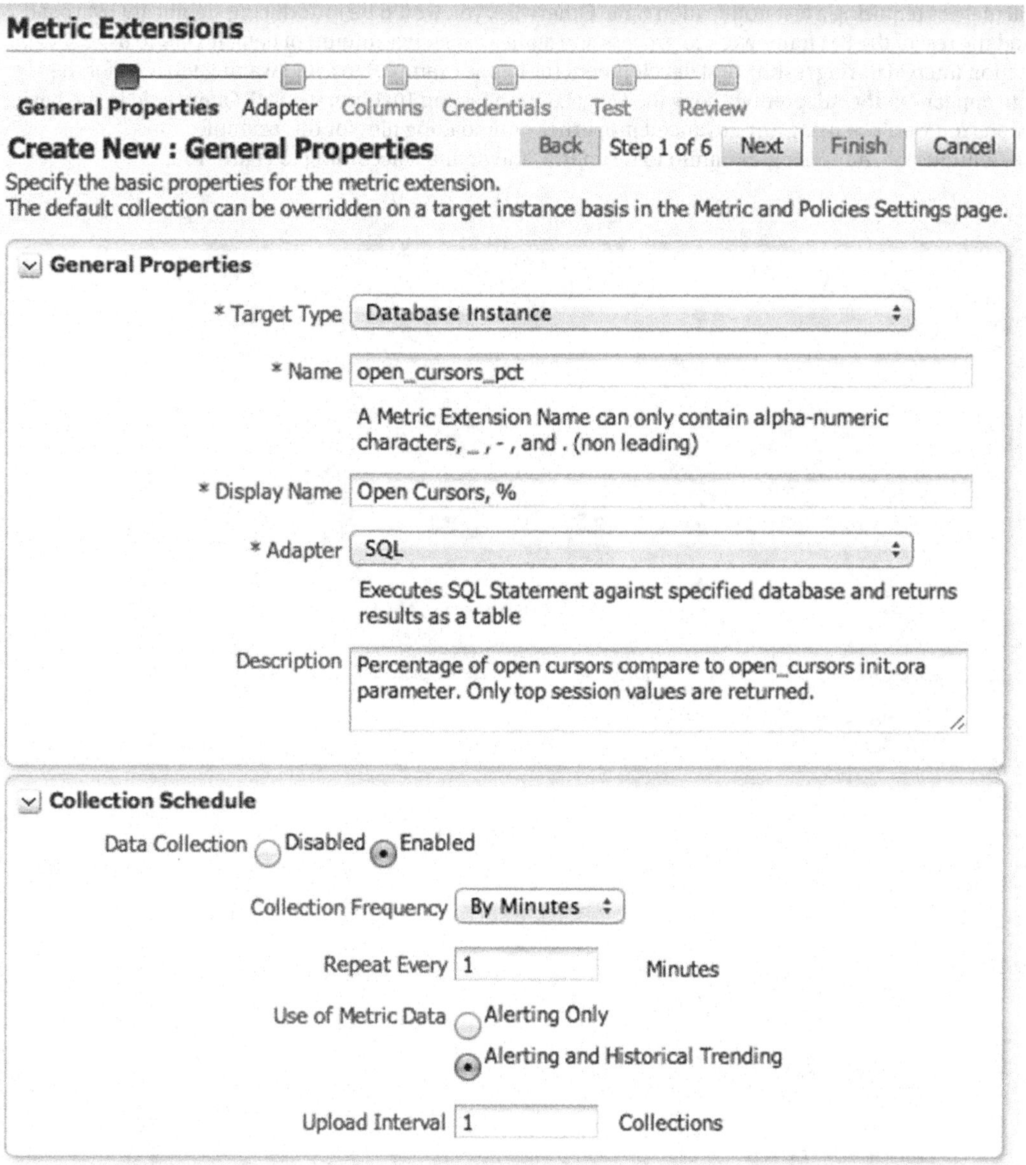

Metric Extensions

General Properties   Adapter   Columns   Credentials   Test   Review

Create New : General Properties   Back   Step 1 of 6   Next   Finish   Cancel

Specify the basic properties for the metric extension.
The default collection can be overridden on a target instance basis in the Metric and Policies Settings page.

▽ General Properties

* Target Type   Database Instance ⬍

* Name   open_cursors_pct

A Metric Extension Name can only contain alpha-numeric
characters, _ , - , and . (non leading)

* Display Name   Open Cursors, %

* Adapter   SQL ⬍

Executes SQL Statement against specified database and returns
results as a table

Description   Percentage of open cursors compare to open_cursors init.ora
parameter. Only top session values are returned.

▽ Collection Schedule

Data Collection ◯ Disabled ◉ Enabled

Collection Frequency   By Minutes ⬍

Repeat Every   1   Minutes

Use of Metric Data ◯ Alerting Only

◉ Alerting and Historical Trending

Upload Interval   1   Collections

Figure 10-2. General properties of open_cursor_pct metric extension

Set the Target Type option to Database Instance so the metric can be deployed on a single-instance database as well as on each instance of a RAC database. If you were to select the metric from a real table or to monitor a global condition such as the number of messages in a queue table, you would set the Target Type to Cluster Database instead of each RAC database instance. Set the Name property to open_cursors_pct. This is the name used by EM internally, and you would use it later if you needed to extract information from the repository—for example, writing a SQL statement for a custom report. Choose SQL as the Adapter and select a collection interval of 1 minute and an upload interval of 1 (indicating an upload on each collection). I recommend that you choose collection intervals carefully and avoid collecting metrics more frequently than 5–15 minutes. You should set the interval below 5 minutes for only a very few critical metrics requiring a fast notification time. Otherwise, you would be introducing significant overhead on the agent and the rest of the EM framework to process and store a excessive amount of data. It's OK to use a 1-minute collection interval during testing and development (as in this example) to avoid waiting too long for the metric history to appear. On the Adapter tab, copy the SQL text from Listing 10-1 into the SQL Query field in the Basic Properties section. You won't be using any advanced properties or uploading files for this example.

Next is the Columns tab. Add a single column to the metric and define it according to Figure 10-3.

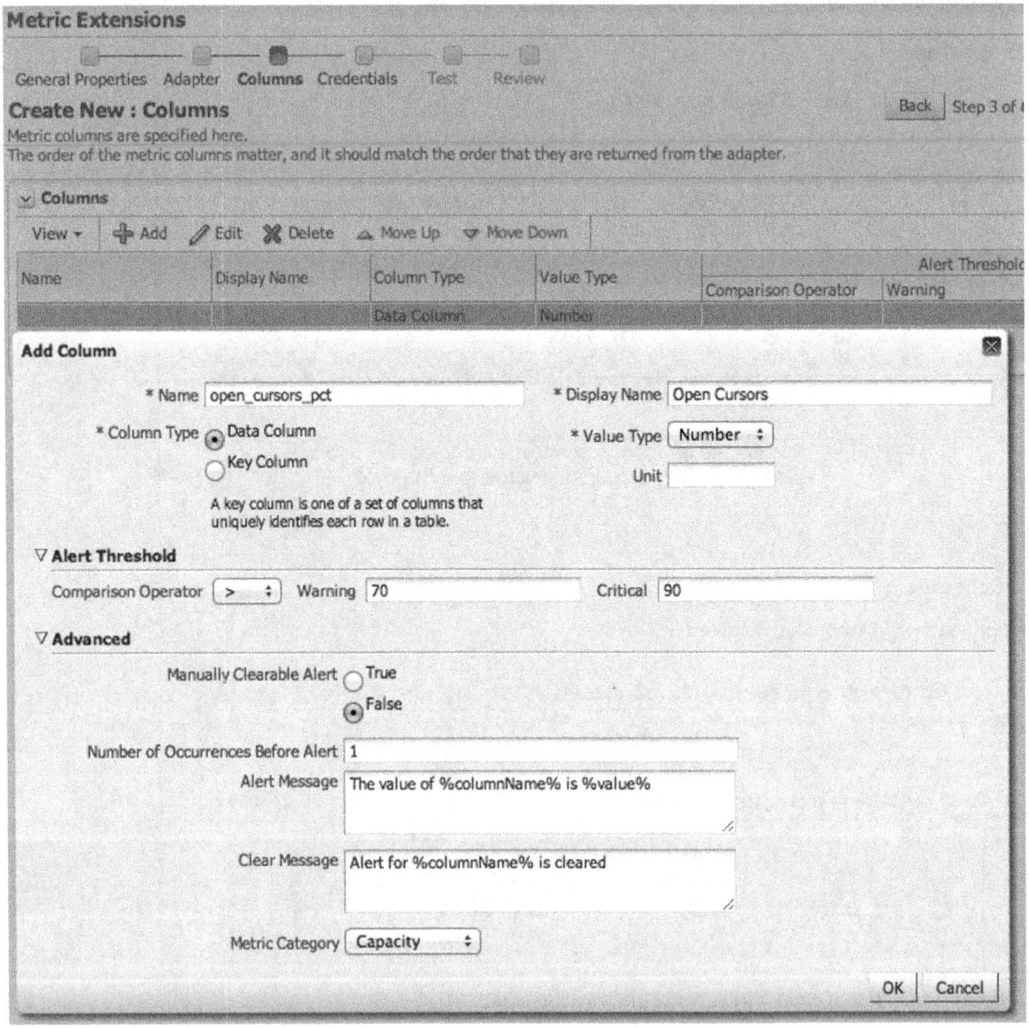

Figure 10-3. *Metric extension column*

In the Alert Threshold section, choose the greater-than (>) comparison operator. Set the default thresholds for warning and critical conditions to 70 and 90 percent, respectively. In the advanced options, you can edit the number of occurrences before an alert as well create a custom message. You can also assign the metric to one of the predefined categories which then enables EM12c Console to group your metrics with other similar metrics.

On the Credentials tab, leave Use Default Monitoring Credentials. Now you are ready to test your metric.

On the Test tab, add one or more databases (remember that you should have View privileges on them if you are not a Super Administrator user). Then click the Run Test button. You should see the collection progress dialog box appear for a short time (unless you selected many database instances), and the collection result is displayed. If you have no error messages and the result is what you expected, you can proceed to completion on the Review tab.

If the metric extension was created successfully after you clicked the Finish button, you will see it on the Metric Extensions home page with the status Editable. You can also see that this metric extension is version 1. Editing the metric extension in Editable status will not increment the version. You can review and edit your metric multiple times, until you get the collection working as you envisioned it in the real-time testing dialog box.

Testing the Metric Extension

If the first draft is working as expected, the next step is to perform test runs on the real targets. Before you can deploy a metric on a target, the metric must be saved as a Deployable Draft. Select your metric and then, from the Actions menu located above the table of metric extensions, choose Save as Deployable Draft. The metric's status changes to Deployable Draft. At this stage, the metric is visible only to you, its owner, unless you explicitly grant permission to other users or roles by using Actions ➤ Manage Access. Also note that you cannot edit a metric extension in Deployable Draft status unless you create a new version, which you will do later.

To ensure that your metric extension behaves as expected, let's deploy it to some targets. This is done by choosing Actions ➤ Deploy to Targets. After you select the targets and submit the deployment jobs, the metric extension will be running in the background. All deployment jobs are asynchronous actions scheduled as jobs in EM12c. Metric extension deployment on one or a few targets is usually pretty quick, so you can click the refresh icon in the top-right corner, and if the job disappears from the list of pending deployments and doesn't show up in the list of failed deployments in the second half of the screen, then deployment was successful. You can also see the deployment progress from the Metric Extensions home page, which indicates the total count of pending and failed deployments, as well as the number of deployed targets for each metric extension in the library, as shown in Figure 10-4.

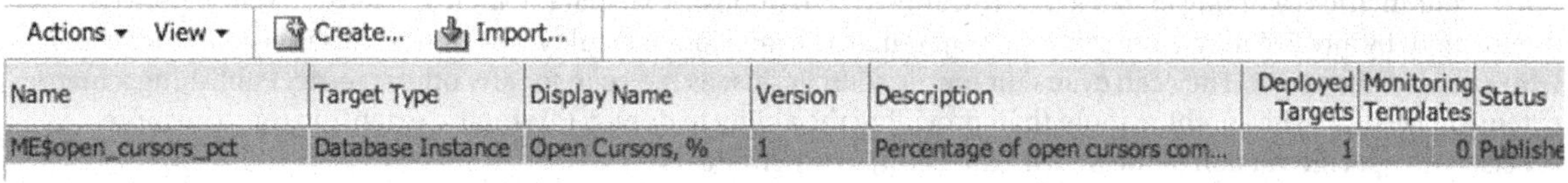

Actions ▾ View ▾	🗂 Create...	⬇️ Import...						
Name	Target Type	Display Name	Version	Description		Deployed Targets	Monitoring Templates	Status
ME$open_cursors_pct	Database Instance	Open Cursors, %	1	Percentage of open cursors com...		1	0	Publishe

Figure 10-4. Metric Extensions home page showing deployment status

Now that the metric extension is deployed, you can use it just like any other out-of-the-box metric that came with the Database Instance target type. After a few hours of collection, you might see data similar to that in Figure 10-5. To get to this screen, you navigate to the target where the metric is deployed and then from the target's menu choose Oracle Database ➤ Monitoring ➤ All Metrics. Note that, unlike user-defined metrics, metric extensions do not have their own view.

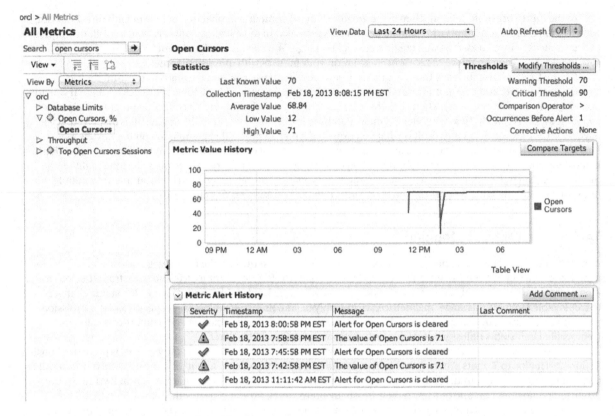

Figure 10-5. *Metric extension details and history*

Publishing the Metric Extension

When your metric is working as expected, you are ready to publish it so that the metric extension is available for deployment by any EM user. Note that a deployed metric extension in Deployable Draft status is visible to all users who can view the target. They can even edit metric settings, just as they can for any other metric. Publishing a metric extension accomplishes nothing more than providing the ability to deploy this metric extension (or to be more precise, this specific version of the metric extension) to other targets.

You can publish a metric extension from the Metric Extensions home page by choosing Actions ➤ Publish Metric Extension. The status changes to Published, and the metric extension becomes available to any EM user. Note that Published metrics can also be included in Monitoring Templates, another important difference from Deployable Draft status.

Now imagine that the metric is working well, but after some time you realize it would be helpful to have additional information about the session. You want to see the highest number of open cursors, and not just how close the open-cursors count is to the limit. Having the SID, username, client machine, client OS user, and client program available in the metric itself would greatly assist in troubleshooting alerts generated by your new metric extension.

Creating a New Version of Metric Extension

Let's improve the metric extension that you just created. From the Metric Extensions home page, select the current version and choose Actions ➤ Create Next Version. Then change the general properties reflecting the changes in the description.

On the Adapter tab, replace the old SQL with that in Listing 10-2, which collects information about the session with the highest number of open cursors.

Listing 10-2. Modified SQL for Open Cursors Metric Extension

```
SELECT ROUND (c.open_cursors / p.value * 100) open_cursors_pct,
       c.open_cursors, c.sid, s.username, s.machine,
       s.program, s.osuser, s.process
  FROM (select * from (SELECT    sid, COUNT (*) open_cursors
             FROM v$open_cursor
         GROUP BY sid
         ORDER BY COUNT (*) DESC)
         WHERE ROWNUM = 1) c,
       v$parameter p, v$session s
 WHERE p.name = 'open_cursors'
   AND s.sid = c.sid
```

On the Columns tab, you need to add new columns. Note that you set a comparison operator only on the open_cursors column, in case somebody wants to use absolute cursor count as a threshold. Other columns can't have any warning or critical conditions set, as they are intended only for informational purposes. See Figure 10-6.

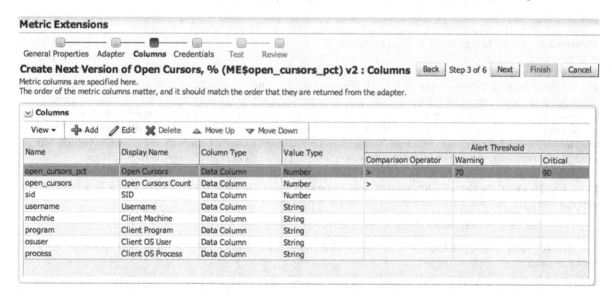

Metric Extensions

General Properties   Adapter   **Columns**   Credentials   Test   Review

Create Next Version of Open Cursors, % (ME$open_cursors_pct) v2 : Columns   Back | Step 3 of 6 | Next | Finish | Cancel

Metric columns are specified here.
The order of the metric columns matter, and it should match the order that they are returned from the adapter.

⌄ Columns

View ▾   ✛ Add   ✎ Edit   ✖ Delete   ▲ Move Up   ▽ Move Down

Name	Display Name	Column Type	Value Type	Comparison Operator	Warning	Critical
open_cursors_pct	Open Cursors	Data Column	Number	>	70	90
open_cursors	Open Cursors Count	Data Column	Number	>		
sid	SID	Data Column	Number			
username	Username	Data Column	String			
machnie	Client Machine	Data Column	String			
program	Client Program	Data Column	String			
osuser	Client OS User	Data Column	String			
process	Client OS Process	Data Column	String			

(Alert Threshold spans Comparison Operator, Warning, Critical)

Figure 10-6. *List of columns for the modified Open Cursors metric extension*

Now test your metric extension. If everything is fine and metric collection works, finish its creation. You will see the next version of the same metric extension with version number 2 appear on the Metric Extensions home page. You can now save version 2 as a Deployable Draft and deploy it to verify that it works as expected. If a previous version of the metric extension was already deployed on that target, it will be upgraded. The final step is to publish the latest version so it's available to all users of EM12c.

When a newer version of the metric extension is published, the upgrade of the older deployment can be done from the screen showing the target deployment. You can access this screen from the Metric Extensions home page: click the link with the number of deployed targets for the previous version of a metric extension and then click the Deploy button (select all targets you want to upgrade first). When that's done, you can see more columns in this metric. The new metric extension collection will look like Figure 10-7.

orcl > All Metrics

All Metrics

Search [open cursors, %] →

Open Cursors, %

Percentage of open cursors compare to open_cursors init.ora parameter.
Only top session values are returned.

View ▾

View By [Metrics ▴▾]

Collection Schedule Every 1 Minute [Modify]
Upload Interval Every Collection
Last Upload Feb 18, 2013 7:37:58 PM EST

▽ orcl
  ▽ ◌ **Open Cursors, %**
    Client Machine
    Client OS Process
    Client OS User
    Client Program
    Open Cursors
    Open Cursors Count
    SID
    Username

Metric	Thresholds	Real Time Value
Client Machine	Not Applicable	em12c2.oracloid.com
Client OS Process	Not Applicable	1234
Client OS User	Not Applicable	oracle
Client Program	Not Applicable	OMS
Open Cursors	Set	70
Open Cursors Count	Not Set	210
SID	Not Applicable	307
Username	Not Applicable	SYSMAN

☑ Data shown in above table is collected in real time.

Figure 10-7. Modified Open Cursors metric extension

Note that you might want to have access to more than a single top session with open cursors—perhaps to the top ten. For this, you need to convert your metric extension to a multirow metric, which requires one or more columns as key columns. In this case, you could use the SID column as a key and then modify the query to return the top ten sessions. Unfortunately, you won't be able to add a key column in the next version of the metric extension but instead need to create a new metric extension. Fortunately, it's easy to clone existing metric extensions by using Actions ➤ Create Like from the Metric Extensions home page. Note that there are other limitations on creating a new metric extension version—for example, you cannot remove or change the sequence of the older columns but can change the Display Name.

Even though the SID (and arguably SERIAL#) is enough for the key column, consider adding other columns in the key. This way, the alert notification can include the key values. The default alert message (see the advanced settings when you edit the metric extension column) is as follows:

The value of %columnName% for %keyValue% is %value%

The key value will be produced as a comma-concatenated string from all keys, so your alert message will look like this:

The value of open_cursors_pct for 260,SYSMAN,em12c2.oracloid.com,OMS,oracle,1234 is 72

You can modify your alert message to be more descriptive. For example, your alert message template could be as follows:

Open cursors is at %value% percent for session %keyValue%
(SID, username,machine,program,osuser,process)

Right from this alert message, you can see which sessions are to blame. Unfortunately, it's currently not possible to refer to the specific key columns of the metric to make the alert message more user-friendly. At least, I haven't found a way to do so.

So far, you have used a SQL adapter to collect metrics. As of the 12.1.0.2.0 EM release, six documented adapters are available for metric extensions, and one undocumented. Although you will most likely be using two adapters (the SQL adapter and OS Command—Multiple Columns adapter), let's review all the available adapters for a more complete picture.

SQL Adapter

The SQL adapter is the one you used in the preceding example. Because you are already familiar with its basic capabilities, let's just review its additional options.

If your SQL is too long, you might prefer to upload a SQL file instead of specifying SQL code inline. The uploaded SQL file is distributed with your metric extension to the agents that collect your metrics, and these agents then run SQL from the file.

If you are selecting a predefined set of name-value measurements, you can use transposed results instead of creating a two-column metric with the name as the key column and value as the data column. For example, say you want to collect four metrics by using the query in Listing 10-3. You would need to create the first column as a key. However, you would have no control of column naming, and alert messages could be only generic.

Listing 10-3. SQL Statement to Collect Physical Reads and Writes

```
select name, value
  from v$sysstat
 where name in ('physical read total IO requests',
                'physical read total bytes',
                'physical write total IO requests',
                'physical write total bytes')
 order by name;
```

NAME	VALUE
physical read total IO requests	2285653
physical read total bytes	21313147392
physical write total IO requests	1245633
physical write total bytes	27849077248

Note that the ORDER BY clause is added to make sure the results are always in the same order (in this case, the same order as in the IN list). Now you just need to create four data columns, and you can specify more-descriptive names such as *Total Physical Read Requests* and a custom alert message:

Total Physical Read Requests is too high - %value% (warning threshold is
%warning_threshold% and critical threshold is %critical_threshold%)

As you can see in this example, you can include the thresholds in your alert message.

You can also specify bind variables in SQL text instead of literals. However, this is useful only if you generate the value of the variable dynamically, and metric extensions don't really provide much flexibility there (other than predefined variables that are not very useful as SQL parameters). If you end up in this situation, you are probably better off to redesign and merge those metric extensions into one by using additional key column(s). However, if you have multiple metric extensions using the same SQL but different literals, then bind variables are the way to go.

It's also possible to use a PL/SQL block returning a cursor (this is what the Out parameter is used for in the advanced properties) instead of plain SQL. It's useful if you need to use dynamic SQL or perform metric collection differently based on certain conditions, such as the Oracle database version or the version of the application you are extracting the data from.

The last example also demonstrates an important limitation of metric extensions: they are not very useful when working with data that requires additional processing based on a number of previous collections (such as the cumulative counters used in the example). We are not really interested in the total number of IO requests since the start of the database instance, but instead in the average number of IO requests over the collection period. Even though the formula would be very simple (the difference between two collected values divided by the collection interval), metric extensions do not provide a way of calculating such ratios. Of course, you can use a PL/SQL block to store previously collected counters and calculate the ratio per interval, but it's not as trivial and also introduces much more significant measurement intrusion when your measurements actually cause the changes to the database.

347

This limitation of cumulative counters exists no matter what adapter you are using for your metric extensions. So far we've focused on the SQL adapter, but let's look at other options.

OS Command Adapters

There are three OS Command adapters, and you may use them even more frequently than the SQL adapter. OS Command adapters differ from one another only in whether they can collect multiple columns and multiple rows:

- OS Command—Multiple Columns

- OS Command—Single Column

- OS Command—Multiple Values

All three OS Command adapters have three basic properties: `Command`, `Script`, and `Arguments`. The agent basically executes the command line, concatenating these three properties. In fact, you can specify them all in a single command property, so we're not sure why there are three properties, other than making properties more readable. You can upload the script (or even multiple scripts, programs, and other required files) and then reference the location of the uploaded files by using the `%scriptsDir%` substitution variable in any of the attributes—for example, `%scriptsDir%/myscript.sh` for the `Script` property.

I strongly recommend using Perl scripts to ensure that your metric extensions are platform independent. Each Oracle Management Agent comes with the same version of Perl, so you won't depend on what Perl version, if any, is installed on the server. Just use `%perlBin%/Perl` in the command property, and it will be automatically substituted with the location of the Perl binary installed with the Oracle Management Agent (usually `<AGENT_HOME>Perl/bin/Perl`).

There are a couple of other ways to pass parameters other than on the command line. This is useful when you want to avoid a long command line or avoid handling different escaping rules that are platform dependent as well as to pass sensitive information such as credentials (because command-line arguments are easily visible to any user on many platforms). One way to pass arguments is by using environment variables. An agent sets the environment variable before calling the OS command, and the program or script can read that variable during executions. An even better way of passing parameters is by using standard input that is then parsed by the program. Oracle refers to that mechanism as *input properties*. The latter is the most secure way to pass credentials to the script, because even environment variables for a process can be retrieved easily on some platforms.

■ **Note**   For more details on environment variables and input properties, refer to the *Oracle Enterprise Manager Cloud Control 12c Administrator's Guide* (Chapter 8, "Metric Extensions," Section 8.4).

OS Command adapters have two sets of credentials: host credentials and input credentials. *Host credentials* are used to log in to the server running an agent for the target type. By default, an OS Command adapter uses default monitoring credentials—the credential used to collect the pre-defined metrics of a target. However, you can choose to create your own host credential sets and then set credentials for the targets where you plan to deploy your metric extensions. For example, you might need to run your collection scripts as a special OS user (for example, ROOT or another application user other than the one running the agent itself). Note that the SQL adapter has the same capability, so you can define a custom database credential set to run as a different database user than the default monitoring user (for example, DBSNMP).

Input credentials are the second type of credentials that can be defined. These credentials are totally independent of host credentials and are passed to the program or script being executed using standard input just like input properties. The advantage of input credentials is that you can set them independent of the metric extension definition. If different targets require different credentials, users of the metric extension can easily define credentials without the need to create a unique metric extension with various passwords hard-coded, which is what you would need to do if using input properties for passing credentials.

■ **Note** An example of using input credentials can be seen in the *Oracle Enterprise Manager Cloud Control 12c Administrator's Guide* (Chapter 8, "Metric Extensions," Section 8.4.1).

Now let's look at each of the OS Command adapters.

OS Command—Multiple Columns

The OS Command—Multiple Columns adapter is the one that you will likely be using most often. The output from the command is parsed by the adapter so that each line is a single row, and then each line itself is tokenized into multiple values. The adapter splits lines correctly, whether the end of line is marked in Unix-like format (single LF) or Windows (CR+LF).

The adapter allows the use of a "Start With" prefix to filter out the lines of output that do not contain metrics. This is a good practice, preventing potential output noise from interfering—for instance, warnings that you didn't expect or just want to ignore. The widely accepted standard for the prefix is em_result=. Listing 10-4 shows an example of output.

Listing 10-4. Sample Output from OS Command Using the em_result= Prefix

```
em_result=<metrics line 1>
This line is ignored
em_result=<metrics line 2>
If em_result= is not at the start of the line, it's ignored too
em_result=<metrics line 3>
```

Note that leading and trailing spaces in the prefix are significant and are not truncated.

The content of the line after the prefix is then tokenized into columns by using a simple delimiter string. The default (and commonly used) delimiter is the pipe symbol (|). However, if your column content might contain that character, you can use any other delimiter and even a multicharacter string to make it truly unique, such as {=-DELIMITER-=} so that a line like this is parsed correctly into three values:

```
em_result=Some common separators are | , % ;{=-DELIMITER-=}123{=-DELIMITER-=}456
```

Spaces have a special meaning in the delimiter strings. First, the leading and trailing spaces are truncated and ignored. The rest of the spaces seem to be splitting the delimiter string into multiple delimiters, but they are applied very inconsistently, so it's difficult to predict the end result. I've tried to create a delimiter to parse lines with comma-separated values and optionally enclosed in double quotes, but I couldn't come up with a reliable delimiter string. I suspect the code simply never was meant to deal with spaces in the delimiter. The documentation says nothing about handling spaces, and their handling seems to be unreliable, so I strongly recommend avoiding spaces in your delimiter strings at this point.

One final note about spaces: the spaces in the collected values are not truncated when they are stored in the repository. However, the EM user interface displays them with leading and trailing spaces truncated. If you are setting conditions on the text columns such as CONTAINS, then leading and trailing spaces are significant in both condition strings and collected metric values, so be careful. I recommend avoiding leading and trailing spaces, if possible, because you don't see them in the user interface, but they are there. (Just check the repository view MGMT$METRIC_CURRENT, for example.)

When defining adapters, you need to define named columns and their attributes. You already went through the preceding examples, so let's just touch on the distinction between data columns and key columns.

Data columns are really the metric values you want to collect. For example, you might want to monitor the size of a staging directory in which files are loaded for subsequent processing. The total size of the files in that directory is the metric you want to calculate—that would be one data column. You might also want to calculate the total number of files in the staging directory—that's another data column. For each of those data columns, you might want to define a comparison operator. In this case, you will most likely want to select the more-than (>) alert condition so you can generate warnings and errors when the size or number of files in the staging directory grows beyond the predefined threshold. Note that it's important to select the right operator during metric development. The thresholds themselves are optional and can be customized by metric extension users for each target. However, the operators can be changed only by the metric extension author, and changing them requires creating a new version of the metric extension.

Imagine now that you want to monitor not one but multiple staging directories—and each of them separately. Instead of defining multiple metric extensions (one per directory), you can combine them into the same metric extension and collect the directory size and the number of files as a separate line and then add a directory path to distinguish the lines. This is when you would use key columns. In this example, the directory path would be the key column, and the size of the files would be a data column. Note that if you are creating a new version of a metric extension, you can't remove any of the existing columns or add any key columns. When it comes to modifications, you can change only some properties of the existing columns, such as display name and comparison operator. However, you can add additional data columns. For example, if you already have a metric monitoring the size of a directory, you can't create a new version and add a key column with a directory path to monitor the sizes of multiple directories. Instead, you will need to clone it as a new metric extension and not just the next version.

The key column (or columns) must be unique for each data collection. Otherwise, an error is raised. If an adapter receives multiple rows, and no key columns are defined for the metric extension, an error is raised as well. Finally, remember to choose the correct column type: String or Number. Remember that only number metrics are displayed on the charts and rolled up or aggregated as collection data aged in EM12c moving from detailed to hourly and daily snapshots. String metrics are displayed only as tables in the EM interface.

OS Command—Single Column

The OS Command—Single Column adapter returns just one value. You should still think of it as a table with one column and one row (EM12c always treats metrics as tables), so you need to define a single column in the Columns tab. The complete output of the command even multiline output—is passed back as a value. I haven't found much use for this adapter, but if you need to pass back a multiline fragment of text, this is the way to go. You can then set up a CONTAINS or MATCH alert condition to test the existence of a substring or regular expression match for this returned text.

Note that this adapter doesn't have Delimiter and Start With properties as OS Command—Multiple Columns does. You can't filter output lines with a prefix. Unfortunately, this adapter is available for only a very limited set of targets, as described later in the section "Adapters and Target Types."

OS Command—Multiple Values

The OS Command—Multiple Values adapter returns multirow results by using the same prefix mechanism as the OS Command—Multiple Columns adapter. It doesn't have the Delimiter property, because the adapter doesn't split the content of the line in multiple values; the content of the whole line after the prefix is passed as the value. The end result is a single-column table. Note that you define only a single data column and no key columns. The adapter basically collects a set of values. So the difference between this adapter and OS Command—Multiple Columns is that OS Command—Multiple Values doesn't require any key columns.

One use for such an adapter is collecting lines from the log file, where you can define a CONTAINS or MATCH condition on the column. Note that if you try to simulate a similar collection with the OS Command—Multiple Columns adapter by using a single key column, you wouldn't be able to define an alerting condition on that column. In addition, duplicate values would produce an error.

SNMP Adapter

While the idea of being able to collect metrics over SNMP (Simple Network Management Protocol) is nice, the current implementation of the SNMP adapter makes it of very limited use for metric extensions. The SNMP adapter is designed to collect metrics from a single SNMP server, normally running locally. However, up to the EM release 12.1.0.2.0, the SNMP adapter is basically broken, because it requires a specific dynamic property of the host target to be evaluated correctly—SNMPHostname—and this property is resolved on only a very few hardware platforms. You can apply a workaround by using the emcli command to manually set that property name, but you can't use the SNMP adapter to collect metrics from multiple devices by using a single host target to deploy the metric extension to.

Note that you will also need to set SNMP credentials in order to use the SNMP adapter. The documentation on this adapter is rather incomplete, so I suggest that you avoid using it at this point. Instead, use OS Command adapters to collect SNMP metrics or use plug-ins (which have a full-featured SNMP metric-collection method, covered in the second part of this chapter).

JMX Adapter

A JMX (Java Management Extensions) adapter is used to collect metrics from Java applications that have JMX-based standard instrumentation embedded in JMX-enabled servers such as Oracle WebLogic, IBM WebSphere, Red Hat JBoss, and even stand-alone JVM (Java Virtual Machine). For more information, refer to the standard documentation, *Oracle Enterprise Manager Cloud Control 12c Administrator's* Guide (Chapter 8, Section 8.4.1).

Although this documentation is admittedly skinny, as you learn about management plug-ins in the rest of this chapter, you will also learn about underlying fetchlets, and the documentation on JMX fetchlets is a bit more descriptive. For more information, see *Oracle Enterprise Manager Cloud Control Extensibility Programmer's Reference* (Chapter 20, "Using Fetchlets." Section 20.11). A more complete example can be found in *Oracle Enterprise Manager Cloud Control 12c Administrator's Guide,* (Chapter 20, "Monitoring Using Web Services and JMX").

Adapters and Target Types

EM12c limits the choice of adapters for each target type. Although the documentation doesn't cover which adapters are available for which target type, you can see the associations from the EM_MEXT_TARGETTYPE_ADAPTERS repository view. From that view, you can also see that a couple of target types have Web Services Adapter support even though it's not documented. You can also see in the EM_MEXT_ADAPTERS view that there are even more adapters available, such as the RESTful Web Wervices Wdapter. However, they are not enabled for any of the target types. I expect that these are provisions for the next releases, as we've seen features that were delivered internally and externalize only in a later version.

Various OS Command adapters are available for some targets but not for others, which really makes little sense. For example, the OS Command—Single Column adapter is available for Automatic Storage Management (but not for Cluster ASM), Cluster Database, Database Instance, and a few other target types. Almost every target type has the OS Command—Multiple Columns adapter available. The OS Command—Multiple Values adapter isn't associated with any of the target types that are available on a system with default plug-ins in release 12.1.0.2.0.

You can find detailed official documentation on the metric extensions adapters in the *Oracle Enterprise Manager Cloud Control 12c Administrator's Guide* (Section 8.4). If you are more interested in the under-the-hood implementation, check out EM_MEXT_% views and tables in the SYSMAN schema. I will get back to some content in those tables when I discuss plug-ins later in this chapter (see the "Under the Hood of Metric Extensions" section).

Chapter 8 of *Oracle Enterprise Manager Cloud Control 12c Administrator's Guide* has more details on other capabilities of metric extensions, such as managing access to metric extensions, using alert options, and exporting/importing metric extensions. There you can also find how to migrate your old user-defined metrics from Grid Control 10g and 11g to the new metric extensions in 12c Cloud Control.

Management Plug-ins

Metric extensions are easy to create and, compared to 10g-style user-defined metrics, are much easier to manage at scale and provide much more flexibility to users. However, they are still very limited when it comes to monitoring more-complex targets and metrics.

The power of plug-ins is in new target types that developers can create. Target types provide the already familiar notion of managed targets for each component of your managed infrastructure. For example, a database instance is a target and so is a listener. Even Oracle homes are presented as targets in EM12c.

If your application runs on a server as a daemon, and there are ten metrics you want to collect, either you can define ten metric extensions and deploy all of them or you can define a new target type in a plug-in and then deploy just one plug-in. Targets also have instance properties that enable configuration of the target according to its deployment parameters. In contrast, metric extensions are not parameterized at all, so if your application is configured differently on each server or you are running multiple instances of the application on the same server, you would have to create a dedicated set of metric extensions for each application.

In addition, plug-ins provide so much more beyond monitoring extensions. They provide full management capabilities so that plug-in developers can implement actions on targets such as starting and stopping an application or retrieving logs for analysis on demand or enabling debug mode. Target pages in the console are also fully customizable. There are ways to define how the new targets can be autodiscovered by EM12c, and many more features are available such as jobs, reports, configuration management, and compliance standards. You will learn about some of them in the remainder of this chapter while reviewing the sample plug-ins.

Getting Started with the Extensibility Framework

As mentioned earlier, the EM12c Extensibility framework is not just an add-on feature as it was in the 10g and 11g versions. Instead, it forms the underlying foundation for all management plug-ins, including those delivered by Oracle, to monitor its core products such as databases, middleware, applications, and engineered systems.

The Extensibility framework contains everything you need to create new, full-featured target types—from advanced metric-collection capabilities down to automated discovery, configuration management, jobs support, and compliance management, as well as full-blown dashboards and fully interactive target-management interfaces.

The Enterprise Manager Extensibility documentation has two guides for plug-in developers:

- *Oracle Enterprise Manager Cloud Control Extensibility Programmer's Guide* is a brief overview of plug-in concepts and how they all fit together. It's useful to read it in full before going to the next guide. A title such as *Management Plug-ins Concepts Guide* would reflect the content better.

- *Oracle Enterprise Manager Cloud Control Extensibility Programmer's Reference* is the documentation that you will be using all the time. It's structured as a guide rather than a simple reference, so think of it as the *Management Plug-ins Developer's Guide*.

This section focuses on the practical aspects of plug-in development and details that are not very clear in the documentation. Because the Extensibility framework has been changed dramatically in EM12c and is not as broadly used as other end-user functionality, its documentation is not as clear and thorough as the rest of the EM12c documentation. However, always make sure to check the latest version of the Oracle documentation, as improvements are released quietly in online documentation from time to time.

Even if you are not planning to develop plug-ins yourself, this section will help you understand some internals of EM12c, so I recommend you go through it anyway.

Before you dive into the details, let's look at the lifecycle of a plug-in:

- *Design and development*: This is where plug-in developers spend most of their efforts.

- *Packaging the plug-in into an Oracle Plug-in Archive (OPAR) file*: This is a single package that can easily be distributed.

- *Deploying the plug-in on the Enterprise Manager system*: EM12c administrators import a plug-in from the OPAR file and deploy it on the OMS, making it available for end users. End users can then add new targets to monitor and manage.

As you go through the examples in this chapter, you will see how to iterate through this cycle during plug-in development. First we'll cover how to set up your development environment.

Development Environment

I recommend that you have a dedicated EM12c plug-in development environment. It's easier to analyze the logs during troubleshooting and to fully isolate the issues you might encounter. Some of your activities as a plug-in developer might cause disruption to the environment, so it's safer to have a development environment than to develop on a shared EM12c system and risk affecting other users.

A single virtual machine (VM) works very well for that purpose. I use two virtual processor cores and 6GB of RAM for my virtual machine on my laptop. You can get away with a single core and 3–4GB of RAM, but make sure you have a reasonable swap size, as you will be using some Java tools in addition to running the EM12c environment itself. If you don't have enough memory or swap, you might experience weird failures while using the empdk command-line tool for packaging a plug-in, for example.

My development VM with Oracle Enterprise Linux hosts the EM repository, OMS, and the agent. I also installed and configured the Extensibility Development Kit (EDK) in that same VM. This way, I have a complete development environment on a single VM. It pays to keep backups of your development VM in case you cause any inconsistencies to your EM12c repository, as you will be creating and deleting objects in the SYSMAN schema as well as some metadata records.

You might want to do the development on your workstation where you have your favorite development tools and editors (mine is vi, so I'm all set on the VM). In this case, you should install the Enterprise Manager Command Line Interface (EMCLI) there before installing the EDK. For detailed instructions on installing EMCLI, refer to Chapter 1 or navigate to Setup ➤ Command Line Interface in your EM12c console.

Extensibility Development Kit

The Extensibility Development Kit (EDK) has several components:

- Plug-in development tool used to verify and package plug-ins.

- Reference documentation that includes PDF versions of the two extensibility guides noted earlier and XML Schema Definition documentation that contains all possible XML elements much more than described in the PDF but description of most of the elements is either missing or very brief so you would be experimenting a lot if you want to use undocumented options.

- Plug-in samples. As of EDK release 12.1.0.2, multiple variations of the same plug-in are provided: the Host Sample plug-in. The versions differ in the functionality they implement, becoming progressively more complex and feature rich. The previous EDK version had only one sample plug-in, and the amount of files, code, and features implemented was simply overwhelming for beginners, so it was really difficult to use it as an example.

The best way to install the EDK is to navigate to the EM12c console: choose Setup ➤ Extensibility ➤ Development Kit, and follow the instructions. In a nutshell, you download a zipped distribution, uncompress it in a folder of your liking, and having set a proper environment, you can call the empdk utility. I usually make sure I have both empdk and emcli in my path. I will refer to the location of EDK as <EDK> when I need to make it part of the path.

Note that you should run EDK only on one of the supported platforms. For example, while most of the functionality works on my Mac OS X, plug-in packaging simply hangs as it's an unsupported platform because EDK uses the Oracle Universal Installer to perform some of its functions.

■ **Note**   The *Oracle Enterprise Manager Cloud Control Extensibility Programmer's Reference* (Chapter 1, Section 1.3) has more-detailed instructions for installing the EDK.

Sample Plug-ins Deployment

Before we proceed, let's package and deploy three sample plug-ins that are shipped with EDK—performing steps 2 and 3 of the plug-in lifecycle described in the previous section. Assuming you are on Unix/Linux, go to `<EDK>/samples/utl` and run `./build_sample_plugin.sh oracle.samples.xsh1`. (You might need to add executable permissions to the script beforehand. And if you are using Windows instead, look inside the shell script and modify it to run on Windows or just call the commands yourself using Windows notation.) This script will create the OPAR package in your home directory: `12.1.0.0.0_oracle.samples.xsh1_2000_0.opar`. Run the script for two other versions of the plug-in, which are more advanced: `xsh2` and `xsh3`. We will deploy them, and you can see how the plug-in evolves during development from simple to more complex. You now have three OPAR files in your home directory.

Note that creating an OPAR archive will call the Oracle Universal Installer behind the scenes, so you will need to comply with its generic requirements, such as having enough free swap space.

Before going further, you need to perform one extra step: configuring a Software Library. (See Chapter 6 for more-detailed Software Library coverage.) This is done only once after you install OMS, and you normally do it for patching and provisioning functionality as well as for EM12c Self Update. One way to do it is to use EMCLI (you can also add it by using the EM12c console). By now you should already have EMCLI working, so log in by using `emcli login -username=SYSMAN`. I also have a habit of syncing EMCLI with the OMS, so I run `emcli sync`, but in practice it doesn't need to run every time. Next, create the Software Library location:

```
emcli add_swlib_storage_location -name=swlib -path=/some/path/on/OMS/server
```

If you think that the Software Library location has already been configured, just run `emcli list_swlib_storage_locations` to verify. You need to have at least one active location.

Now you are ready to upload the OPAR files to the OMS. If your OPAR files are locally on the same server where the OMS is running, upload each file by using the following:

```
emcli import_update -file=<absolute path to .opar file> -omslocal
```

Note that `emcli` doesn't actually upload the file but just sends a command to OMS (a verb in EMCLI terminology) to perform the import action. If an OPAR file is not local to the OMS, you can specify the host and credentials so that OMS can retrieve the file from that remote host. This example can be found in the *Oracle Enterprise Manager Cloud Control Extensibility Programmer's Reference* (Chapter 13, Section 13.5.2).

Now is the time to deploy the plug-in to the OMS. This is when the OMS activates a certain version of the plug-in and makes its target type(s) an integral part of its interface and API, just like the Database Instance target type, for example. You can deploy a plug-in by using the EM12c console, as indicated in the *Oracle Enterprise Manager Cloud Control Extensibility Programmer's Reference* (Chapter 13, Section 13.5.3). However, we will use the command line here because it's more repeatable and quicker to document. We will use EMCLI again:

```
emcli deploy_plugin_on_server -plugin=oracle.samples.xsh1
```

Also deploy `oracle.samples.xsh2` and `oracle.samples.xsh3` in the same way. Note that `emcli` will ask for the SYS password during deployment and not just SYSMAN, presumably because plug-in deployment requires the SYSDBA role. Note that `emcli` actually sends a deployment job in the background, and you can check on the progress by using `emcli get_plugin_deployment_status -plugin_id=oracle.samples.xsh1`.

And, finally, the culmination: adding the target type instances! You will use `emcli` again to avoid long navigation through the EM12c console and multiple screenshots. For each of the three target types, use this command:

```
emcli add_target -name='Sample Host 1' -type=sample_host1 -host=<Existing Host Name>
-properties="sample_host1_username:<OS user>;sample_host1_password:<OS pwd>"
```

`<Existing Host Name>` is where the new plug-in will be deployed. Use the exact spelling that you see in the EM12c console for that host target. For `<OS user>` and `<OS pwd>`, you can use Oracle user credentials (in fact, the sample plug-in provided in EDK 12.1.0.2.0 doesn't use them at all, as it simply runs commands as the OS user running the local management agent). Run this command for the two other plug-in versions, incrementing the index in the name, type, and properties. You will end up with three sample host targets. They are all monitoring the same server (the local server where the agent is running), but each provides incrementally more functionality.

To simulate the host's up/down state, the plug-ins read `/tmp/hostsample_status`. The target is considered up when the content of the file is "up." Please initialize that file on the host where you are deploying by using the command `<echo up>/tmp/hostsample_status`. Otherwise, your Sample Host X targets will be in the Status Pending state indefinitely.

Basic Plug-in Target Types and Metrics

In this section, you will start working with the simplest sample EDK plug-in located in `<EDK>/samples/plugins/oracle.samples.xsh1`. Inside is the `plugin_dist` directory that I refer to as the stage or staging area.

Stage Structure

To package a plug-in using EDK, its files must be organized within a staging area. EDK defines a certain directory structure to be followed. I recommend that you create that directory structure right at the beginning of the development. You will start with the simplest possible structure shown in Figure 10-8.

```
stage/
    plugin.xml
    agent/
        plugin_registry.xml
        default_collection/
                target_type.xml (link to ../../oms/metadata/ default_collection/target_type.xml)
        metadata/
                target_type.xml (link to ../../oms/metadata/targetType/target_type.xml)
        scripts/
                    scripts
    oms/
        metadata/
                default_collection/
                                target_type.xml
                    targetType/
                            target_type.xml
```

Figure 10-8. *Plug-in staging area structure*

The staging root contains `plugin.xml`, a plug-in definition containing the basic plug-in information required by the OMS. The two mandatory subdirectories in the staging root are oms and agent. The oms directory contains all the files used for deployment on the OMS, and the agent directory contains the files for deployment on the agent. You can think of them as agent-side and OMS-side areas. You will see that some files must be included in both areas. The `plugin_registry.xml` file is somewhat similar to the `plugin.xml` file in the staging root directory, but its content is for deployment on the management agent. Think of `plugin.xml` and `plugin_registry.xml` together as the plug-in definition. Note that a single plug-in may contain more than a single target type if it's designed to support a complex system. For example, the Oracle Exadata Plug-in contains ten new target types.

Target type metadata is the key component of a plug-in. The XML target type metadata file is included in both the OMS and the agent areas. I usually place the target type metadata file in `<stage>/oms/metadata/targetType/` and create a soft link to it from `<stage>/agent/metadata/` since my development platform is Linux. While the name of the file itself can be selected freely, the advised practice is to name it after the target type it defines and add the `.xml` extension.

Default collection metadata is tightly coupled with the target type metadata and defines collection schedules and collection-related attributes for all metrics including alert conditions. Just like the target type metadata, the default collection metadata XML file is present in both OMS and agent areas, so I typically use a soft link as well. It's advisable to name the file the same as the target type metadata XML file.

You will learn that there are many more files that you can include in the OMS-side area, but this is the bare minimum you would normally see in any plug-in. Start each new plug-in by creating this basic directory tree.

Plug-in Metadata

A simplified version of `plugin.xml` is shown in Listing 10-5. You will find it in `<stage>/plugin.xml`. Remember that the staging area of our first sample plug-in is `<EDK>/samples/plugins/oracle.samples.xsh1/plugin_dist`.

Listing 10-5. Plug-in Metadata `plugin.xml` for Simple Host Plugin 1

```
<?xml version = "1.0"?>
<Plugin xmlns:xsi="http://www.w3.org/2001/XMLSchema-instance"
    xsi:schemaLocation=
        "http://www.oracle.com/EnterpriseGridControl/plugin_metadata plugin_metadata.xsd"
    xmlns="http://www.oracle.com/EnterpriseGridControl/plugin_metadata">
  <PluginId vendorId="oracle" productId="samples" pluginTag="xsh1"/>
  <PluginVersion value="12.1.0.0.0"/>
  <PluginOMSOSAruId value="2000"/>
  <ShortDescription>Sample Host Plugin 1</ShortDescription>
  <Readme>Sample Host Plugin 1. See Book Expert Oracle Enterprise Manager 12c.</Readme>
  <PluginAttributes Category="Others" DisplayName="Sample Host Plugin 1"/>
  <TargetTypeList>
    <TargetType name="sample_host1" isIncluded="TRUE"/>
  </TargetTypeList>
</Plugin>
```

See the full `plugin.xml` file of the sample for more options, as well as the documentation, the *Oracle Enterprise Manager Cloud Control Extensibility Programmer's Reference* (Chapter 2, Section 2.4). Even more options can be seen in the plug-in metadata reference located at `<EDK>/doc/partnersdk/mrs/emcore/pluginMetadata/`. Here, let's just go through a few mandatory, basic elements. The bulky attributes `xmlns:xsi, xsi:schemaLocation`, and `xmlns` of the root element Plugin have references to various namespaces and XML Schemas. Just make sure you keep them as is from the sample template. The same applies to other XML files that we will use.

The PluginId consists of three parts separated by dots: `vendorId.productId.pluginTag`. The dot notation will be used later in the agent-side definition. Vendor ID and Product ID can be up to eight characters long, while the plug-in tag must be four characters or fewer. For example, Oracle's sample plug-in ID is `oracle.sysman.xsh1`, and for my demo MySQL plug-in, I use the ID `pythian.mysql.demo`.

The plug-in version is indicated by five numbers: a.b.c.d.e. The first two numbers (a.b) should be the same as the EM12c version that you are developing on. The third number (c) should always be 0. The fourth number is what you will be incrementing every time you're publishing the plug-in. Oracle reserves the fifth number (e) for future use and instructs that you always set it to 0. However, I have been using it to identify minor plug-in releases. For example, 12.1.0.1.2 is the current release of the Pythian MySQL plug-in at the time of this writing.

You need to increment versions as you deploy the next versions in your development environment. You could use that last number for development release increments or you can just modify the plug-in ID during development. For example, I use `pythian.mysql.prod` for publicly released versions and `pythian.mysql.test` for development and testing.

The `PluginOMSOSAruId` element defines on which OS the OMS should be running to support this plug-in. A value of 2000 indicates a generic platform, and you will often find that your plug-ins have pretty much no dependency on the OMS server platform but often have a dependency on the agent OS. I won't go into the details of compatibility here (see the documentation referenced earlier) but `plugin.xml` is the place that you can define the compatibility of the plug-in and other EM12c components.

The `ShortDescription` and `Readme` tags are self-explanatory. The `PluginAttributes` element hosts a few basic properties. You can set a few predefined categories for the `Category` attribute, such as Databases, Middleware, and so forth. The `DisplayName` attribute is how your plug-in will be shown in the EM12c user interface.

Finally, there is the `TargetTypeList` element listing all the target types a plug-in contains. A simple plug-in usually contains just one target type, so there is only one `TargetType` child element. The target type name is an internal ID of the target type included in the plug-in. More on ID selection for target types is shown later in this chapter, when I actually define one.

There are also provisions to define plug-in dependencies, version support and compatibility, and a multitude of other attributes such as a "What's New" section. You don't need to get into that now and can always make plug-in metadata more complex later. I generally recommend starting simple and slowly adding features into your plug-in.

While `plugin.xml` contains OMS-side metadata, `plugin_registry.xml` defines the metadata required by the agents where the plug-in is deployed—usually just the list of target type metadata files and default collection metadata files. For a single target type plug-in, there is just one of each. They are defined by using the `TargetTypes` and `TargetCollections` elements, simple containers for one or more `FileLocation` elements. The path in `FileLocation` is relative to the agent directory in the staging area. Listing 10-6 is the simplified `plugin_registry.xml` file from the example.

Listing 10-6. Agent-Side Plug-in Metadata `plugin_registry.xml` for Sample Host Plugin 1

```xml
<?xml version="1.0"?>
<PlugIn ID="oracle.samples.xsh1" Description="Sample Host Plugin 1" Version="12.1.0.0.0"
    xmlns:xsi="http://www.w3.org/2001/XMLSchema-instance"
    xsi:schemaLocation="http://www.oracle.com/EnterpriseGridControl/plugin plugin.xsd" >
  <TargetTypes>
    <FileLocation>metadata/sample_host1.xml</FileLocation>
  </TargetTypes>
  <TargetCollections>
    <FileLocation>default_collection/sample_host1.xml</FileLocation>
  </TargetCollections>
</PlugIn>
```

You can see that the attributes ID, `Description`, and `Version` are replicated from the OMS-side `plugin.xml` file. Note that the ID is a dot-notation version of `PluginId`. More-advanced options are available, but they are still quite poorly documented and not provided in the examples. For example, you can register your own metric collection method by defining a custom fetchlet (you will learn about fetchlets soon) but you won't do that until you become very proficient in plug-in development.

Other than the standard documentation in the Oracle *Enterprise Manager Cloud Control Extensibility Programmer's Reference* (Chapter 2, Section 2.5), more details can be found in the EDK API reference at `<EDK>/doc/partnersdk/mrs/emcore/agentPluginMetadata/`. This XML API documentation is generated from the XML Schema that defines the structure of this XML—what elements can exist where and how many, what their attributes are, and which ones are optional, as well as sparse comments that you would, nevertheless, find useful for elements that are not documented anywhere else.

At this point, there have been enough opportunities already to make plenty of mistakes. Fortunately, the EDK provides validation tools that can help us make sure our definitions are syntactically and semantically correct. For example, it will catch malformed XML files as well as mismatched plug-in IDs. Listing 10-7 demonstrates a sample validation command line and the successful validation output. The output file referenced at the end contains more details. Note that packaging a plug-in into an OPAR file performs explicit validation before packaging.

Listing 10-7. Plug-in Validation Example

```
[oracle@em12c2 oracle.samples.xsh1]$ empdk validate_plugin -stage_dir plugin_dist
Validating Plugin Xml : Passed
Validating Plugin Structure: Passed

Validating Metadata Syntax: Passed
Validating Metadata Semantic: Passed
Validating Embedded SQL strings in meta data: Passed
Plugin Validation : Passed
Validation Report generated to: /home/oracle/edk/samples/plugins/oracle.samples.xsh1/./plugin_
validation_report_121127.txt
```

Note that if you remove the Readme element, for example, the validation will pass with warnings because this element is optional in the XML Schema, so syntactically everything is correct, but the EDK has a semantic rule that this element should be present as a matter of best practices. I use the staging area of the host sample from the EDK, but you can also start your own staging area by using the preceding XML content and go along in parallel.

Now that validation has succeeded, you can move onto creating the core structure: the target type metadata.

Target Type Metadata

Target type metadata defines the basic structure of the plug-in—its properties, metrics, and how to collect them. This is an absolute minimum for creating a new target type. Target type metadata is defined in a single XML file placed in the `<stage>/oms/metadata/targetType` directory. Oracle's most recent recommendation is to name the file after the plug-in ID by using the `vendorID_productID_PluginTag.xml` template. The previous naming convention was after the target type ID with an added `.xml` extension, but in general, it can be any file name. I recommend calling the target type metadata file by using the target type, because you can package more than one target type in the same plug-in. You also need to provide the same XML file in the agent area under the `<stage>/agent/metadata` directory, which is subsequently referenced from `plugin_registry.xml`, as you learned earlier. On Unix/Linux servers, I simply create a symbolic link from the agent area to the master copy in the OMS area. This way, I never forget to sync them up. (If you do forget to synchronize the copies, as I did few times, troubleshooting can be a huge time sink. That's when I moved to symbolic links.)

The general structure of the target type metadata looks like Listing 10-8.

Listing 10-8. <TargetMetadata> Element

```
<TargetMetadata META_VER="1.8" TYPE="sample_host1">
  <Display>...</Display>
  <Metric>...</Metric>
  ......
  <Metric>...</Metric>
  <InstanceProperties>...</InstanceProperties>
</TargetMetadata>
```

The top-level element TargetMetadata includes a unique target type ID "sample_host1" in the TYPE attribute, and metadata version "1.8" as the META_VER attribute. You should change the version number if you change the file. When EM12c detects that the target type version has changed, it will reload the new metadata. I've spent countless hours troubleshooting why my plug-in didn't work after I updated the metadata definition to simply find out later that I missed changing the META_VER attribute. When a newer version of the plug-in is deployed, EM12c analyzes whether the metadata version has changed and skips some updates internally if META_VER is unchanged in the new target type metadata definition.

Note that the examples packaged with the EDK, such as sample_host1, reference the XML DataType Definition (DTD) $OMS_HOME/sysman/admin/dtds/TargetMetadata.dtd in the comments. This is an old definition from 10g/11g Grid Control that is not only old-style but also outdated. Use the XML Schema–based API reference in <EDK>/doc/partnersdk/mrs/emcore/targetType. For example, the TargetMetadata root element is described in <EDK>/doc/partnersdk/mrs/emcore/targetType/noNamespace/element/TargetMetadata.html.

The children of the TargetMetadata element normally include three elements: Display, Metric, and InstanceProperties.

Display

First, let's examine the Display element. This element is used solely for storing properties that indicate how a component defined by the parent element is displayed in the EM12c console. You will see the Display element present under almost any other element of the target type metadata that has some visibility in the user interface. In this case, it's the target type itself, and the Display element defines how the target type is displayed. In its simplest form, the Display element will contain the single element Label with the content used to display the target type in the console, as in Listing 10-9. The optional NLSID attribute of the Label is a unique identifier that can be used for translation of the console user interface associated with this target type to other languages. If you specify it, make a habit of prefixing the NLSID with the target type ID so that it's unique across all possible plug-ins (since your target type ID is unique, you just need to make sure that all your NLSIDs are unique within your own target type). The Display element can have additional elements in it, depending on the context, as you will see later in this chapter.

Listing 10-9. <Display> Element

```
<Display>
  <Label NLSID="hs_displayname">Sample Plugin Host 1</Label>
</Display>
```

Note that the order of the elements in the target type metadata XML file is important; Metric elements must always precede the InstanceProperties element. Next you will look at the InstanceProperties structure, as it will later be useful in understanding metrics and how they are collected.

Instance Properties

InstanceProperties is a required element that has to be placed after all Metric elements. There should be exactly one InstanceProperties descriptor in the root element TargetMetadata. This descriptor consists of one or several InstanceProperty elements and, optionally, DynamicProperties elements, as shown in Listing 10-10. Each InstanceProperty entry specifies an attribute of the target that should be defined by a user in the EM12c console when adding a new target instance (see Figure 10-9). The DynamicProperties element defines attributes that are calculated automatically by the agent instead.

Listing 10-10. <InstanceProperties> Element Structure

```
<InstanceProperties>
        <InstanceProperty NAME="USE_FAKE_DATA" ... </InstanceProperty>
        <InstanceProperty NAME="sample_host1_username" ... </InstanceProperty>
        <InstanceProperty NAME="sample_host1_password" ... </InstanceProperty>
        <DynamicProperties>...</DynamicProperties>
        <DynamicProperties>...</DynamicProperties>
</InstanceProperties>
```

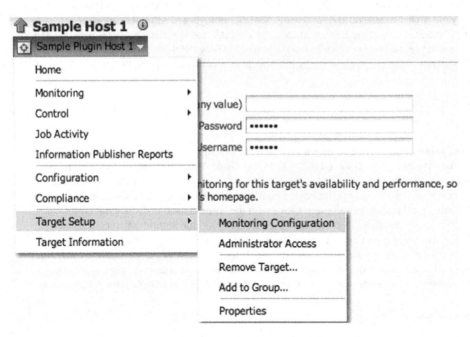

Figure 10-9. Instance properties are set in the target's monitoring configuration in the EM12c console

Instance properties normally represent the configuration of the target instance so that an agent can collect various metrics and calculate dynamic properties. Many targets include credentials in the instance properties—a username and password used to connect to the target and collect information. Other properties often include the path to the installation directory, the port or socket path for communications, or even the hostname if the target is running on a host other than the one the agent is running on.

Because it's a demo plug-in, Oracle includes the property USE_FAKE_DATA so you can set it to TRUE to enable the collection script to return predefined data instead of real gathered metrics. This is a good debugging technique.

Listing 10-11 provides an example of the password property.

Listing 10-11. `<InstanceProperty>` Element for Password

```
<InstanceProperty NAME="sample_host1_password" CREDENTIAL="TRUE" OPTIONAL="TRUE">
  <Display>
    <Label NLSID="host_password">Host Password</Label>
  </Display>
</InstanceProperty>
```

The `NAME` attribute defines the handle you can use later to reference this property when defining metric collections. Setting `CREDENTIAL` to `TRUE` ensures that this property is stored encrypted instead of as clear text, making it more difficult to retrieve passwords by unauthorized users. The `HIDE_ENTRY="TRUE"` attribute makes the EM12c console use a password-style input box in which stars are displayed instead of the real text entered in the browser, for properties marked as credentials. `HIDE_ENTRY` is set to `TRUE` by default, so if you want to have the username part of the credential displayed in clear text, you need to set this attribute to `FALSE`. Another attribute, `NEED_REENTER`, when set to `TRUE` will make the EM12c console display a dual entry for that property—something you often see done for passwords.

The `OPTIONAL` attribute denotes properties that don't have to be defined and, thus, have some default value acceptable in many cases. For example, the default value for the `USE_FAKE_DATA` attribute is an empty string, which signals the plug-in to use real collected metrics.

You can also see that the `InstanceProperty` has a child `Display` element that is already familiar to you. In this case, it defines how this property is displayed in the EM12c console. To see that in action, navigate to your Host Sample 1 target and choose Target Setup ➤ Monitoring Configuration from the target's menu, as shown in Figure 10-9.

Metrics

The set of metrics is the real meat of the target type metadata; they define what information is collected and how. `Metric` is the most important and arguably most complex element of the target type metadata. A target type can (and normally does) contain multiple `Metric` child elements, and they all must be placed before the `InstanceProperties` element. Listing 10-12 shows the `Response` metric from the `sample_host1` target type.

Listing 10-12. Response Metric Definition in XML

```
<Metric NAME="Response" TYPE="TABLE">
  <Display>
    <Label NLSID="hs_response_displayname">Response</Label>
  </Display>
  <TableDescriptor>
    <ColumnDescriptor NAME="Load" TYPE="NUMBER" IS_KEY="FALSE">
      <Display>
        <Label NLSID="hs_response_cpuload">CPU Load</Label>
      </Display>
    </ColumnDescriptor>
    <ColumnDescriptor NAME="Status" TYPE="NUMBER" IS_KEY="FALSE">
      <Display>
        <Label NLSID="hs_response_status">Status (up/down)</Label>
      </Display>
    </ColumnDescriptor>
  </TableDescriptor>
  <QueryDescriptor FETCHLET_ID="OSLineToken">
    <Property NAME="scriptsDir" SCOPE="SYSTEMGLOBAL">scriptsDir</Property>
    <Property NAME="fake" SCOPE="INSTANCE" OPTIONAL="TRUE">USE_FAKE_DATA</Property>
    <Property NAME="perlBin" SCOPE="SYSTEMGLOBAL">perlBin</Property>
```

```
        <Property NAME="command" SCOPE="GLOBAL">%perlBin%/perl</Property>
        <Property NAME="script" SCOPE="GLOBAL">
           %scriptsDir%/sample_host1/data_collector.pl --collect Response --fake "%fake%"
        </Property>
        <Property NAME="startsWith" SCOPE="GLOBAL">em_result=</Property>
        <Property NAME="delimiter" SCOPE="GLOBAL">|</Property>
    </QueryDescriptor>
</Metric>
```

The `Metric` element must have a `NAME` unique within the target type. `TYPE` is most frequently a `TABLE` but can be some other value that I won't be looking at here. Each `Metric` element should include one `TableDescriptor`. A `TableDescriptor` defines columns with names, types, and labels. Finally, a `QueryDescriptor` tag describes how to collect metric values via one of the fetchlets. These are similar to metric extension adapters, but there are many more fetchlet types available, and you have much more flexibility configuring them in XML. The order of the columns in a `TableDescriptor` is important because the fetchlet configured under the `QueryDescriptor` element must return the values in that order.

The `TableDescriptor` element is a simple container for the multiple `ColumnDescriptor` elements (each describing a column in the table, as you might have already guessed). Each column descriptor has the familiar `Display` element describing how this column is displayed in the user interface. Attributes of the column descriptor define column names and types. `STRING` and `NUMBER` are two column types that you will be using most of the time. The `IS_KEY` attribute lets you specify whether this column is part of the unique key for the metrics, returning multiple rows as in the multirow metrics you learned about in the section "Metric Extensions."

For each target type, it's important to define a special metric with the name `Response`, of type `TABLE`, with a column named `Status`. The EM12c framework will use this column for the target's up and down status and historical availability statistics. You also must define a critical condition for this metric, as you will learn later. EM12c knows that the target is down if the `Status` column of the `Response` metric generates a critical alert. One way to get the availability history for a target is via the target's menu: choose the Target Information option and then click the availability percentage. The example availability history for Sample Plug-in Host 1 is shown in Figure 10-10.

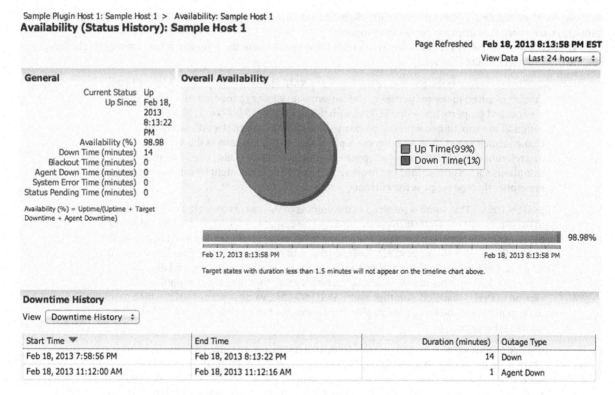

Sample Plugin Host 1: Sample Host 1 > Availability: Sample Host 1
Availability (Status History): Sample Host 1

Page Refreshed   **Feb 18, 2013 8:13:58 PM EST**

View Data   Last 24 hours ‡

General

Current Status	Up
Up Since	Feb 18, 2013 8:13:22 PM
Availability (%)	98.98
Down Time (minutes)	14
Blackout Time (minutes)	0
Agent Down Time (minutes)	0
System Error Time (minutes)	0
Status Pending Time (minutes)	0

Availability (%) = Uptime/(Uptime + Target Downtime + Agent Downtime)

Overall Availability

Up Time(99%)
Down Time(1%)

98.98%

Feb 17, 2013 8:13:58 PM   Feb 18, 2013 8:13:58 PM

Target states with duration less than 1.5 minutes will not appear on the timeline chart above.

Downtime History

View   Downtime History ‡

Start Time ▼	End Time	Duration (minutes)	Outage Type
Feb 18, 2013 7:58:56 PM	Feb 18, 2013 8:13:22 PM	14	Down
Feb 18, 2013 11:12:00 AM	Feb 18, 2013 11:12:16 AM	1	Agent Down

Figure 10-10. *Example availability history for Sample Plug-in Host 1*

You can also collect more columns in the Response metric in addition to Status. It often is easy to collect a few key measurements while checking the status of the target. For example, one measurement might be the response time of the connection request to a database or the host's load average, as is the case with the Sample Plug-in Host 1 target type. This will save on the number of collection calls but won't affect the target's availability. Only the column Status is taken into account for target availability.

Finally, let's move on to the data collection. In the vast majority of cases, you will be using one of the available fetchlets configured by the QueryDescriptor element. The management agent will execute collection methods according to the defined fetchlet and "fetch" values for the metrics.

Other collection options let EM12c calculate metric values by joining or aggregating some of the previously collected metrics. Such a collection is defined by using an ExecutionDescriptor element instead of a QueryDescriptor. Another metrics collection option is to configure an agent to be a passive "listener" for the data sent to it by targets (for example, by using SNMP traps). The available mechanisms are called *receivelets* and are defined by the PushDescriptor. I cover only the use of fetchlets as that's the only mechanism that's fully documented, but you can dig into the XML Schema documentation if you want to try using two other advanced metric-collection mechanisms. The *Oracle Enterprise Manager Cloud Control Extensibility Programmer's Reference* (Chapter 19) describes the use for the SNMP receivelet.

The QueryDescriptor has a single attribute, FETCHLET_ID, that uniquely identifies the fetchlet type used to collect the required information. As the various fetchlets are discussed later, you will see that the metric extension adapters discussed earlier are using nothing else but some of those fetchlets.

Each fetchlet has its own set of required and optional properties with predefined names. You configure a fetchlet by defining the Properties elements with these names. The OSLineToken fetchlet, for example, corresponds to the OS Command—Multiple Columns adapter from the metric extensions. This fetchlet has a required command property as well as a few optional properties, such as startWith and delimiter. You can also specify additional ad-hoc properties that can serve as "helpers" to form fetchlet's pre-defined configuration properties. For example, the perlBin and fake properties are referenced from the command property.

The SCOPE attribute of a Property element defines the context where the property value is resolved. The following are the most important SCOPE options:

> GLOBAL: The value is the content of the Property XML element with placeholder variables that are resolved to the properties of the current QueryDescriptor element. In our example, the command property has scope GLOBAL with the value %perlBin%/Perl. Placeholders within %% are substituted with the property values of the current QueryDescriptor element, such as perlBin. Another example of the GLOBAL property is the script property that references scriptDir and fake properties. GLOBAL scope is also used for constant definitions such as the delimiter property. The name GLOBAL might be misleading, but just remember that the scope is the current QueryDescriptor element.

> SYSTEMGLOBAL: This value is resolved in the context of the emd.properties configuration file in the directory $AGENT_HOME/sysman/config. The content of the Property XML element is the name of the variables from the emd.properties agent configuration file. For example, emd.properties contains perlBin, defining the path to the Perl executable. This is useful if Perl scripts are used to gather metric values, so you can always use the Perl distribution that's installed with the management agent rather than hoping that a compatible system version of Perl is installed. Another useful SYSTEMGLOBAL value is scriptsDir, which points to the path where the scripts for all plug-ins are installed in a subdirectory with the same name as the target type ID.

> INSTANCE: This value is resolved in the context of the target instance (that is, the values of instance properties that are defined when the target is configured). These values are different for each target instance. In our example, you can see how USE_FAKE_DATA is referenced, but not sample_host1_username or sample_host1_password. If metric collections were actually using these properties, they would have been passed to the connection script one way or another.

> ENV: This is the value taken from the environment variable. For example, if your monitoring script requires a special binary to be installed on the server, and that binary is not distributed with the plug-in, you can specify a path to that binary via a certain environment variable set before the agent is started. For example, <Property NAME="mypath" SCOPE="ENV">MYSQL_PATH</Property> will take the value of the environment variable MYSQL_PATH as the value for the property mypath so that you can later refer to it as %mypath% from the command property.

It's possible to set environment variables before the command is run—whether to define requirements or pass parameters. If command-line parameters contain special symbols, they might be handled differently on different platforms. Environment variables seem to be passed reliably on all platforms, including Linux, Windows, and Unix. Passing credentials and other sensitive information via environment variables could be more secure than via the command line, which is often easily observed by any logged-in host user. However, some platforms may expose the content of environment variables of a process to other users, as Linux does via the /proc filesystem. Later in this chapter, you will learn about monitoring credentials, which is a more secure way to pass a login and password to a script.

Let's summarize the definition of the Response metric from Listing 10-12. A Response metric is a single-row metric with the columns Load and Status. It's using the OSLineToken fetchlet that is capable of returning a multirow, multicolumn result set from an OS command. The fetchlet is configured to run a Perl script named data_collector.pl and parses output by separating column values with a pipe symbol (|) and filtering in only the lines prefixed with em_result=.

Default Collection Metadata

Now that you know how the EM12c user can configure new target instances (via the InstanceProperties element) and what metrics target type will collect and how (Metric elements), the only missing bit is to define how often metrics need to be collected and what the alerting conditions are on the metrics. This is defined in the Default Collection metadata XML file placed in <EDK>/oms/metadata/default_collection and linked from <EDK>/agent/default_collection. Use the same naming convention as for the target type metadata file. A sample default collection metadata definition is shown in Listing 10-13. See the default collection definition of the Sample Host 1 target for the complete example.

Listing 10-13. Sample Default Connection Metadata Definition

```
<TargetCollection TYPE="sample_host1">
  <CollectionItem NAME="Response">
    <Schedule>
      <IntervalSchedule INTERVAL="5" TIME_UNIT="Min"/>
    </Schedule>
    <Condition COLUMN_NAME="Status" CRITICAL="1" OPERATOR="LT"/>
  </CollectionItem>
  <CollectionItem NAME="Perf" UPLOAD="1">
    <Schedule>
      <IntervalSchedule INTERVAL="5" TIME_UNIT="Min"/>
    </Schedule>
    <MetricColl NAME="CPUPerf">
      <Condition COLUMN_NAME="non_nice" WARNING="NotDefined" CRITICAL="NotDefined"
        OPERATOR="GE"
        MESSAGE="The value for %columnName% is %value%%%.  It has risen above the
          critical (%critical_threshold%%%) or warning (%warning_threshold%%%) threshold."
        CLEAR_MESSAGE="The value for %columnName% is %value%%%." />
      <Condition ... />
      ...
    </MetricColl>
    <MetricColl NAME="MemoryPerf">...</MetricColl>
    <MetricColl NAME="CPUProcessorPerf">...</MetricColl>
    ...
  </CollectionItem>
  ...
</TargetCollection>
```

The root element is TargetCollection, and its TYPE attribute should match the type attribute of the TargetMetadata root element from the target type metadata XML file (sample_host1). The TargetCollection element contains a number of CollectionItem elements, and each CollectionItem element matches to a Metric element in the target type metadata file. The NAME attribute of CollectionItem should match the metric name.

There is also a way to group the collection of multiple metrics in the same collection item when the same collection frequency or metric collection order is required. This is done by including MetricColl elements (one per metric) inside a CollectionItem (for example, the collection item "Perf"). In this case, the NAME attribute of the child MetricColl elements should match metric names as in the example ("CPUPerf", "MemoryPerf", and "CPUProcessorPerf"). See the *Oracle Enterprise Manager Cloud Control Extensibility Programmer's Reference* (Chapter 3, Section 3.5.1).

For each collection item, we can define a Schedule child element that typically includes an IntervalSchedule child element indicating the frequency of the collection by using the numerical attribute INTERVAL and string attribute TIME_UNIT. The latter can be set to Sec, Min, Hr, or Day, and default to Min. As this is a default collection definition, this setting represents the initial default frequency. EM12c users can modify collection intervals, as for any other metrics, and plug-in developers can set the limits on those settings by using the MIN_INTERVAL and MAX_INTERVAL attributes of the IntervalSchedule element. Other scheduling options are also available, such as running on a certain day of the month or week. They are not documented in the extensibility guides, but you can see the XML Schema documentation from <EDK>/doc/partnersdk/mrs/emcore/default_collection for additional options, and you can also see them in the console when modifying a collection schedule.

If the schedule is not defined for a metric, this metric will not be automatically collected by the agent except when an EM12c user opens the real-time metric view, in which case OMS requests the collection from the agent each time the real-time view is refreshed. Whether or not the initial collection schedule is defined in the default collection file, the schedule can be customized in the EM12c console. You use the All Metrics view of a target, as shown in Figure 10-11 for the collection item named "Perf" (shown earlier in Listing 10-13).

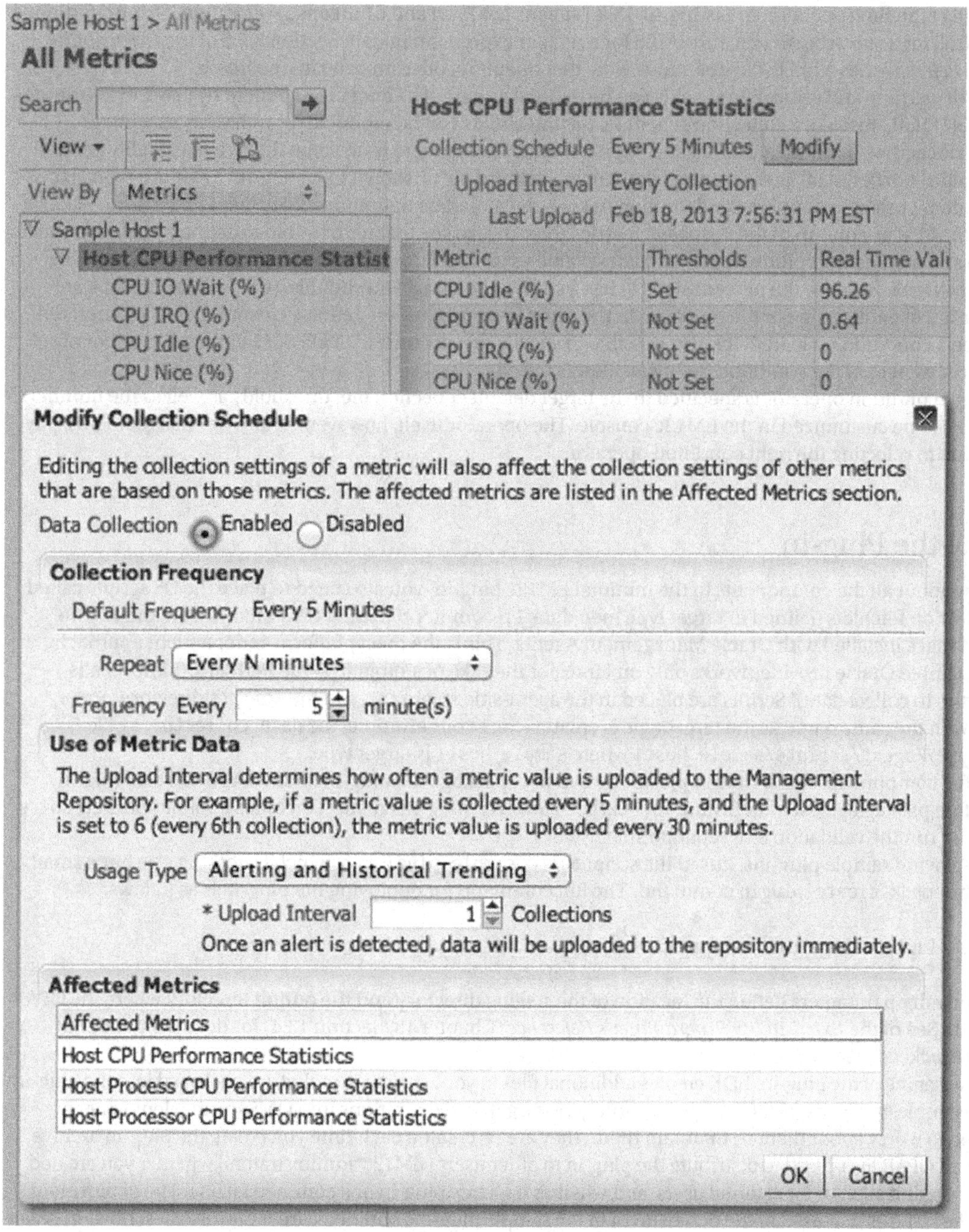

Sample Host 1 > All Metrics

All Metrics

Search [   ] [→]

View ▾   ☰ ☷ ☶

View By [Metrics   ⬍]

▽ Sample Host 1
  ▽ **Host CPU Performance Statist**
    CPU IO Wait (%)
    CPU IRQ (%)
    CPU Idle (%)
    CPU Nice (%)

Host CPU Performance Statistics

Collection Schedule Every 5 Minutes [Modify]
Upload Interval Every Collection
Last Upload Feb 18, 2013 7:56:31 PM EST

Metric	Thresholds	Real Time Val
CPU Idle (%)	Set	96.26
CPU IO Wait (%)	Not Set	0.64
CPU IRQ (%)	Not Set	0
CPU Nice (%)	Not Set	0

Modify Collection Schedule   ☒

Editing the collection settings of a metric will also affect the collection settings of other metrics that are based on those metrics. The affected metrics are listed in the Affected Metrics section.

Data Collection ⦿ Enabled ◯ Disabled

Collection Frequency

Default Frequency Every 5 Minutes

Repeat [Every N minutes   ⬍]

Frequency Every [5 ⬍] minute(s)

Use of Metric Data

The Upload Interval determines how often a metric value is uploaded to the Management Repository. For example, if a metric value is collected every 5 minutes, and the Upload Interval is set to 6 (every 6th collection), the metric value is uploaded every 30 minutes.

Usage Type [Alerting and Historical Trending ⬍]

＊ Upload Interval [1 ⬍] Collections
Once an alert is detected, data will be uploaded to the repository immediately.

Affected Metrics

Affected Metrics
Host CPU Performance Statistics
Host Process CPU Performance Statistics
Host Processor CPU Performance Statistics

[OK] [Cancel]

Figure 10-11. *Customizing the collection schedule*

Each column in a metric can have a condition defined for testing against warning and critical thresholds—one Condition element per column. If you define a collection item per metric, the Condition elements are children of CollectionItem. Otherwise, Condition elements are children of MetricColl. Condition elements have two required attributes: COLUMN_NAME and OPERATOR. The latter defines a comparison operator, which can either be a numerical relation or string matching operator. In Listing 10-13, LT means *less than* and GT means *greater than*. String conditions include CONTAINS for a substring match and MATCH for a regular expression match. Section 3.5.5 of the *Extensibility Programmer's Reference* has a full list of operators. Note that operator codes must be in uppercase.

The default warning and critical thresholds can be defined as part of a Condition element by using the attributes WARNING and CRITICAL. Just like a collection schedule, the thresholds can be modified by an EM12c user. Both warning and critical thresholds are optional and often left undefined if there is no value that is a reasonably good default. The value "NotDefined" is the same as defining no value at all, as shown in Listing 10-13 for the "non_nice" column condition. I prefer to just skip the definition to keep the metadata definition clean, just as there is no WARNING threshold for the Status column of the Response metric. You can also see that it's possible to define a column-specific alert message and include the column name and latest value as well as thresholds by using a placeholder variable such as %columnName%. Because the percent sign (%) has a special meaning, you should use a double percent sign (%%) to include a real percent sign in the message. In the same fashion, you can define a custom message generated in EM12c when a condition is cleared. It's also possible to specify the attribute OCCURRENCES to set the number of consequent occurrences of the condition before an alert is raised.

As long as a condition operator is specified in the target default collection file, thresholds as well as the number of occurrences can be customized in the EM12c console. The operator itself, however, cannot be changed. Thus, pay special attention to selecting the right condition operator.

Packaging the Plug-in

Now you know about all the components of the minimal EM12c plug-in, you also need to place the OS scripts called by metric collection fetchlets defined in target type metadata. I recommend writing OS scripts in Perl and use the version of Perl that's installed with Oracle Management Agents. This is the most platform-independent approach (though the example Oracle provides works only on Linux for the sake of simplicity—the Perl script simply calls some OS utilities to collect data). Scripts are placed in the agent-side staging area in the scripts directory, and a subdirectory with the same name as the target type is created. So, in our example, the data_collector.pl file is placed in <stage>/agent/scripts/sample_host1 where sample_host1 is target type.

With all the components and scripts in place, you can now package the plug-in archive. You can run plug-in validation before packaging, just as in Listing 10-7 earlier. However, plug-in creation includes a validation step, so it's not necessary to run the validation as a separate step.

When deploying sample plug-ins, I used the script build_sample_plugin.sh, which is nothing else but a small wrapper for the empdk create_plugin command. The full command for deploying the plug-in is as follows:

```
empdk create_plugin -stage_dir <stage_dir> -out_dir <output_dir>
```

Two mandatory parameters define the location of the staging directory and the output directory where the OPAR file is produced. See of the *Extensibility Programmer's Reference* (Chapter 13, Section 13.4) for details on optional arguments of empdk create_plugin.

During packaging of the plug-in, EDK creates additional files in your staging area that are packaged into the plug-in archive. For example, it creates PL/SQL code importing the target type definitions into OMS during deployment. You don't need to worry about them or maintain them; they are re-created each time you create the plug-in archive.

The created OPAR file is used to distribute the plug-in to other users (EM12c administrators) whether you created it for your own organization or for external users, and whether it's a free plug-in or a commercial one. The deployment procedure is the same as that used in the deployment of the sample plug-ins outlined earlier and also described in detail in the *Extensibility Programmer's Reference* (Chapter 13, Sections 13.5 and 13.6). The end-user documentation on plug-in management is available in Chapter 22 of the *Oracle Enterprise Manager Cloud Control 12c Administrator's Guide* (refer to the "Importing Plug-In Archives" part of Section 12.4.3.2 if you distribute an OPAR file directly to end users).

For the three host sample plug-ins, all steps have already been done earlier, so the initial samples are already deployed and targets created. Note that the oracle.samples.xsh1 plug-in implements a few more features that you will look into later in this chapter, but what you've learned so far is pretty much the core of any plug-in with new target types.

Agent's Metric Browser

It's often useful to use the agent's Metric Browser interface to view what the agent is actually collecting and even some debugging information on the collected metrics. This is useful during troubleshooting, when it's not clear whether the problem is with the metrics collection on the agent side or occurring during uploading and loading into the repository on the OMS side. To activate the Metric Browser for the agent, run the following as the OS user running the agent:

```
emctl setproperty agent -name _enableMetricBrowser -value true
```

To determine the URL of the Metric Browser, run the command `emctl status agent`. The Agent URL line will display in the format `http://host:port/emd/main/`. Modify this URL by adding the `/browser/` string between `emd` and `main`, like this: `http://host:port/emd/browser/main`. Your agent might have `https` instead of `http` if it's secured, so use the `https` URL in that case.

Using the Metric Browser is especially useful when using transient and computed columns, which are described later. There is also a full Metric Definition XML fragment available with all attributes explicitly defined, even including default values—a great way to learn about some nondocumented options. The Metric Browser lets you access any target type, and not only your own targets, so you can see complete (and often complex) metric definitions from Oracle's own targets that can give you excellent ideas on how to create your own metrics. Other debugging information is available on metric collection but, unfortunately, it hasn't yet been documented in any detail and I haven't had a need to use it so far.

Under the Hood of Metric Extensions

You probably noticed that defining target type metrics is similar to defining metric extensions, but in XML format. In fact, Metric Extensions feature is basically the user interface for adding new metrics to existing targets without the burden of creating completely new plug-ins and target types. Behind the scenes, metric extensions are the same XML metric definitions that you see in target type metadata.

All metric extensions are stored in the table `EM_MEXT_VERSIONS` in the SYSMAN schema in the repository database. The `METADATA_DEFINITION` column stores nothing else but the XML `Metric` element as the definition of the metric extension. The relevant `CollectionItem` element is in the `COLLECTION_DEFINITION` column of that table.

Listing 10-14 contains the XML definition of the very first `"Open Cursors, %"` metric extension I created. It is formatted here for readability.

Listing 10-14. XML Representation of a Metric Extension

```xml
<Metric NAME="ME$open_cursors_pct" TYPE="TABLE">
  <Display>
    <Label NLSID="NLS_METRIC_oracle_databaseME$open_cursors_pct">Open Cursors, %</Label>
    <Description NLSID="NLS_DESCRIPTION_oracle_databaseME$open_cursors_pct">
      Percentage of open cursors compare to open_cursors init.ora parameter.
      Only top session value is returned.</Description>
  </Display>
  <TableDescriptor>
    <ColumnDescriptor NAME="open_cursors_pct" TYPE="NUMBER">
      <Display>
        <Label NLSID="NLS_COLUMN_oracle_databaseME$open_cursors_pctopen_cursors_pct">
          Open Cursors</Label>
        <Unit NLSID="mext_unit_nlsid_ME$open_cursors_pct_open_cursors_pct">%</Unit>
      </Display>
      <CategoryValue CLASS="Default" CATEGORY_NAME="Capacity">
      </CategoryValue>
```

```
  </ColumnDescriptor>
</TableDescriptor>
  <QueryDescriptor FETCHLET_ID="SQL">
    <Property NAME="STATEMENT" SCOPE="GLOBAL" OPTIONAL="TRUE">
    SELECT ROUND (c.open_cursors / p.value * 100) open_cursors_pct
    FROM (SELECT   sid, COUNT (*) open_cursors
               FROM v$open_cursor
         GROUP BY sid
         ORDER BY 2 DESC) c,
         v$parameter p
  WHERE p.name = 'open_cursors' AND ROWNUM = 1;</Property>
    <Property NAME="MachineName" SCOPE="INSTANCE" OPTIONAL="TRUE">MachineName</Property>
    <Property NAME="Port" SCOPE="INSTANCE" OPTIONAL="TRUE">Port</Property>
    <Property NAME="SID" SCOPE="INSTANCE" OPTIONAL="TRUE">SID</Property>
    <Property NAME="UserName" SCOPE="INSTANCE" OPTIONAL="TRUE">UserName</Property>
    <Property NAME="password" SCOPE="INSTANCE" OPTIONAL="TRUE">password</Property>
    <Property NAME="Role" SCOPE="INSTANCE" OPTIONAL="TRUE">Role</Property>
    <CredentialRef NAME="SQLCreds">
  </CredentialRef>
</QueryDescriptor>
</Metric>
```

If you find it challenging to create metric definitions in XML from scratch, you can start by creating a metric extension as a prototype and then simply pick up the XML definition from the repository, copy it into your target type metadata definition XML file, and modify it as needed. The raw XML definition gives you much more flexibility.

EM12c Fetchlets

EM12c comes with more than a dozen documented fetchlets. Here is a brief summary of available fetchlets:

> *OS Command fetchlets*: This family of fetchlets lets you run operating system commands and scripts and pass metric values as the output. You have already looked at examples, and the three OS Command fetchlets have the same functionality as the OS Command adapters you looked at in the "Metric Extensions" section. The OS commands are run by an agent using the same OS user that's running the agent itself on the host where the agent is installed. To ensure platform compatibility as much as possible, I recommend that you use Perl scripts as commands and use Perl that's distributed with the agents. The scripts and any dependencies can be added to the plug-in and can be distributed when a plug-in is deployed on the agents. Note that if dependencies cannot be simply copied, and need compilation or any other configuration on the host, then such dependencies will likely need to be preinstalled on the hosts running agents. This complicates deployment and should be avoided. For example, if you want to connect to a non-Oracle database from a Perl script using DBI, you need to compile required DBD modules such as DBD::MySQL, which needs to be done manually on each agent on the host before the plug-in is deployed. Thus, using Perl native modules is preferred (such as Net::MySQL in this example—this is what I use for the MySQL plug-in).

SQL fetchlet: This fetchlet allows you to run a SQL statement or PL/SQL block against an Oracle database and return a table of values. Multiple input parameters can be specified for both SQL and PL/SQL. In case of a PL/SQL block, a single output parameter must be defined and returned from PL/SQL as a PL/SQL REF CURSOR or as a named type defined as an array of objects. The fetchlet's properties define the database connection and credentials as well as SQL parameters, the inline SQL statement or SQL file to run, and the maximum number of rows to retrieve. This fetchlet cannot be used to run SQL against non-Oracle databases. Some use cases for this fetchlet include collecting application metrics from status tables in the Oracle database or monitoring applications that are running inside the database, such as Oracle Application Express (APEX) applications.

SNMP fetchlet: This fetchlet allows metric collection from SNMP targets. The metric based on the SNMP fetchlet can collect values from multiple object identifiers (OIDs). Each OID can refer to either a single variable or multiple instances (one per network interface, for example). The fetchlet also supports PINGMODE, a simple way of creating a Response metric returning 1 if the SNMP port is responding, and 0 if a time-out occurs. This is better than generating a metric collection error. The fetchlet supports SNMP v1 and v2 protocols based on community strings as well as the more secure v3 protocol that requires credentials rather than a community string. Obvious use cases are for monitoring remote network equipment or remote hosts that are not natively supported by the Oracle agent (such as Ubuntu Linux) or that cannot have an agent installed for some reason. Metric extensions' SNMP adapter is based on this fetchlet, as you might have guessed. However, the SNMP adapter configuration is so limited that it makes it practically useless in metric extensions context.

HTTP Data fetchlets: This family of fetchlets is very similar to the OS Command fetchlets but takes output from an HTTP GET request by using a specified URL instead of executing an OS command. The output can be a raw value or lines of values or a delimiter-based tokenized lines of values—all the same options as for OS Command fetchlets.

URLXML fetchlet: This fetchlet can process an XML response retrieved from an HTTP URL and extract tabular data following predefined pattern matching. It supports HTTP GET requests only and can also be configured with a proxy server similar to HTTP Data fetchlets. Note that a pattern is defined so that it extracts rows from a hierarchical XML structure, because metrics accept tables of values. Each value is a number or a string, so no complex types can be returned and processed. You need to flatten your data collection.

REST fetchlet: This provides a mean of collecting data from RESTful web sources. It supports GET and POST HTTP methods and Basic Authentication. The response can be either in XML or in JavaScript Object Notation (JSON) formats and can be transformed into a tabular presentation for metrics by using either XPath or JSONPath. HTTPS is also supported.

URL Timing fetchlet: This is a useful collection mechanism to test the performance of web applications. It supports a simple proxy and can be used for both HTTP and HTTPS protocols. The fetchlet supports Basic Authentication for HTTP. It has capabilities for defining a connection time-out and retries and is flexible in configuring the metrics it collects. The fetchlet can accept multiple URLs. For each URL, it retrieves not only the page itself but any content required on the page such as images, style sheets, and so forth. It can provide detailed statistics for each URL or per URL. There are couple dozen statistics from obvious ones such as total bytes received and total time to retrieve the page as well as advanced statistics such as DNS resolution time or average time before the first byte is received for each request.

JDBC fetchlet: This is similar to the URL Timing fetchlet because it collects the timing information for running a specified SQL statement against any database supporting JDBC connectivity. It collects such metrics as request status, total time, number of rows retrieved, and other, more fine-grained timings such as separate connect time and fetch time. Unfortunately, this JDBC fetchlet does not return the values retrieved as the result of the SELECT command. It would be more appropriate to call it the JDBC Timing fetchlet to reflect its purpose better, but that's not how the Oracle Extensibility documentation names it.

Web Services and JMX fetchlets: These provide mechanisms for retrieving data by using Web Services or Java Management Extensions (JMX). Both are widely adopted industry standards. While Web Services are a generic distributed messaging and remote execution standard, JMX is a standard that's designed specifically for Java applications manageability. While each Java virtual machine (JVM) implementation normally supports JMX, applications need to be instrumented to report their metrics to the JVM so that they are accessible to the monitoring tools. Oracle's application servers support JMX as well as many other software products such as IBM WebSphere and Red Hat JBoss. Many Apache projects are supporting JMX as well—for example, Apache Tomcat or Apache ZooKeeper from the Hadoop ecosystem. In fact, Hadoop's core NameNode and JobTracker components are instrumented to expose their runtime metrics via JMX. Chapter 20 of the *Extensibility Programmer's Reference* has a detailed walk-through for creating a new target type based on Web Services and JMX.

WBEM fetchlet: This is the collector to retrieve metrics from components supporting the Web-Based Enterprise Management (WBEM) standard. This standard is widely adopted by the industry and is supported by a lot of open source and proprietary software. The WBEM standard is much more advanced than the outdated SNMP protocol, as it includes all the metadata, is more secure, and is much more compatible among different vendors. The WBEM fetchlet is basically a Common Information Model (CIM) client that connects to CIM Object Manager (CIMOM), often called a CIM Server. Windows Management Interface (WMI) is Microsoft's implementation of WBEM/CIM. CIMOM servers can be embedded on the devices or servers (such as some Cisco devices or Windows or HP-UX). There is also a WS-Management fetchlet that's similar to the WBEM fetchlet but is based on WS-Management standards. Microsoft Windows Remote Management (WinRM) is one example of a WS-Management implementation.

DMS Fetchlet: This collector allows using the Dynamic Monitoring Service (implemented, for example, in Oracle Application Server and Fusion Middleware). It allows applications to be instrumented to exhibit runtime metrics via DMS, and then an agent can use very effective collection mechanisms. Unlike using shell script-based metrics, DMS fetchlet collectors don't fork any processes, so it's very effective in terms of resource consumption. The DMS API was submitted to the Java Community Process in 2001 as Java Specification Request 138: Performance Metric Instrumentation. However, it wasn't widely adopted in the industry and was withdrawn in 2010.

■ **Note** You can find a full description of fetchlets in Chapter 20 of the *Extensibility Programmer's Reference*.

In addition, several fetchlets are not documented (and thus, are not guaranteed to work in the future or even current releases). For example, the JDBCSQL fetchlet, unlike the JDBC Timing fetchlet, allows collection of values returned by SQL via a JDBC connection to any database with JDBC drivers, and not just Oracle. However, be careful relying on undocumented fetchlets, as any EM12c patch set or patch might affect functionality or availability of these fetchlets even if they seem to work well at the moment.

Computed Metric Columns

The most reliable and, at the same time, simple collection mechanisms are stateless—returning values derived only from the current state of the monitored target and not taking the previous collection into account. A typical example is the current number of active database sessions. However, we often need to calculate an incremental difference of the metric from the previously collected value. For example, you might want to collect the current value of cumulative counters such as the number of user commits since database instance startup or, as you will see in the host example, the cumulative number of CPU ticks that the CPU core spent doing work in a certain mode (using `vmstat -s` in Linux, for example). Such cumulative values are not useful on their own but are useful in indicating a difference since previous collections.

Let's look at the example of CPU utilization collection from the `sample_host1` target type (see Listing 10-15).

Listing 10-15. Using TRANSIENT and COMPUTE_EXPR Columns

```
<Metric NAME="CPUPerf" TYPE="TABLE">
  <TableDescriptor>
      <ColumnDescriptor NAME="non_nice_t" TYPE="NUMBER" TRANSIENT="TRUE"/>
      <ColumnDescriptor NAME="nice_t" TYPE="NUMBER" TRANSIENT="TRUE"/>
      <ColumnDescriptor NAME="system_t" TYPE="NUMBER" TRANSIENT="TRUE"/>
      <ColumnDescriptor NAME="idle_t" TYPE="NUMBER" TRANSIENT="TRUE"/>
      <ColumnDescriptor NAME="io_wait_t" TYPE="NUMBER" TRANSIENT="TRUE"/>
      <ColumnDescriptor NAME="irq_t" TYPE="NUMBER" TRANSIENT="TRUE"/>
      <ColumnDescriptor NAME="non_nice" TYPE="NUMBER"
                      COMPUTE_EXPR="100.0 * (non_nice_t - _non_nice_t)/(
                                    (non_nice_t - _non_nice_t) +
                                    (nice_t - _nice_t) +
                                    (system_t - _system_t) +
                                    (idle_t - _idle_t) +
                                    (io_wait_t - _io_wait_t) +
                                    (irq_t - _irq_t)
                                    )">
        <Display>...</Display>
      </ColumnDescriptor>
      <ColumnDescriptor NAME="nice" TYPE="NUMBER"
                      COMPUTE_EXPR="100.0 * (nice_t - _nice_t)/(
                                    (non_nice_t - _non_nice_t) +
                                    (nice_t - _nice_t) +
                                    (system_t - _system_t) +
                                    (idle_t - _idle_t) +
                                    (io_wait_t - _io_wait_t) +
                                    (irq_t - _irq_t)
                                    )">
      ...
  </TableDescriptor>
</Metric>
```

First, you will see that the first seven columns are marked with the attribute `TRANSIENT="TRUE"`. This tells the agent that the values of these columns are not actually sent to the OMS to be stored in the repository but collected to be available for calculating values of other columns. The columns with the defined `COMPUTE_EXPR` attribute do not take their values from the fetchlet but instead use that defined expression to compute the value. The compute expression can reference existing columns by name, and those referenced columns must be defined in the `TableDescriptor` before they are referenced in the `COMPUTE_EXPR` because column values are calculated in sequence, from the top down.

To reference the value of the column from the previous collection, the value should simply be prefixed with a single underscore symbol (_). So if the current value is nice_t, the previous collection is _nice_t. Consequently, the difference is nice_t - _nice_t, which is the number of CPU ticks spent executing niced processes in user mode since the previous collection. Summing up all CPU ticks since the last collection would then give us the total number of CPU ticks since the last collection. The percent of time that the CPU was executing niced user processes is the ratio between niced CPU ticks and total ticks, normalized to a percentage by multiplying by 100. The same applies to all other CPU modes such as system or idle CPU.

Let's look at another example: calculating the number of user rollbacks and commits. The Oracle database keeps a counter of commits and rollbacks since database startup, but calculating purely on a cumulative counter isn't useful for monitoring. What's useful is the average number of commits and rollbacks per second between two collection intervals. So if the previous number of commits is c0 collected at time t0, and current collection is c1 collected at t1, then the number of commits per second would be (c1-c0)/(t1-t0). I do not specifically reference timestamps in metric definitions because EM12c adds the timestamp implicitly (there is a way to explicitly collect it, but it's rarely required). Thus, we don't have access to that timestamp value from the COMPUTE_EXPR definition. However, all we need is the interval.

Even though you define an interval in the default collection, you shouldn't hard-code this value in COMPUTE_EXPR because (1) the user can customize it and (2) the real interval might be slightly different, because the configured interval is just a target. Fortunately, EM12c has an embedded variable __interval (note the double-underscore prefix) that returns the number of seconds since the last collection. Thus, a metric with the number of commits and rollbacks per second could look like the one in Listing 10-16.

Listing 10-16. Using __interval in COMPUTE_EXPR Columns

```
<Metric NAME="transactions_stat" TYPE="TABLE">
  <TableDescriptor>
    <ColumnDescriptor NAME="commits" TYPE="NUMBER" TRANSIENT="TRUE"/>
    <ColumnDescriptor NAME="commits_ratio" TYPE="NUMBER"
                      COMPUTE_EXPR="(commits - _commits) / __interval">
      <Display>...</Display>
    </ColumnDescriptor>
    <ColumnDescriptor NAME="rollbacks" TYPE="NUMBER" TRANSIENT="TRUE"/>
    <ColumnDescriptor NAME="rollbacks_ratio" TYPE="NUMBER"
                      COMPUTE_EXPR="(rollbacks - _rollbacks) / __interval">
      <Display>...</Display>
    </ColumnDescriptor>
  </TableDescriptor>
  <QueryDescriptor>...</QueryDescriptor>
</Metric>
```

The example in Listing 10-16 is not from the sample host target, but imagine that the QueryDescriptor uses the SQL fetchlet that returns two columns, the cumulative number of commits and rollbacks for a database instance since startup. Let's say at the first collection, the fetchlet returns 1,000 for the commits column. Because it's the first collection, there was no previous _commits or __interval value, and the computed column isn't calculated yet. At the second collection, which happens 60 seconds later, imagine the fetchlet returning 1,300 for commits. In this case, the commit_ratio column would calculate to (1,300 – 1,000)/60, or 5 commits per second. The same logic applies to rollbacks.

Note that the fetchlet defined in the QueryDescriptor should return values skipping computed columns. It's not required to delay the definition of all computed columns to the very end of TableDescriptor, and you can place computed columns right after the columns they reference. Computed columns are calculated by the agent, and you can clearly monitor the process in the Metric Browser. The agent tracks the values of TRANSIENT columns but doesn't submit them to OMS, so it doesn't bloat the size of the EM12c repository.

Compute expressions are also useful to convert units (say from bytes to kilobytes or megabytes if precision is not needed) or to convert from blocks to actual bytes if some metrics return blocks.

I found it useful to use a trick when working with cumulative counters that can be reset from time to time (just as instance statistics are reset at instance restart), resulting in a negative difference, which in turn will produce huge negative ratios. Instead, such collections should be skipped. This is essential to make your metric collections trustworthy.

COMPUTE_EXPR supports a conditional operator in the form of {cond} ? {true value} : {false value}. If a previously collected value is higher than the current value, then I should return an empty value, which I would prefer instead of 0 since it tells me that the collection is simply missing. Because COMPUTE_EXPR doesn't like to take a NULL (no value) in the formula, I use a trick to produce an empty value for the column: I cause an exception dividing by 0. So my formula looks like _val > val ? 1/0 : (val - _val)/__interval. I learned that EM12c catches the exception and assumes the column value is empty. This has been working since at least Grid Control 10.2 and still works in 12.1.0.2. However, test your metric collection with any new patch sets; because this behavior is not documented, there is no guarantee it won't change. I would love to have an explicit expression to return a NULL-like value.

Key Columns

Just as in metric extensions, it's possible to declare some columns as key columns and process multiple rows returned from the fetchlet as multiple rows in the table. Listing 10-17 demonstrates an example of a metric for statistics per CPU, where the CPU number is defined as a KEY column. The result is the same as with key columns in metric extensions. The complete XML fragment is in the target type metadata of the sample_host1 target type.

Listing 10-17. Key Columns Definition Example

```
<Metric NAME="CPUProcessorPerf" TYPE="TABLE">
  <TableDescriptor>
      <ColumnDescriptor NAME="CPUNumber" TYPE="NUMBER" IS_KEY="TRUE"/>
      <ColumnDescriptor NAME="CPUUser" TYPE="NUMBER" IS_KEY="FALSE"/>
      ...
  </TableDescriptor>
  ...
</Metric>
```

Dynamic Properties

I have covered only static instance properties that are defined by EM12c users when adding target instances. However, there is a mechanism to collect properties dynamically that can later be used in the plug-in configuration for metric collections. For example, you might want to collect the target version or the platform it's running on so that you can then collect platform-dependent metrics (often Linux and Windows platforms are handled differently, for example). You can also use dynamic properties to display on the target home page (something you will learn about later).

Just like static instance properties, dynamic properties are defined under InstanceProperties as a DynamicProperties element. The element structure is similar to that of Metric element but it doesn't have a TableDescriptor. The list of properties is defined in the PROP_LIST attribute as a semicolon-separated list (for example, "prop1;prop2;prop3"). It also has a special format ROW instead of TABLE used normally for metrics. Just like a metric, DynamicProperties includes a QueryDescriptor defining the fetchlet used to collect the properties listed in PROP_LIST. The fetchlet should return just one row with the values corresponding to the PROP_LIST attribute. Listing 10-18 shows a shortened snippet of a dynamic property from the sample_host1 target that we've been using as an example so far.

Listing 10-18. Boot Date Dynamic Property Example from `sample_host1` Target

```
<InstanceProperties>
  <InstanceProperty ...>...</InstanceProperty>
  <DynamicProperties NAME="HostSampleBootDate" PROP_LIST="bootDate" FORMAT="ROW">
    <QueryDescriptor FETCHLET_ID="OSLineToken">
      <Property .../>
      <Property NAME="script" SCOPE="GLOBAL">
          %scriptsDir%/sample_host1/data_collector.pl --collect BootDate --fake "%fake%"
      </Property>
      <Property .../>
    </QueryDescriptor>
  </DynamicProperties>
</InstanceProperties>
```

A dynamic property can then be referenced in the fetchlet configuration for metrics in the `Property` element with `SCOPE="INSTANCE"`—just like any other static property.

You can find more information on `DynamicProperties` in Section 3.3.6.2 of the *Extensibility Programmer's Reference*. However, the official documentation is pretty sparse. You can find more details in the XML Schema documentation under `<EDK>/doc/partnersdk/mrs/emcore/targetType`.

One of the best uses of dynamic properties is to define category properties that are, in turn, used for conditional definitions in the target type metadata using a `ValidIf` element. This element can be defined as a child of several elements such as `Metric` or `QueryDescriptor` so that certain metrics are activated only when the defined category property is matching certain choices. Another use case is to configure different fetchlets to collect metric values depending on the value of category property. Unfortunately, as of EM12c version 12.1.0.2.0, this functionality is not officially documented, so you should be careful relying on it. However, it was available since Grid Control 10g versions, and you can see how it's used in Oracle's out-of-the-box plug-ins (for example, in its rac_database target type). You can find the `rac_database` target type metadata definition in `<AGENT_BASE>/plugins/oracle.sysman.db.agent.plugin_12.1.0.2.0/metadata/rac_database.xml`. Note that Oracle uses XML functionality by including other files' XML content to facilitate the reuse of identical definitions. For example, the database version calculations are the same for the RAC database, the ASM instance, and the database instance, so it's defined in the `dyn_props.xmlp` file that's referred from multiple target type metadata definition files.

Note that Oracle's `sample_host` targets include other dynamic properties defining related links. I believe that this part of the example has not been removed since 10g/11g Grid Control and isn't relevant anymore. Prior to EM12c, the Extensibility framework had very few features to customize the home page of a target, and adding custom links to the related links section on the home page was one of them. EM12c has rich target user interface definition options, and related links via dynamic properties are not used anymore, so this dynamic property in all `sample_host` demo targets is ignored and should have been removed.

Reports

EM12c provides two reporting mechanisms:

Information Publisher: This is the same mechanism that existed in Grid Control 10g/11g versions, which had the Information Publisher PL/SQL API and used to require reports definitions to be created using PL/SQL. EM12c has now XML-based Information Publisher report definitions and the ability to design reports by using the EM12c console and export them by using EMCLI. To have similar capabilities in 10g/11g, I had to create a custom extractor that produced PL/SQL API-based definitions from the reports developed using the console UI. EM12c will still transform XML into PL/SQL calls behind the scenes, but the convenience of XML definitions is huge, compared to long cumbersome PL/SQL definitions that were virtually impossible to validate syntactically without trying to execute them. See Chapter 4 of the *Extensibility Programmer's Reference* for detailed documentation on creating and customizing Information Publisher reports, including details of XML elements.

BI Publisher: EM12c can integrate with Oracle Business Intelligence Publisher for more-advanced reporting capabilities. However, integration with BI Publisher might require licensing Oracle Business Intelligence Publisher, which is holding back the adoption of BI Publisher with EM12c, based on my observation. If you are developing plug-ins for external users and not just for your organization, you probably shouldn't rely on the availability of BI Publisher in the target EM12c environments, so be sure to provide comparable reports by using Information Publisher. Chapter 5 of the *Extensibility Programmer's Reference* provides very brief instructions on creating the BI Publisher reports, but this documentation quality and depth is nowhere close to the documentation ofInformation Publisher API. It also relies on prior knowledge of the Oracle Business Intelligence Publisher product.

Although Chapter 4 of the *Extensibility Programmer's Reference* notes that Information Publisher is deprecated, the reality is that so many existing reports and customers are relying on it, that it will not go anywhere in EM12c or probably the next versions unless Oracle packages BI Publisher with EM12c by default. My personal recommendation for plug-in development is to stick with Information Publisher at the moment, until Oracle provides reporting capabilities that don't require integration with additional products (and licenses). This also ensures that your plug-ins will work with any EM12c installation, whether it's integrated with BI Publisher or not. This section covers only Information Publisher reports. Although Chapter 5 of the *Extensibility Programmer's Reference* covers deploying BI Publisher reports, there are no instructions on how to package them with the plug-in archive.

Creating Information Publisher reports is fairly simple in EM12c. You can study examples of a report packaged with the `sample_host1` target within the `oracle.samples.xsh1` plug-in. Follow these steps to create a new report definition using Information Publisher API and package with your plug-in:

1. When the first version of the plug-in (still without reports) and target type is developed and deployed, create report definitions by using the EM12c console reports wizard. This will require creating SQL and/or PL/SQL to query the repository views and extract information (such as the target's metrics, configuration, and so forth) in the format required by reporting components such as charts, text labels, links, and tables. At this stage, you will get as close as possible to the desired report, iteratively improving your report. You can find documentation about the available repository views in Chapter 18 of the *Extensibility Programmer's Reference*.

2. Use the EMCLI command `emcli export_report` to extract the XML definition of the designed report.

3. You can modify and further customize the extracted XML report definition. The XML format provides the report developer additional design features not available directly in the EM12c console reports wizard. Most of Chapter 4 of the *Extensibility Programmer's Reference* is dedicated to the documentation of XML elements for Information Publisher reports, and you should use that as a reference.

4. Finally, place the created report definition files into `<STAGE>/oms/metadata/reports` and package the new version of the plug-in. EDK will automatically pick up reports during creation of the OPAR file as long as the report definitions are placed in the correct location.

When the plug-in with reports is deployed on the OMS, its reports are available in the EM12c console in the Information Publisher Reports section as SYSTEM reports. These reports cannot be deleted or modified by the EM12c users. However, the reports can be cloned to create a copy that can be customized if required. 10g/11g Grid Control allowed to mark some SYSTEM reports to be available directly on the target's home page in the Reports tab. This tab has been removed from EM12c, because it provides UI customization of the target home page that far supersedes the older capabilities of simply embedding reports.

Two reports in the category Performance Reports of the `oracle.samples.xsh1` plug-in are good examples to study. The configuration report with this plug-in is using dummy data (selecting constants from DUAL table), so that isn't a useful example to study.

It's useful to use the Metadata Registration Service (MRS) to update report definitions directly in the repository without repackaging and redeploying the plug-in. See more details about MRS at the end of this chapter.

Enterprise Configuration Management

The EM12c Extensibility framework has full support for Enterprise Configuration Management (ECM). While 10g/11g Grid Control supported ECM feature, it wasn't documented and officially supported for third-party plug-in developers (even though ECM was used by Oracle's own plug-ins). EM12c added XML metadata definitions to ECM instead of awkward PL/SQL-based definitions, and that allowed simple support for plug-in developers.

There are three steps to adding configuration management capabilities:

1. Determine a configuration that needs to be collected. Organize that configuration in one or more tables, where each table corresponds to a configuration item. Configuration item can be single row or multirow, just like collecting monitoring metrics. If tables defining a configuration have relations between them, it's possible to define the full ECM schema with hierarchical relations. Think of it as ECM metadata describing configuration information to EM12c so that it can be used in the same manner as for out-of-the-box targets. ECM metadata is an XML file placed in the OMS staging area in the `<STAGE>/oms/metadata/snapshotlive` directory. Based on the ECM metadata, EM12c creates custom tables and views in the SYSMAN schema of the repository.

2. Each configuration item is collected as a metric defined in the target type metadata XML file, with special settings required for configuration metrics. Thus, you need to define special collection metrics in the target type metadata.

3. Define special default collection items in the default collection metadata XML file.

Out of three examples provided in the EDK, only the `oracle.samples.xsh3` plug-in contains complete implementation of ECM. The `oracle.samples.xsh1` and `oracle.samples.xsh2` plug-ins do have configuration metrics defined but are missing ECM metadata, so no repository tables are created, which means configuration information gathered by the agent is not actually loaded anywhere. Just ignore the metrics in the first two sample plug-ins. I suspect the developers simply forgot to remove these metrics when splitting the demo plug-in into multiple examples.

Listing 10-19 contains the ECM metadata snippet from the `oracle.samples.xsh3` plug-in. This file should be placed in the staging area in `<STAGE>/oms/metadata/snapshotlive`.

Listing 10-19. ECM Metadata Snippet

```
<METADATAS>
  <METADATA SNAP_TYPE="HostSample3Snap" TARGET_TYPE="sample_host3" VER="1">
    <METADATA_UI_NAME>Hostsample Configuration Data</METADATA_UI_NAME>
    <TABLE NAME="MGMT_EMX_HS_SYSTEM" SINGLE_ROW="Y">
      <UI_NAME>Hostsample System Configuration</UI_NAME>
      <COLUMN NAME="hostname" TYPE="STRING" TYPE_FORMAT="256" IS_KEY="N">Hostname</COLUMN>
      <COLUMN NAME="version" TYPE="STRING" TYPE_FORMAT="256" IS_KEY="N">Version</COLUMN>
    </TABLE>
    ...
    <TABLE NAME="MGMT_EMX_HS_NET" SINGLE_ROW="N">
      <UI_NAME>Hostsample Network Configuration</UI_NAME>
      <COLUMN NAME="net_interface" TYPE="STRING" TYPE_FORMAT="32" IS_KEY="Y">Interface</COLUMN>
      <COLUMN NAME="net_mtu" TYPE="NUMBER" IS_KEY="N">Maximum Transmission Unit (bytes)</COLUMN>
      <COLUMN NAME="net_flag" TYPE="STRING" TYPE_FORMAT="16" IS_KEY="N">Flag</COLUMN>
    </TABLE>
  </METADATA>
</METADATAS>
```

The ECM metadata contains the root element METADATAS, which is just a container for one or more snapshots defined by the METADATA element. One metadata element must match to one CollectionItem in the default collection metadata that I will define later. Think of it as a configuration snapshot.

Each configuration snapshot defines one or more tables, where each table matches to a configuration metric defined in the target type metadata. All configuration metrics also must be included in the matching CollectionItem in the default collection metadata. Columns between configuration tables and configuration metrics must, of course, match. Multirow tables are marked with the SINGLE_ROW="N" attribute and must contain at least one column marked as key by using IS_KEY="Y". Because you are comfortable with metadata definitions, I won't go through each attribute. Most of them are self-explanatory, and you can find full details in Chapter 6 of the *Extensibility Programmer's Reference*.

Note that you need to increment the version of the ECM metadata (VER attribute) every time it's changed, just as for the target type metadata.

The documentation refers to the generate_ecm_resources utility that's presumably a part of the EDK. This utility is supposed to generate a configuration metric template as well as an associated default collection template, so that all table names, columns names, and other items are matching—which I found can be quite confusing to create from scratch. Unfortunately, the utility is missing in the latest EDK distribution that I used (the one coming with the 12.1.0.2 version of EM12c), so I couldn't take advantage of it.

Configuration metrics for the target type metadata need to be created, as shown in Listing 10-20. Note that the listing provides only relevant snippets because the fetchlet configuration in the QueryDescriptor elements is already familiar to you as well as Display elements. The complete XML definitions are available in the EDK sample plug-ins.

Listing 10-20. Configuration Metrics Snippet

```
<Metric NAME="HostConfig" TYPE="RAW" CONFIG="TRUE">
  <TableDescriptor TABLE_NAME="MGMT_EMX_HS_SYSTEM">
    <ColumnDescriptor NAME="hostname" COLUMN_NAME="hostname" TYPE="STRING" IS_KEY="FALSE"/>
    <ColumnDescriptor NAME="version" COLUMN_NAME="version" TYPE="STRING" IS_KEY="FALSE"/>
  </TableDescriptor>
  <QueryDescriptor ...>...</QueryDescriptor>
</Metric>
...
```

```
<Metric NAME="NetConfig" TYPE="RAW" CONFIG="TRUE">
  <TableDescriptor TABLE_NAME="MGMT_EMX_HS_NET">
    <ColumnDescriptor NAME="net_interface" COLUMN_NAME="net_interface"
                      TYPE="STRING" IS_KEY="TRUE"/>
    <ColumnDescriptor NAME="net_mtu" COLUMN_NAME="net_mtu" TYPE="NUMBER" IS_KEY="FALSE"/>
    <ColumnDescriptor NAME="net_flag" COLUMN_NAME="net_flag" TYPE="STRING" IS_KEY="FALSE"/>
  </TableDescriptor>
  <QueryDescriptor ...>...</QueryDescriptor>
</Metric>
```

Configuration metrics should have the CONFIG="TRUE" attribute set. Its type must be set to "RAW", which means that the values are collected directly into a table in the repository schema. The TABLE_NAME property of the TableDescriptor from Listing 10-20 must match the NAME of the corresponding TABLE element from the ECM metadata in Listing 10-19. The attributes NAME and COLUMN_NAME of the ColumnDescriptor element in Listing 10-20 must match the NAME attribute of the column elements in Listing 10-19. I naively assumed that only COLUMN_NAME needs to match, and it caused me long hours of troubleshooting until I realized that the NAME attribute also must be set to the same value. The columns marked as part of the unique key in the tables in the ECM metadata must also be marked as keys in the corresponding configuration metric, as you can see for the net_interface column.

Now that you understand the content of ECM metadata and what's needed in target type metadata, it's time to complete the picture by adding the required CollectionItem to the default collection metadata, as shown in Listing 10-21.

Listing 10-21. CollectionItem for Configuration Snapshot

```
<CollectionItem NAME="HostSample3Snap" UPLOAD_ON_FETCH="TRUE" CONFIG="TRUE">
  <Schedule OFFSET_TYPE="INCREMENTAL">
    <IntervalSchedule INTERVAL="24" TIME_UNIT="Hr"/>
  </Schedule>
  <MetricColl NAME="HostConfig" />
  ...
  <MetricColl NAME="NetConfig" />
</CollectionItem>
```

The NAME of the CollectionItem in Listing 10-21 must match the SNAP_TYPE attribute of the METADATA element from Listing 10-19. The CollectionItem attribute also must be marked as a configuration collection with the CONFIG="TRUE" attribute. Setting the OFFSET_TYPE attribute to incremental is not critical, as it just means that the interval is counted from the end of the last collection rather than between collection start times. For quickly executing collections, that makes no difference. A collection item must include all configuration metrics defined in Listing 10-20, each matching to a table defined in Listing 10-19.

Assuming that the ECM metadata is at the correct location in the staging area, it will be automatically included in the plug-in archive during packaging. Note that if you are tweaking ECM metadata without changing other components, you can normally upload only the ECM metadata by using MRS just as you can for reports. MRS is, again, described at the end of the chapter.

You can find the complete documentation on ECM in Chapter 6 of the *Extensibility Programmer's Reference*. There you can see, for example, how to define indexes on ECM table columns and how to create dependencies between configuration items. Note that unless you are translating ECM captions into other languages, you can ignore the instructions for generating a .dlf file that's placed in <STAGE>/oms/rsc/ecm. (The documentation refers to nonexisting generate_ecm_resources utilities, but the .dlf file itself can be generated by using empdk generate_metadata_resource -service LiveSnapshotRegistration.)

If ECM is defined correctly and configurtion metrics collected, you can navigate via the target's menu to Configuration ➤ Last Collected and see the latest configuration collected, as shown in Figure 10-12. If you need to troubleshoot the configuration information collection, the agent's Metric Browser covered earlier in this chapter is a huge help. Chapter 6 of the *Extensibility Programmer's Reference* contains useful troubleshooting recommendations as well.

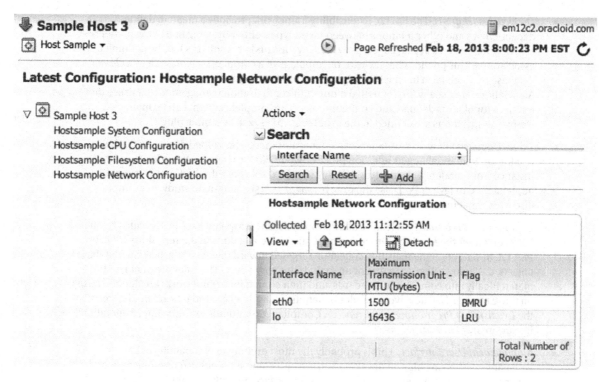

Figure 10-12. Configuration information in the EM12c console

Although defining configuration metrics looks a bit cumbersome, it becomes reasonably clear once you get the hang of it. The good news is that all configuration management features are immediately available, just as for standard Oracle targets, but without any change management licensing options. These features include configuration comparison between different targets or comparison with a saved configuration as well as tracking configuration changes over time.

More-Advanced Features

You've gone through the basic plug-in features as well as some of the advanced features such configuration management, and there are more available. Armed with this basic knowledge and the practical skills you gained by playing with the provided sample, you can consult the documentation for more-advanced features available to you as a plug-in developer. Note that if the documentation is not clear (and you will notice that on several occasions), you can also consult the existing sample plug-ins provided with the EDK, Oracle's own out-of-the-box plug-ins, as well as the XML Schema definitions in the additional documentation coming as part of the EDK.

The following list briefly introduces the features not covered in this chapter and the functionality they provide:

- *Job Types*: Plug-in developers can extend the EM12c job system by defining new job types. The job system is flexible and allows specifying rules how job parameters are defined, which credential should be used, how to control access to jobs, and how to serialize jobs. Job types are defined in the `oracle.samples.xsh2` plug-in.

- *Credentials*: Credentials are needed to support the jobs framework as well as to provide a secure alternative to defining passwords and passing to fetchlets in a more secure way than via instance properties. (Remember that command lines and environment variable content is not protected from other users.) While credentials are already defined in the `oracle.samples.xsh1` plug-in, they are not used until `oracle.samples.xsh2`, so use this plug-in to study Credentials examples.

- *Derived Associations*: The EM12c Extensibility framework provides a mean to define dependencies and other relations between target types, either by using one of the predefined associations (such as deployed_on, provided_by, or cluster_contains), or by defining new associations. This provides EM12c with the topology of a complex system, such as a cluster database or a web farm in which multiple monitored components are interconnected. Associations are usually implemented along with configuration management to ensure that a system topology is defined and configuration of the complete system can be managed. Derived associations are defined in the oracle.samples.xsh2 example plug-in.

- *Target Discovery*: Plug-in developers can enable automatic and guided discovery modes in addition to manual targets addition process where EM12c users must configure a target instance from scratch. This involves defining special discovery rules and scripts generally implemented in Java or Perl. Use the oracle.samples.xsh3 plug-in to study an example discovery implementation.

- *Compliance Standards*: This feature allows you to define compliance rules. The rules can be based on either the existing metrics and configuration collections in the repository (SQL or PL/SQL based) or on the real-time collection targeted toward files, users, processes, database objects, a Windows Registry entry, or an Active Directory entity. The rules are organized hierarchically into compliance standards, and then compliance frameworks are defined based on those standards. Extensive examples of defining compliance standards are in Chapter 12 of the *Extensibility Programmer's Reference*. A Compliance Standards example implementation is in plug-in oracle.samples.xsh3.

- *Management User Interface*: This is probably the most exciting new capability of EM12c Extensibility, allowing plug-in developers to create a completely custom user interface and to control the user experience. The custom user interface not only lets plug-in developers control how collected metrics and configuration information is displayed, but also gives full capabilities for an interactive user interface, including performing administrative actions such as starting and stopping components, killing sessions or users, creating target resources, and pretty much any other action that an administrator might need to perform. There are two ways to create a custom user interface. The easier but more limited method is to use the metadata-based management interface for defining pages, screen layout, and actions purely declaratively via XML constructs. While it's a huge step compared to 10g and 11g, limited interactive features are available. The more complex method is to use the Adobe Flex-based framework, which gives complete control over the user experience and full interactive capabilities, as well as allows you to package custom UI components with the plug-in. A metadata-based declarative UI is implemented in oracle.samples.xsh2. A Flex-based UI is implemented in oracle.samples.xsh3. However, there is only a prebuild Flex component, and I couldn't locate it in the sources. For a more complete Flex-based example, use another example in <EDK>/samples/plugins/HostSample.

- *Customized Incident Management*: This feature allows plug-in developers to customize what you see on the Incident Manager page when selecting an incident. They can add information in the incident details region, customize the diagnostic links, define a new guided resolution region, as well as override the default search expression for My Oracle Support. The documentation refers to registering incident management customizations by using only MRS, but based on the target path where metadata is stored in OMS, empdk should be able to package incident management customizations as part of a plug-in archive if it's placed under either <STAGE>/oms/metadata/events/custmzn or <STAGE>/oms/metadata/custmzn.

Note that the best implementation of a Flex-based UI is in the HostSample demo located in the EDK in <EDK>/samples/plugins/HostSample. A README file explains how to build the plug-in as well as how to use Adobe Flash Builder to open and work with the Flex-based UI, which is a great way to learn advanced UI development with EM12c.

While custom management UI is the most complex area of Extensibility, the documentation is not very clear, and it's difficult to draw the line between metadata-based UI and Flex-based. Thus, learning by example will help you a lot. I've also found that searching for a generic Adobe Flex solution such as charts attributes lets me guess some of the XML attributes for metadata-based UI that I was not able to find in the EM12c Extensibility documentation or EDK.

Metadata Registration Service

During development of the plug-in, you might have to do many iterative adjustments and verify the impact in the EM12c console after each change. Packaging, deploying, and upgrading a plug-in with each small change can be daunting. To reduce this deployment overhead, EM12c provides the Metadata Registration Service (MRS) via the `emctl register oms metadata` command to selectively upload and upgrade specific metadata. MRS is documented in Section 13.7 of the *Extensibility Programmer's Reference*, but at the time of this writing the documentation coverage is spotty.

From my experience, MRS works well for updating definitions of reports on the fly, updating user interface definitions (`mpcui` service), and ECM metadata (`LiveSnapshotRegistration` service). However, registering new target type metadata didn't always succeed for me, possibly because target metadata didn't propagate successfully to the agent.

For example, to update or register a new report definition, you can use the following command:

```
emctl register oms metadata -service report -file report_file.xml -pluginId oracle.samples.xsh1
```

Note that some services require special steps when registering components. For example, registration of the compliance standards service via MRS must be followed by manual execution of the `EM_COMPLIANCE_UTIL.trigger_rule_dependency_job` procedure in the repository database.

MRS also lets you implement some new features—for example, new job types and compliance standards with existing targets—without actually developing any new plug-ins at all. In fact, although most of the time you create plug-ins to package new target types, you can also create plug-ins without any target types and package, for example, just reports or compliance standards.

Summary

In this chapter, you have become familiar with Metric Extensions and most of their features. You learned that while EM12c metric extensions are much more flexible and manageable than Grid Control 10g/11g user-defined metrics, they still lack many features that are essential for collecting metrics from multiple new targets and even existing ones. For example, you can't easily process cumulative counters, create parameterized metric extensions, or use additional collection mechanisms. Later, you also learned that metric extensions are built on top of the EM12c Extensibility framework and are basically converted to similar XML definitions that you create when developing new target types.

In the second part of the chapter, you learned how to set up an environment for plug-in development, where to find documentation and samples, and how to build and deploy those samples. Based on those sample plug-ins, you learned all the basics of plug-in development and some tricks to make your life easier and your plug-in development more efficient. You also drilled into the details of some useful advanced features such as configuration management and learned where to look for sample implementation and documentation.

This chapter has emphasized that many sources are available for learning more about Extensibility and plug-ins—whether using official documentation, XML Schema documentation, or even drilling into Oracle's supplied plug-ins to understand how certain features work. Even if you don't expect to develop plug-ins either for your own use or for distributing externally, the knowledge of the EM12c Extensibility framework should deepen your understanding of EM12c internals, make you a better troubleshooter, and help you find answers to questions even if they're not documented by Oracle. EM12c is there to make you more efficient in managing enterprise infrastructures, and you can automate more tasks and cover a broader IT infrastructure footprint by leveraging the Extensibility framework one way or another.

CHAPTER 11

■ ■ ■

Enterprise Manager Jobs

by Kellyn Pot'Vin

A database job is defined as "a unit of work an administrator defines to automate commonly run tasks." The need for administrators to schedule database maintenance tasks, scripts to maintain or run batch jobs after hours, or backups of the database is obvious; these jobs are a requirement of the DBA role. The EM Job System grants the user scheduling flexibility to run jobs at any time and at any interval. It integrates seamlessly with the EM12c environment, unlike schedulers that are separate from the main database management and monitoring system.

The Enterprise Manager Job System was introduced in Oracle 9i, yet the EM jobs in Enterprise Manager 12c still aren't utilized as often as other features, such as monitoring, alerting, backups, and performance pages.

Throughout my years as a database administrator, I experienced few environments for which the EM Job System had been chosen over other job schedulers and was curious as to why. For all the ease of management, notification, and scheduling that the EM Job System offers, many administrators still appear loyal to their own collection of scripts to manage work performed in the database. Oracle already provides the historically challenged DBMS_JOBS and the more recently introduced and advanced DBMS_SCHEDULER_JOBS, which includes enhancements such as chained jobs and more-defined scheduling. In addition, the operating system cron scheduler allows the administrator to use any language that is available at the operating system (OS) level to script what is needed and schedule it.

Offering more options for scheduling and managing, along with another set of database-level views/tables in regards to support, might seem like overkill. My main task in this chapter is to convince administrators why the EM12c Job System is not just a better choice, but superior to previous versions of the EM job systems and the more enhanced way to manage database jobs in any database environment.

Enhancements include the following:

- Simple interface for job scheduling

- One location to manage all job events in an environment

- Job Library to be utilized as a repository of jobs

- Capability to easily tie in job requirements for blackouts and maintenance

- Simplification of global tasks through job deployment

The EM Job System also supports all areas of the infrastructure in the EM console, executing jobs for many of the tasks occurring transparently to the administrator interacting with the console interface.

Why Use EM12c Jobs

The main question to be answered is why an administrator should switch from their current job management program/scheduler to the Enterprise Manager Job System. When first introduced to an environment with EM12c, I also wanted this question answered. I had always utilized my own suite of shell and Perl scripts that I felt quite comfortable scheduling in the OS cron scheduler. I found the scripts/OS-level scheduler a satisfactory solution after small adjustments to environment variables and code were put in place to take the uniqueness of the server environment into consideration. The choice of the OS-level scheduler still appeared to be the best for ease of database management.

As I began to manage new environments for multiple clients, multiple server platforms, and OS profile designs and preferences, I encountered an intriguing challenge. I now was working in a large database team environment requiring me to quickly become familiar with others' scheduling choices or a new script author's coding style, or when investigating backup and maintenance scripts, I was even unsure of what kind of scheduler had been implemented. When multiple job schedulers were in use, often incorrect assumptions were made about which scheduler was executing which task in regards to monitoring, backup, and alerting.

It was immediately apparent that almost no time was required to acclimate in environments that utilized the job system through Enterprise Manager. The interface was similar no matter whether it was in a 10g or 11g Enterprise Manager or even the new 12c version. Maintaining, changing, "skipping," or any other tasks regarding the job within the Enterprise Manager Jobs interface were easy for administrators to familiarize themselves with. As all jobs were contained within the Enterprise Manager, creating maintenance windows during blackouts was simpler to manage.

The benefits of using the EM12c Jobs interface over other schedulers are as follows:

- Simple or advanced job search feature with wildcard functionality

- Schedule can be viewed for any conflicts with other running jobs across the entire environment

- Choice to skip all jobs during a target blackout or to configure jobs to run even though the target is in a blackout state, simplifying concerns of tasks running during maintenance

- Ability to incorporate scripts into the EM12c Job System to perform any task, providing a uniform scheduling, notification, and alerting system for all job tasks

Enterprise Manager Job Architecture

Three areas, shown in Figure 11-1, are central to the EM Jobs interface for EM12c:

EM Jobs Service: The enterprise management target service that manages all jobs in the Enterprise Manager

Job Library: Repository for jobs

Job Activity: Job interface system to view, create, and manage jobs

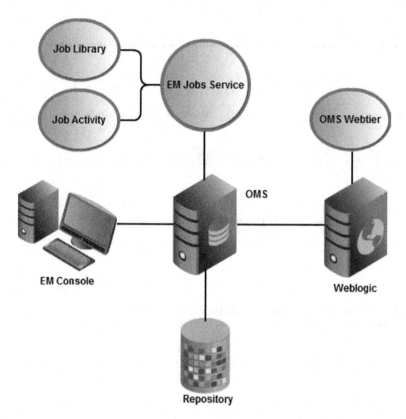

Figure 11-1. *The EM Job System as part of the high-level EM12c architecture*

Previous chapters provided a significant introduction to the Oracle Management Service (Chapter 3), the repository (Chapter 1), and the EM console and the WebLogic server (Chapter 4). Each of the EM Job components—the EM Jobs Service, Job Activity, and Job Library—are explained in further detail in the upcoming pages of this chapter.

EM Job System Components

The EM Job System envelops a large, complex number of components that interact with almost all aspects of the EM12c environment. As you become more familiar with the user jobs, system jobs, and agent jobs managed by the EM Jobs Service, you will see how the continued health and monitoring of the EM12c environment rely on this feature to execute tasks immediately or at scheduled times.

EM Jobs Service

The EM Jobs Service is the running service that controls all jobs processing in an EM12c environment. This interface can be difficult to locate, but is easiest to access by clicking Targets ➤ All Targets, typing **Service** in the Search Target Name box, and clicking the arrow. Then click EM Jobs Service (see Figure 11-2). The EM Jobs Service interface, shown in Figure 11-3, then displays. We will return to this interface repeatedly, as it is an important gateway to the advanced features of the EM12c Jobs Service.

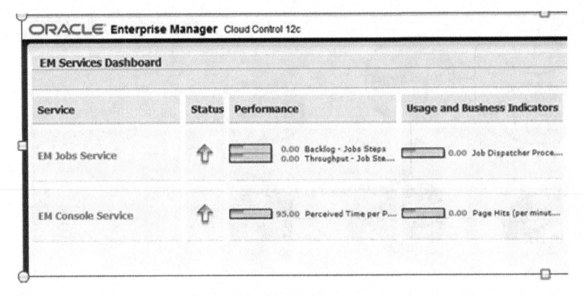

Figure 11-2. *The EM Services Dashboard, including the EM Jobs Service and the EM Console Service, along with status, performance, usage, components, and important service levels*

Figure 11-3. *The EM Jobs Service interface, demonstrating the basic information displayed in the main, left pane, including status, incidents, and uptime*

This console interface allows the user to view the service status, incidents, violations, performance charts, test performance, configuration topology of the job environment, and all other features included in the EM Job System.

You also can locate the EM Jobs Service page (and see how wildcard searches work in EM12c) by clicking Targets ➤ All Targets, typing **%job%** in the Search Target Name box, and clicking the arrow. The agent EM Jobs Service shows in the list and can be accessed by clicking the target name.

Figure 11-4. Wildcard searches are easy in the All Targets view

Monitoring Configuration

The EM Jobs Service interface includes various tabs that provide access to the Job System's functionality. The tab that is perhaps the most frequently used by DBAs is the Monitoring Configuration tab (see Figure 11-5).

EM Service: EM Jobs Service

Home   Charts   Test Performance   System   Monitoring Configuration   Topology

Figure 11-5. The Monitoring Configuration tab is one of the most used in the EM Jobs Service interface

The Monitoring Configuration section of the user interface contains numerous options to interact with features of the EM Jobs Service.

The Root Cause Analysis Configuration option can be used to perform automatic or manual inspection of any EM service upon failure. This analysis can then pinpoint the issue or be uploaded to My Oracle Support to assist with a service request. This feature is very beneficial in saving the administrator time otherwise wasted when manually filling out a service request in the My Oracle Support interface. The service requests covered in this section are for the main EM12c services, including the Enterprise Manager console, the Oracle Management Service, and the EM Jobs Service.

The Performance Metrics link enables you to configure thresholds for EM job-step throughput and job-step backlog. When using the EM Job System as the main job scheduler for a database environment, this can offer a monitoring incentive that is missing from most other job schedulers. Gathering postexecution performance information may not be available in other scheduling/logging methods, but with the EM12c Jobs Service, all data is retained for a default of 31 days.

Another link within the Monitoring Configuration tab, is Service Tests and Beacons. Service tests are an excellent way to test the ability of a web page to complete a simple transaction on a regular interval, to test for uptime, or to log in to a web site and verify that files are available for download at a certain time. Unlike metric extensions (described in Chapter 13), this feature is very URL specific and uses an EM Job to fulfill the task on the requested interval.

This feature has the unique option to record a web session by using an ActiveX plug-in that is then configured as part of an EM job to perform the task during the scheduled interval, checking for successful completion of the recorded steps a user would complete if they were to access the same web site. Figure 11-6 shows a session recording from the web site— successfully signing in, accessing four files, and then signing out. This session will be used by the EM Jobs Service to create the performance test and then continue on to the beacon settings.

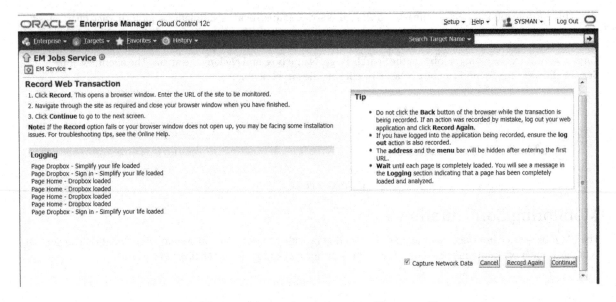

Figure 11-6. A session being recorded for use with a performance test and beacon settings

■ **Note**   To record a web transaction to be used by a performance test, Microsoft's Internet Explorer is the only supported web browser. Options won't appear when attempted with other browsers. In certain instances, the web transaction may fail even through Internet Explorer using the ActiveX plug-in, and the administrator will be directed by My Oracle Support to utilize the Oracle Application Development Framework (ADF) to record web transactions and import into the service test interface as a saved session file.

The Job Activity Page

The Job Activity page enables you to do the following:

- Create a job

- Save jobs that have been scheduled, running, or previously executed to the Job Library to retain for future use

- View or edit an existing job in the activity section

- View results of, edit, create, resume, suspend, stop, or delete a job execution

- Search for jobs by various methods, including job name (wildcards allowed), job type, and status

The Job Activity page, shown in Figure 11-7, can be viewed at the level of the database, cluster, or full monitored environment.

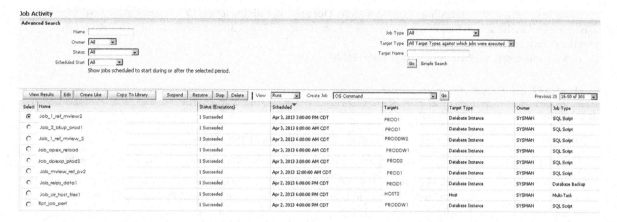

Figure 11-7. *An example of job activity, with the administrator viewing the activity scheduled furthest into the future first, and descending into current and past activity by scrolling down*

When searching and viewing the Job Activity page, keep in mind the following terminology in Table 11-1.

Table 11-1. *Important Job Activity Terms*

Job Activity	Description
Job execution	A single job execution in EM12c—often attributed to one target, but can have multiple targets or none at all, depending on the task.
Job run	A summary of all executions of a specific job

When searching job executions and job runs, you can use a wildcard (%) in the job name search options, as shown in Figure 11-8. This wild card can be used for any of the fields requiring you to enter a value (rather than those offering drop-down choices).

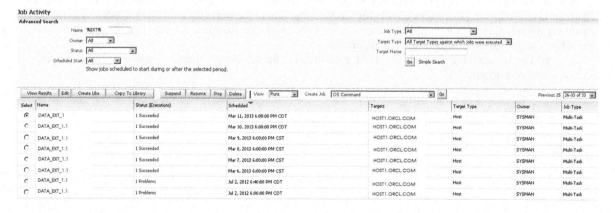

Figure 11-8. *Job activity search using a wildcard option*

The job search in the preceding example searched for any job with the letters EXTR in the name. No distinction was requested in the search for job type (scheduled, succeeded, problem, and so forth), so all jobs were returned that met the search criteria.

EM Job supports the job operations listed in Table 11-2.

Table 11-2. *Job Activity Actions*

Job Action	Description
Create	Create an OS or SQL script, along with other types of jobs.
Edit	Update the existing job and change scheduled time, interval, parameters, and so forth.
Create Like	Create a job from an existing one, with options to edit the existing parameters, schedule, and so forth. (Backup jobs and certain other maintenance jobs may not allow the Create Like option.)
Delete	Remove either a single scheduled/failed job or remove all instances of the job from the EM Job Activity view. (Any library copies will be retained.)
Suspend	Place the job "on hold" until it is resumed, enabling the existing schedule to continue.
Resume	Resume a suspended schedule for a job. Jobs must be resumed individually.
Retry on Failure	Retry the job if it is in the allowed list of job types.

The Enterprise Manager Job Library

The Enterprise Manager Job Library allows the repository of jobs that can be submitted to the EM Job scheduler. This repository contains all the jobs created by an administrator outside of backups and EM console processing. The library retains only what has been saved to it and must be kept up-to-date with changes in active jobs. An exporter that would create a snapshot of current jobs to the library would be beneficial, but unfortunately does not exist at this time. Therefore, it is important to always save any changed jobs, including simple execution time changes, from the Job Activity page to the library. If for any reason you must refer to the library to re-create the job, this will ensure a correct resubmission of the job to the scheduler.

For users of earlier 10g and 11g EM jobs, there was no migration process for jobs to a new EM12c environment. This feature is also missing in the new EM12c version, but plans are in the works for Oracle to include one in an upcoming release. This feature should have multiple benefits, not just for migrations, but as part of upgrades, secondary options for backup/recovery, and replication.

The Job Library interface, shown in Figure 11-9, is similar to the Job Activity page and uses many similar options, including Edit and Access.

Figure 11-9. *An example of a production Job Library for the EM12c console*

EM Job Schema

More than 70 JOB tables exist in the SYSMAN schema, but only a few are involved in the major components of the EM Job System and require a basic understanding. You can execute queries against these tables for a more difinitive view of the EM Job environment. Figure 11-10 shows two main tables, along with the relationships between objects.

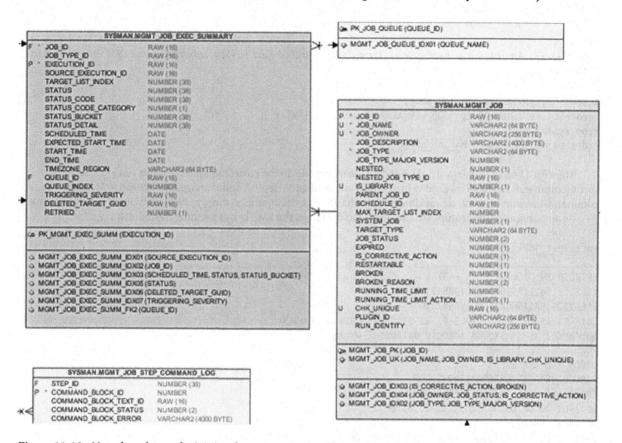

Figure 11-10. *Note the columns for joining the most common objects in the EM Job System part of the SYSMAN schema*

The following example queries will report against job data. The MGMT_JOB table, which is often used in the upcoming queries, contains both the Job Library and the job_activity information, so this must be kept in mind when querying, as shown in Figure 11-11. Often this data is essential if at any time the EM Job Activity or Job Library interface is unsuccessful at managing a job and the Enterprise Manager Command Line Interface (EMCLI) must be used.

SYSMAN	BACKUP_APEX	JOB_LIBRARY
SYSMAN	BACKUP_APEX.1	JOB_ACTIVITY
SYSMAN	BACKUP_APEX_DEV	JOB_LIBRARY
SYSMAN	BACKUP_APEX_DEV.1	JOB_ACTIVITY
SYSMAN	BACKUP_EM12REP	JOB_ACTIVITY
SYSMAN	BACKUP_EM12REP_000044	JOB_ACTIVITY
SYSMAN	BACKUP_REMOVE_ARCHLOGS	JOB_LIBRARY

Figure 11-11. *An example of backup job information for both the active jobs (submitted) and the jobs retained in the library*

```
select  mj.job_owner, mj.job_name,
decode(mj.is_library, 1, 'JOB_LIBRARY', 0, 'JOB_ACTIVITY')
from sysman.mgmt_job mj
order by mj.job_owner, mj_job_name;
```

The EMCLI can also be used to gather data regarding jobs in the environment. This utility has its own set of verbs (commands) that are invoked to query, execute, configure, deploy, and manage the Enterprise Manager from a command-line interface, often providing more-enhanced capabilities than the graphical interface of the EM console.

As an example of this feature, we can query job data from the EMCLI by executing the following:

```
emcli get_jobs
```

```
REFRESH_MV_ORCL.MV_DEVA_PART.1             SQLScript
416E2CE166724F53BCF3ECD798E1759B
B16A12D945A1466C871B99E1A5226309
2013-01-21 07:00:00   2013-01-21 07:02:22America/Chicago
Succeeded  5    SYSJOB  oracle_database  ORCL5
```

```
ORCL5_MFC_APP_REF.1                        SQLScript
F39C0BE9B9F74F758FFDA95392778CDF
E088B023C23048E79768BC4FEC2888B3
2013-01-20 06:00:00   2013-01-20 06:00:23
America/Chicago
Succeeded  5    SYSJOB  oracle_database  ORCL5
```

The JOB_ID column is one of the most common columns to join on in this schema, as it identifies the job in question. In the preceding results, you can see that two jobs were returned that included the job name, job type, job ID, and target GUID, along with execution information, including times, time zone, and whether the job successful.

In the next example, MGMT_JOB_EXEC_SUMMARY is joined to the MGMT_JOB table to display the most recent history and verify the job status.

```
select mj.job_name, mjes.start_time,  mjes.end_time,
DECODE(mjes.status,
  1, 'SCHEDULED', 2, 'RUNNING', 3, 'FAILED INIT',
  4, 'FAILED', 5, 'SUCCEEDED', 6, 'SUSPENDED',
  7, 'AGENT DOWN', 8, 'STOPPED', 9, 'SUSPENDED/LOCK',
  10, 'SUSPENDED/EVENT', 11, 'SUSPENDED/BLACKOUT',
  12, 'STOP PENDING', 13, 'SUSPEND PENDING', 14, 'INACTIVE',
  15, 'QUEUED', 16, 'FAILED/RETRIED', 17, 'WAITING', 18, 'SKIPPED',status) "Execution STATUS"
from sysman.mgmt_job mj, sysman.mgmt_job_exec_summary mjes
```

```
where mj.job_id=mjes.job_id
and mj.job_name ='BACKUP_EM12REP_000044'
order by mjes.start_time desc;
```

The output from this query will result in backup job information on the database repository. Both the current running job, along with the historical jobs information, can be seen in Figure 11-12.

🗒 JOB_NAME	🗒 START_TIME	🗒 END_TIME	🗒 Execution STATUS
BACKUP_EM12REP_000044	18-SEP-12	(null)	RUNNING
BACKUP_EM12REP_000044	18-SEP-12	18-SEP-12	SUCCEEDED
BACKUP_EM12REP_000044	18-SEP-12	18-SEP-12	SUCCEEDED
BACKUP_EM12REP_000044	18-SEP-12	18-SEP-12	SUCCEEDED
BACKUP_EM12REP_000044	18-SEP-12	18-SEP-12	SUCCEEDED

Figure 11-12. *Querying job status information*

We can then query the data from the last 24 hours that meets the following criteria: not requiring corrective action—is_corrective_action = 0, has a status of in standard job history—status IN (5,4,3,18,8), and has required—retried is not null.

```
SELECT mjes.job_id, mj.job_name, mjes.retried
FROM MGMT_JOB_EXEC_SUMMARY mjes, MGMT_JOB mj
WHERE mjes.job_id = mj.job_id AND mj.is_corrective_action = 0
AND mjes.status IN (5,4,3,18,8)
AND  mjes.start_time > sysdate-1
and mjes.retried is not null;
```

JOB_ID	🗒 JOB_NAME	🗒 RETRIED
BFC7CAEC5756D963E04014AC080046B1	BACKUP_APEX_DEV.1	1
C61282120F595658E043080014ACBC49	BACKUP_EM12REP	1

Figure 11-13. *The results for jobs that have experienced at least one retry*

These basic queries offer examples of how to join the tables and how to report on the EM Job System from SQL*Plus. This data can then help you troubleshoot, or you can use this information at the EMCLI to address an issue or perform a task outside the EM console.

Knowing who has the right to create and manage jobs is essential. Jobs should be owned by individual users, with preferred credentials set to this level to ensure accountability for the use of those credentials.

By creating the EM12c administrator logins and setting them up securely, you can see who ran a job and who edited a job, ensuring that those creating, executing, and even deleting jobs are tracked effectively in the Enterprise Manager access log. As the user is not the repository owner (SYSMAN), this eliminates security issues that could arise by the extensive roles and grants given to this user by default in the EM12c environment.

To see who has credentials to run and manage jobs, you can run a simple query to show who has what privileges (see Figure 11-14), along with how those credentials compare to those owned by the SYSMAN schema (see Figure 11-15). Figure 11-16 provides a diagram for reference.

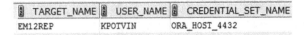

TARGET_NAME	USER_NAME	CREDENTIAL_SET_NAME
EM12REP	KPOTVIN	ORA_HOST_4432

Figure 11-14. *Users with target credentials from a query to the EM SYSMAN schema*

TARGET_NAME	USER_NAME	CREDENTIAL_SET_NAME
EM12REP	SYSMAN	ORA_EM12C_NC12543

Figure 11-15. *Example of SYSMAN credentials that might appear in an environment*

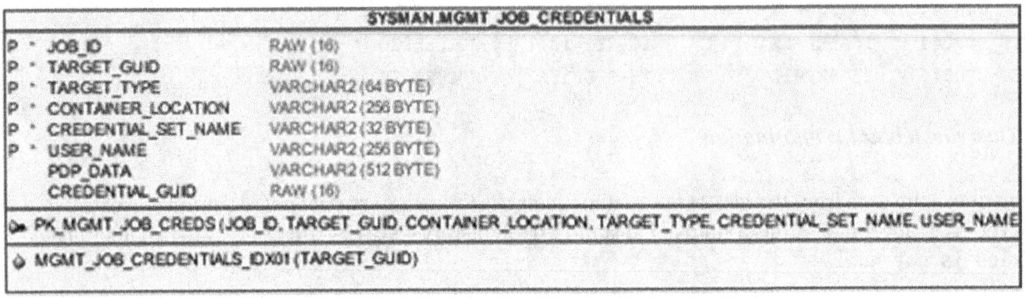

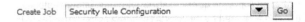

Figure 11-16. *Credential, job command, and job info tables to be used for granular queries on job activity*

```
SELECT mt.target_name, mtc.user_name, mtc.credential_set_name
FROM MGMT_TARGET_CREDENTIALS mtc, MGMT_TARGETS mt
WHERE mtc.TARGET_GUID=mt.target_GUID;

SELECT mt.target_name, mtc.user_name, mtc.credential_set_name
FROM MGMT_TARGET_CREDENTIALS mtc, MGMT_TARGETS mt
WHERE mtc.TARGET_GUID=mt.target_GUID
And mtc.USER_NAME='SYSMAN';
```

The MGMT_JOB_CREDENTIALS table contains all the job credential data and can be queried on its own or joined to MGMT_JOB and other tables for more information.

Job Creation

The job creation interface has remained similar to previous versions of Enterprise Manager. However, because of the interface's complexity, this section provides a clear example of job creation. In this example, we will create a simple security job that will check on who has privileges to the DBA_* views.

From the Job Activity menu, click the Create Job drop-down menu and select Security Rule Configuration. Then click Go (see Figure 11-17).

Create Job   Security Rule Configuration   ▼   Go

Figure 11-17. *Starting the job creation*

This opens the job creation page. Starting with the General tab, fill in the name and a description (if desired). Then select a target type (for this example, choose Database Instance) and click Add to choose a database target.

After the target is selected in the Add Target window, you return to the main screen, which now displays information similar to that in Figure 11-18.

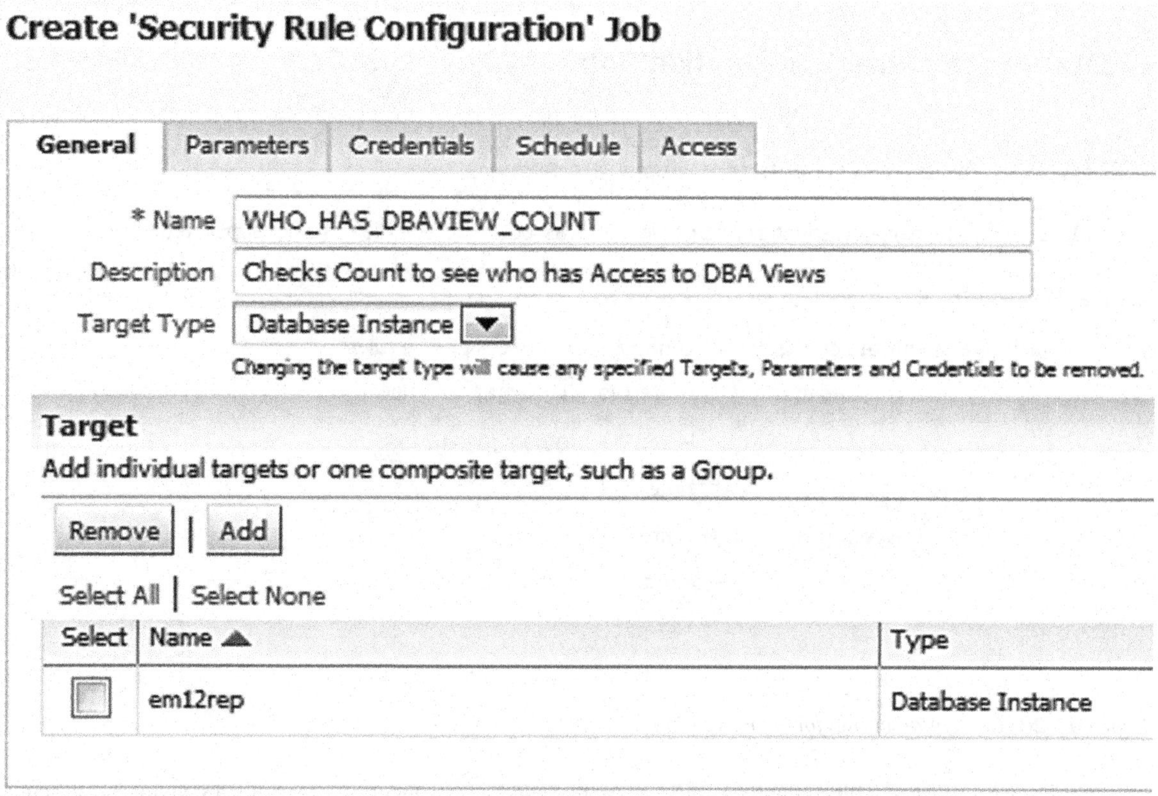

Create 'Security Rule Configuration' Job

| General | Parameters | Credentials | Schedule | Access |

* Name `WHO_HAS_DBAVIEW_COUNT`

Description `Checks Count to see who has Access to DBA Views`

Target Type `Database Instance ▼`

Changing the target type will cause any specified Targets, Parameters and Credentials to be removed.

Target

Add individual targets or one composite target, such as a Group.

`Remove` | `Add`

Select All | Select None

Select	Name ▲	Type
☐	em12rep	Database Instance

Figure 11-18. *The General tab configured for a new job*

You now have successfully filled out the General tab and can move on to the Parameters tab.

Choose the Access to DBA_* Views option from the Security Rule drop-down list. For the maximum number of rows to be returned, enter **All** (see Figure 11-19).

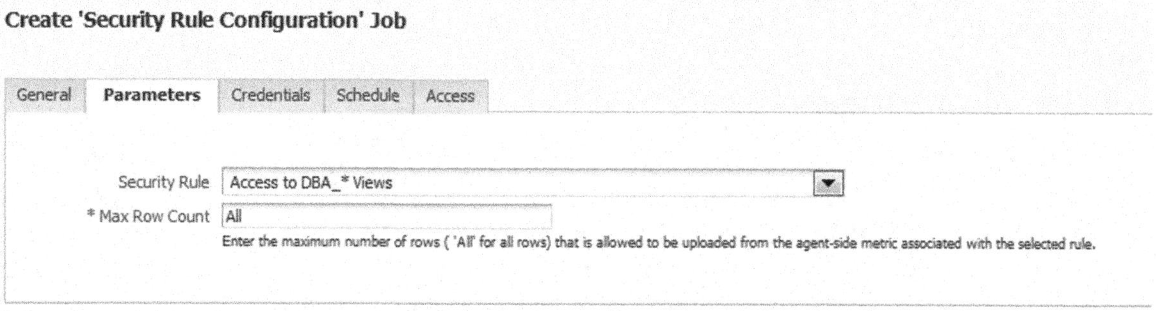

Create 'Security Rule Configuration' Job

| General | Parameters | Credentials | Schedule | Access |

Security Rule `Access to DBA_* Views                    ▼`

* Max Row Count `All`

Enter the maximum number of rows ('All' for all rows) that is allowed to be uploaded from the agent-side metric associated with the selected rule.

Figure 11-19. *Parameter settings to check access to DBA_* views*

Next, click the Credentials tab. For this example, Named is selected for the Credential option (see Figure 11-20). We will fill out the details to give a clear understanding of the interface, but it is always preferable to have Preferred Credentials set up beforehand for ease of management.

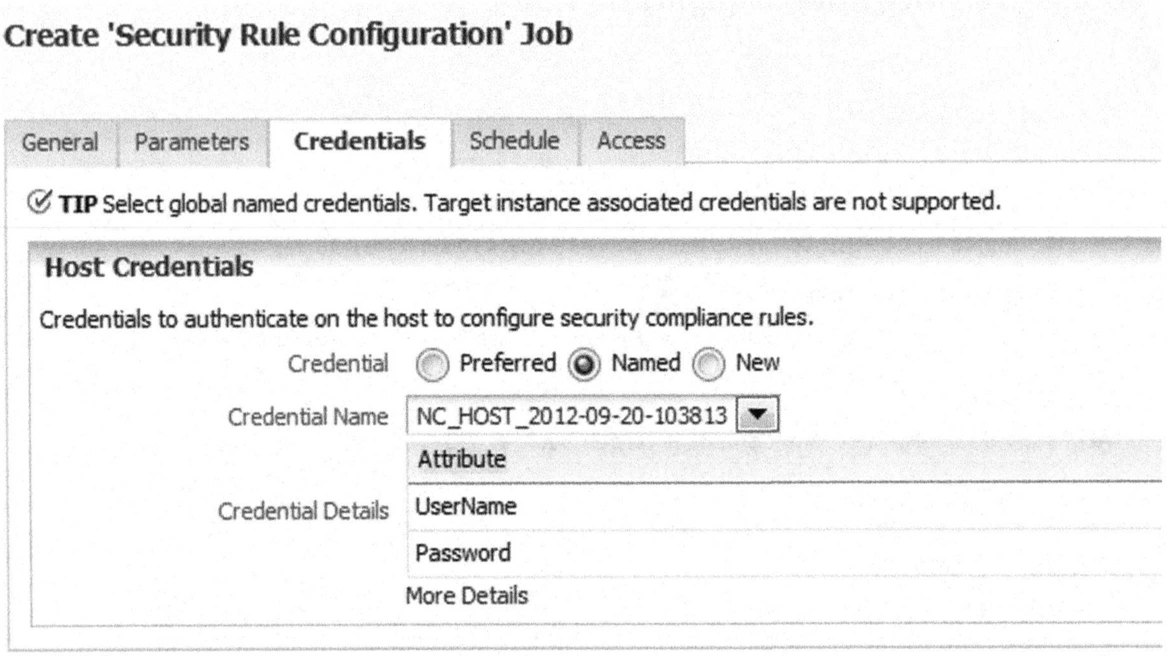

Create 'Security Rule Configuration' Job

General   Parameters   **Credentials**   Schedule   Access

✓ **TIP** Select global named credentials. Target instance associated credentials are not supported.

Host Credentials

Credentials to authenticate on the host to configure security compliance rules.

Credential	◯ Preferred ◉ Named ◯ New
Credential Name	NC_HOST_2012-09-20-103813 ▼

Credential Details	Attribute
	UserName
	Password
	More Details

Figure 11-20. Credential settings for a job creation

When you are finished with credentials, move on to the Schedule tab. Figure 11-21 shows a schedule set to send the report each Monday at 9:30AM and to never expire or to have an end-date grace period.

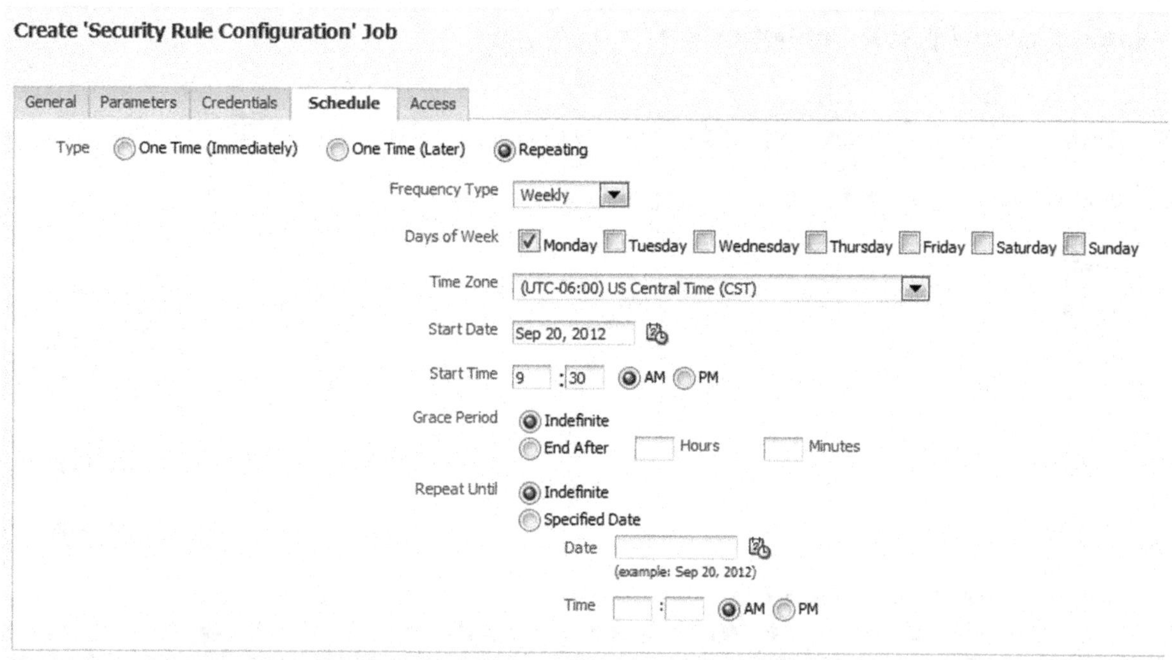

Create 'Security Rule Configuration' Job

| General | Parameters | Credentials | **Schedule** | Access |

Type   ◯ One Time (Immediately)   ◯ One Time (Later)   ◉ Repeating

Frequency Type   Weekly ▼

Days of Week   ☑ Monday ☐ Tuesday ☐ Wednesday ☐ Thursday ☐ Friday ☐ Saturday ☐ Sunday

Time Zone   (UTC-06:00) US Central Time (CST) ▼

Start Date   Sep 20, 2012 📅

Start Time   9 : 30   ◉ AM ◯ PM

Grace Period   ◉ Indefinite
                ◯ End After   [   ] Hours   [   ] Minutes

Repeat Until   ◉ Indefinite
                ◯ Specified Date
                Date [   ] 📅
                (example: Sep 20, 2012)

                Time [   ] : [   ]   ◉ AM ◯ PM

Figure 11-21. *Setting up the scheduling for the new job*

Next you have the option to set each of the administrators (outside of the owner) to view or manage the job, as shown in Figure 11-22. The administrators can also be removed from the access list by placing a check mark in the box under the Remove column (which is not shown in Figure 11-22, but is at the far right).

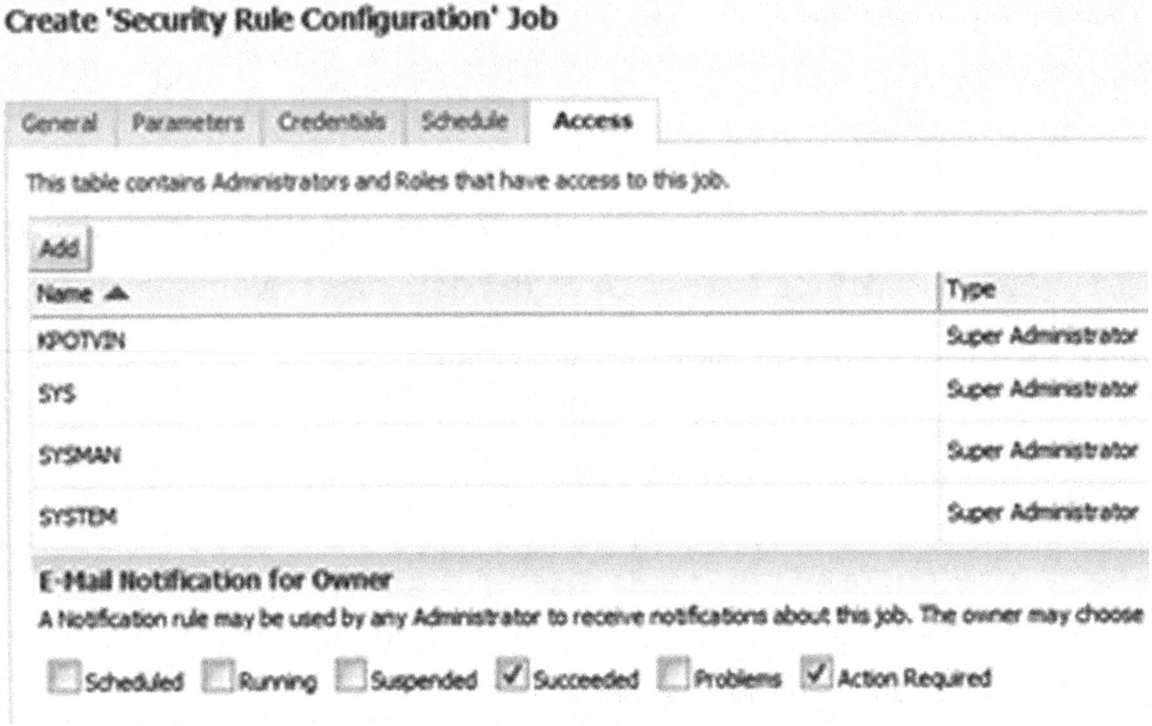

Create 'Security Rule Configuration' Job

| General | Parameters | Credentials | Schedule | **Access** |

This table contains Administrators and Roles that have access to this job.

Add

Name ▲	Type
KPOTVIN	Super Administrator
SYS	Super Administrator
SYSMAN	Super Administrator
SYSTEM	Super Administrator

E-Mail Notification for Owner

A Notification rule may be used by any Administrator to receive notifications about this job. The owner may choose

☐ Scheduled ☐ Running ☐ Suspended ☑ Succeeded ☐ Problems ☑ Action Required

Figure 11-22. *Who has access and what notifications will be sent*

Below the Security Rule Configuration section is the E-Mail Notification section. Here you choose the following notification options:

> *Scheduled*: The job is scheduled to run.

> *Running*: The job is executing.

> *Suspended*: The job has been suspended from running.

> *Succeeded*: The job has completed successfully.

> *Problems*: The job has encountered failures or problems in a step or overall.

> *Action Required*: Intervention by an administrator is required. This includes jobs with a status of skipped.

Because the job is owned by the user KPOTVIN, any e-mail addresses identified with that user and configured in the EM console will receive notifications according to the settings. This user also has the ability to view, manage, and monitor the job

Types of Jobs

The Enterprise Manager has extended its support of job types in version 12c. Although OS Command, SQL Script, and RMAN may be prevalent, dozens of jobs are now supported by the EM Job environment:

Application Development Protocol (ADP): Job protocol used by the Oracle ADF.

Agent Configuration and Control Operations: These two are the first of a number of Enterprise Manager scheduled jobs types. These jobs are created as part of an agent configuration or control request in the EM console.

ASM Scripts: Many tasks in Automatic Storage Management are scheduled as a job in the EM console. This is another EM console created job, as opposed to a job created through the EM Jobs interface.

Clone Home: One of the most anticipated additions, this new job type allows you to easily clone an existing Oracle home to a new Oracle home.

Database Configuration: Another EM console job type, this updates a database configuration without requiring you to perform the task on the target server.

Deployments: A new EM12c feature, this job is deployed from the EM console to targets for monitoring and configuration.

Discovery of Specific Oracle Components: Jobs are also scheduled to discover Oracle components on designated Oracle targets through the EM console. This autodiscovery saves time and effort by dynamically pulling configuration and target information directly from the server to ensure correct configuration of any target.

Log Rotation: Logs, trace files, and Enterprise Manager logs can become difficult to manage if they become too large. This job type can be created in the EM Jobs interface to manage many of the database logs that you access and monitor on a regular basis.

OPatch Updates: Another new job type to EM12c, automated OPatch updates ensure that you have the latest version of the OPatch utility installed on each target monitored through the EM12c environment.

OS Commands: This job type allows you to migrate existing OS scripts from a cron scheduler or other OS-level scheduler and into a single scheduler within the Enterprise Manager console. By migrating to the EM Jobs interface, there is no further need to manage through a second scheduler in times of EM blackouts, as all can be managed through a single interface.

RMAN: All Recovery Manager jobs, although created through the RMAN interface in the EM console, will show as scheduled jobs in the Job Activity interface. These job types are unable to be saved to the library and have limited editing capabilities in the Job Activity interface.

Security: This job type involves the security interface accessed from the Setup ➤ Security section in the EM console. These jobs include those for administrators, roles, credentials, and audit data.

SQL Scripts: The most common job type involving EM jobs, this allows you to execute SQL, procedures, and any other taskthat would be performed from a SQL*Plus session.

Multitask Jobs: For jobs that have multiple steps required to complete a process, this is a new feature in EM12c. In the past, you had to script out complex, multistep processes. Now, the EM12c Jobs interface makes it simple to create jobs with multiple steps, including those with logic requests of success on each step.

It is simple enough to locate the common and new job types that are supported by the EM12c Jobs Service. The following query shows not just the job types supported, but also the job type ID that is used for EMCLI execution.

```
select * from sysman.MGMT_JOB_TYPE_INFO
where job_type_category=0
and editable=1
and agent_bound=1
and job_type not like '%Obsolete%'
and job_type_default is not null;
```

Figure 11-23 shows the query results, with the job type from the SYSMAN schema in the OMS repository database and any pertinent information about each. This data clearly shows job types that are supported for the front-end (job_type_category=0), able to be edited post job creation (that is, backup jobs cannot be edited once created outsidethe backup and recovery scheduler), and are all available to an agent (agent_bound vs. an OMS-level job.) As you can see in the figure, all obsolete job types are skipped but are still listed in the repository.

JOB_TYPE_ID	JOB_TYPE	JOB_TYPE_OWNER	JOB_TYPE_CATEGORY	LAST_MODIFIED_BY
BFC71D34736A9B93E04014AC08001B7D	SQLScript	(null)	0	(null)
BFC71D34736E9B93E04014AC08001B7D	OSCommand	(null)	0	(null)
BFC71D34737B9B93E04014AC08001B7D	HostCommand	(null)	0	(null)
BFC71D34739F9B93E04014AC08001B7D	SwlibUploadFiles	(null)	0	(null)
BFC71D3473A19B93E04014AC08001B7D	EntityTransferAndExecute	(null)	0	(null)
BFC71D34750E9B93E04014AC08001B7D	EsaProp	(null)	0	(null)
BFC71D347EEE9B93E04014AC08001B7D	Log Rotation	(null)	0	(null)
BFC71D347F329B93E04014AC08001B7D	WebLogic Control	(null)	0	(null)
BFC71D347F4E9B93E04014AC08001B7D	JavaEEAppCompUpload	(null)	0	(null)
BFC71D3483A19B93E04014AC08001B7D	Backup	(null)	0	(null)
BFC71D3484149B93E04014AC08001B7D	RMANScript	(null)	0	(null)

Figure 11-23. Results in job type information, showing some of the specific job types available to the system

Effective Monitoring and Job Status

The status of any given job running in the EM Job System is extremely important, as notifications and alerts are based on this status. Because a job may contain more than one step, the status changes as each step is executed, and events can be triggered to alert administrators to the different statuses of the job run. This job status can be monitored, alerted, and managed through job events.

Job events return the reporting status and alert the responsible party. You can set these up manually, as job events are not enabled by default. This is done so as not to overload the system with event monitoring.

Job events are as follows:

All: Report on all statuses of any job.

Scheduled: The job has been scheduled to run.

Action Required: An administrator is required for the job to run to completion. This includes jobs that are skipped because of a scheduled blackout.

Suspended: The job has been suspended and therefore is unable to execute its regular schedule.

Succeeded: The job has executed successfully.

Problems: A failure has occurred in one or more job steps.

Job events can be configured via the Job Events Generation Criteria page. You access this page from the EM console by choosing Setup ➤ Incidents ➤ Job Events, as shown in Figure 11-24. The Step 1 page appears, shown in Figure 11-25. Here you can decide which events by default will send alert notifications, and these can be narrowed down by target or group.

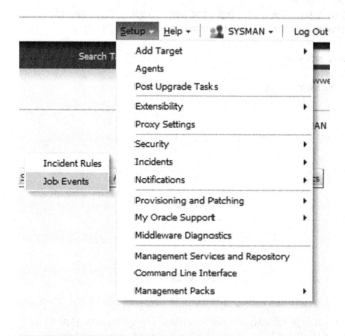

Figure 11-24. *Reaching the Job Events feature from the Setup menu in the EM console*

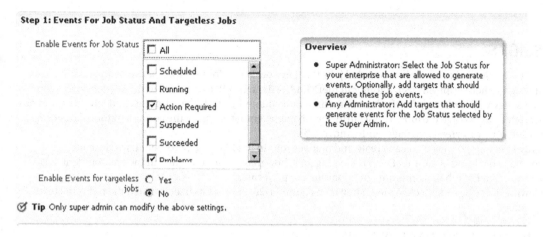

Figure 11-25. *Setting up default options for alerting and notifications on all jobs in an EM12c environment*

Some administrators choose to be notified of job run successes (Succeeded). Based on my professional experience, I recommend not configuring jobs to perform this notification. The largest amount of time spent by an administrator on alerts is caused not by too little monitoring, but too much. If Enterprise Manager is configured to include emailed "success" notifications, you become accustomed to receiving them, knowing that they do not require response, and this may result in critical issue notifications missed.

For those administrators who want to shut off individual success messages and simply report these andjob failures once a day, a secondary job can be set up to report and eliminate unnecessary inividual notifications.

```
select mj.job_id, mj.job_name, mjes.start_time, mjes.end_time,
mjes.status_detail, mjes.retried
from sysman.mgmt_job mj, sysman.mgmt_job_exec_summary mjes
where mj.job_id=mjes.job_id
and mjes.start_time >= sysdate-1
and mj.job_status!=0
and mj.expired=0;


JOB_ID
---------------------------------
JOB_NAME                                                          START_TIM
----------------------------------------------------------------- ---------
END_TIME   STATUS_DETAIL    RETRIED
---------  -------------  ----------
285DCE9F51ED4E6D843974116963EDC3
DPEXP_ORCL_1230                                                   31-DEC-12
31-DEC-12                0
```

The preceding output shows a job that failed, was not expired, and was never retried. The query reequested any job that was run in the last day, had not failed (successful=0), and was not expired (0 is actively scheduled jobs). This information can be used instead of reporting on each individual job. The choice is up to the administrator, but knowing how to find information about a job is essential when default options are not to the administrator's preference.

Permissions

Many times I've experienced conflicts in scheduled jobs that have occurred, for example, between one task that was scheduled through a shell script via cron, another in theDBMS_SCHEDULER, and a third in the EM Job scheduler. The EM12c Jobs Service provides a job scheduler that can handle numerous task script formats and job types, and has a single job interface to manage the jobs. The security for job management is part of the administrator creation steps, securing the users who can create, manage, and remove jobs.

There are many ways to view who can create and manage jobs in the EM12c environment. Because the administrator may not always be aware of who is creating jobs, how many, and how often in the environment, it is essential to ensure that EM job demands are not impairing the performance of the system.

The following query provides a clear view, shown in Figure 11-26, of who has been granted the rights to create and schedule jobs.

```
SELECT grantee  from SYSMAN.MGMT_PRIV_GRANTS
WHERE PRIV_NAME='SUPER_USER';
```

GRANTEE
KPOTVIN
SYS
SYSMAN
SYSTEM

Figure 11-26. *EM12c Super Users may also create and manage EM jobs*

EM Jobs Service Charts and Metrics

The EM Jobs Service interface, shown in Figure 11-27, enables you to easily assess the health of your EM Job environment. The tabs at the top of the interface allow quick access to the Jobs Service's advanced features. These tabs can be reached by choosing Targets ➤ All Targets, performing a wildcard search for **%Service%**, and then clicking EM Jobs Service.

Figure 11-27. *EM Jobs Service home page, showing high-level statistics and incident information*

From this interface, you can view details about performance, usage, and incidents.

EM Jobs Service Charts

Making decisions on how many jobs are too many in a given time frame became much easier with the performance charts in the EM12c EM Jobs Service. These charts are accessed through the Charts tab.

The EM Jobs Service charts show information regarding the performance of the job dispatcher, backlog of job steps, and throughput (see Figure 11-28). This graphical view of the data enables you to quickly ascertain whether there is an issue with job performance in the EM12c environment.

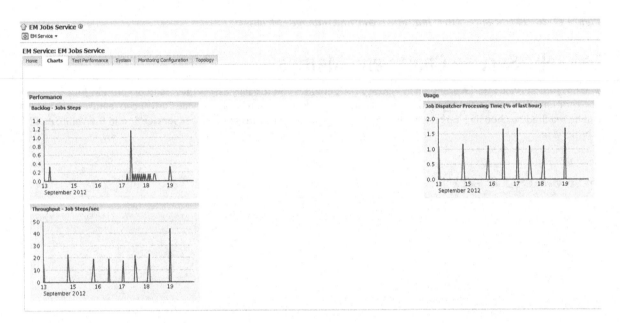

Figure 11-28. *Three preconfigured EM job perfomance charts*

You can create further monitoring enhancements for "job heavy" environments on the Monitoring Configuration tab of the EM Jobs Service. You can then view this chart for heavy resource usage, as the data is broken down effectively into three parts: Job Steps, Processing Time, and Throughput (Job Steps/Sec).

Performance Metrics

Performance metrics enable you to set up metrics specifically tied to a feature, in this case, EM jobs. The default metrics are set for a standard database environment, leaving you to edit them in the existing interface if needed, although that is rarely required. Two crucial metrics require only minimal configuration because of the uniqueness of most database environments:

- Throughput—Job Steps/Sec

- Backlog—Jobs Steps

These two metrics, once configured for the value that is desired for the environment, will alert when the throughput for a job is above the amount set per second or when the quantity of job steps backlogged is above the threshold.

Usage Metrics

One metric is preset in the list: Job Dispatcher Processing Time (% of Last Hour). You can also add and configure specific usage metrics to the environment. These are set up very similarly to the performance metrics and should be tested thoroughly, based on the information gathered in the performance charts shown previously in Figure 11-28.

The Usage Metrics area can be accessed by choosing Targets ➤ All Targets ➤ EM Jobs Service ➤ Metric Configurations ➤ Usage Metrics. Alternatively, you can access these metrics via a link on the Monitoring Configuration tab (see Figure 11-29).

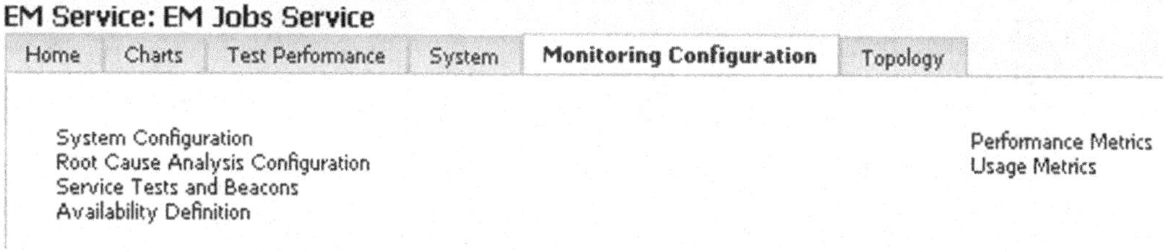

Figure 11-29. *The Usage Metrics option is located at the lower right area of the Monitoring Configuration tab*

You can add, edit, or delete metrics from the Usage Metrics interface. In the following example, we will add a systems usage metric by simply clicking the Add button and proceeding with the wizard. Figure 11-30 and Figure 11-31 show different parts of the first wizard page.

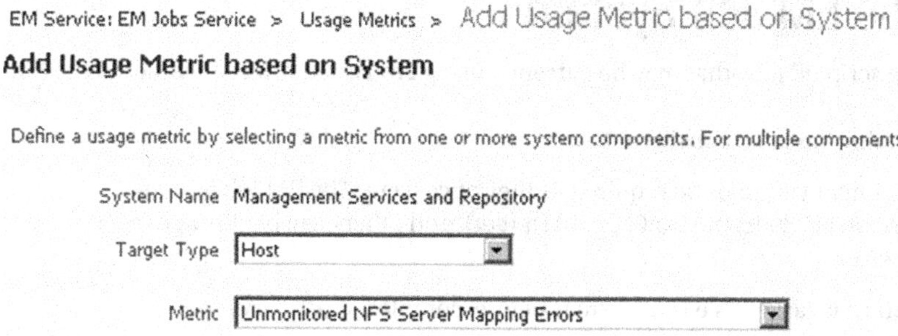

Figure 11-30. *Adding a usage metric o check for NFS server mapping errors on a target host's unmonitored NFS server*

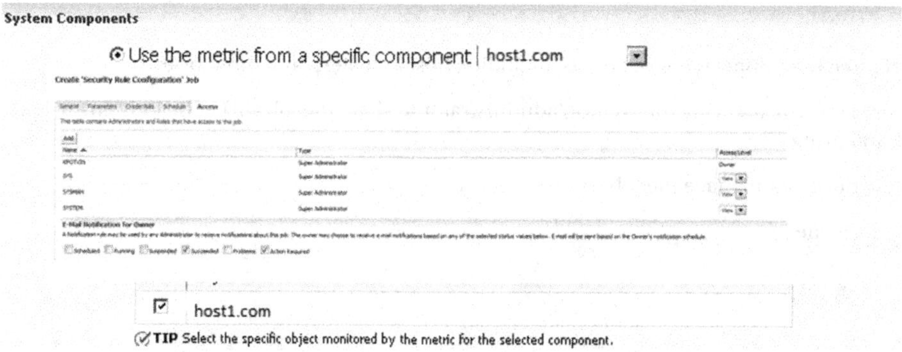

Figure 11-31. *Choosing the correct system component settings for the configuration of the storage-free usage metric*

In this example, we will add a usage metric to monitor for mapping errors on an unmonitored NFS server (see Figure 11-30).

Set the Target Type option to Host and the Metric option to Unmonitored NFS Server Mapping Errors. Then you choose the host target you wish to base ithe metric on and choose whether to allow EM12c to monitor each disk separately or by the average of total storage free on the specific disk (see Figure 11-31).

Next, you click Continue and proceed to name your usage metric and set warning and critical thresholds (see Figure 11-32). Then click OK to save the new usage metric.

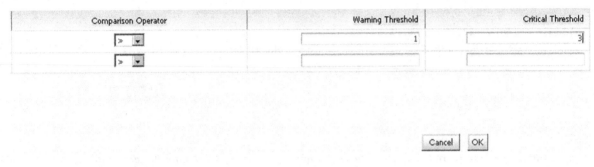

Figure 11-32. *After giving the usage metric a descriptive title, set reasonable thresholds*

This metric is now available for use and can be accessed from the All Metrics section of the EM console.

Migrating Scripts to the EM Job System

It is a simple process to migrate existing scripted jobs that may be currently using cron or another scheduler to the EM Job System.

These changes to the preexisting scripts must be considered:

- No longer will many environment variables be required as they once were. The EM Job System will already know what the ORACLE_HOME, the ORACLE_SID (target), and others will be through the EM and the target properties.

- Submitting a job against multiple targets is easy, whereas before, complex, cross-server authentication may have been required.

- Maintenance and other jobs can be submitted against target groups in EM, allowing for ease of database management. If the group is updated, the job will then address the changes to the group as well.

- Jobs can be attributed to multiple types of targets, including hosts, clusters, and directories.

EM Job privileges are very granular, allowing the creator/administrator to share the job with other administrators. These privileges include the following:

- Full access to edit, delete, or manage the job.

- Viewing the results of the job

Managing EM12c Jobs

Previous sections of this chapter provided clear descriptions of the EM12c Job System and the EM Jobs Service components. The next step— although less in depth because of the similarity in basics to other sections—is to understand how to properly manage jobs.

Job management is performed through the Job Activity page and accessed at the EM12c summary or target-specific level. To access the page directly from any of these options, go to the Database tab and select Jobs ➤ Job Activity. Depending on the task at hand, various choices are available; this section covers the following topics:

- Viewing job results

- Editing

- Stopping

- Suspending

- Copying to the library

- Deleting

Viewing Job Results

Having the ability to view job results clearly and with access to execution log information has remained almost unchanged since EM10g. This data still has relevance and value to today's administrator when required to manage and be notified of issues with an EM Job. Figure 11-33 shows the Job Activity interface.

Figure 11-33. *Viewing jobs from the Job Activity interface*

If we choose to view information about the Backup_APEX_DEV.1 job, for example, we can simply click its radio button if it is not already selected and then click the View Results button just above it.

Any output from the job then displays, as shown in Figure 11-34.

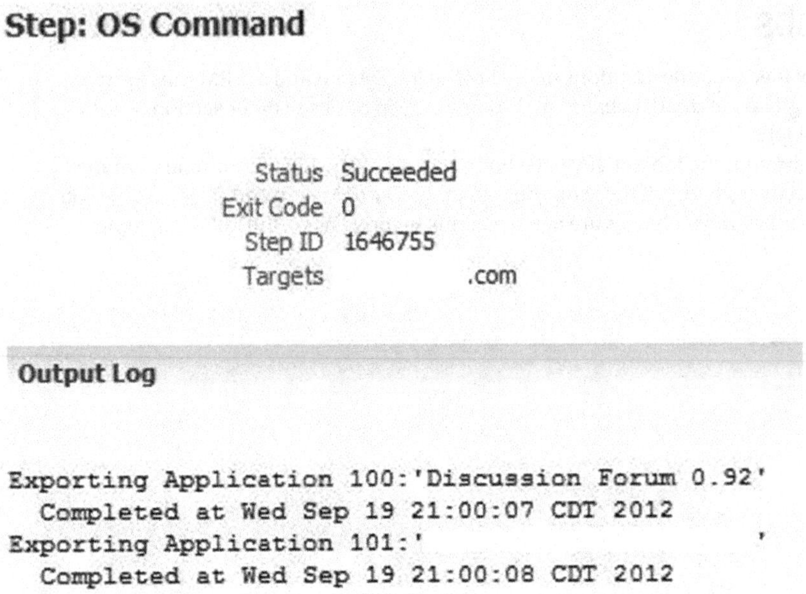

Step: OS Command

```
        Status  Succeeded
     Exit Code  0
       Step ID  1646755
       Targets            .com
```

Output Log

```
Exporting Application 100:'Discussion Forum 0.92'
  Completed at Wed Sep 19 21:00:07 CDT 2012
Exporting Application 101:'                        '
  Completed at Wed Sep 19 21:00:08 CDT 2012
```

Figure 11-34. EM Job log output

Editing Jobs from the Activity View

Jobs that are scheduled to run, as well as jobs that have already executed, are available for editing. (Depending on the job type, such as backups, only minor changes can be made.) Jobs that have executed previously can then be resubmitted as new jobs. When you update a new job with changes, they are submitted to any future intervals of the job as well. This is an important distinction to make, because if a job needs a one-time change, then a single Create Like of an existing job, with a single, scheduled execution, may be the better choice to ensure that regular execution times are not impacted.

■ **Note** Any edited job from the Job Activity view won't automatically save to the library. Any permanent changes that should be retained in the library should be saved in the Job Library view.

Stopping a Running Job

Clicking the Stop button stops the job and all subsequent runs of the job. No future scheduling of the job will occur.

Suspending Jobs

Clicking the Suspend button is the proper way to put a job "on hold" for maintenance that will place the target out of service. You can then restart the job at a later time.

Copying to the Library

The Copy to Library option copies the chosen job to the library to be accessed later, edited, submitted, and so forth. Backup jobs, data pump jobs, and other miscellaneous jobs cannot be retained in the library and will fail if you attempt to save them. These jobs can be retained through backup and recovery of the EM12c, but at this time, no library exists for the backup and data pump jobs.

Deleting Jobs

Deleting a job offers the option to delete the specific run of the job or to delete all jobs, including history, from the Job System. Ensure that if you choose to remove all job history, this will not violate any retention information required by the business. Upon deletion, the job is removed from the scheduler and must be resubmitted. Therefore, ensuring that jobs are retained in the library is important if you delete all history and the job information is required for future use.

Managing the Manager

EM12c release 2 has an additional Job System page titled Managing the Manager (MTM). This page enables you to perform tasks similar to those found on the Job Activity, Job Library, and Job Health Monitor pages, but provides a more enhanced, complete view of the job environment.

The MTM displays the following:

- Standard health of the EM Job System

- Job status

- Diagnostics information

- Agent management

- Tracked upload intervals and notifications

Although not available until EM12c release 2, the Health Overview page now incorporates the overall load and activity of the environment and job load (target specific).

Troubleshooting the EM12c Job System

If there is an issue beyond a simple failed job due to incorrect syntax or configuration of a job that is trapped in the EM console interface log files, you might need to use the Enterprise Manager Diagnostics Kit, also known as EMDIAG.

This data is not only valuable but also required for most service requests through My Oracle Support.

The EMDIAG basic repository kit comes with EM12c. The other two kits are available via download through My Oracle Support. Documentation for the EMDIAG kit is available via MOS Note: *MOS ID#* 421053.1 The three kits are as follows:

repvfy: Included in the EM12c installation, this kit pulls data directly from the OMS repository.

agtvfy: Cloud Control-specific kit to maintain and diagnose issues.

omsvfy: Specific kit to diagnose and maintain the OMS database repository.

Performing the Installation

Perform the steps in this section to install EMDIAG.

1. First, you will change to the newly created directory, where you will install EMDIAG, so cd
   to the EMDIAG home (a new directory you have chosen to unzip the files into):

   ```
   cd $EMDIAG_HOME/bin
   ```

2. In the bin directory are three common files—the executable, the batch file for windows
   support, and the Perl script that supports both:

   ```
   -rwxrwxr-- 1 oracle dba   3331 Feb 23  2012 repvfy.bat
   -rwxrwxr-- 1 oracle dba 198800 Aug 31 18:57 repvfy.pl
   -rwxrwxr-x 1 oracle dba   7195 Aug 31 18:57 repvfy
   ```

   Initiate the installation by performing the following:

   ```
   ./repvfy install -tns em12rep -pwd password
   ```

3. The installation commences, and you end with the following:

   ```
   PL/SQL procedure successfully completed.
   COMPONENT               INFO
   --------------------    --------------------
   EMDIAG Version          2012.0831
   Repository Version      12.1.0.1.0
   Database Version        11.2.0.3.0
   Test Version            2012.0926
   Repository Type         CENTRAL
   Verify Tests            381
   Object Tests            157
   Deployment              SMALL
   8 rows selected.
   Disconnected from Oracle Database 11g Enterprise Edition Release 11.2.0.3.0 - 64 bit
   Production With the Partitioning, OLAP, Data Mining and Real Application Testing options
   ```

4. Check the installation and verify the version:

   ```
   $ ./repvfy version -tns em12rep version
   ```

   Enter the SYSMAN password when prompted. The following output results:

   ```
   Component                       Version
   ------------------------------  ---------------
   repvfy                              2012.0831
   EMDIAG                                   12cR1
   Database                            11.2.0.3.0
   Repository                          12.1.0.1.0
   Tests                                2012.0926
   Linux                                   2.6.18
   ```

```
x86_64-linux-thread-mult
PERL                              5.10.0
SQL*Plus                     11.2.0.3.0
Agent Zip                            3.0
Agent Unzip                         6.00
----------------------------  ---------------
```

Using the EMDIAG with EM12c

Numerous diagnostic reports can be run, depending on the arguments that are submitted. The EMDIAG kit is a full diagnostic suite that will assist the administrator and My Oracle Support in diagnosing issues when they arise in the EM12c environment.

Job-Level Diagnostics

The following query from Enterprise Manager will gather data that is required to then run the diagnostics for job-level reports. This example uses a backup job for Apex.

From SQL*Plus as a user with select privileges to the SYSMAN schema, perform the following:

```
select mj.job_id, mj.job_name, mjh.execution_id, mjh.step_id
from sysman.mgmt_job mj, sysman.mgmt_job_history mjh
where mj.job_id = 'BFC78F41009876F3E04014AC08003231'
and mj.job_id=mjh.job_id
and mjh.start_time > sysdate-1;
```

Figure 11-35 shows the output.

```
JOB_ID
--------------------------------
JOB_NAME
--------------------------------------------------------------
EXECUTION_ID                     STEP_ID
--------------------------------  ----------
BFC78F41009876F3E04014AC08003231
BACKUP_APEX.1
D622E12D59B9111DE043080014AC52F6     4739278
```

Figure 11-35. *Output from the preceding query*

Using the job name, we can perform some diagnostics report gathering on the job itself. Because of the large amount of diagnostic data that is offered, redirecting the output to a file is recommended.

```
$ cd $EMDIAG_HOME/bin
./repvfy dump job -name BACKUP_APEX.1 -pwd w0rldw1d3 -tns em12rep > ./rep_apex_job.lst
```

The output file then shows you a full report on the job, starting with the information about the diagnostic tool, the database, test, and repository. Figure 11-36 shows this information. Figure 11-37 shows some of the job parameters. Figure 11-38 shows parameter arguments. Figure 11-39 shows the job source and target.

```
COMPONENT            INFO
------------------   -------------------
EMDIAG Version       2012.0831
Repository Version   12.1.0.1.0
Database Version     11.2.0.3.0
Test Version         2012.0926
Repository Type      CENTRAL
```

Figure 11-36. *Verions and EMDIAG information about the repository*

```
LEVEL JOB_ID                          JOB_NAME                        JOB_TYPE
           JOB_OWNER                        JOB_STATUS        TARGET_TYPE           SCHEDULE_ID
              EXP      NST      LIB SYS                    RST       CA   BRK REASON
---------- ---------- ---------- ---------- ---------- -------------------- ---------- ---------- ---------- ------------------------------------
           ---------- ---------- ---------- ---------- -------------------- ---------- ---------- ---------- ------------------------------------
---------- ---------- ---------- ---------- ---------- -------------------- ---------- ---------- ---------- ------------------------------------
         1 BFC78F41009876F3E04014AC08003231 BACKUP_APEX.1                        OSCommand
               SYSMAN                      0-Job Active      host                              BFC78F41009976F3E04014A
C08003231      0        0        0 0-User job                1        0          0
```

Figure 11-37. *From here, the report steps into information about the job's runtime, time zone, and other details*

```
PARAMETER_NAME                                          PARAMETER_TYPE              SCALAR_VALUE
           VECTOR_VALUE
---------- ----------------------------------------     ----------------------------   ----------------------------
---------- ----------------------------------------     ----------------------------   ----------------------------
args                                                    Scalar                      /home/oracle/enkitec/backup_
apex_apps.sh
command                                                 Scalar                      %job_default_shell%
user_command                                            Scalar                      /home/oracle/enkitec/backup_
apex_apps.sh
```

Figure 11-38. *Parameter arguments for job steps in EM12c from the EMDIAG job report*

```
ENTITY_GUID                HOST_NAME                                        ENTITY_NAME
                ENTITY_TYPE                  ACTIVE TIMEZONE_REGION              TYPE_MET BROKEN_REASON
-------------------------- ----------------------------------------- ---------- ------------------------------ ---------------------------------------
-------------------------- ----------------------------------------- ---------- ------------------------------ -------- -------------
EFD92E6468B02696B602A650E085B5A9 db1.wwex.com                                            db1.wwex.com
                host                                          1 America/Chicago                   4.1                      0
```

Figure 11-39. *GUID information about the host running the job*

The next section then lets you know who owns the job and who has grants, along with what kind of grants, on the job. Because this job is simply owned and run by the SYSMAN user only, only this user shows in our example report.

The next section of the report, shown in Figure 11-40, presents the last ten runtimes in history, including elapsed time, retries, and success information about the job.

```
[----- MGMT_JOB_EXEC_SUMMARY ------------------------------------------------]


EXECUTION_ID                    STATUS                      TLI  QUEUE_ID                TIMEZONE_REGION
SCHEDULED_TIME      EXPECTED_START_TIME  START_TIME          END_TIME                RETRIED
------------------- -------------------- -------------------- ---------- ------------------------------- ----------   ------------------------------
D622E12D59B9111DE043080014AC52F6 17-Waiting                     1                                                     America/Chicago
03-MAR-2013 01:00:00 03-MAR-2013 07:00:00 03-MAR-2013 07:00:00                                          0
D60EC331ECD62440E043080014AC72F3 01-Scheduled                   1                                                     America/Chicago
27-FEB-2013 01:00:00 27-FEB-2013 07:00:00 27-FEB-2013 07:00:00                                          0
D5BE6FA34C23798CE043080014ACBAF7 05-Succeeded                   1                                                     America/Chicago
23-FEB-2013 01:00:00 23-FEB-2013 07:00:00 23-FEB-2013 07:00:05 23-FEB-2013 07:04:00                     0
D56D33BBC6641E0DE043080014AC0322 05-Succeeded                   1                                                     America/Chicago
19-FEB-2013 01:00:00 19-FEB-2013 07:00:00 19-FEB-2013 07:00:01 19-FEB-2013 07:03:59                     0
D4ECF565BBEA50DBE043080014ACE1DF 05-Succeeded                   1                                                     America/Chicago
15-FEB-2013 01:00:00 15-FEB-2013 07:00:00 15-FEB-2013 07:00:04 15-FEB-2013 07:04:09                     0
D4CB032C2F0D4435E043080014AC855A 05-Succeeded                   1                                                     America/Chicago
11-FEB-2013 01:00:00 11-FEB-2013 07:00:00 11-FEB-2013 07:00:01 11-FEB-2013 07:04:08                     0
D3F4A50189B87D1EE043080014ACA703 05-Succeeded                   1                                                     America/Chicago
07-FEB-2013 01:00:00 07-FEB-2013 07:00:00 07-FEB-2013 07:00:02 07-FEB-2013 07:04:05                     0
D39F918782366228E043080014AC1AF4 05-Succeeded                   1                                                     America/Chicago
03-FEB-2013 01:00:00 03-FEB-2013 07:00:00 03-FEB-2013 07:00:01 03-FEB-2013 07:04:02                     0
D3C655AAB5D26CD0E043080014AC4ED5 05-Succeeded                   1                                                     America/Chicago
30-JAN-2013 01:00:00 30-JAN-2013 07:00:00 30-JAN-2013 07:00:02 30-JAN-2013 07:04:01                     0
D38990D9E0362007E043080014AC71B4 05-Succeeded                   1                                                     America/Chicago
26-JAN-2013 01:00:00 26-JAN-2013 07:00:00 26-JAN-2013 07:00:02 26-JAN-2013 07:04:04                     0
```

Figure 11-40. *Displaying the historical data regarding the job runs in the EM Jobs Service*

In this example, the EMDIAG indicates that one job is in a waiting state. The recent history in Figure 11-41 shows that all jobs have been successful. However, there is one level-17 job, signifying that one run did have to wait because of some undisclosed issue that isn't shown in the execution summary.

```
STATUS                  STATUS_DETAIL        CNT
----------------------- -------------- ----------
01-Scheduled                        0          1
05-Succeeded                        0          8
17-Waiting                          0          1
```

Figure 11-41. *Values of job run status and the summary counts for the historical report*

If there were any errors in the job analysis, this is saved for the last section of the report. Our example compiled successfully and showed no issues, and so the output results in what you see in Figure 11-42.

```
[----------------------------------------------------------------------------]
[----- Job Analysis ---------------------------------------------------------]
[----------------------------------------------------------------------------]

analyzeJob

PL/SQL procedure successfully completed.
```

Figure 11-42. *Successful completion of the analysis of the job, with no errors presented at the end of the report*

If a job has more than one step and you wish to gather detailed diagnostic information about that step only, a secondary report can be generated by running the following:

```
./repvfy dump -tns <oms_sid> step -id <step_id>
```

GUID Target Diagnostics

For our next scenario, we are going to utilize the GUID for our EM12rep (the OMS repository for the EM12c) and gather EM environment data:

```
./repvfy dump -tns <oms_sid> execution
-guid EFD92E6468B02696B602A650E085B5A9 -pwd <pwd>
> ./rep_guid.lst
```

By running the GUID-level command you get a one-stop-shop kind of diagnostic report about your EM Jobs Service health. (GUID is your target GUID and dumps out information on all the jobs, from all the targets.)

The report starts out very similarly to the job-level report, listing repository and EM information. However, you will notice a distinct difference as you get to target info, especially if your EM environment is large.

If there are any background jobs submitted by the EM Jobs Service that are experiencing issues, they are clearly reported in their own section, as shown in Figure 11-43.

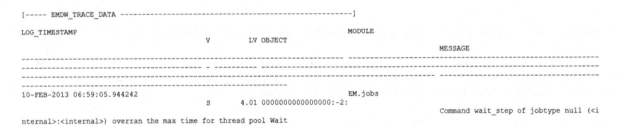

Figure 11-43. Trace data about an error in the job execution

My only complaint at this time is that the BP1 version of the EM12c, when the EMDIAG is run against it at a full environment level, experiences an error at the Job Analysis Summary step. You can see that error in Figure 11-44.

```
[------------------------------------------------------------------------]
[----- Job Analysis ----------------------------------------------------]
[------------------------------------------------------------------------]

   INTO   job
          *
ERROR at line 6:
ORA-06550: line 6, column 10:
PLS-00321: expression 'JOB' is inappropriate as the left hand side of an assignment statement
ORA-06550: line 7, column 3:
PL/SQL: ORA-00904: : invalid identifier
ORA-06550: line 5, column 3:
PL/SQL: SQL Statement ignored
```

Figure 11-44. Single error from the OMS diagnostic-level EMDIAG

Therefore, if you are still using a BP1 version and need to pull this level of diagnostic data, I hope that you have your issue narrowed down to a single job or target as the focus of the report, subsequently avoiding this error. Release 2 has corrected the problem.

Global Diagnostics

In this example, we will run a level-9 diagnostic, which will run a report against the whole of the Enterprise Manager environment, checking the health and other issues:

```
./repvfy -tns em12rep verify -level 9 –detail
```

The first thing this level of diagnostic does is check the version of EMDIAG you are using and whether a newer version is available as an update.

The diagnostics then proceed to perform a full verification of the EM environment, as shown in Figure 11-45, before logging in to SQL*Plus to perform the secondary diagnostics on the EM testing, the installation information about the EM system, and internal jobs and alerts from the EM environment.

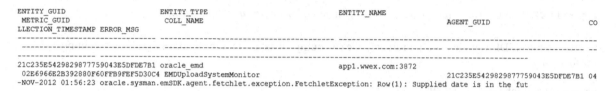

Figure 11-45. *Global-level diagnostics displaying metric collection issues from the EMDIAG*

The diagnostic proceeds through all promoted and unpromoted targets, makes recommendations on changes, and then ends the report by verifying any nonstandard EM users, as demonstrated in Figure 11-46.

```
verifyUSERS
=====================================================================
6001. Non-standard EM system administrators accounts
---------------------------------------------------

no rows selected
```

Figure 11-46. *Recommendations to verify users for nonstandard EM system accounts*

We can query the data from the MGMT_JOB table again in the SYSMAN schema to look at backup jobs that are not one-time jobs (status<>2).

```
select job_name, job_id
from SYSMAN.MGMT_JOB
where job_name like '%BACKUP%'
and job_status <> 2;
```

Figure 11-47 shows the results of the query.

JOB_NAME	JOB_ID
BACKUP_REMOVE_ARCHLOGS	BFC78F41007C76F3E04014AC08003231
BACKUP_APEX.1	BFC78F41009876F3E04014AC08003231
BACKUP_APEX_DEV.1	BFC7CAEC5756D963E04014AC080046B1
BACKUP_EM12REP_000044	C6128211FBF25658E043080014ACBC49
BACKUP_EM12REP	C61282120F595658E043080014ACBC49
BACKUP_WWDEV_000064	C5EA6EFDD4703EA1E043080014AC37D0
BACKUP_APEX_DEV	C0BE73F1C8DB9094E04014AC080029C9
BACKUP_APEX	BFD0BC13028FE173E04014AC0800706B

Figure 11-47. Results of a sample query, displayingall jobs with a name including BACKUP

Using the EMDIAG utility commandrepvfy, we can dump all data from the job into a log file by executing the following:

```
$repvfy dump job –name  BACKUP_APEX.1
```

Or again, we can query from SQL*Plus to gather the STEP_ID with data from the original query:

```
select mj.job_id, mj.job_name, mjh.execution_id, mjh.step_id
from sysman.mgmt_job mj, sysman.mgmt_job_history mjh
where mj.job_id = 'BFC78F41009876F3E04014AC08003231'
and mj.job_id=mjh.job_id
and mjh.start_time > sysdate-1;
```

Figure 11-48 shows an example of JOB_ID, EXECUTION_ID, and STEP_ID that can be used as we proceed through the EMDIAG steps to dump data to the log files.

JOB_ID	JOB_NAME	EXECUTION_ID	STEP_ID
BFC78F41009876F3E04014AC08003231	BACKUP_APEX.1	C979658693B409C9E043080014ACD94B	1554906
BFC78F41009876F3E04014AC08003231	BACKUP_APEX.1	C979658693B409C9E043080014ACD94B	1554905
BFC78F41009876F3E04014AC08003231	BACKUP_APEX.1	C979658693B409C9E043080014ACD94B	1554907
BFC78F41009876F3E04014AC08003231	BACKUP_APEX.1	C9C1AE6F09461288E043080014AC07D8	1554908

Figure 11-48. An example of JOB_ID, EXECUTION_ID, and STEP_ID

We then can use the STEP_ID and proceed to dump to log files more data about the job in question:

```
$repvfy dump step –id 1554907
```

The STEP_ID is also located in the last occurrence of the error in the emoms.trc file, located in the $OMS_HOME/gc_inst/em/EMGC_OMS1/sysman/log. This trace file will direct you to the target and job information if for some reason the information did not return in the query from SQL*Plus.

The EXECUTION_ID, also shown in Figure 11-48, can be then used to gather more information on the failure from the execution steps, which will then be dumped to another log file, located in the same $EMDIAG_HOME/logs directory as an execution log:

```
$repvfy dump execution –guid C979658693B409C9E043080014ACD94B
```

The output from an EMDIAG execution is quite extensive. If you are not familiar with it, or if you feel uncomfortable with your own analysis of the data, you should not hesitate to open a service request with My Oracle Support and upload the files for a technical representative from Oracle to review.

The logs for the output from these reports will then be generated to the <EMDIAG_HOME>/log directory to be reviewed or uploaded to My Oracle Support. I do prefer to redirect the screen output to a file for easy review, as seen in the preceding examples. This data should help you answer questions regarding your EM12c environment without having to always open an SR, but if the need arises, this valuable diagnostic data can then be generated to save time and effort so that the you can perform tasks other than just answering My Oracle Support questions.

Blackouts and EM12c Job Impact

Issuing a blackout from any of the blackout creation entry points in the EM12c environment is often performed during maintenance windows so as to not produce nonessential notifications and alerts. When job notifications are set up for individual jobs, the EM Job System can cause significant alerting compared to setting up blackouts through job events.

You have two choices for jobs when setting up a blackout: the jobs can be skipped during the blackout or the jobs can continue to run, alerting only during the time the target is unavailable to the job.

The default is to continue to run jobs during the blackout, so you must deselect the check box to stop jobs from running.

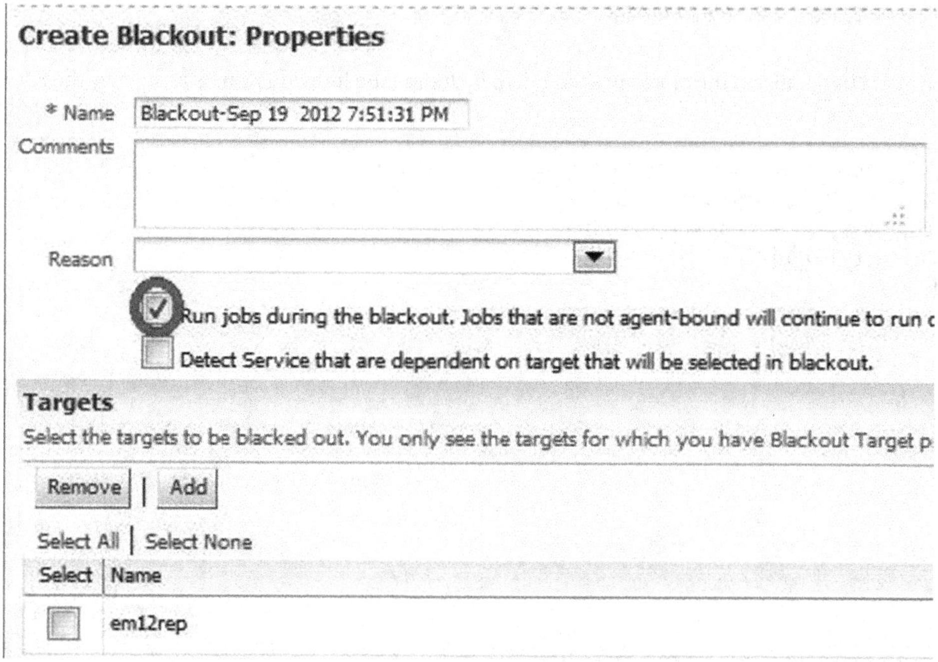

Figure 11-49. If you don't want to attempt job runs, you must deselect the default checkbox to skip job execution during the blackout

There are two considerations when making the choice:

- If you allow jobs to continue to run during the blackout and the target becomes unavailable at the very end of the job, when the target agent would send a successful execution code back to the Jobs Service, the job will continue to show as running, and any subsequent runs of the job will be skipped.

- If you stop jobs from running during the entire blackout, jobs will be skipped during that blackout. If the job is set to notify on Action Required, notifications will be sent for every scheduled job that is skipped.

As blackouts are also issued as jobs, but run in the background, you can view these by querying tables in the database as well. The following query examples show how first, a join between the three tables of MGMT_JOB, MGMT_JOB_EXEC_SUMMARY, and MGMT_BLACKOUTS results in information regarding any existing blackout scheduled.

```
SELECT mj.job_name, mj.job_id, mje.status, mje.scheduled_time
FROM    MGMT_JOB mj, MGMT_JOB_EXEC_SUMMARY mje, MGMT_BLACKOUTS mb
WHERE   mb.start_job_id=mj.job_id
AND     mj.job_id=mje.job_id;
```

```
JOB_NAME
----------------------------------------------------------------------
JOB_ID                                  STATUS  SCHEDULED
------------------------------------    ------  ---------
BLK_START_JOB8B622FDB951541AEBE79557C9CE2588C
25448A0E45BD48FC86E7A7E4A5A44B63             1  17-JAN-13
```

Figure 11-50. *Output from querying a blackout in EM12c*

The next query then offers us details on the blackout scheduled, including the individual steps as seen by the EM Jobs Service.

```
SELECT  mje.step_id, mje. step_name, mje .step_type, mje. step_status,
mje .start_time,  mje .output_id,  mje .error_id
FROM    MGMT_JOB_EXECUTION mje,  MGMT_BLACKOUTS mb
WHERE   mje.job_id=mb.start_job_id
ORDER BY mje.step_id;
```

```
   STEP_ID STEP_NAME
-- -------- -----------------------------------------------------------------
STEP_TYPE STEP_STATUS START_TIM OUTPUT_ID
--------- ----------- --------- -----------------------------------------------
ERROR_ID
-------- -----------------------------
     88654 BLK_START_JOB8B622FDB951541AEBE79557C9CE2588C
         7              1 17-JAN-13


     88655 main
         2              1 17-JAN-13


     88656 ProcessStart
         1              1 17-JAN-13
```

Figure 11-51. *Detailed information regarding a blackout submitted in the EM12c environment*

These queries are also helpful, because blackouts may be planned/scheduled for the future, and not visible in the EM console. You can query the database to ensure that the agent has issued communications required to the OMS, verifying that a blackout exists or is reporting correctly

Controlling Multiple Management Agents Through EM Jobs

Systemwide maintenance can be a daunting task that can be simplified with the use of the EM Jobs interface. Management agents enable you to submit job tasks to multiple targets with one job. This can be used to black out multiple targets, shut down instances, apply patches, and a multitude of other common tasks. To submit a task that can be used by multiple agents, the jobs must be created correctly

To access the Management Agent setup page, shown in Figure 11-52, you choose Setup ➤ Agents.

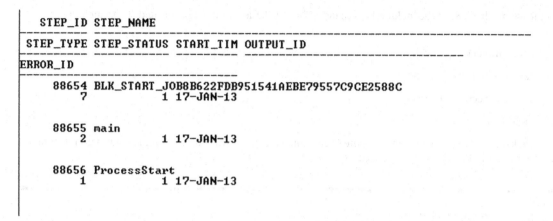

Figure 11-52. *Management agents in EM12c*

Select the agents that need to be included in the task. Then click the task to be performed. Tasks include the following:

- Block/Unblock

- Start U/Shut Down/Restart

- Resecure/Secure/Unsecure

- Properties

You can click one of these task buttons, and the Create Job page then asks you to submit the standard information for an EM Job (see Figure 11-53).

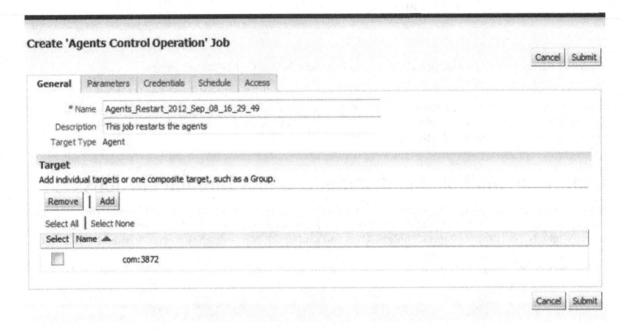

Figure 11-53. *General information about an Agent Control job*

This is an excellent feature to assist with repetitive maintenance tasks that require agents to be shut down and then restarted, eliminating the need for you to log on to each of the consoles to perform the tasks individually.

You can then use EM Jobs through the Agents interface to configure multiple agents in one job execution.

This includes changing the time zone, setting a proxy host, or even performing regular security tasks such as changing the repository password.

Summary

The EM Job System is a mature feature in the enhanced EM12c product line that offers administrators a more integrated scheduler option for the database environment. Its ability to support the database and server environment's job requirements make it the obvious choice, considering the monitoring EM12c design. The benefits to moving all jobs, including scripting, multistep jobs, advanced logic checks, and service tests, are all worthwhile to the administrator of today, who is expected to perform the demanding role of database specialist.

▪ ▪ ▪

CHAPTER 12

Incident Management

by Pete Sharman

The goal of incident management is to enable administrators to monitor and resolve service disruptions that may be occurring in their data centers as quickly and efficiently as possible. Instead of managing the numerous discrete events that may be raised as the result of any of these service disruptions, we want to manage a smaller number of more-meaningful incidents, and to manage them based on business priority across the lifecycle of those incidents.

To do this, EM12c provides a centralized incident console called Incident Manager that enables an administrator to track, diagnose, and resolve these incidents, as well as providing features to help eliminate the root causes of recurrent incidents. Incident Manager also includes features to tie in to Oracle expertise via relevant My Oracle Support knowledge base articles and documentation to enable administrators to accelerate the process of diagnosing and resolving incidents and problems. Finally, Incident Manager also offers the ability to do lifecycle operations for incidents, so you can assign ownership of an incident to a specific user, acknowledge an incident, set a priority for an incident, track an incident's status, escalate an incident, or suppress it so you can defer it to a later time. You can also raise notifications on an incident or open a help-desk ticket via the help-desk connectors.

Because Incident Manager is brand new functionality in EM12c, this chapter provides the following:

- An explanation of the new terminology, including events, incidents, and problems
- An introduction to the user interface so you will be able to set up Incident Manager
- Some suggested guidelines on how to get the most out of this new functionality

Incident Manager Terminology

Before drilling into how you use the Incident Manager functionality, you need to understand some of the new terminology. Let's start with looking at events and incidents, and how they are differentiated.

Events and Incidents

Enterprise Manager continues to be the primary tool for managing and monitoring the Oracle data center, so it manages and monitors Oracle applications as well as the application stack, from application servers to databases to hosts, and the operating system. When Enterprise Manager detects issues in any of this infrastructure, it raises events. The *events* might be any of the following:

> *Metric alerts*: These alerts (for example, CPU utilization or tablespace usage alerts) indicate that a critical threshold you set has been crossed.

> *Job events*: These could be caused by a failure in a job as you are using the job system. An event is raised to signal the failure of a particular job.

Standards violations: If you are using compliance standards, and any of the targets that are being monitored violate any of those standards, a standards violation event could be raised.

Availability events: If Enterprise Manager detects that a target is down, an availability event can be raised.

Other events: Other types of events can occur as well, such as an SLA alert or High Availability and Connector External Class. Of course, users can define their own event types and cause an event to be raised.

All these events signal that particular issues have occurred in the Oracle data center. Across all these events, you really want to be able to determine which are significant and, from these significant events, be able to correlate those that are related to the same underlying issue. At the end of the day, what you as an administrator want to manage is a smaller number of significant incidents. You may have a performance incident that amalgamates a number of performance events, another incident related to space, and a different incident based on availability problems. The goal for incident management is therefore to not manage individual numerous events but the smaller set of more-meaningful incidents. An incident could be a significant event (such as a target being down, for example) or a combination of events that all relate to the same issue (for example, running out of space could be detected by Enterprise Manager as separate events raised from the database, host, and storage target types).

Events are significant occurrences in your IT infrastructure that Enterprise Manager detects and raises. Each event has a set of attributes indicating the type of event, its severity (Fatal, Critical, and so on), the object or entity on which the event is raised (typically a target, but possibly a job or some other object), the message associated with the event, the timestamp at which it occurred, as well as the functional category (such as availability, security, and so forth).

Associated with these events are event severities. The first of these, Fatal, is a new severity level in Enterprise Manager specifically associated with the target availability event type that means the target is down. Critical and Warning events have the same meaning as they had in previous releases. Next, the Advisory level is typically associated with compliance standards violation events. The Informational level is used to indicate simply that an event has occurred, but there is no need to do anything about it.

As noted previously, an incident can contain one or more events. Let's look at the details of an incident with one event. Figure 12-1 shows an incident with one availability event.

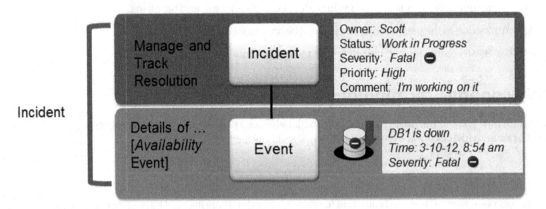

Figure 12-1. *Incident with one event*

The event signals that the database DB1 is down and includes a timestamp indicating when the event was raised. Because this is a target availability event and the database is down, the severity is marked as Fatal. An incident can be created for that event, so the incident contains only one event. In order to manage and track the resolution of the incident, the incident has other attributes such as owner (the Enterprise Manager user who is working on the incident), status, incident severity (which is based on the event severity), priority, and a comment field.

Incidents can also contain multiple events; those events would be related and point to the same underlying cause. The example in Figure 12-2 shows two metric alert events on a host target—a memory utilization metric alert event and a CPU utilization metric alert event because the host is starting to suffer from a heavy load. We have a Warning severity memory utilization metric alert event, and a short time later a Critical severity CPU utilization metric alert event.

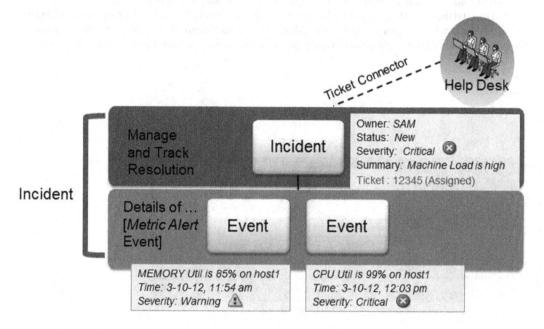

Figure 12-2. *Incident with multiple events*

An incident can be created containing both events in order to manage and track the resolution of the entire incident. Again, we have additional attributes associated with the incident, as in the previous example. Enterprise Manager automatically assigns the incident severity, based on the worst-case event severity of all the events contained in the incident. Since the worst event severity is Critical, the incident severity is also set to Critical. Finally, the incident has a summary, which is a short description of what the incident is about. The individual events are indicating the machine load is high, so you can set the summary to that. Alternatively, you can set the incident summary to be the same as the event messages.

If you are using one of the help-desk connectors to interface to a help-desk system, an incident might also result in a help-desk ticket, which can allow the help-desk analyst to work on the incident. Within Enterprise Manager, you'll be able to track both the ticket number and the status of that particular ticket.

Problems

A *problem* is the underlying root cause of an incident. In Enterprise Manager terms, a problem is specifically related to an Automatic Diagnostic Repository (ADR) incident or Oracle software incident. Enterprise Manager automatically creates a problem whenever it detects that an ADR incident has been raised. An ADR incident can be thought of as a critical Oracle software problem typically requiring contacting Oracle Support, opening a service request, and possibly receiving a patch for that problem.

Whenever an ADR incident is raised, we generate one incident in Enterprise Manager for that ADR incident, and we also automatically generate a problem object as well. All the ADR incidents that have the same problem signature (that is, the same root cause) will be linked into a single problem object (for example, ADR incidents for an ORA-0600 error that have the same arguments to the ORA-0600 error will be linked into a single problem object). The administrator can manage the problem in Incident Manager in the same way as you would manage an incident, so you can assign an owner to the problem, track the resolution, and so on. In addition, there are in-context links to Support Workbench functionality that allow the administrator to package the diagnostic material, open a service request, and view the status of diagnostic activity such as the SR number and ultimately bug number (if one is generated) within the user interface.

Figure 12-3 illustrates how incidents and problems are related. In this example, two ADR incidents (two ORA-600 errors) have occurred in a database. Both of these incidents are of Critical severity. Enterprise Manager Cloud Control automatically creates a problem object containing those incidents. Within the Incident Manager user interface, you can link to the Support Workbench to open a service request that you can then track from Incident Manager.

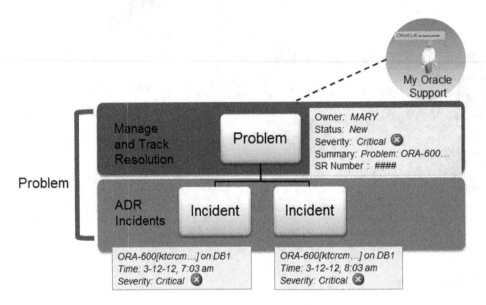

Figure 12-3. *Incidents and problems*

Incident Rule Sets

Incident rule sets are the replacement of and an enhancement to notification rules. They provide a way to automate actions related to events, incidents, or problems. Some of the common scenarios, or use cases, for incident rule sets include creating an incident based on an event, sending notifications such as e-mails or pages, opening help-desk tickets, and automating incident workflow actions (such as automatically assigning the owner of an incident or escalating an incident after it has been open for some time).

There are two types of incident rule sets in Enterprise Manager Cloud Control 12.1: an enterprise rule set and a private rule set. An *enterprise rule set* is meant to be used to implement your operational practices when it comes to managing events and incidents. All the actions we discussed earlier, such as creating an incident, sending a notification, and opening a ticket, are supported within an enterprise rule set type. Because these are actions that affect all types of incidents and problems, the user who creates these rule sets requires the Rule Set resource privilege. Once an enterprise type rule set is created, it is visible to all Enterprise Manager users. When you create a rule set, further development of that rule set can be done in a collaborative manner, so each rule set can basically have multiple authors (that is, multiple Enterprise Manager users) who can edit that particular rule set. A *private rule set*, on the other hand, is designed only to send e-mail notifications to yourself. As a result, no special privileges are required to create a private rule set.

A rule set is defined as a set of one or more rules that are applied to a common set of objects such as targets (including groups) or jobs. Within a group, you can specify a set of heterogeneous targets (that is, a group of different target types) for a rule set to be applied to. The idea of a rule set is to enable you to logically combine different rules that relate to the same object into a single manageable unit. This is one of the enhancement requests that we have heard many times for notification rules in earlier releases, where administrators have often created multiple notification rules based on the target type that at the end of the day operate on the same group. Logically combining these rules into one unit is a natural progression from the earlier functionality to make it easier to track and manage these multiple rules.

The rules within a particular rule set are executed in a specific order. By default, the rules are executed in the order they are created, but you can change that at any time. The rule sets themselves can also be executed in a specific order. Again, by default this is the order in which the rule sets are created, but that can be changed as well.

Some out-of-the-box rule sets that are provided with Enterprise Manager Cloud Control 12.1 automatically create incidents for what Oracle Corporation believes are meaningful events as well as automating event deletion. You can use these rule sets as is, but you can't edit them. You can, however, create your own versions by using the Create Like functionality, and the originals can be disabled if they do not meet your requirements.

Rules are part of rule sets. A *rule* is basically an instruction to EM12c that indicates how to automate actions when an event, incident, or problem occurs. Rules do not operate retroactively, so a rule operates on events, incidents, or problems that occur only after the rule is created.

A rule consists of two parts: the criteria and the action. The *criteria* specify the events, incidents, or problems that the rule applies to. The *action* tells EM12c what operations you want it to perform on those specified events, incidents, or problems. Each operation, in turn, can have some additional conditions. Let's look at a couple of examples of how this works:

- If the rule criteria is a specific metric alert (for example, CPU utilization or tablespace percent used crosses a certain threshold of either Warning or Critical severity), the action could be to create an incident.

- Another rule could operate on incidents that are of either Warning or Critical severity, and the action is to send a notification. In this case, there could be an additional condition that if the rule condition is Severity = Critical, then the action is to notify by page, while if Severity = Warning, the action is to notify by e-mail.

- Another example of a rule might be for incidents that have been open longer than seven days, where the rule action is to set the escalation level to 1 (esclation levels can range from 1 to 5).

Let's now look at an example of a rule set. Figure 12-4 shows an enterprise rule set that operates on the Production group, PROD-GROUP.

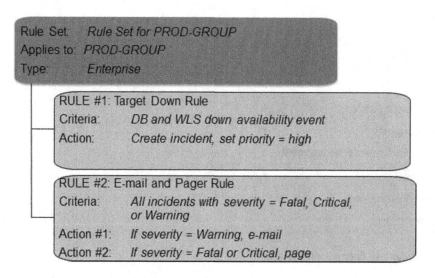

Figure 12-4. *An incident rule set*

This heterogeneous group consists of a set of targets that includes hosts, databases, and WebLogic servers. This rule set has two rules. The first is a Target Down rule; the criteria for the rule are any database or WebLogic servers that are down. In this case, the action is to automatically create an incident and set its priority to high. The second rule within this rule set has to do with sending notifications. The criteria for this rule are for any incident on the targets within PROD-GROUP that has a severity of Fatal, Critical, or Warning. The actions here are to send an e-mail only if the severity is set to Warning, or to send a page if the severity is set to either Fatal or Critical.

Incident Manager User Interface

Now that you understand the basic terminology and concepts behind incident management, let's spend a bit of time introducing the Incident Manager user interface. The user interface has two parts:

- The incident rule setup interface, used to create your own incident rules to automate responses for incidents and events

- The Incident Manager console, which is used to search for, view, and manage outstanding incidents, events, and problems

Let's look at creating your own incident rules first.

Creating Incident Rules

To create an incident rule, you need to click the Setup menu from the upper right of any screen and then choose Incidents ä Incident Rules, as shown in Figure 12-5.

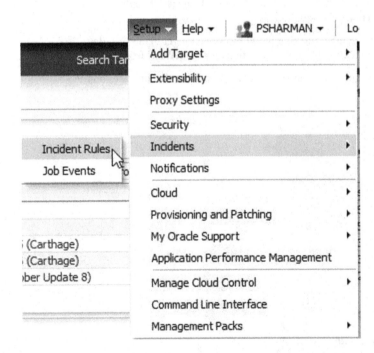

Figure 12-5. *Accessing the Incident Rules - All Enterprise Rules page*

This takes you to the Incident Rules - All Enterprise Rules page, where you can view, edit, or delete existing rule sets, or create your own. In this example, you're going to define a rule in a rule set that creates an incident and e-mails you when the USERS tablespace for the orcl database is close to running out of space. To get this rule to execute, you change the default setup of the USERS tablespace to not autoextend when it runs out of space, and also change the critical threshold for the tablespace to be triggered at 90 percent full. These operations are done outside the creation of the rule set (that part is left out of the following screenshots). Click the Create Rule Set button, shown in Figure 12-6, to start the process of creating a new rule set.

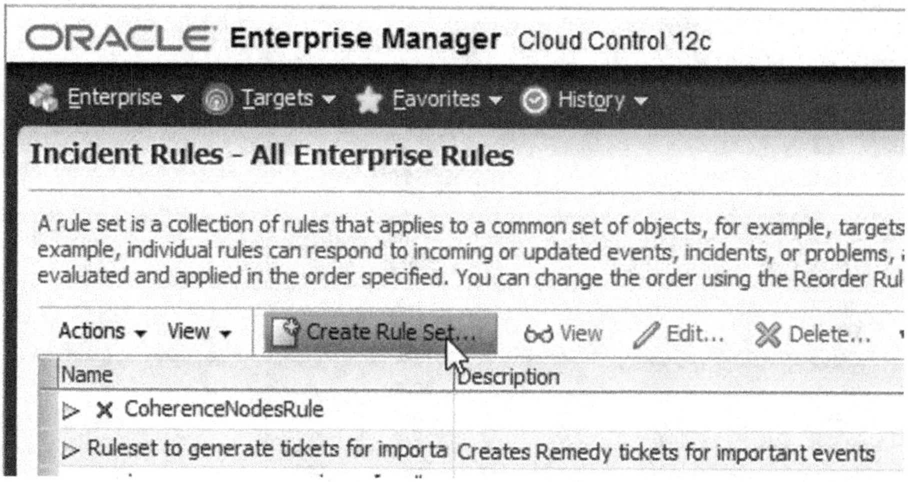

Figure 12-6. *First step in creating a rule set*

The important part of the Create Rule Set page is the bottom, where you specify the targets the rule applies to and the rules that make up the rule set (see Figure 12-7). Fill in the rule set name (a mandatory field) and provide a description for the rule set. The rule set type defaults to Enterprise. (Private is used when you want to be notified about something that is not a standard business practice; the only action it can perform is to send an e-mail.) Next click the Add button, as shown in Figure 12-7, to add a group this rule set will apply to (while specific targets can also be added, the full power of this tool is used when rule sets are applied to multiple targets at one time).

Figure 12-7. *Adding targets to a rule set*

The Search and Select: Targets pop-up appears, provided you have disabled the pop-up blocker in your browser (if you haven't, allow pop-ups for the site and retry the operation). From here, you can select the different targets for this rule set. In the example shown in Figure 12-8, you choose the group HQ GROUP, which you know contains the orcl database.

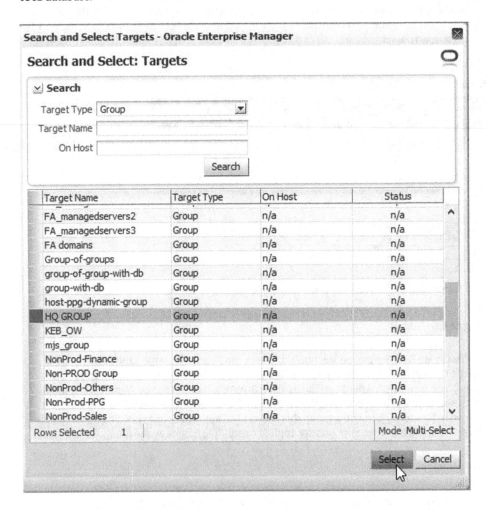

Figure 12-8. *The Search and Select: Targets screen*

Once the target group is selected, you need to add the relevant rules to the rule set. To start this operation, click the Rules tab. Then click the Create button, shown in Figure 12-9.

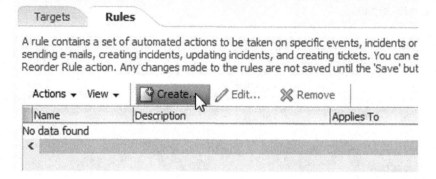

Figure 12-9. *Adding rules to a rule set*

Because rules can apply to events, incidents, or problems, you need to select the type of rule you are creating. In this example, as shown in Figure 12-10, you're creating a rule on the Tablespace Full metric alert event, so you choose the first option on the Select Type of Rule to Create pop-up.

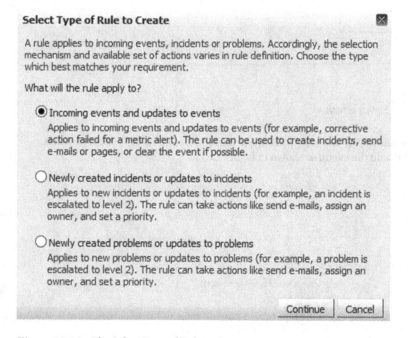

Figure 12-10. *The Select Type of Rule to Create screen*

Next you need to specify the type of event by choosing Metric Alert from the drop-down list (see Figure 12-11).

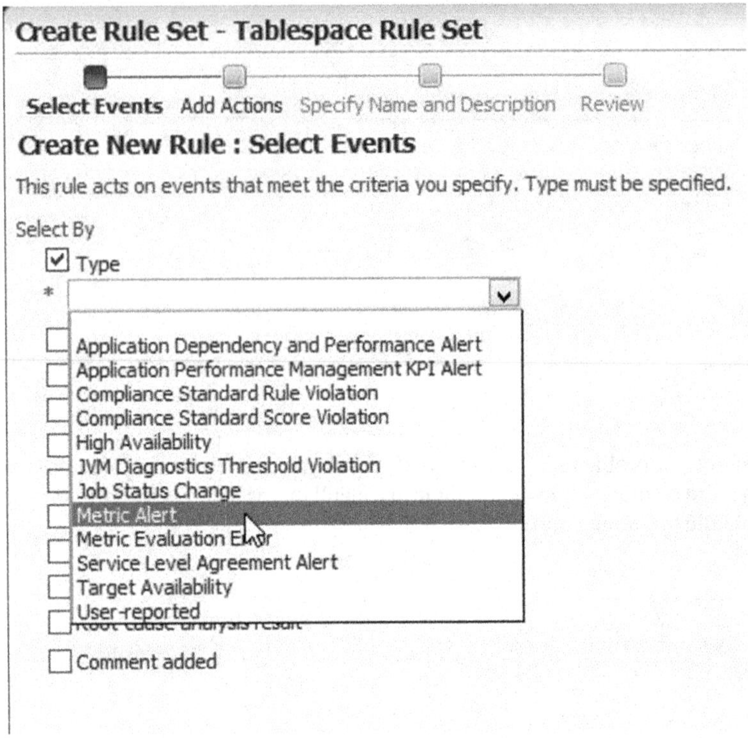

Figure 12-11. *The Create New Rule: Select Events screen*

You want this rule to act on only specific metric alerts, so you choose the Specific Events of Type Metric Alert radio button. Then click the Add button to add the event, as shown in Figure 12-12.

Figure 12-12. *Adding metric alert events to a rule*

Select a Target Type of Database Instance. Then search for all metrics that contain *Tablespace* in their name to minimize the list (see Figure 12-13).

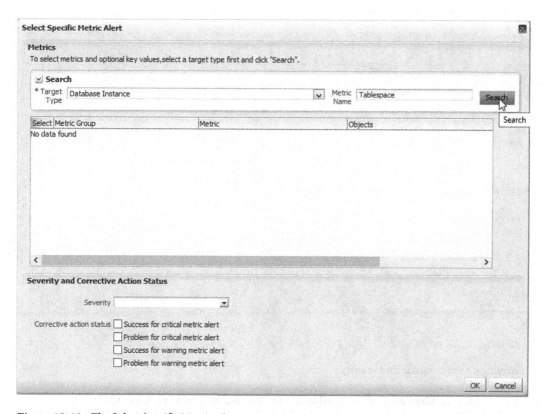

Figure 12-13. The Select Specific Metric Alert screen

In this case, as shown in Figure 12-14, you want to use the Tablespace Free Space (MB) metric, and restrict the rule to the USERS tablespace, specifically for the Critical severity case.

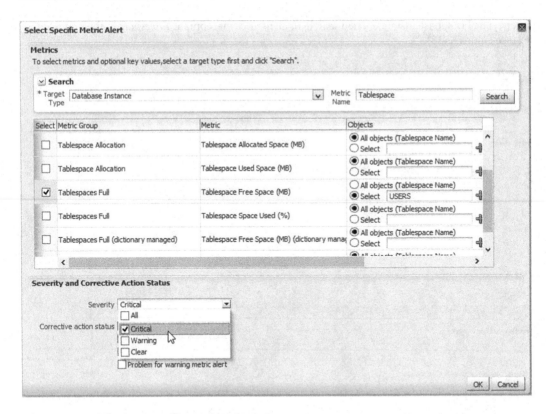

Figure 12-14. *Selecting a specific metric and severity*

When finished, click the Next button. Now you need to add the relevant actions, so click the Add button, as shown in Figure 12-15.

Figure 12-15. *Adding an action to a rule*

Now you need to tell the rule to create an incident (assigned to your EM administrator name), set the priority to urgent, and also e-mail you to ensure that you get the notification, as shown in Figure 12-16.

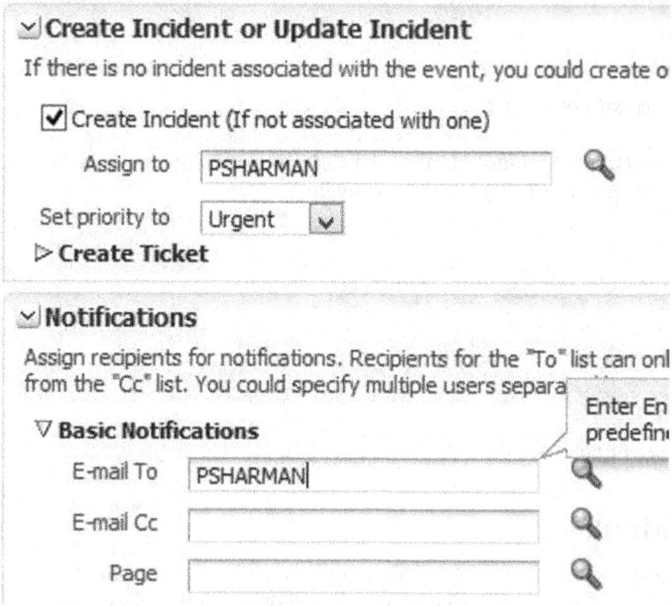

∨ Create Incident or Update Incident

If there is no incident associated with the event, you could create o

☑ Create Incident (If not associated with one)

Assign to   PSHARMAN

Set priority to   Urgent ∨

▷ **Create Ticket**

∨ Notifications

Assign recipients for notifications. Recipients for the "To" list can onl from the "Cc" list. You could specify multiple users separa

Enter En
predefin

▽ **Basic Notifications**

E-mail To   PSHARMAN|

E-mail Cc

Page

Figure 12-16. Adding notifications to a rule

Once this is done, click the Continue button and then click the Next button. Provide a name and description for the rule and click Next, as shown in Figure 12-17.

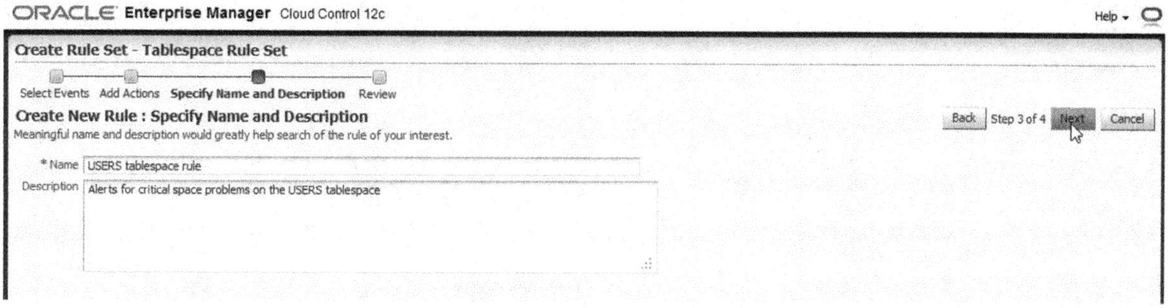

ORACLE Enterprise Manager Cloud Control 12c   Help ▾

Create Rule Set - Tablespace Rule Set

Select Events   Add Actions   **Specify Name and Description**   Review

Create New Rule : Specify Name and Description   Back | Step 3 of 4 | Next | Cancel
Meaningful name and description would greatly help search of the rule of your interest.

* Name USERS tablespace rule

Description Alerts for critical space problems on the USERS tablespace

Figure 12-17. Specifying a rule name and description

Click the Continue button. On the next screen, click the OK button, and then click Save to save the rule set. Finally, click OK to acknowledge the rule set creation message, as shown in Figure 12-18.

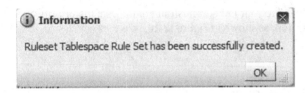

Information

Ruleset Tablespace Rule Set has been successfully created.

OK

Figure 12-18. Window confirming a ruleset was successfully created

You should now start seeing incidents generated in the Incident Manager console, as shown in Figure 12-19. This may take up to 30 minutes, depending on the frequency of checking for the event.

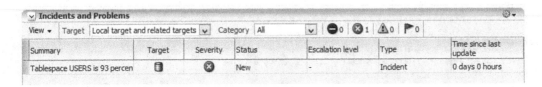

Figure 12-19. Tablespace Full alerts in the Incident Manager console

Looking at the Details of an Incident

Now let's move on to looking at the details for a particular incident, using the example rule set we just created. The first step is to scroll through the list of open incidents until you find the relevant incident. (In this case, Tablespace USERS is 93 percent full.)

When you select the row containing that incident by clicking anywhere in it, the bottom half of the screen swaps to the details for that incident, as you would see in a normal master-detail form. Figure 12-20 shows an example.

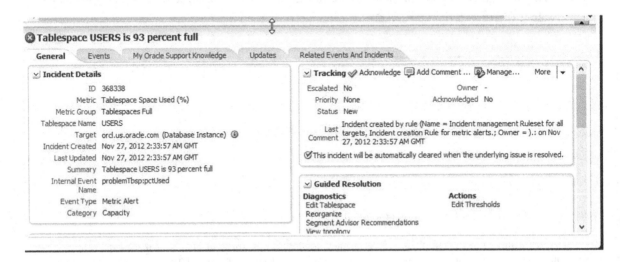

Figure 12-20. Details of an incident

As is standard in EM12c, you can change the layout of the screen by hovering over the separation between its two parts (as you can see in the top middle of the screen in Figure 12-20) and then dragging the cursor to show you more information without scrolling. The General tab, shown in Figure 12-21, shows you specific details about the incident and the metrics data that generated it, a guided resolution region to walk you through resolving the incident, as well as a tracking region we'll come back to after looking at the other tabs.

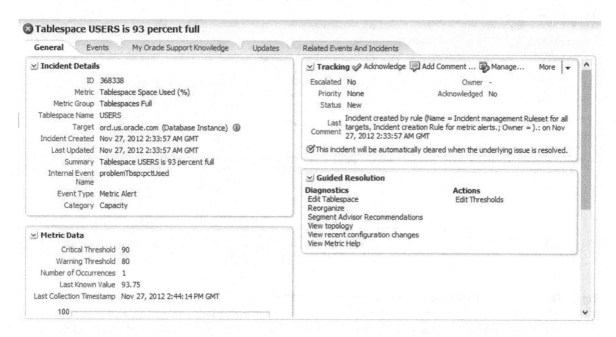

Figure 12-21. *The General tab in Incident Manager*

By clicking the Events tab, you can see all the events that have generated this incident. In this particular case, there is only one event, as shown in Figure 12-22.

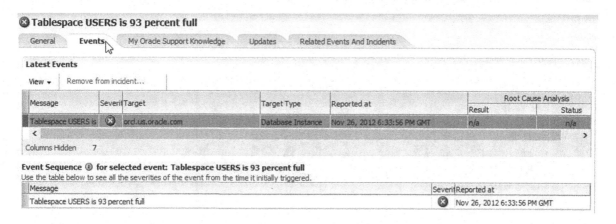

Figure 12-22. *The Events tab in Incident Manager*

Moving over to the next tab, My Oracle Support Knowledge (shown in Figure 12-23), you can see information that has been pulled from My Oracle Support and may be relevant in helping to resolve the issue. The information is ranked on relevance, so hopefully the more relevant articles will help with the resolution.

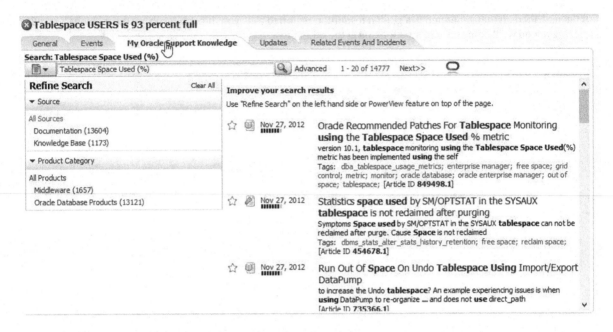

Figure 12-23. *The My Oracle Support Knowledge tab in Incident Manager*

The Updates tab shows information on any updates that have been made to the incident. (In this example, there haven't been any updates, so the screenshot is not included.) You can also see any related events and incidents by clicking the final tab (again, not shown here as there are none yet for this particular incident).

Let's move now to the Tracking region on the General tab. Here you can acknowledge the incident, add a comment to it, or manage it (which also allows acknowledging the incident or adding a comment to it). Click the Manage button to access the screen shown in Figure 12-24.

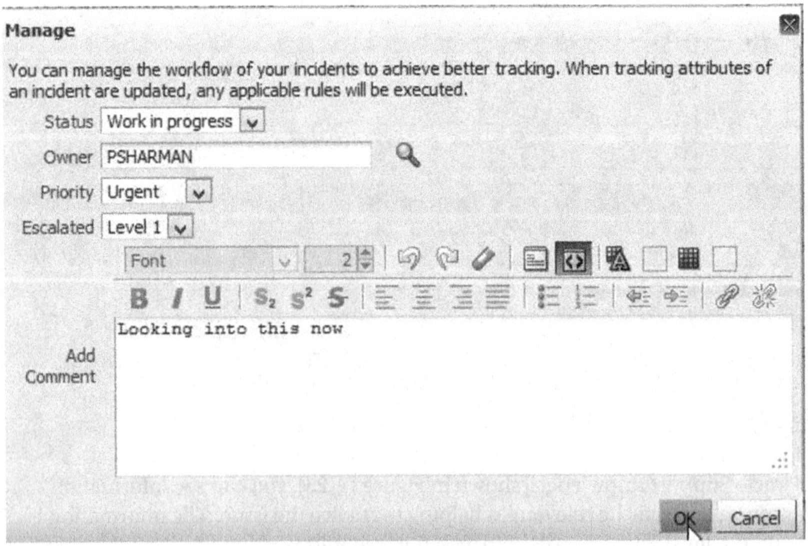

Figure 12-24. *Managing the workflow for an incident*

In the example shown in Figure 12-24, I've changed the status of the incident to Work in Progress, added a priority and comment, and also escalated the incident to level 1 (as indicated earlier, five levels of escalation are allowed). This shows any other administrators in the system that this incident is being worked on.

Creating a Custom View

You may have noticed with the screenshot you first saw of the Incident Manager console that in a complex environment, you can see a very large number of open incidents, and finding the ones you are specifically interested in isn't easy. Thankfully, EM12c enables you to build a custom view to restrict the number of incidents you see to something more manageable. To do this, click the Create button in the left-hand Views pane on the Incident Manager console, as shown in Figure 12-25.

Figure 12-25. *Starting to create a custom view*

For this particular example, you want to build a view of the open incidents and problems in the past 24 hours, so you choose the relevant values for the different fields here. As seen in Figure 12-26, you can then click the Get Results button to ensure that this does display what you want to see.

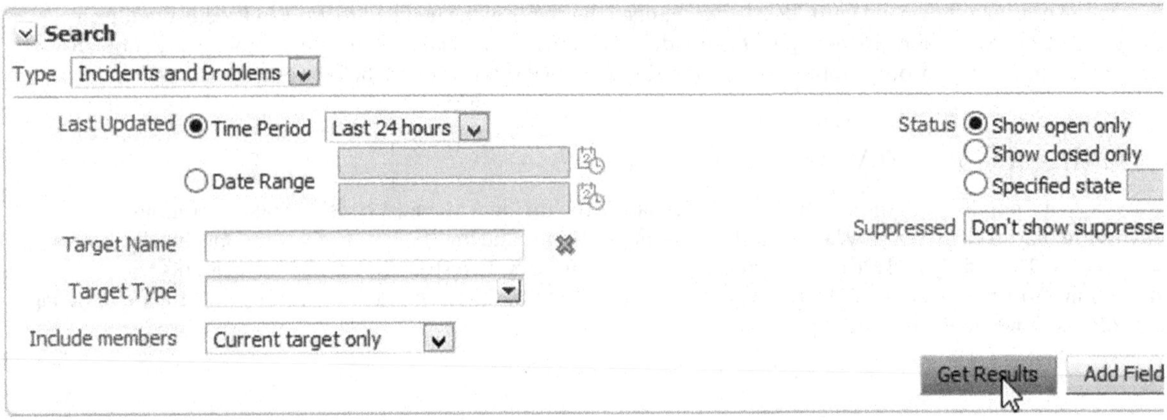

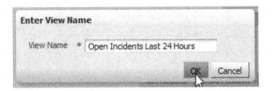

Figure 12-26. *Searching for incidents that match the custom view*

Once you're happy with the results, click the Create View button.

When prompted, provide a meaningful name for the custom view, as shown in Figure 12-27.

Enter View Name

View Name * | Open Incidents Last 24 Hours |

OK   Cancel

Figure 12-27. *Entering a view name for the custom view*

Now you will see the view in the list of custom views on the left side, as shown in Figure 12-28.

Figure 12-28. *Selecting the custom view you just created*

Prioritization of Rules and Notifications

In certain scenarios, your EM12c site might be under heavy load. In these cases, more important events and incidents are processed ahead of others. Two factors are taken into account when determining the processing priority.

The first is the lifecycle status of the target, with the priority based on the following order: Mission Critical targets have the highest priority, followed by Production, Stage, and Test, and then Development targets have the lowest. As an administrator, one of the responsibilities you have is to set the lifecycle status of each target appropriately. The statuses shown here are the ones shipped out of the box with the product.

The second factor is the type of event or incident. Any events or incidents that have to do with availability, such as target down, are always set as highest priority. Next, any events or incidents that are for critical or warning severities are handled, and finally any events that are informational only are treated as the lowest priority.

This prioritization is taken into account only when the system is under heavy load. When the system is under normal load, events and incidents are handled as they arrive.

Backward Compatibility

As far as backward compatibility is concerned, when you migrate from earlier releases to EM12c, backward compatibility for notifications is provided. If you have created any notifications based on PL/SQL, operating system scripts, or SNMP traps, these notification methods will be migrated and continue to work in EM12c.

However, Oracle does encourage you to create new versions of these notification methods by using the new event model so you can leverage the new features we have been discussing. If you have created notification rules in earlier releases, Oracle will migrate those to incident rule sets in the new release as part of the upgrade process.

Let's look at an example of how this mapping of notification rules to incident rule sets is done. Figure 12-29 shows an Enterprise Manager 11.1 notification rule that applies to the group PROD-GROUP and the database target in that group.

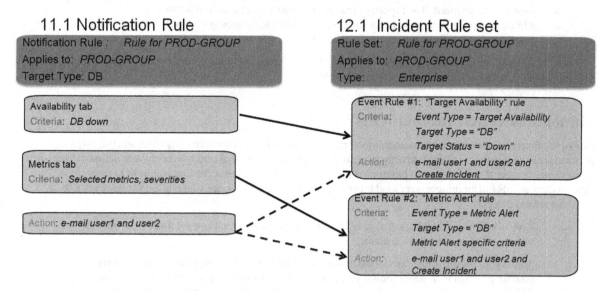

Figure 12-29. *Mapping a notification rule to an incident rule set*

If you're familiar with notification rules in the earlier release, you'll be aware of the tabs in the notification rule setup. In our example, the Availability tab shows the criteria of Database Down chosen, and the Metric tab shows selected metrics of interest and their severity. Finally, the action is set to e-mail two users, user1 and user2.

When this is migrated to an incident rule set in EM12c, the rule set is applied to the same target (the group PROD-GROUP) and it will be of type Enterprise. An event rule will be created in the rule set to cover the criteria for the target availability specified in the notification rule. In the notification rule, the criterion is Database Down. In the incident rule set, that translates to criteria where the event type is target availability, the target type is database, and the target status is down, and because the action in the notification rule is to e-mail the users, that action is carried over into the incident rule set as well. In addition, an incident object is created for this particular event. For the metrics you may have selected on the Metrics tab in your notification rule, a metric alert rule is created where the criteria is as follows: event type is metric alert, target type is database, and specific criteria are set for the metric alerts as well. The action here again is carried over to e-mail the users, and in addition an incident is created for this event.

Incident Manager Guidelines

Now that you've seen how to use the Incident Manager functionality in the EM12c release, let's examine some suggested guidelines on how to get the most out of this functionality. Before we do that, however, it is best to define some goals that you might want to reach to ensure scalable, smarter monitoring with Incident Manager. At a high level, these goals might be defined as follows:

- Meeting your monitoring requirements. These will, of course, vary from customer to customer, but in general terms, this means that appropriate notifications must be sent and incident management operational processes must be followed. The easiest way of doing this is by deploying monitoring standards.

- Comply with security practices. Ensure that you follow the principle of least privilege when granting target privileges. In other words, grant only the level of privilege that is needed to perform the required monitoring.

- Ease of management. It is important that your infrastructure does not become an administrative headache, so make the best use of administrative groups so you can manage "many as one," while requiring minimal effort to monitor new targets.

Setting up target monitoring and roles for target privileges have been covered in Chapter 7, so let's just look at suggested guidelines for setting up rules to manage incidents.

Managing Events and Incidents

One of the first considerations when managing events and incidents is to control events at the source. Just as in performance management, where you want to ensure that only the work that needs to be done is actually done, in Incident Manager it makes sense to have only those events and incidents occur that you want to respond to. Unnecessary events put an unnecessary load on your system. The following are some things you may want to consider toward this end:

- Review your metric settings. It may seem obvious, but ensure that you set thresholds only on metrics that you actually care about.

- Adjust your metric thresholds based on metric trends. One of the more important actions you can perform with your monitoring system is to track metric trends for some period of time (how long will depend on how much history you might already have, as well as how frequently metrics are measured) so you can take some intelligent decisions on what metrics are important (which can then feed back into the previous bullet) as well as what levels your thresholds should be set at.

- Set the number of occurrences appropriately. If some events occur only once or twice, for example, you might not need to be notified of them. You can set the number of occurrences of a metric that must be reached before you are notified.

- Use corrective actions to autoclear metric alerts. Depending on the metric itself, you may be able to define a corrective action that will take place automatically to resolve the issue. This will autoclear the metric alert so you do not need to take action. You might also want to consider creating a rule that clears events for all metric alerts if the event has been open for a certain number of days.

- Disable metric collection for those metrics that you might not care about. Once you have the history information discussed in the second bullet, you can use that to not only set metric thresholds but to disable those metrics that may not be important in your particular environment.

- Define metric settings in monitoring templates, and use those templates in monitoring collections. This will allow you to take full advantage of administration groups, lessening the amount of work involved for you when new targets are added to your environment or when threshold values need to be adjusted.

Rule Set Recommendations

In terms of recommendations for rule sets, let's start off with some general recommendations. First, as just discussed, it is strongly recommended to use a group as the target for a rule set. You want to put together all the rules that pertain to members of that group in the same rule set. Then as much as possible, take advantage of the fact that you can control the execution order of the rules within the rule set.

When you create a rule in a rule set within EM12c, you'll notice three types of rules. Let's look at specific recommendations on how you would use these types. For rules that operate on events, the use case is to create incidents for the alerts or events that are managed in Enterprise Manager. If you want to use a ticketing connector in Enterprise Manager to create tickets for these incidents, use rules on events to do so, by using the rule actions to first create an incident on the event and then create a ticket for the incident. Another use case for rules on events would be to simply send events to third-party management systems using event connectors. The final scenario would be to only send notifications on events rather than creating incidents, as you could in earlier releases.

For rules that operate on incidents, one of the primary use cases is to automate operations that pertain to incident workflow (such as automatically assigning owners to incidents), to set priority for an incident or set its escalation level, or to send notifications for incidents. You can also as another use case create tickets based on incident conditions, such as creating a ticket when an incident is escalated to level 2.

Rules are used on problems to automate the management of problem workflows in much the same way as for incidents. For example, you can automatically assign owners to problems, set the priority or escalation level for a problem, or send notifications for problems.

Incident rule sets can be easily used for automation and workflow management. For example, you might do the following:

- Auto-assign incidents for faster resolution. When incidents are created, assign an incident owner automatically. Alternatively, create a separate rule to assign ownership based on specific criteria. In either case, this saves having to manually assign the incident to a specific owner.

- Automate your escalation processes. You may want to set the escalation level for an incident based on the length of time the incident has been open and unresolved. If you do not auto-assign incidents as discussed in the first bullet, you may want to escalate unassigned important incidents.

- Send notifications for escalated incidents or problems. When an incident or problem is escalated, you can send an e-mail notification, assign an owner, or set a priority for the incident or problem.

- Auto-assign priority levels. Just as with ownership, you can assign a priority level automatically when an incident is created. You can then sort by priority in the Incident Manager console and work on high-priority incidents first.

Summary

Incident Manager provides administrators with a central point of control for managing events, incidents, and problems within the infrastructure detected by Enterprise Manager. It allows you to monitor and resolve service disruptions quickly and efficiently, and provides a way to manage a smaller number of meaningful incidents rather than numerous discrete events. Using its integration with My Oracle Support allows you to access integrated Oracle expertise to accelerate incident and problem diagnosis and resolution.

■ ■ ■

CHAPTER 13

High Availability, Backup, and Recovery

by Leighton Nelson

This chapter explores three levels of architecture required for setting up a highly available Oracle Enterprise Manager Cloud Control 12c environment. It also covers backup and recovery methods for the components of the system, including the repository database, management service, and agents.

Enterprise Manager Cloud Control 12c provides a complete infrastructure management solution for databases, applications, and hardware. Having such a key component in the enterprise naturally leads to concerns about redundancy and high availability. If something does go wrong within the configuration, recovery should occur in the shortest possible time, thus minimizing disruptions to manageability and monitoring of the enterprise infrastructure. Maintenance will also be required to apply patches to the Enterprise Manager software components (that is, database, management service, agents, and operating systems). It is with these concerns in mind that Oracle Enterprise Manager has been designed to meet the desired service and operating levels by using different high-availability mechanisms.

High Availability

Each component within the Enterprise Manager architecture should be made highly available to enable a complete high-availability configuration. The main components to be considered, shown in Figure 13-1, are as follows:

> *Management Agent*: Runs on targets and communicates with and sends metrics to the OMS
>
> *Management Server*: The heart of the Enterprise Manager that provides Management Services
>
> *Repository*: Stores persistent data from the monitored targets in an Oracle database
>
> *Software Library*: Stores files for patching, provisioning, and agent and plug-in deployment

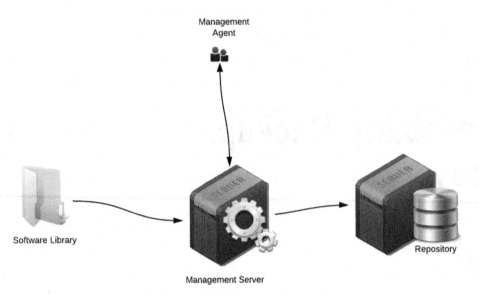

Figure 13-1. *Enterprise Manager Cloud Control 12c architecture*

Different levels of high availability can be configured for each component with varying levels of complexity and cost. When considering your high-availability requirements, there should be minimal trade-offs in cost, complexity, performance, and data loss. Generally, the complexity and level of high availability are proportional to each other.

The Oracle Management Agent should be configured to start on boot. This ensures that no manual intervention will be required after a server reboots and quickly enables targets to be monitored after a service disruption. On Unix and Linux operating systems, a script called `gcstartup` is placed in `/etc/init.d` and made to run at certain runlevels. On Microsoft Windows, a service is created to start automatically on boot.

Oracle has defined four levels of high availability for Enterprise Manager Cloud Control. These are summarized in Table 13-1. Only levels 1 to 3 are covered in this chapter.

Table 13-1. *Levels of Enterprise Manager High Availability*

Level	Description	Load Balancer Required	Cost
1	OMS and repository on separate hosts. No redundancy.	No	$
2	OMS installed on shared storage with VIP used in active/passive failover. Repository database using local Data Guard.	No	$$
3	Multiple OMSs in active/active configuration. Repository using RAC database with local Data Guard.	Yes, at primary site	$$$
4	Primary OMS in active/active configuration with RAC repository database. Standby OMS at DR site in active/active configuration. Standby RAC database at DR site.	Yes, at primary and standby sites	$$$$

Oracle Management Agent

The Oracle Management Agent is responsible for sending metrics and pending alerts for hosts on which it is installed. To provide high availability, the following features should be enabled for the agent:

- Enable the agent to start automatically on OS boot up. This should be configured automatically after running the root.sh script.

- Install the agent on redundant storage. This includes a RAID-configured storage back end.

- Configure restart parameters for the agent watchdog process. The watchdog process is responsible for restarting the agents based on the following environment variables:

  - EM_MAX_RETRIES indicates the maximum number of times the watchdog process will attempt to restart the agent within the EM_MAX_RETRY_WINDOW. The default is set to 3.

  - EM_RETRY_WINDOW indicates the time interval that is used with EM_MAX_RETRIES before trying to start the management agent. The default is set to 600 seconds.

After installing the Enterprise Manager agent, the <AGENT_HOME>/root.sh script should be executed. This will create the following scripts on Linux and some Unix operating systems that control the startup of the management agent.

- /etc/init.d/gcstartup

- /etc/init/gcstartup

- /etc/rc.d/init.d/gcstartup

If these files are not present, make sure the <AGENT_HOME>/root.sh script has been executed.

Loss or corruption of the agent will result in loss of monitoring and metric data uploads for its associated targets. Likewise, if the agent is down, targets will not be able to communicate with the management server, resulting in loss of manageability.

Management Repository

The repository is the persistent store for monitoring data uploaded by agents. It stores metrics and configuration data from all monitored targets. Loss of the repository will result in management server failure. It is recommended to enable database high-availability features such as Real Application Clusters (RAC) or RAC One Node, Automatic Storage Management (ASM) for data file storage (depending on redundancy levels and back-end RAID configuration),and Data Guard for the repository. Additionally, the management service should be configured to use the Single Client Access Name (SCAN) and a nondefault RAC service name if the repository is configured as a RAC database. The following is an example of configuring the management service for use with a RAC database:

```
emctl config oms -store_repos_details -repos_conndesc "
(DESCRIPTION= (ADDRESS=(PROTOCOL=TCP)
(HOST=emrep-scan.example.com)(PORT=1521) )
(CONNECT_DATA=(SERVER=DEDICATED) (SERVICE_NAME = emrep)))"
-repos_user sysman
```

Figure 13-2 shows an example of an OMS configured with a RAC repository database using the SCAN name. For additional details on configuring SCAN, see the *Oracle Clusterware Administration and Deployment Guide 11g Release 2 (11.2)*.

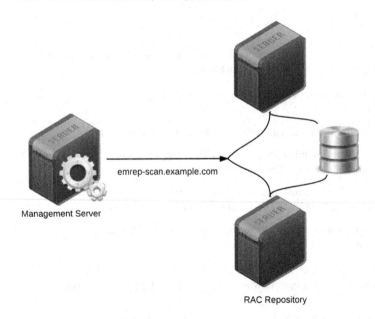

Management Server

emrep-scan.example.com

RAC Repository

Figure 13-2. Repository database configured using RAC database

Consider using the Maximum Availability Architecture[1] (MAA) Advisor in Enterprise Manager Cloud Control 12c to configure additional HA components, including the following:

- Enable `ARCHIVELOG` mode so that consistent hot backups of the database can be performed.

- Enable block checksums to enable Oracle to detect corruption due to physical disks or storage systems. Set the `DB_BLOCK_CHECKSUM` parameter to `TYPICAL` or `FULL`.

- Configure the size of redo log files and groups appropriately. Optimize I/O throughput and performance of the database so that log switches do not occur too frequently. Use of the Redo Log Sizing Advisor (enabled by setting `FAST_START_MTTR_TARGET`) can help determine the optimal sizes.

- Use a Fast Recovery Area[2] to store recovery-related files such as redo logs and archive logs. Oracle can then use suggested backup mechanisms that use the Fast Recovery Area.

- Enable Flashback Database to enable faster database recovery using flashback logs.

- Use fast-start fault recovery to control the instance-recovery time. Set the initialization parameter `FAST_START_MTTR_TARGET` to specify the number of seconds that instance recovery should take.

- Enable database block checking to enable early detection and prevention of data and memory corruption. Set `DB_BLOCK_CHECKING` to `TRUE` or `FULL`.

After configuring the components, you can monitor the status of each by using the High Availability Console, shown in Figure 13-3.

---

[1] Maximum Availability Architecture (MAA) is a set of Oracle-recommended practices based on high-availability features. These recommendations are based on product development validations and experiences of customers running Oracle products.
[2] The Fast Recovery Area was previously called Flash Recovery Area in pre-11.2 Oracle databases.

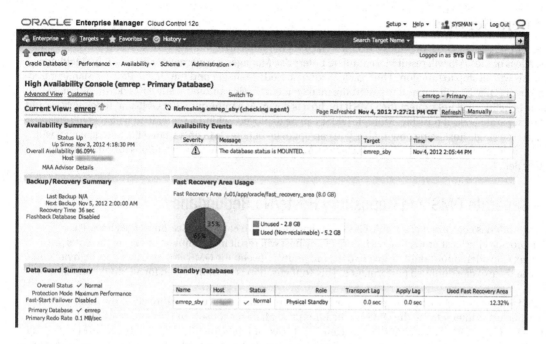

Figure 13-3. *Enterprise Manager Cloud Control 12c High Availability Console*

■ **Note** The management repository should be configured in its own database to ensure that operations on the repository do not affect other applications, and vice versa.

A physical standby database is recommended to provide disaster recovery in case of a failure at the primary site. Data on the primary repository will be kept in sync with the standby database. When configuring a physical standby for the repository database, use similar hardware and resources as the primary site so that there aren't any performance implications in the event of a failover/switchover. Use Enterprise Manager to create a standby database from the primary database. Determine the network mode that you want to use to synchronize the standby database based on your network bandwidth and recovery objectives:

> *Maximum Protection*: Synchronous writes to standby
>
> *Maximum Availability*: Synchronous writes to standby
>
> *Maximum Performance*: Asynchronous writes to standby

■ **Note** Enterprise Manager can create only a single-instance standby database. You can use the Convert to RAC feature in Enterprise Manager to convert the single-instance physical standby database to RAC.

Management Service

The management service, or OMS, provides a user interface via the Enterprise Manager console and processes data from agents. A loss of the OMS will result in a complete Enterprise Manager outage: agent uploads, jobs, incidents, and notifications will all stop to function. The Oracle WebLogic Node Manager and the Oracle Process Manager and Notification Server (OPMN) will attempt to restart the management service automatically if it is down. Although this provides some benefit, it will not protect the OMS if the host is down. At a minimum, the OMS and repository should be installed on separate hosts if possible. Multiple OMSs can be deployed behind a server load balancer to provide protection against a single host being down. Also, you can opt to install the OMS on a shared filesystem, which will provide passive failover in case of the loss of a single host. You will look at each of these options for protecting the OMS in further detail.

Level 1—Separate OMS and Repository Hosts/No Redundancy

A level 1 configuration is composed of a single OMS and repository, with each installed on its own host. This configuration provides the least protection, as failure of any host will result in a complete outage of the Enterprise Manager system. Consideration should be given to the proximity between the OMS and repository, as high network latency between the two can diminish performance. This configuration is recommended for all but the smallest of configurations.

Figure 13-4 is a diagram of a level 1 high-availability configuration. Agents upload directly to the management service host, while users interact with the OMS via the Enterprise Manager console or the command-line EMCLI directly to the physical OMS host. If either the management service or repository database hosts become unavailable, a complete outage will occur, resulting in loss of monitoring for targets. Keeping each component on its own server reduces the likelihood of their impacting each other due to resource overhead. For example, increasing the database parameters sga_max_size and sga_target could lessen the performance of the OMS because doing so reduces the amount of memory available to the operating system. In addition, it lays the basis for a scalable environment as business requirements dictate.

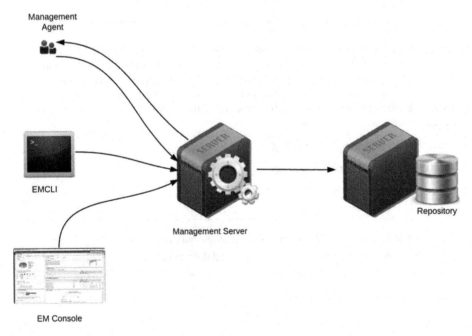

Figure 13-4. *Level 1 high-availability configuration with OMS and repository on separate servers*

Level 2—Active/Passive OMS and Data Guard Repository

To reduce OMS downtime during a planned or unplanned outage, some redundancy should be introduced into the configuration. A level 2 configuration uses a shared filesystem for the management service to achieve an active/passive, or cold, failover cluster solution. The filesystem is shared between two or more hosts and is active on only one host at a time.

The following steps should be performed as a prerequisite to a level 2 high-availability configuration:

1. The shared filesystem for the OMS can be installed on a general-purpose cluster file system including NFS, Oracle Cluster File System (OCFS2), and Oracle Automatic Storage Management Cluster File System (ACFS). If NFS is used as the shared storage, ensure that the correct mount options are set in /etc/fstab (/etc/filesystems on AIX) to prevent potential I/O issues. Specifically, rsize and wsize should be set.

    The following example shows an entry in the /etc/fstab file on a Linux server; the NFS share is mounted on a filer named filer1 under the /vol1/oms_share directory.

    ```
    filer:/vol1/oms_share /u01/app/oms_share nfs rw,bg,rsize=32768,wsize=32768,
    hard,nointr,tcp,noac,vers=3,timeo=600 0 0
    ```

2. Install binaries for the OMS, along with the inventory, on the shared filesystem.

3. Set up the virtual hostname and IP address (VIP) by using Oracle Clusterware or third-party software and hardware. Failover is achieved by using the virtual hostname for the OMS along with a unique IP address that resolves to the hostname.

4. Configure the repository database by using a local physical standby with Data Guard (see Figure 13-5).

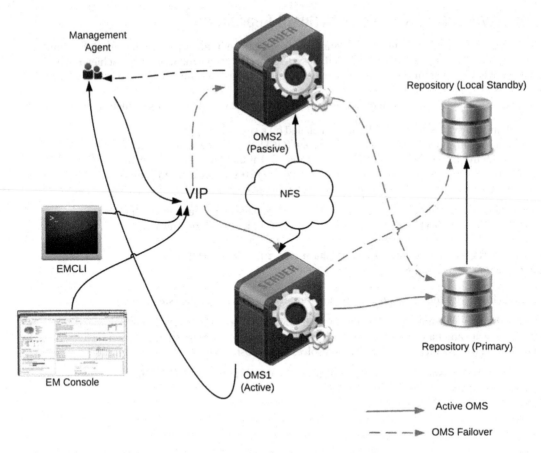

Figure 13-5. Level 2 Enteprise Manager Cloud Control 12c high-availability configuration with active/passive OMS and local standby

In our example, we will use Oracle Clusterware to create and manage the virtual hostname as well as perform failover of the application. OCFS2 is chosen as the shared filesystem.

■ **Note**   OCFS v1 is not supported as shared storage for the OMS.

You should configure the following prerequisites on all hosts before installing the management service:

1. Ensure that the OS user ID is identical on each host where the OMS will be installed.

■ **Note**   For Red Hat Enterprise Linux and Oracle Linux operating systems, install the `oracle-validated` or `oracle-preinstall-11gr2` package to enable consistent UIDs and GIDs.

```
[oracle@oms1 ~]$ id -a
uid=1101(oracle) gid=1000(oinstall) groups=1000(oinstall),1021(asmdba),1032(dba)
```

2. Set environment variables.

    a. Operating System Time Zone variable, TZ:[3]

        ```
        export TZ='America/New_York'
        ```

    b. The PERL5LIB variable should be unset to avoid being associated with the incorrect
        PERL libraries.

3. Install Oracle Clusterware on both servers (see the Oracle Grid Infrastructure Installation
    Guide).

4. Install and configure OCFS2.

5. Prepare the database for use with OMS (see Chapter 2 for more information).

Before installing the OMS, a virtual hostname that maps to a unique static IP address should be available (which means an IP address that is currently not used, in the same subnet as the other Enterprise Manager components). A VIP is configured on the public subnet used for accessing the server. If the server that hosts the VIP goes down, it is relocated to an available member of the cluster by Oracle Clusterware. Likewise, if maintenance needs to be performed on a server hosting the VIP, it can be relocated to another server in the cluster.

A VIP can be created in the same way as any other Clusterware resource. However, Oracle recommends that you use the appvipcfg utility in Oracle Clusterware 11gR2 to create application VIPs. The VIP is created with a set of predefined settings suitable for an application VIP, such as a placement policy and failback[4] option. See *Oracle Clusterware Administration and Deployment Guide11gR2* documentation for details on using appvipcfg.

Using the following steps, create an application VIP for the OMS:

1. After installing Oracle Clusterware 11gR2, log in as the ROOT user and issue the following
    command:

    ```
    GRID_HOME/bin/appvipcfg create -network=1 \
            -ip=192.168.1.0 \
            -vipname=omsvip \
            -user=root
    ```

    An example output of running appvipcfg is as follows:

    ```
    [root@oms1 bin]# /u01/app/11.2.0/grid/bin/appvipcfg create -network=1 \
    -ip=192.168.1.0 \
    -vipname=omsvip \
    -user=root
    Production Copyright 2007, 2008, Oracle.All rights reserved
    2012-10-28 03:30:29: Creating Resource Type
    2012-10-28 03:30:29: Executing /u01/app/11.2.0/grid/bin/crsctl add type
    app.appvip_net1.type -basetype ora.cluster_vip_net1.type -file
    /u01/app/11.2.0/grid/crs/template/appvip.type
    2012-10-28 03:30:29: Executing cmd: /u01/app/11.2.0/grid/bin/crsctl add type
    app.appvip_net1.type -basetype ora.cluster_vip_net1.type -file
    ```

---

[3] The format for the TZ environment variable will depend on your operating system. For more information on setting the TZ variable, see your operating system documentation.

[4] The default value of the failback is set to 0, which means that the VIP and its dependent resources will not automatically fail back to the original node after it becomes available again.

```
/u01/app/11.2.0/grid/crs/template/appvip.type
2012-10-28 03:30:37: Create the Resource
2012-10-28 03:30:37: Executing /u01/app/11.2.0/grid/bin/crsctl add resource
omsvip -type app.appvip_net1.type -attr
"USR_ORA_VIP=192.168.1.0,START_DEPENDENCIES=hard(ora.net1.network)
pullup(ora.net1.network),STOP_DEPENDENCIES=hard(ora.net1.network),
ACL='owner:root:rwx,pgrp:root:r-x,other::r--,user:root:r-x',
HOSTING_MEMBERS=oms1.example.com,APPSVIP_FAILBACK="
2012-10-28 03:30:37: Executing cmd: /u01/app/11.2.0/grid/bin/crsctl add
resource omsvip -type app.appvip_net1.type -attr
"USR_ORA_VIP=192.168.1.0,START_DEPENDENCIES=hard(ora.net1.network)
pullup(ora.net1.network),STOP_DEPENDENCIES=hard(ora.net1.network),
ACL='owner:root:rwx,pgrp:root:r-x,other::r--,user:root:r-x',
HOSTING_MEMBERS=oms1.example.com,APPSVIP_FAILBACK="
```

This creates a VIP on network 1, which is defined as IP address 192.168.1.0. The VIP name is omsvip and it is owned by the ROOT user.

2. Next you need to allow the Oracle Grid Infrastructure software owner (for example, GRID) to run the script to start the VIP. As ROOT, execute the following:

```
GRID_HOME/bin/crsctl setperm resource omsvip -u user:grid:r-x
```

3. Start the VIP as the GRID user.

```
GRID_HOME/bin/crsctl start resource omsvip
```

For example:

```
[grid@oms1 ~]$ $GRID_HOME/bin/crsctl start resource omsvip
CRS-2672: Attempting to start 'omsvip' on 'oms1'
CRS-2676: Start of 'omsvip' on 'oms1' succeeded
```

4. Check the status of the VIP.

```
GRID_HOME/bin/crsctl status resource omsvip
```

The status of the output should be similar to the following:

```
NAME=omsvip
TYPE=app.appvip_net1.type
TARGET=ONLINE
STATE=ONLINE on oms1
```

5. The virtual hostname is defined in DNS, and should resolve to the application VIP address created using the preceding steps. Check whether the virtual hostname and VIP are resolvable by using nslookup or the dig command.

```
$ nslookup omsvip
```

This should resolve to a unique IP address of the virtual hostname on every node in the cluster.

6. Also do a reverse lookup of the IP address.

```
$nslookup <virtual IP address>
```

7. Verify that the IP address returned from the nslookup output is running on the OMS host.

```
ifconfig -a|grep <virtual IP address>
```

8. After you have verified that the virtual hostname and VIP have been configured correctly, you can then proceed with the OMS installation. The following should be performed before starting the installer:

   a. Create a new ORACLE_HOME for the OMS on the shared storage on all nodes in the cluster:

   ```
   $ mkdir -p /u01/app/oms_share
   ```

   b. Create an Oracle inventory directory under the ORACLE_HOME for the OMS on all nodes:

   ```
   $ mkdir /u01/app/oms_share/oraInventory
   ```

   c. Create the inventory pointer in the oraInventory directory:

   ```
   $ vi oraInst.loc
   ```

   The oraInst.loc file should contain the path to the inventory and the group of the software owner for the OMS. For example:

   ```
   inventory_loc=/u01/app/oracle/oms_share/oraInventory
   inst_group=oinstall
   ```

9. Next, you proceed with the installation by specifying the ORACLE_HOSTNAME environment variable as your virtual hostname and pointing to the shared inventory location.

```
runInstaller -invPtrloc /u01/app/oms_share/oraInst.loc \
ORACLE_HOSTNAME=omsvip.example.com -debug
```

10. Install the OMS on the first host by following the installation steps as described in the *Oracle Enterprise Manager Cloud Control 12c Basic Installation Guide*. You need to complete the installation only once. Because the location is shared, the binaries will be accessible from another host that shares the filesystem.

After the OMS has been successfully installed and is up and running, if the host were to go down, then the VIP would be automatically relocated to another node. The management service can then be manually started on any remaining node in the cluster on which the VIP is running.

1. To manually relocate the VIP to another host in the cluster, issue the following command:

```
[grid@oms1 ~]$ crsctl relocate res omsvip
CRS-2673: Attempting to stop 'omsvip' on 'oms1'
CRS-2677: Stop of 'omsvip' on 'oms1' succeeded
CRS-2672: Attempting to start 'omsvip' on 'oms2'
CRS-2676: Start of 'omsvip' on 'oms2' succeeded
```

2. Check whether the IP address associated with the VIP is running on the relocated host.

    ```
    ifconfig -a|grep <vip>
    ```

    The repository database should be reachable from other hosts in the cluster, and the listener should be up and running.

3. Set the ORACLE_HOSTNAME environment variable to the virtual hostname. Continuing with our example, we use the following command:

    ```
    export ORACLE_HOSTNAME=omsvip.example.com
    ```

4. Start the OMS on the new node.

    ```
    $OMS_HOME/bin/emctl start oms
    ```

Alternatively, Oracle Clusterware can be configured to fully manage the OMS by creating start, check, stop, clean, and abort routines that tell it how to operate on the OMS. Details on this configuration are outside the scope of this chapter. See the *Oracle Clusterware Administration and Deployment Guide 11gR2* for details.

With a cold-failover solution in place for the OMS, you are protected from the failure of a single host. However, time to perform failover could range from a few minutes to hours, depending on whether it is done manually or automated via Oracle Clusterware or other methods. The repository also needs to be protected, as it is now a single point of failure. As mentioned earlier, a local Data Guard setup consisting of a single physical standby is highly recommended. The standby database should be configured on a separate host from the management servers and primary database. However, it may be possible to create both the primary and the physical standby on another OMS host to keep costs down. In the event of a planned or unplanned outage of the primary repository, the physical standby can be switched or failed over to the standby on a remaining host. Please note that the host will now become a single point of failure.

As a prerequisite to creating a standby database using Enterprise Manager, the destination host should have an Oracle Management Agent installed and should be monitored by Enterprise Manager. Also, if ASM is used as database storage, it should be monitored along with the listener.

To create a standby database using Enterprise Manager, use these steps:

1. Navigate to the repository database home page and choose Availability ä Add Standby from the menu.

2. Back up the primary database (see Figure 13-6). Data Guard uses RMAN to create the standby database based on either a new or existing backup. An online backup requires that the database be in ARCHIVELOG mode.

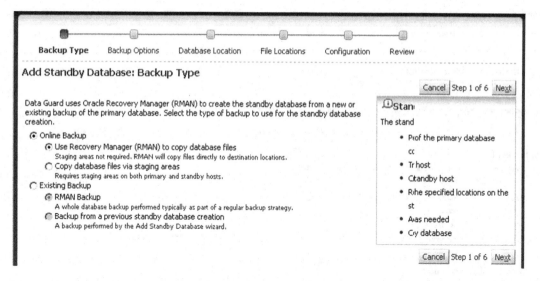

Figure 13-6. *Adding a standby database by using a RMAN online backup*

If using the online method, perform the backup at a time outside peak hours so that performance of Enterprise Manager Cloud Control is not negatively impacted. When using this method, you can also decide to use RMAN's feature to copy backups directly to the destination host using Oracle Net Services or stage the backups before copying. The latter option requires additional storage at both the primary and secondary sites. If there is an existing backup as a result of routine backup procedures or from a previous Add Standby Database operation, it may be used as well.

3. Next you'll select a backup option. As you can see in Figure 13-7, you provide the degree of parallelism RMAN will use, as well as the credentials for the primary host. The standby database will require standby redo logs for real-time apply. They will be created on the primary database as well in the event of a role transition. You may use OMF for the standby redo logs (default) or manually specify the log files. For databases using ASM, supply the disk group name.

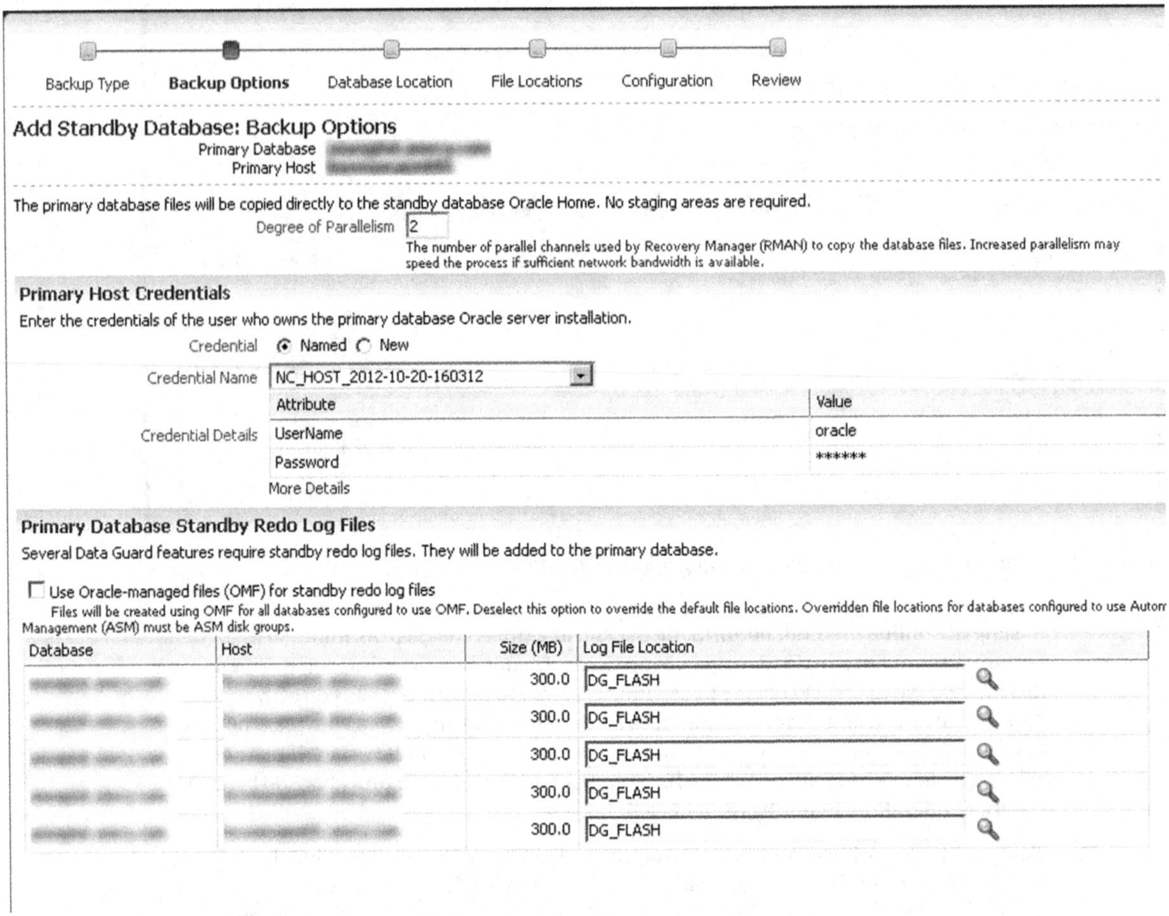

Figure 13-7. *Add Standby Database, Backup Options*

4. Add the file locations for storing database files and the Fast Recovery Area on the standby, as shown in Figure 13-8. If using ASM, specify the disk groups.

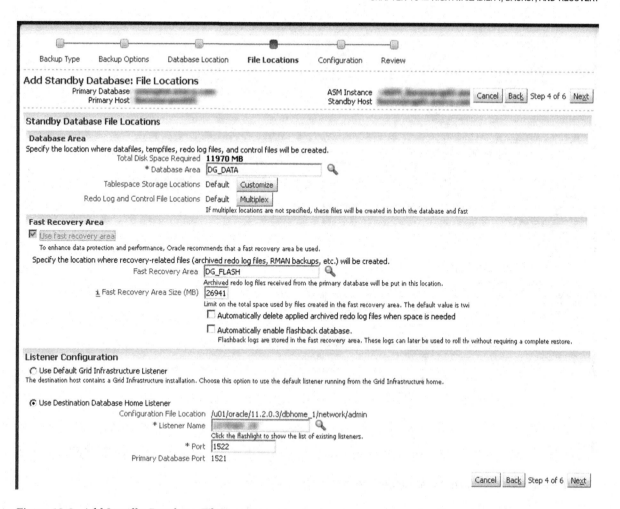

Figure 13-8. *Add Standby Database, File Locations*

5. Choose configuration properties of the standby database, as shown in Figure 13-9.

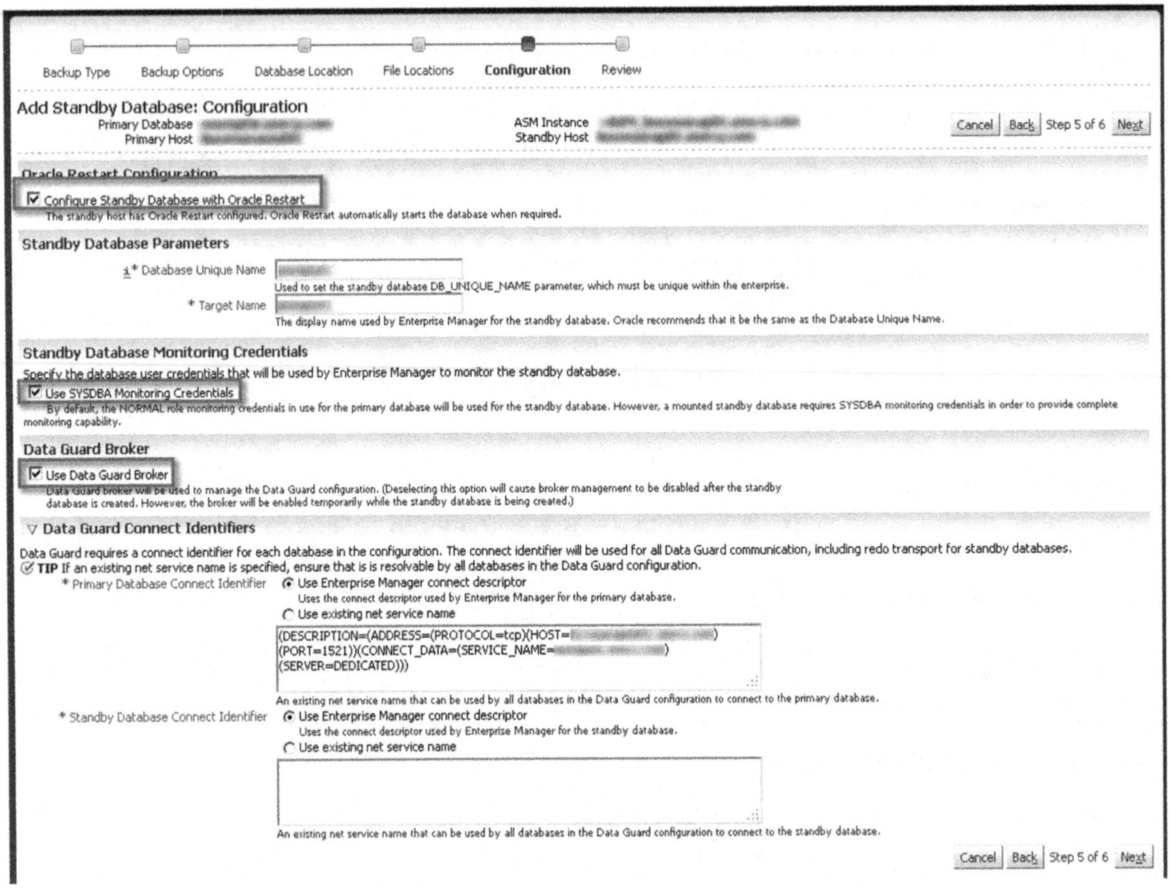

Figure 13-9. *Add Standby Database, Configuration*

If Oracle Restart[5] is configured on the standby server, enable it for the configuration:

a. Provide a unique name for the standby database and a name for the target in Enterprise Manager.

b. Specify the monitoring credentials to be used by Enterprise Manager by selecting the Use SYSDBA Monitoring Credentials check box. This is because the standby database will be in mounted state while the redo is being applied. Using the SYSDBA role will enable more monitoring information to become available.

c. Select the Use Data Guard Broker check box to enable management of the primary and standby using the Data Guard Broker. It simplifies the management of primary and standby databases in a Data Guard configuration, including role transitions and health checks. A connect identifier is required by Data Guard for all communication with the primary and standby databases. Provide a connect descriptor to be used by Data Guard. Either the Enterprise Manager connect descriptor or an existing service name can be used.

---

[5] Oracle Restart is the single-instance high-availability feature of Oracle Database 11gR2. It provides high availability by restarting database instances, services, and listeners in the event of a failure. It also restarts the database components on bootup of the server.

6. Review your options on the next screen, shown in Figure 13-10, and then click the Finish button.

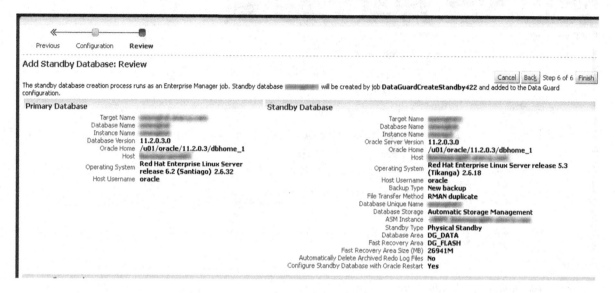

Figure 13-10. *Add Standby Database, Review*

7. A job is created to build the standby database. Click the job name to view the steps and output, as shown in Figure 13-11.

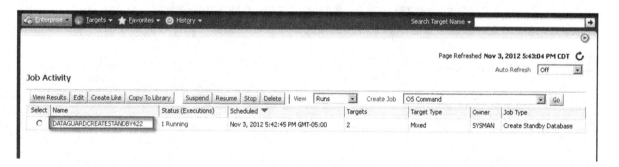

Figure 13-11. *Data Guard job creation*

After the standby database has been successfully created, you will be able to manage it via the Enterprise Manager console. From the repository database home page, choose Availability ➤ Data Guard Administration, as shown in Figure 13-12.

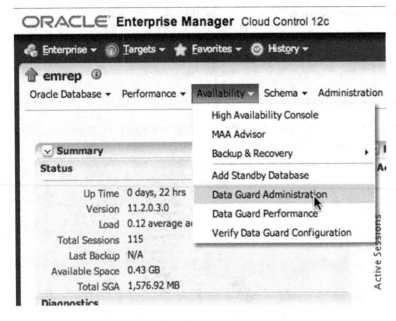

Figure 13-12. *Data Guard Administration option*

The Data Guard screen presents an overview of the Data Guard status as well as configuration information about the primary and standby databases, as shown in Figure 13-13.

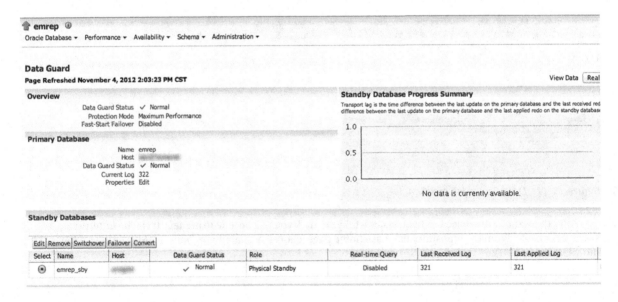

Figure 13-13. *Data Guard status*

By default, the standby was created by using Maximum Performance protection mode.[6] This mode ensures that if a network connectivity problem exists between the primary and the standby databases, it will not impact the primary database's performance. However, this has the potential for data loss. Because we are using a local Data Guard, it may be feasible to enable Maximum Availability protection mode. This will also not impact the availability and performance of the primary database if a network connectivity issue arises, but provides a higher level of data protection. Change the protection mode to Maximum (see Figure 13-14).

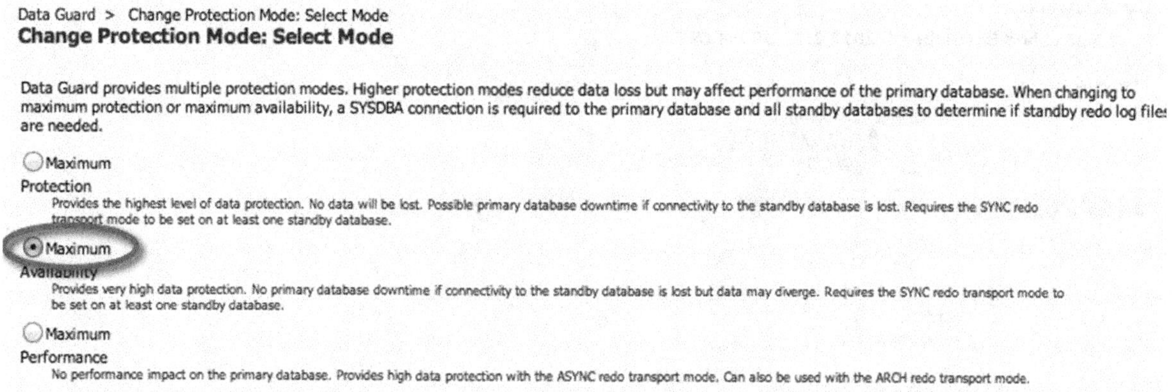

Data Guard > Change Protection Mode: Select Mode
Change Protection Mode: Select Mode

Data Guard provides multiple protection modes. Higher protection modes reduce data loss but may affect performance of the primary database. When changing to maximum protection or maximum availability, a SYSDBA connection is required to the primary database and all standby databases to determine if standby redo log files are needed.

○ Maximum
Protection
> Provides the highest level of data protection. No data will be lost. Possible primary database downtime if connectivity to the standby database is lost. Requires the SYNC redo transport mode to be set on at least one standby database.

◉ Maximum
Availability
> Provides very high data protection. No primary database downtime if connectivity to the standby database is lost but data may diverge. Requires the SYNC redo transport mode to be set on at least one standby database.

○ Maximum
Performance
> No performance impact on the primary database. Provides high data protection with the ASYNC redo transport mode. Can also be used with the ARCH redo transport mode.

Figure 13-14. *Changing the Data Guard protection mode*

The protection mode changes will be reflected in the console, as seen in Figure 13-15. Changing from Maximum Performance to Maximum Availability will also change the redo transport mode from Asynchronous (ASYNC) to Synchronous (SYNC).

---

[6]*Protection mode* refers to the accepted potential data loss in event of primary database failure. The three available modes are Maximum Performance, Maximum Availability, and Maximum Protection.

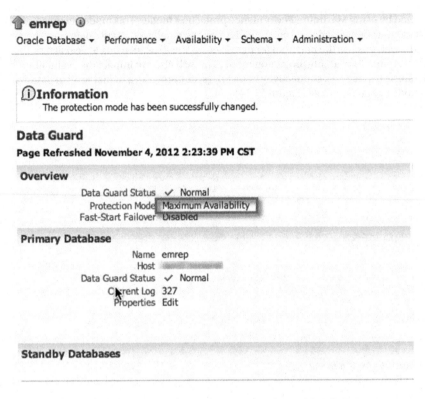

Figure 13-15. *Data Guard Maximum Availability protection mode*

In addition, we recommend to use Data Guard Broker to manage the Data Guard operations such as failover, switchover, and health checks. The Data Guard Broker simplifies the management of databases in such a configuration by providing a GUI interface via Enterprise Manager or the command-line utility Data Guard Broker Line Manager, dgmgrl. A full discussion of Data Guard and Data Guard Broker is outside the scope of this chapter. See the *Oracle Data Guard Concepts and Administration 11g Release 2 (11.2)* documentation for details. In order to manage role-change operations for the Enterprise Manager repository, the latter method should be used, as the Enterprise Manager Cloud Control 12c system would not be available to complete the operations.

It is also possible to configure the management service so that no configuration changes are required after the repository database changes roles (that is, during switchover/failover). Using Oracle Database 11gR2, you can configure services by using the srvctl command-line utility that will be active only when the database is assuming the primary role. The following example illustrates the steps for configuring a database service in a Data Guard configuration for use with the OMS:

1. Create a database service called emrepsrvc on the primary database emrepprim for use with OMS.

    ```
    $ srvctl add service -d emrepprim -s emrepsrvc -l PRIMARY -q FALSE -e NONE -m NONE
    -w 0 -z 0
    ```

2. Verify the configuration of the service.

    ```
    $ srvctl config service -d emreptst -s emrepsrvc
    Service name: emrepsrvc
    Service is enabled
    ```

```
Cardinality: SINGLETON
Disconnect: false
Service role: PRIMARY
Management policy: AUTOMATIC
DTP transaction: false
AQ HA notifications: false
Failover type: NONE
Failover method: NONE
TAF failover retries: 0
TAF failover delay: 0
Connection Load Balancing Goal: LONG
Runtime Load Balancing Goal: NONE
TAF policy specification: NONE
Edition:
```

3. Start and check the status of the service on the primary.

```
$ srvctl start service -d emreptst -s emrepsrvc
$ srvctl status service -d emreptst -s emrepsrvc
Service emrepsrvc is running
```

4. Create the same service on the standby database for use when the role changes to a primary.

```
$ srvctl add service -d emrepsby -s emrepsrvc -l PRIMARY -q FALSE -e NONE -m BASIC
-w 0 -z 0
$ srvctl config service -d emrepsby -s emrepsrvc
Service name: emrepsrvc
Service is enabled
Cardinality: SINGLETON
Disconnect: false
Service role: PRIMARY
Management policy: AUTOMATIC
DTP transaction: false
AQ HA notifications: false
Failover type: NONE
Failover method: BASIC
TAF failover retries: 0
TAF failover delay: 0
Connection Load Balancing Goal: LONG
Runtime Load Balancing Goal: NONE
TAF policy specification: NONE
Edition:
```

5. Reconfigure the OMS to use the new service in the connect descriptor.

```
$OMS_HOME/bin/emctl config oms -store_repos_details -repos_conndesc
'(DESCRIPTION=(FAILOVER=ON)(ADDRESS_LIST=(ADDRESS=(PROTOCOL=TCP)(HOST=oemhost1)
(PORT=1521))
(ADDRESS=(PROTOCOL=TCP)(HOST=oemhost2)(PORT=1521)))(CONNECT_DATA=(SERVICE_NAME=emrepsrvc.
smrcy.com))(FAILOVER_MODE=(TYPE=select)(METHOD=basic)))' -repos_user sysman
```

```
Oracle Enterprise Manager Cloud Control 12c Release 2
Copyright (c) 1996, 2012 Oracle Corporation.  All rights reserved.
Enter Repository User's Password :
Successfully updated datasources and stored repository details in Credential Store.
If there are multiple OMSs in this environment, run this store_repos_details command on
all of them.
And finally, restart all the OMSs using 'emctl stop oms -all' and 'emctl start oms'.
```

6. Stop and Restart the OMS.

   a. To stop the OMS, use emctl stop oms -all:

```
$emctl stop oms -all
Oracle Enterprise Manager Cloud Control 12c Release 2
Copyright (c) 1996, 2012 Oracle Corporation.  All rights reserved.
Stopping WebTier...
WebTier Successfully Stopped
Stopping Oracle Management Server...
Oracle Management Server Successfully Stopped
AdminServer Successfully Stopped
Oracle Management Server is Down
```

   b. To restart, use emctl start oms:

```
$emctl start oms
Oracle Enterprise Manager Cloud Control 12c Release 2
Copyright (c) 1996, 2012 Oracle Corporation.  All rights reserved.
Starting Oracle Management Server...
Starting WebTier...
WebTier Successfully Started
Oracle Management Server Successfully Started
Oracle Management Server is Up
Verify that the new DG connection string is in use
$emctl config oms -list_repos_details
Oracle Enterprise Manager Cloud Control 12c Release 2
Copyright (c) 1996, 2012 Oracle Corporation.  All rights reserved.
Repository Connect Descriptor : (DESCRIPTION=(FAILOVER=ON)(ADDRESS_
LIST=(ADDRESS=(PROTOCOL=TCP)(HOST=oemhost1)(PORT=1521))
(ADDRESS=(PROTOCOL=TCP)(HOST=oemhost2)(PORT=1521)))(CONNECT_DATA=(SERVICE_
NAME=emrepsrvc.smrcy.com))(FAILOVER_MODE=(TYPE=select)(METHOD=basic)))
Repository User : sysman
```

Level 3—Active/Active OMS with SLB and RAC Data Guard Repository

In the previous section, we determined that there would be some downtime while the OMS is failed over to another host. Some environments cannot tolerate such downtime, and so an increased level of availability is required. Fortunately, this can be achieved by using multiple management servers coupled with a RAC database as a repository.

RAC provides both high availability and scalability for the database. You could also consider an active/passive RAC One Node[7] configuration. Additionally, a local physical standby is used to protect the database in the event of a database storage failure. The management services are located behind a Server Load Balancer (SLB). The SLB then directs traffic from the Enterprise Manager console and management agents to an available OMS. Each management server can be installed on separate hosts from the RAC nodes (see Figure 13-16). However, you may need to balance the costs of having separate servers and the level of protection needed for such a configuration. The management servers and repository databases should be in close proximity to each other to reduce network latency. This may dictate that the management servers and RAC database instances coexist on the servers.

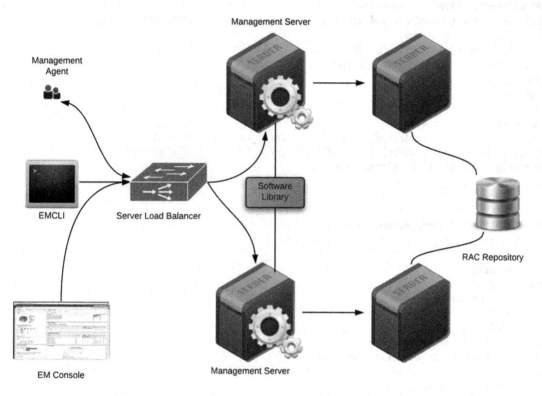

Figure 13-16. *Level 3 high availability with multiple OMSs configured behind a Server Load Balancer and a RAC database management repository*

This level of availability also provides the ability to scale based on business requirements. More OMS servers can be added to scale out, while nodes can be added to the RAC database to scale the repository.

The steps required in setting up a level 3 high-availability configuration are listed here:

1. Install the primary OMS.

2. Configure the SLB.

3. Add repository targets.

---

[7] Oracle RAC One Node is a new option available with Oracle Database 11g Release 2. Oracle RAC One Node is a single instance of an Oracle RAC-enabled database running on one node in a cluster.

4. Configure the Software Library.

5. Add a second OMS.

6. Create a standby database.

7. Convert the standby database to RAC.

After an initial installation of the first OMS, the agents and users connect via the physical hostname:

```
$ $OMS_HOME/bin/emctl status oms -details
Oracle Enterprise Manager Cloud Control 12c Release 2  Copyright (c) 1996, 2012 Oracle
Corporation.  All rights reserved.
Enter Enterprise Manager Root (SYSMAN) Password :
Console Server Host       : oem1.example.com
HTTP Console Port         : 7790
HTTPS Console Port        : 7803
HTTP Upload Port          : 4890
HTTPS Upload Port         : 4904
EM Instance Home          : /u01/app/oracle/Middleware/gc_inst/em/EMGC_OMS1
OMS Log Directory Location : /u01/app/oracle/Middleware/gc_inst/em/EMGC_OMS1/sysman/log
OMS is not configured with SLB or virtual hostname
Agent Upload is locked.
OMS Console is locked.
Active CA ID: 1
Console URL: https://oem1.example.com:443/em
Upload URL: https://oem1.example.com:4904/empbs/upload

WLS Domain Information
Domain Name       : GCDomain
Admin Server Host: oem1.example.com

Managed Server Information
Managed Server Instance Name: EMGC_OMS1
Managed Server Instance Host: oem1.example.com
WebTier is Up
Oracle Management Server is Up
```

When a Server Load Balancer is configured, agent and console traffic is directed to multiple management services by the SLB. The SLB configuration should be done after the installation of the first OMS.

Server Load Balancer Configuration

The configuration of the SLB may vary depending on the manufacturer of the device. However, there are several requirements for the SLB, which are listed here:

> *Virtual server ports*: Four ports should be configured—Secure Upload, Agent Registration, Secure Console and Unsecure Console. If the OMS is configured for only secure upload and agent traffic, then only the Secure Upload and Secure Console virtual server ports are required.

Persistence: HTTP and HTTPS traffic between the Enterprise Manager console and OMS require persistence or "stickiness" so that requests sent to one OMS don't switch to another during the same session. Not having persistence could result in users constantly having to log in as their sessions are handled by different management services.

Application monitoring: Checks the health of the management services so that requests aren't sent to one that is either unavailable or degraded.

In addition to these requirements, some devices may also require additional settings such as F5 BIG-IP TCP Profiles. Table 13-2 shows an example management port configuration using only Secure Upload and Secure Console ports.

Table 13-2. *Management Service Ports*

Cloud Control Service	TCP Port	Monitor Name	Persistent	Pool Name	Load Balancing	Virtual Server Name	Virtual Server Port
Secure Upload	4899	mon_ccsu4899	None	pool_cssu4899	Round Robin	vs_ccsu4899	4899
Secure Console	7803	mon_cssc7803	Source IP	pool_cssc7803	Round Robin	vs_cssc7803	443

The preceding configuration assumes that the Secure Upload port was configured using port 4899 and that the Secure Console port was configured using port 7803. The ports are configured during the OMS installation. Verify that you provide the same ports used during the Enterprise Manager Cloud Control 12c installation. A virtual hostname and IP address are also registered in DNS to allow clients to connect to the SLB.

Next you need to create the following items:

Pools: Groups of two or more OMS servers that are load balanced, with each pool running a different management service

Health monitors: Determines that the service is running and available to accept connections

Virtual servers: A unique IP address and port that represents a pool of servers

After the SLB has been configured, the next step is to configure the OMS to use the SLB. To do this, you need to resecure the management service to regenerate the certificate.

```
emctl secure oms -sysman_pwd <sysman_password> \
     -reg_pwd <agent_reg_password> \
     -host <virtualhostname> \
     -secure_port 4899 \
     -slb_port 4899 \
     -slb_console_port 443 \
     -console \
     -lock_console
```

The following example illustrates securing the OMS with the SLB virtual hostname by using the HTTPS Upload using port 4904 and HTTPS Console port 443. The console is also locked to prevent non-HTTPS traffic from accessing it.

```
$OMS_HOME/bin/emctl secure oms -sysman_pass \
-reg_pwd regpass \
-host slb.example.com \
-secure_port 4904 \
```

```
-slb_port 4904 \
-slb_console_port 443 \
-reset \
-console \
-lock_console
Oracle Enterprise Manager Cloud Control 12c Release 2
Copyright (c) 1996, 2012 Oracle Corporation.  All rights reserved.
Securing OMS... Started.
Securing OMS... Successful
Restart OMS
```

After running these commands, the OMS will need to be restarted.

```
emctl stop oms -all
```

```
emctl start oms
```

To verify that the OMS has been successfully secured, issue the following command:

```
emctl status oms -details
```

The output of this command should indicate that SLB or virtual hostname as well as the ports for the SLB HTTPS Upload and HTTPS Console.

```
$ $OMS_HOME/bin/emctl status oms -details
Oracle Enterprise Manager Cloud Control 12c Release 2  Copyright (c) 1996, 2012 Oracle
Corporation.  All rights reserved.
Enter Enterprise Manager Root (SYSMAN) Password :
Console Server Host      : oem1.example.com
HTTP Console Port        : 7790
HTTPS Console Port       : 7803
HTTP Upload Port         : 4890
HTTPS Upload Port        : 4904
EM Instance Home         : /u01/app/oracle/Middleware/gc_inst/em/EMGC_OMS1
OMS Log Directory Location : /u01/app/oracle/Middleware/gc_inst/em/EMGC_OMS1/sysman/log
SLB or virtual hostname: slb.example.com
HTTPS SLB Upload Port : 4904
HTTPS SLB Console Port : 443
Agent Upload is locked.
OMS Console is locked.
Active CA ID: 1
Console URL: https://slb.example.com:443/em
Upload URL: https://slb.example.com:4904/empbs/upload

WLS Domain Information
Domain Name      : GCDomain
Admin Server Host: oem1.example.com

Managed Server Information
Managed Server Instance Name: EMGC_OMS1
Managed Server Instance Host: oem1.example.com
WebTier is Up
Oracle Management Server is Up
```

Users can now access the server by using the virtual hostname https://slb.example.com. Port 443 is the default HTTPS port, so it is not necessary to specify the port number. If another port is selected as the secure port, it should be specified as part of the URL. Any agents that were previously deployed and configured to upload to the physical hostname of the OMS will be required to be resecured also. Use the following command to resecure the agents:

```
emctl secure agent -emdWalletSrcUrl https://slb.example.com:4899/em
```

After securing the agent, check the status to verify that it is uploading to the SLB Upload port by checking the REPOSITORY_URL property.

```
$ $AGENT_HOME/core/12.1.0.2.0/bin/emctl status agent
Oracle Enterprise Manager Cloud Control 12c Release 2
Copyright (c) 1996, 2012 Oracle Corporation.  All rights reserved.
----------------------------------------------------------------
Agent Version      : 12.1.0.2.0
OMS Version        : 12.1.0.2.0
Protocol Version   : 12.1.0.1.0
Agent Home         : /u02/app/oracle/agent12c/agent_inst
Agent Binaries     : /u02/app/oracle/agent12c/core/12.1.0.2.0
Agent Process ID   : 19494
Parent Process ID  : 19454
Agent URL          : https://oem1.example.com:3872/emd/main/
Repository URL     : https://slb.example.com:4904/empbs/upload
Started at         : 2012-11-03 12:44:10
Started by user    : oracle
Last Reload        : (none)
Last successful upload                       : 2012-11-03 12:47:04
Last attempted upload                        : 2012-11-03 12:47:05
Total Megabytes of XML files uploaded so far : 1.09
Number of XML files pending upload           : 44
Size of XML files pending upload(MB)         : 0.64
Available disk space on upload filesystem    : 44.63%
Collection Status                            : Collections enabled
Heartbeat Status                             : Ok
Last attempted heartbeat to OMS              : 2012-11-03 12:46:09
Last successful heartbeat to OMS             : 2012-11-03 12:46:09
Next scheduled heartbeat to OMS              : 2012-11-03 12:47:09


----------------------------------------------------------------
Agent is Running and Ready
```

Likewise, if EMCLI was previously configured, it also needs to be reconfigured to use the SLB:

```
emcli setup -url=https://slb.example.com/em -username=sysman
```

Additional OMS Installation

The next step is to install additional management services. This can be done by using either the Add Additional OMS Deployment Procedure (recommended) or Silent Mode. See the *Oracle Enterprise Manager Cloud Control Advanced Installation and Configuration Guide* for details on using Silent Mode installation.

The deployment procedure simplifies the process of deploying additional management servers to meet high-availability requirements. It automates the steps required to prepare and install additional management services by collecting input via a wizard-driven interface. It will clone the existing middleware home, including the OMS configuration based on the collected input. Any additional servers should also meet the same requirements for installing an OMS. See Chapter 8 of the *Oracle Enterprise Manager Cloud Control Basic Installation Guide 12c Release 2* for prerequisites for the additional management service.

■ **Note** Any new servers that are intended to be used as an OMS should already have the agent deployed. The deployment procedures will not clone an agent to the target.

Follow these steps to install an Additional OMS

1. From the Enterprise Manager console, choose Enterprise ➤ Provisioning and Patching ➤ Procedure Library, as shown in Figure 13-17.

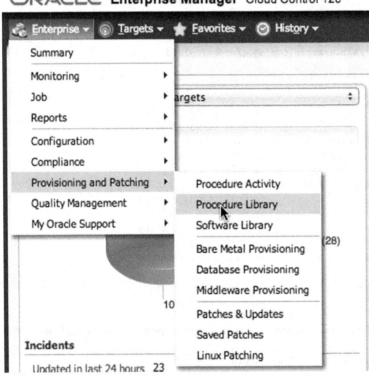

Figure 13-17. *Accessing the Procedure Library*

2. Select the Add Management Service radio button and click Launch (see Figure 13-18). You can sort the columns by the name of the Procedure by clicking if the procedure is not visible in the list.

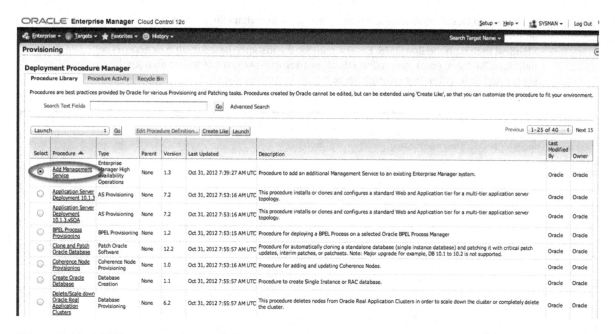

Figure 13-18. *Add Management Service deployment procedure*

3. The next screen, shown in Figure 13-19, lists the prerequisites that should be met before continuing with the procedure. Select all the check boxes associated with the prerequisites already met. If any are not met, you should resolve them first before continuing with the processors. Click Next when you are finished.

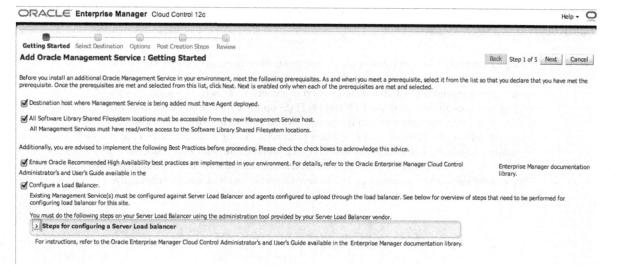

Figure 13-19. *Add Oracle Management Service prerequisite checks*

4. On the Select Destination screen, choose a managed host that will be used as the additional OMS, as shown in Figure 13-20. The path for the Middleware home will be identical to that on the first OMS. Enter a path for the instance base location or accept the defaults. Choose or enter the credentials of the user who owns the software on both the source and destination (for example, `oracle`).

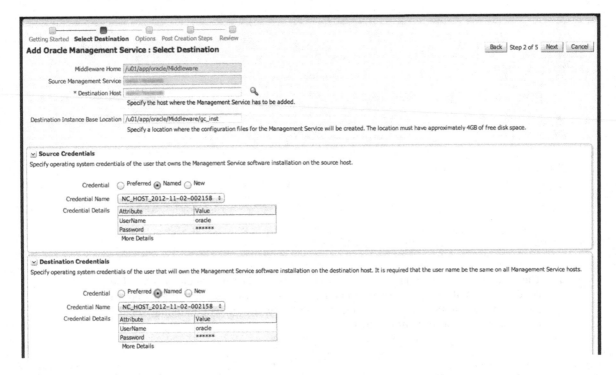

Figure 13-20. *Add OMS, Select Destination*

5. Next you will choose how to transfer the cloned home from the source OMS host to the destination host and select the staging locations (see Figure 13-21). The staging locations should have a minimum of 4GB free. If a shared filesystem such as NFS is selected, no staging locations are required. For FTP and HTTP(S) options, there also needs to be 8GB of free space in the operating system temporary location (`/tmp` in Unix or Linux or `C:\Temp` in Windows). See Chapter 9 of the *Oracle Enterprise Manager Cloud Control Basic Installation Guide 12c Release 2* for details on specifying the temporary location. In addition, you need to provide the ports to be used for the destination management service. They will default to the source management service ports. We recommend keeping the ports on all management services identical if possible.

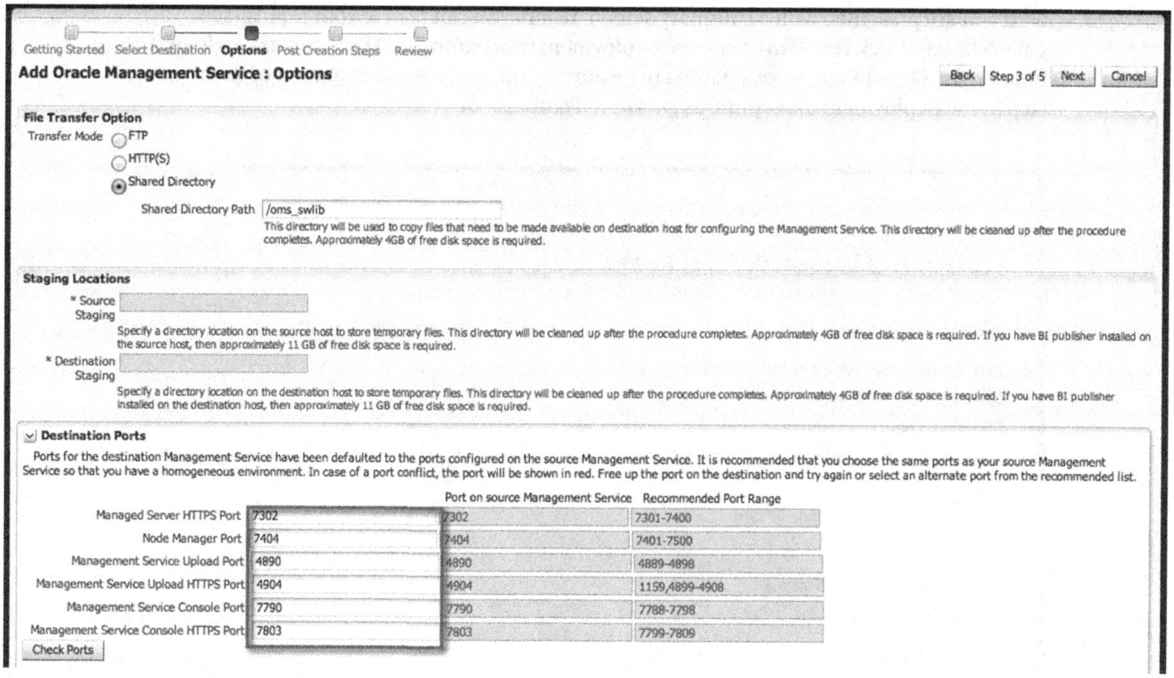

Figure 13-21. *Add OMS, Options*

6. The Post Creation Steps screen, shown in Figure 13-22, lists the requirements for setting up the SLB to include the new OMS host if that has not been done. The root.sh script also must be executed. Optionally, you may provide an e-mail address to receive post-installation steps.

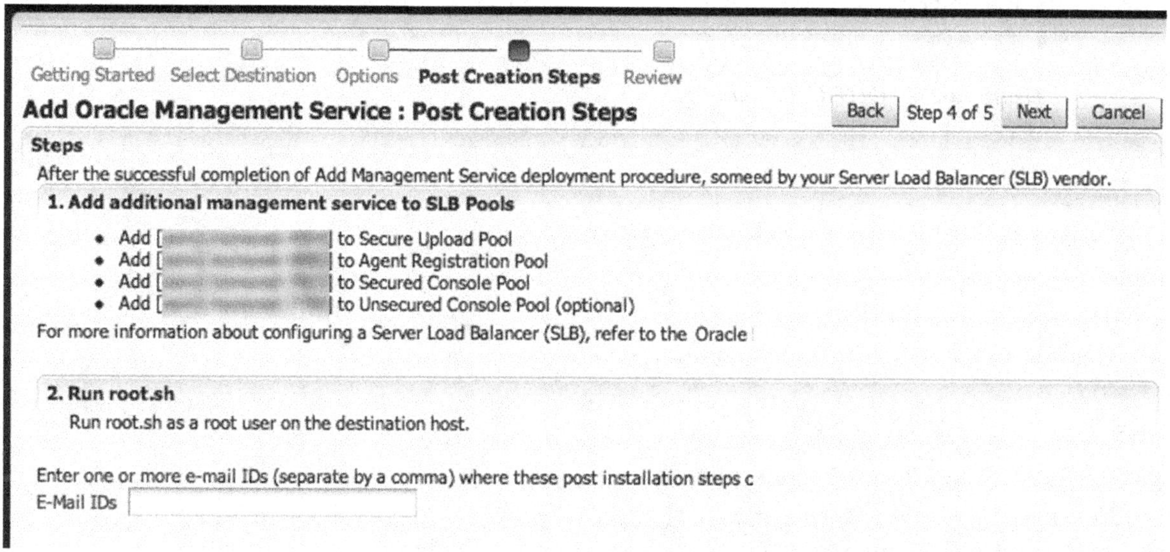

Figure 13-22. *Add OMS, Post Creation Steps*

7. Next you are presented with a summary screen, where you can review your inputs (see Figure 13-23). Click Finish to create the deployment procedure job. This could take a long time to run, depending on your hardware resources. You can view the progress of each step in the deployment procedure, as shown in Figure 13-24.

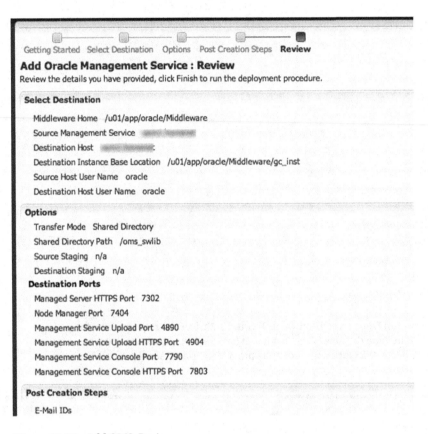

Figure 13-23. *Add OMS, Review*

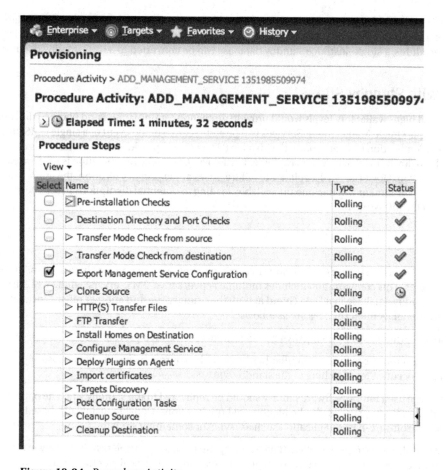

Figure 13-24. *Procedure Activity*

If any step fails, you should review it and perform the necessary corrective actions before resuming or retrying. If you provided an e-mail address for the post-installation steps notification, you will be provided with steps to configure the SLB with the newly added OMS and to execute the root.sh script.

The following new targets are discovered automatically in the Enterprise Manager console:

- Oracle WebLogic Server

- Oracle Web Tier

- Application deployments

- Oracle Management Service

- Oracle Management Agent

- Enterprise Manager Cloud Control host

Any other existing targets on the host should be promoted via Add Manual Target or Auto Discovery Results.

After the additional management service has been configured, the next step in the high-availability configuration is to use Data Guard to create a local physical standby database for the repository. The Oracle MAA architecture recommends a RAC physical standby, but a single-instance standby can be used as well. The standby database will protect against storage, media corruption, or any incident that results in a loss of the primary database.

The standby database can be added by using the same procedure as described in the level 2 high-availability section of this chapter. Using Enterprise Manager Cloud Control, it is not possible to create a RAC standby. However, using deployment procedures, a single-instance standby database can be converted to a RAC standby database.

Level 4—MAA with Standby Site

The previously described high-availability levels would provide protection for unplanned and planned downtime. Using an SLB with multiple Oracle Management Services will provide service in the event of a single OMS becoming unavailable. Using Real Application Clusters coupled with a local Data Guard provides the highest levels of availability for the repository with no downtime if a host is unavailable. If a failover or switchover operation is performed, minimal downtime will occur. However, if a complete site failure arises at the primary location, the entire Enterprise Manager Cloud Control environment will become unavailable, leading to potential disruptions in service for other applications that rely on the infrastructure.

Prerequisites

Configuring a standby Enterprise Manager Cloud Control system at a separate site provides high availability and protects against site failures. This configuration includes multiple active/active OMS servers behind a SLB in addition to a RAC primary and standby database in a Data Guard at both the primary site and another off-site location. Prerequisites for standby management services are as follows:

- Configure the primary site by using MAA configuration, as described previously.

- Configure the standby site by using similar hardware and resources to ensure that no loss of performance occurs after switching to the standby site.

- Shared storage used for the Software Library should be replicated to the standby site. The path for the Software Library should also be identical at both locations. Consider using disk-based replication or software-based replication such as rsync[8] or something similar.

- A second SLB should also be deployed at the standby site to ensure complete redundancy in a disaster recovery environment. Use vendor solutions that provide VIP failover from primary to standby sites.

After these prerequisites have been met, install and configure the standby management services by using instructions in the *Oracle Enterprise Manager Cloud Control 12c Administrator's Guide*.

Standby Management Server Installation

To install a standby management server, you perform a software-only installation by using either a modified version of the Add Management Service deployment procedures from the Procedure Library or Oracle Universal Installer. The next example walks you through the steps used in the former method.

If a firewall exists between the primary and standby sites, it should be configured to allow communication for the HTTP Console, HTTPS Console, HTTP Agent Upload, and HTTPS Agent Upload ports as well as the Admin Server and Node Manager ports.

---

[8] rsync is software that enables replication of files and directories from one system to another while minimizing data transfer through the use of deltas.

The following deployment procedure provides a step-by-step workflow for cloning the primary Enterprise Manager software including plug-ins and patches to another server:

1. Copy the emkey to the management repository by running this command on the first management service (with the Admin Server running):

```
$ $OMS_HOME/bin/emctl config emkey -copy_to_repos
Oracle Enterprise Manager Cloud Control 12c Release 2
Copyright (c) 1996, 2012 Oracle Corporation.  All rights reserved.
Enter Enterprise Manager Root (SYSMAN) Password :
The EMKey has been copied to the Management Repository. This operation will cause
the EMKey to become unsecure.
After the required operation has been completed, secure the EMKey by running
"emctl config emkey -remove_from_repos".
```

2. Export the configuration from the first management service on the primary site. Use a shared filesystem if possible to eliminate transferring files remotely.

```
$ $OMS_HOME/bin/emctl exportconfig oms -sysman_pwd oracle12c -dir /u02/backup
Oracle Enterprise Manager Cloud Control 12c Release 2
Copyright (c) 1996, 2012 Oracle Corporation.  All rights reserved.
ExportConfig started...
Machine is Admin Server host. Performing Admin Server backup...
Exporting emoms properties...
Exporting secure properties...
Exporting configuration for pluggable modules...
Preparing archive file...
Backup has been written to file: /u02/backup/opf_ADMIN_20121227_131133.bka

The export file contains sensitive data.
Please ensure that it is kept secure.

ExportConfig completed successfully!
```

3. Install a management agent on the target standby host if one does not already exist.

4. Perform a software-only installation of the Enterprise Manager software by using the modified Add Standby Management Service deployment procedure.

   a. From the menu, choose Enterprise ➤ Provisioning and Patching.

   b. Choose the Add Management Service procedure and click Create Like, as shown in Figure 13-25.

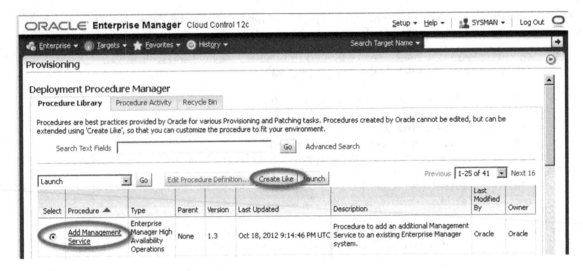

Figure 13-25. *Creating a deployment procedure for the standby management service*

    c.   Enter a new name for the procedure, such as **Add Standby Management Service**. See Figure 13-26.

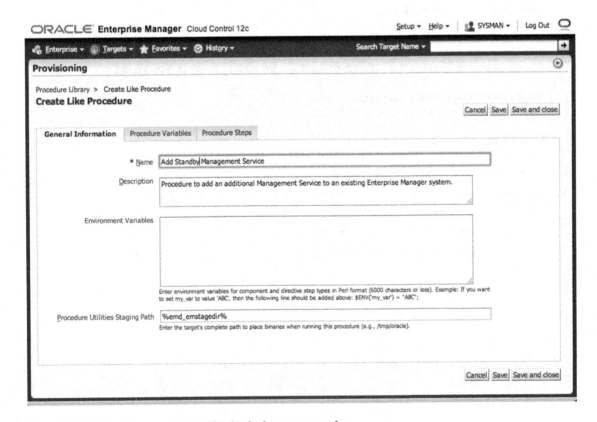

Figure 13-26. *Providing a new name for the deployment procedure*

d. Navigate to the Procedure Step tab and disable the steps (see Figure 13-27):

- Configure Management Service

- Targets Discovery

- Post Configuration Tasks

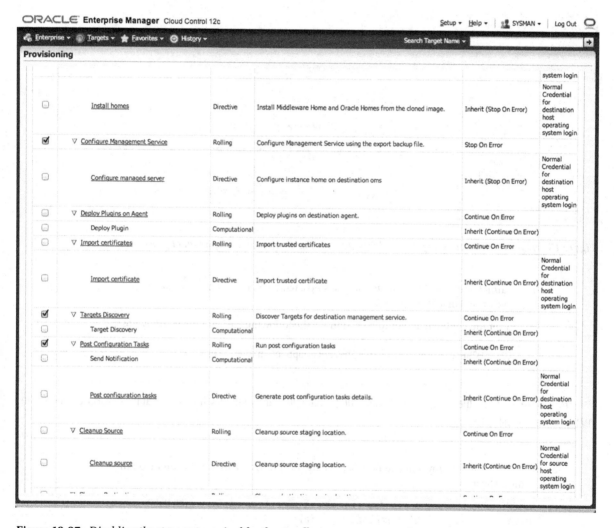

Figure 13-27. *Disabling the steps not required for the standby management service*

e. Save the deployment procedure. The new procedure should appear similar to Figure 13-28.

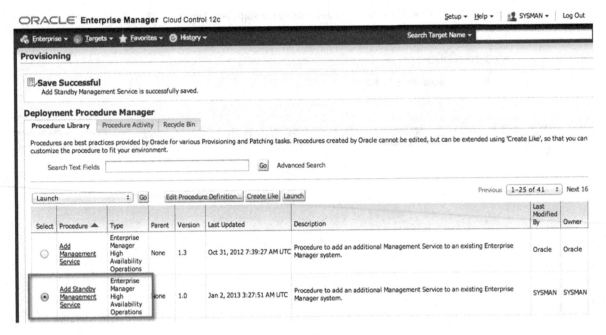

Figure 13-28. *Successful creation of the Add Standby Management Service deployment procedure*

f.   Launch the procedure and follow the steps, which will be identical to the ones performed in adding an OMS.

g.   After the deployment completes, remove the following file from the standby host:

```
<OMS_HOME>/sysman/config/emInstanceMapping.properties
```

■ **Note**   Make sure that the `/tmp` filesystems on the primary and target standby hosts have at least 4GB free. If not, the OMS installation will fail.

---

5.   Configure the standby management service by running `omsca` in standby mode on the standby host.

```
$ $OMS_HOME/bin/omsca standby -EM_DOMAIN_NAME GCDomainStby -NM_USER \
nodemanager -AS_USERNAME weblogic -nostart
Oracle Enterprise Manager Cloud Control 12c Release 12.1.0.2.0
Copyright (c) 1996, 2012, Oracle. All rights reserved.

Enter Admin Server Host Name[oem3.example.com]:
Enter Admin Server HTTPS Port[7101]:
Enter Admin Server user password:
Confirm Password:
Enter EM instance host [oem3.example.com]:
Enter Upload HTTP PORT[4889]:
Enter Upload HTTPS PORT[4899]:
```

```
Enter location for OMS config files[/u01/oracle/gc_inst]:/u01/oracle/Middleware/gc_inst
Enter Node Manager Password:
Confirm Password:
Enter Repository database host name:oem.example.com
Enter Repository database listener port:1521
Enter Repository database SID:oemprd1
Enter Repository database user password:
Enter Agent Registration password:
Confirm Password:
Doing pre requisite checks ......
Pre requisite checks completed successfully

Doing infrastructure setup ......
Infrastructure setup of EM completed successfully.

Doing pre deployment operations ......
Pre deployment of EM completed successfully.

Deploying EM ......
Deployment of EM completed successfully.

Configuring webtier ......
Configuring webTier completed successfully.

Securing OMS ......
EM Key is secured and is backed up at /u01/oracle/Middleware/oms/sysman/config/emkey.ora
Adapter created successfully: emgc_USER
Adapter created successfully: emgc_GROUP
Post "Deploy and Repos Setup" operations completed successfully.

Performing Post deploy operations ....
Total 0 errors, 0 warnings. 0 entities imported.
pluginID:oracle.sysman.core
Done with csg import
pluginID:oracle.sysman.core
Done with csg import
Post deploy operations completed successfully.

EM configuration completed successfully.
EM URL is:https://oem.example.com:7799/em
```

6. Configure plug-ins by running this command:

```
pluginca -action deploy -isFirstOMS true -plugins <plugin-list> -oracleHome
<oms oracle home> -middlewareHome <wls middleware home>
```

- The following query should be used to get the list of plug-ins:

```
SELECT epv.plugin_id, epv.version FROM em_plugin_version epv,
       em_current_deployed_plugin ecp
```

```
WHERE epv.plugin_type NOT IN ( 'BUILT_IN_TARGET_TYPE' , 'INSTALL_HOME')
      AND ecp.dest_type='2'
      AND epv.plugin_version_id = ecp.plugin_version_id;
```

- The plug-ins should be a comma-separated list of this format:

```
<plugin-id>=<plugin-version>,<plugin-id>=<plugin-version>,...
```

- A query such as the following can be used to extract the plug-ins in the required format:

```
SELECT listagg(epv.plugin_id||'='||epv.version,',')
      within group (order by epv.plugin_id)
FROM em_plugin_version epv, em_current_deployed_plugin ecp
WHERE epv.plugin_type NOT IN ( 'BUILT_IN_TARGET_TYPE' , 'INSTALL_HOME')
      AND ecp.dest_type='2'
      AND epv.plugin_version_id = ecp.plugin_version_id;
```

- The results of the query can then be used as the plugins argument in pluginca:

```
$ $OMS_HOME/bin/pluginca -action deploy -isFirstOMS true -plugins "oracle.sysman.
db=12.1.0.2.0,oracle.sysman.emas=12.1.0.3.0,oracle.sysman.mos=12.1.0.2.0,
oracle.sysman.xa=12.1.0.3.0" -oracleHome $OMS_HOME -middlewareHome $MW_HOME
pluginca - Plugin Configuration Tool
Oracle Enterprise Manager 12c Release 2 Grid Control
Copyright (c) 1996, 2012 Oracle Corporation. All rights reserved.
Log file: /u01/oracle/Middleware/oms/cfgtoollogs/pluginca/gcinstall/configplugin_
deploy_2013-01-02_14-42-39.log
Trace file: /u01/oracle/Middleware/oms/cfgtoollogs/pluginca/gcinstall/configplugin_
deploy_2013-01-02_14-42-39.trc
Initializing PluginCA.
Options passed: -loglevel debug -action deploy -isfirstoms true -plugins oracle.
sysman.db=12.1.0.2.0,oracle.sysman.emas=12.1.0.3.0,oracle.sysman.mos=12.1.0.2.0,
oracle.sysman.xa=12.1.0.3.0 -oraclehome /u01/oracle/Middleware/oms –middlewarehome
/u01/oracle/Middleware
Starting Deployment
Invoking pre deploy callbacks.
OMS state could be found. It is down
Performing Midtier deconfig
Performing Midtier config
Performing Opss deconfig
Performing Opss config
Performing Post metadata registration
Performing Midtier update oh prop
Performing Post config module
Invoking post deploy callbacks.
Completed Deployment
```

7. Import the configuration exported from the primary management service in step 2. If the configuration was exported to a local filesystem, copy it over to the standby host first.

```
$OMS_HOME/bin/emctl importconfig oms -file /u02/backup/opf_ADMIN_20121227_131133.bka
Oracle Enterprise Manager Cloud Control 12c Release 2
Copyright (c) 1996, 2012 Oracle Corporation.  All rights reserved.
ImportConfig started...
Enter Enterprise Manager Root (SYSMAN) Password :
Enter Agent Registration Password:
Processing export file...
Checking OS and OMS Versions...
OS check passed.
OMS version check passed.
Proceed with oms import...
Backing up the OMS before import...
Pre-import backup of OMS failed...
Error: null

Do you wish to continue with import? (y/n)
y
Continuing with Importconfig...
Updating OMS properties...
Configuring emoms.properties...
Processing zipped files...

If you have software library configured
please make sure it is functional and accessible
from this OMS by visiting:
 Setup->Change Management->Software Library

Resecure the OMS...
OMS secured!
ImportConfig completed successfully!
```

8. Stop the standby OMS.

```
emctl stop oms
```

9. From the primary Enterprise Manager console, add the WebLogic Domain and associated targets by using the Add Manual Targets Guided Discovery to discover Fusion Middleware targets on the standby host.

10. Configure Single Sign On on the standby if previously configured on the primary. This includes Active Directory authentication for Enterprise Manager Cloud Control administrators.

11. Perform configuration of any additional components such as BI Publisher or Real User Experience Insight if configured on the primary.

Standby Management Server Post-Installation

One caveat of having a standby site is the additional administrative overhead required. The standby site has to be kept in sync with the primary site after the initial configuration. For the repository database, Data Guard handles synchronization automatically. Patches applied to the software homes on the primary also need to be applied at the standby site. Any database scripts executed on the primary as part of the patching process are handled by Data Guard and should not be executed again on the standby site. Plug-ins deployed or updated on the primary site are also required to be deployed and updated on the standby site. Failing to do so will cause the OMS to fail to start up if a switchover is attempted. See the *Oracle Enterprise Manager Cloud Control Administrator's Guide 12c Release 2* for details on plug-in deployment and upgrades on the standby site.

In addition to the preceding changes, the SYSMAN credentials should be kept in sync on the primary and standby sites. If this is not done, role transitions will fail on the standby OMS. To change the SYSMAN credentials on the primary and standby OMS, follow these steps:

1. Change the SYSMAN password on the primary OMS.

```
$ emctl config oms -change_repos_pwd
Oracle Enterprise Manager Cloud Control 12c Release 2
Copyright (c) 1996, 2012 Oracle Corporation.  All rights reserved.
Enter Repository User's Current Password :
Enter Repository User's New Password :

Changing passwords in backend ...
Passwords changed in backend successfully.
Updating repository password in Credential Store...
Successfully updated Repository password in Credential Store.
Restart all the OMSs using 'emctl stop oms -all' and 'emctl start oms'.
Successfully changed repository password.
```

2. Stop the OMS, including Admin Server.

```
$ emctl stop oms -all
Oracle Enterprise Manager Cloud Control 12c Release 2
Copyright (c) 1996, 2012 Oracle Corporation.  All rights reserved.
Stopping WebTier...
WebTier Successfully Stopped
Stopping Oracle Management Server...
Oracle Management Server Already Stopped
AdminServer Successfully Stopped
Oracle Management Server is Down
```

3. Start the OMS.

```
$ emctl start oms
Oracle Enterprise Manager Cloud Control 12c Release 2
Copyright (c) 1996, 2012 Oracle Corporation.  All rights reserved.
Starting Oracle Management Server...
Starting WebTier...
WebTier Successfully Started
Oracle Management Server Successfully Started
Oracle Management Server is Up
```

4. Change the SYSMAN password on the standby OMS.

```
$ emctl config oms -change_repos_pwd -use_sys_pwd -sys_pwd <sys_password>
Oracle Enterprise Manager Cloud Control 12c Release 2
Copyright (c) 1996, 2012 Oracle Corporation.  All rights reserved.
Enter Repository User's New Password :
```

```
Changing passwords in backend ...
Passwords changed in backend successfully.
Updating repository password in Credential Store...
Successfully updated Repository password in Credential Store.
Restart all the OMSs using 'emctl stop oms -all' and 'emctl start oms'.
Successfully changed repository password.
```

5. Stop the OMS, including the Admin Server.

```
$ emctl stop oms -all
Oracle Enterprise Manager Cloud Control 12c Release 2
Copyright (c) 1996, 2012 Oracle Corporation.  All rights reserved.
Stopping WebTier...
WebTier Successfully Stopped
Stopping Oracle Management Server...
Error occurred while trying to stop Oracle Management Server
AdminServer Successfully Stopped
Oracle Management Server is Down
```

6. Start the Admin Server.

```
$ emctl start oms -admin_only
Oracle Enterprise Manager Cloud Control 12c Release 2
Copyright (c) 1996, 2012 Oracle Corporation.  All rights reserved.
Starting Admin Server only...
Admin Server Successfully Started
```

Software Library

The Software Library is used for patching, agent deployment, provisioning, and self-updating. It should be installed on shared storage so that multiple management servers can access it. Any of the following options can be used for shared storage:

- NFS

- OCFS2

- DBFS

- ACFS

Because the Software Library is so critical, it should be located on a highly available file system. This means using a RAID (mirrored and striped) back-end storage system.

The Software Library can be configured by logging into the Enterprise Manager console and choosing Setup ➤ Provisioning and Patching ➤ Software Library. Choose a location on a shared filesystem that has been mounted on the OMS for the Software Library (see Figure 13-29). Multiple locations can also be added.

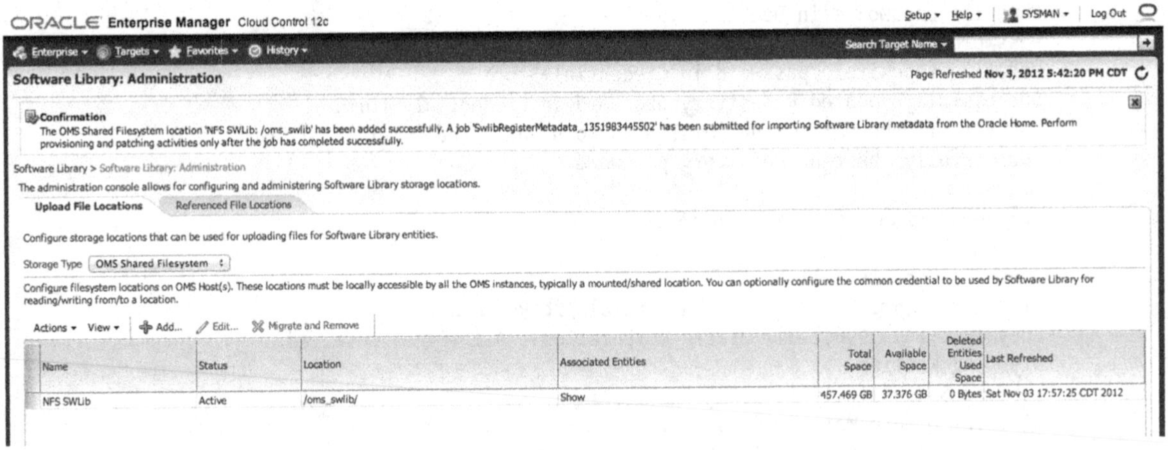

Figure 13-29. *Software Library setup*

Backup

In a highly available Enterprise Manager Cloud Control configuration, the three components—OMS, repository, and agent—are individually configured to reduce downtime. Although we recommend that the highest level of availability be implemented, the associated costs and required resources may be prohibitive. Also, in any IT framework, failure of components is likely to happen over time. As such, no high-availability architecture is complete without discussing backup and recovery strategies.

Backing up the Enterprise Manager ecosystem requires a solution that encompasses the repository, OMS, and agents. Each component is individually backed up based on its available methods. The management repository database stores metrics and data provided by agents. It should be backed up according to recommended backup strategies for Oracle databases using RMAN.

Repository Backup

The first step in configuring a backup strategy for the repository database is to ensure that it is in ARCHIVELOG mode. This will allow consistent online backups to be taken and also facilitates point-in-time recovery of the database. Hot backups should be taken regularly using recommended backup strategies. Database high-availability features such as the Fast Recovery Area and flashback database should also be enabled to allow for faster recovery of the database in the event of a failure. Backups can be configured by using the Enterprise Manager Cloud Control console. Consider using Enterprise Manager's Recommended Backup Strategy option to back up the repository database.

To schedule a database backup using Enterprise Manager, follow these steps:

1. Go to the repository database home page and choose Availability ➤ Backup & Recovery ➤ Schedule Backup.

2. Log in as a user with SYSDBA credentials.

3. Click the Schedule Oracle-Suggested Backup button to create a fully automated backup strategy based on the destination for the backups (Disk, Tape, and so forth), as shown in Figure 13-30. The Oracle-suggested backup is based on an incrementally updated backup strategy. It will schedule a full backup first, after which incremental backups will be scheduled. Based on the backup, a recovery to any point in a day will be possible.

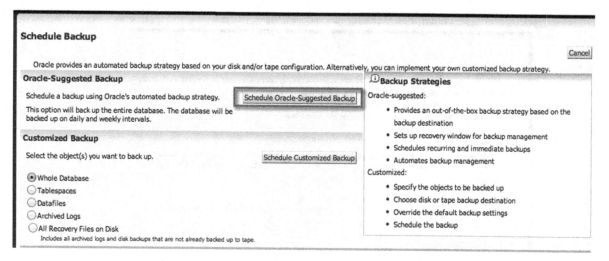

Figure 13-30. *Scheduling an Oracle-suggested backup*

■ **Note** If a disk-based backup strategy is used, Oracle recommends using the Fast Recovery Area to enable faster recovery.

---

4. Select the destination media for the backup, as shown in Figure 13-31.

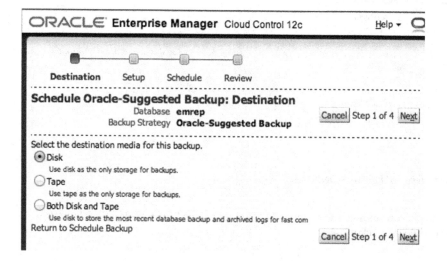

Figure 13-31. *Scheduling a backup destination type*

5. Enter the location for the backup, as shown in Figure 13-32. In a disk-based backup strategy, the default is to use the Fast Recovery Area if it has been configured.

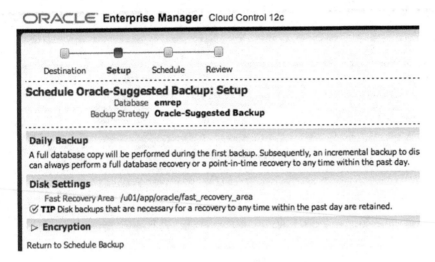

Figure 13-32. *Choose the Fast Recovery Area as the disk-based backup location*

6. Enter a schedule for the recurring backup, as shown in Figure 13-33.

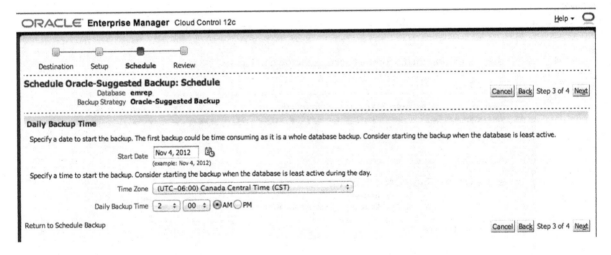

Figure 13-33. *Oracle-suggested backup schedule*

7. Review the Backup Settings and generated RMAN script (see Figure 13-34). Click Submit Job to schedule the backup.

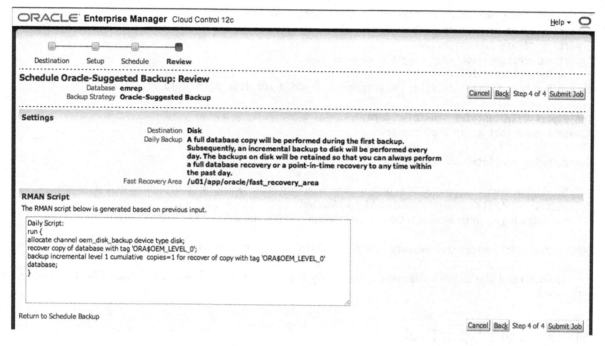

Figure 13-34. *Oracle-suggested backup settings*

Using Oracle Enterprise Manager Cloud Control to schedule the backup job also enables you to receive notifications about the job status as well as view backup information including run times and time of last backup.

Oracle Management Service Backup

The Oracle Management Service is responsible for communicating with management agents and uploading data to the management repository. It includes the Oracle Fusion Middleware home, the OMS home, and the Web Tier (OHS) Oracle home in addition to plug-in homes. The OMS filesystem should be backed up periodically to preserve any changes such as patches, updates, or configuration changes. Use the `exportconfig` command to back up the OMS instance home (`MW_HOME/gc_inst`) including the WebLogic Server, Web Tier, and Administration Server. To create a backup of the instance and all subcomponents, use the following syntax:

```
emctl exportconfig oms [-sysman_pwd <sysman password>]
    [-dir <backup dir>]        Specify directory to store backup file
    [-oms_only]                Specify OMS-only backup on Admin Server host
    [-keep_host]               Specify to backup hostname if no slb defined
                               (Use this option only if recovery will be done
                                 on machine that responds to this hostname)
```

The following example backs up the OMS configuration to a shared directory. An archive is created with a `.bka` extension.

```
$ $OMS_HOME/bin/emctl exportconfig oms -sysman_pwd oracle12c -dir /mnt/backup
Oracle Enterprise Manager Cloud Control 12c Release 2
Copyright (c) 1996, 2012 Oracle Corporation.  All rights reserved.
ExportConfig started...
```

```
Machine is Admin Server host. Performing Admin Server backup...
Exporting emoms properties...
Exporting secure properties...
Exporting configuration for pluggable modules...
Preparing archive file...
Backup has been written to file: /mnt/backup/opf_ADMIN_20121104_224806.bka

The export file contains sensitive data.
Please ensure that it is kept secure.

ExportConfig completed successfully!
```

In addition to backing up the OMS configuration, a backup of the Oracle inventory and output of the opatch lsinventory -detail command should also be performed.

The following example generates the opatch inventory output and writes it to a shared filesystem.

```
$OMS_HOME/OPatch/opatch lsinventory -detail > /mnt/backups/opatch_bkup.log
```

The backup of the OMS can either be done manually or scheduled via the Enterprise Manager Cloud Control Job System.

Management Agent Backup

The management agents are stateless, so no backups are necessary. Instead, a reference gold image of the agent should be created for all platforms being monitored. Any patches and customizations should be included in the gold configuration. In the event that a management agent is lost, it should be installed from the reference gold image.

Recovery

Performing regular backups of each Enterprise Manager Cloud Control component is important. However, of even more significance is the ability to restore the components successfully if needed. Enterprise Manager recovery may require recovery of several components including the repository, management service, and agents depending on the nature of the problem. For example, recovering the management service in a scenario where the host is lost may require additional steps compared with restoring the management service to the original host. You will examine these scenarios in the following sections.

Repository Recovery

The Cloud Control console will be unavailable in the event that the OMS is down. To restore the repository database, the RMAN command-line utility should be used. With RMAN, you can restore the database by using either a full recovery or a point-in-time recovery (see the *Oracle Database Backup and Recovery Guide*). In the case of the latter, you may need to resynchronize agents that are out of sync with the repository. To resynchronize the agent by using EMCTL, use the following syntax:

```
emctl resync repos (-full|-agentlist "agent names")
[-name "resync name"]
[-sysman_pwd "sysman password"]
```

This command should be executed after the management repository has been restored and before starting the OMS.

The steps required to make Enterprise Manager Cloud Control operational after restoring the repository database will vary depending on whether a full or incomplete recovery is performed as well as whether the recovery was done on the same host or a different host. Table 13-3 summarizes the steps required for the different recovery scenarios. In each scenario, the repository database should be recovered after stopping the OMS.

Table 13-3. Recovery Scenarios for OMS, Repository, and Agent

	Full Recovery on Same Host	Incomplete Recovery on Same Host	Full Recovery on Different Host	Incomplete Recovery on Different Host
Repository resync	No	Yes	No	Yes
OMS reconfig	No	No	Yes	Yes
Relocate Management repository target	No	No	Yes	Yes
OMS and repository monitoring reconfig	No	No	Yes	Yes

OMS reconfiguration is required whenever the repository database is recovered on a different host. This stores the new database connection description in the OMS. We use the following command to reconfigure the repository database in the OMS:

```
emctl config oms -store_repos_details (-repos_host <host> -repos_port <port> -repos_sid
<sid> | -repos_conndesc <connect descriptor>) -repos_user <username> [-repos_pwd <pwd>]
```

Follow these steps to reconfigure the OMS:

1. Stop all the OMSs.

   ```
   emctl stop oms
   ```

2. Reconfigure the repository connection string on each of the OMSs.

   ```
   emctl config oms -store_repos_details
   ```

3. Restart Admin Server and all the OMSs by using the following:

   ```
   emctl stop oms -all
   emctl start oms
   ```

Recovering the repository on a different host also requires relocating the management repository database target to a different agent running on the new host. This can be done only if an agent already exists on the host and no other database has been discovered by it. Use the following syntax to relocate the target to a new host:

```
emctl config repos [-sysman_pwd <sysman password>]
       [-agent <new agent>]    Specify new destination agent for repository target
       [-host <new host>]      Specify new hostname for repository target
       [-oh <new oracle home>] Specify new OracleHome for repository target
```

```
[-conn_desc [<jdbc connect descriptor>]]
                         Update Connect Descriptor with value if specified,
                         else from value stored in emoms.properties
[-ignore_timeskew]       ignores timeskew on agent
```

The monitoring configuration for the OMS and repository target should also be updated by using this command:

```
emctl config emrep [-sysman_pwd <sysman password>]
      [-agent <new agent>]    Specify new destination agent for emrep target
      [-conn_desc [<jdbc connect descriptor>]]
                              Update Connect Descriptor with value if specified,
                              else from value stored in emoms.properties
      [-ignore_timeskew]      ignores timeskew on agent
```

After the database has been recovered and reconfiguration performed, the next step would be to log in to the Enterprise Manager Cloud Control console and verify that all operations have been restored.

Oracle Management Service Recovery

Recovering an OMS requires recovery of both the software homes (Fusion Middleware) and the instance homes (gc_inst). The software homes can either be recovered from a filesystem backup or be reinstalled using the Install Software Only option on the same or a different host using the Enterprise Manager Cloud Control 12c installer. The OMS home must be in the same location as the OMS home being recovered.

All plug-ins that existed in the OMS are required to be installed for the recovery to succeed. The following SQL query should be run as the SYSMAN user:

```
SELECT epv.display_name, epv.plugin_id, epv.version, epv.rev_version,decode(su.aru_file,
null, 'Media/External', 'https://updates.oracle.com/Orion/Services/download/'
||aru_file||'?aru='||aru_id||chr(38)||'patch_file='||aru_file) URL
FROM em_plugin_version epv, em_current_deployed_plugin ecp, em_su_entities su
WHERE epv.plugin_type NOT IN ('BUILT_IN_TARGET_TYPE', 'INSTALL_HOME')
AND ecp.dest_type='2'
AND epv.plugin_version_id = ecp.plugin_version_id
AND su.entity_id = epv.su_entity_id;
```

The following example output shows the plug-ins, versions, revisions, and URLs. The URL will display if downloaded via Self Update. Otherwise, the status will be Media/External.

```
SQL>
```

DISPLAY_NAME	PLUGIN_ID	VERSION	REV_VERSION	URL
Oracle MOS (My Oracle Support)	oracle.sysman.mos	12.1.0.2.0	0	Media/External
Oracle Fusion Middleware	oracle.sysman.emas	12.1.0.3.0	0	Media/External
Oracle Database	oracle.sysman.db	12.1.0.2.0	20120804	Media/External
Oracle Exadata	oracle.sysman.xa	12.1.0.3.0	0	Media/External

If any additional plug-ins are listed, they should be downloaded into a single directory; then rename the extensions from .zip to .opar. Use the Install Software Only option to install the Middleware and OMS Oracle home components if not restoring from a filesystem backup. After the software has been reinstalled or restored, the next step is to install the additional plug-ins (if any). Execute the PluginInstall.sh script located in

OMS_HOME/sysman/install by specifying the -PluginLocation flag to select the location where the downloaded plug-ins are kept. In the case of a Software Only installation, all patches previously applied will have to be redone.

After restoring the software homes, the next step would be to restore or re-create the OMS. This is done by using the omsca utility and specifying the path of the backup generated by the emctl exportconfig command.

```
omsca recover -as -ms -nostart -backup_file <exportconfig file>
```

The steps required to recover the OMS may vary depending on whether an SLB is in use or multiple management services are configured as well as whether recovery is done on the same host or a different host. The following steps are required for restoring a single OMS on the same host without an SLB. The OMS instance will be recovered by using the OMS configuration backup taken by emctl exportconfig.

1. Clean up the failed host.

2. Verify that the Software Library is available.

3. Restore the software home by restoring a backup of the filesystem or run the installer's Software Only option. (See the *Oracle Enterprise Manager Cloud Control Advanced Installation and Configuration Guide Release 2*).

4. Execute omsca in recovery mode and specify the location of the backup file taken previously.

5. Recover agents if necessary.

6. Start the OMS.

7. Verify that the OMS is working.

See the *Oracle Enterprise Manager Cloud Control 12c Administrator's Guide* for details on other OMS recovery scenarios.

Management Agent Recovery

The recovery of the management agent requires reinstalling it, preferably from a reference install, or performing a filesystem restore from a previous backup. The agent should be cloned with the existing patches and customizations. The agent should also be installed by using the same port. After it has been reinstalled, a resynchronization should be performed from the Agent Resynchronization page in Enterprise Manager Cloud Control.

■ **Note** The agent is blocked by the OMS after reinstallation to prevent targets from overwriting data from previous configurations. Use the Resynchronize Agent button to resynchronize and unblock the agent.

Agent recovery in a typical scenario usually follows these steps:

1. Remove the existing agent Oracle home by using the Oracle Universal Installer (OUI) to clean up the inventory.

2. Install a new agent or clone from the reference install, using the same port and path. The filesystem can also be restored from a previous backup.

3. Perform Agent Resynchronization from the Enterprise Manager Cloud Control Agent home page.

4. Reconfigure user-defined metrics if necessary.

5. Verify the status of the agent.

   ```
   emctl status agent
   emctl upload agent
   ```

Switchover and Failover

Both the management service and repository can be switched over and failed over independently when using level 2, 3, or 4 high-availability configurations. Switchover is usually done during planned maintenance, including operating system and software patching, while a failover normally occurs during unplanned maintenance such as hardware or software failure.

In a level 2 configuration, the switchover and failover of the management service follow the same procedure. As mentioned earlier, this requires relocating the OMS virtual hostname and VIP to another host and then starting the OMS manually or using Clusterware to automate the relocation. In level 2, 3, or 4 configurations that utilize a physical standby database for the Enterprise Manager repository, the database has to be switched over (planned) or failed over (unplanned). The OMS does not require any action in level 3 high availability because multiple management services are involved. The SLB will monitor the management services and detect when one has failed and route traffic to the available OMS.

To switch over the management repository using Data Guard, use the DGMRL command-line utility as the Enterprise Manager console will not be able to switch over the repository. Follow these steps to do a switchover of the management repository with a management service that has not been switched over:

1. From the Enterprise console, choose Availability ä Data Guard Administration.

2. Check that the Redo Apply process is up-to-date. Verify the ApplyLag status is zero as shown in Figure 13-35.

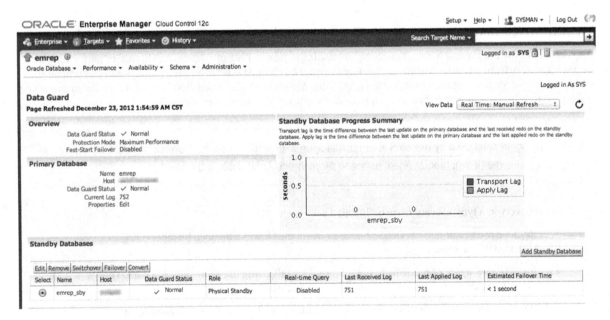

Figure 13-35. *Data Guard administration showing ApplyLag and TransportLag status*

3. Stop the management services on the primary site by running the following command. If multiple management services are being used, this should be done on each OMS.

```
emctl stop oms -all
```

4. Switch over to the standby database by using the DGMGRL command-line utility. This can be done on either the primary or standby site in the case of a switchover. Verify the Data Guard configuration and databases before doing a switchover. The following example illustrates these steps.

   a. Verify the Data Guard configuration and databases before doing a switchover:

```
$ dgmgrl
DGMGRL for Linux: Version 11.2.0.3.0 - 64bit Production

Copyright (c) 2000, 2009, Oracle. All rights reserved.

Welcome to DGMGRL, type "help" for information.
DGMGRL> connect sys/<password>
Connected.
DGMGRL> show configuration

Configuration - emrep

  Protection Mode: MaxPerformance
  Databases:
    emrep  - Primary database
    emrep2 - Physical standby database

Fast-Start Failover: DISABLED

Configuration Status:
SUCCESS

DGMGRL> show database emrep

Database - emrep

  Role:             PRIMARY
  Intended State:   TRANSPORT-ON
  Instance(s):
    emrep

Database Status:
SUCCESS

DGMGRL> show database emrep2

Database - emrep2

  Enterprise Manager Name: emrep_sby
  Role:                    PHYSICAL STANDBY
  Intended State:          APPLY-ON
```

```
         Transport Lag:           0 seconds
         Apply Lag:               0 seconds
         Real Time Query:         OFF
         Instance(s):
           emrep2

     Database Status:
     SUCCESS
```

b.   Issue the SWITCHOVER command:

```
DGMGRL> switchover to emrep2;
Performing switchover NOW, please wait...
New primary database "emrep2" is opening...
Operation requires shutdown of instance "emrep" on database "emrep"
Shutting down instance "emrep"...
ORACLE instance shut down.
Operation requires startup of instance "emrep" on database "emrep"
Starting instance "emrep"...
Unable to connect to database
ORA-12514: TNS:listener does not currently know of service requested in connect
descriptor

Failed.
Warning: You are no longer connected to ORACLE.

Please complete the following steps to finish switchover:
        start up and mount instance "emrep" of database "emrep"
```

■ **Note**   Additional steps may be required after issuing the switchover command depending on the current state of the Data Guard configuration. In the example shown, the new standby database should be started and mounted manually.

c.   Verify the status of the Data Guard configuration to see that the roles have been switched:

```
DGMGRL> connect sys/<password>
Connected.
DGMGRL> show configuration;

Configuration - emrep

  Protection Mode: MaxPerformance
  Databases:
    emrep2 - Primary database
    emrep  - Physical standby database

Fast-Start Failover: DISABLED

Configuration Status:
SUCCESS

DGMGRL> show database emrep2;
```

```
Database - emrep2

  Enterprise Manager Name: emrep_sby
  Role:                    PRIMARY
  Intended State:          TRANSPORT-ON
  Instance(s):
    emrep2

Database Status:
SUCCESS

DGMGRL> show database emrep;

Database - emrep

  Role:            PHYSICAL STANDBY
  Intended State:  APPLY-ON
  Transport Lag:   0 seconds
  Apply Lag:       0 seconds
  Real Time Query: OFF
  Instance(s):
    emrep

Database Status:
SUCCESS
```

Here you can see that the role of the database has been successfully changed. The next step is to reconfigure the OMS to use the new primary database.

5. Start the Admin Server if it is not already running.

```
emctl start oms -admin_only
```

6. Configure the OMS with the new primary database repository.

```
$OMS_HOME/bin/emctl config oms -store_repos_details -repos_conndesc
"(DESCRIPTION=(ADDRESS_LIST=(ADDRESS=(PROTOCOL=TCP)(HOST=oem3)(PORT=1522)))
(CONNECT_DATA=(SID=emrep2)))" -repos_user sysman
Oracle Enterprise Manager Cloud Control 12c Release 2
Copyright (c) 1996, 2012 Oracle Corporation.  All rights reserved.
Enter Repository User's Password :
```

7. Start the OMS.

```
emctl start oms
```

8. Relocate the management repository target. The management agent on an OMS monitors the OMS and management repository targets. After the switchover, the repository target needs to be updated to reflect the switched-over repository database, which is the new primary.

```
emctl config emrep -agent <central_agent_name> -conn_desc <conn_desc_of_new_primary>
```

Failover of the management repository using Data Guard is similar to a switchover, except the command issued using DGMGRL would be `failover to <standby_db_name>`.

In addition to using the preceding manual steps, you can automate the failover of the OMS and management repository by using Data Guard fast-start failover:

- Fast-start failover determines when a failover to a standby is necessary by using an Observer process that runs on another host independent of both primary and standby servers. If the Observer cannot contact the primary site after a certain configurable period, it will automatically fail over to the standby database.

- After failover occurs, a database event called `DB_ROLE_CHANGE` is fired.

- The `DB_ROLE_CHANGE` event causes a trigger to be fired, which in turn starts up the Enterprise Manager Application tier.

A script can be created that will automate these steps. Using the sample script provided in the `<OMS_HOME>/sysman/ha` directory, create a script that will configure the OMS to point to a new primary database and start up all management services. Listing 13-1 is an example of a script that will start up the standby OMS and reconfigure the OMS with the new primary management repository database that has been switched over in a Data Guard configuration.

Listing 13-1. Sample Script to Start EM Tier on Standby Site

```sh
#!/bin/sh
LOGFILE="/oms_swlib/em/failover/em_failover.log"
OMS_ORACLE_HOME="/u01/app/oracle/Middleware/oms"
CENTRAL_AGENT="oem2.example.com:3872"
SYSMAN_PWD="oracle12c"

#log message
echo "#############################" >> $LOGFILE
date >> $LOGFILE
echo $OMS_ORACLE_HOME >> $LOGFILE
id >>  $LOGFILE 2>&1

#switch all OMS to point to new primary and startup all OMS
$OMS_ORACLE_HOME/bin/emctl config oms -store_repos_details -repos_conndesc
"(DESCRIPTION=(ADDRESS_LIST=(ADDRESS=(PROTOCOL=TCP)(HOST=oem1)(PORT=1521)))
(CONNECT_DATA=(SID=emrep2)))" \
-repos_user sysman -repos_pwd $SYSMAN_PWD >> $LOGFILE 2>&1
$OMS_ORACLE_HOME/bin/emctl sync_opss_policy_store \
 -sysman_pwd oracle12c >> $LOGFILE 2>&1
$OMS_ORACLE_HOME/bin/emctl stop oms >>  $LOGFILE 2>&1
$OMS_ORACLE_HOME/bin/emctl start oms >>  $LOGFILE 2>&1

#relocate Management Services and Repository target
#to be done only once in a multiple OMS setup
#allow time for OMS to be fully initialized
$OMS_ORACLE_HOME/bin/emctl config emrep -agent $CENTRAL_AGENT \
-conn_desc -sysman_pwd $SYSMAN_PWD >> $LOGFILE 2>&1

#always return 0 so that dbms scheduler job completes successfully
exit 0
```

The sample script in Listing 13-2 creates a trigger that will be fired whenever the DB_ROLE_CHANGE event occurs during a switchover or failover operation. This trigger will then call the preceding script to start the Enterprise Manager tier.

Listing 13-2. Sample Database Role-Change Trigger

```
--
--
-- Sample database role change trigger
--
--
CREATE OR REPLACE TRIGGER FAILOVER_EM
AFTER DB_ROLE_CHANGE ON DATABASE
DECLARE
    v_db_unique_name varchar2(30);
    v_db_role varchar2(30);
BEGIN
    select upper(VALUE) into v_db_unique_name
    from v$parameter where NAME='db_unique_name';
    select database_role into v_db_role
    from v$database;

    if v_db_role = 'PRIMARY' then

        -- Submit job to Resync agents with repository
        -- Needed if running in maximum performance mode
        -- and there are chances of data-loss on failover
        -- Uncomment block below if required
        -- begin
        --   SYSMAN.setemusercontext('SYSMAN', SYSMAN.MGMT_USER.OP_SET_IDENTIFIER);
        --   SYSMAN.emd_maintenance.full_repository_resync('AUTO-FAILOVER to '||
        --     v_db_unique_name||'- '||systimestamp, true);
        --   SYSMAN.setemusercontext('SYSMAN', SYSMAN.MGMT_USER.OP_CLEAR_IDENTIFIER);
        -- end;

        -- Start the EM mid-tier
        dbms_scheduler.create_job(
            job_name=>'START_EM',
            job_type=>'executable',
            job_action=> '/oms_swlib/em/failover/' || v_db_unique_name|| '_start_oms.sh',
            enabled=>TRUE
        );
    end if;
EXCEPTION
WHEN OTHERS
THEN
    SYSMAN.mgmt_log.log_error('LOGGING', SYSMAN.MGMT_GLOBAL.UNEXPECTED_ERR,
SYSMAN.MGMT_GLOBAL.UNEXPECTED_ERR_M || 'EM_FAILOVER: ' ||SQLERRM);
END;
/
```

Summary

This chapter presented the main components of an Enterprise Manager Cloud Control system—Oracle Management Service, Oracle Management Repository, Oracle Management Agent, and Software Library—that need to be configured for high availability. Each of these components needs to be protected by using a different method.

Repository database high availability requires the use of database high-availability features including ASM, RAC, and Data Guard. Each should be configured using Oracle-recommended best practices where appropriate. RAC provides scalability and protects against the failure of a single host with seamless failover. Data Guard protects against host and storage failure with minimal downtime (typically less than a minute) during role changes. In its most highly configurable form, the repository database is deployed on a RAC database with a local RAC physical standby using Data Guard. A standby site with identical configuration is also available to provide services in the event of a loss of the primary site.

The Oracle Management Service can use various techniques to enable high availability, each differing in cost and complexity. The simplest technique involves separating the OMS host from the repository host. You also looked at an active/passive, or cold, failover solution in which multiple hosts share a single OMS on a shared filesystem, with only one active at any given point in time. This uses the concept of a VIP to enable failover in the event of the loss of one host in the cluster. Manual failover is required, and some downtime occurs as the OMS is restarted on another host. The next level sets up multiple management services behind a load balancer. This enables a seamless failover solution in the event of the loss of a single OMS. In an MAA configuration, a standby site is configured with a similar configuration as the primary site. This obviously costs the most. However, it not only offers single-site availability but also protects against disasters.

Management agents are made highly available by configuring reference images in the software library. This makes the agents easier to recover using deployment procedures.

A key aspect of highly available architecture is its backup and recovery strategy. Each component in the Enterprise Manager Cloud Control system should follow recommended best practices where appropriate to ensure recoverability to meet business recovery point and recovery time objectives thus causing minimal disruptions to the business.

In addition to the four levels of high availability discussed in this chapter, other technology solutions can provide varying levels of high availability. These include but are not limited to virtualization software such as Oracle VM Server, data replication technology including Oracle GoldenGate and Oracle Streams, and storage-level replication solutions. The choice of a solution hinges on business requirements, resources, and costs.

Index

■ P, Q